# THE AMERICAN REVOLUTION RE

The American Revolution Reader is a collection of leading essays on the American revolutionary era from the eve of the imperial crisis through George Washington's presidency. Articles have been chosen to represent classic themes, such as the British–colonial relationship during the eighteenth century, the political and ideological issues underlying colonial protests, the military conflict, the debates over the Constitution, and the rise of political parties. The volume also captures how the field has been reshaped in recent years, including essays that cover class strife and street politics; the international context of the Revolution; the roles of women, African Americans, and Native Americans; as well as the reshaping of the British Empire after the war.

With essays by Gordon S. Wood, Mary Beth Norton, T.H. Breen, John M. Murrin, Gary B. Nash, Woody Holton, Rosemarie Zagarri, John Shy, Alan Taylor, Maya Jasanoff, and many other prominent historians, the collection is ideal for classroom use and for any student of the American Revolution.

**Denver Brunsman** is Assistant Professor of History at George Washington University. He is the author of *The Evil Necessity: British Naval Impressment in the Eighteenth-Century Atlantic World* and an editor of *Colonial America: Essays in Politics and Social Development*, Sixth edition (Routledge).

**David J. Silverman** is Professor of History at George Washington University. He is the author of *Red Brethren: The Brothertown and Stockbridge Indians and the Problem of Race in Early America* and an editor of *Colonial America: Essays in Politics and Social Development*, Sixth edition (Routledge), among other books.

# Routledge Readers in History

# THE AMERICAN REVOLUTION READER

Edited by
DENVER BRUNSMAN
and
DAVID J. SILVERMAN

Routledge
Taylor & Francis Group

NEW YORK AND LONDON

First published 2014
by Routledge
711 Third Avenue, New York, NY 10017

Simultaneously published in the UK
by Routledge
2 Park Square, Milton Park, Abingdon, Oxon OX14 4RN

*Routledge is an imprint of the Taylor & Francis Group, an informa business*

*Library of Congress Cataloging in Publication Data*
The American Revolution reader / edited by Denver Brunsman and
David J. Silverman.
   pages cm. – (Routledge readers in history)
   Includes bibliographical references.
   1. United States – History – Revolution, 1775–1783. I. Brunsman,
   Denver Alexander, 1975– II. Silverman, David J., 1971–
   E208.A4397 2013
   973.3–dc23                                      2013006057

ISBN: 978-0-415-53756-8 (hbk)
ISBN: 978-0-415-53757-5 (pbk)

Typeset in Amasis
by HWA Text and Data Management, London

Printed and bound in the United States of America by Sheridan Books, Inc. (a Sheridan Group Company).

For John M. Murrin

# CONTENTS

# PREFACE

*The American Revolution Reader* is a collection of leading essays on the history of the American revolutionary era from the eve of the imperial crisis with Britain through the ratification of the Constitution and George Washington's presidency. It is the first major edited anthology of its kind in more than a decade. After an explosion of academic scholarship on the Revolution during the bicentennial period from the late 1960s to the late 1970s, there was a drought for much of the 1980s and 1990s. This volume reflects a current resurgence of interest in the Revolution, drawing the majority of its selections from work in the new millennium while including a handful of classic treatments of particular topics. A single collection of this sort can hardly be comprehensive in its coverage of an event as far-reaching as the American Revolution. Instead, our goal is to represent current interpretations of timeless issues and new trends in scholarship over the past generation.

Classic themes explored here include the British–colonial relationship during the eighteenth century, the political and ideological issues underlying colonial protests against imperial reforms, the patriot–loyalist divide, the military conflict, the debate over drafting and ratifying the Constitution, and precedents established during Washington's presidency. At the same time, this volume reflects more recent trends in the field, including class strife during the revolutionary era, the British consumer revolution, the Revolution in global context, the roles of white women, African Americans, and American Indians, and the reshaping of the British Empire after the war. In sum, the collection incorporates the diverse range of subjects, old and new, prominent in the current study of the Revolution.

New approaches to the Revolution are consistent with changes that have influenced the broad discipline of history since the 1960s. The analytical categories of race, class, and gender have reinvigorated a wide range of fields, including the American Revolution, by opening new perspectives beyond that of white male elites. As the essays in this volume attest, it is now possible to identify multiple social revolutions that took place during the revolutionary era. American independence opened new avenues of freedom for blacks even as it failed to end slavery, provided women with an enhanced role in the American polity and political language to contend for future rights, and secured a measure of social equality for poor white men unknown in the colonial era. The Revolution inspired generations of men and women of all backgrounds to pursue social advancements that were inconceivable before 1776.

At the same time, it fell woefully short in fulfilling the stirring pronouncement in the Declaration of Independence that "all men are created equal." Southern whites turned to slave labor as never before after the Revolution, driven by the new profitability of cotton. The new nation facilitated this re-entrenchment of racial slavery in a number of ways. The Constitution, especially the three-fifths clause, gave southern states political power to defend slavery disproportionate to the number of white citizens in those states. The South would largely control the presidency and the Supreme Court, and boast an equal voice in the Senate, up to the Civil War. Moreover, the federal government's acquisition of new territory from Indians, Spain, and France, opened up millions of fresh acres for the spread of slavery. In this, Indians were losers too. The creation of a new democratic empire answerable to white men who wanted Indian land without Indians on it, was an unmitigated disaster for indigenous people. Indians still held most of the continent on the eve of the Revolution. A century later, the nation was confining them to reservations. The Revolution even fell short in fulfilling the ambitions of many white Americans. White women still lacked the vote in the new political order despite their many sacrifices during the War for Independence. Many white men, perhaps a majority, opposed ratification of the Constitution because they judged that it granted the federal government a dangerous amount of power and consolidated that power in elite hands. Suffice it to say, for a large percentage of Americans, white, black, or Indians, the Revolution was at best a disappointment and at worst a catastrophe.

In the past generation, study of the Revolution has further transformed due to changes in the field of colonial American studies. Until quite recently, scholars of the colonial era lamented that the Revolution overshadowed their period. The creation of the American nation-state made it impossible to study the colonial era on its own terms. Put simply, all colonial roads – whether African, Dutch, English, French, German, Indian, Spanish, Swedish, or Russian – led to the founding of the United States. But as study of the American Revolution waned during the 1980s and 90s, the colonial period received new attention from scholars. With this new emphasis, scholarship on the Revolution began to take cues from the colonial field. The two most significant developments in colonial studies have been the emergence of Atlantic history and the expanded study of Indians and colonialism in the American interior. Similarly, in recent years, some of the most vibrant work on the Revolution has considered the event, including its causes and consequences, in broad Atlantic and North American continental contexts.

Essays in this volume prominently feature these trends. An Atlantic perspective changes the very way that we think of the Revolution. Rather than a movement that spawned solely from American soil, we now appreciate the protests of the 1760s and 1770s as deeply conditioned by the thriving British Empire in which they took place. Unlike many political revolutions that have followed it, the American Revolution was not a product of growing nationalist sentiment. Rather, Americans firmly identified themselves as British subjects, even as they resisted British imperial policies. A separate American identity only emerged during and after the Revolution. In turn, the political turmoil and invention that took place in North America had sweeping consequences across the globe.

The view from Indian country has also changed how we understand the Revolution. Most notably, the experience of Native Americans forces us to acknowledge the devastating consequences of America's victory over Britain. In the Treaty of Paris of 1783, Britain surrendered to the United States millions of acres of land still occupied by native peoples in the Ohio River Valley, Great Lakes region, and southeast, thus setting the stage for decades of warfare over this territory. Moreover, with its commitment to territorial expansion and teeming numbers of western settlers, the new United States had the fullest intention of occupying those lands. For Indians, then, the U.S. was not an enlightened nation manifestly destined to possess the continent, but a new and unprecedentedly powerful imperial threat. White settlers in Indian country also challenge triumphal narratives of the American founding. They at once distrusted eastern elites and the power of the federal government, even as they called upon those resources to wrest territory from Indians, the British, and the Spanish. America's democratic and imperial impulses played out in especially dramatic form along its western edge.

Taken together, these various influences have turned the American Revolution into a more stimulating subject of study than it was a generation or even a decade ago. We have organized this volume to highlight new perspectives without neglecting important traditional topics and viewpoints. Part I, Imperial Context, establishes the British Atlantic background for understanding American colonial resistance to British policies following the Seven Years' War in 1763. Part II, Imperial Crisis, explores the escalating nature of American resistance that culminated in independence. Part III, War and the Home Front, looks at the Revolutionary War and its connections to various elements of American society. Part IV, American Constitutionalism and Nation-Building, depicts different struggles over what has been termed the "American Revolutionary Settlement" – the lasting institutional and social outcomes of the Revolution. Part V, A Social Revolution?, attempts to answer this question by profiling the experiences of African Americans, Indians, white women, and non-elite white men in the wake of the Revolution. Part VI, Legacies, traces the longer-term impact of the Revolution on the British Empire and the American republic.

We invite readers to consider, question, and even contest the riveting arguments and issues presented in the essays that follow. Doing so engages in a project as timeless as the American Revolution itself – interpreting what exactly the event meant for the diverse inhabitants of North America and the world.

Denver Brunsman
David J. Silverman
*Washington, D.C.*

# ACKNOWLEDGMENTS

We thank our students at George Washington University who served as the ideal test audience for this collection. It has been a pleasure to work again with Kimberly Guinta and her outstanding editorial team at Routledge. We appreciate the anonymous reviewers for offering generous feedback on earlier incarnations of this volume. Without financial assistance from George Washington University, the book would not be possible. We are especially grateful to the History Department's chairman, William Becker, and its administrator, Michael Weeks, for supporting the project. Our families have provided additional support in ways too numerous to count. Finally, we thank John M. Murrin, to whom this volume is dedicated, for showing the way.

# PART I

# IMPERIAL CONTEXT

# 1
# LIBERTY, PROVINCE, AND EMPIRE
*Ned C. Landsman*

## Introduction

In this selection, Ned C. Landsman introduces one of the great ironies of the American revolutionary era: on the eve of their fierce protests against British policies of the 1760s and 1770s, American colonists did not aspire to political independence or even identify themselves as American. Rather, colonists were proud members of the British Empire and increasingly thought of themselves as provincial Britons. They felt on par with residents of other provincial sectors of the empire outside London, including Lowland Scots, Protestant Irish, and inhabitants of England's growing provincial towns and ports, such as Liverpool, Newcastle, and Whitehaven. Whereas their ancestors in the seventeenth century had viewed themselves as painfully remote from Europe, colonists in the eighteenth century understood themselves as integral parts of a larger British Atlantic world.

If anything, Landsman contends, the American colonies outpaced the mother country in celebrating the most prized British cultural value – liberty. Liberty was a protean concept with multiple definitions, ranging from legal protections, such as the right to private property, to a particular notion of religious freedom associated with Protestantism. British subjects throughout the Atlantic contrasted their Protestant empire – and its promotion of liberty – with the supposed tyrannical and absolute Catholic rule of Britain's chief rival, France. On a local level, American colonists connected liberty to the self-government provided by their individual colonial assemblies. In the eighteenth century, the assemblies, modeled on parliament, developed into the most powerful political institutions in British North America. Notably, colonists did not view their self-rule as a violation of their membership in the British Empire, but instead as the highest expression of their Britishness. Pursuing independence was not on the political agenda for these provincial Britons, for they already considered themselves the freest people on earth.

- By the 1760s, the British had constructed the strongest empire of the time, yet the central government exerted minimal direct control over its colonial territories. What were some of the factors that contributed to British imperial success? Was the lack of central oversight a weakness or virtue of the empire?

- Landsman notes that Britons defined liberty in opposition to slavery, which was considered its exact opposite. How could white colonists celebrate a polity based on liberty that depended so heavily on slavery? How might nonwhites, particularly enslaved Africans and Indians, have viewed membership in the British Empire? Consider the essays later in this volume by Ira Berlin and Colin G. Calloway for insights.

- Accepting that Landsman's argument is correct and American colonists self-identified as provincial Britons, how do we account for the American Revolution? Did the British values of colonists encourage or hinder resistance to British policies? Despite their British identity, did colonists manifest any values or characteristics that would later come to be regarded as especially American?

In February of 1746, Charles Chauncy mounted his pulpit in Boston to perform what was then a traditional New England rite: the delivery of a sermon of thanksgiving, this one for the defeat of a recent and dangerous rebellion. The uprising to which he alluded had been fought principally in Scotland and led by the Catholic prince Charles Edward Stuart, "Bonnie Prince Charlie," in the last of many attempts to restore to his father what had once been his grandfather's crown. New Englanders had not had much use for Stuart kings while they held the throne, and they certainly were not about to support them now: the Stuarts' Catholicism, their connections to the French court, and their past history of authoritarian rule all made them anathema to a British and Protestant populace. Thus Chauncy celebrated the recent defeat of the Jacobite armies, which had posed the specter of *"Popery* and *Slavery"* and threatened Britons in "the Enjoyment of their *Rights* and *Liberties,* which distinguish them from the other Nations of the Earth."[1]

In his preaching on the subject of liberty, the Old Light Chauncy sounded much like the evangelical Samuel Davies of Princeton in Davies's sermon on the death of George II. Even Chauncy's most frequent antagonist, Jonathan Edwards, who was then composing the many works that challenged what he deemed the unsound theological positions of his rival, had no quarrel with the Bostonian's opinions of the Jacobite threat to Protestant liberties. Indeed, upon first hearing of the threat, Edwards expressed fear that the rebellion itself might represent a divine punishment to "the nations of Great Britain" for their sinful ways, although recent providential intervention in the New Englanders' attack on the French bastion at Louisbourg on Cape Breton made him hopeful that God remained on the side of Protestants and liberty.[2]

If a single catchword can represent most of what provincials valued within their world, that word would have to be *liberty.* To the extent that the Enlightenment signified the reconception

of secular history in a progressive direction, liberty was the end toward which it moved. The term was nearly ubiquitous throughout the eighteenth-century British world, turning up in countless contexts in many realms of life. As with most terms that seem to capture collective aspirations at any given point in time, its meaning is hard to define with precision. It meant many things to many people. At the simplest level, liberty meant freedom from arbitrary restraint, the term *arbitrary* being the most critical one here. It certainly did not mean the absence of all regulation, which was not liberty in eighteenth-century understandings but anarchy or licentiousness; rational restraint was basic to civil society and to social well-being and, in short, to what eighteenth-century men and women referred to as social "happiness."

What distinguished arbitrary restraint was its absolute quality, the total subjection to another, or others, unrelated to any overriding social imperative. The term for that subjection was *slavery,* the very opposite of liberty. Slavery, in a political sense, signified the complete dependence on the will of another rather than simply the system of forced labor that we associate with the term. People living under arbitrary governments could bemoan their enslavement without implying that they lived under a system of bondage; slaveholders themselves could and did complain of their slavery, as we shall see.[3]

Liberty was part of many realms of life. In politics, liberty meant principally freedom from arbitrary rule and in particular from that of absolute monarchs, which was what Britons considered most of the world's rulers to be. In civil life, liberty signified the presence of specific legal protections, such as the right to hold property, for those who either had it or could aspire to it, and the established protections of the legal system for those entitled to it—in short, freedom from arbitrary punishment. In the religious culture of British Protestants, liberty meant the right to follow one's conscience in accordance with the word of God as revealed in Scripture, and freedom from arbitrary human authorities that tried to impose their wills above biblical commands; it was the creation of just such a human authority that rendered Catholicism an unfit religion in the minds of most Protestants and a threat to liberty of conscience. In cultural matters, liberty signified freedom of enquiry, without interference from church or state and without the tyrannical authority of superstition or ancient learning. Socially, liberty increasingly came to mean the right of citizens to pursue their fortunes without unnecessary hindrance from the authority of the state, or even from the tyranny of birth. Genteel origins might indeed provide privileges to those who possessed them but ought not to prevent the peaceful pursuit of prosperity and happiness among those of every station in life.

Some of the meanings of liberty varied from place to place and from group to group. Within the rural confines of Congregationalist New England, for example, liberty for many was often associated with the authority of local communities to conduct their own affairs without interference from the outside—even if those "outsiders" were merely claiming the liberty to worship in their own way. In Tidewater Virginia, liberty in its fullest sense was the property of the gentry, of male landowners, who claimed the right to govern, represent, and speak for their communities and their households—including wives, children, slaves, and servants—without restraint from the government of the colony or the empire. For mid-Atlantic farmers, liberty meant something like the ability to own or at least possess their farms, to be secure from rapacious landlords or onerous taxes from church or state. And nearly everywhere in the British colonies, liberty would come to be associated with a significant degree of provincial control over provincial affairs.[4]

There was little to distinguish the concept of liberty as it emerged in America from the mainstream of British thinking on political matters, unless it was the existence of a somewhat narrower range of meanings across the political spectrum; it was, after all, British liberty whose protection provincials claimed. Rather than departing from the core of British political ideas, provincials on the whole were rather close to the center, and there were few representations of the extremes of political thinking found in Britain itself. Not many Americans could be found on the extreme political right, which viewed liberty as deriving from aristocratic or at least gentle birth and protected by kings who held their authority by divine right. Although recent historians have found considerable support in many parts of Britain for the continuing claims of the Stuart dynasty to a legitimate right to the British throne, there were few avowed Jacobites in America.[5] The rebellion of 1715 attracted little conspicuous support in the colonies, that of 1745 almost none. Those movements derived the bulk of their support from Britain's farthest outlying regions—northern England, northern Scotland, and Celtic Ireland—not among the commercial towns and Protestant citizenries of provincial England and Lowland Scotland, the areas with which provincial Americans maintained their closest connections.

Neither were many Americans positioned on what might be considered the far left of the British political spectrum in the middle years of the eighteenth century—the emerging republican politics of radical groups in London and among the provincial Dissenters—at least not before 1760. To be sure, colonials voiced considerable support for London's John Wilkes in his ongoing battle against the British ministry. But Americans saw Wilkes principally as simply a defender of liberty against tyranny—"Wilkes and liberty" was the slogan associated with his supporters—rather than as a representative of any particular radical position. Moreover, the general weakness of royal authority in the colonies worked against the establishment of truly radical stances on political matters before the 1760s, as did the relative absence of urban centers of the sort that fostered them. Thus colonials viewed sympathy for Wilkes as entailing significant protest not against the system in general but only against abuses. To most provincial citizens, Wilkes could be defended on the basis of a British liberty that was firmly rooted in Protestantism, the common law, and the inherent safeguards of the British Constitution, all safely within the mainstream of British thinking.[6]

If one had asked a typical provincial British citizen of the eighteenth century the reasons for the blessing of liberty that he and his neighbors possessed, the questioner would likely have received one of several answers. One would have referred to religion, to British Protestantism and the freedom of enquiry it claimed to promote; civil and religious liberty were widely believed to be inextricably interconnected. A second would likely have been British virtue, the spirited defense of liberty that Britons had actively exhibited over the years against repeated attacks from the monarchy, especially by the Stuarts during the 1640s and the 1680s; such a spirit was at least partly attributed to Protestant independence as well.[7]

A third set of answers would have cited British institutions: the heritage of the English common law and the system of government established after the Revolution of 1688 and summarized by the phrase "the British Constitution." Unlike the Constitution of the United States, the British Constitution was not a written document. The phrase referred instead to the structure of government, the way the government conducted itself, and the powers that it held, deriving from traditional practice and from such revered documents as the Magna Charta and the Bill of Rights. At the heart of the Constitution was the tripartite system of government by a combination of crown, lords, and commons, working not through separation of powers but jointly in what was called "mixed government." That system met the twin goals of moderation and balance on the one hand—so resonant for partisans of the "moderate Enlightenment"— and of popular participation on the other.

Liberty, so conceived, was far from universal. If it seemed to most Britons to be the particular inheritance of Protestants, many doubted that it

was safe to extend its blessings to others, who would likely commit to destroying the religion on which those liberties rested. Nor was liberty necessarily incompatible with the institution of slavery, despite what seems to us a contradiction in terms; liberty was the property of citizens and certainly did not belong to those whose interests ran counter to those of civil society. Even John Locke's famous triad of life, liberty, and property allowed for the institution of slavery in the case of captives in just wars, whose lives could otherwise have been forfeited. Liberty could be a prized possession without carrying implications that it had to belong to everyone.

In fact, liberty and bonded slavery seemed to be intimately connected everywhere in the colonial world. To the plantation owners in the southern provinces, the economic independence they derived from the profits of slave labor provided the very foundation of their liberties. And even the economic liberties that mid-Atlantic family farmers so highly valued—the opportunity to profit from the surplus produce of independent family farms—depended in large part on the ready market for that surplus that existed in the plantation economies to the south or in the West Indies, with their abundant supply of slave labor. Few provincials, with the exception of such attentive Quakers as John Woolman, thought much about that connection.[8]

As the persistence of slavery in the colonial world illustrates, the context in which provincial ideas of liberty developed differed from that which Britons experienced. The necessities of colonial society, and in particular the need for population, extended the reach of liberties from being the possession of a restricted class of property holders to a broader component of both propertied and nonpropertied white society. The political status of the American colonies also differed from that of Britain, and American provincials would come to root their liberties to an unusual degree in the particular legal forms of their colonial charters. More generally, the connotations of liberty that emerged there would be distinctive, as many provincials came to identify liberty in the broadest sense as both the natural state and as one of the principal advantages of provincial society.

## Liberty, Virtue, and the Independent Reflector

Some of the meaning that liberty held for provincial citizens can be observed in the *Independent Reflector,* a series of polite essays offered to the New York citizenry by the New York lawyer William Livingston along with his associates William Smith Jr. and John Morin Scott. In style, the paper was something of a hybrid. In part it cultivated the polite style of the *Spectator* and of such literary journals as the *Gentleman's Magazine,* but its concerns were never "meerly literary," in Livingston's words. Rather, the paper's principal design, he announced in the first issue, was to vindicate the *"civil and religious* RIGHTS of my Fellow-Creatures" while exposing "publick *Vice* and *Corruption."* The *Reflector,* invoking a popular phrase, refused to be a "silent Spectator" where "the Rights of the Community are infringed, or violated"; it would devote itself instead to "displaying the amiable Charms of Liberty, with the detestable Nature of *Slavery* and *Oppression."*[9]

In its devotion to the cause of liberty, the *Independent Reflector* most closely resembled the essays by the English opposition writers of the early eighteenth century, John Trenchard and Thomas Gordon, especially those essays that appeared in the *London Journal* between 1720 and 1723 under the title *Cato's Letters,* although the name of their publication was drawn from Trenchard and Gordon's earlier *Independent Whig.* The reputation of the Roman patriot Cato as a defender of liberty was enhanced by Joseph Addison's popular play of that name, and both the play and the essays were widely read in the colonies. The essays were regularly reprinted or excerpted in the colonial press almost from their first appearance; one on the liberty of the press appeared in the *New England Courant* as early as 1722.[10]

The *Reflector's* debt to the work of Trenchard and Gordon suggests an important aspect of the meaning of liberty in provincial America. Neither man was a great thinker, and their contributions have been overshadowed by those of such seminal writers as their predecessor John Locke, whose *Two Treatises on Government,* with its allocation to the government of the protection of life, liberty, and property, has long stood as a classic of political thought. Yet if such luminaries as Locke have left us a legacy to which historians of political theory must ever return, such popular writers as Trenchard and Gordon still have much to tell us about the meaning of political liberty to British citizens in the eighteenth century.[11]

Locke's works on politics have long been regarded as perhaps the classic statement of liberal theory, a theory of politics that emphasizes the rights of individuals and freedom from governmental interference with those rights. Trenchard and Gordon's work is based at least in part on a different tradition in political theory traceable to the work of the seventeenth-century writer James Harrington, author of *Oceana,* and, before him, to such humanist and classical writers as Machiavelli and even Aristotle. That tradition, called "civic humanism," viewed man as exercising his full liberty through civic participation; liberty here signified the freedom to participate in civic life—although not necessarily for everyone— more than it meant freedom from its authority. It valued public action over private interest and deemed the vigorous pursuit of the public welfare as essential to liberty's preservation. The term for that pursuit was *virtue,* and its presence among the citizenry was essential for preventing corruption, political decay, and the inevitable loss of liberty that would follow. It was thus a philosophy that valued public engagement over private tranquillity.[12]

As was the case with Cato's essays, the primary aim of the *Reflector* was to promote public virtue, or watchfulness, and especially to guard against abuses in public life. As Livingston wrote in the first *Reflector,* "Public Abuses are, in their own

Nature, progressive; and tho' easily removed in their Origin, acquire Strength by their Duration, and at last become too potent to be subdued." Defenders of liberty had to remain always on their guard, because a failure to resist even "the least Invasion of civil or religious Liberty, is an encouragement to greater, and presages mightier Evils to come; while a seasonable Opposition might not only have vanquished the present, but discouraged all future Abuses of the like Nature."[13] Liberty was always under attack, a theme Cato enunciated in "Cautions against the natural Encroachments of Power," in which he contended that, "because Liberty chastises and shortens Power, therefore Power would extinguish Liberty; and consequently Liberty has too much cause to be exceeding jealous, and always upon her Defence."[14] And liberty, once lost, was very difficult to regain.

The guarding of liberty seemed especially important to eighteenth-century Britons because, from their perspective, it was not only fragile but rare. As Britons looked beyond their borders, they saw, or thought they saw, a world of absolutist monarchies, such as France and Spain were deemed to be. Beyond those lay a still-larger world full of what were generally referred to as "Oriental despotisms." Only in small, isolated pockets of Europe did liberty thrive, and except in Britain, it was largely restricted to such small and weak states as Switzerland or the Netherlands. Moreover, liberty was often under attack from abroad as well as at home, leading the *Reflector* to consider not simply domestic political abuses but also "the dangerous vicinity of the French to the British Plantations."[15]

Liberty in this sense also demanded that citizens place the public interest above their own, which was, in essence, the principal meaning of political virtue in the eighteenth century. That is a sense of the word *virtue* that has nearly been lost in our time, as we live under a system that maintains that the good of the whole is best attained when each individual promotes his or her own interest. Since the nineteenth century, the term *virtue* has been applied principally to

the activities of individuals in private life, and especially to women; as we have seen, in the eighteenth century it was already basic to the vocabulary of such evangelical women as Esther Burr and to other Enlightened women. But in the eighteenth century the term also retained a very public meaning; virtue in that sense was essentially a masculine trait, employed in defense of an otherwise defenseless liberty whose connotations were, in that sense, feminine.[16]

The principal part of virtue was public spirit, the promotion of the community's interests above self-interest or even above the interest of one's family or neighbors. The pursuit of such "partial" interests was roundly condemned in this view, under the labels of *faction* or *party*. Neither was a term of approbation. The *Reflector*, for instance, included a whole paper on the subject of "Party-Divisions," which discussed how "zeal for the common Good" was "gradually extinguished by the predominating Fervor of a Faction."[17]

One reason that factious behavior was rendered so unsavory in the eighteenth century was its association with the passions. As the *Reflector* explained, "From the Moment that Men give themselves wholly up to a Party, they abandon their *Reason,* and are led Captive by their *Passions."* Their own cause "presents such bewitching Charms, as dazzle the Judgment," the other side "such imaginary Deformity, that no Opposition appears too violent."[18] People were drawn to factions for base reasons, such as the love of power or wealth. Such motives induced them to act against their better selves, against their reason, against the common good, as well as against principles of Christian charity. A well-ordered commonwealth thus resembled a well-ordered mind: the placing of the faculties in their appropriate order would lead to both individual and social happiness.

Yet if the *Reflector* generally denounced factious behavior, its antipathy to faction itself was not absolute. In other essays, the authors began to bring into their pages a different view of faction that was then emerging, one more often associated with liberal views than with civic ones, in which faction and the pursuit of individual interest could have positive as well as negative effects. At one point Livingston described the division of New York into "so great a Variety of Opinions and Professions" as an advantage, with "the Jealousy of all Parties combating each other," producing "a perfect Freedom for each particular Party."[19]

The *Reflector's* argument, it has been noted, anticipated that offered by James Madison in his famous *Federalist* essay #10 in 1787, which has been variously interpreted as exemplifying both liberal and civic ideals. There Madison also revealed his distaste for faction—indeed, Madison contended, one of the principal arguments for a new federal government was its ability to "break and control the violence of faction." Yet it was the violence of factions rather than factions themselves that Madison sought to break. Factions themselves had their advantages. The great number of factions that would emerge in the extensive territory that encompassed the new United States, Madison believed, and within the enlarged territorial districts from which representatives would be elected, would prevent any single interest from attaining too large a foothold in the government.

However clear the distinctions between the civic and liberal traditions may have seemed to historians of political thought, they were less carefully maintained by contemporaries. In fact, both Locke and Cato held honored places in the pantheon of Whig heroes that emerged in British and British-American discussion; also revered were the seventeenth-century radical and martyr Algernon Sydney, the eighteenth-century Tory critic Henry St. John, Viscount Bolingbroke, and the popular schoolmaster and essayist James Burgh, whose writings drew on all of those traditions. British political culture was a composite of many different views, linked only by the pervasive belief that all helped to advance liberty, the hallmark of an Enlightened age.[20]

That composite heritage allowed Britons and Americans both to celebrate monarchy at the same time that they lauded the accumulated restraints on monarchical power established in the Magna Charta and the Bill of Rights; kings as well as commons had a role to play in the history of liberty, serving as mutual checks on one another. The king and only the king, in theory, shared the interests of the whole nation and was not susceptible to those of any one group or faction. Kings were the protectors of the people, not only against invasion from abroad but also against corruption from within. This role of the king as protector led Americans, including Samuel Davies, to valorize George II on his death in 1760 and to await so eagerly the reign of George III. To celebrate monarchs as bastions of liberty was an important mechanism for promoting British and provincial identities.[21]

Thus Americans in the eighteenth century possessed a mixed political heritage, one that combined a civic fear of faction with a liberal attachment to interest, a reverence for kings with a devotion to popular government. What they shared was the conviction that theirs was in fact a nation of liberty in a world of tyrannies, whether they attributed that fact to the limitations on the British monarchy, to its system of balanced power through mixed government, to ancient tradition, to the Common Law, or to the Protestant heritage. Thus would the *Reflector* claim for itself "the Privilege of a free Briton, to expose the Abuses of Government; and, when Occasion offers, to animadvert on the lawless Conduct of his Superiors." He would do so, indeed, with "the Spirit peculiar to an Englishman."[22]

The rhetoric of liberty played a prominent role in provincial politics. It was employed by what came to be called the "popular" party, led by Elisha Cooke, that rose up in Massachusetts under the new charter, which opposed the prerogatives of governors and officeholders and, at least in Boston, regularized such practices as the employment of explicit instructions by the town meeting to its elected representatives. It was part of the appeal of a series of repeated populist attacks on the Pennsylvania proprietorship David Lloyd undertook. In New York, claims of liberty had formed a component of ethnic politics even during the seventeenth century; in some instances, the claim of English liberties was used to suppress traditional Dutch political practices. In the next century, James Alexander and William Smith would oppose Governor Cosby through the instrument of John Peter Zenger's *New-York Weekly Journal*. In their first essay, they defended both the liberty of the press and the importance of guarding the liberties of the people from attack by entrenched powers.[23]

The politics of liberty was well suited to opposition styles, especially when joined to the emerging political press, which claimed the role of public watchman; indeed, William Livingston and his associates used the name "The Watch-Tower" for a series of essays that succeeded the *Reflector* in the *New-York Mercury*. *Cato's Letters*, published originally in the *London Journal*, proved so widely adaptable in the colonies expressly because of that union. Benjamin Franklin published an excerpt from Cato on the freedom of speech as "inseparable from Publick Liberty" in 1722 in response to his brother's imprisonment in Boston. In New York, James Alexander and Lewis Morris, the aristocratic opponents of Governor Cosby, also employed Trenchard and Gordon's writings in their attack on executive prerogatives published in the *New-York Weekly Journal*.[24]

## Liberty, Provinciality, and Prosperity

What made the preservation of liberty seem so compelling to provincials in the eighteenth century was its apparent connection to nearly every other element of prosperity and social happiness. As the *Reflector* observed in a passage that was echoed countless times in the colonies, in absolute monarchies "the whole Country is overspread with a dismal Gloom. *Slavery* is stamp'd on the Looks of the Inhabitants; and *Penury* engraved on their Visages. ... To prevent Complaints, the *PRESS* is prohibited. ...

The liberal Sciences languish: The politer Arts droop their Heads. ... The Fields lie waste and uncultivated: Commerce is incumbered with supernumerary Duties: The Tyrant riots in the Spoils of his People; and drains their Purses, to replenish his insatiate Treasury."[25]

The situation under a system of liberty was altogether different. "The Subjects of a free State, have something open and generous in their Carriage; something of Grandeur and Sublimity in their Appearance, resulting from their Freedom and Independence. ... They can think for themselves; publish their Sentiments, and animadvert on Religion and Government, secure and unmolested." Under such a system, "[a]griculture is encouraged, and proves the annual Source of immense Riches to the Kingdom: The Earth opens her fertile Bosom to the Ploughshare, and luxuriant Harvests diffuse Wealth and Plenty thro' the Land." The *Reflector* went on to ask whether the "rising Prosperity of Pennsylvania," the "Admiration of the Continent," was not the result of "the impartial Aspect of their Laws upon all Professions," which led to a "vast Importation of religious Refugees, to their Strength and their Riches."[26]

Liberty promoted not only prosperity but enlightenment, through the exercise of free inquiry. "The Restraint of civil Authority, in different Countries and Ages, upon the free Exercise of human Reason, has ever been attended with a Decay of all valuable Knowledge and Literature. It is as impossible for the Sciences to grow and flourish under the Frowns and Terrors of Oppression, as for a People to breath Liberty under the savage Administration of a Tyrant. The Advancement of Learning depends upon the free Exercise of Thought; it is therefore absurd to suppose, that it should thrive under a Government that makes it Treason even for a Man to think."[27]

Here again, Livingston and his colleagues drew from Trenchard and Gordon, who had pronounced liberty "the divine Source of all human Happiness." They continued, "to possess, in Security, the Effects of our Industry, is the most powerful and reasonable Incitement to be industrious. ... where Property is precarious, labour will languish." Indeed, liberty would "increase Mankind, and the Happiness of Mankind. ... Liberty naturally draws new People to it," and therefore "countries are generally peopled in Proportion as they are free."[28]

Such ideas were given additional force by what provincial Americans saw around them. During the first half of the eighteenth century, the British colonies in North America found themselves in a period of dramatic demographic and economic growth. Between 1700 and 1750, the settler population of the British colonies increased perhaps fourfold—to more than a million people, including slaves—a rate of growth that was surprisingly close to that imagined by provincials. American wealth and trade were also perceived to be growing at a heady rate.[29]

Provincials were not unaware of the growth that surrounded them, which they began to attribute to the relatively unconstrained nature of the colonial economy, or, as they viewed it, the effects of economic liberty. As New York's Archibald Kennedy observed, "liberty and encouragement" were the cornerstones of colonial prosperity.[30] From that perspective, within the context of provincial society, prosperity, which traditional moral economists had portrayed as threatening to moral welfare, could be portrayed instead as its confirmation.[31]

From those observations, provincial commentators developed some particular perspectives on their economy. Perhaps the most famous was Benjamin Franklin's 1751 essay on population, entitled "Observations Concerning the Increase of Mankind, Peopling of Countries, &c."[32] Franklin hypothesized that the availability of land and the prevalence of opportunity in the American colonies was allowing for a dramatic growth of population, which he reckoned was doubling every 25 years. Such growth was likely to continue, in Franklin's view, as long as colonials did not fall prey to the dangers of overcrowding, the loss of trade, or the

importation of "foreign luxuries and needless manufactures."

Franklin's work was both original and influential, but it was not without precedent. Some of his suggestions about population, for example, including his famous estimate that colonial population was doubling every 25 years, were anticipated by his friend and correspondent Archibald Kennedy in an essay written the year before.[33] Perhaps more importantly, Franklin's concern with population growth in particular was part of a much larger philosophical inquiry into the causes and ramifications of population growth that was then taking place in the British world. That discussion, largely the work of Scots and Dissenters, fit with their general concerns about the likely condition of Britain's outlying regions in the face of the continuing acquisition of wealth and power by metropolitan interests. Among the most important contributions to that discussion was the famous population "debate" that took place between David Hume and Robert Wallace in the Philosophical Society of Edinburgh during the 1740s. It is likely that Franklin had access to their debate before Wallace's tract was published in 1753; he became a member of the Edinburgh society shortly thereafter.[34]

The interest in population growth provincials and Dissenters demonstrated generally reflected the developing perception that in both population and trade, provincial growth was outpacing that of England itself. That perception was part of the inspiration for the new science of political economy, which is often dated from the 1776 publication of Adam Smith's *Inquiry into the Nature and Causes of the Wealth of Nations*. In fact the *Wealth of Nations* developed out of a larger discussion of the principles of economics that formed an important part of Enlightenment science and of the Scottish Enlightenment in particular. It included contributions not only from academics and philosophers but from a wide variety of merchants and government officials at all levels. In Britain, its most important practitioners were Scots: Adam Smith, David

Hume, Sir James Steuart, and a host of lesser figures, all concerned in their works with such basic questions as the effect on provinces and poorer trading partners of their ever-growing commercial relationships with wealthier and more powerful neighbors, as in the case of provinces within the empire. In that sense, provincial political economy was substantially devoted to assessing the future commercial and political prospects of outlying regions.[35]

Despite the variety of contributions to the provincial discussion of commerce, several common themes emerged. One was the substantial consensus in favor of the general principles of free trade. Free trade in that context meant something considerably less than the full operation of the free market, or *laissez-faire,* a position that even Adam Smith never fully endorsed. Rather, it signified the liberty to buy and sell on the open market free from undue constraint from entrenched interests. In particular it meant freedom from excessive metropolitan control such as that exerted over the American provinces by the Navigation Acts—unfairly, in the opinion of many—and especially from unfair competition from the chartered metropolitan trading companies, such as the British East India Company, which were linked to the corruptions and luxuries of the court. Free trade, so defined, was not incompatible with the closing of imperial markets to foreign merchants, which served to maintain guaranteed markets for the raw materials that the colonies produced.[36]

Free trade in that sense was not necessarily deemed inconsistent with a form of structured trading, as long as it was designed to promote general economic interests and not to restrict unduly the particular commercial opportunities of any single part. It was antithetical to much of the British mercantile system, however, which under the Navigation Acts restricted numerous sectors of provincial commerce in favor of metropolitan trading interests. Thus Benjamin Franklin came to argue that the key to unifying the empire was to elevate the colonies to positions of equality with the metropolis in all their affairs—politically,

through incorporation into an enlarged imperial parliament to which the colonies would send members, and economically, through repeal of all trade regulations that discriminated against the colonies.[37]

Political economists began to portray the flow of commerce itself as a positive good. In purely economic terms, increased trade came to seem the key to the creation of wealth. Such reasoning was part of the logic behind colonial efforts to create land banks, which were controversial in New England and elsewhere during the first half of the eighteenth century. Land banks were intended to use the wealth in land, which provincials possessed in abundance, to back paper money in a traditionally cash-poor economy. The Congregationalist minister John Wise, among the leading supporters of the land bank in Massachusetts, argued that such a bank would lead to a more rapid circulation of money and thus to increased population and development. Opposed to the bank were other merchants and leading citizens who decried its inflationary tendencies and the instability it would promote.[38]

At stake in the matter of land banks was the perennial issue of growth and opportunity versus stability and order. Well-established proponents of order opposed the land bank; provincial men on the make supported it. In that sense, the land bank controversy paralleled divisions in the region over the Regular Singing controversy, the Awakening, and other matters. But whichever side provincials took on the land bank issue, they shared the assumption that the circulation of money through trade would lead to an increase in money. Moreover, for many, the creation of prosperity—whether orderly or rampant—more than the quest for religion and virtue per se, was now the principal standard towards which the society ought to move. Indeed, prosperity would increasingly be portrayed as necessary to religion and virtue.[39]

The development of the science of political economy coincided with a significant shift in the rhetoric of social analysis, one in which morality and the market came to be almost inextricably intertwined. If earlier generations of theologians had commonly cited remarkable providences, or incidents that seemed to suggest the suspension of the common or natural order, as evidence of divine favor or disfavor, by the middle of the eighteenth century conformity to that order was increasingly equated with the providential plan. In that rhetorical shift, the metaphor of the market loomed large: the market, as it was being redefined by political economists, came to represent a grand mechanism for reconciling competing needs and goals in harmony with the natural order. Represented in that fashion, the market served to promote the balance and order so valued by adherents to the moderate Enlightenment; in fact, the market constituted an important tool in promoting harmony, peace, and civility. For similar reasons, prosperity and commercial expansion would come to serve as moral justifications for any social action, in effect demonstrating its conformity to nature and to the divine order.[40]

Such a shift had significant ramifications for the provincial world. If eighteenth-century analysts believed that one of the benefits of liberty was prosperity, so also did the evident prosperity of the provincial world implicitly endorse the nature of provincial society and the conditions of relative political and economic liberty in which it prospered. Thus would William Livingston cite Pennsylvania's prosperity as evidence of the rightness of that colony's policy of toleration and religious pluralism. So also would Benjamin Franklin use the colonies' growth and wealth as a confirmation of the virtues of a social order based on frugality and industry.[41]

In the provincial setting in particular, provincials came to assert, liberty, although far from universal, could expand beyond the privileged few to take in the bulk of a white settler population committed to the goal of economic development. Provincial liberty was the source of prosperity, of freedom of enquiry, of Enlightenment, and even of a pure form of religiosity. Thus in the provinces in particular, liberty, piety, prosperity, and Enlightenment all seemed to be strongly interconnected.

## Liberty, Legislature, and Locality: The Rise of the Assembly

If provincial Americans almost uniformly praised the system of liberty in which they lived, few of them participated in that system at the imperial level. Most colonial business was transacted at court through hired colonial agents residing in the metropolis. For the overwhelming majority of even the voting population of the American colonies, politics was experienced no higher than at the provincial level.[42]

As late as the 1680s, the status of provincial politics, and even of the provincial governments, had been very much in doubt. In creating the Dominion of New England out of the northern colonies, the Stuart governments had revoked the original charters of several of those provinces; had the Glorious Revolution not intervened, they might have suppressed the rest. In the matter of their royal charters, few doubted that what the king gave, the king could also take away.

As late as the 1680s, colonials as subjects could be certain of few rights. In Massachusetts, those who protested the loss of the charter and resisted the newly organized Dominion of New England were told by one judge that they were mistaken in assuming that English liberties followed them "to the ends of the Earth." In fact, they had "no more Privileges left" than that they were not "bought and sold for slaves."[43] Colonials on the whole were likely to disagree. Already in 1687, the Congregational minister John Wise persuaded his town to insist on "their liberty as freeborne English subjects of his majesty" in opposing the arbitrary claims of the Dominion.[44]

If the Glorious Revolution stood for anything in the colonies, it was the right of Americans to be treated as something other than pure dependents, or provincial slaves. Liberty, property, and Protestantism were to be as secure in the colonies as elsewhere in the empire. But to say that they had rights was not the same as establishing precisely what those rights were or how far they extended. When, after that revolution, Increase Mather had sought a reissue of the Massachusetts charter, the king had demurred and granted instead a new, modified charter for the colony. Henceforth, Massachusetts was dependent on a royal governor. Equally important, the charter itself retained the status of a royal gift.

Over the next 60 years, charters gradually became much more secure. In part such security was simply the result of the passage of time; tradition and the constant exercise of authority were matters that held considerable weight in British constitutional theory.[45] In part it was an unanticipated consequence of changes in British politics after the Glorious Revolution: the augmented authority of Parliament and the lessening of the royal prerogative diminished the king's ability to alter the terms of charters at will.

Those same 60 years saw the various colonies adopt more uniform structures of government. Nearly all of the colonies moved toward a tripartite form that included a royal governor appointed by the Crown, a council working with the governor, and an elected lower house of assembly. Moreover, those elected assemblies almost everywhere dramatically increased their powers and posed a real challenge to the authority of often equally assertive royal governors, a phenomenon referred to as the "rise of the assemblies."[46]

The rise was more a matter of circumstance and practice than of positive law. It resulted in part from structural weaknesses in the office of the royal governors, who held positions that were, in theory, analogous to that of the king in British politics but without any of the mystique, and many of the actual powers, of that figure. Royal governors were hardly revered figures; even the most popular and powerful were commoners and career officials who received none of the respect or adulation accorded the monarch. Many were far from popular in any event.[47]

Royal governors also did not possess many of the powers of patronage and appointment that the king was able to use to influence legislators. Moreover, they lacked permanence and could be removed by the king at will, which often made their positions precarious. Those who bowed to the will of the assembly risked the monarch's displeasure, and even those who scrupulously followed royal policy rarely achieved job security in the process. Governors who alienated their assemblies by firm adherence to royal instruction often found themselves sacrificed by court officials seeking to mollify discontented colonials.[48]

However much provincials celebrated monarchy, they were far less complacent about the positions of the king's representatives in the colonies. Those officials lacked either a permanent interest in or a connection with the societies they administered. Most seemed to be there for their own benefit rather than for that of their societies; as one pamphleteer wrote, "[T]he chief End of many Governours coming to the Plantations" was "to get Estates for themselves."[49] They were therefore perfect subjects for the watchfulness of virtuous provincials.

The assemblies also rose in power because they were adaptable to the colonies' varying circumstances. In Virginia and elsewhere in the plantation south, the assembly was the principal forum for a planter elite serving as spokesmen for their society on the model of the virtuous, civic-minded landowner. In Congregational New England, the General Court represented not plantations but towns, who chose their representatives in town meetings to speak for the local community in the provincial government. In the heterogeneous mid-Atlantic, where the general conduct of politics seemed considerably more factious, the assembly often provided a focus for opposition factions such as that of Morris and Alexander to challenge the administration of Governor Cosby.

Although British political theory characterized the legislatures as the democratic branch of government, the rise of the assembly was not necessarily democratic in its implications.

Because that body asserted its position as spokesmen for the colony against possible assaults from imperial officials, assemblymen often emphasized harmony and unity over contention. The result was often unchallenged elite control. Certainly those Virginia gentlemen who represented their colony so eloquently in the House of Burgesses were anything but spokesmen for the common person; on the contrary, virtually all belonged to a unified and interlocking group of families that comprised the colonial elite. Elsewhere, the assemblies were dominated by competing elite factions throughout the provincial period.[50]

Nor did the rise of the assembly signify a growing antipathy to monarchy. Provincials distrusted imperial officials far more than they did the kings who appointed them. Indeed, the attack on such officials was part of the ritual by which provincial citizens celebrated monarchy; it fit very neatly the fiction that although the king could do no wrong, his advisers and appointees could and did. Provincials implicitly contrasted patriotic and benevolent kings with the corrupt and profit-seeking men who served them.[51]

The rise of the assembly better reflected a stage in the phenomenon that the historian Edmund Morgan has called the "invention of the people," or, more specifically, the idea of the sovereignty of the people. Morgan contends that the idea of popular sovereignty came not from the people but from their leaders, who developed the concept of popular rule in order to exercise it themselves as representatives. Provincial leaders also promoted the authority of the lower or democratic houses of the legislature in order to assert their authority over provincial affairs against the interference of imperial officials, so that the rise of the assembly was synonymous with the consolidation of authority by a provincial elite.[52]

Thus the concept underlying the rise of the assemblies was never truly democratic. Even the most powerful assemblies constituted only one branch in a mixed political system. Within any mixed system, it is the officers of government,

rather than the people they represent, who govern. In that sense, eighteenth-century ideas were not so far removed from those of the seventeenth-century Massachusetts minister John Cotton, who had asked the then-rhetorical question, "if the people be governors," then "who shall be governed?"[53]

On the surface, the rise of the assembly seemed compatible with the leading principles of British politics. The ascendancy of the lower houses of the colonial governments mirrored the rise of Parliament, and both apparently reflected the triumph of popular rule following the Glorious Revolution. But the analogy was again more a matter of practice than of law; it was never clear how secure the assemblies' authority was. Moreover, their rise created something of a paradox in the British system, since the charters from which their statutory authority derived had been granted not by Parliament but by the Crown. In that sense, the rise of the assemblies and of the royally chartered governments they represented and the ascendancy of Parliament were implicitly opposed. Of course, hardly anyone noticed the discrepancy before mid-century, and British policy during that period has been characterized by the term "salutary neglect." After 1760, however, the contest between Parliament and the assemblies would be a major factor in bringing on the Revolution.

By the middle years of the eighteenth century, two views of the colonial governments emerged in the British world. From the British point of view, the colonial governments represented local and inferior political units fully subordinate to a British Parliament under a British constitution that represented the source of British liberties everywhere. Yet exactly what the British constitution said about the colonial governments was less clear. Jack P. Greene has recently pointed out that tradition was at least as important as statutory law in that constitution, and for many years the colonial governments did not really behave as inferior units at all. Rather, the assemblies and the charters were the principal bastions of colonial liberty, which was experienced as something very much like home rule for the provinces. In that sense, political liberty to American provincials implied the general system of British liberties restricted by only a minimal exertion of metropolitan power.[54]

By that time, the power of the assemblies in fact, if not in theory, was almost universally acknowledged. Not everyone considered such power to be a good thing. Many royal governors and other imperial officers complained repeatedly about the assemblies' excessive powers, which seemed to them a direct violation of the principle of balance that comprised "the strength and beauty of the British Constitution," in the words of South Carolina's James Glen. Instead, "all the Weights that should trim and poise it [were] by different Laws thrown into the Scale of the People." The people hurt themselves by weakening the power of the Crown, in Glen's view, as "every deviation from the Constitution" represented a threat to stability, order, and virtue.[55]

## Provincial Imperialists

Glen and a few of his fellow governors were one group that did challenge the growing initiatives of the assemblies, assisted by other imperial officials who found their administrative tasks in the colonies difficult to accomplish in the face of resistance from intractable lower houses. During the middle third of the eighteenth century, those officials began to send a steady stream of letters to London complaining of the virtual independence of the assemblies and seeking redress from Britain. After 1748, when the Earl of Halifax became president of the Board of Trade, those complaints began to produce an extensive rethinking of the relationship between the provinces and the empire, reflected especially in the many and varied plans for restructuring the method of governing the colonies that were submitted to the board at about that time.[56]

It is tempting to think of all of those governors and other imperial officials simply as outsiders, representing a foreign interest in America, which was how the colonial assemblies often portrayed

them. Such a portrayal is a bit misleading. A number of those most active in colonial affairs had long-term relationships with the colonies and lived in one or several of them for many years. James Abercromby for instance, one of those most active in the movement to restructure the imperial relationship, resided in South Carolina from 1731 to 1744 and served for many years thereafter as colonial agent in London for North Carolina and Virginia. Although he was not born in the colonies, it would be inaccurate to portray him as simply an outsider. Other leading officials involved in the effort to restructure that relationship, such as New York's Archibald Kennedy, were permanent residents of America.

Many of those men had provincial origins themselves. Several of the most prominent governors who led the call for curbing the power of the assemblies were Scots, including James Glen of South Carolina and Robert Dinwiddie of Virginia. Others, such as Arthur Dobbs of North Carolina and Henry Ellis of Georgia, were Ulster men. Other imperial officials in America prominent in that effort included the Scots Henry McCulloh, John Rutherfurd, James Abercromby, Archibald Kennedy, and James Alexander, along with the Ulster native William Knox.

Those men have often been misunderstood. They have been castigated with names such as "Tory-Imperialist"; nearly all have been described as partisans of imperial interests who had no respect for colonial needs.[57] To the extent that they considered colonial government to be out of balance, with excessive and essentially unchecked powers residing in the local assemblies, such views are correct. Yet for many among them, their principal goal was less to extend metropolitan control over provincial affairs than to reconstruct imperial relations in a manner that would solidify imperial ties on the basis of extended commercial ties and mutual advantage. In that sense, their ideas were compatible with decidedly provincial views of the political economy of empire.

The reality of their situations was a good deal more complicated than might be supposed.

Those men were well connected with many of the most prominent leaders of colonial society, some of whom would establish reputations as defenders of American liberties, including Benjamin Franklin and William Livingston. The plans they offered reflected their positions as members of provincial elites. As men of the Enlightenment, they shared some basic Enlightenment values, such as harmony and balance, liberty, and the moderating and civilizing influence of commercial ties.[58]

One of the most persistent of those officials was Henry McCulloh, who came to North Carolina in 1741 attached to a fellow Scot and associate, Governor Gabriel Johnstone, and speculated in land at the same time that he participated in politics and revenue collections. Around 1750, McCulloh began to write about imperial affairs. In a series of pamphlets and tracts appearing over the next several years, McCulloh advocated the establishment of a firm alliance with the northern Indians to repel the threat of French invasion and a reconstruction of provincial governments, including restraints on the assemblies, a firmer structure for intercolonial relations, and ominously, a stamp tax to pay the increased costs of administration. Yet McCulloh blamed the inefficiency of colonial government not on provincials but rather on lax and greedy officials, and the union he proposed for the colonies would have created a powerful provincial assembly of a sort that imperial officials in London would later reject. He suggested that any new measures be mild enough that colonials "should not have too great a temptation to resist." Even the stamp tax he proposed was designed to leave provincial matters in provincial hands; McCulloh suggested that revenues be directed into a dedicated fund that would be reserved for the colonies' exclusive use. He would oppose the stamp tax that the British Parliament finally passed in 1765.[59]

Another important figure was James Abercromby, sometime rival of McCulloh's, also a Scotsman and a longtime colonial agent and revenue official for several southern colonies. In 1752, Abercromby drafted a new plan for the regulation of the colonies, entitled "An Examination of the Acts of Parliament Relative to the Trade and the Government of our American Colonies." That proposal placed considerably more blame on the colonists than did McCulloh for the intractability of their governments, and Abercromby rejected most colonial claims to political rights within the empire. Nonetheless, he rejected wholesale changes in the powers colonials exercised, whether they held a right to them or not, unless they were absolutely necessary "to make them a part Depending on the Whole, for the good of the whole." He argued instead for aligning imperial relations with the growing "wealth and strength" of the colonies, a phrase he used three times.[60]

In the year 1754, amid threats of a new war with France originating from border conflicts along the western frontiers of British America, a congress of delegates, which included some of the most prominent leaders in the British colonies, met at Albany for the purpose of securing the Iroquois alliance and coordinating their defensive efforts. Together, the men sketched a plan for political union based upon a model suggested by Benjamin Franklin for aiding in their administration, diplomacy, and defense.

Such prominent provincial leaders as Benjamin Franklin, Archibald Kennedy, and James Alexander actively promoted the plan, but it stood little chance. It was ignored by Parliament, which was wary of vesting any new powers in what would be a purely provincial body. The plan proved equally unpopular in the colonial legislatures, where the new framework appeared a threat to the continuing autonomy of their provincial governments.[61] Franklin later contended that the plan had represented the best chance at establishing a permanent framework for colonial participation in the empire, but it was not to be. Its existence suggested considerable common ground among the most cosmopolitan of provincial and imperial elites. For those groups, liberty in the empire signified something like the opportunity for provincial citizens to prosper in a firm but balanced imperial union.

To a considerable degree, both the officials' call for imperial integration and the colonial resistance their plans engendered were traceable to a growing sense of provincial competence and confidence. That growth, which was as obvious to imperial officials as it was to colonials, led to fears that the colonies were on a road to breaking away from Britain; that was in part the implication of James Abercromby's repeated remarks on the colonies' growing "wealth and strength." Such suspicion also accounted for the tone of alarm that characterized the reports of such officials as James Glen that colonial legislatures were exercising virtual independence. The irony is that it was almost always British officials who envisioned the colonies breaking away; provincials uniformly discounted such predictions.[62]

Provincial Americans were no less aware of the developments on which such predictions were based. By mid-century, few Americans doubted that the colonial population and its trade were likely to grow faster than Britain's. Similarly, few doubted the reason: it was attributed to the relatively unconstrained colonial economy and to the air of liberty one found there, which impelled eager emigrants to seek out homes there. As New York's Archibald Kennedy observed, "liberty and encouragement" were the cornerstones of colonial prosperity.[63]

Two different visions of provincial liberty thus underlay those provincial reactions to the Albany Plan. Those who supported it shared a basic Enlightened vision of ordered liberty, of liberty guaranteed by harmony and moderation, by balanced government, and by the civilizing influences of expanded commercial ties. Its opponents evidenced a different vision of liberty, one rooted in local autonomy, with local leadership as the principal bulwark against grasping power and the potential for distant tyranny. Both versions were amply represented in provincial culture. Both were substantially rooted in provincial claims to the rights of

citizenship and to the pursuit of provincial interests with the same legitimacy as those promoted from the metropolis.

A third set of ideas about liberty was also beginning to emerge in the provincial world in the eighteenth century, one that was increasingly populist in tone and might be called, for lack of a better term, a democratic form of liberty. That variety found few adherents among the provincial elite. Instead, its principal proponents were found among a diverse group that included some small farmers in the western sections of several colonies who resented eastern leadership, as in the case of the "Regulator" movements against the eastern monopolization of political power that appeared in the Carolinas; radical evangelicals who moved beyond the New Side wing of the established churches into Separate, Baptist, and other dissenting communions while attacking the claims to knowledge and authority of the settled clergy; urban tradesmen who viewed the claims of the right to leadership maintained by their social betters as nothing more than self-interest; and the merchant seamen of the leading port towns. It was evident, in varying measures, in the antiauthoritarian sentiment that was emerging in some—though not all—areas of the culture of the backcountry. Those varied groups shared no clear set of beliefs but some common sentiments. Those sentiments were diversely expressed, but in their different ways, each of those groups came to believe that the way to protect their liberties was to remove them from the hands of traditional leadership into more common hands. They shared with their fellow provincials the insistence on the principle of equity in political arrangements and—for some—a belief in locality as the remedy for oppression.[64]

Sentiments of that sort found their most overt political expression in the artisanal communities in the cities of New York, Philadelphia, and Boston and often resembled the emerging republican ideas that appeared among the tradesmen of such British cities as London and Glasgow. As was the case with radical religious ideas, they were somewhat less visible in the more restricted urban sector of provincial America than in its larger British equivalent. Moreover, many of the recorded expressions we have of antielite sentiment emanated from other elites, such as the populist appeals of David Lloyd and William Keith in Pennsylvania; Lloyd, in fact, was attacked by James Logan for his constant raising of the "rattle of rights and privileges" against the proprietary. But in seeking to undermine their opponents' power, those men appealed to artisans and other common sorts in a language of equality; William Keith's "Leather-Apron" club was one such example. The goal of those men was invariably not to unleash the populace but to use popular support to bolster their own power. Yet popular participation, once started, sometimes developed its own momentum.[65]

So it was with the political movement started by the religious awakening. Despite their occasional antiestablishment rhetoric, most evangelical leaders were not especially concerned with changing the political order; their concerns were religious, not political. Yet the separate churches and institutions that resulted, and the principles of equality and fellowship they embodied, helped spur political opposition as well. There was a clear connection, for example, between New Light radicalism and political opposition in frontier Connecticut and between the passionate call to action that appeared in the oratory of Patrick Henry and the evangelical preaching that emerged in the western Virginia counties in which he was raised. Nor is it simply coincidence that a politician such as Herman Husband, who appeared in such varied political agitations as the Carolina Regulation and later Pennsylvania's Whiskey Rebellion was raised in the culture of the Awakening in its most radical forms.[66]

In 1765, in response to the passage of the Stamp Act, those several varieties of liberty substantially came together in opposition to a tax that threatened the authority of the provincial legislatures, the principle of equity in the empire, and the local autonomy of rural farming communities. Even such imperial spokesmen as Henry McCulloh and Thomas

Hutchinson expressed reservations about the act. Eventually provincials holding those differing positions divided over the relationship of empire and liberty. Whereas defenders of provincial authority generally supported American independence, those who took an imperial perspective ended up on both sides of the issue, often after considerable personal conflict. In the aftermath of the Revolution, Americans would divide yet again when confronted with the need to develop a workable central authority under a new and stronger constitution.[67]

## Notes

1. Chauncy, *The Counsel of Two Confederate Kings to Set the Son of Tabeal on the Throne, Represented As Evil* (Boston, 1746), 43.

2. Jonathan Edwards to "a Correspondent in Scotland," 10 November 1745, in *Jonathan Edwards' Apocalyptic Writings* (New Haven: Yale University Press, 1977), 444–60.

3. On the related but changing meanings of liberty and slavery, see the works of David B. Davis, especially *The Problem of Slavery in Western Culture* (Ithaca, N.Y.: Cornell University Press, 1966).

4. Excellent discussion of the varied meanings of liberty can be found in Michael Kammen, *Spheres of Liberty: Changing Perceptions of Liberty in American Culture* (Madison: University of Wisconsin Press, 1986), and David Hackett Fischer, *Albion's Seed: Four British Folkways in America* (New York: Oxford University Press, 1989).

5. J. C. D. Clark, *English Society, 1688–1832* (New York: Cambridge University Press, 1985), and Paul Kleber Monod, *Jacobitism and the English People, 1688–1788* (New York: Cambridge University Press, 1989).

6. Pauline Maier, "John Wilkes and American Disillusionment with Britain," *WMQ*, 3d ser., 20 (1963): 373–95; George Rude, *Wilkes and Liberty* (New York: Oxford University Press, 1962).

7. For a general discussion of the ideology of liberty in eighteenth-century Britain, see H. T. Dickinson, *Liberty and Property: Political Ideology in Eighteenth-Century Britain* (London: Holmes and Meier, 1977).

8. The best treatment of the connection between slave labor and concepts of American liberty is

Edmund S. Morgan, *American Slavery, American Freedom: The Ordeal of Colonial Virginia* (New York: Norton, 1975).

9. *The Independent Reflector, or Weekly Essays on Sundry Important Subjects More Particularly Adapted to the Province of New-York*, ed. Milton M. Klein (Cambridge, Mass.: Harvard University Press, 1963), 55–60.

10. Many of Trenchard and Gordon's essays have been republished in *The English Libertarian Heritage*, ed. David L. Jacobson (1965; reprint, San Francisco: Fox and Wilkes, 1994).

11. The role of Trenchard and Gordon has been highlighted in such works as Caroline Robbins, *The Eighteenth-Century Commonwealthman: Studies in the Transmission, Development and Circumstance of English Liberal Thought from the Restoration of Charles II Until the War with the Thirteen Colonies* (Cambridge, Mass.: Harvard University Press, 1959); Bernard Bailyn, *The Ideological Origins of the American Revolution* (Cambridge, Mass.: Harvard University Press, 1967); and J. G. A. Pocock, *The Machiavellian Moment: Florentine Political Thought and the Atlantic Republican Tradition* (Princeton, N.J.: Princeton University Press, 1975), among many others.

12. Pocock, *Machiavellian Moment.*

13. *Independent Reflector,* 58.

14. *English Libertarian Heritage,* 86.

15. *Independent Reflector,* 444.

16. Ruth H. Bloch, "The Gendered Meanings of Virtue in Revolutionary America," *Signs: Journal of Women in Culture and Society* 13 (1987): 37–58.

17. *Independent Reflector,* 143–50.

18. Ibid., 143. See also Daniel W. Howe, "The Political Psychology of *The Federalist,*" *WMQ,* 3d ser., 44 (1987): 485–509.

19. *Independent Reflector,* 195.

20. See especially Isaac Kramnick, *Bolingbroke and His Circle: The Politics of Nostalgia in the Age of Walpole* (Cambridge, Mass.: Harvard University Press, 1968), and "James Burgh and 'Opposition' Ideology in England and America," in *Republicanism and Bourgeois Radicalism: Political Ideology in Late Eighteenth-Century England and America* (Ithaca, N.Y.: Cornell University Press, 1990), 200–69.

The term *Whig* arose originally in seventeenth-century Scotland referring to the opponents of the Episcopal regime of the Stuarts. By the eighteenth century, Whiggery had come to stand for all supporters of the privileges of Parliament and opponents of the royal prerogative. They ranged from court Whigs identified with the powerful ruling regime under the government headed by the longtime "Prime Minister" Sir Robert Walpole to their critics, the opposition or "radical" Whigs, such as Trenchard and Gordon.

21. Richard L. Bushman, *King and People in Provincial Massachusetts* (Chapel Hill: University of North Carolina Press, 1985), 14–17.

22. *Independent Reflector,* 74–75.

23. Gary B. Nash, *The Urban Crucible: Social Change, Political Consciousness, and the Origins of the American Revolution* (Cambridge, Mass.: Harvard University Press, 1979), 140 ff.; Patricia U. Bonomi, *A Factious People: Politics and Society in Colonial New York* (New York: Columbia University Press, 1971); John M. Murrin, "English Rights as Ethnic Aggression: The English Conquest, the Charter of Liberties of 1683, and Leisler's Rebellion in New York," in *Authority and Resistance in Early New York.* ed. William Pencak and Conrad Edick Wright (New York: New-York Historical Society, 1988), 56–94.

24. See especially Michael Warner, *The Letters of the Republic: Publication and the Public Sphere in Eighteenth-Century America* (Cambridge, Mass.: Harvard University Press, 1990), 49 ff.; [Trenchard and Gordon], "Of Freedom of Speech: That the Same Is Inseparable from Publick Liberty," in *English Libertarian Heritage,* 38–44.

25. *Independent Reflector,* 78–79.

26. Ibid., 183.

27. Ibid., 315.

28. *English Libertarian Heritage,* 133–34.

29. John J. McCusker and Russell R. Menard, *The Economy of British America, 1607–1789* (Chapel Hill: University of North Carolina Press, 1985), chap. 10. Provincial population estimates are discussed below.

30. Archibald Kennedy, *Observations on the Importance of the Northern Colonies under Proper Regulations* (New York, 1750), 12.

31. J. E. Crowley, *This Sheba, Self: The Conceptualization of Economic Life in Eighteenth-Century America* (Baltimore: Johns Hopkins University Press, 1974); J. G. A. Pocock, "Virtue and Commerce in the Eighteenth Century,"

*Journal of Interdisciplinary History* 3 (1972): 119–34; see also his *Virtue, Commerce, and History: Essays on Political Thought and History, Chiefly in the Eighteenth Century* (New York: Cambridge University Press, 1985).

32. *The Papers of Benjamin Franklin*, ed. Leonard W. Labaree, Whitfield J. Bell Jr., et al. (New Haven: Yale University Press, 1959– …), vol. 4, 227–34. See Drew McCoy "Benjamin Franklin's Vision of a Republican Political Economy for America," *WMQ*, 3d ser., 35 (1978): 605–28.

33. Kennedy, *Observations on the Importance of the Northern Colonies*, 3–4.

34. Robert Wallace, *A Dissertation on the Numbers of Mankind in Ancient and Modern Times* (1753; reprint, New York: A. M. Kelley, 1969); David Hume, "Of the Populousness of Ancient Nations," in *David Hume: Writings on Economics*, ed. Eugene Rotwein (Madison: University of Wisconsin Press, 1970), 108–83; and Janet Ann Riesman, "Origins of American Political Economy," (Ph.D. diss., Brown University, 1983), chap. 2. On the Philosophical Society of Edinburgh, see the first two articles in a trio of papers by Roger L. Emerson in *British Journal for the History of Science* 12 (1979): 154–91; 14 (1981): 133–76.

35. Istvan Hont, "The 'Rich Country-Poor Country' Debate in Scottish Classical Political Economy," in *Wealth and Virtue: The Shaping of Political Economy in the Scottish Enlightenment*, ed. Istvan Hont and Michael Ignatieff (New York: Cambridge University Press, 1983), 271–315.

36. Examples of the latter include Benjamin Franklin, *The Interest of Great Britain Considered. With Regard to Her Colonies, and the Acquisitions of Canada and Guadaloupe* (London, 1760), in *Papers of Benjamin Franklin*, vol. 9, 53–8; David Loch, *Essay on the Trade, Commerce, and Manufactures of Scotland* (Edinburgh, 1775).

37. Loch, *Essay on the Trade of Scotland:* Franklin, *Interest of Great Britain Considered.*

38. Riesman, "Origins of American Political Economy," chap. 4; John L. Brooke, *The Heart of the Commonwealth: Society and Political Culture in Worcester County, Massachusetts, 1713–1861* (New York: Cambridge University Press, 1989), 55–65; Richard L. Bushman, *From Puritan to Yankee: Character and the Social Order in Connecticut, 1690–1765* (Cambridge, Mass.: Harvard University Press, 1967), 115–34.

39. The parallel between the land bank and revival discussions has been noted in a number of places, especially Brooke, *The Heart of the Commonwealth,* chaps. 2–3. Also see Rosalind Remer, "Old Lights and New Money: A Note on Religion, Economics, and the Social Order in 1740 Boston," *WMQ*, 3d ser., 47 (1990): 566–73; Mark Hessler, "Providence Lost: A Study of Epistemology and Religious Culture among New England Puritans, 1630–1730," (Ph.D. diss., State University of New York at Stony Brook, 1992); and Crowley, *This Sheba, Self.*

40. Nicholas Phillipson, "Adam Smith as Civic Moralist," in *Wealth and Virtue*, ed. Hont and Ignatieff, 179–202; Jean-Christophe Agnew, *Worlds Apart: The Market and the Theater in Anglo-American Thought, 1550–1750* (New York: Cambridge University Press, 1986).

41. *Independent Reflector,* 183; McCoy, "Benjamin Franklin's Vision of a Republican Political Economy."

42. Alison Gilbert Olson, *Making the Empire Work: London and American Interest Groups, 1690–1790* (Cambridge, Mass.: Harvard University Press, 1992).

43. Quoted in T. H. Breen, *The Character of the Good Ruler: A Study of Puritan Political Ideas in New England, 1630–1730* (New Haven: Yale University Press, 1970), 145.

44. Ibid., 144.

45. Jack P. Greene, *Peripheries and Center: Constitutional Development in the Extended Polities of the British Empire and the United States, 1607–1788* (Athens: University of Georgia Press, 1986).

46. Jack P. Greene, *The Quest for Power: The Lower Houses of Assembly in the Southern Royal Colonies, 1689–1776* (Chapel Hill: University of North Carolina Press, 1963).

47. Richard Bushman, *King and People in Provincial Massachusetts* (Chapel Hill: University of North Carolina Press, 1985).

48. Bernard Bailyn, *The Origins of American Politics* (New York: Alfred A. Knopf, 1967).

49. *An Essay upon the Government of the English Plantations on the Continent of America* (1701), quoted in Bushman, *King and People,* 99.

50. Charles S. Sydnor, *Gentleman Freeholders: Political Practices in Washington's Virginia* (Chapel Hill: University of North Carolina Press, 1952), is the classic survey.

51. Bushman, *King and People*, 91–99.

52. Edmund S. Morgan, *Inventing the People: The Rise of Popular Sovereignty in England and America* (New York: Norton, 1988).

53. "Copy of a Letter from Mr. Cotton to Lord Say and Seal," quoted in E. Brooks Holifield, *The Era of Persuasion: American Thought and Culture, 1521–1680* (Boston: Twayne Publishers, 1989), 140.

54. Greene, *Peripheries and Center.*

55. James Glen to Board of Trade, 10 October 1748, in *Great Britain and the American Colonies, 1606–1763*, ed. Jack P. Greene (Columbia: University of South Carolina Press, 1970), 261–67.

56. See especially Jack P. Greene, "'A Posture of Hostility': A Reconsideration of Some Aspects of the Origins of the American Revolution," *American Antiquarian Society Proceedings* 87 (1977): 27–68.

57. Max Savelle, *Seeds of Liberty: The Genesis of the American Mind* (New York: Alfred A. Knopf, 1948), 292–305.

58. Ned C. Landsman, "The Legacy of the British Union for the North American Colonies: Provincial Elites and the Problem of Imperial Union," in *A Union for Empire: Political Thought and the British Union of 1707*, ed. John Robertson (Cambridge: Cambridge University Press, 1995), 297–317.

59. Henry McCulloh, *A Miscellaneous Essay Concerning the Courses Pursued by Great Britain in the Affairs of the Colonies* (London, 1755), esp. 85–86.

60. *Magna Charta For America: James Abercromby's An Examination of the Acts of Parliament Relative to the Trade and the Government of our American Colonies* (1752), ed. Jack P. Greene, Charles F. Mullett, and Edward C. Papenfuse Jr. (Philadelphia: American Philosophical Society, 1986), 158, 162, passim.

61. Alison Gilbert Olson, "The British Government and Colonial Union: 1754," *WMQ*, 3d ser., 17 (1960): 22–34.

62. J. M. Bumsted, "'Things in the Womb of Time': Ideas of American Independence, 1633 to 1763," *WMQ*, 3d ser., 31 (1974): 533–564; John Murrin, "A Roof without Walls: The Dilemma of American National Identity," in *Beyond Confederation: Origins of the Constitution and American National Identity*, ed. Richard Beeman, Stephen Botein, and Edward C. Carter II (Chapel Hill: University of North Carolina Press, 1987), 333–48.

63. Kennedy, *Observations on the Importance of the Northern Colonies*, 12.

64. Nash, *Urban Crucible;* Marcus Rediker, *Between the Devil and the Deep Blue Sea: Merchant Seamen, Pirates, and the Anglo-American Maritime World, 1700–1750* (New York: Cambridge University Press, 1987); David S. Lovejoy, *Religious Enthusiasm in the New World: Heresy to Revolution* (Cambridge, Mass.: Harvard University Press, 1985); Rhys Isaac, "Evangelical Revolt: The Nature of the Baptists' Challenge to the Traditional Order in Virginia, 1765–1775," *WMQ* 31 (1974): 345–68; Marvin L Michael Kay, "The North Carolina Regulation, 1766–1776: A Class Conflict," in *The American Revolution: Explorations in the History of American Radicalism,* ed. Alfred F. Young (Dekalb, Ill.: University of Northern Illinois Press, 1976), 71–123. For a markedly exaggerated but still informative analysis of backcountry culture, see Fischer, *Albion's Seed.* For a more balanced summary based on an extensive and growing literature, see Gregory H. Nobles, "Breaking into the Backcountry: New Approaches to the Early American Frontier," *WMQ*, 3d ser., 46 (1989): 641–70.

65. Gary B. Nash, *Quakers and Politics: Pennsylvania, 1681–1726* (Princeton: Princeton University Press, 1968); Nash, *Urban Crucible,* 93–101, 148–66.

66. Patricia Bonomi, *Under the Cope of Heaven;* Rhys Isaac, "Preachers and Patriots: Popular Culture and the Revolution in Virginia," in *The American Revolution: Explorations in the History of American Radicalism,* 125–56; Herman Husband, *Some Remarks on Religion, with the Author's Experience in Pursuit Thereof* (Philadelphia, 1761), excerpted in *The Great Awakening: Documents Illustrating the Crisis and Its Consequences,* ed. Alan Heimert and Perry Miller (New York: Bobbs-Merrill, 1967), 636–54.

67. Thomas P. Slaughter, "The Tax Man Cometh: Ideological Opposition to Internal Taxes, 1760–1790," *WMQ*, 3d ser., 41 (1984): 566–91; Landsman, "Legacy of the British Union."

# 2
# THE NATION ABROAD
*The Atlantic Debate over Colonial Taxation*

## Eliga H. Gould

## Introduction

With hindsight, the British decision to levy taxes on the American colonies following the Seven Years' War in 1763 appears disastrous. The policy led to widespread resistance in the colonies that ultimately blossomed into revolution and American political independence. Yet, one task of the historian is to suspend hindsight in order to bring understanding to the choices facing contemporaries of any historical moment. Eliga H. Gould accomplishes this balance masterfully in the following essay by exploring the debate over taxation in the British Atlantic in the aftermath of Britain's momentous victory over France in the war. He shows that there was widespread support within Britain's political classes for leaving troops stationed in areas of North America formerly held by the French. In 1763, Pontiac's Rebellion, an Indian uprising against British authority in western lands, only reinforced the perceived need for troops. There was equal consensus in Britain that the colonies should share in the cost of their own defense. Therefore, the primary question raised during the final passage of the Stamp Act in 1765 was not whether the tax was constitutional, but why Parliament had not passed similar legislation much earlier.

For their part, American colonists participated fully in the Atlantic debate over taxation. They urged British statesmen to preserve the status quo in which Parliament left colonial assemblies in charge of taxes on anything other than overseas commerce. Colonists never accepted Parliament's authority to tax internally (within the colonies), which they famously condemned as "taxation without representation." Still, Gould illustrates that there was much goodwill on both sides – at least initially. The colonies did not reject their obligation to contribute to the empire's coffers, but insisted that they already provided more than enough through external trade and revenue from the Navigation Acts. Similarly, the British argument that the colonists were "virtually" represented in Parliament was not born of malice; it reflected reality in England, where a large percentage of inhabitants were not represented directly by a single member of Parliament. Finally, the British decision to tax the colonists was not so much a punishment as it was a sign of respect that the colonies had matured into equal, or near equal, members of the British Empire. The debate over taxes demonstrated that when colonists pleaded for "the rights of Englishmen," they had to be careful what they asked for.

- Gould's essay forces us to reconsider old assumptions about the American Revolution. For instance, in the realm of taxation, at least, it seems that the true radicals were not the American colonists, as is commonly assumed, but British policy-makers. Which side did more to alter the traditional and highly successful imperial relationship between Britain and America that existed before 1763?
- Consider Gould's essay in relation to the previous essay by Ned C. Landsman. Did American reactions to British policy proposals after the Seven Years' War prove or disprove their British identity and patriotism?
- Were there viable policy alternatives that could have allowed Britain and the American colonies to escape the imperial crisis over taxation and sovereignty?

Britain's prospects had never seemed brighter than they did in 1763. In every quarter of the globe, France's ambitions were in ruins while the British had made substantial acquisitions in Africa, India, the Caribbean, and—most importantly of all—North America, where the crown had gained control over French Canada, Spanish Florida, and the immense wilderness bounded by the Appalachian Mountains and the Mississippi River. As William Pitt boasted in the House of Commons, Britain "had over-run more world" in three years than the Romans had "conquered in a century." Thomas Turner was only slightly more circumspect, noting in his diary the "pleasure" that it gave "every true Briton to see with what success it pleases Almighty God to bless His Majesty's arms with, they having success at this time in Europe, Asia, Africa and America." Oliver Goldsmith even claimed that France was now "sensible of one truth, which, however seemingly inconsistent, is founded on reason and experience; we mean, that Great Britain is stronger, fighting by herself and for herself, than if half Europe were her allies." "It is enough to read the Treaty of Paris," concluded the comte de Vergennes, "to realize the ascendancy which England has acquired over France and to judge how much that arrogant nation savours the pleasure of having humiliated us."[1]

For all the public elation over Britain's triumph, however, the restoration of peace also brought with it a host of new expectations and anxieties. According to many observers (including, it was rumored, some of the new king's closest advisers) the most pressing challenge confronting the nation in 1763 was to disengage from the Continent in the manner envisioned by patriots during the first half of the eighteenth century, using the strategic advantages gained during the Seven Years' War. Although no one denied the importance of remaining on good terms with the other states of Europe, more than a few commentators hoped Britain's rulers would finally make the affairs of the empire their primary concern and, in so

doing, adopt "a plan of policy, which is neither Austrian, Prussian, nor even Hanoverian, but English." The fact that the British possessed in George III a young and vigorous monarch who shared none of his predecessors' affection for Hanover only heightened these patriotic expectations. Indeed, the king himself appeared to promise as much when he brashly claimed in his first speech to Parliament in 1760 "to glory in the name of Briton." As an indication of this concern for Britain's welfare, the king's first two prime ministers—Lord Bute and George Grenville—soon began formulating measures like the Sugar Act (1764), the Currency Act (1764), and the American Mutiny Act (1765), all of which were meant to remedy decades of neglect by enhancing Whitehall's administrative efficiency on the far shores of the Atlantic. Although the day might come when Britain would once again be called to defend the liberties of Europe, the new king's subjects could hope that a proper attention to imperial affairs would free them to fulfill their obligations, not through endless negotiations and useless alliances on the Continent, but as the metropolitan head of a self-sufficient maritime empire.[2]

If the British were to realize these new goals, though, one issue demanded the government's immediate attention: how to defray the costs of defending an empire that was no longer confined to colonies governed by Protestant settlers from Britain and Ireland but that now included a Catholic majority in Quebec, a large indigenous population in the lands west of the Appalachians, and the Indian province of Bengal. Indeed, within a month of the war's end, the government announced that it would expand the army in order to create an unprecedented peacetime establishment of some ten thousand regulars in North America. Although few people doubted that the British ought to bear most of this new burden, a growing number of observers worried that the military and naval expenditures necessary to secure their overseas dominions would eventually bankrupt the Treasury without some contribution from the other members

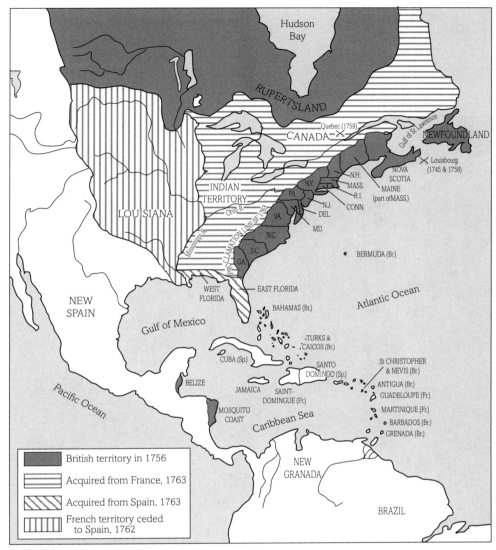

**Figure 2.1** British North America, 1763

of the empire, particularly the older English-speaking colonies in the West Indies and on the North American seaboard. With the grand purpose of raising such a revenue, the ministry of George Grenville enacted the Stamp Act in 1765, committing the British to a fateful series of attempts to tax the colonies in Parliament without their explicit consent. As we shall see, the public support in Britain for Grenville's reform, as well as for the Townshend Revenue Act (1767), reflected a widespread perception that the neglect of colonial affairs under the first two Hanoverian monarchs had been anything but salutary and that the victories of the Seven Years' War had brought their maritime empire to a critical juncture that no true patriot could afford to leave unresolved.[3]

As both Grenville and his supporters were well aware, raising a colonial revenue by parliamentary appropriation represented a significant innovation. Although Parliament had used port duties to regulate the colonies' external trade since the first Navigation Act (1652), metropolitan responsibility for most areas of provincial administration—including the management of colonial defense—still resided, as it had since the seventeenth century, in the relatively powerless hands of the king, his privy councillors, and the governors of the various colonies in America. An unintended effect of this dependence on the royal prerogative was to give colonial legislatures extraordinary control over matters like raising troops and levying taxes. Yet few people doubted that it was within Parliament's authority to change this relationship, nor were there many metropolitan observers, least of all among Grenville's colleagues at Westminster, who questioned the wisdom of doing so in order "to reconcile the regulation of commerce with an increase of revenue." As Grenville assured the House of Commons on presenting his initial proposal in March of 1764, "We have expended much in America. Let us now avail ourselves of the fruits of that expence."[4]

There were several reasons why the metropolitan public found Grenville's request so "unexceptional"—as "Anti-Sejanus" described the Stamp Act to readers of the *London Chronicle* toward the end of 1765. The first was the extent of Britain's conquests in North America and the perception that preserving the strategic gains of the Seven Years' War would require a larger naval and military establishment than the crown had maintained before the war. Although the army's overall size occasioned some comment during the early 1760s, a broad section of the British public, within Parliament as well as without, appeared to accept without question the wisdom of using ten thousand regulars to defend the lands seized from France and Spain.[5] As Thomas Whately, Grenville's treasury secretary and chief political confidant, explained in his defense of the government's military policy, "the Addition of an immense Territory in *North America,* and a very valuable one in the *West Indies"* had expanded the army "a little beyond former Peace Establishments," but he was sure that the nation had "all the reason in the World to hope the burthen will be well compensated both in Profit and Security, and that it will grow lighter

every Day." In the words of another pamphlet, the "present army" was not only "suitable to our situation in Europe" but was "likely to prevent any insults, and to maintain an honourable and advantageous peace." As an indication of the prevalence of such views, the most serious criticism of the proposed establishment came from William Pitt, now in opposition, who worried, not that "the American force" was too numerous, but that it was "hardly sufficient for so large an extent of country."[6]

These attitudes had a good deal to do with the expectation that placing troops in North America would bring stability to the vast frontier beyond the borders of the older American colonies, including Quebec, Nova Scotia, East and West Florida, and—most significantly of all—the Indian lands of the trans-Appalachian interior, from which new settlers were excluded by the Proclamation of 1763. In keeping with contemporary European attitudes, the British tended to think of the territory to the west of the Proclamation Line as *terra nullius*—empty space, inhabited by Indians, French trappers, and British traders, none of whom had much appreciation for the finer points of English jurisprudence or the European law of nations. As both the Americans and their English apologists were quick to point out, the individual colonies had traditionally managed relations in this extensive marchland, negotiating treaties with neighboring Indians, raising temporary levies in time of war, and relying on local militias for their other defensive needs. According to the proponents of imperial reform, however, it was inconceivable that such policies could bring order to the unsettled territories for which the British government was now responsible. Not only did the European settlers in this region seem to be "the outcasts of all Nations, and the refuse of Mankind" (as the British commanding officer at Detroit, Major Henry Bassett, assured a correspondent in 1769) but most people also assumed that only a standing army could fulfill remote obligations like occupying conquered and potentially hostile territory, ensuring that relations with the Indians remained peaceful, and garrisoning distant points in the immense wilderness between the Gulf of Mexico and the Great Lakes.[7]

Furthermore, despite the legendary prowess of colonial Indian fighters like Major Robert Rogers and his dissolute Rangers, most commentators insisted that British regulars were essential for securing the older colonies and those parts of North America designated for immediate settlement. "I am of opinion," declared an anonymous pamphleteer in 1763, that "there ought to be a proper force kept in our new acquisitions, for the protection of the settlers." As Thomas Whately put the issue, the presence of regular troops was certain to "promote the Settlement of the new Colonies; for Planters will value Property there much higher, and be more sollicitous to acquire it, when they observe that … measures are taken for putting those Provinces in a State of Defence." For many people, the central part that British regulars played in the conquest of Canada only enhanced this impression, suggesting that personal military service was no more popular in the settled regions of North America than it was in England, Scotland, and Wales. Likewise, the colonists' largely ineffective response to Pontiac's Rebellion (1763–1766)—the Indian insurrection that took hundreds of lives in Pennsylvania, New York, and the Ohio Valley— provided additional evidence that the Americans were neither willing nor able to assume primary responsibility for their own defense. Although people were willing to concede the military prowess of Americans when they were placed under regular discipline, professional soldiers now seemed to be every bit as necessary for the security of Britain's European settlements as they were on the near shores of the Atlantic.[8]

Finally, according to many, having troops in America promised to discourage both France and Spain from avenging their recent losses. Although not all Britons accepted Pitt's belief that the recent peace amounted to little more than a "temporary truce," many assumed that they would eventually have to fight another colonial war with one or both of the Bourbon powers.[9] Indeed, in the years immediately following the Treaty of Paris (1763), both Versailles and Madrid gave ample evidence of their warlike intentions, with imperial reforms that included raising new colonial taxes, replacing militias with regular troops, and rebuilding their decimated navies. Although such activities were cause for concern, however, many Britons remained hopeful that the combination of their naval superiority in the West Indies and the army in North America would enable the government to treat the neighboring possessions of both rivals as hostages for their good behavior. "Should the Enemy presume, in future, to disturb us in our legal Possession in any Quarter of the Globe," observed one defender of the ministry's colonial policy, "with what Facility may we pour Vengeance upon them, when our *American* Continent [is] conveniently placed … to controul the Islands of the *West-Indies?*" "*The* definitive Treaty is now Public," wrote another pamphleteer; "the many new countries in *America,* added to what we formerly had, will in Time secure us from the future Insult of *France* or *Spain.*" Few people doubted that Britain's European rivals would eventually recover from their current "distress," as George Grenville reminded the House of Commons upon presenting his initial proposal for a colonial stamp tax. With adequate defensive arrangements in North America, however, the British might finally bring lasting security to their Atlantic empire.[10]

In other words, there were sound blue water arguments for keeping a standing army in North America, which explains why both George Grenville and his apologists were so quick to invoke the patriotic rhetoric of the early 1750s to justify their colonial policies. In the opening sections of *The Regulations Lately Made,* for example, Thomas Whately presented the government's activities in North America as a tangible sign that the corrupt Hanoverianism of earlier reigns had finally yielded to a virtuous attention to matters of national concern. Using the same logic, William

Knox, the Irishman whose five years as an official in Georgia apparently gave him authority in such matters, claimed that Britain's dominance in North America had "put it in our power to wage another war with equal efficacy, and with infinitely less expence." By improving the trade and security of the crown's overseas possessions, the Grenville administration could plausibly claim to have ended what yet another apologist termed *"the age of treaties and guarantees,"* and to be substituting "the resources of a strict oeconomy" for the Continental system of *"guarantees, subsidies, extras, quotas,* and *dedommagements"* that had characterized Whig foreign policy since the Glorious Revolution. Although Britain would undoubtedly remain active in the affairs of Europe, the defenders of Grenville's policies hoped that its rulers would do so without falling back on the discredited strategies of the last half-century.[11]

Given these claims, the lack of English opposition to the government's plan to help finance the costs of the American establishment with a colonial revenue is not surprising. As Soame Jenyns, then in his eleventh year at the Board of Trade, put the question during Parliament's final consideration of the Stamp Act: "Can there be a more proper Time to force [the colonies] to maintain an Army at their Expence, than when that Army is necessary for their own Protection, and we are utterly unable to support it?" Thomas Whately struck a similar note: the growing costs of imperial defense, the perpetual nature of the public debt, and the disproportionate burden that both placed on ordinary people in Britain made it inconceivable that the colonists who benefited from this system should not assume some of the expense. Although the few members with colonial experience—notably William Beckford and the cashiered army officer Isaac Barré—raised some telling objections, the parliamentary debates that preceded the measure's final approval revealed broad support for the course of reform charted by the king's ministers. By attempting to tax the American colonists, the British government was obviously departing from the policies of earlier reigns. But it was doing so on the assumption that the troops this revenue would help support were essential if the British were to secure the strategic advantages that they had just fought an expensive war to preserve.[12]

The second reason many of Grenville's supporters gave for taxing the Americans involved the supposition that a perpetual revenue of some sort, whether based on tariffs, the land tax, or excise duties, represented an unavoidable political obligation. This belief reflected the nature of the fiscal bargain that the English had struck with the crown during the second half of the seventeenth century and that half a century of Whig rule had turned into one of the main foundations of Parliament's metropolitan authority. As William Blackstone described it in the first volume of his *Commentaries on the Laws of England* (1765), the current "perfection" of the British constitution was in large measure a result of the Restoration Parliament's decision to provide Charles II with a more certain revenue in exchange for the abolition of personal military tenures. In keeping with his own Tory background, Blackstone lamented the way this system of finance had enhanced the crown's informal power, enabling every monarch since William III to borrow apparently limitless funds in order to wage "long wars" for goals that often had little to do with Britain's own maritime and imperial interests. Because servicing this debt required a constant revenue, however, the crown had come in turn to depend "on the liberality of parliament for it's necessary support and maintenance." In other words, the dynamics of deficit finance and perpetual taxation fostered a symbiotic relationship between king and Parliament, which created obligations that were in practice mandatory. With careful management, the government might reduce some of this fiscal burden, but the idea of "the total abolition of taxes" struck Blackstone as "the height of political absurdity."[13]

Whether Blackstone was thinking of the developing controversy over colonial taxation when he wrote these words is hard to say. To many Britons, though, the political imperatives that made permanent taxation compulsory in Britain created equally pressing obligations in America. In *The Regulations Lately Made,* for example, Whately insisted that the protection that the British state bestowed on American shipping throughout the world had given rise to fiscal obligations that were every bit as extensive. Two years later, Grenville's secretary Charles Lloyd based his own defense of the Stamp Act on the fact that "the Americans, under the shade and protection of Great-Britain, have made rapid advances in population, commerce and wealth." In fact, some people argued that Parliament was under no obligation to confine the proceeds from the Stamp Act to the defense of the American frontier but might just as readily use colonial funds to meet general costs like the naval estimates that benefited the British Empire as a whole. In the words of the former governor of Massachusetts Thomas Pownall:

> It cannot but be observed, that as there are in each respective colony services which regard the support of government, and the special exigencies of the state and community of that colony, so there are general services which regard the support of the crown, the rights and dominions of Great Britain in general:—That as lands, tenements, and other improved property within the colony, considered as the private especial property of that community, should be left to the legislatures of those colonies unincumbered by parliament … so revenues by imposts, excise, or a stamp duty, become the proper fund whereon the parliament of Great Britain may, with the utmost delicacy and regard to the colonies power of taxing themselves, raise those taxes which are raised for the general service of the crown.[14]

What made the Stamp Act seem so urgent, however, was the crushing debt that commentators were sure would otherwise descend on the British themselves. Indeed, according to many of the Stamp Act's defenders, the signs of economic hardship that followed the war's end—including labor unrest in London, massive resistance to the cider tax in the West Country, and grain riots across much of northern England—signaled that the common people of "Great Britain [were] sufficiently exhausted already." During the debates over the Stamp Act's repeal, Lord Lyttleton claimed that only an American revenue could alleviate the "dreadful" burdens on "the gentry and people of this Kingdom." Using the same logic, Whately spoke of the need to safeguard "the Consumption of the Poor," and William Knox was sure that the effects of failing to tax the colonies "already begin to shew themselves in the increased price of labour and the necessities of life." There were even writers for whom the attempt to tax the colonists demonstrated the government's paternal concern for the welfare of ordinary people. In the words of the fictitious John Ploughshare, it was "neither fair nor honest" for the colonists to refuse to make a modest contribution toward maintaining "that army which defends them against the savages." "If the Americans … would judge with candour," another British polemicist put the issue in 1769, "they would readily acknowledge that their brethren on this side the Atlantic lie under much more pressing burdens than themselves."[15]

In addition to such concerns, most apologists gave as a final reason for taxing the colonists their firm belief that Parliament's authority was every bit as extensive in the settled regions of North America and the West Indies as it was in England, Scotland, and Wales. The definitive statement came from Whately, who argued in *The Regulations Lately Made* that Parliament "virtually" represented the American colonists in the same manner that it represented those Britons—including all women and most men— who did not have a direct say in choosing its members. Indeed, because Parliament theoretically spoke for the nation as a whole,

Whately maintained, "all *British* Subjects are really in the same [condition]; none are actually, all are virtually represented in Parliament; for every Member of Parliament sits in the House, not as Representative of his own constituents, but as one of that august Assembly by which all the Commons of *Great Britain* are represented." Whately acknowledged that the existence of provincial legislatures meant that Parliament would "not often have occasion to exercise its Power over the Colonies." When it came to matters that concerned the welfare of the whole, however, Britain and America together constituted "one Nation" whose subjects all had to "be govern'd by the same supreme Authority."[16]

The most striking feature of this formulation was Whately's assumption that the colonists were subject to Parliament by virtue of a common nationality that owed nothing to the exercise of positive political rights. Although not everyone was quite so confident that Westminster could tax the colonies without allowing for some sort of consultation, the fact that active participation played so little role in the patriotism of ordinary men and women in Britain made the denial of such rights to America seem much less anomalous. During the debates that preceded the Stamp Act's eventual repeal, both the measure's supporters and many of its opponents pointed to the numerous occasions in English history when Parliament had taxed individuals and groups that did not have a direct vote for its members. Until the second half of the seventeenth century, Grenville's defenders claimed, the counties palatinate of Durham and Chester had both been taxed by Parliament without sending representatives to the House of Commons. In a similar manner, the succession of wars since the Glorious Revolution had turned the taxation of those without a direct vote into a permanent feature of Parliament's metropolitan sovereignty. "There were twelve millions of people in England and Ireland who were not represented," noted Lord Mansfield during the

debates over the Stamp Act, yet every one of them paid taxes levied in Parliament. William Knox made the same point with a series of rhetorical questions:

> When the tax was laid upon hops, did the people who were to pay the tax, viz. the hop-growers, consent to it, either by themselves or their distinct representatives? Did the people in the cyder counties, or their distinct representatives, consent to the tax upon cyder? Is the land-tax kept up at three shillings with the consent of all the land-owners in the kingdom, or that of all the knights of shires, their distinct representatives? What tax is it indeed to which those who pay it, or their distinct representatives, have all consented? … If this be the case, he must be a patriot indeed who pays any tax whatever, since he can so easily discharge himself from it, by only saying he does not choose to pay it.[17]

Even after reports of the massive riots that greeted the Stamp Act began to appear in the metropolitan press, British observers continued to use such arguments. During the winter of 1765–1766, pamphlets frequently compared the protests in America with the initial unpopularity of the excise in the outlying regions of England and Scotland.[18] Similarly, both Lord Mansfield and Fletcher Norton reminded their colleagues of the plebeian crowds that had defied Parliament over the English Militia Act less than a decade before; by taxing the colonists without their consent, Norton insisted, "we use North America as we use ourselves." Indeed, many members of Parliament acquiesced in the gradual move toward using military force that began during the summer of 1768, on the assumption that regular troops would be able to deal with the popular opposition to taxation in America in the same way they did excise riots in Britain. No less a figure than the Secretary at War, Lord Barrington, held this view. As he assured Sir William Draper:

The present commotions at Boston are such as we see almost every day in our own country: in both there are always men who prefer their own interest to the obedience which every good subject owes to the laws, and factious people who avail themselves of every clamour which arises ... . For a time the laws are without efficacy, unless supported by a proper degree of legal force: when such a force appears at Boston, I am persuaded the Magistrates will be easily enabled to do their duty; and wholesome example will secure future obedience to the laws in all parts of America.[19]

Events would soon show just how mistaken such assumptions were. As the full extent of Grenville's miscalculation impressed itself on the British public, the Stamp Act began to draw criticism from many of the same groups that had rallied to William Pitt's imperial standard a decade before: middle-class patriots, merchants and manufacturers with interests in North America, and parliamentary politicians bent on cultivating a reputation for popularity. Long after the difficulties of raising a colonial revenue had become clear, however, Grenville's apologists continued to insist that, in attempting to secure the gains of the Seven Years' War, the government had asked for nothing from America that the Whig regime did not already expect as a matter of course at home. Moreover, although members of Parliament had adopted the Stamp Act with only the vaguest sense of what their constituents thought, such arguments carried weight with the general public. Indeed, the principal reason why the standoff between Parliament and the colonies proved so intractable was the continued assumption that the various conditions that made for the perfection of the British constitution in England, Scotland, and Wales operated in equal measure throughout the other settled regions of the empire. As the governor of Massachusetts, Sir Francis Bernard, reminded the members of the provincial assembly during the summer of 1765:

In an empire, extended and diversified as that of Great Britain, there must be a supreme legislature, to which all other powers must be subordinate. It is our happiness that the supreme legislature, the parliament of Great Britain, is the sanctuary of liberty and justice; and that the prince, who presides over it, realizes the idea of a patriot King. Surely then, we should submit our opinions to the determinations of so august a body; and acquiesce in a perfect confidence, that the rights of the members of the British empire will ever be safe in the hands of the conservators of the liberty of the whole.[20]

## II. AN AMERICAN THEORY OF EMPIRE

If officials like Bernard regarded the creation of an American revenue as a natural expression of Parliament's authority, Grenville's reforms struck the colonists (and their metropolitan sympathizers) in an entirely different light. Following the lead of the Virginia House of Burgesses, most assemblies insisted on their own competence in matters of "internal Polity and Taxation" and denied the legality of any revenue measure that had not received "their own Consent." At the same time, merchants in ports up and down the North American seaboard organized boycotts of British goods, and more radical groups began planning the popular resistance that convulsed Boston, New York, and a number of other ports during the summer of 1765. "It is enough to break the heart of the Patriot," wrote a contributor to the *New York Mercury,* "to find [his country] fainting and despairing, hourly expecting to be utterly crush'd by the iron rod of power." In the words of the resolves adopted by the Sons of Liberty in Wallingford, Connecticut, "the late act of Parliament called the Stamp-Act, is unconstitutional, and intended to enslave the true subjects of America." And the town of Wilmington, North Carolina, warned that "moderation ceases to be a virtue, when the liberty of British subjects is in danger." "I mean not … to exaggerate things," wrote Pennsylvania attorney John Dickinson in an open letter to William Pitt, but it was "certain, that an unexampled and universal Jealousy, Grief and Indignation [had] been excited in the Colonists by the Conduct of the Mother Country since the Conclusion of the last War."[21]

Although American historians have tended to emphasize the "radical" character of the Stamp Act crisis of 1765, colonial polemicists were quick to assert that their opposition did not mean they disputed the general principle of Parliament's imperial sovereignty; nor, they insisted, did they object to contributing to the costs of government in Britain. In fact, throughout the imperial crisis, one of the mainstays of the American response was the large, though indirect, subsidies that the crown's overseas dominions already made through their compliance with the navigation laws. In the words of the declaration that John Dickinson drafted for the Stamp Act Congress, Britain's monopoly on the "trade of these colonies" meant that "they eventually contribute very largely to all supplies granted there to the crown." Benjamin Franklin made the same point in his famous testimony before the House of Commons: although the colonists denied Parliament's right to impose internal taxes, they readily conceded that "the sea is yours." "You maintain, by your fleets, the safety of navigation in it, and keep it clear of pirates; you may have therefore a natural and equitable right to some toll or duty on merchandizes carried through that part of your dominions." As John Morgan explained in an essay that won him the College of Philadelphia's Sargent Prize in 1766:

> The whole trade of America to all parts of the globe employs, one year with another, above two thousand sail of English ships, by which treasures of greater wealth are conveyed to Britain, than are derived [by Spain] from Mexico or Peru … . From the commodities of America, chiefly

manufactured in England, and conveyed through innumerable channels of trade to every quarter of the globe, Great-Britain acquires immense wealth, keeps up a spirit of industry among her inhabitants, and is enabled to support mighty fleets, great in peace and formidable in war.[22]

One reason for this emphasis on the navigation laws was to refute charges that colonists opposing the Stamp Act had committed acts of rebellion or were in any way challenging the British constitution. "Nothing can be more cruel and absurd," commented a sympathetic pamphleteer in England, "than to pronounce a whole people rebellious, because a few unavowed rioters get together and burn a coach." Indeed, American polemicists insisted that they were, in the main, a loyal and patriotic people. "If I have one ambitious wish," wrote Massachusetts assemblyman James Otis, "it is to see Great-Britain at the head of the world, and to see my King, under God, the father of mankind." John Dickinson echoed these sentiments in his public letter to the planters of Barbados, insisting that "every drop of blood in my heart is *British.*" As Franklin assured the House of Commons, the Americans had long regarded the British constitution as "the best in the world":

> They submitted willingly to the government of the crown, and paid, in all their courts, obedience to acts of parliament. Numerous as the people are in the several old provinces, they cost you nothing in forts, citadels, garrisons or armies, to keep them in subjection. They were governed by this country at the expence only of a little pen, ink and paper. They were led by a thread. They had not only a respect, but an affection for Great-Britain, for its laws, its customs and manners, and even a fondness for its fashions, that greatly increased the commerce.[23]

While demonstrating their allegiance to the present regime, the colonists' compliance with the Navigation Acts also enabled their apologists to draw attention to the part that the monopoly on American commerce had played in making Britain the preeminent maritime power in Europe. As William Pitt reminded the House of Commons, profits from "the trade of the colonies" currently amounted to some "two millions a year" and had provided the bulk of the "fund that carried you triumphantly through the last war." In the words of another observer, there were some that had "treated the Americans with great freedom and contempt, yet it should be remembered that Britain owes her present importance and power to them alone." Perhaps betraying an early indication of the madness that would end his career, James Otis even predicted that "the next universal monarchy" would be British and that the world was about to witness "the highest scene of earthly power and grandeur that has been ever yet displayed to the view of mankind." Indeed, the Stamp Act's opponents frequently noted that the Americans already contributed far more to maintaining British naval power than the sixty thousand pounds that Grenville had expected the new measure to yield. "As long as this globe continues moving," wrote John Dickinson in 1766, "may [Great Britain] reign over its navigable part"—adding, for good measure, "and may she resemble the ocean she commands, which recruits without wasting, and receives without exhausting."[24]

The following decade would show that the American distinction between Parliament's sovereignty over their external trade and its right to tax internally for revenue was unsustainable. Within months of the Stamp Act's repeal, in fact, a new ministry led by none other than William Pitt, now earl of Chatham, was once again considering measures for raising an American revenue, this time through the commercial tariffs that polemicists like Franklin had insisted the colonists did not mind paying.[25] Yet even after the Townshend Revenue Act touched off a fresh round of protests in the colonies, American patriots continued to insist that they had no objection to the substantial benefits that

the British gained from Parliament's regulation of their maritime trade. As the Massachusetts House of Representatives assured Lord Chancellor Camden in early 1768: "The subjects in this province, and undoubtedly in all the colonies, however they may have been otherwise represented to his Majesty's ministers, are loyal: They are firmly attached to the mother state: They always consider her interest and their own as inseparably interwoven, and it is their fervent wish that it may ever so remain."[26]

Although no one doubted that the colonists were obligated to contribute to the British crown directly, however, Americans were sure that their own provincial assemblies were the only legislative bodies with the right to approve such financial grants. In the words of the petition that the Stamp Act Congress presented to George III, the colonists readily conceded a general duty "to grant to your Majesty such Aids as are required for the Support of your Government over them, and other public Exigencies," but the only way they could give their consent was through the assemblies of their respective provinces. Even the crowds in American ports, whose anger over parliamentary taxation occasionally betrayed an impatience with their own elected leaders, signaled their acceptance of this principle by limiting their violence to politicians who refused to denounce the Stamp Act. Benjamin Franklin explained the colonists' position on taxation and representation to the House of Commons:

> Their opinion is, that when aids to the crown are wanted, they are to be asked of the several assemblies, according to the old established usage, who will, as they always have done, grant them freely ... . The granting aids to the crown, is the only means they have of recommending themselves to their sovereign, and they think it extremely hard and unjust, that a body of men, in which they have no representatives, should make a merit to itself of giving and granting what is not its own, but theirs, and deprive them of a right they esteem of the utmost

value and importance, as it is the security of all their other rights.[27]

As Franklin's choice of words suggested, colonial polemicists assumed that their assemblies enjoyed such exclusive powers of taxation partly as a matter of right. In order to substantiate this point, Americans often drew on the history of England's relations with the outlying regions of the British Isles, noting—as Maryland attorney Daniel Dulany did in 1766—that English monarchs had customarily secured the consent of provincial representatives before asking them "to perform or pay anything extrafeudal." As Lord Camden observed during the debates over the Stamp Act's repeal, there was "not a blade of grass" anywhere in Britain "which when taxed, was not taxed by the consent of the proprietor," and Camden insisted, despite contrary assertions by the Stamp Act's supporters, that neither the Welsh nor the inhabitants of counties palatinate like Durham and Chester had been subject to parliamentary taxation before they were granted representation in the House of Commons. Indeed, where Grenville's defenders claimed that the Glorious Revolution had given Parliament unlimited authority over the rest of the empire, American apologists virtually took it for granted that the same settlement that had secured the principle of legislative sovereignty in England provided equally firm guarantees for their own provincial assemblies. In the words of the Declaration of Rights and Grievances adopted by the Stamp Act Congress in October 1765, it was "inseparably essential to the freedom of a people, and the undoubted rights of Englishmen, that no taxes should be imposed on them, but with their own consent, given personally, or by their representatives."[28]

For all their certainty, however, the colonists did not claim the right to be taxed by their own representatives only as a matter of principle. As American commentators never tired of pointing out, this decentralization of fiscal authority owed at least as much to the colonies' well-documented history of providing for their own defensive needs through temporary levies and provincial militias. "I cannot help remarking," wrote the former Massachusetts agent William Bollan in 1765, "that, for one hundred years past, whilst Canada and Louisiana were in the hands of France, the colonies wanted no such defence or security from England; but, on the contrary, they defended themselves." According to the governor of Rhode Island, Stephen Hopkins, there was no precedent for either a standing army or a parliamentary revenue in America, since most colonies had been settled entirely "at the expence of the planters themselves" and had been left "to the protection of heaven and their own efforts" during the long wars with the French and Indians. During Parliament's preliminary consideration of the Stamp Act, Isaac Barré went even further, urging the House of Commons to consider whether the colonies really had been "planted by your care," "nourished by *your* indulgence," and "protected by *your* arms"—or whether settlers had gone to America because of "your oppressions," had grown "by your neglect," and now merited nothing more than Britain's thanks for remaining "as truly loyal as any subjects the King has." As Jared Ingersoll of Connecticut, who witnessed Barré's performance from the Commons gallery, later confided, "I own I felt Emotions that I never felt before."[29]

These alone were adequate reasons to oppose paying a tax that the Stamp Act's supporters depicted as necessary to provide a peacetime army for the colonies' defense. But most commentators carried the issue further still by insisting that the colonists' military self-sufficiency had ultimately made them far more effective participants in Britain's wars with France than if they had been reduced to supporting a permanent revenue of the sort that Grenville's apologists had in mind. The achievements of the New England provincials during the Cape Breton expedition of 1745 often featured with particular prominence in such accounts. "Everyone knows the importance of *Louisbourg,* in the consultations of *Aix la Chapelle,"* wrote James Otis, and Massachusetts clergyman Amos Adams insisted that the "success of the New-England arms" had supplied the *"single* equivalent for all the conquests of France" and Cape Breton "the price that purchased the peace of Europe."[30] In addition, polemicists argued that the level of American participation during the Seven Years' War was comparable to that within Britain itself. "This house may appeal to the nation, that the utmost aid of the people has been chearfully given when his Majesty required it" was the way the members of the Massachusetts assembly put the issue in their famous 1768 letter to Lord Chatham. "Can there then be a necessity for so great a change, and in its nature so delicate and important that instead of having the honour of his Majesty's requisitions laid before their representatives here, as has been invariably the usage, the parliament should now tax them without their consent?"[31]

Probably the most striking feature of this account of Westminster's relations with the colonies was the emphasis that American apologists placed on personal military service. As William Bollan argued in 1765, Americans would be only too "glad to see those red coats embark for England, since they can be of no use to the colonies, whose real defence and protection is received from the British navy, and the valour of their own native militia." Elsewhere, polemicists insisted that, although a standing army might be the appropriate way to secure a conquered province like Quebec, the right of self-defense represented one of the chief benchmarks of English liberty in the older colonies. Indeed, because the regular army was entirely subject to the fiscal control of Parliament, the only legal way for the colonists to fulfill their military obligations was by maintaining local militias and raising temporary levies in times of emergency. As observers described it, the result was a system of military obligation that guaranteed North America would remain a ready source of recruits even as it made Parliament's attempts at taxation both unnecessary and inadvisable.

"How easily are Fleets or Armies recruited for an *American* or *West Indian* Expedition, from two Millions of People just upon the Spot?" asked the English Quaker and royal physician Dr. John Fothergill in 1765. In the words of another essayist:

> Here is a fund of hardy, brave soldiers, inured to fatigue and frugality, ready to engage in the service of *Great-Britain,* whenever she thinks proper to require them. From this fruitful, this increasing source, her armies and navies may receive constant supplies, not of mercenary hirelings ready to engage in the service of the highest bidder, but faithful, dutiful children, animated with becoming fortitude, freedom and loyalty. These, if encouraged, cherished and protected, will indeed prove "Of *Britain's* empire the support and strength."[32]

The American response to the Stamp Act thus highlighted a fundamental schism between metropolitan and provincial definitions of patriotism. Although Grenville and his supporters had insisted otherwise, their attempt to tax the colonists demonstrated that the conditions that made it possible for Parliament to assume final responsibility for all questions of political obligation in Britain simply did not exist in the colonies. Not surprisingly, the Townshend Revenue Act (which included paying the salaries of royal governors among the purposes for which Parliament might tax the colonists) only intensified this conflict. As William Johnson, who acted as the agent for Connecticut in London during the later 1760s, wrote on learning of the new measure, empowering Parliament to assume such extensive responsibilities would eventually deprive the colonists of any political influence whatever, making it unnecessary for "an American Governor ... [to] know whether his government is in that country or in Indostan, in Bengal or at the Cape of Good Hope." John Dickinson made the point even more forcefully in his celebrated *Letters from a*

*Farmer in Pennsylvania* (1768), warning—in a pointed response to Governor Pownall—that once Parliament assumed such powers colonial assemblies would cease to enjoy even the "puny privileges of French parliaments."

> When the charges of the "administration of justice," the "support of civil government," and the expenses of "defending, protecting and securing" us, are provided for, I should be glad to know, upon *what occasions* the crown will ever call our assemblies together. Some few of them may meet of their own accord, by virtue of their charters. But what will they have to do, when they are met? To what shadows will they be reduced? The men, whose deliberations heretofore had an influence on every matter relating to the *liberty* and *happiness* of themselves and their constituents, and whose authority in domestic affairs at least, might well be compared to that of *Roman* senators, will *now* find their deliberations of no more consequence, than those of *constables*.[33]

Largely as a result of these concerns, a growing number of observers insisted that the only way to safeguard the principle of voluntary obligation in the colonies was to reconceptualize Britain's Atlantic empire as a confederation of sovereign states bound together, not by Parliament's unlimited authority, but by allegiance to a common monarch. In some ways, of course, this shift amounted to little more than a belated recognition that Britain's relations with the colonies were not all that different from those with subsidiary allies like Portugal or Hanover. "If Britain has protected the property of America," wrote a pamphleteer in 1769, "it does not constitute her the owner of that property. She has, for her own sake, protected, in their turns, almost every country in Europe, but that does not make her the proprietor of those countries, or give her a power of taxation over them." At the same time, though, introducing the law of nations into what British theorists

continued to depict as a civil dispute carried undeniably subversive implications. In a reply to William Knox's "review" of the imperial controversy, for example, Edward Bancroft, an American-born physician resident in London, argued that, because England's tide to North America during the first age of settlement had been vested in the person of Queen Elizabeth, the colonies owed allegiance to "the *English* Crown" but were under no obligation to obey any act of Parliament, *"even for regulating our Commerce."* Thomas Jefferson employed a similar argument in his famous appeal to George III to "resume the exercise of his negative power" by checking the despotic pretensions of Parliament. As Jefferson insisted in an analogy that English readers must have found particularly offensive, the confederal nature of the 'crown's imperial authority gave provincial assemblies the same right to prevent the king's ministers from stationing British regulars in the colonies that Parliament exercised when it required the king (as German elector) to obtain its consent before deploying Hanoverian troops in Britain.[34]

Even as chances for reaching a mutually satisfactory resolution to the standoff over colonial taxation receded, most American polemicists continued to affirm the need for an imperial union to safeguard what John Dickinson termed "the common good of all." With growing determination, however, the colonists also insisted on preserving the consensual basis of the two most important powers of government, the right to levy taxes and the right to raise troops. Speaking in 1774 of the colonial requisition system that the Stamp Act destroyed, Franklin's convictions on this score were only too clear:

Had this happy method been continued (a method which left the King's subjects in those remote countries the pleasure of shewing their zeal and loyalty, and of imagining that they recommended themselves to their Sovereign by the liberality of their voluntary grants) there is no doubt but all the money that could reasonably be expected to be raised from them, in any manner, might have been obtained from them, without the least heart-burning, offence, or breach of the harmony of affections and interest that so long subsisted between the two countries.

Despite the palpable sense of loss and regret, Franklin's words highlighted the extent to which Parliament's attempt to tax the Americans without their consent had given rise to a theory of empire fundamentally different from the one that most Britons had envisioned from their triumphant perch in 1763.[35]

## III. THE PLUNGE OF LEMMINGS

By the time Franklin wrote this passage, of course, Britain's position no longer seemed nearly as unassailable as at the close of the Seven Years' War. Not only was there the prospect of armed insurrection in Boston—to say nothing of the rest of the American seaboard—but a vocal group of "disaffected patriots" in the environs of London and Westminster seemed bent on making the colonists' cause their own. Furthermore, despite the widespread hope that George Ill's accession would end the party divisions of his predecessor's reign, the period from 1768 onward witnessed the emergence of a new, extraparliamentary opposition centered on the notorious libertine and former militia officer John Wilkes. Given the gravity of these problems, the government's refusal to make any real concession to the colonists' wishes has often looked like an inexplicable act of self-destruction, a stubbornness in the face of disaster that the great twentieth-century historian Sir Lewis Namier likened to the plunge of lemmings hurtling blindly toward the ocean and certain death. If most Britons failed to grasp the full extent of their predicament, however, growing numbers—including many who continued to accept Parliament's imperial authority—feared that the government was losing its hold over the very possessions that the British had just fought a costly war to protect.[36]

These concerns reflected several related developments, the first being the increasingly coercive methods with which the ministers of George III seemed determined to enforce Parliament's colonial requisitions in North America, especially Massachusetts. Although there was nothing unusual about professional troops assisting the civil magistrates at home, many people regarded the army's occupation of Boston during the summer of 1768 as an especially troubling demonstration of Britain's inability to fulfill even the most rudimentary functions of government in North America—let alone raise the sort of revenue envisioned by politicians like George Grenville and Charles Townshend. As John Wilkes wrote the Boston Sons of Liberty in 1769, the king's ministers seemed to be treating the city "as if it were the capital of a province belonging to our enemies, or in the possession of rebels." "Asiatic despotism," Wilkes assured his correspondents, "does not present a picture more odious in the eye of humanity." Elsewhere, those sympathetic to the colonists' situation charged that the British were governing them "as a conquered people," that the army in Boston was acting independently of the civil magistrates, even—as the earl of Chatham warned the House of Lords in early 1775—that Britain had "changed her civil power and salutary laws for a *military code*" and was on the verge of transferring "her seat of empire to Constantinople." History showed, insisted the London politician and Virginia native Arthur Lee, that "the liberties of the subject, which [ought to be] the constant care and provision of the Law and Constitution, could not exist" under such a regime; Chatham went so far as to mention the possibility of amending the English Declaration of Rights to prohibit either the crown or Parliament from maintaining regular troops in any colony without the consent of its representative assembly.[37]

As if the situation in America were not bad enough, commentators also worried about the increasingly tumultuous nature of England's own politics. Nothing caused greater concern on this score than the House of Commons' expulsion of John Wilkes following his election to Parliament in March 1768. Although Wilkes was technically a fugitive from the law when he stood for the London constituency of Middlesex, he already enjoyed a reputation as a popular champion. For those who worried about developments in America, the government's response to the election—including throwing Wilkes in jail and "massacring" a dozen of his riotous supporters at St. George's Field in London— seemed to confirm a disturbing authoritarian trend. Indeed, the House of Commons' repeated refusal in early 1769 to recognize the results of the Middlesex election and its controversial decision to seat one of the losing candidates struck even Wilkes's detractors as an unwarranted abuse of parliamentary privilege no less likely to weaken Britain's liberal underpinnings than what was happening on the far shores of the Atlantic. In the words of a petition submitted by the county of York (one of dozens of English addresses that together garnered some fifty-five thousand signatures), Parliament's treatment of Wilkes "threaten[ed] to impair that equal state of Legal Liberty for which this Nation has long been respected abroad and by which it hath been made Happy at Home." Elsewhere, pamphleteers and publicists claimed that Wilkes's expulsion was but the latest manifestation of a sinister plot to make Parliament absolute, the first signs of which had appeared with Parliament's approval of the Stamp Act. "The government of England is a government of law," declared the celebrated Junius to readers of the *Public Advertiser* in 1771. "We betray ourselves, we contradict the spirit of our laws and we shake the whole system of English jurisprudence, whenever we intrust a discretionary power over the life, liberty or fortune of the subject, to any man, or set of men whatsoever."[38]

On top of everything else, Britain's rulers appeared to be pursuing these misguided policies to the exclusion of all other considerations, including the need to remain vigilant against the reviving ambitions of France and Spain. From the standpoint of the government's critics, the summer of 1768 provided an especially disturbing illustration of this trend, as the king's ministers refused—at the very moment when they were sending troops to Boston and preparing the case against Wilkes—to take firm action against France for its flagrant annexation of the Mediterranean island of Corsica. "What has been your enemy's conduct, what your own?" demanded Colonel Isaac Barré in the House of Commons. "You have been confining yourself to the lowest business, that of pursuing little, low criminals, instead of giving laws to the world." According to Francis Webb, Britain's internal difficulties had made it impossible for the king to "stand forth as the defender of his people's violated rights, and his own dignity." A few commentators even claimed during the Corsica crisis that the Bourbon powers were actively encouraging the British government's despotic tendencies—that, in the words of Stephen Sayre of New York, Britain's foreign rivals had embarked on a policy of "forming dissentions, stirring up prejudices, disaffection, disagreement, and divisions" in order to "bring us to a fatal civil war." "Let us not say we do not feel the discontent in America," warned Sir Hercules Langrishe. "We feel it in the insults of our natural enemies; we feel it in our impotence or our fear to check the progress of their usurpation, and the extension of their empire;—we feel it in the sacrifice of our generosity and of our glory,—we feel it in the wounds of an illustrious people, and the contempt of all Europe."[39]

Wherever they looked during the later 1760s and early 1770s, the British thus found cause for concern. There were even people who affected to believe Parliament's actions threatened to reduce Britain's "empire of liberty" to the same condition of slavery that had characterized the "universal monarchies" of despots like Emperor Charles V, Philip II of Spain, and Louis XIV. To the ministry's supporters, of course, this sounded like an irresponsibly wild, self-serving allegation. For some Britons, though, the parallels with these historic tyrants seemed compelling enough. As Arthur Lee insisted in 1774, those who defended the government's policies in America seemed to have forgotten there was "no magic or efficient power in the world" that could make the laws of Parliament sovereign "in all cases whatsoever." The English naval officer John Cartwright went even further in his precocious call for American independence, noting darkly that, "while Lewis the XIVth was intoxicated with the drunken fancy of universal monarchy, his courtiers did not fail to satisfy him … that he had an undoubted right" to the same sort of authority in Europe that Britain was now claiming in America. Indeed, the Welsh Presbyterian minister, Richard Price, whose *Observations on the Nature of Civil Liberty* sold approximately sixty thousand copies during the first half of 1776, claimed to see no difference between Britain's imperial pretensions in America and the pope's claim to be "the supreme head on earth of the Christian church." For a reading public that would shortly make Edward Gibbon's *Decline and Fall of the Roman Empire* (1776) one of the century's best-selling histories, it went without saying that rulers who succumbed to such pernicious temptations invariably ended by squandering the very dominions they so desperately sought to preserve and expand.[40]

Historians of the American Revolution have devoted a good deal of attention to those Britons who shared these libertarian sentiments. Convinced of its own invincibility and limitless authority, the British government seemed bent on its own destruction in ways right-minded men and women could only lament. For all the evident concern on this account, however, the British were no less troubled by what might happen if Parliament relented on the question of colonial taxation. As even the colonists' critics admitted, safeguarding Westminster's fiscal rights was bound to unsettle a people accustomed to thinking of themselves as the freest in the world—a people, after all, who were supposed to be as solicitous of the liberties of friends and neighbors in Europe and beyond as they were of their own rights and privileges. Yet most Britons also feared that weakening Parliament's imperial authority would give rise

to an unacceptable degree of colonial autonomy. Indeed, just as the government's actions in Boston raised the specter of universal monarchy, the Americans' increasingly radical response threatened to turn Britain's Atlantic empire into a loose-knit confederation not unlike the ineffective alliances from which its people had only recently begun to extricate themselves in Europe. If they bowed to the colonists' demands, the British might well purchase a brief period of prosperity and repose—but it was a repose that people feared would come with the long-term cost of escalating deficits and crushing taxes.

This impression was enhanced by Britain's growing preoccupation with the racially diverse territories gained at the end of the Seven Years' War. In the case of the Indian lands to the west of the Appalachian Mountains, for example, the Stamp Act crisis carried implications for Britain's imperial authority that were no less grave than the unrest in Boston or New York. According to the plan formulated by the Bute and Grenville ministries, the proceeds from the new taxes had been meant for the use of the regular troops stationed in the Ohio and Mississippi Valleys. In the wake of the act's repeal, however, the British faced a difficult choice between bearing the costs of this army themselves or pulling back their garrisons. Although successive ministries from 1766 onward opted for the latter course, British officials routinely warned against the effects of leaving the Indians and frontier settlers at each other's mercy—and of leaving such extensive lands vulnerable to French or Spanish encroachments.[41] Furthermore, Whitehall maintained just enough of a military presence in the Great Lakes region—chiefly at Fort Niagara and Detroit—to make it seem as though the colonists were giving the British sole responsibility for what should have been the "common cause" of all. Within an empire defined by ethnically diverse and geographically remote territories, the American insistence on regarding taxes as voluntary contributions— which their assemblies might refuse whenever they saw fit—increasingly looked like nothing more than a selfish scheme to avoid the most fundamental national obligation of all.[42]

To compound matters, the Americans' resistance to parliamentary taxation stood in stark contrast to the government's relations with the East India Company, whose proprietors reluctantly agreed in 1767 to award the crown an annual subsidy of £400,000 in exchange for Parliament's recognition of their new role as de facto rulers of the Mughal emperor's northeastern province of Bengal. Although there were important differences between the London-based company's governing board and the colonial assemblies in North America, English jurists generally regarded both as "corporations" with special rights and privileges, but nonetheless subject to Parliament's controlling authority. As such, the company's landmark agreement made the American position on taxation look that much more exceptional. In the words of Alexander Dalrymple, the East Indian subsidy showed that no "part of this Nation, whether in a Corporate or Individual Capacity, is independant of the Supreme Jurisdiction of Parliament." As William Knox stated in 1769, Parliament's unlimited sovereignty extended to all British subjects, regardless of their political condition or distance from the metropolis:

> There is no material difference between the grant of the crown to the proprietor of Maryland, and the grant to the proprietors of the countries to the East of the Cape of Good Hope, save in the article of trade. The inhabitants, therefore, of the East-India company's possessions, are equally bound with the people of Maryland to contribute to the burdens of the state; and the sovereign's power over the whole empire, is equally obliged to require them so to do, according to their ability.[43]

For most Britons, though, what sealed the case for colonial taxation was the widespread belief that the colonies along the North American seaboard together constituted an increasingly important part of the greater British nation and that surrendering Parliament's fiscal rights in Massachusetts and Virginia would set a dangerous precedent for the government of English settlers in places as scattered as Ireland, Jamaica, and Bengal. In the words of the aging John Shebbeare, the controversy over colonial taxation ultimately turned on the question of whether "all the subjects of the same realm should, according to their respective abilities, pay their *legal* contributions." "Should the parliament give way to the pretensions of the Americans," wrote Matthew Wheelock in 1770, "the national credit would be immediately affected, as then great Britain *alone* would become responsible for the national debt." Indeed, national ties between Britain and America seemed so pronounced that even friends of America like John Wilkes claimed that it was hard to differentiate "between an inhabitant of Boston in Lincolnshire, and of Boston in New England." According to the colonists' metropolitan sympathizers, of course, this common nationality tended to reinforce the case for allowing them to fulfill their fiscal obligations by obeying the navigation laws and approving wartime requisitions. For a broad swath of the British public, however, the fact that even the colonists' friends in England regarded them as "British subjects" only strengthened the prevailing impression that freeing them from the duty to pay parliamentary taxes would constitute "a system of misgovernment not to be paralleled."[44]

Given the extent of Britain's obligations in the Atlantic and Asia, many people naturally concluded that the Americans' refusal to contribute directly to the national revenue would eventually make the unacceptable costs long associated with war in Europe a permanent feature of British politics. Even Adam Smith, whose defense of free trade in *Wealth of Nations* (1776) gave him a measure of sympathy for the colonists, found the idea of surrendering Parliament's fiscal supremacy indefensible on these grounds. Although Smith hardly shared the polemical purposes of court apologists like

Whately or Knox, his analysis of the imperial crisis seconded many of their positions, including the need to maintain professional troops in outlying provinces like Scotland and the American colonies, the inevitability of deficit finance in times of war, and the unavoidable obligation to pay taxes levied by a centrally constituted sovereign. Smith also insisted on the benevolent effects of modern military and fiscal practice, noting how borrowing funds against future revenue had enabled the governments of Europe to wage expensive wars without imposing extortionate taxes or universal military service on their subjects. But most important of all, he was sure that, unless such debts were serviced by an adequate revenue, they bred enthusiasm of the worst sort, permitting governments to lay out vast expenditures even in times of peace, frequently on the most ephemeral projects and far-fetched schemes. It seemed to Smith that, in the absence of a colonial revenue, Britain's empire in America had become just such a costly project, an imaginary dominion that the general public mistakenly thought contributed to the general prosperity but that actually cost them millions in uncompensated expenditures. As he wrote in the treatise's concluding paragraph:

> The rulers of Great Britain have, for more than a century past, amused the people with the imagination that they possessed a great empire on the west side of the Atlantic. This empire, however, has hitherto existed in imagination only. It has hitherto been, not an empire, but the project of an empire; not a gold mine, but the project of a gold mine; a project which has cost, which continues to cost, and which, if pursued in the same way as it has been hitherto, is likely to cost, immense expense, without being likely to bring any profit.[45]

For a handful of observers—Smith included—this realization was enough to make them ponder whether keeping the colonists in the empire was worth the expense.[46] But for the vast majority of Britons, the spiraling debts, unrealistic expectations, and general lack of direction that the nation's experience with confederations in Europe had invariably produced simply reinforced the case for preserving Parliament's jurisdiction over every aspect of colonial finance. As William Knox insisted in his review of the imperial controversy, "There is no alternative: either the Colonies are a part of the community of Great Britain, or they are in a state of nature with respect to her." Samuel Johnson was equally scathing in his savage attack on the Americans and the self-styled patriots who defended them in Britain. "To suppose," wrote Dr. Johnson, that colonists did not have to "contribute to their own defense, but at their own pleasure" and that they should be freed from "the general system of representation" as it existed in Britain involved "such a degree of absurdity, as nothing but the shew of patriotism could palliate." Even Edmund Burke, no friend of taxing the Americans, dismissed the idea of colonial requisitions, remarking that "the empire of Germany" raised "the worst revenue and the worst army in the world" in just such a manner. As the king's Scottish painter Allan Ramsay observed in 1776, there were "sixteen separate Provinces, upon the continent of America, and about the same number of governments in the American islands," all of which could claim the right to tax themselves. If the British permitted the colonists to exercise this right, it was entirely possible that "the East might be at war, while the West was out of danger; and the North might be lost, for want of the assistance of the South." "This would create a general weakness in the state" was Ramsay's depressing conclusion; "separate interests would actuate every part of the British empire, and nothing but confusion, and destruction, would ensue."[47]

For the same reasons that they had found the patriotic, blue water rhetoric of the 1750s so compelling, the British thus chose to reaffirm the empire's unitary character by giving the fiscal authority of Parliament priority over all other considerations.[48] No doubt this is why the ministry of Lord North took such care in early 1775 to depict the impending war in America as an internal contest over the colonists' obligations to contribute to the national revenue. According to the conciliatory proposition that the government laid before the House of Commons on February 20, the ministry stood ready to rescind all penalties from any colony whose legislature came forward with a regular subsidy for the common defense of the empire, the only stipulation being that the disposition of such grants be left entirely to the discretion of Parliament. As Lord North himself admitted, such a proposal was not likely to meet with approval in America. According to the *London Evening Post,* though, the prime minister claimed that the mere fact that the offer had been extended would not *"fail of doing Good in England":* first by standing "as an eternal monument of the wisdom and clemency, of the humanity and justice, of British Government"; second, by demonstrating the moderation of Parliament to "the traders and manufacturers of England"; and finally, by animating "the officers and soldiers we send out to America to a vigorous and manly exertion of their native courage, without doubt or scruple, when they are assured they no longer fight for a phantom, and a vain, empty point of honour, but for a substantial benefit to their country, which is to relieve her in her greatest exigencies."[49]

As Bernard Bailyn observed some two hundred years later, the "ideological origins" of the American Revolution ultimately lay in an inexorable "logic of rebellion," which led the colonists to believe that Parliament's actions were so diabolical and menacing that their only chance for lasting freedom and prosperity was to sever all remaining ties to the British people and their government. To a greater extent than is sometimes realized, the Revolution's British origins reflected an equally terrifying set of fears and apprehensions, some that could be traced back to the military and fiscal bargain the English had struck at the close of the seventeenth century, others that arose from more recent developments like the growing animus toward

Britain's European allies. Whether these made the American Revolution inevitable is impossible to say. For most Britons who sought to make sense of the looming imperial crisis, however, the government seemed to have little choice. In a letter describing the terms of the Boston Port Act (1774), which Parliament was currently debating, Arthur Lee confessed to Benjamin Franklin, "The highest and lowest Ranks of People in this Country [seemed] so totally debauched and dissipated" that the vast majority accepted the necessity of taking a firm line against the Americans. But according to John Shebbeare, the war in America was likely to be the first ever undertaken solely for the benefit of "the common people." Although the wisdom of attempting to coerce the colonies would come to seem a good deal less obvious, Britons were sure that a contest for the preservation of Parliament's independent authority in the fullest sense possible was preeminently for the welfare of the nation.[50]

## Notes

1. R. C. Simmons and P. D. G. Thomas, eds., *Proceedings and Debates of the British Parliaments respecting North America, 1754–1783,* 6 vols. (Millwood, White Plains, N.Y., 1982–1986), I, 305; David Vaisey, ed., *The Diary of Thomas Turner, 1754–1765* (Oxford, 1984), 191; [Oliver Goldsmith], *The Martial Review; or, A General History of the Late Wars …* (London, 1763), 237; C. B. A. Behrens, *The Ancien Régime* (London, 1967), 158.

2. *The Political Balance, in Which the Principles and Conduct of the Two Parties Are Weighed* (London, 1765), 61; The King's Speech, as quoted in the *Annual Register,* III (1760), 248. According to some accounts, the king said "Britain" rather than "Briton." For a contemporary interpretation of the speech as an explicit rejection of the first two Hanoverian monarchs' Continental policies, see *A Letter to the Whigs, with Some Remarks on a Letter to the Tories* (London, 1762), 15: "What terrors can the most wayward imagination form of predilection and partiality to any foreign interests in the bosom of a Sovereign, who has so

sensibly expressed his affection for this country, when he boasted of his being born a Briton?" For the blue water commitments of George Ill's court, see Nicholas Tracy, "The Gunboat Diplomacy of the Government of George Grenville, 1764–1765: The Honduras, Turks Island, and Gambian Incidents," *Historical Journal,* XVII (1974), 711–731; Philip Lawson, *George Grenville: A Political Life* (Oxford, 1984), 203–207; H. M. Scott, *British Foreign Policy in the Age of the American Revolution* (Oxford, 1990), chaps. 3–5. As Scott rightly notes, the Bute and Grenville administrations remained committed to the "Old System" of cultivating Continental alliances in order to resist French ambitions in Europe (41–50). As he also points out, though, none of George III's early ministries proved willing to renew the peacetime subsidies that had undergirded Whig diplomacy during the 1740s and 1750s and that blue water patriots like Bolingbroke had found so repulsive (50). This alone represented a substantial departure from the Continental policies of George II.

3. The definitive account of the British army in North America is still John Shy, *Toward Lexington: The Role of the British Army in the Coming of the American Revolution* (Princeton, N.J., 1965). For the decision on the peacetime army in 1763, see also John L. Bullion, " 'The Ten Thousand in America': More Light on the Decision on the American Army 1762–1763," *William and Mary Quarterly,* 3rd Ser., XLIII (1986), 646–657; Bullion, "Security and Economy: The Bute Administration's Plans for the American Army and Revenue," *William and Mary Quarterly,* 3rd Ser., XLV (1988), 499–509.

4. P. D. G. Thomas, ed., "Parliamentary Diaries of Nathaniel Ryder, 1764–7," *Camden Miscellany,* XXIII (Camden 4th Ser., VII) (London, [1969]), 234 (hereafter cited as Thomas, ed., "Diaries of Ryder"). The genesis of the Stamp Act is the subject of a considerable literature, including P. D. G. Thomas, *British Politics and the Stamp Act Crisis: The First Phase of the American Revolution, 1763–1767* (Oxford, 1975), chap. 3; John L. Bullion, *A Great and Necessary Measure: George Grenville and the Genesis of the Stamp Act, 1763–1765* (Columbia, Mo., 1982), chap. 1; Lawson, *George Grenville: A Political Life,* 187–202. For the imperial relationship before 1763, see Jack P. Greene, *Peripheries and Center: Constitutional*

*Development in the Extended Polities of the British Empire and the United States, 1607–1788* (Athens, Ga., 1986), 7–76.

5. Letter by "Anti-Sejanus", *London Chronicle,* XVIII, 523 (Nov. 28–30, 1765), in Edmund S. Morgan, ed., *Prologue to Revolution: Sources and Documents on the Stamp Act Crisis, 1764–1766* (New York, 1973), 100; Thomas, *British Politics and the Stamp Act Crisis,* 100. For the tendency in the press to criticize the general size of the peacetime establishment but not the deployment of troops in America, see esp. [David Hartley], *The Budget: Inscribed to the Man, Who Thinks Himself Minister …,* 6th ed. (London, 1764), 5, 9; see also *A Letter to the Right Hon. the Earl of Temple, on the Subject of the Forty-fifth Number of the North-Briton …* (London, 1763), 17; [John Butler], *Serious Considerations on the Measures of the Present Administration …* (London, 1763), 15–18; [Butler], *An Address to the Cocoa-tree, from a Whig, and a Consultation on the Subject of a Standing-Army …* (London, 1763), vii, 25, 30–31, 50–52.

6. [Thomas Whately], *Remarks on the Budget; or, A Candid Examination of the Facts and Arguments Offered to the Public in That Pamphlet* (London, 1765), 6; *A Second Letter to the Right Honourable Charles Townshend, Occasioned by His Commendation of the Budget …* (London, 1765), 13–14; Simmons and Thomas, eds., *Proceedings and Debates,* I, 441.

7. On the adequacy of existing defensive strategies in America, see [James Otis], *Considerations on Behalf of the Colonists, in a Letter to a Noble Lord* (London, 1765), 29; [William Bollan], *The Mutual Interest of Great Britain and the American Colonies Considered …* (London, 1765), 10–11; [John Fothergill], *Considerations relative to the North American Colonies* (London, 1765), 9. The quote by Major Bassett comes from Jack M. Sosin, *Whitehall and the Wilderness: The Middle West in British Colonial Policy, 1760–1775* (Lincoln, Nebr., 1961), 218. Sosin's book is still the best treatment of British policy toward the new dominions, but see also the Report of the Board of Trade, June 18, 1763, in Adam Shortt and Arthur G. Doughty, eds., *Documents Relating to the Constitutional History of Canada, 1759–1791,* 2d ed. rev., 2 vols. (Ottawa, 1918), I, 139–140, 143; Fernand Ouellet, "The British Army of Occupation in the St. Lawrence Valley, 1760–74: The Conflict

between Civil and Military Society," trans. A. Kern, in Roy Prete and A. Hamish Ion, eds., *Armies of Occupation* (Waterloo, Ont., 1984), 17–54; Philip Lawson, *The Imperial Challenge: Quebec and Britain in the Age of the American Revolution* (Montreal, 1989).

8. *An Address to Sir John Cust, Bart., Speaker of the House of Commons; in Which the Characters of Lord Bute, Mr. Pitt, and Mr. Wilkes, Appear in a New Light* (London, 1761), 39; [Thomas Whately], *The Regulations Lately Made concerning the Colonies* ... (London, 1765), 22. On the role of Pontiac's Rebellion in persuading British officials of the need for troops in America, see esp. Shy, *Toward Lexington,* 121–125.

9. The persistence of such tensions is covered in Scott, *British Foreign Policy,* 48–50. As Scott notes, Britain's rivalry with France and Spain was at least as intense after 1763 as it had been in the period before the war. The most serious confrontations included France's occupation of the Turks Islands in the West Indies in 1764, its seizure of Corsica in 1768, and the Falkland Islands dispute with Spain in 1771.

10. *Reflections on the Terms of Peace* ... (London, 1763), 31; *Impartial Observations, to Be Considered on by the King, His Ministers, and the People of Great Britain* ([London?, 1763]), 26 (inscribed in hand on the cover of the copy at the Huntington Library [Pamphlet 32435]: "Wrote 25th March 1763 for Lord Egremont [President of the Board of Trade]"); Thomas, ed., "Diaries of Ryder," 234. The author of *Impartial Observations* took it as a matter of course that the government's plans for North America ought to include maintaining regular troops and that these forces should be paid through an increase in tariffs (13).

11. [Whately], *The Regulations Lately Made,* 31 ("There have been Ministers ignorant of the Importance of the Colonies; others, have impotently neglected their Concerns; and others again have been diverted by meaner Pursuits from attending to them: But happily for this country, the Real and Substantial, and those are the Commercial Interest of Great Britain, are now preferred to every other Consideration"); [William Knox], *The Present State of the Nation: Particularly with respect to Its Trade, Finances, Etc, Etc.* (London, 1768), 12; *The Political Balance,* 34, 46, 60–61. For a trenchant critique of these claims, see *The Late*

*Occurrences in North America, and Policy of Great Britain, Considered* ... (London, 1766), 30–31.

12. [Soame Jenyns], *The Objections to the Taxation of Our American Colonies, by the Legislature of Great Britain, Briefly Consider'd* (London, 1765), 12; [Whately], *The Regulations Lately Made,* 56–57. The consensus in Parliament on the need to raise an American revenue is established in Thomas, *British Politics and the Stamp Act Crisis,* 55–57, 61, 85–100. For the objections of Beckford and Barré, see Simmons and Thomas, eds., *Proceedings and Debates,* II, 11–17.

13. William Blackstone, *Commentaries on the Laws of England,* 4 vols. (1765–1769), ed. Stanley N. Katz et al. (Chicago, 1979), I, 296–297, 315, 323, 325. For more on Blackstone's analysis of English constitutional development, see Eliga Hayden Gould, "War, Empire and the Language of State Formation: British Imperial Culture in the Age of the American Revolution" (Ph.D. diss., Johns Hopkins University, 1993), 127–130.

14. The *Commentaries* make no mention of the specific issue of colonial taxation; Blackstone's parliamentary statements on the question all concerned Parliament's legal right to impose taxes rather than the necessity or utility of doing so (see esp. Blackstone's speech of Feb. 3, 1766, in Simmons and Thomas, eds., *Proceedings and Debates,* II, 140, 147–148); [Whately], *The Regulations Lately Made,* 51–52, 57; [Charles Lloyd], *The Conduct of the Late Administration Examined, relative to the American Stamp Act,* 2d ed. (London, 1767), 136; Thomas Pownall, *The Administration of the Colonies,* 2d ed. (London, 1765), 90. For the broader uses of the proceeds from the stamp tax, see the parliamentary speeches of Grenville and Charles Townshend during the debate of Feb. 6, 1765, in Simmons and Thomas, eds., *Proceedings and Debates,* II, 10, 13; [Whately], *The Regulations Lately Made,* 56, 101–104.

15. *The Justice and Necessity of Taxing the American Colonies, Demonstrated* ... (London, 1766), 10; *Protest against the Bill to Repeal the American Stamp Act, of the Last Session* ([London], 1766), 9; [Whately], *The Regulations Lately Made,* 56–57; [Knox], *The Present State of the Nation,* 30; John Ploughshare, "I Am for Old England," *London Chronicle* (Feb. 20, 1766), in Morgan, ed., *Prologue to Revolution,* 103; *The True Constitutional Means for*

*Putting an End to the Disputes between Great-Britain and the American Colonies* (London, 1769), 31.

16. [Whately], *The Regulations Lately Made,* 40, 109, 112. The last passage quoted concludes: "Their connexion would otherwise be an Alliance, not a Union; and they would be no longer one State, but a confederacy of many: Local Purposes may indeed be provided for by local Powers, but general Provisions can only be made by a Council that has general Authority; that Authority vested by indefeasible right in Parliament over all the Subjects of Great-Britain."

17. Thomas Pownall, *The Administration of the Colonies,* 4th ed. rev. (London, 1768), 140; Simmons and Thomas, eds., *Proceedings and Debates,* II, 129–133, 568; [William Knox], *The Controversy between Great-Britain and Her Colonies Reviewed* ... (London, 1769), 87–88. Some members of Parliament—notably Edmund Burke and the Rockingham Whigs—opposed the Stamp Act for pragmatic reasons but nonetheless accepted the principle of parliamentary sovereignty; see Paul Langford, "Old Whigs, Old Tories, and the American Revolution," *Journal of Imperial and Commonwealth History,* VIII (1980), 106–130. On the parallels between the American colonies and England's counties palatinate, see Lord Mansfield's speech in the upper house on Feb. 3, 1766 (Simmons and Thomas, eds., *Proceedings and Debates,* II, 129–133); Pownall, *The Administration of the Colonies,* 4th ed. 140.

18. *Considerations on the American Stamp Act, and on the Conduct of the Minister Who Planned It* (London, 1765), 30–31; [William Knox], *A Letter to a Member of Parliament, Wherein the Power of the British Legislature, and the Case of the Colonists, Are Briefly and Impartially Considered* (London, 1765), 1–2; *The Justice and Necessity of Taxing the American Colonies, Demonstrated* ... , *Together with a Vindication of the Authority of Parliament* (London, 1766), 13.

19. Simmons and Thomas, eds., *Proceedings and Debates,* II, 169 (for Mansfield's reference to the militia, see 130); Barrington to Draper, Sept. 1, 1768, Papers of William Wildman, Viscount Barrington, Suffolk Record Office (hereafter Barrington Papers), HA 174/Acc 1026/107, 112–113. See also Barrington to General Thomas Gage, Aug. 1, 1768, Barrington Papers, HA 174/Acc 1026/107, 107–108, in which he reminded the commander of the British forces in America

that "Riotous Englishmen in New England must be treated as their fellows in Old England, they must be compelled to obey the law and the civil magistrate must have troops to enforce that obedience."

20. [John Almon, ed.], *A Collection of Papers relative to the Dispute between Great Britain and America, 1764–1775* (1777; New York, 1971), 8–9 (hereafter cited as Almon, ed., *Prior Documents*).

21. "The Virginia Resolves" (May 30, 1765), in Jack P. Greene, ed., *Colonies to Nation, 1763–1789: A Documentary History of the American Revolution* (1967; New York, 1975), 61; *New-York Mercury,* Oct. 21, 1765; *Connecticut Courant* (Hartford), Dec. 30, 1765; "Address of the Mayor and Gentlemen of Wilmington to Governor Tryon," July 28, 1766, in Almon, ed., *Prior Documents,* 112; Dickinson to Pitt, in Morgan, ed., *Prologue to Revolution,* 119.

22. "Declaration of the Stamp Act Congress" (Oct. 19, 1765), in Greene, ed., *Colonies to Nation,* 64; "Examination of Benjamin Franklin" (Feb. 13, 1766), in Almon, ed., *Prior Documents,* 73; John Morgan, "Dissertation I," *Four Dissertations, on the Reciprocal Advantages of a Perpetual Union between Great-Britain and Her American Colonies* ... (London, 1766), 17.

23. *Considerations on the American Stamp Act,* 30; James Otis, *The Rights of the British Colonies Asserted and Proved,* 2d ed. (London, 1766), 61; [John Dickinson], *An Address to the Committee of Correspondence in Barbados* ... (Philadelphia, 1766), in Paul Leicester Ford, ed., *The Writings of John Dickinson,* I, *Political Writings, 1764–1774* (Historical Society of Pennsylvania, *Memoirs,* XIV), (Philadelphia, 1895), 267; "Examination," in Almon, ed., *Prior Documents,* 67.

24. [William Pitt, earl of Chatham], *The Celebrated Speech of a Celebrated Commoner,* [London, 1766], 15; *The Necessity of Repealing the American Stamp-Act Demonstrated; or, A Proof That Great-Britain Must Be Injured by That Act* ... (London, 1766), 29; [Dickinson], *An Address to the Committee in Barbados,* in Ford, ed., *Writings of Dickinson,* 267. The passage containing Otis's quote merits citation in full:

> The cards are shuffling fast through all Europe. Who will win the prize is with God. This however I know, *detur degniori.* The next

universal monarchy will be favourable to the human race, for it must be founded on the principles of equity, moderation and justice. No country has been more distinguished for these principles than Great Britain, since the revolution.

Otis, *The Rights of the British Colonies*, 61. See also [John Dickinson], *The Late Regulations, respecting the British Colonies on the Continent of America Considered* ... (London, 1766), 32: "I think it may justly be said, that the foundations of the power and glory of great britain are laid in america."

25. Thomas, *British Politics and the Stamp Act Crisis*, chap. 16; Lawrence Henry Gipson, *The Coming of the Revolution, 1763–1775* (New York, 1962), chap. 11. The notion that Americans would accept "external" taxes, which ministerial apologists used to justify the Townshend duties, reflected a widespread misunderstanding of what Franklin had actually said in his testimony to Parliament. According to the published version of his statement, Franklin only claimed that it was "the opinion of every one [in the colonies], that we could not be taxed in a parliament where we were not represented. But the payment of duties laid by act of parliament, as regulations of commerce was never disputed" (Almon, ed., *Prior Documents*, 68).

26. Letter dated Jan. 29, 1768, in [Thomas Hollis, ed.], *The True Sentiments of America ... Contained in a Collection of Letters Sent from the House of Representatives of the Province of Massachusetts Bay to Several Persons of High Rank in this Kingdom. Together with Certain Papers relating to a Supposed Libel on the Governor of That Province* (London, 1768), 36.

27. "A Petition to the King from the Stamp Act Congress" (Oct. 19, 1765), in Ford, ed., *Writings of Dickinson*, 194; "Examination," in Almon, ed., *Prior Documents*, 72. For the constitutional principles of rioters protesting the Stamp Act, see Pauline Maier, *From Resistance to Revolution: Colonial Radicals and the Development of American Opposition to Britain, 1765–1776* (1972; New York, 1991), chap. 3; Gary Nash, *Urban Crucible: The Northern Seaports and the Origins of the American Revolution* (Cambridge, Mass., 1979), chap. 6.

28. [Daniel Dulany], *Considerations on the Propriety of Imposing Taxes in the British Colonies for the Purpose of Raising a Revenue* ... (Annapolis, 1765), in Bernard Bailyn and Jane N. Garrett, eds., *Pamphlets of the American Revolution, 1750–1776* (Cambridge, Mass., 1965–), I, 613; Simmons and Thomas, eds., *Proceedings and Debates*, II, 322; "Declaration," in Greene, ed., *Colonies to Nation*, 64. For a fuller discussion of the "imperial constitution" as the colonists understood it, see Greene, *Peripheries and Center*, chaps. 4, 5.

29. [Bollan], *The Mutual Interest of Great Britain and the American Colonies Considered with respect to an Act Passed Last Session of Parliament for Laying a Duty on Merchandise, Etc. with Some Remarks on a Pamphlet, Intitled, "Objections to the Taxation of the American Colonies, Etc. Considered." In a Letter to a Member of Parliament*, 10; [Stephen Hopkins], *The Grievances of the American Colonies Candidly Examined* ... (London, 1766), 38–39; Simmons and Thomas, eds., *Proceedings and Debates*, II, 16; *The Fitch Papers: Correspondence and Documents during Thomas Fitch's Governorship of the Colony of Connecticut, 1754–1766*, II (Jan. 1759–May 1766), *(Collections of the Connecticut Historical Society*, XVIII) (1920), 322–323.

30. Otis, *The Rights of the British Colonies*, 87; Amos Adams, *A Concise, Historical View of the Difficulties, Hardships, and Perils Which Attended the Planting and Progressive Improvements of New England* (London, 1770), 49. For additional references to the Cape Breton expedition, see [Bollan], *The Mutual Interest of Great Britain and the American Colonies Considered*, 10; [Hopkins], *Grievances of the American Colonies*, 38–39; Massachusetts House of Representatives to the earl of Chatham, Feb. 2, 1768, in [Hollis, ed.], *The True Sentiments of America*, 39; [Stephen Sayre], *The Englishman Deceived: A Political Piece, Wherein Some Very Important Secrets of State Are Briefly Recited* ... (London, 1768), 34–35; [John Erskine], *Shall I Go to War with My American Brethren?* ... (London, 1769), 31; *A Brief Review of the Rise and Progress, Services and Sufferings, of New England, Especially the Province of Massachuset's-Bay* (London, 1774).

31. Letter dated Feb. 2, 1768, in [Hollis, ed.], *The True Sentiments of America*, 39. On the alleged levels of American participation in the Seven Years' War, see [Israel Mauduit], *Some Thoughts on the Method of Improving and Securing the Advantages Which Accrue to Great-Britain from the Northern Colonies* (London, 1765), 13–14; *Four*

*Dissertations on the Reciprocal Advantages of a Perpetual Union,* 18, 86–87; *The Crisis; or, A Full Defence of the Colonies* (London, 1766), 21–22; *The Necessity of Repealing the American Stamp-Act,* 8; [Dulany], *Considerations on Imposing Taxes,* in Bailyn and Garrett, eds., *Pamphlets of the American Revolution,* 622.

32. [Bollan], *The Mutual Interest of Great Britain and the American Colonies Considered,* 11; [Fothergill], *Considerations relative to the North American Colonies,* 8; *Four Dissertations, on the Reciprocal Advantages of a Perpetual Union,* 87. On the relationship between militias and colonial autonomy, see also Massachusetts House of Representatives to Dennis DeBerdt, Jan. 12, 1768, in [Hollis, ed.], *The True Sentiments of America,* 72–74; William Pitkin to William Samuel Johnson, June 6, 1768, in "Letters of Dr. William Samuel Johnson," *Trumbull Papers* (Massachusetts Historical Society, *Collections,* 5th Ser., IX [1895]), 276–284 (hereafter cited as *Trumbull Papers*); Sir Francis Bernard to Lord Hillsborough, Sept. 16, 1768, in *Letters to the Ministry, from Governor Bernard, General Gage, and Commodore Hood* ... (London, 1769), 72–74; [Dulany], *Considerations on Imposing Taxes,* in Bailyn and Garrett, eds., *Pamphlets of the American Revolution,* I, 642–643; *The Necessity of Repealing the American Stamp-Act,* 12–13.

33. Letter to Governor William Pitkin, July 13, 1767, in *Trumbull Papers,* 239; [John Dickinson], *Letters from a Farmer in Pennsylvania, to the Inhabitants of the British Colonies* (Philadelphia, 1768), in Ford, ed., *Writings of Dickinson,* 369, 373.

34. *The Case of Great Britain and America, Addressed to the King, and Both Houses of Parliament,* 2d ed. (London, 1769), 29; [Edward Bancroft], *Remarks on the Review of the Controversy between Great Britain and Her Colonies* ... (London, 1769), 40, 119; [Thomas Jefferson], *A Summary View of the Rights of British America* (London, 1774), 28, 39–42.

35. [Dickinson], *Letters from a Farmer in Pennsylvania,* in Ford, ed., *Writings of Dickinson,* 312; [Benjamin Franklin], *The Causes of the Present Distractions in America Explained* ... (New York, 1774), 2.

36. Sir Lewis Namier, *England in the Age of the American Revolution,* 2d ed. (New York, 1961), 41. See also Thomas, *British Politics and the Stamp Act Crisis,* 364–371; J. G. A. Pocock, "1776: The Revolution against Parliament," in *Virtue, Commerce, and History: Essays on Political Thought and History, Chiefly in the Eighteenth Century* (Cambridge, 1985), 73–88.

37. John Wilkes to the Committee of the Sons of Liberty in Boston, Mar. 30, 1769, BL Add. MSS 30,870, 135; John Hope, *Letters on Certain Proceedings in Parliament during the Sessions of the Years 1769 and 1770* ... (London, 1772), 16; Simmons and Thomas, eds., *Proceedings and Debates,* III, 270–296; [William Pitt], *The Speech of the Right Honourable the Earl of Chatham, in the House of Lords, on Friday the 20th of January 1775* ... (London, 1775), 13; [Arthur Lee], *A Speech, Intended to Have Been Delivered in the House of Commons, in Support of the Petition from the General Congress at Philadelphia* ... (London, 1775), 2; William Pitt, first earl of Chatham, *A Plan Offered by the Earl of Chatham, to the House of Lords, Entitled, A Provisional Act, for Settling the Troubles in America* ... (London, 1775), 6–7. Having raised the possibility of amending the Declaration of Rights, Chatham immediately rejected it as an unacceptable encroachment on parliamentary sovereignty.

38. John Brewer, *Party Ideology and Popular Politics at the Accession of George III* (Cambridge, 1976), 179; "Petition of the County of York," presented Jan. 5, 1770, P.R.O., H.O. 55/2/2; Letter XLVII to the *Public Advertiser* (May 25, 1771), in John Cannon, ed., *The Letters of Junius* (Oxford, 1978), 243. For connections between Wilkes and the government's actions in America, see *A Letter to the Right Honourable George Grenville, Occasioned by His Publication of the Speech He Made in the House of Commons* ... (London, 1769), 46–49; [Matthew Dawes], *A Letter to Lord Chatham, concerning the Present War of Great Britain against America* ... (London, 1776), 58.

39. Simmons and Thomas, eds., *Proceedings and Debates,* III, 227; [Francis Webb], *Thoughts on the Constitutional Power, and Right of the Crown, in the Bestowal of Places and Pensions* ... (London, 1772), 62; [Stephen Sayre], *The Englishman Deceived: A Political Piece, Wherein Some Very Important Secrets of State Are Briefly Recited* ... (London, 1768), 3; [Sir Hercules Langrishe], *Considerations on the Dependencies of Great Britain, with Observations on a Pamphlet Intitled, the Present State of the Nation* (London, 1769),

83. See also the editorial remarks of Francis Blackburne in his *Memoirs of Thomas Hollis, Esq. F.R. and A. S.S.,* 2 vols. (London, 1780), 1, 180: "British administration have reaped this advantage from not interfering with the French in their attempts on Corsica, that they may say to them, 'We left you to complete your conquest of Corsica at your leisure: why will you obstruct our conquest of America?'"

40. [Arthur Lee], *An Appeal to the Justice and Interests of the People of Great Britain* ... (London, 1774), 32; [John Cartwright], *A Letter to Edmund Burke, Esq., Controverting the Principles of American Government, Laid Down in His Lately Published Speech on American Taxation* ... (London, 1775), 21; Richard Price, *Observations on the Nature of Civil Liberty, the Principles of Government, and the Justice and Policy of the War with America,* 8th ed. (1776), in Richard Price, *Two Tracts on Civil Liberty, the War with America, and the Debts and Finances of the Kingdom* (1778; New York, 1972), 36, 44–45; the estimate of the pamphlet's sales comes from Bernard Peach, ed., *Richard Price and the Ethical Foundations of the American Revolution: Selections from His Pamphlets, with Appendices* (Durham, N.C., 1979), 9. For the American acceptance of this perception, see Bernard Bailyn, *The Ideological Origins of the American Revolution* (Cambridge, Mass., 1967); Maier, *From Resistance to Revolution.*

41. Army officers routinely referred to the European settlers and traders that increasingly encroached on Indian rights as "banditti" and "vagabonds," and often complained of their "licentiousness" in dealings with native representatives (Sosin, *Whitehall and the Wilderness,* 218).

42. For the general problem, see Sosin, *Whitehall and the Wilderness,* esp. chaps. 3, 4, 6–9; Shy, *Toward Lexington,* 52–68, 192–204, 223–231; Lawson, *Imperial Challenge,* chaps. 2, 5, 6; Peter Marshall, "Colonial Protest and Imperial Retrenchment: Indian Policy 1764–1768," *Journal of American Studies,* V (1971), 1–17.

43. [Alexander] Dalrymple, *A General View of the East-India Company, Written in January, 1769* ... (London, 1772), 61; [Knox], *The Present State of the Nation,* 39–40 (pagination sequence repeats for two pages in original). For the relationship between Parliament's scrutiny of the East India Company and the attempt to tax the American colonies, see H. V. Bowen, *Revenue and Reform: The Indian Problem in British Politics, 1757–1773* (Cambridge, 1991), 24–27, 85, 187–188; P.J. Marshall, "Britain and the World in the Eighteenth Century: I, Reshaping the Empire," *Transactions of the Royal Historical Society,* 6th Ser., VIII (1998), 1–18.

44. John Shebbeare, *An Essay on the Origin, Progress, and Establishment of National Society* ... , 2d ed. (London, 1776), 127; [Matthew Wheelock], *Reflections Moral and Political on Great Britain and Her Colonies* (London, 1770), 41; Wilkes to Junius, Nov. 6, 1771, BL Add. MSS 30, 881, 27; [John Gray], *The Right of the British Legislature to Tax the American Colonies Vindicated, and the Means of Asserting That Right Proposed* ... (London, 1774), 37–38.

45. Adam Smith, *An Inquiry into the Nature and Causes of the Wealth of Nations* (1776), ed. Edwin Cannan, 2 vols. (1904; Chicago, 1976), II, 85, 103, 212–228, 442–465, 483, 486. See also John Robertson, *The Scottish Enlightenment and the Militia Issue* (Edinburgh, 1985), 212–215.

46. Two other notable members of this group were Josiah Tucker and Richard Price. For the emergence of a sustained critique of empire during the 1770s, see Bernard Semmel, *The Liberal Ideal and the Demons of Empire: Theories of Imperialism from Adam Smith to Lenin* (Baltimore, 1993), chaps. 1–4; Peter N. Miller, *Defining the Common Good: Empire, Religion, and Philosophy in Eighteenth-Century Britain* (Cambridge, 1994), chap. 6; Anthony Pagden, *Lords of all the World: Ideologies of Empire in Spain, Britain, and France, c. 1500–c. 1800* (New Haven, Conn., 1995), chaps. 6, 7.

47. [Knox], *Controversy between Great-Britain and Her Colonies Reviewed,* 50–51; [Samuel Johnson], *The Patriot: Addressed to the Electors of Great Britain* (London, 1774), 22–23; Edmund Burke, *The Speech of Edmund Burke, Esq., on Moving His Resolutions for Conciliation with the Colonies, March 22, 1775,* 3d ed. (London, 1775), 99; [Allan Ramsay], *A Plan of Reconciliation between Great Britain and Her Colonies* ... (London, 1776), 49–51. See also Smith, *Wealth of Nations,* ed. Cannan, II, 134: "The assembly of a province, like the vestry of a parish, may judge very properly concerning the affairs of its own particular district; but can have no proper

means of judging concerning those of the whole empire."

48. To be sure, commentators often conceded the existence of important differences between the Americans' political condition and that of their fellow subjects in England, Scotland, or Wales. As an indication of this, Thomas Pownall, Adam Smith, and William Knox each argued that the surest way to secure Parliament's imperial sovereignty would be to grant the colonists the privilege of sending representatives to the House of Commons. Even without such a representation, however, all three continued to think of the Americans as integral parts of a greater British nation that Parliament could tax. For proposals to create an American representation, see Pownall, *The Administration of the Colonies*, 4th ed., 174; Smith, *Wealth of Nations*, ed. Cannan, II, 471; [Knox], *The Present State of the Nation*, 39–40.

49. Simmons and Thomas, eds., *Proceedings and Debates*, V, 435–436; *London Evening Post*, Feb. 25, 1775, quoted in Simmons and Thomas, eds., *Proceedings and Debates*, V, 436.

50. Bailyn, *Ideological Origins*, chap. 4, "The Logic of Rebellion"; Lee to Franklin, London, June 1, 1774, P.R.O., CO. 5/118/27 (Lee observed that the one exception to this support for the government was in "the middling ranks, where you have many friends"); Shebbeare, *Essay on the Origin, Progress, and Establishment of National Society*, 127.

# PART II

# IMPERIAL CRISIS

# 3
# "BAUBLES OF BRITAIN"

*The American and Consumer Revolutions of the Eighteenth Century*

## *T.H. Breen*

## Introduction

During the 1760s and 1770s, Britain and its American colonies experienced three separate crises that together helped to produce the larger imperial crisis that became the American Revolution: the Stamp Act Crisis (1764–66), the Townshend Acts Crisis (1767–70), and the Tea Act/Coercive Acts Crisis (1773–76). Historians have long struggled to answer how American colonists, who lived in diverse and separate geographic regions, managed to unite and forge formidable resistance movements against British policies during these crises. In this now-classic essay, T.H. Breen poses the compelling answer that colonists communicated through a common language of consumption. The one thing that colonists shared, even if they agreed on little else, was an affinity for British goods. In the eighteenth century, British "baubles" – including ceramics, textiles, and metal wares – flooded the colonial marketplace. Items manufactured in England rapidly replaced locally made goods, creating an increasingly homogenous British material culture in America.

Breen argues that this shared material culture became a foundation for the political mobilization of American colonists during the revolutionary era. An unintended consequence of Parliament's various taxes of the 1760s and 1770s was the politicization of consumer goods. A broad cross-section of colonists came together in nonimportation (or boycott) movements against the British products that they had once so loved. According to Breen, nonimportation could advance the revolutionary cause even if local committees rarely succeeded in enforcing complete boycotts of British baubles. The movements mobilized more average people during the revolutionary era than any other cause until the war; in addition, for many colonists nonimportation served as a gateway to republican ideology. The path to American nationhood went through the shared consumption and later rejection of British consumer goods.

- Perhaps the primary problem that Breen considers is how the highly diverse American colonists could communicate across cultural and regional lines. What does he mean by claiming that the world of consumer goods provided a "language" through which colonists could address one another?
- Would Breen's findings about the influence of British "baubles" hold as well for Dutch or German colonists in British North America as they do for English colonists? What about for Indians and African Americans?
- Does Breen exaggerate the value of nonimportation movements in mobilizing American colonists against British policies? How else might have colonists organized without consumer boycotts?

Something extraordinary occurred in 1774. Thousands of ordinary American people responded as they had never done before to an urban political crisis. Events in Boston mobilized a nation, uniting for the first time artisans and farmers, yeomen and gentlemen, and within only a few months colonists who had earlier expressed neutrality or indifference about the confrontation with Great Britain suddenly found themselves supporting bold actions that led almost inevitably to independence.

At mid-century almost no one would have predicted such an occurrence. Some two million people had scattered themselves over an immense territory. They seemed to have little in common. In fact contemporary observers concluded that should the colonists ever achieve political independence, they would immediately turn on each other. "In short", declared one English traveller in 1759, "such is the difference of character, of manners, of religion, of interest, of the different colonies, that I think … were they left to themselves, there would soon be a civil war from one end of the continent to the other".[1] John Adams agreed. Reflecting in 1818 on the coming of revolution, he marvelled that the Americans had ever managed to unite. Their own separate histories seemed to have conspired against the formation of a new nation. The colonies, Adams explained, had evolved different constitutions of government. They had also experienced:

> so great a variety of religions, they were composed of so many different nations, their customs, manners, and habits had so little resemblance, and their intercourse had been so rare, and their knowledge of each other so imperfect, that to unite them in … the same system of action, was certainly a very difficult enterprise.

Very difficult indeed! And yet in 1776 these colonists surprised the world by successfully forming a new nation. In Adams's words, "Thirteen clocks were made to strike together".[2]

Somehow Americans had found a means to communicate effectively with each other, to develop a shared sense of political purpose, to transcend what at mid-century had appeared insurmountable cultural and geographic divisions. The mobilization of strangers in a revolutionary cause eroded the stubborn localism of an earlier period. In other words, it was a process that heightened awareness of a larger social identity. In Benedict Anderson's wonderful phrase, these men and women "imagined" a community, a national consciousness which while not yet the full-blown nationalism of the nineteenth century was nevertheless essential to the achievement of political independence.[3]

Efforts to explain this political mobilization have foundered on an attempt to establish the primacy of ideology over material interest.[4] This is not a debate in which the truth lies somewhere between two extremes. Neither the intellectual nor the economic historian can tell us how Americans of different classes and backgrounds and living in very different physical environments achieved political solidarity, at least sufficient solidarity to make good their claim to independence. Economic explanations – those that analyse an individual's political loyalties in terms of poverty or profits, absence of business opportunities or decline of soil fertility – are not only reductionist in character but also narrowly focused upon the experiences of specific, often numerically small groups in colonial society. Though we learn, for example, why certain urban workers in Boston or Philadelphia might have been unhappy with parliamentary taxation, we never discover how such people managed to reach out to – indeed even to communicate with – northern farmers and southern planters. In other words, the more we know about the pocket-book concerns of any particular eighteenth-century American community, the more difficult it becomes to understand a spreading national consciousness which accompanied political mobilization.

Intellectual historians encounter a different, though equally thorny set of problems. They transform the American Revolution into a mental event. From this perspective, it does not matter much whether the ideas that the colonists espoused are classic liberal concepts of rights and property, radical country notions of power and virtue or evangelical Calvinist beliefs about sin and covenants. Whatever the dominant ideology may have been, we find that a bundle of political abstractions has persuaded colonists living in scattered regions of America of the righteousness of their cause, driving them during the 1760s and 1770s to take ever more radical positions until eventually they were forced by the logic of their original assumptions to break with Great Britain. Unfortunately, intellectual historians provide no clear link between the everyday world of the men and women who actually became patriots and the ideas that they articulated. We are thus hard-pressed to comprehend how in 1774 wealthy Chesapeake planters and poor Boston artisans – to cite two obvious examples – could possibly have come to share a political mentality. We do not know how these ideas were transmitted through colonial society, from class to class, from community to community.

These interpretive issues – those that currently separate the materialists from the idealists – may be resolved by casting the historical debate in different terms. Eighteenth-century Americans, I shall argue, communicated perceptions of status and politics to other people through items of everyday material culture, through a symbolic universe of commonplace "things" which modern scholars usually take for granted but which for their original possessors were objects of great significance.[5] By focusing attention on the meanings of things, on the semiotics of daily life, we gain fresh insight into the formation of a national consciousness as well as the coming of the American Revolution.[6]

The imported British manufactures that flooded American society during the eighteenth century acquired cultural significance largely within local communities. Their meanings were bound up with a customary world of face-to-face relations. Within these localities Americans began to define social status in relation to commodities. This was, of course, an expression of a much larger, long-term transformation of the Atlantic world. And though this process differentiated men and women in new ways, it also provided them with a common framework of experience, a shared language of consumption.

But in America something unusual occurred during the 1760s and 1770s. Parliament managed to politicize these consumer goods, and when it did so, manufactured items suddenly took on a radical, new symbolic function. In this particular colonial setting the very commodities that were everywhere beginning to transform social relations provided a language for revolution. People living in scattered parts of America began to communicate their political grievances *through* common imports. A shared framework of consumer experience not only allowed them to reach out to distant strangers, to perceive, however dimly, the existence of an "imagined community", but also to situate a universal political discourse about rights and liberties, virtue and power, within a familiar material culture. In this context the boycott became a powerful social metaphor of resistance, joining Carolinians and New Englanders, small farmers and powerful merchants, men and women in common cause.[7]

This interpretive scheme gives priority neither to ideas nor experience. Some Americans undoubtedly boycotted British imports because of political principle. By denying themselves these goods they expressed a deep ideological commitment. Other colonists, however, gave up consumer items because their neighbours compelled them to do so. They were not necessarily motivated by high principle, at least not initially. But the very experience of participating in these boycotts, of taking part in increasingly elaborate rituals of non-consumption, had an unintended effect. It served inevitably to heighten popular awareness of the larger constitutional issues at stake. In this sense, the boycott for many Americans was an act of ideological discovery. These particular colonists may not have destroyed tea because they were republicans, but surely they learned something fundamental about republican ideas by their participation in such events. Questions about the use of tea in one's household forced ordinary men and women to choose sides, to consider exactly where one stood. And over time pledges of support for non-importation publicly linked patriotic individuals to other, like-minded individuals. Decisions about the consumer goods tied local communities to other communities, to regional movements and, after 1774, to a national association. Neither the consumer revolution nor the boycott movement can in itself explain an occurrence so complex as the American Revolution. That argument would amount to a new form of reductionism. The aim here is more limited: to explore the relation between the growth of national consciousness and the American rejection of the "baubles of Britain".

# I

The eighteenth century witnessed the birth of an Anglo-American "consumer society". Though the Industrial Revolution was still far in the future, the pace of the British economy picked up dramatically after 1690. Small manufacturing concerns scattered throughout England began turning out huge quantities of consumer goods – cloth, ceramics, glassware, paper, cutlery – items that transformed the character of everyday life. Merchants could hardly keep up with expanding demand. The domestic market hummed with activity. People went shopping, gawking at the wares displayed in the "bow-windows" that appeared for the first time along urban streets. Advertisements in the provincial English journals fuelled consumer desire, and to those middling sorts who wanted to participate in the market but who did not possess sufficient cash, tradesmen offered generous credit.[8]

Americans were quickly swept up in this consumer economy. These were not the self-sufficient yeomen of Jeffersonian mythology. Eighteenth-century colonists demanded the latest British manufactures. Few would have disagreed with the members of the Maryland general assembly who once announced, "We want the British Manufactures".[9] In order to pay for what they imported, the Americans harvested ever larger crops of tobacco, rice and indigo. Northern farmers supplied the West Indian plantations with foodstuffs. Economic historians have traditionally concentrated on this flow of American exports or, more precisely, on the production of staple commodities in response to European market conditions. The problem with this perspective is that it depreciates the role of consumer demand in shaping the colonial economy. At a time when the American population was growing at an extraordinary rate, per capita consumption of British imports was actually rising. In other words, more colonists purchased more manufactured goods every year. Since this was a young population – half of the colonists were under the age of sixteen – one must assume that adults were responsible for this exploding demand. Their consumption raised per capita rates for the entire society. After mid-century the American market for imported goods took off, rising 120 per cent between 1750 and 1773. Throughout the colonies the crude, somewhat impoverished material culture of the seventeenth century – a pioneer world of homespun cloth and wooden dishes – was swept away by a flood of store-bought sundries.[10]

These ubiquitous items transformed the texture of everyday life in provincial America. Even in the most inaccessible regions people came increasingly to rely on imports. One English traveller discovered to her surprise that in rural North Carolina women seldom bothered to produce soap. It was not a question of the availability of raw materials. Good ashes could be had at no expense. But these rural women were consumers, and they preferred to purchase Irish soap "at the store at a monstrous price".[11] In more cosmopolitan environments, the imports were even more conspicuous.

Eighteenth-century Americans situated other men and women within a rich context of British manufactures. John Adams betrayed this habit of mind when he visited the home of a successful Boston merchant:

> Went over [to] the House to view the Furniture, which alone cost a thousand Pounds sterling. A seat it is for a noble Man, a Prince. The Turkey Carpets, the painted Hangings, the Marble Table, the rich Beds with crimson Damask Curtains and Counterpins, the beautiful Chimny Clock, the Spacious Garden, are the most magnificent of any Thing I have ever seen.[12]

Like other Americans, Adams had obviously developed a taste for British imports.

How does one make sense out of this vast consumer society? There is much that we do not know about eighteenth-century colonial merchandizing. Still, even at this preliminary stage of investigation, it is possible to discern certain general characteristics that distinguished the colonial market-place at mid-century: an exceptionally rapid expansion of consumer *choice,* an increasing *standardization* of consumer behaviour and a pervasive *Anglicization* of the American market.

Of these three, the proliferation of choice is the most difficult to interpret. We simply do not know what it meant to the colonial consumer to find himself or herself suddenly confronted by an unprecedented level of variety in the market-place. Perhaps it was a liberating experience? Perhaps the very act of making choices between competing goods of different colour, texture and quality heightened the individual's sense of personal independence? After all, the colonial buyer was actively participating in the consumer economy, demanding what he or she wanted rather than merely taking what was offered.

Whatever the psychological impact of this change may have been, there is no question that Americans at mid-century confronted a range of choice that would have amazed earlier generations. A survey of New York City newspapers revealed, for example, that during the 1720s merchants seldom mentioned more than fifteen different imported items per month in their advertisements. The descriptions were generic: cloth, paper, ceramics. But by the 1770s it was not unusual during some busy months for New York journals specifically to list over nine thousand different manufactured goods. And as the number of items expanded, the descriptive categories became more elaborate. In the 1740s New York merchants simply advertised "paper". By the 1760s they listed seventeen varieties distinguished by colour, function and quality. In the 1730s a customer might have requested satin, hoping apparently that the merchant had some in stock. By the 1760s merchants advertised a dozen different types of satin. No carpets were mentioned in the New York advertisements before the 1750s, but by the 1760s certain stores carried carpets labelled Axminster, Milton, Persian, Scotch, Turkey, Weston and Wilton. One could purchase after the 1750s purple gloves, flowered gloves, orange gloves, white gloves, rough gloves, chamois gloves, buff gloves, "Maid's Black Silk" gloves, "Maid's Lamb Gloves", and even "Men's Dog Skin Gloves". There is no need to continue. Everywhere one looks, one encounters an explosion of choices.

If, as many scholars currently argue, human beings constitute external reality through language, then the proliferation of manufactures during the eighteenth century may have radically altered how Americans made sense out of everyday activities. The consumer market provided them with an impressive new vocabulary, thousands of words that allowed them not only to describe a changing material culture but also to interpret their place within it. Adams demonstrated this point when in his diary he recorded his reactions to the possessions of the wealthy Boston merchant. This language of goods was shared by all who participated in the market. It was not the product of a particular region or class, and thus furnished colonists with a means of transmitting experience across social and geographic boundaries. As we have seen, a visitor could engage the women of North Carolina in a discourse about imported soap. It was a conversation that the women of Virginia and Massachusetts would also have understood.

An example of this kind of cultural exchange occurred in a Maryland tavern in 1744. A travelling physician from Annapolis witnessed a quarrel between an innkeeper and an individual who by his external appearance seemed "a rough spun, forward, clownish blade". The proprietor apparently shared this impression, because she served this person who wore "a greasy jacket and breeches and a dirty worsted cap" a breakfast fit "for some ploughman or carman". The offended customer vehemently protested that he too was a gentleman and to prove his status, pulled a linen hat out of his pocket. He then informed the embarrassed assembly that "he was able to afford better than many who went finer: he had good linnen in his bags, a pair of silver buckles, silver clasps, and gold sleeve buttons, two Holland shirts, and some neat night caps; and that his little woman att home drank tea twice a day". What catches our attention is not the man's clumsy attempt to negotiate status through possessions – people have been doing that for centuries – but rather that he bragged of owning specific manufactured goods, the very articles that were just then beginning to transform American society. He assumed – correctly, in this case – that the well-appointed stranger he encountered in a country tavern understood the language of shirts, buckles and tea.[13]

This expanding consumer world of the mid-eighteenth century led almost inevitably to a *standardization* of the market-place. To be sure, as the previous anecdote suggests, Americans had begun to define status in relation to commodities. In this they were not especially unique. Throughout the Atlantic world choice created greater, more visible marks of distinction. Nevertheless by actually purchasing manufactured imports as opposed to making do with locally produced objects, by participating in an expanding credit network and by finding

oneself confronted with basically the same types of goods which were now on sale in other, distant communities, Americans developed a common element of personal experience.

One can only speculate, of course, why colonial shoppers purchased certain items. They may have been looking for status, beauty, convenience or price. Whatever the justification may have been, the fact remains that people living in different parts of America were exposed to an almost identical range of imported goods. In part, this standardization of the market-place resulted from the manufacturing process; after all, there were only so many dyes and glazes and finishes available during this period. The Staffordshire ceramics, for example, that sold in Charleston were of the same general shapes and colours as the Staffordshireware that sold in the shops of Philadelphia, New York and Boston. Indeed an examination of newspaper advertisements in these colonial ports reveals no evidence of the development of regional consumer taste.[14] British merchants sent to America what they could obtain from the manufacturers; the colonists bought whatever the merchants shipped. It is not surprising, therefore, to discover a Virginian in 1766 exclaiming, "Now nothing are so common as Turkey or Wilton Carpetts".[15] As we have already discovered, carpets of the same description had just made their appearance in the newspaper advertisements in New York and in the home of the Boston merchant described by John Adams.

The standardization of taste affected all colonial consumers. This is an important point. It is easy for modern historians to concentrate on the buying habits of the gentry.[16] Their beautiful homes – many of which are now preserved as museums – dominate our understanding of the character of daily life in eighteenth-century America. This interpretive bias is not a problem peculiar to the colonial period. The consumer behaviour of the wealthy has always been more fully documented than that of more humble buyers. But however much we are drawn to the material culture of the colonial élite, we should realize that the spread of the consumer market transformed the lives of ordinary men and women as fundamentally as it did those of their more affluent neighbours. Though wealthy Americans purchased goods of superior quality, poorer buyers demanded the same general range of imports. Rural pedlars, urban hawkers, Scottish factors responded to this eager clientele, providing farmers and artisans with easy credit, the ticket to participation in this consumer society. These people became reliant on imported manufactures, so much so in fact that Francis Fauquier, lieutenant-governor of Virginia, could note in 1763, "These imports daily encrease, the common planters usually dressing themselves in the manufactures of Great Brittain [*sic*] altogether".[17]

Tea provides an instructive example of the standardization of consumer taste. Early in the eighteenth century this hot drink became the preferred beverage in gentry households. Polite ladies – perhaps as a device to lure gentlemen away from tavern society – organized elaborate household rituals around the tea service. In fact the purchase of tea necessitated the acquisition of pots, bowls, strainers, sugar-tongs, cups and slop-dishes. One writer in a New York newspaper suggested the need for a school of tea etiquette. The young men of the city, finding themselves "utterly ignorant in the Ceremony of the Tea-Table", were advised to employ a knowledgeable woman "to teach them the Laws, Rules, Customs, Phrases and Names of the Tea Utensils".[18]

Though less well-to-do Americans did not possess the entire range of social props, they demanded tea. As early as 1734 one New Yorker reported:

> I am credibly informed that tea and china ware cost the province, yearly, near the sum of L10,000; and people that are least able to go to the expence, must have their tea tho' their families want bread. Nay, I am told, they often pawn their rings and plate to gratifie themselves in that piece of extravagance.[19]

It did not take long for this particular luxury to become a necessity. "Our people", wrote another New York gentleman in 1762, "both in town and country, are shamefully gone into the habit of tea-drinking".[20] And when Israel Acrelius visited the old Swedish settlements of Delaware at mid-century, he discovered people consuming tea "in the most remote cabins".[21] During the 1750s even the inmates of the public hospital of Philadelphia, the city poor-house, insisted on having bohea tea.[22] All these colonists drank their tea out of imported cups, not necessarily china ones, but rather ceramics that had originated in the English Midlands where they had been fired at very high temperature and thus made resistant to the heat of America's new favourite drink.

Ordinary Americans adopted tea for reasons other than social emulation. After all, it was a mild stimulant, and a hot cup of tea probably helped the labouring poor endure hard work and insubstantial housing. Nevertheless in some isolated country villages the desire to keep up with the latest consumer fads led to bizarre results, the kind of gross cultural misunderstanding that anthropologists encounter in places where products of an alien technology have been introduced into a seemingly less-developed society.[23] In 1794 a historian living in East Hampton, New York, interviewed a seventy-eight-year-old woman. "Mrs. Miller", he discovered, "remembers well when they first began to drink tea on the east end of Long Island". She explained that none of the local farmers knew what to do with the dry leaves: "One family boiled it in a pot and ate it like samp-porridge. Another spread tea leaves on his bread and butter, and bragged of his having ate half a pound at a meal, to his neighbor, who was informing him how long a time a pound of tea lasted him". According to Mrs. Miller, the arrival of the first tea-kettle was a particularly memorable day in the community:

> It came ashore at Montauk in a ship, (the *Captain Belt)*. The farmers came down there on business with their cattle, and could not

find out how to use the tea-kettle, which was then brought up to old "Governor Hedges". Some said it was for one thing, and some said it was for another. At length one, the more knowing than his neighbors, affirmed it to be the ship's lamp, to which they all assented.

Mrs. Miller may have been pulling the historian's leg, but whatever the truth of her story, it reveals the symbolic importance of tea in this remote eighteenth-century village.[24]

Standardization of consumer goods created a paradoxical situation. As Americans purchased the same general range of British manufactures – in other words, as they had similar consumer experiences – they became increasingly Anglicized. Historians sometimes refer to this cultural process as "the colonization of taste".[25] The Anglo-American consumer society of the eighteenth century drew the mainland colonists closer to the culture of the mother country. In part, this was a result of the Navigation Acts which channelled American commerce through Great Britain, a legislative constraint that made it difficult as well as expensive for Americans to purchase goods from the Continent. There is no reason to believe, however, that parliament passed these acts in a conscious attempt to "colonize American taste". That just happened. And during the eighteenth century this process is easy to trace. For most people, articles imported from the mother country carried positive associations. They introduced colour and excitement into the lives of the colonists. Their quality was superior to that of locally made goods, silverware and furniture being two notable exceptions. It is not surprising that the demand for British manufactures escalated so quickly after mid-century. The market itself created new converts. Advertisements, merchants' displays, news of other people's acquisitions stoked consumer desire and thereby accelerated the spread of Anglicization. Booksellers – just to note one example – discovered that colonial readers preferred an English imprint to an American

edition of the same title. "Their estimate of things English was so high", reports one historian, "that a false London imprint could seem an effective way to sell a local publication".[26]

Anglicized provincials insisted on receiving the "latest" English goods. They were remarkably attuned to even subtle changes in metropolitan fashion. "And you may believe me", a young Virginia planter named George Washington lectured a British merchant in 1760, "when I tell you that instead of getting things good and fashionable in their several kinds[,] we often have Articles sent Us that could have been usd [sic] by our Forefathers in the days of yore".[27] Washington may have envied his neighbours in Maryland. According to one visitor to Annapolis:

> The quick importation of fashions from the mother country is really astonishing. I am almost inclined to believe that a new fashion is adopted earlier by the polished and affluent American than by many opulent persons in the great metropolis [London] … In short, very little difference is, in reality, observable in the manners of the wealthy colonist and the wealthy Briton.[28]

No doubt this man exaggerated, but as he well understood, after mid-century American consumers took their cues from the mother country. Certainly that was the case of the people whom William Smith observed in New York. "In the city of New-York", he wrote in 1762, "through the intercourse with the Europeans, we follow the London fashions".[29] Benjamin Franklin saw this development in a favourable light; at least he did so in 1751. "A vast Demand is growing for British Manufactures", he marvelled, "a glorious market wholly in the Power of Britain".[30] The colonists belonged to an empire of goods. The rulers of the mother country could well afford to let the Americans drift politically for much of the eighteenth century, following a policy that has sometimes been labelled "salutary neglect". Like Franklin, the ablest British administrators must have sensed that the bonds of loyalty depended upon commerce, upon the free flow of goods, and not upon coercion.[31]

Let me summarize the argument to this point. Before the 1760s most Americans would not have been conscious of the profound impact of consumption upon their society. They were like foot-soldiers who witness great battles only from a narrow, personal perspective and thus cannot appreciate the larger implications of thousands of separate engagements. Of course, the colonists were aware of the proliferation of choice, but for most of them the acquisition of British imports was a private act, one primarily associated with one's own social status within a community or household. Manufactured goods shaped family routines; they influenced relationships within a particular neighbourhood. In symbolic terms these articles possessed local meanings. Certainly before the Stamp Act crisis – a few extreme evangelicals like James Davenport to the contrary notwithstanding – the Americans developed no sustained public discourse about goods.[32]

Nevertheless the totality of these private consumer experiences deeply affected the character of eighteenth-century provincial society, for in a relatively short period following 1740 this flood of British manufactures created an indispensable foundation for the later political mobilization of the American people. Though these highly Anglicized men and women were not fully aware of this shared experiential framework, it would soon provide them with a means to communicate across social and spatial boundaries. Only after political events beyond their control forced them to form larger human collectivities – as was the case after 1765 – did they discover that a shared language of goods was already in place.

## II

The importation of British goods on such a vast scale created social tensions that the colonists were slow to appreciate. The very act of purchasing these articles – making free choices

from among competing possibilities – heightened the Americans' already well-developed sense of their own personal independence. The acquisition of manufactures also liberated them from a drab, impoverished, even insanitary folk culture of an earlier period. But consumption inevitably involved dependency. The colonists came increasingly to rely upon British merchants not only for what they now perceived as the necessities of daily life but also for a continued supply of credit. So long as the Anglo-American economy remained relatively prosperous and stable, it was possible to maintain the fiction of personal independence in a market system that in fact spawned dependence. But those days were numbered. An increasingly volatile international economy coupled with parliament's apparent determination to tax the colonists sparked an unprecedented debate about the role of commerce within the empire. Comfortable relations and familiar meanings were no longer secure. That was the burden of John Dickinson's troubled remark in 1765, "under all these restraints and some others that have been imposed on us, we have not *till lately* been unhappy. Our spirits were not depressed".[33]

As Dickinson's observation suggests, the colonists' experiences as consumers no longer yielded the satisfaction that they had at an earlier time. The rising level of personal debt made the Americans' growing dependence upon British merchants increasingly manifest, and in this context of growing consumer "disappointment", the meaning of imported goods began to shift.[34] A semiotic order was changing. Articles that had been bound up with local cultures, with individual decisions within households, were gradually thrust into public discourse, and during the constitutional crisis with Great Britain these "baubles" were gradually and powerfully incorporated into a general moral critique of colonial society that traced its origins in part to radical country pamphleteers such as John Trenchard and Thomas Gordon and in part to the evangelical preachers of the Great Awakening.[35] In other words, a constitutional crisis transformed private consumer acts into public political statements. Britain's rulers inadvertently activated a vast circuit of private experience and in the process created in the American colonies what they least desired, the first stirrings of national consciousness.

To understand the process of symbolic redefinition one must remember that the merchants of the mother country bore as much responsibility as did the members of parliament for the growing unhappiness of the American consumers. To be sure, during the Stamp Act crisis British merchants petitioned the House of Commons in support of the colonists. But at the same time these businessmen pushed upon the American market more goods and credit than it could possibly absorb. Indeed their aggressive, though short-sighted drive to maximize returns not only substantially increased colonial indebtedness but also alienated American wholesalers who had traditionally served as middlemen between the large British houses and the American shopkeepers.[36] As Governor Francis Bernard of Massachusetts explained to the earl of Shelburne in 1768:

> for some years past the London merchants, for the sake of increasing their profits, have got into dealing immediately [directly] with the retailers … Instead of dealing with respectable houses[,] the London merchants are engaged in a great number of little shops, and for the sake of advantages derived from trading with people who cannot dispute the terms … they have extended their credit beyond all bounds of prudence, and have … glutted this country with goods.[37]

Parliament exacerbated these structural tensions within the American market. Though its efforts to raise new revenues after 1764 did not cripple the colonists' ability to purchase imported goods, parliament did remind the Americans of their dependence. If the colonists continued to purchase items such as glass, paper and paint from British merchants – which seemed quite likely since they could not produce these articles themselves – then the Americans would inevitably have to pay unconstitutional taxes. As Dickinson noted sarcastically in his influential *Letters from a Farmer,* "I think it evident, that we *must* use paper and glass; that what we use *must* be *British;* and that we *must* pay the duties imposed, unless those who sell these articles are so generous as to make us presents of the duties they pay".[38]

Considering the growing ambivalence of the colonists towards consumer goods – these items were immensely desirable, but also raised unsettling questions about economic dependency – it is not surprising that the Stamp Act crisis sparked a boycott of British manufactures.[39] During the anxious months of 1764 and 1765 urban Americans endorsed non-importation as the most likely means to bring about the Stamp Act's repeal and alleviate the burden of personal debt. As "Philo Publicus" explained to the readers of the *Boston Gazette,* "We have taken wide Steps to Ruin, and as we have grown more Luxurious every Year, so we run deeper and deeper in Debt to our Mother Country". After observing how extravagantly the people of Boston decorated their parlours, how they piled their sideboards high with silver plate, how they collected costly china, this writer concluded, "I wonder not that my Country is so poor, I wonder not when I hear of frequent Bankruptcies".[40]

The boycott seemed an almost reflexive reaction to constitutional crisis. Of course, in 1765 angry Americans had little other choice. After all, there was no colonial Bastille for them to storm; George III and his hated ministers lived in safety on the other side of the Atlantic.

But however circumscribed the range of responses may have been, the boycott served the colonists well. Participation in these protests provided Americans with opportunities to vent outrage against the policies of a distant government – much as Americans and others who boycott South African goods do today –

and though it was not clear whether anyone in the mother country actually listened, the very act of publicly denying themselves these familiar imports began to mobilize colonists of different regions and backgrounds in common cause.

The success of this first boycott should not be exaggerated. Most activities were restricted to urban centres, and though non-importation momentarily upset the flow of Anglo-American trade, it did not bring the British economy to its knees. Nevertheless, however limited its economic impact may have been, this initial confrontation reveals a mental process at work which in time would acquire extraordinary significance. As early as 1765 many colonists had begun to realize that patterns of consumption provided them with an effective language of political protest. In that sense, Americans discovered political ideology through a discussion of the meaning of goods, through observances of non-consumption that forced ordinary men and women to declare where exactly they stood on the great constitutional issues of the day. British manufactures thus took on a new symbolic function, and the boycott became a social metaphor of political resistance. If the mainland colonies had not already been transformed into a consumer society, the Stamp Act protesters would have found it extremely difficult to communicate effectively with each other at this moment of political crisis. The purchase of British manufactures was the one experience that most of them shared, and by raising the possibility that they could do without these goods patriotic Americans strained the bonds of Anglicization.

Revolution did not occur in 1765. The bonds of empire withstood the challenge, and as soon as parliament repealed the Stamp Act the Americans returned to the import shops. The confrontation with the mother country had eroded but not destroyed the traditional meaning of consumer goods. Newspaper advertisements carried the familiar words "just imported from England", a clear indication that many colonists still took their cultural cues from

Great Britain. Until that connection could be severed, independence was out of the question. This does not mean that Americans deserted the political principles that they had mouthed during the Stamp Act protest; most certainly they were not hypocrites. The boycott had provided colonists with a behavioural link between a political ideology and local experience, and when it was abandoned ideas about liberty and representation, slavery and virtue were temporarily dissociated from the affairs of daily life.

The Townshend Act of 1767 returned consumer goods to the centre of American political discourse. This ill-conceived statute levied a duty upon imported glass, paper, tea, lead and paint.[41] Patriotic leaders throughout the colonies advocated a campaign of non-consumption, and though this boycott would ultimately disappoint some of its more fervent organizers, it revealed the powerful capacity of goods in this society not only to recruit people into a political movement but also to push them – often when they were unaware of what was happening – to take ever more radical positions. As in the Stamp Act crisis, imported British manufactures provided a framework in which many colonists learned about rights and liberties.

During the period of protest against the Townshend Act, roughly between 1767 and 1770, colonists began to speak of consumer goods in a highly charged moral language. Of course, these Americans were not the first people to condemn the pernicious effects of luxury and self-indulgence. That concern had vexed moralists for centuries. Nevertheless during the Stamp Act crisis a dominant theme of the political discourse had been debt. The purchase of British manufactures undermined the personal independence of the American consumers and thus made them fit targets for tyrannical conspirators. But after 1767 the thrust of patriotic rhetoric shifted from *private* debt to *public* virtue. By acquiring needless British imports the colonial consumer threatened the liberties of other men and women. "Every

Man who will take Pains to cultivate the Cost of Homespun", advised a writer in the *Boston Gazette,* "may easily convince himself that his private Interest, as well as [that of] the Publick, will be promoted by it".[42] In other words, how one spent one's own money became a matter deserving public scrutiny.

The artefacts of a consumer culture took on new symbolic meaning within a fluid political discourse, and before long it was nearly impossible for Americans to speak of imported goods without making reference to constitutional rights. The politicization of consumption was clearly evident in the 22 December 1767 instructions of the Boston town meeting to its representatives in the general assembly. We, your constituents, they announced, are worried about "the distressed Circumstances of this Town, by means of the amazing growth of Luxury, and the Embarrassments of our Trade; & having also the strongest apprehensions that our invaluable Rights & Liberties as Men and British Subjects, are greatly affected by a late Act of the British Parliament"; they urged their representatives "to encourage a spirit of Industry and Frugality among the People".[43] Colonists living in different parts of America called for a boycott not just of those few imports specifically taxed by the Townshend Act but, rather, a long list of British manufactures, everything from clocks to carriages, hats to house furniture, even mustard.[44] The lists contained scores of items, a virtual inventory of the major articles of the mid-century consumer culture. The colonists seemed determined to undo patterns of consumption that had taken root in the 1740s, to return perhaps to a simpler period of self-sufficiency, which in fact had never existed, but which in this political crisis seemed the best strategy for preserving liberty. In this social context it made sense for colonial writers to declare: "Save your money and you can save your country".[45]

The Townshend boycotts – ineffective though they may have been in forcing parliament to back down – helped radical colonists to distinguish friends from enemies. Strangers communicated ideology through the denial of consumer goods. Rhetoric was not enough. One had to reveal where one stood. The non-consumption movement forced individuals to alter the character of their daily lives, and as they did so, they formed collectivities of like-minded colonists, acts which inevitably reinforced their own commitment to radical politics. The leaders of Windham, a small village in south-eastern Connecticut, scheduled a town meeting in response to correspondence they had received from Boston. This letter from the outside urged the people of Windham to join in a boycott; in other words, to think of politics in terms that extended far beyond the boundaries of the community. This invitation caused the villagers to take note of their "surprising fondness … for the use and consumption of foreign and British manufactures". After a full discussion of the issues, they publicly pledged "to each other that we will discourage and discountenance to the utmost of our power the excessive use of all foreign teas, china ware, spices and black pepper, all British and foreign superfluities and manufactures". This covenant helped the townspeople to sort themselves out. One group of Windham inhabitants was now prepared to expose another group as "Enemies to their Country", and once this decision had been taken, both sides probably thought more deeply about political loyalties than they had ever done before. And the villagers spread word of their resolution, appointing a committee "to correspond with committees from the several towns in the County in order to render the foregoing proposals as extensive and effectual as may be". The confrontation with British imports was extending the political horizons of ordinary people in this small Connecticut village. Though they could not possibly correspond directly with distant Americans, they expressed their "earnest desire that every town in this Colony and in every Colony in America would explicitly and publicly disclose their sentiments relating to the Non-importation Agreement and the violations thereof".[46] Without question, one encounters in Windham the makings of an "imagined community", the seeds of national consciousness.

By mobilizing people ordinarily excluded from colonial politics, the non-consumption movement of this period greatly expanded the base of revolutionary activities. The Townshend boycott politicized even the most mundane items of the household economy and thereby politicized American women. Decisions about consumption could not be separated from decisions about politics. Within this electric atmosphere mothers and wives and daughters monitored the ideological commitment of the family. Throughout the colonies women altered styles of dress, wove homespun cloth and stopped drinking tea. At one wedding in Connecticut, countrywomen appeared in garments of their own making and insisted upon having "Labrador tea", a concoction brewed from indigenous herbs. Other women in New England participated in spinning and weaving competitions, community rituals of great symbolic complexity. The actual homespun was invested with political significance. But so too were the women themselves. Their efforts at the wheel, like those of Mahatma Gandhi in another era, became local representations of a general ideology that connected the people of these communities – at least in their political imaginations – to unseen men and women in other American communities.[47]

The boycott of consumer goods also drew young people into the political debate. The students of Harvard, Yale and the College of Rhode Island, for example, appeared at commencement during the late 1760s wearing homespun suits.[48] Though such displays irritated royal officials – that was the fun of it – they also transmitted political meanings through non-consumption to other young people. This was an important element in the process of developing a national consciousness. In a society in which the average age was about sixteen, the young could not be taken for granted. A large percentage of the American population in 1776 had not even been born at the time of the Stamp Act crisis,

and if college students had not been recruited into the boycott movement, they might not later as adults have appeared at Bunker Hill.

The circle of participation widened to include even the poorer members of colonial society, the kinds of people who were as dependent upon the consumer society as were their gentry neighbours. They collected rags required for the manufacture of "patriotic" paper. Goods – or in this case the denial of goods – were mobilizing an entire populace. Peter Oliver, the Boston loyalist who later wrote an acerbic history of the Revolution, noted that during the protest against the Townshend duties, the city's radicals circulated:

> A Subscription Paper … Enumerating a great Variety of Articles not to be imported from *England,* which they supposed would muster the Manufacturers in *England* into a national Mob to support their Interests. Among the various prohibited Articles, were *Silks, Velvets, Clocks, Watches, Coaches & Chariots;* & it was highly diverting, to see the names & marks, to the Subscription, of Porters & Washing Women.[49]

Oliver found the incident amusing, an example of how a few troublemakers had duped the poorer sorts. But the porters and washerwomen of Boston knew what they were doing.[50] Affixing one's signature or mark to a document of this sort was a personal risk that they were willing to accept. Like the village women and the graduating students, these people had been mobilized through goods; it is difficult to see how independence could have been achieved without them.

The protest against the Townshend duties generated group activities that might best be termed "rituals of non-consumption". These were focused moments in the life of a community during which continuing social relations were often, quite suddenly politicized. The spark for these events was usually a letter sent by some external body urging the villagers to support the boycott. In some towns large numbers of men and women took oaths before their neighbours swearing not to purchase certain items until parliament repealed the obnoxious taxes. These ceremonies possessed a curious religious character, much like the covenant renewals in the early Congregational churches of New England. In other communities specially selected committee-men carried subscription papers from house to house.[51] In Boston the "Subscription Rolls, for encouraging Oeconomy, Industry, our own Manufactures, and the disuse of foreign Superfluities" were kept in the office of the town clerk. According to a notice in the *Boston Gazette,* "The Selectmen strongly recommend this Measure to Persons of *all ranks,* as the most honorable and effectual way of giving *public* Testimony of their Love to their Country, and of endeavouring to save it from ruin".[52] Whether they lived in Boston or an inland village, ordinary colonists were obviously under considerable pressure to sign. But the decision was theirs to make. By pledging to support non-consumption they reaffirmed their moral standing in the community. They demonstrated that they were not "enemies to their country" – a country that in fact they were only just beginning to define.

Perhaps the most effective political ritual associated with non-consumption, at least in New England, was the funeral. More than any other event connected with the life cycle, the funeral in eighteenth-century America had become an occasion of conspicuous consumption. Wealthy families distributed commemorative rings. Gloves were given out, and custom mandated that all attendants wear mourning dress made of the best imported cloth that they could afford. Indeed opulent funerals were in themselves an indication of the spread of the consumer society. "Such was the fashion", one colonist explained, that bereaved families imagined that if they disappointed their friends and neighbours, "they should have made themselves obnoxious to the censures of an ill-natured and malicious world,

who would have construed their frugality into niggardliness".[53]

During the protest against the Townshend duties, such extravagant displays suddenly seemed inappropriate. A shift in the symbolic meaning of British imports called forth a change in funeral etiquette. And since these were highly visible events, they inevitably confronted those persons who had not thought deeply about imperial politics with an ideological message. The freeholders and inhabitants of Boston agreed "not to use any Gloves but what are manufactured here, nor any new Garments upon such Occasion but what shall be absolutely necessary".[54] Everywhere one saw signs of retrenchment at funerals, a trend that one anonymous writer declared "affected every true patriot with particular satisfaction".[55] As might be expected, the loyalist historian, Peter Oliver, denounced the politicization of funerals. He saw the hand of the radicals behind these restrictions. "Under Pretence of Oeconomy", he announced, "the Faction undertook to regulate Funerals, that there might be less Demand for English Manufactures". Oliver recognized that expensive funerals had at an earlier time "ruined some Families of moderate Fortune", but from his perspective the patriot funeral raised even greater problems. "One Extreme was exchanged for another. A Funeral now seemed more like a Procession to a *May Fair,* and Processions were lengthened, especially by the Ladies, who figured a way … to exhibit their Share of Spite, & their Silk Gowns".[56] Funerals had moved from the private to the public realm, and as was recently the case in the black townships of South Africa, they became powerful political statements. It is perhaps not surprising, therefore, that the members of the Continental Congress enthusiastically endorsed this particular means of mobilizing mass support, pledging in September 1774 that:

> on the death of any relation or friend, none of us, or any of our families will go into any further mourning-dress, than a black crape

or ribbon on the arm or hat, for gentlemen, and a black ribbon and necklace for ladies, and we will discontinue the giving of gloves and scarves at funerals.[57]

The repeal of the Townshend Acts in 1770 retarded the growth of national consciousness in the American colonies. Parliament's apparent retreat on the issue of taxation revealed the symbolic function that consumer goods had played in the constitutional discourse. As political tensions within the empire eased, these articles no longer carried such clear ideological meanings. Repeal, in fact, unloosed a frenzy of consumption. Though the tax on tea remained, the colonists could not be deterred from buying British manufactures. Between 1770 and 1772 they set records for the importation of foreign goods. Radical leaders such as Samuel Adams warned the Americans that the threat to their political liberties had not been removed. He begged them to continue their resistance, to maintain the boycott. But few listened. Commerce returned to the old channels, and as it did so, goods again became associated with the Anglicization of American society. It is no wonder that Adams grumbled in a letter to his friend Arthur Lee that the colonial newspapers were once again filled with advertisements for "the Baubles of Britain".[58]

The non-importation movement of the late 1760s had in fact been only a partial success. The merchants of Philadelphia accused the merchants of Boston of cheating. People everywhere found it more difficult than they had anticipated to do without the thousands of items imported from the mother country. The most notable successes of the period had been local, something that had occurred within regionally clustered communities. For all the rhetoric, it had proved hard to communicate to very distant strangers.[59] George Mason understood the problem. "The associations", he explained, "almost from one end of this continent to the other, were drawn up in a hurry and formed upon erroneous principles". The organizers of these boycotts had expected parliament to back

down quickly, certainly within a year or two, but that had not happened. The results did not discourage Mason, however, for as he explained in December 1770, "had one general plan been formed exactly the same for all colonies (so as to have removed all cause of jealousy or danger of interfering with each other) in the nature of a sumptuary law, restraining only articles of luxury and ostentation together with the goods at any time taxed", the results might have been different.[60] Americans had not yet discovered how to communicate continentally.

In 1773 parliament stumbled upon an element of mass political mobilization that had been missing during the Townshend protest. By passing the Tea Act, it united the colonists as they had never been before. The reason for this new solidarity was not so much that the Americans shared a common political ideology, but rather that the statute affected an item of popular consumption found in almost every colonial household. It was perhaps *the* major article in the development of an eighteenth-century consumer society, a beverage which, as we have seen, appeared on the tables of the wealthiest merchants and the poorest labourers. For Americans, therefore, it was not difficult to transmit perceptions of liberty and rights through a discourse on tea. By transforming this ubiquitous element of daily life into a symbol of political oppression, parliament inadvertently boosted the growth of national consciousness. "Considering the article of tea as the detestable instrument which laid the foundation of the present sufferings of our distressed friends in the town of Boston", the members of the Virginia house of burgesses declared in August 1774, "we view it with horror, and therefore resolve that we will not, from this day, either import tea of any kind whatever, nor will we use or suffer, even such of it as is now at hand, to be used in any of our family".[61] And in the northern colonies, people now spoke of tea-drinkers not simply as enemies of our country – a term which in the 1760s had referred to one's colony or region – but as enemies "to the liberties of America".[62]

The public discourse over tea raised issues about the political effects of consumption that had been absent or muted during the previous decade. The language of goods became more shrill, hyperbolic. During the Stamp Act crisis, colonists associated consumption chiefly with personal debt. After parliament passed the Townshend duties, they talked more frequently in a moral vocabulary. By denying themselves the "baubles" of the mother country, they might thereby preserve their virtue. But in 1774 they spoke of tea as a badge of slavery, as a political instrument designed by distant tyrants to seize their property. "A WOMAN" argued in the *Massachusetts Spy* that:

> in the present case the use of tea is considered not as a *private* but as a *public* evil … we are not to consider it merely as the herb tea, or what has an ill-tendency as to health, but as it is made a handle to introduce a variety of public grievances and oppressions amongst us.

Tea, A WOMAN concluded, is a sign of "enslaving our country".[63] In an impassioned appeal to the citizens of Charleston, South Carolina, one speaker – probably Christopher Gadsden – insisted that a non-importation agreement would "prove a means of restoring our liberty". "Who that has the spirit of a man", he asked:

> but would rather forego the elegancies and luxuries of life, than entail slavery on his unborn posterity to the end of time? … Nothing but custom makes the curl-pated beau a more agreeable sight with his powder and pomatum, than the tawney savage with his paint and bear's grease. Too long has luxury reigned amongst us, enervating our constitutions and shrinking the human race into pigmies.[64]

And finally, another writer in this period bluntly reminded newspaper readers in New England that "the use of Tea is a political evil in this country".[65]

Throughout America the ceremonial destruction of tea strengthened the bonds of political solidarity. Once again, we must look to local communities for the embryonic stirrings of national consciousness. It was in these settings that a common commodity was transformed into the overarching symbol of political corruption. By purging the community of tea leaves – an import that could be found in almost every American home – the colonists reinforced their own commitment to certain political principles. But they did more. The destruction of the tea transmitted an unmistakable ideological message to distant communities: we stand together. The Boston Tea Party is an event familiar to anyone who has heard of the Revolution.[66] In many villages, however, the inhabitants publicly burned their tea. Everyone was expected to contribute some leaves, perhaps a canister of tea hidden away in a pantry, a few ounces, tea purchased long before parliament passed the hated legislation, all of it to be destroyed in flames that purged the town of ideological sin. "We hear from [the town of] Montague", reported the *Massachusetts Spy*:

> that one of the inhabitants having inadvertently purchased a small quantity of tea of a pedlar, several of the neighbours being made acquainted therewith, went to his house and endeavoured to convince him of the impropriety of making any use of that article for the present, while it continues to be a badge of slavery.

The visiting committee easily persuaded the man "to commit it to the flames". The group then ferreted the pedlar out of the local tavern, seized his entire stock of tea and "carried [it] into the road, where it was burnt to ashes".[67] In Charleston, Massachusetts, the town clerk announced that he would oversee the collection of all tea in the community: "And that the tea so collected, be destroyed by fire, on Friday next at noon day, in the market place". He declared that any persons who failed to participate in this activity "are not only inimicable to the liberty of America in general, but also show a daring disrespect to this town in particular".[68] From Northampton County on Virginia's eastern shore came news that a committee had collected 416 pounds of tea. Moreover "Some gentlemen also brought their Tea to the Court House, and desired it might be publickly burnt, in which reasonable request they were instantly gratified".[69] And from Wilmington, North Carolina, a traveller reported, "the Ladies have burnt their tea in a solemn procession".[70]

The seizure and destruction of tea became an effective instrument of political indoctrination, forcing the ignorant or indifferent people of these communities publicly to commit themselves to the cause of liberty while at the same time reinforcing the patriots' commitment to a radical ideology. The individuals involved were often ordinary men and women. Had they not become associated with tea, they might have remained anonymous colonists, going about their business and keeping their political opinions to themselves. But they were not so lucky. Early in 1774 Ebenezer Withington, a "labourer" living in Dorchester, allegedly found some tea on a road that ran along the ocean. Soon thereafter he was called before a meeting of "Freeholders and other Inhabitants" where Withington confessed in writing before his neighbours that:

> I found said Tea on Saturday, on going round the Marshes; brought off the same thinking no Harm; returning I met some Gentlemen belonging to the Castle [the British fort in Boston Harbour], who asked me if I had been picking up the Ruins? I asked them if there was any Harm; they said no except from my Neighbours. Accordingly, I brought Home the same, part of which I Disposed of, and the Remainder took from me since.

The townspeople decided that Withington had not realized the political significance of his act.

The people who had purchased tea from him were warned to bring it to the village authorities immediately for destruction or risk having their names published as enemies of the country.[71] The Dorchester committee – and committees in other towns as well – performed the same political function that local militia units would serve during the Revolution. They provided ideological instruction, and by so doing made it difficult even for the poorest persons either to remain neutral or retain old loyalties.[72]

Sometimes tea sparked an incident that mobilized an entire village. By their own admission, the inhabitants of Truro, an isolated village on Cape Cod, had not kept informed about the gathering political storm in Boston. Then, one day, some tea apparently washed ashore near Provincetown, and the men who discovered it sold small quantities to a few Truro farmers. That purchase precipitated a crisis. A town committee questioned these persons and concluded "that their buying this noxious Tea was through ignorance and inadvertance, and they were induced thereto by the base and villainous example and artful persuasions of some noted pretended friends to government from the neighbouring towns; and therefore this meeting thinks them excusable with acknowledgement".

But individual confession was not sufficient to exonerate the community. The people of Truro had failed to educate themselves about the dangers to their constitutional liberties and, of course, had left themselves vulnerable to scheming persons who peddled tea, the symbol of oppression. The town meeting decided, therefore, to form a special committee which would draft a resolve "respecting the introduction of Tea from Great Britain subject to a duty, payable in America". After deliberating for half an hour, the members of this committee returned with a statement which was at once defensive and radical:

> WE the inhabitants of the town of Truro, though by our remote situation from the centre of public news, we are deprived

of opportunities of gaining so thorough a knowledge in the unhappy disputes that subsist between us and the parent state as we could wish; yet as our love of liberty and dread of slavery is not inferior (perhaps) to that of our brethren in any part of the province, we think it our indispensable duty to contribute our mite in the glorious cause of liberty and our country.

People asked immediately what in fact they could do to demonstrate that their ideological hearts were in the right place. "We think", the committee responded, "that most likely method that we can take to aid in frustrating those inhuman designs of administration is a disuse of that baneful dutied article Tea".[73] The inhabitants of this village communicated their political beliefs not only to the radical leaders of Boston and to the members of the Massachusetts general assembly but also to themselves through tea. By dropping this popular import they overcame the peculiarities of local experience and linked up with other Americans, distant strangers whose crucial common bond with the farmers of Truro at this moment was their participation in an eighteenth-century consumer society.

During the summer of 1774 patriot spokesmen throughout America called for some form of boycott. Boston's leaders, for example, urged the people of Massachusetts to sign a Solemn League and Covenant pledging to break off "all commercial connection with a country whose political Councils tend only to enslave them".[74] Loyalists castigated this "infernal Scheme". In this atmosphere almost any manufactured article could spark a dispute. The League in fact threatened to bring the political battles of the street into the home, "raising a most unnatural Enmity between Parents & Children & Husbands & Wives".[75] People living in other parts of America now looked to the Continental Congress for guidance. As George Mason had recognized in 1770, a successful boycott required the united and co-ordinated efforts of all the colonists. When the congressional

delegates convened in September 1774, they passed legislation almost immediately, creating the Association, a vast network of local committees charged with enforcing non-importation. This was a truly radical act. In an attempt to halt further commerce with Great Britain, Congress authorized every county, city and town in America to establish a revolutionary government.[76] As Henry Laurens explained in September 1774:

> From the best intelligence that I have received, my conclusions are, that So. Carolina, No. Carolina, Virginia, Maryland, Pensylvania [*sic*], New Jersey, New York, Connecticut, Rhode Island, Massachusets [*sic*], New Hampshire, one chain of Colonies extending upwards of 1,200 Miles & containing about three Millions of White Inhabitants of whom upwards of 500,000 [are] Men capable of bearing Arms, will unite in an agreement to Import no goods from Great Britain, the West India Islands, or Africa until those Acts of Parliament which Strike at our Liberties are Repealed.[77]

The colonists responded enthusiastically to the call. The committees monitored consumption, identifying local patriots by the garments they wore and by the beverages they drank, and demanding public confessions from those who erred. In Virginia counties everyone was expected to sign the Association, a promise before one's neighbours – almost a statement of one's new birth as a consumer – not to purchase the despised manufactures of the mother country. According to James Madison, these signings were "the method used among us to distinguish friends from foes and to oblige the Common people to a more strict observance of it [the Association]".[78] As in earlier boycotts, people sorted themselves out politically through goods. A committee in Prince George's County announced, "That to be clothed in manufactures fabricated in the Colonies ought to be considered as a badge and distinction of respect and true patriotism".[79] The local associations also educated ordinary men and women about the relation between consumer goods and constitutional rights, in other words, about the relation between experience and ideology. A committee in Anne Arundel County, Maryland, helped Thomas Charles Williams understand that by importing tea he had "endangered the rights and liberties of America". Proceedings against Williams were dropped, after he proclaimed that he was "sincerely sorry for his offense".[80] Silas Newcomb of Cumberland, New Jersey, was more stubborn. The members of the local association failed to convince the man of his error in drinking "East-India Tea in his family", and they were finally compelled "to break off all dealings with him, and in this manner publish the truth of the case, that he may be distinguished from the friends of American liberty".[81]

## III

The colonists who responded to Boston's call in 1774 were consciously repudiating the empire of goods. Within barely a generation the meaning of the items of everyday consumption had changed substantially. At mid-century imported articles – the cloth, the ceramics, the buttons – had served as vehicles of Anglicization, and as they flooded into the homes of yeomen and gentry alike, they linked ordinary men and women with the distant, exciting culture of the metropolis. By participating in the market-place, by making choices among competing manufactures, the colonists became in some important sense English people who happened to live in the provinces. By taxing these goods, however, parliament set in motion a process of symbolic redefinition, slow and painful at first, punctuated by lulls that encouraged the false hope that the empire of goods could survive, but ultimately straining Anglicization to breaking-point. Americans who had never dealt with one another, who lived thousands of miles apart, found that they could communicate their political grievances through goods or, more precisely, through the denial of goods that had held the

empire together. Private consumer experiences were transformed into public rituals. Indeed many colonists learned about rights and liberties through these common consumer items, articles which in themselves were politically neutral, but which in the explosive atmosphere of the 1760s and 1770s became the medium through which ideological abstractions acquired concrete meaning.

When the colonists finally and reluctantly decided that they could do without the "baubles of Britain", they destroyed a vital cultural bond with the mother country. "The country", explained James Lovell to his friend Joseph Trumbull in December 1774, "... seems determined to let England know that in the present struggle, commerce has lost all the temptations of a bait to catch the American farmer".[82] Lovell may have exaggerated, but he helps us to understand why in 1774 the countryside supported the cities. Consumer goods had made it possible for the colonists to imagine a nation; the Association made it easier for Americans to imagine independence.

## Notes

Earlier drafts of this essay were presented at "Of Consuming Interests: The Style of Life in the Eighteenth Century", a conference organized by the United States Capitol Historical Society, Washington, D.C., 20 March 1986; and at a workshop for the Anthropology Department, Univ. of Chicago, 19 January 1987. I would especially like to acknowledge the suggestions of Marshall Sahlins, Michael Silverstein, Bernard Cohn, James Oakes and Josef Barton.

1  Andrew Burnaby, *Travels through North America* (New York, 1904), pp. 152–3.
2  *The Works of John Adams,* ed. S. F. Adams, 10 vols. (Boston, 1850–6), x, p. 283, John Adams to Hezekiah Niles, 13 Feb. 1818.
3  Benedict Anderson, *Imagined Communities: Reflections on the Origin and Spread of Nationalism* (London, 1983); Linda Colley, "Whose Nation? Class and National Consciousness in Britain, 1750–1830", *Past and Present,* no. 113 (Nov. 1986), pp. 97–117; Geoff Eley, "Nationalism

and Social History", *Social Hist.,* vi (1981), pp. 83–107; Richard L. Merritt, *Symbols of American Community, 1735–1775* (New Haven, 1966). See also T. H. Breen, "Persistent Localism: English Social Change and the Shaping of New England Institutions", *William and Mary Quart.,* 3rd ser., xxxii (1975), pp. 3–28.

4 I discuss this historiographic debate in *Tobacco Culture: The Mentality of the Great Tidewater Planters on the Eve of Revolution* (Princeton, 1985), ch. 1. See also Gordon S. Wood, "Rhetoric and Reality in the American Revolution", *William and Mary Quart.,* 3rd ser., xxiii (1966), pp. 3–32.

5 See Mihaly Czikszentmihalyi and Eugene Rochberg-Halton, *The Meaning of Things: Domestic Symbols and the Self* (Cambridge, 1981). Though this is a study of contemporary society, it provides historians with valuable insight into how people interpret the material objects of daily life.

6 See Lynn A. Hunt, *Politics, Culture and Class in the French Revolution* (Berkeley, 1984); Anthony Giddens, *The Constitution of Society: Outline of the Theory of Structuration* (Berkeley, 1984); Marshall Sahlins, *Islands of History* (Chicago, 1985).

7 The Swadeshi movement in late nineteenth-century and early twentieth-century India provides some intriguing parallels to the American experience. As C. A. Bayly explains, "After 1905, the import of British-made cloth into India and the ensuing destruction of Indian handicraft production became the key theme of Indian nationalism. In the hands first of Bengali leaders and later of Mahatma Gandhi and his supporters, the need to support *swadeshi* (home) industries and boycott foreign goods was woven through with notions of neighbourliness, patriotism, purity, and sacrifice, all of which provided unifying ideologies more powerful than any single call for political representation or independence": C. A. Bayly, "The Origins of Swadeshi (Home Industry): Cloth and Indian Society, 1700–1930", in Arjun Appadurai (ed.), *The Social Life of Things: Commodities in Cultural Perspective* (Cambridge, 1986), p. 285. Also Sumit Sarkar, *The Swadeshi Movement in Bengal, 1903–1908* (New Delhi, 1973); Bernard S. Cohn, "Cloth, Clothes and Colonialism: India in the 19th Century" (paper for the Wenner-Gren Foundation, symposium, 1983).

8 The literature on the development of an Anglo-American consumer society during the eighteenth century is quite large. Works that were particularly helpful for this investigation include Charles Wilson, *England's Apprenticeship, 1603–1763* (Cambridge, 1965); Ralph Davis, *A Commercial Revolution in English Overseas Trade in the Seventeenth and Eighteenth Centuries* (London, 1967); Roy Porter, *English Society in the Eighteenth Century* (Harmondsworth, 1982); Harold Perkin, *The Origins of Modern English Society* (London, 1969); Neil McKendrick, John Brewer and J. H. Plumb, *The Birth of a Consumer Society: The Commercialization of Eighteenth-Century England* (Bloomington, 1982); Eric Jones, "The Fashion Manipulators: Consumer Tastes and British Industries, 1660–1800", in Louis P. Cain and Paul J. Uselding (eds.), *Business Enterprise and Economic Change: Essays in Honor of Harold F. Williamson* (Kent, Ohio, 1973), pp. 198–226; Lorna Weatherill, "A Possession of One's Own: Women and Consumer Behaviour in England, 1660–1740", *Jl. Brit. Studies,* xxv (1986), pp. 131–56; Joanna Innes, "Review Article: Jonathan Clark, Social History and England's 'Ancien Regime'", *Past and Present,* no. 115 (May 1987), pp. 165–200.

9 *Archives of Maryland, lix: Proceedings and Acts of the General Assembly of Maryland, 1764–1765,* ed. J. Hall Pleasants (Baltimore, 1942), p. 210.

10 I have reviewed the literature of consumer behaviour in eighteenth-century America in "An Empire of Goods: The Anglicization of Colonial America, 1690–1776", *Jl. Brit. Studies,* xxv (1986), pp. 467–99. See also John J. McCusker and Russell R. Menard, *The Economy of British America, 1607–1789* (Chapel Hill, 1985), ch. 13; Carole Shammas, "How Self-Sufficient Was Early America?", *Jl. Interdisciplinary Hist.,* xiii (1982), pp. 247–72; Gloria Mam, "The Standard of Living in Colonial Massachusetts", *Jl. Econ. Hist.,* xliii (1983), pp. 101–8; Lorena S. Walsh, "Urban Amenities and Rural Sufficiency: Living Standards and Consumer Behavior in the Colonial Chesapeake, 1643–1777", *Jl. Econ. Hist.,* xliii (1983), pp. 109–17; Marc Egnal and Joseph A. Ernst, "An Economic Interpretation of the American Revolution", *William and Mary Quart.,* 3rd ser., xxix (1972), pp. 3–32. An interpretation of the character of the eighteenth-century American economy that differs substantially from the one advanced here can be found in James A. Henretta, "Families and Farms: *Mentalité in* Pre-

Industrial America", *William and Mary Quart.*, 3rd ser., xxxv (1978), pp. 3–32.

11 [Janet Schaw], *Journal of a Lady of Quality … 1174 to 1776,* ed. Evangeline W. and Charles M. Andrews (New Haven, 1921), p. 204.

12 *Diary and Autobiography of John Adams,* ed. L. H. Butterfield, 4 vols. (New York, 1964), i, p. 294.

13 Alexander Hamilton, *Gentleman's Progress: Itinerarium of Dr. Alexander Hamilton,* ed. Carl Bridenbaugh (Chapel Hill, 1948), pp. 13–14.

14 Observations about the character and content of eighteenth-century American advertising found in this essay are based on extensive research in the newspapers of Boston, New York, Philadelphia, Williamsburg and Charleston, carried out by the author and Rebecca Becker of Northwestern University.

15 John Hemphill, "John Wayles Rates his Neighbors", *Virginia Mag. Hist, and Biography,* lxvi (1958), p. 305.

16 See Richard L. Bushman, "American High Style and Vernacular Cultures", in Jack P. Greene and J. Pole (eds.), *Colonial British America: Essays in the New History of the Early Modern Era* (Baltimore, 1984), pp. 345–83.

17 Public Record Office, London, C.O. 5/1330, Francis Fauquier, "Answers to the Queries Sent to Me by the Right Honourable the Lords Commissioners for Trade and Plantation Affairs", 30 Jan. 1763. See also Breen, "Empire of Goods", pp. 485–96.

18 Cited in Esther Singleton, *Social New York under the Georges, 1714–1776* (New York, 1902), pp. 380–1.

19 *Ibid.,* p. 375.

20 William Smith, *The History of the Late Province of New-York … 1762* (New York Hist. Soc. Collections, iv, pt. 2, 1829), p. 281.

21 Cited in Rodis Roth, "Tea Drinking in Eighteenth-Century America: Its Etiquette and Equipage", in *Contributions from the Museum of History and Technology,* paper 14 (U.S. National Museum, ccxxv, Washington, D.C., 1961), p. 66.

22 Billy G. Smith, "The Material Lives of Laboring Philadelphians, 1750 to 1800", *William and Mary Quart.,* 3rd ser., xxxviii (1981), p. 168.

23 See, for example. H. A. Powell, "Cricket in Kiriwina", *Listener,* xlviii (1952), pp. 384–5.

24 Henry P. Hedges, *A History of the Town of East-Hampton* (Sag-Harbor, 1897), p. 142.

25 Bayly, "Origins of Swadeshi", pp. 303–11. See also Nicholas Phillipson, "Politics, Politeness and the Anglicisation of Early Eighteenth-Century Scottish Culture", in R. A. Mason (ed.), *Scotland and England, 1286–1815* (Edinburgh, 1987), pp. 226–46.

26 Stephen Botein, "The Anglo-American Book Trade before 1776: Personnel and Strategies", in William L. Joyce *et al.* (eds.), *Printing and Society in Early America* (Worcester, Mass., 1983), p. 79.

27 *The Writings of George Washington,* ed. John C. Fitzpatrick, 39 vols. (Washington, D.C., 1931), ii, p. 350, George Washington to Robert Cary and Co., 28 Sept. 1760.

28 William Eddis, *Letters from America,* ed. Aubrey C. Land (Cambridge, Mass., 1969), pp. 57–8.

29 Smith, *History of the Late Province of New-York,* p. 277.

30 Benjamin Franklin, "Observations Concerning the Increase of Mankind" (1751), in *The Papers of Benjamin Franklin,* ed. Leonard W. Labaree, 25 vols. (New Haven, 1959 and continuing), iv, p. 229.

31 See Breen, "Empire of Goods".

32 D. D. Hall, "Religion and Society: Problems and Reconsiderations", in Greene and Pole (eds.), *Colonial British America,* pp. 337–8. The most famous evangelical of the period, George Whitefield, embraced the latest merchandizing techniques, literally selling the revival to the American people. The crowds flocked to hear Whitefield, while his critics grumbled about the commercialization of religion. One anonymous writer in Massachusetts noted that there is "a very wholesome law of the province to discourage Pedlars in Trade" and it seems high time "to enact something for the discouragement of Pedlars in Divinity also": *Boston Weekly News-Letter,* 22 Apr. 1742. For connections between the consumer revolution and the Great Awakening, see Frank Lambert, "'Pedlar in Divinity': George Whitefield and the Great Awakening, 1737–1745" (Graduate seminar paper, Northwestern Univ., 1987).

33 John Dickinson, "The Late Regulations Respecting the British Colonies" (1765), in *The Writings of John Dickinson,* ed. Paul Leicester Ford, 2 vols. (Philadelphia, 1895), i, p. 217 (my emphasis).

34 The psychological implications of economic "disappointment" are imaginatively discussed

in Albert O. Hirschman, *Shifting Involvements: Private Interest and Public Action* (Princeton, 1982). See also Tibor Scitovsky, *The Joyless Economy: An Inquiry into Human Satisfaction and Consumer Dissatisfaction* (New York, 1976).

35  Bernard Bailyn, *The Ideological Origins of the American Revolution* (Cambridge, Mass., 1967); Gordon Wood, *The Creation of the American Republic, 1776–1787* (Chapel Hill, 1969); Edmund S. Morgan, "The Puritan Ethic and the American Revolution", *William and Mary Quart.,* 3rd ser., xxiv (1967), pp. 3–43.

36  William T. Baxter, *The House of Hancock: Business in Boston, 1724–1775* (Cambridge, Mass., 1945), pp. 239–42; Egnal and Ernst, "Economic Interpretation of the American Revolution"; Breen, *Tobacco Culture,* chs. 3–5.

37  Cited in William Pencak, *War, Politics and Revolution in Provincial Massachusetts* (Boston, 1981), p. 164.

38  John Dickinson, *Letters from a Farmer in Pennsylvania* (1768), in *Writings of John Dickinson,* ed. Ford, i, p. 355. Also "The Pitkin Papers", *Colls. Connecticut Hist. Soc.,* xix (1921), p. 74, William Pitkin to Richard Jackson, 14 Feb. 1767.

39  See Edmund S. and Helen M. Morgan, *The Stamp Act Crisis: Prologue to Revolution* (Chapel Hill, 1953).

40  *Boston Gazette,* 1 Oct. 1764. Also Arthur M. Schlesinger, *The Colonial Merchants and the American Revolution, 1763–1776* (Columbia Univ. Studies in History, Economics and Public Law, lxxviii, no. 182, New York, 1918), pp. 63–5; Charles M. Andrews, "Boston Merchants and the Non-Importation Movement", *Trans. Colonial Soc. Massachusetts,* xix (1916–17), pp. 182–91. For a discussion of the cultural meaning of debt in this period, see Breen, *Tobacco Culture.*

41  Merritt Jensen, *The Founding of a Nation: A History of the American Revolution, 1763–1776* (New York, 1968), pp. 237–344; Andrews, "Boston Merchants", pp. 191–252.

42  *Boston Gazette,* 11 Jan. 1768.

43  *A Report of the Record Commissioners of the City of Boston Containing the Boston Town Records, 1758 to 1769* (Boston, 1886), pp. 227–8.

44  *Ibid.,* p. 221. Also "Virginia Nonimportation Resolutions, 1769", in *The Papers of Thomas Jefferson,* ed. Julian P. Boyd, 22 vols. (Princeton, 1953), i, pp. 28–9.

45  Cited in Andrews, "Boston Merchants", p. 92.

46  Cited in Ellen D. Larned, *History of Windham County, Connecticut,* 2 vols. (Worcester, Mass., 1880), ii, pp. 116–19.

47  Andrews, "Boston Merchants", pp. 193–4. Also Linda K. Kerber, *Women of the Republic: Intellect and Ideology in Revolutionary America* (Chapel Hill, 1980), pp. 38–41.

48  Andrews, "Boston Merchants", pp. 195–7.

49  *Ibid.,* p. 197; Peter Oliver, *Origin and Progress of the American Revolution: A Tory View,* ed. Douglass Adair and John A. Schutz (Stanford, 1961), p. 61.

50  See Alfred F. Young, "George Robert Twelves Hewes, 1742–1840: A Boston Shoemaker and the Memory of the American Revolution", *William and Mary Quart.,* 3rd ser., xxxviii (1981), pp. 561–623.

51  Andrews, "Boston Merchants", pp. 209–14; Schlesinger, *Colonial Merchants,* ch.3.

52  *Boston Gazette,* 30 Nov. 1767 (my emphasis).

53  *Massachusetts Spy,* 6 Jan. 1774. Also Robert A. Gross, *The Minutemen and their World* (New York, 1976), p. 33.

54  *Report of the Record Commissioners,* p. 224. Also Andrews, "Boston Merchants", p. 196; Morgan, *Stamp Act Crisis,* pp. 247–8.

55  *Massachusetts Spy,* 6 Jan. 1774.

56  Oliver, *Origin and Progress of the American Revolution,* p. 62.

57  "The Association", 20 Oct. 1774, in *Documents of American History,* ed. Henry Steele Commager (New York, 1949), p. 86.

58  *The Writings of Samuel Adams,* ed. Harry Alonzo Cushing, 4 vols. (New York, 1904–8), ii, p. 267.

59  Jensen, *Founding of a Nation,* chs. 10–12.

60  Kate Mason Rowland, *The Life of George Mason, 1725–1792,* 2 vols. (New York, 1892), i, pp. 148–9.

61  "Virginia Non-Importation Agreement", 1 Aug. 1774, in *Documents of American History,* ed. Commager, p. 80.

62  "New York Sons of Liberty Resolutions on Tea", 29 Nov. 1773, *ibid.,* p. 70.

63  *Massachusetts Spy,* 6 Jan. 1774; also *ibid.,* 13, 20 Jan., 25 Aug. 1774.

64  "To the Inhabitants of the Province of South Carolina, about to Assemble on the 6th of July", 4 July 1774, in *American Archives,* comp. Peter Force, 4th ser., 6 vols. (Washington, D.C., 1837–53), i, p. 511.

65  *Massachusetts Spy,* 23 Dec. 1773.

66 See Benjamin Woods Labaree, *The Boston Tea Party* (New York, 1964).

67 *Massachusetts Spy,* 17 Feb. 1774.

68 *Ibid.,* 6 Jan. 1774.

69 *American Archives,* comp. Force, 4th ser., i, pp. 1045–6.

70 [Schaw], *Journal of a Lady of Quality,* p. 155.

71 *Massachusetts Spy.* 13 Jan. 1774.

72 On the responsibility of the colonial militias to indoctrinate citizens, see John W. Shy, *A People Numerous and Armed: Reflections on the Military Struggles for American Independence* (New York, 1976), pp. 193–224.

73 *Massachusetts Spy,* 31 Mar. 1774.

74 *American Archives,* comp. Force, 4th ser., i, pp. 397–8; Jensen, *Founding of a Nation,* pp. 468–75; Schlesinger, *Colonial Merchants,* pp. 319–26; Gross, *Minutemen,* pp. 47, 50–1.

75 Oliver, *Origin and Progress of the American Revolution,* p. 104.

76 Jensen, *Founding of a Nation,* pp. 506–7.

77 *The Papers of Henry Laurens,* ed. George C. Rogers, Jr., 10 vols. (Columbia, S.C., 1981), ix, p. 552, Henry Laurens to Peter Petrie, 7 Sept. 1774.

78 *Papers of James Madison,* ed. W. T. Hutchinson and William M. E. Rachal, 3 vols. (Chicago, 1962), i, p. 135, James Madison to William Bradford, 20 Jan. 1775.

79 *American Archives,* comp. Force, 4th ser., i, p. 494.

80 *Ibid.,* p. 1061.

81 *Ibid.,* ii, p. 34.

82 Cited in Jensen, Founding of a Nation, p. 561.

# 4
# 1776: THE COUNTERCYCLICAL REVOLUTION
*John M. Murrin*

## Introduction

In this essay, John M. Murrin takes a broad view of the British imperial crisis, concluding that the American Revolution was a "countercyclical" event. By this, he means that the Revolution went against the existing trends of the era, which, if anything, suggested a greater British role in American colonial society, not political separation. Murrin rejects various attempts by other historians to explain the Revolution as an event decades in the making. Instead, in multiple areas – from patterns of religious worship to inheritance and other legal customs – the American colonies became increasingly Anglicized, or British, over the course of the eighteenth century. Before the American Revolution, the British Empire thrived because of the affection felt by colonists for the mother country.

Alternately, according the Murrin, the Revolution can be understood as a process of increasing *disaffection* for British imperial rule. His close reading of the British imperial policies during the three major imperial crises (Stamp Act, Townshend Acts, and Tea Act/Coercive Acts) leads him to conclude that colonists entered the revolutionary era accepting of British imperial rule in external affairs, particularly trade, but jealously guarded the sovereignty of their colonial assemblies over internal matters, especially taxes. Therefore, it was no surprise that colonists waged the fiercest resistance against the Stamp Act (1765), an internal tax, and the Massachusetts Government Act (1774), which violated the very principle of colonial self-government. In Murrin's telling, the American Revolution is a story of unintended, even shocking, consequences. By 1775, a great empire that had once flourished from the voluntary actions of its colonial subjects relied upon military coercion to retain only a fraction of its previous authority.

- In describing the workings of the British Empire, Murrin places heavy emphasis on the distinction between policies that affected the internal and external affairs of the American colonies. Consider the difference for the daily lives of colonists. Could the British have avoided an imperial crisis if Parliament had limited its legislation to external matters?
- Murrin credits riots with helping to advance the American cause of defeating unpopular British policies, especially the Stamp Act. Compare his account with T.H. Breen's in the previous essay, which downplays the role of crowd action. Are the two accounts of popular mobilization incompatible, or did American protests vary according to particular British policies?
- As Murrin details, the American colonies grew at a feverish pace in the eighteenth century. If the Revolution had not happened when it did, is it possible to imagine other more "cyclical" means by which America might have separated from the British Empire?

"I shall burn all my Greek and Latin books," exclaimed the jubilant Horace Walpole in 1762 when he heard of the capture of Martinique; "they are histories of little people. The Romans never conquered the world, till they had conquered three parts of it, and were three hundred years about it; we subdue the globe in three campaigns; and a globe, let me tell you, as big again as it was in their days."[1] In five years beginning in 1758, the British Empire crushed New France, took Guadeloupe and Martinique from France, nearly drove the French out of India, brutally punished the Cherokees for entering the North American war in 1760, and when Spain finally intervened in the struggle in 1762, conquered Havana and Manila before the Peace of Paris ended the fighting in 1763.[2] Nothing in the history of the British people prepared them for so awesome a triumph. And yet, just twelve years later, British soldiers clashed with Massachusetts militia at Lexington and began another world war. Both France and Spain intervened, and by 1783 Britain had to concede the independence of the United States of America.

The irony was overwhelming. It still is. To many contemporaries, including both the duc de Choiseul and the comte de Vergennes (that is, the French foreign minister who negotiated the peace treaty and his successor who gave America the French alliance in 1778), Britain's spectacular triumph over its imperial rivals by 1763 all but guaranteed the revolt of the mainland colonies in the years that followed. With no French or Spanish enemy nearby to threaten them, the colonists would discover, both men predicted, that they no longer needed British protection and would soon throw off British rule.[3]

Choiseul and Vergennes saw the Canada cession as a master stroke of French policy. Many loyalists and historians have agreed with them. Had Canada remained French, lamented Governor Thomas Hutchinson of Massachusetts in 1773, "none of the spirit of opposition to the Mother Country would have yet appeared & I think the effects of [the Canada cession] worse

than all we had to fear from the French or Indians."[4]

Yet the argument does not hold up under analysis. The mainland colonies remained vulnerable to assault from the sea, and only Britain could give them naval protection. Although the French army had left Canada, the *habitants* remained behind, and the colonists still feared them. Parliament's Quebec Act of 1774 terrified patriots in the British colonies because they understood its potential. It marked a serious effort to placate the French settlers on their own terms on the eve of conflict between Britain and the thirteen colonies. The First Continental Congress denounced the Quebec Act for encouraging the French settlers "to act with hostility against the free Protestant colonies, whenever a wicked ministry shall chuse so to direct them." Once the fighting began, the Second Continental Congress, fearing that the governor of Quebec "is instigating the people of that province and the Indians to fall upon us," launched its own preemptive invasion of Canada in 1775. The patriots escalated their resistance into armed conflict with Britain not because the Gallic Peril had disappeared but despite their recognition that it had revived.[5]

Britain was unable to convert its gigantic triumph over its imperial rivals into a successful postwar policy for North America. That failure is still, after more than two centuries, the enigma at the core of the American Revolution. Unless we can account for it, we still cannot explain why the Revolution happened at all. In my judgment, the scholarship of the past two or three decades, as wonderful and imaginative as much of it has been, has only deepened this central problem. Old explanations, such as the Canada cession and the rise of a sense of American national identity within the British Empire, have collapsed.[6] Other studies have been giving us an empire that was becoming much more tightly integrated in the three or four decades before independence. We can see similar patterns whether we look at transatlantic migration, the late imperial economy, the rise of evangelical religion, colonial political culture, or the willingness of colonists to embrace a larger British and imperial identity.

The achievement of American independence was a countercyclical event. It ran against the prevailing integrative tendencies of the century. The American Revolution was a crisis of imperial *integration* that the British state could not handle.

# I

Beginning around 1730, when the population of the mainland colonies was only about 630,000 settlers and enslaved Africans, transatlantic migration soared to peaks that, in absolute numbers, had never been achieved before. This volume was probably a higher percentage of the existing settler population than any colony had known since its founding generation. About 248,000 enslaved Africans and 284,000 Europeans landed in the thirteen colonies between 1730 and 1775. When the fighting began in 1775, about 10 percent of the residents had arrived in North America since 1760. The British Empire had become a remarkably efficient redistributor of people who took advantage of the demand for labor or the availability of land thousands of miles away. Land in North Carolina, Pennsylvania, New York, or even Nova Scotia could start thousands of people moving across the ocean on quite short notice – close to 10,000 a year by the early 1770s.

But if transatlantic migration was binding ever more people together ever more tightly, the whole process could seem like a disaster to some of those left behind, particularly Irish or Scottish landlords who faced a serious risk of losing most of their tenants and their rental income. Wills Hill, Earl of Hillsborough, owned 100,000 acres of land on his Irish estates and faced constant pressure from emigration. As president of the Board of Trade, he supported the Proclamation of 1763, which created at least a temporary barrier to the settlement of most western lands in North America. He became the first secretary of state for the American colonies

in 1768 and again used all his influence to prevent the creation of new colonies in the West. When speculators won over even the king to their Vandalia project, he resigned in frustration in 1772. But the British government did adopt one of his major ideas. It began interviewing emigrants as a way of gauging the seriousness of the problem and, perhaps, as a prelude to a statutory limitation of emigration from the British Isles.[7]

Similar patterns characterized the late imperial economy. It became much more dynamic and efficient after 1730 or 1740, to the great benefit of most colonial consumers and to the pain of some merchants who found that increased competition could seriously reduce their profit margins. The colonial population doubled about every twenty-five years, which meant an automatic increase in demand for British products. But British imports increased even more rapidly than population in the last three to five decades (depending on the colony) before independence and contributed immensely to the growing refinement of life in the half century before independence. And because growing European demand kept the prices of American exports high, while the prices of imports from Britain were falling, partly in response to the first phase of the industrial revolution, the settlers were, in short, getting more for their money. As Glasgow absorbed an ever larger share of the tobacco trade, Scotland also achieved a level of prosperity it had never known before. To a significant degree, Chesapeake tobacco provided the material base for the Scottish Enlightenment, the most exciting intellectual movement of the era.[8]

# II

The Great Awakening and internal colonial politics, for very different reasons, have often been invoked to explain why the Revolution happened. On the surface, both seem to provide compelling arguments. Nearly all evangelicals in the thirteen colonies supported the Revolution.

Nearly all loyalists, except in Nova Scotia, rejected revivalism. Similarly, the resistance movement after 1764 had strong support within colonial assemblies. It began by affirming the principle of "no taxation without representation," which expanded to "no legislation without consent" by 1774, both of which were strong affirmations of each colony's right to self-government through its elective assembly.

Yet the Great Awakening never pitted North American churches against their British counterparts across the Atlantic. Nothing comparable to the antebellum split of evangelical churches along sectional lines occurred within the British Empire before the Revolution. Instead, the revivals divided communities within themselves and sent both factions looking for allies in other colonies and across the ocean. Beginning with George Whitefield's spectacular tour of the colonies in 1739–1740, the Awakening brought distant peoples into contact with one another who otherwise might never have heard of each other. The College of New Jersey – a Presbyterian institution and the first colonial college founded specifically to propagate vital piety – paid its own homage to the geographical extent of the revivals by taking its first president from Long Island, its second from New Jersey, its third (Jonathan Edwards) from Congregational Massachusetts, its fourth from Virginia, its fifth from Maryland, and its sixth from Scotland. And even though evangelicals gave overwhelming support to the Revolution, antievangelicals were by no means a loyalist phalanx. They can be found all along the political spectrum of the era from Thomas Paine and Thomas Jefferson on the left, to George Washington and James Madison in the center, and to Joseph Galloway and Thomas Hutchinson on the right. Except in Connecticut and New Jersey, evangelicals seldom achieved positions of political leadership. Antirevivalists directed events on both sides of the revolutionary divide.[9]

Underlying trends in colonial public life show similar patterns and ambiguities. In seventeenth-century Virginia, the orthodox colonies of New England, and the Dutch areas of New York, jury trials for noncapital crimes were rare before the Glorious Revolution. Only in the eighteenth century did the colonies fully embrace the jury ideology that had taken shape in England under the later Stuarts.[10] In histories of colonial politics, the most misleading assumption has been that of a teeter-totter. If the assembly was rising, royal government must have been declining. Beyond any doubt the assemblies played an increasing role in provincial life throughout the century. They sat longer, passed more laws, and drew on a more elite segment of the population for their membership. But royal government also became measurably stronger in the middle decades of the century. In every colony except New York, the most effective royal governors served sometime between 1720 and the 1760s. In Virginia, South Carolina, and Georgia, they succeeded through a highly ritualized form of persuasion and flattery that the assembly reciprocated. The Virginia House of Burgesses had only one public quarrel with a royal governor in the forty-five years between 1720 and the Stamp Act of 1765. In New Hampshire, Massachusetts, New York, and New Jersey, successful governors used patronage and influence to build majorities in the assembly. And even though all the assemblies helped organize resistance to the Stamp Act and the Townshend Acts, many of them stopped well short of revolution after Parliament passed the Coercive Acts in 1774. In the five colonies from New York through Maryland, no legal assembly ever repudiated the Crown. All of them had to be pushed aside by popularly elected provincial congresses. When the Revolution finally came, much of its thrust was directed at the assemblies, not through them.[11]

Even the language of revolution was a fairly recent British import. Seventeenth-century colonists spoke of their "liberties," not of "rights," much less "natural rights," a phrase that John Locke finally turned into a commonplace expression. The language of natural rights took hold quite late in North America, only during the adult years of the resistance leaders of the

1760s. In the colonies it mixed, sometimes uneasily, with that other heritage from the English Commonwealth tradition, the conviction that public life presents an eternal struggle between power and liberty, that power nearly always wins over time, and that corruption is its most effective weapon. For Bernard Bailyn, this "Country" ideology has become the necessary and sufficient explanation for the Revolution. In the colonies, he argues, formal royal prerogatives were stronger than in Britain, where the Crown, for example, no longer vetoed bills or dismissed judges. But the governors' informal powers, especially their patronage, were never sufficient to manage the assemblies as effectively as Sir Robert Walpole controlled Parliament. This gap between formal and informal constitutions was filled by angry factions who denounced the corruption of royal officials. As early as the 1730s, Bailyn believes, the colonists were primed for revolution. Parliament had only to provide the stimulus to set the process in motion.[12]

The Declaration of Independence did unite the language of natural rights with a formal indictment of George III for a systematic conspiracy to undermine liberty in the colonies, mostly through corruption. Without this pervasive fear, the Revolution of 1776 would not have happened. But for most of the provincial era, the languages of politics had functioned quite differently. Natural rights and English rights were interchangeable terms until the early or mid-1770s. The colonists believed that the English constitution embodied their natural rights.[13]

When the language of corruption was invoked, it often reflected a governor's strength, not, as Bailyn's argument assumes, his weakness. In northern colonies those who attacked corruption were opposition leaders unable to win majority support in the legislature, such as Lewis Morris during the John Peter Zenger affair in New York in the 1730s or the Boston opposition to Governor William Shirley in the late 1740s. In other words, this language replicated its role in British politics in the age of Sir Robert Walpole,

who dominated the government between 1721 and 1742. In southern colonies, this "Country" paradigm was not even oppositional after the 1720s. Rather, both governors and planters believed that their colonies had achieved an ideal constitutional balance, and they used the tension between power and liberty to celebrate their own accomplishment, a government without corruption that achieved its goals through mutual trust and cooperation. Maryland's governor, by contrast, had more patronage than any other colonial executive. It never gave him the political effectiveness or stability that Virginia, South Carolina, and Georgia achieved through their stylized politics of harmony.[14]

The Seven Years' War, or what Lawrence Henry Gipson called the Great War for the Empire, brought these integrative tendencies to a culmination. After Britain's very rocky start through 1757, William Pitt took charge of the war effort, sustained about 30,000 redcoats in America, and raised about 20,000 provincial troops for each campaign from 1758 until the fall of Montreal in 1760. The mainland colonies then raised thousands more for the West Indian campaigns of 1761 and 1762. So massive and successful was this overall effort that both Old Lights and New Lights discovered millennial significance in the global triumph of British liberty. The Presbyterian Church, rent by a schism over the revivals in 1741, healed the breach at the height of the war in 1758. When George III succeeded his grandfather as king in 1760, his North American subjects responded warmly to his call for the restoration of virtue and piety to public life. Throughout North America, the colonists gloried in their British identity.[15]

## III

We are back where we started. The British Empire by 1763 achieved a level of integration it had never known before, and the result was equally unprecedented – total victory over New France. Yet even though the colonies had been anglicizing their societies for decades, important differences remained between them and the mother country. The most significant involved the household. The English practice of primogeniture had never taken deep hold in America. The head of the household expected to pass his own status down to all his sons and to enable all his daughters to marry men of comparable standing in the community. This pattern dated back to the reforms of the London Company, which made landholding a reasonable ambition for most Virginia settlers after 1618, and Plymouth also made land available to male settlers from the 1620s. Compared with Britain, North America had been a paradise for younger sons for a century and a half. But after about 1750, many households, even if they added a craft to their main occupation of farming, had difficulty sustaining this level of opportunity. Some fathers responded by privileging sons over daughters and older sons over younger ones. In Virginia most tidewater land had been entailed by the 1760s – that is, the owner could not divide the estate for sale in separate parcels or bequeath it to more than one heir, although he could set up other sons on land somewhere else. At this level the basic anglicizing tendencies of the century had to seem like a foreclosure of opportunity to many settlers.[16]

Ceaseless expansion became the American answer to this dilemma, and Indians paid the heaviest price for the ambitions of ordinary settlers. And yet the demand for expansion does not get us very far in trying to explain the onset of the revolution against Britain. The British did slow the process, more for speculators than for actual settlers, and the eagerness of settlers (or squatters) to move west probably helped radicalize great planters who began to despair of the Crown's willingness to grant titles to lands that they claimed. But after Hillsborough's resignation as American secretary in 1772, the British government was also moving toward the settlement of the Ohio Valley. The Revolution erupted because of confrontations along the eastern seaboard, not in the West, although tensions there also contributed to the alienation

of affection that fatally undermined British authority.[17]

We are left with the oldest tool available to historians for explaining anything: narrative. We have to tell the story of the three imperial crises that undermined the British Empire despite all the advantages it had won by 1763. The Stamp Act Crisis of 1764–1766 began when George Grenville, the prime minister, tried to address the empire's needs for defense and revenue. In the process he polarized the very real needs of the empire with the traditional rights of the colonists, especially the right to be taxed only through the consent of their assemblies. After Grenville rejected the relevance of this argument, colonial mobs nullified the Stamp Act by compelling the stamp distributors in each colony to resign.

The colonists blamed Grenville's ministry, not Parliament or the Crown, for the crisis, and they rejoiced heartily when George III replaced Grenville with the new ministry of the Marquess of Rockingham in the summer of 1765. Rockingham decided that repeal was the only alternative to a civil war in North America, but he needed a better argument than colonial riots to build a parliamentary majority for repeal. Even before news of colonial nonimportation agreements reached London, he encouraged British merchants and manufacturers to petition for repeal on the grounds that the Grenville program had deranged their trade. This argument then persuaded the colonists that their own nonimportation agreements had been decisive in converting the ministry to repeal, a misconception that would again make nonimportation central to resistance to Britain from 1768 to 1775 as well as from 1806 to 1812. Apparently no one stopped to reflect that the Stamp Act itself, once stamps became unavailable, imposed nonexportation on the colonies for several months. Merchants refused to send ships to sea lest they be confiscated for lack of stamped clearance papers after they reached their destinations. The crisis ended when Parliament repealed the Stamp Act, which had levied taxes on legal documents, pamphlets, and newspapers; but Parliament only amended the Sugar Act of 1764 by lowering the duty on imported molasses from three pence to one penny per gallon while extending the tax to British West Indian as well as foreign molasses. That duty, disguised in the statute's preamble as a regulation of trade, brought in more than £30,000 per year until Lexington.[18]

The colonists believed that they had vindicated their rights as Englishmen. But the resolution of the crisis revealed another gap, this one structural, that hardly anyone but Benjamin Franklin understood. In the debate over the Stamp Act, both sides had rejected the distinction between "internal" taxes, such as excises on the consumption of goods or stamp duties on legal documents, and "external" taxes, or port duties imposed on oceanic commerce. Grenville never doubted that Parliament could lay duties on colonial trade, something that it had been doing since 1673, and he argued that if it possessed that power, it could impose internal taxes as well. Colonial spokesmen denied that Parliament could impose any duties for revenue, either internal or external, but they acknowledged that Parliament could levy port dudes for the regulation of trade. Most colonial spokesmen did concede the *power* of Parliament to do all three, but they insisted that Parliament's exercise of the power to tax would deprive them of their rights as Englishmen. The Sons of Liberty, by taking to the streets and nullifying the Stamp Act before it could go into effect, demonstrated – violently but effectively – that whatever Parliament's claim of right, it lacked the power to collect an internal tax. As the Revenue Act of 1766 also demonstrated, it certainly did have that power over American trade, whether or not the colonists conceded the right. Significantly, hardly anybody objected strenuously to the penny duty on molasses. Most merchants saw it as an opportunity to do within the law what they had been doing through smuggling ever since the Molasses Act of 1733.

In short, the Stamp Act crisis was debated along an ideological axis of legislation (the regulation of trade, a power that was conceded to Parliament) versus taxation (which was denied). But the crisis was resolved along the internal-external axis, which both sides claimed was meaningless (see Figure 4.1). The Stamp Act was repudiated, but the duty on molasses became more lucrative than ever. Only Benjamin Franklin grasped how the empire had actually been working for the previous century. As he told the House of Commons in 1766, "[T]he sea is yours; you maintain, by your fleets, the safety of navigation in it, and keep it clear of pirates; you may have therefore a natural and equitable right to some toll or duty on merchandizes carried through that part of your dominions, towards defraying the expence you are at in ships to maintain the safety of that carriage." He also thought that elementary prudence would prevent Parliament from abusing this power. Excessive duties would kill trade, not increase revenue. The Townshend Crisis (1767–1770) would change his mind about the underlying decency and wisdom of British imperial policy.[19]

## IV

Imperial authority was indeed recovering after repeal of the Stamp Act, but then Charles Townshend launched the second imperial crisis when he persuaded Parliament to pass the Townshend Revenue Act in 1767. It addressed no real problem. It created many new ones. It did not pretend to meet the empire's serious need for revenue to support an army in the West. It took off excises in England that brought in twice as much revenue as Townshend expected to gain from the new duties that he imposed on tea, lead, glass, painters' colors, and paper, to be collected in American ports. That revenue would be used primarily to pay the salaries of colonial governors and judges in northern royal colonies, thus eliminating any dependence they still had on the assemblies. Parliament also created the American Board of Customs Commissioners. In a choice that suggested his desire for a confrontation, Townshend located

| Internal taxes (1765)<br>   Stamp Act | External taxes (1767-1770)<br>   Sugar Act (1764)<br>   Revenue Act of 1766<br>   Townshend Revenue Act (1767) |
| Internal legislation (1774)<br>   The Massachusetts Government Act showed that this quadrant was the most sacred one to the colonists. | External legislation (1776)<br><br>   The Navigation Acts made this quadrant the most sacred one to the British. |

**Ideology**

**Geography**

In this figure, the horizontal axis represents ideology, or something in people's minds—for the colonists, the effort to achieve consistency by distinguishing between parliamentary legislation (permissible) and parliamentary taxation (illegitimate). The vertical axis stands for something physical and real, the coastline of North America, which marked the internal-external dichotomy in the debates of the period. To most contemporaries, this dichotomy seemed a matter of expediency, not principle. In fact, it marked the power axis of the empire, the boundary of effective parliamentary action. Parliament could exercise power over oceanic commerce. It never succeeded in extending that power to the internal affairs of the colonies.

Note that while the Stamp Act was contested in terms of the taxation-legislation dichotomy, the crisis was resolved along the internal-external axis. The colonists stopped rioting when the Stamp Act was repealed, even though the Sugar Act remained in place and, as amended by the Revenue Act of 1766, became much more blatantly a revenue measure, not a regulation of trade.

Note also that the intersection of the two axes creates four quadrants that can also reveal what the primary issue became in each successive crisis—internal taxation in 1765–1766, external taxation from 1767 to 1770, and internal legislation in 1774–1775. Only with independence did the colonists repudiate the Navigation Acts (external legislation), under which they had lived for more than a century.

**Figure 4.1** Geography and ideology in the coming of the revolution

the headquarters of the new board in Boston, the most violent North American city during the Stamp Act riots, rather than in centrally located Philadelphia, which had been much quieter in 1765.

The colonists reacted much more slowly to the Townshend Revenue Act than they had to the Stamp Act. John Dickinson and other writers realized that whatever Townshend's real objectives had been (he died suddenly in September 1767 before his legislation took effect), it did mark a direct challenge to government by consent in the colonies, but effective resistance to an "external tax" proved difficult to organize. The Massachusetts House of Representatives sent a circular letter to the other assemblies in February 1768 urging a concerted resistance, but not much happened. The southern colonies already paid fixed salaries to their governors and were much less alarmed than Massachusetts by the new use of parliamentary revenue under the

Townshend Act. Many merchants balked at the call for another round of nonimportation, and effective agreements did not take hold in the major northern ports until early 1769, more than a year after the Revenue Act went into effect, and then only in response to subsequent British provocations.

If the new measures had been prudently managed, the ministry could probably have gotten through the next few years without creating a serious intercolonial crisis. But in March 1768, raucous (though nonviolent) demonstrations in Boston on the anniversary of the Stamp Act's repeal frightened the Customs Commissioners into a demand for military support, and the violent riot in June that followed the seizure of John Hancock's sloop *Liberty* for smuggling led to a second call for troops. Hillsborough turned these minor incidents into a major crisis. He ordered the Massachusetts House to rescind its circular letter, forbade any other assembly to receive it favorably, and dispatched four regiments of redcoats to Boston. In this way local incidents mushroomed into a confrontation involving all the mainland colonies. Reacting to favorable responses to the circular letter, the governor in every royal province was forced to dissolve his assembly until government by consent really did seem threatened by 1769. The confrontation between the army and Boston led to violence and the deaths of five civilians when soldiers fired in self-defense on an angry crowd on March 5, 1770. As Franklin had warned in 1766 when asked whether soldiers could enforce the Stamp Act, "They will not find a rebellion; they may indeed make one."[20]

Lord North broke up colonial resistance by repealing all the Townshend duties except the one on tea, which had, in fact, provided over 70 percent of the revenue collected under the act. Although British tea continued to be boycotted, the broader nonimportation agreements fell apart by the end of 1770, and colonial spokesmen harshly condemned those colonies, such as Rhode Island and New York, that were first to capitulate. As gratifying as these outbursts must have been to imperial officials, another trend was more significant. Nobody celebrated. The Sons of Liberty knew they had lost a major encounter. The simultaneous failure of the Wilkite reform movement in England, in which about a fourth of the voters signed petitions calling for new parliamentary elections, persuaded many observers that government by consent was indeed under siege throughout the empire.[21]

The real significance of the Townshend Crisis is that it never ended and that it made a conspiracy thesis quite credible to American settlers. Sober colonists now suspected that Parliament itself, not just one particular ministry, was deeply corrupt and still planning to deprive them of their liberties. Why else would it insist on retaining the tea tax? Many colonists were also losing confidence in the integrity of the king, who never responded to any of their petitions. The most significant casualty during the second imperial crisis was the erosion of the mutual confidence, or what colonists called the "affection," that had bound the largely voluntaristic societies of North America together with the hierarchical kingdom of Great Britain into an effective empire. The *Gaspée* affair of 1772, in which Rhode Islanders destroyed a marauding customs vessel, illustrated how far mutual trust had disintegrated by then. When Britain tried to identify the perpetrators and ship them to England to stand trial for their lives, no one in Rhode Island would name them, and even more ominously for imperial harmony, twelve colonies – all but Pennsylvania – created legislative committees of correspondence to keep in touch with one another and *anticipate* the next assault of the British government on colonial liberties. The coming of the Revolution is really a story of growing colonial disaffection, the destruction of the one bond that had held very different societies together despite the inability of nearly all leaders to explain adequately how the imperial system actually worked.[22]

## V

In 1773, Lord North revised his colonial policy around a seemingly sensible but disastrously mistaken assumption. Nobody, he reasoned, would start a revolution if the government *lowered* the price of tea in the colonies. In response to a major credit crisis and the possible bankruptcy of the East India Company, Britain's largest corporation, the company, seconded by Franklin, asked North to repeal the Townshend duty in America and thus open the whole continent to British tea. North rejected that suggestion in favor of something more clever. He repealed the remaining import duties on the company's tea within Britain but kept the Townshend duty in America. That change would permit the company to undersell smuggled Dutch tea in both Britain and the colonies. The Tea Act also granted the company and its small number of consignees a monopoly on shipping the tea to America and selling it there to consumers.

These monopolistic features gave the Sons of Liberty the leverage they needed to nullify the act. They did not have to try to police the entire waterfront to enforce nonimportation, as during the Townshend Crisis. They could concentrate their attention on the small number of vessels carrying the tea. They pressured consignees to resign and forced the specially chartered tea ships to depart without landing their cargoes. These tactics worked everywhere but Boston, where Governor Thomas Hutchinson protected the consignees in Castle William in Boston harbor and then refused to grant clearance papers to the tea ships. On the night before the duties would have to be paid, the patriots dumped 342 chests of tea into Boston harbor rather than allow cheap but dutied tea to get loose among Massachusetts consumers and thus establish a precedent for broader parliamentary taxation of the colonies.[23]

Parliament responded with the Coercive Acts. The Boston Port Act, passed in March 1774 and implemented on June 1, closed the port of Boston (including Charlestown) until the town paid for the tea. Britain enforced it ruthlessly and, obviously, the Royal Navy had the power to do so. By the end of June numerous public calls had been issued for a Continental Congress to meet in Philadelphia in September, and it was already clear that any such congress would adopt major trade sanctions against Britain. But then the Massachusetts Government Act, passed in May and implemented in August, transformed the charter government of Massachusetts without the colonists' consent, mostly by making the Council, or upper house, appointive instead of elective and by restricting the powers of town meetings. The result was massive refusal to obey. Jurors would not take oaths under the new arrangements, and county conventions met to close the royal law courts and take charge of local affairs.

Because the new governor, General Sir Thomas Gage, refused to recognize the traditional House of Representatives that had gathered in Salem, the towns elected their own Provincial Congress, which was already convening in Concord, and it created its own Committee of Public Safety as its informal executive body. North's ministry assumed that Gage and his soldiers would be able to intimidate the whole province of Massachusetts Bay. Instead the colonists confined his power to the town of Boston. Taxes went to the Provincial Congress in Concord, not to Gage in Boston. Each county's militia purged itself of untrustworthy officers and accepted leadership from Concord. Stunned, Gage warned North in September that he would need 20,000 redcoats to carry out his mission. He was discovering that the alternative to government by consent was not a more authoritarian and effective structure under the Crown but rather the utter disintegration of British authority in the colony. In January, North replied by dispatching some reinforcements and by ordering Gage to send an expedition to Concord. The Revolutionary War broke out not over the "external" legislation of the Port Act but in a hopeless attempt to enforce another inland measure, the Massachusetts Government Act.[24]

Once the fighting began and the king rejected even the very moderate Olive Branch Petition of the Second Continental Congress, the conspiracy theses prevalent on both sides of the Atlantic turned into self-fulfilling prophecies. The king believed that the colonists had been plotting independence at least since 1765. The colonists concluded that the 30,000 redcoats and Hessians heading for America proved that the British state was determined to crush their liberties. The last bond of empire to yield was the underlying colonial affection for the British people, who stood condemned in American eyes by their acquiescence in the war and in the king's use of foreign mercenaries. As Thomas Jefferson put it in a passage that did not make the final draft of the Declaration of Independence,

> [T]hese facts have given the last stab to agonizing affection; and manly spirit bids

us to renou[n]ce forever these unfeeling brethren. [W]e must endeavor to forget our former love for them, and to hold them, as we hold the rest of mankind, enemies in war, in peace friends. [W]e might have been a free & a great people together, but a communication of grandeur and of freedom, it seems, is below their dignity. [B]e it so, since they will have it. [T]he road to happiness and to glory is open to us too; we will climb it apart from them and acquiesce in the necessity which denounces our eternal separation.[25]

The colonies declared their independence in July, and the British then inflicted on them the bloodiest war in their history to that time. Even two centuries later, the Revolution has been exceeded only by the Civil War in the percentage of casualties suffered by its participants.[26]

## VI

The coming of the Revolution is mainly a story of growing popular disaffection. But that pattern does not explain the new political order that arose after independence. To become effective republics, the newly independent states would have to experience internal revolutions that would redefine their public lives in remarkable ways. By 1776 the British made the colonists choose "whether they would be men and not English or whether they would be English and not men," as Edmund S. Morgan has nicely put it.[27] The transition from the rights of Englishmen to the rights of man meant a rejection of the British model of constitutionalism and had truly revolutionary implications. The earliest state constitutions, however, did seem to create something like sovereign legislatures within their borders, even as they groped to find some adequate way to institutionalize what they were beginning to call the separation of powers. At first, in nearly every state, the legislature itself defined the fundamental rights of its citizens, even though, as critics pointed out, any subsequent

legislature could then repeal or change them. Rights defined through conventional legislation were not "fundamental" because they could be repealed at any time.

The Massachusetts Constitution of 1780 found an answer to this dilemma. It was drafted by a convention elected only for that purpose, and the constitution was then ratified by the citizens assembled in their town meetings. This procedure drew a sharp distinction between the sovereign people, who alone had the power to make a constitution, and the legislature elected under that constitution. In 1787 the Philadelphia Convention extended that process to the emerging American nation when it insisted that the new Federal Constitution be ratified by state conventions summoned only for that purpose. Popular sovereignty thus took hold as the underlying myth that still organizes public life in the United States.[28]

In France, the Revolution very nearly became the nation, which defined itself as a passionate repudiation of the past. Americans, by contrast, did not reject the Gregorian calendar or the boundaries of their states as they had been laid out under British colonial rule. In Eric Van Young's terms, they launched the most successful creole revolution of the era, an accomplishment made possible because, unlike their Latin American counterparts, they seldom had to listen to the voices of indigenous peoples or of their own enslaved Africans. The muted protests of these "others" enabled the settlers to participate fully in the transatlantic revolution that soon spread from North America to France. But unlike the French, the American public did not even debate the nation or the shape it ought to assume until the ratification struggle that followed the Philadelphia Convention of 1787. In the United States the Revolution was a military struggle for independence that inspired republican experiments at the state level, but a sense of American national identity emerged only gradually, mostly as a consequence of independence and a recognition, especially among Federalists, that if the Union collapsed, the results could be catastrophic. Americans set about defining their national identity because most of them realized that they were not yet a nation. Why else would some men, two decades after the ratification struggle, have organized an Association of American Patriots for the Purpose of Forming a National Character?[29]

Two aspects of America's countercyclical revolution remain surprising. First, it did remarkably little long-term damage to Great Britain, which soon discovered that it could retain most of the economic benefits of the old imperial system without assuming the costs of defense. Second, although Americans had lived under British rule for a century and a half almost without even contemplating independence, once they repudiated George III, they did not look back. There has never been a serious movement since 1776 to restore monarchy in the United States, and no central government of the United States has ever claimed the powers of a sovereign parliament. From the perspective of most Indians, the new republic was more imperial than the old empire. The Revolution generated irresistible pressure to open the West to settlement and vastly expanded the public role of ordinary householders. But among the victors in the revolutionary struggle, the biggest gainers were middling white householders who won an unprecedented share of public power. The lower houses of the legislature grew much larger and became open to men of modest wealth, the suffrage expanded, and, as the political parties took hold nationally after 1790, voter turnout sometimes reached extraordinary levels.[30]

In the twelve years after ratification, the Federalist Party tried to turn the American republic into a purified version of the British state by funding the national debt at par, chartering the Bank of the United States (modeled on the Bank of England) to handle government finance, and creating a professional army and navy. Their Democratic-Republican opponents denounced them as mad anglophiles who would probably restore monarchy if they could, a charge that all but a few Federalists denied in good conscience.

But only after the so-called revolution of 1800, which brought Jefferson and the Democratic-Republicans to power on the national level, did the American Revolutionary Settlement take permanent hold. Jefferson reduced the army and navy to token strength, set about paying off the national debt (without repudiating it), and rejoiced when the charter of the Bank of the United States expired in 1811. The Louisiana Purchase, meanwhile, doubled the land area of the nation.

Jefferson's republic became the embodiment of American exceptionalism. Jeffersonians rejected active participation in Europe's balance of power. They set out to achieve hegemony within North America, not in the conventional European manner of building enormous armies and fleets sustained by a huge burden of taxation but by encouraging American citizens to take physical possession of the continent from the Atlantic to the Pacific, to the terror of its Indian occupants and of the republics Mexican neighbors. (Canadians fared better because they still had British protection.) The Monroe Doctrine extended these ambitions to the entire Western Hemisphere. No other society has ever tried anything of the kind.[31]

In 1838, young Abraham Lincoln, in his first major public address, spelled out some of the implications of this achievement:

> All the armies of Europe, Asia, and Africa combined, with all the treasure of the earth (our own excepted) in their military chest; with a Buonaparte for a commander, could not by force, take a drink from the Ohio, or make a track on the Blue Ridge, in a trial of a thousand years.
>
> … If destruction be our lot, we must ourselves be its author and finisher. As a nation of freemen, we must live through all time, or die by suicide.[32]

The success of the United States made the republic unique and probably gave it the ability to hold the loyalties of its citizens through its most severe crisis, the Civil War. One wonders how often Lincoln recalled these words during that struggle.

But American exceptionalism has also had a price. No other society has ever been able to imitate it. Others can borrow from our constitutions and bills of rights and have often combined them with some version of parliamentary government derived from Britain. But no one else has ever aspired to hegemony over an entire hemisphere, sustained without a serious military establishment only through the everyday economic activities of its citizens. That accomplishment became the most distinctive legacy of 1776 and, for most Americans, defined their national identity until the world wars of the twentieth century forced the United States to create an army, navy, and air force that could match any others on the planet. The long-term consequences of this transformation are still unfolding. Most spokesmen for the revolutionary generation would warn us to be on guard. Global empire and liberty do not easily reinforce one another.

## Notes

1. Horace Walpole to George Montague, March 22, 1762, *The Yale Edition of Horace Walpole's Correspondence*, ed. W. S. Lewis et al., 43 vols. (New Haven, Conn.: Yale University Press, 1937–1983), 10: 22.

2. To regain Havana, Spain ceded Florida to Britain and agreed to pay an enormous ransom for Manila. Britain returned Guadeloupe and Martinique to France.

3. For the prophecies of Choiseul and Vergennes, see Edward Channing, A *History of the United States,* 6 vols. (New York: Macmillan, 1905–1925), 2: 602–3.

4. See especially Lawrence Henry Gipson, "The American Revolution as an Aftermath of the Great War for the Empire, 1754–1763," *Political Science Quarterly* 65 (March 1950): 86–104, esp. 104.

5. For a fuller discussion, see John M. Murrin, "The French and Indian War, the American Revolution, and the Counterfactual Hypothesis: Reflections on Lawrence Henry Gipson and John Shy," *Reviews in American History* 1 (September 1973): 307–18. The quotations are from "The Association" (October 1774) and the "Declaration of the Causes and Necessities of Taking Up Arms" (July 1775), *Journals of the Continental Congress, 1774–1789*, ed. Worthington Chauncey Ford, 34 vols. (Washington, D.C.: U.S. Government Printing Office, 1904–1937), 1: 76; 2: 152.

6. See my "A Roof without Walls: The Dilemma of American National Identity," in *Beyond Confederation: Origins of the Constitution and American National Identity,* ed. Richard Beeman, Stephen Botein, and Edward C. Carter II (Chapel Hill: University of North Carolina Press, 1987), 333–48, and T. H. Breen, "Ideology and Nationalism on the Eve of the American Revolution: More Revisions in Need of Revising," *Journal of American History* 84 (June 1997): 13–39.

7. Aaron Fogleman, "Migrations to the Thirteen North American Colonies, 1700–1775: New Estimates," *Journal of Interdisciplinary History* 22 (spring 1992): 691–709, esp. table 1 on p. 698; Bernard Bailyn, *Voyagers to the West: A Passage in the Peopling of America on the Eve of the Revolution* (New York: Knopf, 1986), esp. 29–36 on Hillsborough; and Bernard Bailyn and Philip D. Morgan, eds., *Strangers within the Realm: Cultural Margins of the First British Empire* (Chapel Hill: University of North Carolina Press, 1991).

8. Some of the most relevant studies, within a huge literature, are James F. Shepherd and Gary M. Walton, *Shipping Maritime Trade, and the Economic Development of Colonial North America* (Cambridge: Cambridge University Press, 1972); John W. Tyler, *Smugglers and Patriots: Boston Merchants and the Advent of the American Revolution* (Boston: Northeastern University Press, 1986); Thomas M. Doerflinger, *A Vigorous Spirit of Enterprise: Merchants and Economic Development in Revolutionary Philadelphia* (Chapel Hill: University of North Carolina Press, 1986); T. H. Breen, "'Baubles of Britain': The American and Consumer Revolutions of the Eighteenth Century," *Past and Present* 119 (May 1988): 73–104; Cary Carson, Ronald Hoffman, and Peter J. Albert, eds., *Of Consuming Interests: The Style of Life in*

*the Eighteenth Century* (Charlottesville: University Press of Virginia, 1992); Richard L. Bushman, *The Refinement of America: Persons, Houses, Cities* (New York: Knopf, 1992); Jacob M. Price, "The Rise of Glasgow in the Chesapeake Tobacco Trade, 1707–1775," *William and Mary Quarterly* 11 (April 1954): 179–99; Istvan Hont and Michael Ignatieff, eds., *Wealth and Virtue: The Shaping of Political Economy in the Scottish Enlightenment* (New York: Cambridge University Press, 1983); Richard B. Sher and Jeffrey R. Smitten, eds., *Scotland and America in the Age of Enlightenment* (Princeton, N.J.: Princeton University Press, 1990); and Ned C. Landsman, *From Colonials to Provincials: American Thought and Culture, 1680–1760* (New York: Twayne, 1997).

9. For a fuller discussion, see John M. Murrin, "No Awakening, No Revolution? More Counterfactual Speculations," *Reviews in American History* 11 (June 1983): 161–71.

10. John M. Murrin and A. G. Roeber, "Trial by Jury: The Virginia Paradox," in *The Bill of Rights: A Lively Heritage*, ed. John Kukla (Richmond: Virginia State Library and Archives, 1987), 108–29, and John M. Murrin, "Magistrates, Sinners, and a Precarious Liberty: Trial by Jury in Seventeenth-Century New England," in *Saints and Revolutionaries: Essays on Early American History,* ed. David Hall, John M. Murrin, and Thad W. Tate (New York: Norton, 1984), 152–206, and "English Rights as Ethnic Aggression: The English Conquest, the Charter of Liberties of 1683, and Leisler's Rebellion in New York," in *Authority and Resistance in Early New York,* ed. William Pencak and Conrad Edick Wright (New York: New-York Historical Society, 1988), 56–94. My own research into the court records of nine New England counties for anywhere between three and eight decades after the Glorious Revolution shows that jury trials for noncapital crimes became routine by the early eighteenth century and that acquittal rates rose sharply above what they had been during the Puritan era. For the pattern in eighteenth-century New York, see Julius Goebel Jr. and T. Raymond Naughton, *Law Enforcement in Colonial New York: A Study in Criminal Procedure (1664–1776)* (New York: Commonwealth Fund, 1944).

11. The classic arguments for the rise of the assembly and the decline of royal government were made by Leonard W. Labaree, *Royal Government in America* (New Haven, Conn.: Yale University Press, 1930), and Jack P. Greene, *The Quest for Power: The Lower Houses of Assembly in the Southern Royal Colonies, 1689–1776* (Chapel Hill: University of North Carolina Press, 1963). For the growing impact of royal governors, see John M. Murrin, "Political Development," in *Colonial British America: Essays in the New History of the Early Modern Era,* ed. Jack P. Greene and J. R. Pole (Baltimore: The Johns Hopkins University Press, 1984), 408–56.

12. See James H. Hutson, "The Emergence of the Modern Concept of a Right in America: The Contribution of Michel Villey," *American Journal of Jurisprudence* 39 (1994): 185–224; John M. Murrin, "From Liberties to Rights: The Struggle in Colonial Massachusetts," in *The Bill of Rights and the States: The Colonial and Revolutionary Origins of American Liberties,* ed. Patrick Conley and John P. Kaminski (Madison, Wis.: Madison House, 1992), 63–99; T. H. Breen, "The Lockean Moment: The Language of Rights on the Eve of the American Revolution," (lecture, University of Oxford, May 15, 2001); and Bernard Bailyn, *The Ideological Origins of the American Revolution* (Cambridge, Mass.: Belknap Press, 1967), and *The Origins of American Politics* (New York: Knopf, 1968).

13. Jeremy Stern, in a Princeton dissertation (still in progress) on the Townshend Crisis in Massachusetts, is paying close attention to the radicalization of language, including the shift toward an emphasis on John Locke and natural rights.

14. For a fuller discussion of political culture in the colonies, see Jack P. Greene, "Political Mimesis: A Consideration of the Historical and Cultural Roots of Legislative Behavior in the British Colonies in the Eighteenth Century," with a comment by Bernard Bailyn and a reply by Greene, *American Historical Review* 75 (December 1969): 337–67, and Murrin, "Political Development," in Greene and Pole, eds., *Colonial British America,* 408–56. Two excellent studies of northern governors are Jere R. Danieli, "Politics in New Hampshire under Governor Benning Wentworth, 1741–1767," *William and Mary Quarterly* 23 (January 1966): 76–105, and John A. Schutz, *William Shirley, King's Governor*

*of Massachusetts* (Chapel Hill: University of North Carolina Press, 1961). For "Country" politics in southern colonies, see David Alan Williams, "Anglo-Virginia Politics, 1690–1735," in *Anglo-American Political Relations, 1675–1775,* ed. Alison G. Olson and Richard M. Brown (New Brunswick, N.J.: Rutgers University Press, 1970), 76–91; Robert M. Weir, "'The Harmony We Were Famous For': An Interpretation of Pre-revolutionary South Carolina Politics," *William and Mary Quarterly* 26 (October 1969): 473–501; and W. W. Abbot, *The Royal Governors of Georgia, 1754–1775* (Chapel Hill: University of North Carolina Press, 1959). For a spectacular glimpse of the ruthless and dysfunctional tone of Maryland politics, see Cecilius Calvert to Governor Horatio Sharpe, March 17, 1761, *Archives of Maryland,* ed. William Hand Browne et al., 72 vols. (Baltimore: Maryland Historical Society, 1883–1972), 14: 1–13.

15. For a superb study of the conflict, see Fred Anderson, *Crucible of War: The Seven Years' War and the Fate of Empire in British North America, 1754–1766* (New York: Knopf, 2000). His earlier book, *A People's Army: Massachusetts Soldiers and Society in the Seven Years' War* (Chapel Hill: University of North Carolina Press, 1984), is primarily a study of 1756, when tensions between British officers and provincial soldiers reached their peak. Harold E. Selesky, *War and Society in Colonial Connecticut* (New Haven, Conn.: Yale University Press, 1990), emphasizes the growing professionalism of provincial soldiers as the war progressed, including their willingness to reenlist. For millennialism and imperial patriotism, see Nathan O. Hatch, *The Sacred Cause of Liberty: Republican Thought and the Millennium in Revolutionary New England* (New Haven, Conn.: Yale University Press, 1977). Eleven sermons were published in the colonies to celebrate the accession of George III. Dozens more celebrated the capture of Louisbourg, Quebec, and Montreal and the Peace of Paris of 1763.

16. See especially Toby L. Ditz, "Ownership and Obligation: Inheritance and Patriarchal Households in Connecticut, 1750–1820," *William and Mary Quarterly* 47 (April 1990): 235–65; Gloria L. Main, "Inequality in Early America: The Evidence from Probate Records of Massachusetts and Maryland," *Journal of*

*Inter-disciplinary History* 7 (spring 1977): 559–81; Gordon S. Wood, *The Radicalism of the American Revolution* (New York: Knopf, 1992), esp. chap. 3; and Holly Brewer, "Entailing Aristocracy in Colonial Virginia: Ancient Feudal Restraints' and Revolutionary Reform," *William and Mary Quarterly* 54 (April 1997): 307–46.

17. Marc Egnal, *A Mighty Empire: The Origins of the American Revolution* (Ithaca, N.Y.: Cornell University Press, 1988), tries to link revolutionaries with expansion and loyalists with opposition to expansion. In my judgment, his argument is too teleological. Eric Hinderaker, *Elusive Empires: Constructing Colonialism in the Ohio Valley, 1673–1800* (New York: Cambridge University Press, 1997), is a brilliant contrast of French, British, and American imperialism in the Ohio Valley. See also Woody Holton, "The Ohio Indians and the Coming of the American Revolution in Virginia," *Journal of Southern History* 60 (August 1994): 453–78, and, more generally, *Forced Founders: Indians, Debtors, Slaves and the Making of the American Revolution in Virginia* (Chapel Hill: University of North Carolina Press, 1999).

18. P. D. G. Thomas, *British Politics and the Stamp Act Crisis: The First Phase of the American Revolution* (Oxford: Clarendon Press, 1975); Paul Langford, *The First Rockingham Administration, 1765–1766* (Oxford: Oxford University Press, 1973); Jean-Yves LeSaux, "Commerce and Consent: Edmund Burke's Imperial Vision and the American Revolution" (Ph.D. diss., Princeton University, 1992). LeSaux shows that, although all British spokesmen accepted parliamentary sovereignty, they could mean very different things when they invoked it.

19. The best study is still Edmund S. Morgan and Helen M. Morgan, *The Stamp Act Crisis: Prologue to Revolution*, 3rd ed. (Chapel Hill: University of North Carolina Press, 1995). For the Franklin quotation, see Edmund S. Morgan, ed., *Prologue to Revolution: Sources and Documents on the Stamp Act Crisis, 1764–1766* (Chapel Hill: University of North Carolina Press, 1959), 145.

20. Morgan, *Prologue to Revolution,* 144.

21. George Rudé, *Wilkes and Liberty: A Social Study of 1763 to 1774* (Oxford: Clarendon Press, 1962); P. D. G. Thomas, *John Wilkes: A Friend to Liberty* (Oxford: Clarendon Press, 1996).

22. Easily the best narrative history of these events is Merrill Jensen, *The Founding of a Nation: A History of the American Revolution, 1763–1776* (New York: Oxford University Press, 1968), 186–433. Pauline Maier, *From Resistance to Revolution: Colonial Radicals and the Development of American Opposition to Britain, 1765–1776* (New York: Knopf, 1972), is a very perceptive study of the process of disaffection, which was a much stronger word in the eighteenth century than it is today. See also Pauline Maier, "John Wilkes and American Disillusionment with Britain," *William and Mary Quarterly* 20 (July 1963): 373–95, and "Coming to Terms with Samuel Adams," *American Historical Review* 81 (February 1976): 12–30. Richard D. Brown, *Revolutionary Politics in Massachusetts: The Boston Committee of Correspondence and the Towns, 1772–1774* (Cambridge, Mass.: Harvard University Press, 1970), is an essential study of the cumulative process of disaffection.

23. The standard study is Benjamin W. Labaree, *The Boston Tea Party* (New York: Oxford University Press, 1964).

24. David Ammerman, *In the Common Cause: American Response to the Coercive Acts of 1774* (Charlottesville: University Press of Virginia, 1974); David Hackett Fischer, *Paul Revere's Ride* (New York: Oxford University Press, 1994).

25. Pauline Maier, *American Scripture: Making the Declaration of Independence* (New York: Knopf, 1997), 240–41.

26. Howard H. Peckham, *The Toll of Independence: Engagements and Battle Casualties of the American Revolution* (Chicago: University of Chicago Press, 1974), esp. 131–34.

27. Morgan and Morgan, *The Stamp Act Crisis,* 119.

28. Edmund S. Morgan, *Inventing the People: The Rise of Popular Sovereignty in England and America* (New York: Norton, 1988). For a superb, brief account of the development of American constitutionalism in these years, see Robert R. Palmer, *The Age of the Democratic Revolution: A Political History of Europe and America, 1760–1800,* 2 vols. (Princeton, N.J.: Princeton University Press, 1959–1964), 1: 213–35.

29. See Isaac Kramnick, "The 'Great National Discussion': The Discourse of National Politics in 1787," *William and Mary Quarterly* 45 (January 1988): 3–32, and, for the Association of American Patriots, Joyce Appleby, *Inheriting the Revolution: The First Generation of Americans* (Cambridge, Mass.: Belknap Press, 2000), 196. For a subtle argument that American leaders understood the importance of the Union but that hardly anybody made its survival his top priority, see James E. Lewis Jr., *The American Union and the Problem of Neighborhood: The United States and the Collapse of the Spanish Empire, 1783–1829* (Chapel Hill: University of North Carolina Press, 1998).

30. Gordon S. Wood, *The Creation of the American Republic, 1776–1787* (Chapel Hill: University of North Carolina Press, 1969); Jackson Turner Main, "Government by the People: The American Revolution and the Democratization of the Legislatures," *William and Mary Quarterly* 23 (July 1966): 354–67; Stanley Elkins and Eric McKitrick, *The Age of Federalism: The Early American Republic* (New York: Oxford University Press 1993).

31. For fuller discussions of the American Revolution Settlement and of American exceptionalism, see John M. Murrin, "The Great Inversion, or, Court versus Country: A Comparison of the Revolution Settlements in England (1688–1721) and America (1776–1816)," in *Three British Revolutions: 1641, 1688, 1776,* ed. J. G. A. Pocock (Princeton, N.J.: Princeton University Press, 1980), 368–453, and "The Jeffersonian Triumph and American Exceptionalism," *Journal of the Early Republic* 20 (spring 2000): 1–25.

32. "Address before the Young Men's Lyceum of Springfield, Illinois, January 27, 1838," In *The Collected Works of Abraham Lincoln,* ed. Roy P. Basler et al., 11 vols. (New Brunswick, N.J.: Rutgers University Press, 1953–1990), 1: 109.

# 5
# "REBEL AGAINST REBEL"

*Enslaved Virginians and the Coming of the American Revolution*

## Woody Holton

### Introduction

Few Americans realize that more than a year passed between the battles of Lexington and Concord and the Declaration of Independence. That period saw bloody fighting between the colonies and Britain, as in the colonies' failed invasion of Canada, the Siege of Boston, and the opening stages of the Battle of New York. It also was a time of landmark political developments, such as in the Continental Congress's Olive Branch Petition and the king's declaration that the colonies were in a state of rebellion. Simultaneously, colonists debated whether a political settlement with Britain was possible or desirable. Many colonies outside New England were reluctant to vote for independence until the summer of 1776.

In this provocative essay, Woody Holton argues that the ultimate factor which led Virginia, in particular, and the southern colonies, more generally, to support independence was the decision of Virginia's royal governor, Lord Dunmore, to offer freedom to slaves who would take up arms in support of the king. With no sense of irony, white Virginians considered this threat to their slave system to be the most glaring example of British tyranny. Not coincidentally, the Declaration of Independence, lead-authored by Virginian Thomas Jefferson, prominently featured this grievance in its list of kingly offenses justifying American rebellion, as Robert G. Parkinson discusses in this volume.

Holton insists that we must consider the central role of slavery and of slaves themselves in the American Revolution, for slavery and the fear it caused permeated American society, particularly in the South. His essay, alongside that of Ira Berlin, raises a number of tantalizing questions.

- In what ways did slaves themselves demand that they too were entitled to the natural rights trumpeted by white revolutionaries?
- Were white Americans hypocrites for holding slaves even while they denounced British tyranny and defended their liberty? How would they have answered this question?
- Militarily, politically, and symbolically, what was the significance of the British offering freedom to slaves who fought for the British standard, in the short term and, potentially, in the long term both for the North American colonies and the British Empire as a whole?

For more than six months after the battles of Lexington and Concord, the fighting between British and patriot troops was confined to the northern colonies. Then on 26 October 1775, a squadron of British naval vessels attacked the town of Hampton, Virginia. The Revolutionary War had come to the South.[1] The battle of Hampton resulted partly from the actions of a "small mulatto man" named Joseph Harris. Only four months earlier, Harris had been a resident of Hampton and the property of another Hamptonian, Henry King, whom he served as a pilot on the Chesapeake Bay. Harris, it was said, was "well acquainted with many creeks on the *Eastern* Shore, at *York, James* River, and *Nansemond,* and many others." All in all, he was "a very useful person."[2]

Harris's knowledge gave him an opportunity to gain his freedom. On 8 June 1775, Virginia's last royal governor, John Murray, fourth Earl of Dunmore, fearing an attack from the increasingly belligerent patriots, fled Williamsburg and took refuge on HMS *Fowey.* There he set about assembling a small squadron to fight the patriots. To accomplish his designs he needed people who knew the bay, so when Harris slipped off one night in July and presented himself to the skipper of the *Fowey,* he was welcomed and immediately put to work as a pilot. When the *Fowey* left the Chesapeake a short time later, Harris transferred to a tender called the *Liberty.*

On the night of 2 September 1775, a hurricane swept through Tidewater Virginia and drove the *Liberty* ashore near Hampton. On board Harris's vessel when it went aground was Matthew Squire, captain of the *Liberty's* mother ship, the *Otter.* Harris obtained a canoe from a slave, and he and Squire managed to get across Hampton Roads to the *Otter,* which was anchored off Norfolk. Their escape was fortunate, because white leaders had threatened to execute slaves like Harris who fled to the British. Meanwhile, the beached *Liberty* fell into the hands of the rebels, who helped themselves to the sails and other equipment (including seven swivel guns) and then set the boat ablaze. The *Liberty* "was

burnt by the people thereabouts," the *Virginia Gazette* reported, "in return for [Squire's] harbouring gentlemen's negroes, and suffering his sailors to steal poultry, hogs, &c." Captain Squire was furious. He demanded that Hampton at least return the *Liberty's* stores. The rebel committee that ruled the town said it would be happy to comply with the captain's request – as soon as Squire returned Harris and other black crewmen to their former owners. This Squire refused to do, prompting a patriot newspaper to note with sarcasm the "singular ATTACHMENT AND LOYALTY to his sovereign" of Squire's "Ethiopian director."[3]

Eventually deciding that the contest could not be resolved peacefully, Squire attacked Hampton on 26 October with six small craft. The little squadron came under deadly long arms fire. Some nine blacks and other British sailors were killed, and Squire had to retreat. One of his vessels, the *Hawke,* went aground, and its crew was captured. The white prisoners, including Joseph Wilson, an indentured servant who had escaped from George Washington, were "treated with great humanity," a patriot newspaper reported. The black crewmen were "tried for their lives."[4]

The engagement at Hampton was the first battle of the Revolutionary War south of Massachusetts. Just as the earlier fighting in New England had helped poison relations between Britain and all the rebel colonies, so the battle of Hampton helped embitter white Virginians against their king. Thomas Jefferson reported that the armed confrontation had "raised our country into perfect phrensy." The story of the battle would have been very different if Joseph Harris had not made his dash for freedom. Perhaps Hampton whites would never have come into conflict with Captain Squire at all.[5]

Harris was but one of thousands of enslaved Virginians who found opportunity within the breach that opened between loyalist and patriot whites in 1775. A majority of those who reached British lines ended up worse off than before. Many were killed in battle, and hundreds died of disease. Others were recaptured and subjected to worse working conditions than before, in Chiswell's Mines, which supplied rebel soldiers with lead, or on sugar plantations in the West Indies. In the single year 1776, however, 400 former slaves sailed away from Virginia to freedom. The aspirations and actions of enslaved Virginians during the American Revolution have been ably chronicled by several scholars.[6] Now that the struggle for black freedom during the revolutionary era is coming into focus, we can begin to assess its effect on white Virginians. One result of the slaves' struggle was political: In seeking their own freedom, black Virginians indirectly helped motivate white Virginians to declare independence from Britain.

In August 1774 most white Virginians were angry at Parliament for adopting the acts they called Intolerable. These colonists, however, were content to express their outrage by cutting off trade with Britain. It was a long way from the boycott of 1774 to the revolution of 1776. What happened during the crucial year 1775 to convert mere boycotters into revolutionaries? Some of the factors that turned white Virginians against Britain were geographically or temporally remote; the colonists were incensed that the British army had invaded far-off Massachusetts, and they feared that the king's troops might invade Virginia as well. A third source of the white Virginians' anger was not remote at all; they were irate at Governor Dunmore for first threatening to ally with enslaved Virginians and then, later, actually doing so.

Neither Dunmore's threat in April 1775 to emancipate Virginia's slaves nor his offer of freedom in November of that year to patriots' bondspeople who joined his army would have carried much significance if black Virginians had remained entirely passive during the revolutionary crisis. But slaves were not passive. Perhaps a thousand of them took advantage of Dunmore's offer of emancipation in November 1775. Even before the governor published his proclamation, however, scores of slaves had joined his little army or undertaken their own

resistance to white rule. Even earlier, before Dunmore first threatened to offer freedom to the slaves, bondspeople in different parts of Virginia had gathered to discuss how to take advantage of the growing rift among whites. And the opposition of 1774 and 1775 was only the culmination of a tradition of black resistance that was as old as Virginia slavery itself.[7]

Afro-Virginians were most often the victims, not the perpetrators, of interracial violence, but they struck back often enough to maintain a permanent undercurrent of fear in the minds of most whites in the Chesapeake. Although it has been estimated that fewer than 1 percent of enslaved Virginians killed whites in the eighteenth century, it is likely that by the 1760s almost every white person in the eastern counties knew of a free person who had been killed by a slave.[8] At the same time that the black percentage of the population increased, the percentage of slaves who killed whites (as opposed to fellow slaves) also grew.[9]

If individual whites had nightmares about waking up amid flames or feeling the first spasms of a stomach contorted by poison, whites as a group frequently worried about servile insurrection. Slave plots seemed to be especially rife during the Seven Years' War (1755–63).[10] In July 1755 Charles Carter reported to Lieutenant Governor Robert Dinwiddie that enslaved workers in Lancaster County had gathered near his son's home, possibly with a view to allying with the Native American and French foes who had just defeated General Edward Braddock's army near Fort Duquesne. Dinwiddie replied on 18 July. "The Villany of the Negroes on any Emergency of Gov't is w't I always fear'd," he told Carter. "I greatly approve of Y'r send'g the Sheriffs with proper Strength to take up those y't apear'd in a Body at Y'r Son's House." If the slaves were "found guilty of the Expressions mention'd," Dinwiddie said, " … an Example of one or two at first may prevent those Creatures enter'g into Combinat[ion]s and wicked Designs."[11] Later in the war, Richard Henry Lee told the House of Burgesses that slaves, "from the nature of their situation, can never feel an interest in our cause, because … they observe their masters possessed of liberty which is denied to them."[12]

White Virginians became especially alarmed about their slaves during Pontiac's War, the Indian uprising of 1763–64. For the first time in recent memory, Indians spared the lives of blacks at the settlements they attacked; gentlemen wondered why. "As the Indians are saving & Carressine all the Negroes they take," militia lieutenant William Fleming told Lieutenant Governor Francis Fauquier in July 1763, "should it be productive of an Insurrection it may be attended with the most serious Consequences." The following month, a Virginia clergyman reported that Indians had "carried a great number of women and children, as well as some men, and (for the first time too) a good many negroes, into captivity."[13]

Although the slave-Indian alliance that so frightened white Virginians never materialized, bondspeople continued to plan insurrections after the war. A group in Loudoun County revolted in early 1767 and killed an overseer named Dennis Dallis. Three of them were hanged. In neighboring Fairfax County that same year, enslaved workers poisoned several overseers. "[S]ome of the negroes have been taken up, four of whom were executed about three weeks ago, after which their heads were cut off, and fixed on the chimnies of the court-house," a Boston newspaper reported, "and it was expected that four more would soon meet with the same fate." Frederick County slaves also reportedly plotted a rebellion in the 1760s.[14] In Stafford County in May 1769, some of John Knox's slaves "barbarously murdered" him. Suspicion fell on two fugitives named Phill and Winny, and Knox's brothers offered a reward of £105 for their capture and conviction. Within a month both had been apprehended and put to death, along with one of the "house wenches," who had not initially been a suspect in her master's death.[15] Around Christmas of the same year, the bondsmen on Bowler Cocke's plantation in nearby Hanover County attacked

the steward, his assistant, and a neighbor and beat each severely. When a band of whites arrived to suppress the insurrection, Cocke's slaves "rushed upon them with a desperate fury, armed with clubs and staves." The whites saved themselves by shooting dead two of the rebels and nearly decapitating a third.[16]

As Lieutenant Governor Dinwiddie had said in 1755, "any Emergency" that divided white Americans could give blacks the opportunity to launch rebellions.[17] The American Revolution was such an emergency. By Christmas 1774, some enslaved Virginians had begun to discuss how to exploit the widening rift between white colonists and the royal governor and navy. "In one of our Counties lately," James Madison reported in November 1774, "a few of those unhappy wretches met together & chose a leader who was to conduct them when the English Troops should arrive." Enslaved workers in other colonies also met to consider how to profit from the imperial conflict. In St. Andrew's Parish, Georgia, slaves rebelled in December 1774 and killed four whites before they were captured and burned alive. An account of a plot in Ulster County, New York, appeared in the *Virginia Gazettes* in mid-March 1775; the scheme had been uncovered when a white man overheard two enslaved conspirators planning to obtain gunpowder and shot.[18]

The fears that these plots induced in white Virginians were heightened by the rumor that the British government might encourage slave insurrections as a way of suppressing the patriot movement.[19] Late in 1774, William Draper, who had just returned to London from an extended tour of America, published a pamphlet arguing that one way to put down the patriot rebellion would be to "Proclame *Freedom* to their Negroes." Arthur Lee, who was living in London, had obtained a copy of Draper's pamphlet by early December 1774, when he mentioned Draper's "proposal for emancipating your Negroes … & arming them against you" to his brothers in Virginia. Lee reported the plan "meets with approbation from ministerial People."[20] James

Madison heard in early 1775 that a bill freeing the slaves had been introduced in Parliament. No such bill has been found, but Edmund Burke noted on the floor of the House of Commons in March that many pro-government members favored "a general enfranchisement of [the] slaves."[21] During spring 1775, many Virginians believed that these proposals were about to be implemented. According to a House of Burgesses report, British officials contemplated "a Scheme, the most diabolical," to "offer Freedom to our Slaves, and turn them against their Masters." A similar accusation was made in an anonymous letter that appeared in Alexander Purdie's *Virginia Gazette* in June. The writer alluded to recent rumors of slave conspiracies and then added: "From some hints, it was inferred that the negroes had not been without encouragement from a Gentleman of the Navy" – probably Captain Henry Colins of HMS *Magdalen*.[22]

Enslaved Virginians did not wait for British "encouragement" to intensify their activism. In spring 1775 several groups of slaves in the James River watershed reportedly assembled to plan rebellions. On 15 April 1775 Toney, a slave in Prince Edward County, was charged with insurrection and conspiracy to commit murder; he received fifteen lashes.[23] Three days later whites in nearby Chesterfield County were "alarm'd for an Insurrection of the Slaves," trader Robert Donald reported. Slave patrols were usually somewhat lax in Virginia, but the one in Chesterfield was quickly revived. "[W]e Patrol and go armed – a dreadful enemy," Donald wrote on 18 April.[24] Three more days passed. Then "Sentence of death [was] passed upon two Negroes … tried at Norfolk, for being concerned in a conspiracy to raise an insurrection in that town," the *Virginia Gazette* reported. One of the accused blacks in Norfolk was Emanuel de Antonio. The other was called simply Emanuel, and he was the property of Matthew Phripp, the militia lieutenant for Norfolk County.[25] On 21 April, the very day that the two Emanuels were sentenced to die, Edmund Pendleton reported that the free half of Williamsburg's population

had been frightened by "some disturbances in the City, by the *Slaves*."[26]

It is possible that the two Emanuels in Norfolk and Toney in Prince Edward County were not in touch with each other, with the Williamsburg plotters, or with those in Chesterfield County. Many white Virginians, however, thought that the alleged occurrence in different parts of the James River watershed of four slave conspiracies during the third week of April 1775 – the largest number in such a short time before Gabriel's Rebellion in 1800 – was no coincidence. They believed that what they were facing was not just a few scattered outbreaks but a coordinated attack. Edward Stabler, a Williamsburg Quaker, noted in May that during the previous month "[t]here had been many Rumours here of the Negroes intending to Rise." Although Stabler considered the rumor of a wide-ranging slave conspiracy "without much foundation," it was real enough to terrify many of his fellow citizens. An anonymous newspaper essayist stated in June that "various reports of internal insurrections" had circulated throughout the spring. "Whether this was general, or who were the instigators, remains as yet a secret," he said.[27]

It was in this context of rising aspirations among blacks and mounting fears among whites that Governor Dunmore decided to put Virginia's major ammunition cache out of the reach of patriot militiamen. Early on Friday morning, 21 April, he had a detachment from HMS *Magdalen* remove fifteen half barrels of gunpowder from the colonial magazine in the center of Williamsburg and secure them on the warship. Many white Virginians believed that the governor's timing was no coincidence, that he intentionally removed the powder amid the swirl of rumors of servile insurrection in order to abandon them to the fury of their slaves. Many years later, Edmund Randolph, who had lived in Williamsburg in April 1775, pronounced the transfer of the powder "not far removed from assassination." He concluded that the governor "designed, by disarming the people, to weaken the means of opposing an insurrection of the slaves … for a protection against whom in part the magazine was at first built."[28]

In 1774 Dunmore had led an attack against the Shawnee and Mingo nations that forced them to cede all the land east of the Ohio River to Virginia; in March 1775 a patriot convention unanimously praised the earl "for his truly noble, wise and spirited Conduct on the late Expedition against our Indian Enemy."[29] As late as 20 April, despite the anti-British currents sweeping over the American colonies, Dunmore remained what Norfolk merchant James Parker pronounced him in January 1775 – "as popular as a Scotsman can be among weak prejudiced people." Overnight the relocation of the gunpowder turned him into a villain. By dawn on 21 April, most of white Williamsburg, having learned of the removal of the powder, gathered on the town green near the governor's palace. Many carried weapons. The people in the crowd meant to force the governor to return the gunpowder, but they agreed to stand down while the town council and provincial leaders first gave Dunmore a chance to give up the powder peacefully. A delegation met with him and surprised everyone by agreeing to let the powder stay on board the *Magdalen*. Returning to the green, the leaders persuaded the crowd to disperse.[30]

Williamsburg lapsed into "perfect tranquility." But then "a Report was spread by his Excellency's throwing out some threats respecting the Slaves."[31] The report was true. On 22 April, the day after he removed the gunpowder, Dunmore reignited the crisis. He gave Dr. William Pasteur, a member of the Williamsburg town council, a message for Peyton Randolph, the Speaker of the House of Burgesses: If any high-ranking British official was harmed, Dunmore "would declare Freedom to the Slaves, and reduce the City of *Williamsburg* to Ashes."[32]

It became clear at once what probably had prompted Speaker Randolph and other white leaders to back off so quickly from their demand the previous day that Dunmore immediately return the powder. They did not want to provoke

him to employ a weapon far more lethal than fifteen half barrels of gunpowder, the more than 180,000 Virginians who were enslaved.[33] A day later, Dunmore went beyond whatever subtle hints he may have dropped in his meeting with white leaders; he explicitly threatened to free Virginia's slaves.

Dunmore's posture frightened white Virginians. In Williamsburg, the town fathers doubled the nightly slave patrol. In Amelia, the patriot committee, fearful "for the internal security of the county," ordered "that patrollers in every neighbourhood be constantly kept on duty."[34]

Dunmore's suspiciously timed seizure of the gunpowder and his threat to free the slaves coincided with the battles of Lexington and Concord. White Virginians interpreted the initiatives of General Thomas Gage in Massachusetts and Governor Dunmore in Virginia as part of a concerted ministerial plot to disarm them. The government's scheme seemed likely to have its most dire consequences in the slave colonies. White Virginians debated how best to respond. Provincial leaders in Williamsburg believed the safest strategy was to avoid antagonizing Dunmore. In the countryside, however, independent military companies mustered and prepared to march to the capital. At least seven counties that had not yet formed independent companies hastily did so.[35]

Although the clash at Lexington and Concord was clearly one reason that so many white Virginians turned their attention to military preparedness at this time, they were also concerned about events in their own colony. The Sussex County committee explicitly linked its decision to establish an independent company to Dunmore's oddly timed relocation of the gunpowder. The governor, the Sussex committee asserted, had attempted "to render (at least as far as in his power so to do) this colony defenceless, and lay it open to the attacks of a savage invasion, or a domestick foe." His actions made it "absolutely necessary that this county be put into the best posture of defence possible." More than six hundred members of independent companies converged on Fredericksburg by 29 April and made ready to march south to the capital. Among their goals, a Virginia historian recalled many years later, was "to seize the governor and crush at once the seeds of insurrection."[36]

The men who assembled for the march to Williamsburg no doubt expected whites in the capital to be comforted to hear that reinforcements were on the way. Instead, white Williamsburg residents were terrified. The moment colonial treasurer Robert Carter Nicholas and Speaker Peyton Randolph learned that the independent companies had gathered, they began "writing letters over all the country to prevent those meetings." according to Norfolk merchant James Parker.[37] Speaker Randolph warned the Fredericksburg encampment that "violent measures may produce effects, which God only knows the consequence of." His fears were not unfounded. On 28 April, the day after Dunmore learned that the independent companies intended to march against him, he reiterated his threat to raise the slaves. The governor drew a line in the sandy Tidewater soil. He told Pasteur that "if a large Body of People came below *Ruffin's Ferry* (a place about thirty Miles from this City) that he would immediately enlarge his plan, and carry it into Execution." If any whites had dared to hope that Dunmore's earlier warning had been only the product of momentary passion, by repeating it he set them straight. During "this alarming crisis," a group of Williamsburg slave patrollers said, "even the whispering of the wind was sufficient to rouze their fears." The governor underscored that he would not strike the first blow; Pasteur reported that he "more than once did say, he should not carry these Plans into Execution unless he was attacked."[38]

Fearful gentry' leaders managed to persuade most of the independent volunteer companies to disband – most, but not all. The Albemarle County volunteers voted on 29 April to march to Williamsburg "to demand satisfaction of

Dunmore for the powder, and his threatening to fix his standard and call over the negroes," the company's first lieutenant noted.[39] Apparently the Albemarle troops had second thoughts and turned back, but the company from Hanover County, led by Patrick Henry, decided on 2 May to march on. The Hanover men, who were soon joined by volunteers from other counties, feared that Dunmore's suspiciously timed removal of the gunpowder would lead to "calamities of the greatest magnitude, and most fatal consequences to this colony," presumably including a slave revolt.[40] Speaker Randolph and other leaders tried to persuade Henry's followers that by attacking Dunmore they would provoke him to create the very "calamities" and "fatal consequences" they meant to prevent.[41]

The leaders' assessment of the governor's intentions was correct. As Henry's band headed toward Williamsburg, "several negroes" went to the governor's palace and "made a tender of their services." Dunmore turned them away, but he told Attorney General John Randolph that if the Hanover volunteers attacked him and "Negroes on that Occasion offered their Service they would be received."[42] On 3 May, Dunmore issued a proclamation. He demanded that free Virginians cease all resistance to his authority, and he took the occasion to remind them of their vulnerability to a slave or Indian uprising. This veiled warning may have helped persuade Henry and Receiver General Richard Corbin to reach a face-saving compromise in which Corbin paid Henry for the gunpowder – which remained on board the *Magdalen*.[43]

The powder magazine incident is one of the chestnuts of Virginia history. It marked the first time since Bacon's Rebellion in 1676 that a large number of Virginians had taken up arms to attack a royal governor. It served also "to widen the unhappy breach between Great Britain and her colonies," as the soldiers encamped at Fredericksburg declared. All over the colony, county committees proclaimed that Dunmore had "highly forfeited all title to the confidence of the good people of Virginia."[44] In the midst of the crisis, Patrick Henry recognized that the episode would foster patriotism in Virginia. As the Hanover independent company marched toward Williamsburg, he observed that the removal of the gunpowder "was a fortunate circumstance, which would rouse the people from North to South."[45]

The growth of anti-British sentiment in Virginia in May 1775 is usually ascribed simply to the battles of Lexington and Concord and to Dunmore's decision to seize the gunpowder.[46] But the governor learned from Benjamin Waller, a member of Williamsburg's patriot committee, that Dunmore had forfeited "the Confidence of the People not so much for having taken the Powder as for the declaration he made of raising and freeing the Slaves." Louisa County trader Thomas Mitchell noted "that the Governor's Declaration to give Freedom to the Slaves greatly inflamed the Minds of those who believed it," although not everyone did. It is possible that many patriots only pretended to believe the stories about Dunmore's "stiring up the Negroes to Rebellion" (as Rawleigh Downman put it in July) because the rumors furnished a good pretext for anti-British activities.[47] Because Dunmore's opponents had backed down, however, no one knew what he would have done if they had called his bluff and attacked him. Patriots may have exaggerated their anger at Dunmore's tactics of intimidation, but they did not invent it.

Racial tensions escalated the imperial conflict in another way as well. One of the charges that whites lodged against Dunmore was that he had chosen to remove the powder at the very moment when reports of slave conspiracies poured into Williamsburg. The slave revolt scare in April 1775 was the crucial context of Dunmore's seizure of the gunpowder. It was not only his decision to "remov[e] the powder from the magazine" but also "the several circumstances attending the same" that angered the Richmond County committee. Others agreed. The Fredericksburg encampment considered the relocation of the gunpowder "ill timed." A

South Carolina newspaper described the racial context of the transfer and then observed, "The monstrous absurdity that the Governor can deprive the people of the necessary means of defense at a time when the colony is actually threatened with an insurrection of their slaves … has worked up the passions of the people there almost to a frenzy."[48]

Despite the reality of Dunmore's threat to free the slaves and his decision to remove the gunpowder during this tense period, the possibility must be considered that patriots publicly exaggerated their fear in order to cast further odium on the royal governor. White Virginians, however, seem to have been sincere when they said they feared a slave insurrection at the time Dunmore removed the powder. Loyalists such as James Robison, the chief factor for William Cuningharne & Company of Glasgow, agreed with patriots that "an insurrection … was dreaded" in Virginia during the spring of 1775.[49] If one suspects that the *Virginia Gazette's* account of the "conspiracy to raise an insurrection" in Norfolk was only patriot propaganda, one need only consult the minute book of the Norfolk County court, in which the trial of the two Emanuels is recorded.[50] The death of one of the alleged conspirators, Matthew Phripp's Emanuel, can be traced in the Norfolk County tithable lists, from which he disappeared between the taking of the 1774 and 1778 enumerations.[51] The trial of Toney in Prince Edward County is also a matter of record. It is possible that the Williamsburg town council's allegation on 21 April that Dunmore had removed the gunpowder amid "various reports" of slave plots "in different parts of the country" was just rhetoric,[52] but whites' fears as recorded in the private letters of Edmund Pendleton, Edward Stabler, and Robert Donald were almost certainly not fabricated.

If anything, white Virginians may have understated their apprehensions of slave revolt in their public pronouncements. In November 1774, when James Madison told a Princeton classmate that slaves in the Piedmont had planned to take advantage of the expected British invasion, he judged it "prudent such attempts should be concealed as well as suppressed." A year later, when editor John Pinkney printed a letter from South Carolina in his *Virginia Gazette,* he omitted part of it. "This letter goes on farther," Pinkney informed his readers, "and relates a great deal about the negroes in South Carolina: but we think it prudent to suppress the account." Although nothing was certain in this murky world of "exaggeration, distortion, [and] censorship," it seems likely that white Virginians' anger at Governor Dunmore for taking their gunpowder was intensified by the context in which he took it. The earl seized the stores at the end of the third week of April 1775, when white Virginians circulated more reports of slave conspiracies than they had during any previous week in the colony's history.[53]

Some white Virginians expressed their growing rage at Dunmore in jokes about his relations with black women. There had long been talk about the governor's philandering, but during the summer of 1775, for the first time, his concubines were said to include blacks. On 1 June 1775, Pinkney's *Virginia Gazette* sarcastically predicted that "The BLACK LADIES" would "be jollify entertained at the p[alac]e." A year later, after Dunmore had assembled a mostly black army to battle the patriots, Purdie's *Virginia Gazette* maintained that the diminutive Dunmore and his forces celebrated their landing on Gwynn's Island "with a promiscuous ball, which was opened, we hear, by a certain spruce little gentleman, with one of the black ladies." The next month, Landon Carter of Richmond County heard a story about a patriot cannonball passing between Dunmore's legs. Carter joked in his diary that perhaps the "shot cooled his latitudinous virility for that night at least."[54]

Accounts of the Virginia slave plots, the removal of the gunpowder, and the possibility that Dunmore would ally with slave conspirators soon spread throughout the South. At the same time, the same routes of communication carried reports of the battles of Lexington and Concord and rumors from London about an emancipation bill being proposed in Parliament. All of this news led many southerners of every race and condition to believe that the British government might soon forge some sort of alliance with enslaved Americans. Dunmore's threat on 22 April to "declare Freedom to the Slaves" was ambiguous – perhaps deliberately so. Had the governor meant he would liberate only those slaves he could enlist in the British army – or all of them? Many southerners believed during the late summer of 1775 that Britain might adopt "an Act of Grace" by which enslaved Americans would "be all set free," as Charleston merchant Josiah Smith, Jr., reported on 18 May. A group of Charleston slaves had apparently contemplated a rebellion since April. The news from Virginia, Massachusetts, and London persuaded many South Carolinians that the new governor, Lord William Campbell, who was due to arrive in June, was going to free the slaves and "encourage an insurrection," as the governor himself later reported. The rumor kept white South Carolinians on tenterhooks from early May until 19 June, when Campbell landed without incident.[55]

In North Carolina, too, reports from London, Massachusetts, and Virginia contributed to talk that the British government might soon incite a slave revolt. In early July, when a widespread slave conspiracy was discovered in Pitt, Craven, and Beaufort counties, whites suspected that British officials had conferred with the conspirators about strategy and made certain promises to them. Allegedly the plan was for blacks to start a rebellion on the night of 8 July. They were to kill their owners and then move westward toward the backcountry, where "they were to be received with open arms by a number of Persons there appointed and armed by [the] Government for their Protection," according to Colonel John Simpson of Pitt County.[56]

Many enslaved Americans carried the rumors about British aid for black insurrection one step farther: They believed that the whole purpose of the expected British invasion of the

South was to liberate them. In South Carolina, a slave reported that Thomas Jeremiah, a free black fisherman and harbor pilot who hoped to help the British troops link up with rebel slaves, told bondspeople "the War was come to help the poor Negroes." Farther south in St. Bartholomew Parish at about the same time, a black preacher named George told gatherings of slaves 'That the Young King, meaning our Present One, came up with the Book, & was about to alter the World, & set the Negroes Free." George was executed.[57] The widespread belief among many black southerners that their freedom was Britain's chief war aim was detected by some whites. John Drayton wrote many years after the Revolution that Arthur Lee's assertion that the London government meant to incite an insurrection was "the more alarming; because, it was already known, [bondsmen] entertained ideas, that the present contest was for obliging us to give them their liberty."[58]

The report that freeing the slaves was one of Great Britain's objectives — perhaps even the primary one — may have been fabricated by black leaders in the hope that it would serve as a self-fulfilling prophecy. If a real slave revolt crystallized around the apocryphal story of a British army of liberation, British statesmen might indeed be drawn into an alliance with the slave rebels.

An additional source of anxiety for white leaders, and of hope for blacks, was the possibility that a large number of poor whites might cast their lots with the slaves and the British. About a month after Dunmore removed the Williamsburg gunpowder and threatened to emancipate the slaves, John Simmons of Dorchester County, Maryland, boasted: "[I]f I had a few more white people to join me I could get all the negroes in the county to back us, and they would do more good in the night than the white people could do in the day." He added, "[I]f all the gentlemen were killed we should have the best of the land to tend."[59] During July, Thomas Cox, a white inhabitant of York County, Virginia, was accused of trying to incite slaves to

rebel. He was found innocent of this charge but guilty of breach of the peace.[60]

The deepest fears of white leaders, and the highest hopes of blacks, were not realized. Dunmore did not proclaim a general emancipation, nor did he lead a rebellion of slaves and poor whites. During the summer, however, he began assembling a small fleet to confront the patriots. The governor soon welcomed such fugitive slaves as the pilot Joseph Harris, and the sanctuary that he offered runaways changed the whole calculus of race relations in Virginia. Previously, fugitive slave advertisements appearing in the *Virginia Gazette's,* commonly surmised that the escapee had gone to visit family. By September 1775, however, advertisers began to conjecture that their slaves had fled slavery by joining the British.[61]

The story of one fugitive illustrated how the meaning of escape had changed. On 10 February 1775, a fifteen-year-old girl (whose name is not known) was purchased by Virginia's official vintner, Andrew Estave. The teenager may have been one of the many young Virginians who were sold far away from their families as they reached adulthood; in any event, she found life with Estave so intolerable that in her first few months as his property, she ran away three times. Each time the girl was recaptured and suffered forty lashes. The punishment did not have its desired effect, so Estave suspended it and assumed that the fifteen-year-old would be thereby reconciled to her fate. She was not. Early in the summer of 1775, as Estave told readers of the *Virginia Gazette,* another of the women he owned "found my child, together with this cruel and unnatural wretch, concealed behind my barn, among the bushes, with her thumb thrust into the private parts of my poor child." Estave was summoned. "During the confusion," the fifteen-year-old escaped and fled — to the governor's palace in Williamsburg, where she hoped to cast her lot with Dunmore. The governor had himself recently fled to a British warship, and the teenager was soon returned to her master for punishment. First she suffered "eighty lashes, well laid on." Then Estave poured fire embers on her back.[62] Although the teenager's escape attempt was unsuccessful, it is significant that she sought refuge in the building that until recently had symbolized the enforcement, not the evasion, of white rule.[63]

The new opportunities produced by the conflict among white Virginians inspired activism even among those slaves who did not try to reach Dunmore. During the summer of 1775, the number of enslaved workers brought before the county courts for criminal trials reached a record level.[64] No doubt many white Virginians blamed the crime wave on Governor Dunmore.

In the fall of 1775, Dunmore gave white Virginians additional reasons to hate him and the government he represented. On 15 November at Kemp's Landing south of Norfolk, his outnumbered force, made up largely of former slaves, defeated 170 members of the Princess Anne County militia. Several militiamen were killed, and the rest were put to flight. The patriot commander, Joseph Hutchings, was captured by one of his own former bondsmen.[65] Kemp's Landing persuaded Dunmore that fugitive slaves could be valuable allies indeed. The governor "was so ela[ted] with this Victory," John Page, vice-chairman of the Committee of Safety, reported, that he immediately published his famous emancipation proclamation.[66] About 1,000 slaves escaped their owners and joined Dunmore. Enlisted in an "Ethiopian Regiment" and wearing uniforms that pointed up the hypocrisy of liberty-seeking patriots by proclaiming "Liberty to Slaves," former bondsmen soon made up the major part of the loyalist troops.[67] In order to glimpse the psychological effect of emancipation on the people who reached Dunmore, it may be sufficient to notice the case of a man whites called Yellow Peter. He escaped one day in 1775 or 1776 and was later seen "in Governor Dunmore's regiment with a musquet on his back and a sword by his side." He had changed his name to Captain Peter.[68]

Although Dunmore apparently meant to limit his offer of emancipation to able-bodied men (he addressed it to servants and slaves "able and willing to bear Arms"), half of those who joined him and survived the war were women and children.[69] Among them was Francis Rice's slave, Mary, One night in spring 1776, Mary, a resident of Hampton, snatched up her three-and-a-half-year-old daughter Phillis and made a dash for the British lines. The two got in safely, lived through the Revolution, and settled afterward in Nova Scotia.[70]

Still, for the 99 percent of slaves who did not escape to Dunmore, his emancipation proclamation was in many ways a disappointment. During summer 1775, many Virginians anticipated that the British government might make the abolition of slavery a goal of the war. Instead, Dunmore offered freedom only to individuals and formed a conventional army to pursue the limited strategy of taking and holding ground. Even as Dunmore's decision to fight a traditional war destroyed the hopes of many black Virginians, it emboldened whites. To them, a black regiment in the British army was a frightening thing indeed, but it was nothing like a British promise of general emancipation. By August 1776, patriots forced Dunmore's vastly outnumbered army to retreat to New York City.

The relief that white Virginians experienced when Dunmore chose to fight a conventional war did not diminish their anger at him for allying with slaves. As early as May 1775, free subjects had begun literally to demonize their governor. In November, when he published his declaration of emancipation, this process intensified. Citizens denounced Dunmore's "Diabolical scheme" and all "'his infernal tribe." "Our Devil of a Governor goes on at a Devil of a rate indeed," Benjamin Harrison commented after reading the Virginia news.[71]

The deterioration in white Virginians' affection for Dunmore was not the only political result of his proclamation. Thomas Jefferson spoke for other white Americans when he stated in the Declaration of Independence that

Dunmore's emancipation proclamation was a major cause of the Revolution.[72] Throughout Virginia, observers noted that the governor's pronouncement turned neutrals and even loyalists into patriots. "The Inhabitants of this Colony are deeply alarmed at this infernal Scheme." Philip Fithian recorded in his journal as he passed through the Virginia backcountry in late November. "It seems to quicken all in Revolution to overpower him at any Risk." Richard Henry Lee told Catharine Macauley that "Lord Dunmores unparalleled conduct in Virginia has, a few Scotch excepted, united every Man in that large Colony." Archibald Cary agreed. "The Proclamation from Lord D[unmore], has had a most extensive good consequence," he wrote; white "Men of all ranks resent the pointing a dagger to their Throats, through the hands of their Slaves." Cary noted that by endangering loyalists as well as patriots, Dunmore's decision converted many of the former into the latter.[73]

These patriot writers' comments on the governor's declaration may have reflected some measure of wishful thinking about its effect on undecided and loyalist whites, but Dunmore's pronouncement did transform many neutrals and loyalists into patriots. It even pushed two members of the colony's powerful executive council, Robert "Councilor" Carter and William Byrd III, from the loyalist to the patriot camp. During summer 1775, Byrd had offered to lead British troops. Both he and Carter, however, became patriots after Dunmore confirmed his alliance with black Virginians. Byrd then tendered his services to the patriot forces.[74]

Some of William Byrd's fellow conservatives initially believed that as soon as Dunmore's superiors in London learned about his emancipation proclamation, they would repudiate it and recall him. At the end of 1775, Landon Carter assured his diary that it was "not to be doubted" that Dunmore would soon receive "some missive commission to Silence all his iniquities both male and female." (This was yet another reference to Dunmore's alleged

miscegenation.)[75] But the winter of 1775–76 came and went with no evidence that anyone at Whitehall objected to Dunmore's decision to offer freedom to the slaves.

It was not just in Virginia that Dunmore's emancipation proclamation helped alienate whites from Britain. In Maryland, loyalist William Eddis observed that Dunmore's "measure of emancipating the negroes has excited an universal ferment." He speculated that the declaration would "greatly strengthen the general confederacy." Edward Rutledge of South Carolina expected that the "proclamation issued by Lord Dunmore" would tend "more effectually to work an eternal separation between Great Britain and the Colonies, – than any other expedient, which could possibly have been thought of." In Philadelphia, a play depicting Dunmore welcoming black recruits became part of the library of anti-British propaganda. In the play, *The Fall of British Tyranny* by Philadelphia silversmith John Leacock, Lord Kidnapper (Dunmore) congratulates himself on raising "rebel against rebel" and says he expects his emancipation proclamation "will greatly intimidate the rebels – internal enemies are worse than open foes."[76]

Although Dunmore was the only royal governor who made a formal offer of freedom to his colony's slaves before 4 July 1776, other British leaders informally cooperated with bondspeople and thereby helped motivate white Americans to declare independence. In North Carolina in June 1776, patriot James Iredell stated that when royal officials encouraged enslaved Americans "to cut our throats," they "added spurs to our Patriotism."[77]

White Americans also denounced British cooperation with American Indians. Here, too, Dunmore was one of the most popular targets. In November 1775 Dunmore sent his associate John Connolly to Detroit and the Ohio country to recruit an army of Indian warriors that would join forces with the governor's Anglo-black army at Alexandria in spring 1776. Connolly was captured as he rode west through Maryland,

and his plot was revealed. It infuriated white Americans. In John Leacock's *Fall of British Tyranny,* Lord Kidnapper muses: "[I]f we can stand our ground this winter, and burn all their towns that are accessible to our ships, and Colonel Connolly succeeds in his plan … we shall be able to make a descent where we please, and drive the rebels like hogs into a pen."[78]

As previously noted, a man named Emanuel disappeared from Matthew Phripp's tithables between the recording of the 1774 and 1778 lists. He was one of the two slaves executed in Norfolk in April 1775 "for being concerned in a conspiracy to raise an insurrection in that town."[79] Emanuel was not the only enslaved worker whom Phripp lost in the early years of the American Revolution. Other names also vanished from his tithable list during the war. About most of these people we know nothing, but we do know what became of several of them. When the British army and navy evacuated New York City in 1783, about 3,000 slaves went with them. Before leaving, navy captains made a list of their formerly enslaved passengers. On board the *Danger,* anchored near Staten Island (and not far from the little island where the Statue of Liberty would rise a century later), the compilers of the list recorded the presence of "James Tucker. 55 years, almost worn out … Formerly slave to Capt. [M.] Fipps. Norfolk, Virginia; left him in 1776 with Lord Dunmore."[80] When the *Danger* cleared New York harbor, bound for Nova Scotia, James Tucker was on board. He might have been "almost worn out," but he was headed to freedom.

We do not know how James Tucker had spent the years between 1776 and 1783, but it is clear that he was able to wring a larger measure of freedom from the American Revolution than did any of the white colonists who had revolted against British tyranny. If slaves such as Matthew Phripp's Emanuel had not made their own efforts to win freedom in 1774 and 1775, Governor Dunmore might never have published the emancipation proclamation that resulted not only in the freedom of hundreds of Virginians such as Phripp's James but also in the deterioration of relations between white Virginians and the British government.

Although the effect of Dunmore's cooperation with slaves on white Virginians' decision to declare independence is often mentioned by scholars who write about the Revolution, it is generally underestimated.[81] One reason for this minimization is that students of the origins of the Revolution often do not mention enslaved Virginians until November 1775, when Dunmore issued his famous emancipation proclamation. Actually, as several social historians have shown, the governor's declaration culminated a process that had begun much earlier. Slaves had always resisted their condition. In 1774, while Dunmore was still one of the colony's most popular governors, enslaved Virginians began conspiring to exploit the opportunities presented to them by the imperial crisis. The following April, as rumors of the planning of a wide-ranging insurrection circulated, a group of slaves literally knocked on the governor's door and offered to cast their lots with his.[82] And slaves kept knocking all through the summer and into the fall. Andrew Estave's fifteen-year-old bondswoman presented herself at the governor's palace early in the summer, after Dunmore had taken refuge on a British warship. She was recaptured, but other slaves did reach the earl and served him as sailors, raiders, and soldiers.[83] It was not until after the series of black initiatives culminating in the victory at Kemp's Landing on 15 November that Dunmore officially offered freedom to the slaves.[84] The slaves' insurgency played an important role in persuading Dunmore to ally with them – and thus in prodding white Virginians farther along the road to independence.

If black Virginians really did help push whites into independence, how does that change our understanding of the Revolution in Virginia? At least to some extent, we must agree with an anonymous resident of Williamsburg who assessed the situation in November 1775, shortly after Dunmore published his emancipation proclamation. "Whoever considers well the meaning of the word Rebel," he wrote, "will discover that the author of the Proclamation is now himself in actual rebellion, having armed our slaves against us, and having excited them to an insurrection."[85] In modern terms, this author might have said that white Virginians' struggle against Dunmore and his Ethiopian Regiment was not a revolution but a counterrevolution.

The war in Virginia pitted two classes, slave owners and slaves, against each other. At least in this one aspect of Virginia's multifaceted revolutionary experience, therefore, Virginia fits the Progressive historians' interpretation of the Revolution as a dual conflict over both home rule and who would rule at home. For years students of the origins of the American Revolution in Virginia, taking as an article of faith the "relative docility of the poorer farmers" in that colony, found almost no value in the Progressives' hypothesis that class conflict helped cause the Revolution.[86] More recently, the assumption that small farmers were tractable has been challenged.[87] And if enslaved Virginians are considered a class – which surely they must be – then there certainly was class conflict in Virginia during the prerevolutionary period, and that antagonism did help bring on the American Revolution. In fact, judging from the frenzied white reaction to Dunmore's decision to forge an alliance with black Virginians, it may be that Virginia was the colony in which class conflict gave the biggest push to the movement for independence.

## Notes

Woody Holton is an assistant professor of history at Bloomsburg University. The author wishes to thank the following groups and individuals for useful comments on earlier drafts of this essay: Fred Anderson, the Bloomsburg University Social Studies Club. Edward Countryman. John d'Entremont. Emory G. Evans. Marjoleine Kars. Staughton Lynd. Michael A. McDonnell, John Murrin, Michael Lee Nicholls, Julie Richter, John E. Selby, Jon Sensbach, Brent Tarter, Thad W. Tate. Fredrika J. Teute, the outside readers for the *Virginia Magazine of History and Biography,* and especially Peter H. Wood. Research for this essay was funded in part by fellowships from the Virginia Historical Society and the Virginia Foundation for the Humanities.

1 Howard H. Peckham, ed., *The Toll of Independence: Engagements & Battle Casualties of the American Revolution* (Chicago and London, 1974), 9.

2 George Gray, deposition, 4 Sept 1775, in William J. Van Schreeven, Robert L. Scribner, and Brent Tarter, eds., *Revolutionary Virginia: The Road to Independence* (7 vols.; Charlottesville, 1973–83), 4:70 (first quotation); George Montague to Matthew Squire, 20 July 1775, in Peter Force. comp., *American Archives: Consisting of a Collection of Authentick Records, State Papers. Debates, and Letters and Other Notices of Publick Affairs* … 4th ser. (6 vols.; Washington. D.C., 1837–46), 2: 1692 (second and third quotations).

3 *Virginia Gazette* (Purdie), 8 Sept. 1775; *Virginia Gazette* (Dixon and Hunter), 23 Sept. 1775. Joseph Harris appears on the muster role of the *Otter* during this time: see Admiralty 36/7763, Public Record Office. Kew, England (hereafter cited as PRO), Virginia Colonial Records Project, survey report 8793.

4 Lund Washington to George Washington, 3 Dec. 1775, in W. W. Abbot et al., eds., *The Papers of George Washington: Revolutionary War Series* (7 vols. to date; Charlottesville, 1985–), 2:479: *Virginia Gazette* (Purdie), 3 Nov. 1775 (quotation); John Page to Thomas Jefferson, 11 Nov. [1775], in Julian P. Boyd et al., eds., *The Papers of Thomas Jefferson* (26 vols. to date: Princeton, 1950–), 1:257. The fate of the *Hawke's* black crewmen is not known.

5 Thomas Jefferson to John Randolph, 29 Nov. 1775. Archibald Cary to Thomas Jefferson, 31 Oct. 1775, in Boyd et al., eds., *Jefferson Papers,* 1:269 (quotation), 249; Edmund Randolph, *History of Virginia,* ed. Arthur H. Shaffer, Virginia Historical Society Documents, 9 (Charlottesville, 1970), 227–29. George Montague, captain of the *Fowey,* stated that Joseph Harris was free (George Montague to Matthew Squire. 20 July 1775, in Force, comp., *American Archives,* 4th ser., 2:1692). The captain's comment implies that Harris was already legally free before he joined the crew of the *Fowey.* Certainly there were

free blacks in prerevolutionary Hampton, but it is not known whether Harris was one of them. Every other reference to Harris indicates he was a fugitive slave. See, for example, Sarah Shaver Hughes, "Elizabeth City County, Virginia, 1782–1810: The Economic and Social Structure of a Tidewater County in the Early National Years" (Ph.D. diss., College of William and Mary, 1975), 32.

6  See, for example, Benjamin Quarles, *The Negro in the American Revolution* (Chapel Hill, 1961); Sylvia R. Frey, "Between Slavery and Freedom: Virginia Blacks in the American Revolution." *Journal of Southern History* (hereafter cited as *JSH*) 49 (1983): 375–98; Sylvia R. Frey, *Water from the Rock: Black Resistance in a Revolutionary Age* (Princeton, 1991); Robert A. Olwell, "'Domestick Enemies': Slavery and Political Independence in South Carolina, May 1775–March 1776," *JSH* 55 (1989): 21–48; and Charles W. Carey, Jr., "'These Black Rascals': The Origins of Lord Dunmore's Ethiopian Regiment," *Virginia Social Science Journal* 31 (1996): 65–77. Earlier studies of African Americans in the Revolution include William Tittamin, "The Negro in the American Revolution" (M.A. thesis, New York University, 1939); Herbert Aptheker, *The Negro in the American Revolution* (New York, 1940); and Luther P. Jackson, "Virginia Negro Soldiers and Seamen in the American Revolution," *Journal of Negro History* (hereafter cited as *JNH*) 27 (1942): 247–87.

7  Quarles, *Negro in the Revolution;* Frey, "Between Slavery and Freedom"; Peter H. Wood, "'The Dream Deferred': Black Freedom Struggles on the Eve of White Independence," in Gary Y. Okihiro, ed., *In Resistance: Studies in African, Caribbean, and Afro-American History* (Amherst, Mass., 1986), 166–87; Peter H. Wood, "'Liberty Is Sweet': African-American Freedom Struggles in the Years before White Independence," in Alfred F. Young, ed., *Beyond the American Revolution: Explorations in the History of American Radicalism* (DeKalb. Ill., 1993), 149–84.

8  Philip J. Schwarz, *Twice Condemned: Slaves and the Criminal Laws of Virginia, 1705–1865* (Baton Rouge, 1988), 144. For examples of violence, see Richard Bland and William Fleming, petition, 5 Nov. 1764. James Boyd, petition, 7 Nov. 1764, in John Pendleton Kennedy, ed., *Journals of the House of Burgesses of Virginia, 1761–1765* (Richmond, 1907), 237, 239; Daniel Hamlin, petition, 25 Feb. 1772, in John Pendleton Kennedy, ed., *Journals of the House of Burgesses of Virginia, 1770–1772* (Richmond, 1906), 189; Thomas Patterson, petition, 12 May 1774, Committee of Public Claims, report, 13 May 1774, in John Pendleton Kennedy, ed., *Journals of the House of Burgesses of Virginia, 1773–1776 …* (Richmond, 1905), 92, 98; Augusta County Order Book, 11 Apr. 1772, in Lyman Chalkley, ed., *Chronicles of the Scotch-Irish Settlement in Virginia, Extracted From the Original Court Records of Augusta Country, 1745–1800* (3 vols.: Rosslyn, Va., 1912–13),1:167; John Davis, *Travels of Four Years and a Half in the United States of America During 1798, 1799, 1800, 1801 and 1802* (1803: New York 1909), 414; Henry Lee to Richard Lee, 16 Feb. 1767, Richard Bland Lee Letterbook, Custis-Lee Papers, Manuscripts Department, Library of Congress, Washington. D.C. (hereafter cited as DLC); David John Mays, *Edmund Pendleton, 1721–1803: A Biography* (2 vols.: Cambridge, Mass., 1952), 1:22, 35; Freeman H. Hart, *The Valley of Virginia in the American Revolution, 1763–1789* (Chapel Hill, 1942), 15; Schwarz. *Twice Condemned,* pp. ix–x, chap. 6: and William Waller Hening, ed., *The Statutes at Large: Being a Collection of All the Laws of Virginia …* (13 vols.: Richmond. Philadelphia, and New York, 1809–23), 6:104–12.

9  Schwarz, *Twice Condemned,* p. 143. Edmund S. Morgan draws a connection between slavery and the American Revolution that is very different from the one drawn in this essay. He argues that elite Virginians felt secure enough to embrace republicanism because they had solved "the problem of the poor" by creating "a society in which most of the poor were enslaved." By holding the poorest Virginians in bondage, he says, gentlemen "removed them from the political equation." Morgan's argument is undermined by a growing body of evidence showing that slaves consistently resisted their condition and thus remained, at the same time that they were among their owners' largest sources of income, a "problem" for them. (It also appears that very few Virginia gentlemen embraced republicanism with the enthusiasm ascribed to them by Morgan.) See Edmund S. Morgan, *American Slavery, American Freedom: The Ordeal of Colonial*

*Virginia* (New York, 1975), 381 (first and second quotations), 380 (third quotation).

10  Herbert Aptheker, *American Negro Slave Revolts* (New York, 1943), pp. 18–208; Thad W. Tate, *The Negro in Eighteenth-Century Williamsburg* (Charlottesville, 1965), 109–13: Theodore Allen, "'… They Would Have Destroyed Me': Slavery and the Origins of Racism," *Radical America* 9 (1975): 56; Schwarz, *Twice Condemned,* pp. 171–74: Mays, *Edmund Pendleton,* 1:119–20.

11  Dinwiddie advised Carter to keep "Patrollers out for the Peace of Y'r Co[un]ty" and to instruct sheriffs to "seize all Horses used by Negroes in the Night Time" (Robert Dinwiddie to Charles Carter, 18 July 1755, in R. A. Brock, ed., *The Official Records of Robert Dinwiddie … .* Collections of the Virginia Historical Society, new ser., 3, 4 [2 vols.: Richmond, 1883–84], 2:104–5). Cf. Mark J. Stegmaier, "Maryland's Fear of Insurrection at the Time of Braddock's Defeat." *Maryland Historical Magazine* 71 (1976); 467–83; Wood, "'Liberty Is Sweet,'" 154.

12  Richard Henry Lee, speech, n.d., in Richard H. Lee. ed., *Memoir of the Life of Richard Henry Lee, and His Correspondence With the Most Distinguished Men in America and Europe …* (2 vols.: Philadelphia, 1825), 1:18.

13  William Fleming to Francis Fauquier, 26 July 1763, in George Reese, ed., *The Official Papers of Francis Fauquier, Lieutenant Governor of Virginia, 1758–1768,* Virginia Historical Society Documents, 14, 15, 16 (3 vols.; Charlottesville, 1980–83), 2:998; Peter Fontaine to Moses and John Fontaine and Daniel Torin, 7 Aug. 1763, in Ann Maury, ed., *Memoirs of a Huguenot Family* (New York, 1872), 372. Cf. Benjamin Johnston, advertisement, in *Virginia Gazette* (Rind), 16 Dec. 1773.

14  *Boston Chronicle,* 11–18 Jan. 1768, quoted in Aptheker, *American Negro Slave Revolts,* pp. 198–99; Frederick County militia, accounts, 23 Mar. 1767. Committee of Public Claims, report, 23 Nov. 1769, in John Pendleton Kennedy, ed., *Journals of the House of Burgesses of Virginia, 1766–1769* (Richmond, 1906), 91, 286; Schwarz, *Twice Condemned,* 146–47.

15  Robert Knox and William Knox, advertisement, in *Virginia Gazette* (Rind), 15 June 1769 (first quotation): *Virginia Gazette* (Rind), 20 July 1769 (second quotation).

16  *Virginia Gazette* (Rind), 25 Jan. 1770.

17  Robert Dinwiddie to Charles Carter, 18 July 1755, in Brock, ed., *Dinwiddie Records.* 2:104 (quotation); Aptheker, *American Negro Slave Revolts,* 4.

18  James Madison to William Bradford, Jr., 26 Nov. 1774, in William T. Hutchinson et al., eds., *The Papers of James Madison* (17 vols.: Chicago and Charlottesville, 1962–91). 1:130 (quotation); Wood. "'Liberty Is Sweet,'" 161–63.

19  Jonathan Boucher, *A Letter from a Virginian to the Members of the Congress …* ([New York], 1774), 32; Henry Cruger to Ralph Izard, 21 Mar. 1775, in *Correspondence of Mr. Ralph Izard, of South Carolina …* (New York, 1844), 58.

20  "Viator" [William Draper], *The Thoughts of a Traveller Upon Our American Disputes* (London, 1774), 21; Arthur Lee to [Richard Henry Lee?], 6 Dec. 1774, Lee Family Papers, 1638–1867, Virginia Historical Society, Richmond. Lee continued: "Do not laugh at it, till you are sure it woud be vain. If you apprehend it woud bc dangerous take proper precautions against it."

21  William Bradford, Jr., to James Madison, 4 Jan. 1775, in Hutchinson et al., eds., *Madison Papers.* 1:132: Edmund Burke, speech on conciliation with the colonies, 22 Mar. 1775, in Edmund Burke, *Speeches and Letters on American Affairs,* Everyman's Libran, 340 (London and New York, 1908), 102.

22  House of Burgesses, address to John Murray, earl of Dunmore, 19 June 1775, in *JHB, 1773–76,* 256; *Virginia Gazette* (Purdie), 16 June 1775. Cf. Virginia convention of 1775, "A Declaration of the Delegates … ," 26 Aug. 1775, in Van Schreeven, Scribner, and Tarter, eds., *Revolutionary Virginia,* 3:501. The rumor that the British government intended to arm enslaved Americans against their masters circulated in other colonies as well. During the critical month of April 1775, Philadelphia Quaker James Kenny reported that "a great Woman in London" had written a Philadelphian saying several members of the House of Lords had informed her of a "secret Plan." "[A]rms &c" were "to be given to all the … Negros to act against the Collonie" (James Kenny to Humphry Marshall, 25 Apr. 1775 [typescript], Humphry and Moses Marshall Papers, William L. Clements Library, University of Michigan, Ann Arbor).

23  Schwarz, *Twice Condemned,* 182, 184.

24  Robert Donald to Patrick Hunter, 18 Apr. 1775, in *Buchanan and Milliken* v. *Robert Donald,* 1794, U.S. Circuit Court. Virginia District, Ended Cases (restored). Box 6, Vi.

25  *Virginia Gazette* (Dixon and Hunter), 29 Apr. 1775 (supplement): Norfolk County Minute Book, 21 Apr. 1775, Vi.

26  Edmund Pendleton to George Washington, 21 Apr. 1775, in David John Mays, ed., *The Letters and Papers of Edmund Pendleton, 1734–1803,* Virginia Historical Society Documents 7, 8 (2 vols.: Charlottesville, 1967), 1:102.

27  Edward Stabler to Isaac Pemberton, 16 May 1775, Pemberton Papers, 27:144, Historical Society of Pennsylvania, Philadelphia (microfilm, Colonial Williamsburg Foundation. Williamsburg. Va. [hereafter cited as ViWC]): *Virginia Gazette* (Purdie), 16 June 1775. Cf. unnamed merchants, note at the foot of Archibald Cary to James Lyle et al., 12 June 1775, Colonial Office 5/1353, ff. 129–31, PRO (microfilm, p. 401. Lamont Library. Harvard University, Cambridge, Mass.). Certainly a conspiracy this extensive was possible. Twenty-five years later, in 1800, organizers of Gabriel's Rebellion recruited clusters of supporters in counties throughout the Tidewater and Piedmont. See Gerald W. Mullin, *Flight and Rebellion: Slave Resistance in Eighteenth-Century Virginia* (New York, 1972), 140–63; Philip J. Schwarz, "Gabriel's Challenge: Slaves and Crime in Late Eighteenth-Century Virginia," *Virginia Magazine of History and Biography* (hereafter cited as *VMHB*) 90 (1982): 283–309: and Douglas R. Egerton, *Gabriel's Rebellion: The Virginia Slave Conspiracies of 1800 and 1802* (Chapel Hill and London, 1993).

28  Randolph, *History of Virginia,* p. 219. Cf. Sussex County committee, resolution. 8 May 1775, Virginia convention of 1775. "A Declaration of the Delegates … ." 26 Aug. 1775, in Van Schreeven. Scribner, and Tarter, eds., *Revolutionary Virginia,* 3:107, 501; John Murray, carl of Dunmore, to William Legue, earl of Dartmouth. 1 May 1775, in K. G. Davies, ed., *Documents of the American Revolution, 1770–1783* (21 vols.: Shannon, Ireland, 1972–81), 9:109.

29  Virginia convention of 1775, resolution, 25 Mar. 1775, in Van Schreeven, Scribner, and Tarter, eds., *Revolutionary Virginia,* 2:376. On Dunmore's War, see Jack M Sosin, "The British Indian Department and Dunmore's War," *VMHB* 74 (1966): 34–50; Turk McCleskey. "Dunmore's War," in Richard L. Blanco, ed., *The American Revolution, 1775–1783: An Encyclopedia* (2 vols.; New York and London, 1993), 1:492–97; Michael N. McConnell, *A Country Between: The Upper Ohio Valley and Its Peoples, 1724–1774* (Lincoln, Nebr., 1992), 268–79; and Woody Holton, "The Ohio Indians and the Coming of the American Revolution in Virginia," *JSH* 60 (1994): 453–78.

30  James Parker to Charles Steuart, 27 Jan. 1775, Charles Steuart Papers, MSS 5025, National Library of Scotland, Edinburgh (microfilm. Vi); John E. Selby, *The Revolution in Virginia, 1775–1783* (Charlottesville, 1988), 1–2.

31  John Dixon, deposition, quoted in Committee on the Late Disturbances, report, 14 June 1775, in *JHB, 1773–76,* 233 (quotations); Randolph. *History of Virginia,* 220.

32  William Pasteur, deposition, quoted in Committee on the Late Disturbances, report, 14 June 1775, in *JHB, 1773–76,* 231.

33  Peter H. Wood, "The Changing Population of the Colonial South: An Overview by Race and Region. 1685–1790," in Peter H. Wood, Gregory A. Waselkov, and M. Thomas Hatley, eds., *Powhatan's Mantle: Indians in the Colonial Southeast,* Indians of the Southeast (Lincoln. Nebr., 1989), 38.

34  Benjamin Waller and John Dixon, depositions, quoted in Committee on the Late Disturbances, report, 14 June 1775, in *JHB, 1773–76,* 232–33: Amelia County committee, minutes, 3 May 1775, in Van Schreeven, Scribner, and Tarter, eds., *Revolutionary Virginia,* 3:83.

35  The counties were Mecklenburg, New Kent, Chesterfield, Louisa, Essex, Henrico, and Nansemond. See Randolph, *History of Virginia,* 220; James Lyle and Robert Donald, Thomas Mitchell, Archibald Ritchie, Archibald Bryce, and Andrew Sprowle et al., depositions, quoted in Committee on the Late Disturbances, report, 14 June 1775, in *JHB, 1773–76,* 234–37; Mecklenburg County committee, resolution, 8 May 1775, New Kent County committee, minutes, 3 May 1775, in Van Schreeven, Scribner, and Tarter, eds., *Revolutionary Virginia,* 3:105, 85: Mays, *Edmund Pendleton,* 2:353n: and Dale E. Benson, "Wealth and Power in Virginia, 1774–

1776: A Study of the Organization of Revolt" (Ph.D. diss., University of Maine, 1970), 173.

36 Cumberland County committee, minutes, 1 May 1775, in Van Schreeven, Seribner, and Tarter. eds., *Revolutionary Virginia*, 3:75; Sussex County committee, resolution, 8 May 1775, in ibid., 3:107; Selby, *Revolution in Virginia*, p. 4: John Burk, Skelton Jones, and Louis Hue Girardin, *The History of Virginia, From its First Settlement to the Present Day* (4 vols.: Petersburg, Va., 1804–16), 3:410.

37 Parker said Nicholas had found "it more difficult to extinguish a flame than kindle it" (James Parker to Charles Steuart, 6–7 May 1775, Charles Steuart Papers [microfilm, Vi]).

38 Peyton Randolph and the "Corporation of the City of Williamsburg" to Mann Page. Jr., Lewis Willis, and Benjamin Grymes, Jr., 27 Apr. 1775, in Van Schreeven, Scribner, and Tarter, eds., *Revolutionary Virginia*, 3:64; Charles Campbell, *History of the Colony and Ancient Dominion of Virginia* (Philadelphia, 1860), 609; William Pasteur, deposition, quoted in Committee on the Late Disturbances, report, 14 June 1775, in *JHB, 1773–76*, 231: *Virginia Gazette* (Pinkney), 4 May 1775.

39 George Gilmer, diary and memoranda, in Van Schreeven, Scribner, and Tarter, eds., *Revolutionary Virginia*, 3:52 n. 2 (quotation); Albemarle County independent company of volunteers, minutes, [29 Apr. 1775], in ibid., 3:69–70: *Virginia Gazette* (Pinkney), 30 June 1775.

40 It has generally been believed that the Hanover men sought only the return of the gunpowder to the Williamsburg munitions depot. But Hanover's patriot committee said the men marched to Williamsburg because they had heard that white inhabitants of the capital felt "apprehension for their persons and property" (Hanover County committee, minutes, 9 May 1775, in Van Schreeven, Scribner, and Tarter, eds., *Revolutionary Virginia*, 3:111, 179n).

41 *Virginia Gazette* (Pinkney), 11 May 1775, in Van Schreeven, Scribner, and Tarter, eds., *Revolutionary Virginia*, 3:117; George Dabney to William Wirt, 14 May 1805, Patrick Henry Papers. DLC: Campbell. *History of Virginia*, 612.

42 *Virginia Gazette* (Pinkney), 4 May 1775: John Randolph, deposition, quoted in Committee on the Late Disturbances, report, 14 June 1775, in *JHB, 1773–76*, 232.

43 *Virginia Gazette* (Pinkney), 4 May 1775; Randolph, *History of Virginia*, 220.

44 Spotsylvania council, minutes, 29 Apr. 1775, in Van Schreeven, Scribner, and Tarter, eds., *Revolutionary Virginia*, 3:71 (first quotation); Mecklenburg County committee, resolution, 13 May 1775; New Kent County committee, resolutions, 3 May 1775; Gloucester County committee, resolutions, 26 Apr. 1775; Richmond County committee, resolutions, 12 May 1775; Orange Country committee, resolutions and address, 9 May 1775, in ibid., 3:124 (second quotation), 85, 61, 121, 112. On 20 April, the day before Dunmore removed the gunpowder, Robert Munford had said that he intended to ask the voters of his county to endorse a loyalist address that he had written. After learning of the gunpowder incident and Dunmore's threat to free the slaves. Munford decided not to present his petition. In fact, he became a major in the patriot army (Robert Munford to William Byrd III, 20 Apr. 1775, in Marion Tinling, ed., *The Correspondence of the Three William Byrds of Westover, Virginia, 1684–1776*, Virginia Historical Society Documents, 12, 13 [2 vols.: Charlottesville, 1977], 2:806, 806 n. 3).

45 Quoted in George Dabney to William Wirt, 14 May 1805, Patrick Henry Papers.

46 See, for example, H. J. Eckenrode, *The Revolution in Virginia* (Boston and New York, 1916), 49–54; Virginius Dabney, *Virginia: The New Dominion* (Garden City. N.Y., 1971), 128–29; and Warren M. Billings, John E. Selby, and Thad W. Tate, *Colonial Virginia: A History* (White Plains, N.Y., 1986), 342.

47 Benjamin Waller, deposition, quoted in Committee on the Late Disturbances, report, 14 June 1775, in *JHB, 1773–76*, 232: Thomas Mitchell, deposition, quoted in Committee on the Late Disturbances, report, 14 June 1775, in ibid., 234; Rawleigh Downman to Samuel Athawes, 10 July 1775, Rawleigh Downman Letterbook, DLC, as quoted in Michael A. McDonnell, "The Politics of Mobilization in Revolutionary Virginia: Military Culture and Political and Social Relations, 1774–1783" (D.Phil, thesis, Oxford University, 1995), 37–38.

48 Richmond County committee, resolutions, 12 May 1775, in Van Schreeven, Scribner, and Tarter, eds., *Revolutionary·Virginia*, 3:121; Spotsylvania council,

minutes, 29 Apr. 1775, in ibid., 3:71; *South Carolina Gazette and Country Journal,* 6 June 1775, quoted in Peter H. Wood, "'Taking Care of Business' in Revolutionary South Carolina: Republicanism and the Slave Society," in Jeffrey J. Crow and Larry E. Tise. eds., *The Southern Experience in the American Revolution* (Chapel Hill, 1978), 282.

49  James Robison to William Cuninghame & Company, 3 May 1775, in T. M. Devine, ed., *A Scottish Firm in Virginia, 1767–1777: W. Cuninghame and Co.* (Edinburgh, 1984), 187.

50  The newspaper accounts of the Norfolk insurrection do not mention the leaders' names, and the Norfolk County court did not specify the felony for which Emanuel and Emanuel de Antonio were convicted. One might be tempted to conclude, therefore, that the two Emanuels were not necessarily the leaders of the slave revolt mentioned in the newspaper – that they were hanged for some lesser offense. But we can conclude that the accusation against the two Emanuels was indeed insurrection, because they were hanged only one week after their trial. Under Virginia law, the execution of slaves had to be stayed for at least ten days – unless the condemned were insurrectionists (Hening, ed., *Statutes at Large,* 6:106).

51  Lists for the intervening years have not survived. The other alleged conspirator, Emanuel de Antonio, also disappeared from the Norfolk tithable lists between 1774 and 1778 – but so did all of the other slaves owned by James Campbell & Company, a loyalist firm whose principal left Virginia early in the Revolution. See Elizabeth B. Wingo and W. Bruce Wingo, *Norfolk Counts, Virginia, Tithables, 1766–1780* (Norfolk, Va., 1985), 230, 242, 261.

52  Municipal Common Hall of Williamsburg to John Murray, earl of Dunmore, 21 Apr. 1775, in Van Schreeven, Scribner, and Tarter, eds., *Revolutionary Virginia,* 3:55.

53  James Madison to William Bradford, Jr., 26 Nov. 1774, in Hutchinson et al., eds., *Madison Papers,* 1:130: *Virginia Gazette* (Pinkney), 6 Dec. 1775; Aptheker, *American Negro Slave Revolts,* esp. chap. 7. Several recent retellings of the story do not mention its black participants. See, for example, Billings, Selby, and Tate, *Colonial Virginia,* 342; and Rhys Isaac, *The Transformation of Virginia, 1740–1790* (Chapel Hill, 1982), 256–58.

Even Herbert Aptheker, a careful searcher for evidence of slave conspiracies, believed that there was no plot in Virginia in April 1775 (Aptheker, *American Negro Slave Revolts,* 204). His skepticism regarding Dunmore's assertion that he moved the gunpowder in order to protect whites from a rumored slave plot was justified, because Dunmore himself acknowledged in a letter to the earl of Dartmouth, the secretary of state, that the plot was not the real reason for the relocation of the powder. The governor, however, sincerely believed the rumor itself, because he stated in the same letter that whites in Williamsburg were "apprehensive of insurrections among their slaves (some reports having prevailed to this effect)" (John Murray, earl of Dunmore, to William Legge, earl of Dartmouth, 1 May 1775, in Davies, ed., *Documents of the American Revolution.* 9:107–8).

54  *Virginia Gazette* (Pinkney), 1 June 1775; *Virginia Gazette* (Purdie), 31 May 1776; Jack P. Greene, ed., *The Diary of Colonel Landon Carter of Sabine Hall, 1752–1778,* Virginia Historical Society Documents, 4, 5 (2 vols.; Charlottesville, 1965) 2:1058 (16 July 1776). Still later Adam Stephen predicted that Dunmore would participate in a rumored British invasion of Virginia "in order to add some more oderiferous beauties to his Ethopian seraglios" (Adam Stephen to Richard Henry Lee, 22 Apr. 1777, quoted in Harry M. Ward, *Major General Adam Stephen and the Cause of American Liberty* [Charlottesville, 1989], 168).

55  Robert Beverley to William Fitzhugh, 20 July 1775, Robert Beverley Letterbook, DLC: Josiah Smith, Jr., to James Poyas, 18 May 1775; Josiah Smith, Jr., to George Appleby, 16 June 1775, Josiah Smith Letterbook, Southern Historical Collection, University of North Carolina, Chapel Hill; Wood, "'Liberty Is Sweet,'" 166–68; Wood, "'Taking Care of Business,'" 280–87; Robert M. Weir, *Colonial South Carolina: A History* (Millwood, N.Y., 1983), 200–203.

56  Wood. "'The Dream Deferred,'" 175 (quotation); Alan D. Watson, "Impulse toward Independence: Resistance and Rebellion among North Carolina Slaves, 1750–1775," *JNH* 63 (1978): 317–28.

57  Quoted in Frey, *Water from the Rock,* pp. 58, 62.

58  John Drayton, *Memoirs of the American Revolution From Its Commencement to the Year 1776. Inclusive: As Relating to the State of South-Carolina …* (2 vols.; Charleston, 1821), 1:231.

59 Quoted in Ronald Hoffman, *A Spirit of Dissension: Economics. Politics, and the Revolution in Maryland,* (Baltimore and London, 1973), 147.

60 York County Order Book, 17 July 1775 (microfilm and typescript), ViWC; Schwarz. *Twice Condemned,* p. 183. In July 1775 a rumor circulated in York County that British troops were about to land, and Cox's accusers may have thought he was working with slaves to prepare for the invasion. See William Reynolds to George Flowerdewe Norton, 16 July 1775, William Reynolds Letterbook, DLC. My thanks to Julie Richter for sharing her research on Thomas Cox.

61 Mullin, *Flight and Rebellion,* 132–33. White servants, especially convicts, also ran away and headed to the British naval squadron. See, for example, Francis Smith and James Tutt. advertisements, in *Virginia Gazette* (Pinkney) 27 July 1775; and John Murray, earl of Dunmore, to William Legge, earl of Dartmouth, 25 June 1775, in Davies, ed., *Documents of the American Revolution,* 9:202–3.

62 This story is based entirely on a newspaper notice that Estave published in order to justify what some of his white neighbors had called his "cruel and inhuman treatment" of the enslaved teenager (*Virginia Gazette* [Pinkney], 20 July 1775). We can only imagine how the story would change if we had testimony from the fifteen-year-old.

63 If the teenager had reached the governor's palace before Dunmore left it, he might have been able to grant her sanctuary (charter of Williamsburg, in *William and Mary· Quarterly,* 1st ser., 10 [1901–2]: 87). My thanks to Brent Tarter and John M. Hemphill II for this reference.

64 John Bailey's slaves Phil and Mial "received guilty verdicts in Southampton County conspiracy trials" (Schwarz, *Twice Condemned,* 181, 183 [quotation], 184). On 3 July 1775, William Johnson's slave Gloster was sentenced to death for burglary "but broke out of jail and vanished" (William Johnson, petition, 14 June 1776, Caroline County, calendared in Randolph W. Church, ed., *Virginia Legislative Petitions: Bibliography, Calendar, and Abstracts from Original Sources, 6 May 1776–21 June 1782* [Richmond, 1984], 24–25).

65 Robert Honyman, diary, 2 Jan. 1776, DLC: Selby. *Revolution in Virginia,* 64.

66 John Page to Thomas Jefferson, 24 [Nov.] 1775, in Boyd et al., eds., *Jefferson Papers,* 1:265.

67 *Virginia Gazette* (Dixon and Hunter), 2 Dec. 1775. Slaves also answered later calls from British generals. North of Virginia, bondsmen were allowed to join the Continental army in return for their freedom – but only with their owners' permission (Quarles, *Negro in the Revolution,* chaps, 4–5).

68 Edmund Taylor, debt owed to Thomas Banks, 1 Sept. 1776. abstracted in "British Mercantile Claims, 1775–1803," *Virginia Genealogist* 16 (1972): 104–5.

69 John Murray, earl of Dunmore, proclamation Nov. 1775, in Van Schreeven, Scribner. and Tarter, eds., *Revolutionary Virginia,* 4:334; Graham Russell Hodges, ed., *The Black Loyalist Directory: African Americans in Exile after the American Revolution* (New York, 1996). Cf. Quarles, *Negro in the Revolution,* 172: and the list of fifty formerly enslaved "Women [who] embarked at Mill Point" with Dunmore's fleet, printed in the *Virginia Gazette* (Dixon and Hunter)1 Aug. 1776, and analyzed in Sarah Stroud, "Tracing Runaway Slaves from Norfolk County, Virginia, during the American Revolutionary War" (seminar paper, Randolph-Macon Woman's College, 1995).

70 Hodges, ed., *Black Loyalist Directory,* p. 201. During the American Revolution, many of the enslaved women who ran away took their children with them – an occurrence that was very rare before and after the war (Sara M. Evans, *Born for Liberty: A History of Women in America* [New York and London, 1989], 52). For accounts of other black Americans who joined the British and settled after the Revolution in Nova Scotia and Sierra Leone, see Gary B. Nash, "Thomas Peters: Millwright and Deliverer," in David G. Sweet and Gary B. Nash, eds., *Struggle and Survival in Colonial America* (Berkeley and Los Angeles, 1981), 69–85; Ellen Gibson Wilson, *The Loyal Blacks* (New York, 1976); and James W. St. G. Walker, *The Black Loyalists: The Search for a Promised Land in Nova Scotia and Sierra Leone, 1783–1870* (New York, 1976).

71 Thomas Nelson, Jr., to Mann Page, Jan. 1776, Francis Lightfoot Lee to Landon Carter, 12 Feb. 1776, Benjamin Harrison to Robert Carter Nicholas, 17 Jan. 1776, in Paul H. Smith et al., eds., *Letters of Delegates to Congress, 1774–1789*

(23 vols, to date: Washington. D.C., 1976–), 3:30 (first quotation), 237 (second quotation), 107 (third quotation). A rumored British design to ally with Native Americans was also described as "diabolical" and "infernal" (George Washington to John Augustine Washington, 13 Oct. 1775, Richard Henry Lee to George Washington, 13 Nov. 1775, George Washington to Richard Henry Lee, 26 Dec. 1775, in Abbot et al., eds., *Washington Papers: Revolutionary War Series* 2:161, 363, 611).

72 Page Smith, *A New Age Now Begins: A People's History of the American Revolution* (2 vols.: New York. St. Louis, and San Francisco, 1976), 1:704; Garry Wills, *Inventing America: Jefferson's Declaration of Independence* (Garden City, N.Y., 1978), 71, 75.

73 Robert Greenhalgh Albion and Leonidas Dodson, eds., *Philip Vickers Fithian: Journal, 1775–1776* (Princeton, 1934), 135 (28 Nov. 1775); Richard Henry Lee to Catharine Macauley, 29 Nov. 1775; Archibald Cary to Richard Henry Lee, 24 Dec. 1775, in Paul P. Hoffman and John L. Molyneaux, eds., The Lee Family Papers, 1742–1795 (microfilm: Charlottesville, 1966), Reel 2.

74 William Byrd III to Sir Jeffery Amherst, 30 July 1775, in Tinling, ed., *Byrd Correspondence* 2:812–13; Greene, ed., *Carter Diary,* 2:989 (25 Feb. 1776); Van Schreeven, Scribner, and Tarter, eds., *Revolutionary Virginia,* 5:386n–87n; Selby, *Revolution in Virginia,* 66; Thomas Jefferson to William Wirt, 29 Sept. 1816, in *Reminiscences of Patrick Henry in the Letters of Thomas Jefferson to William Win* (Philadelphia, 1911), 29.

75 Greene, ed., *Carter Diary,* 2:960 (n.d. 1775); John Page to Richard Henry Lee, 20 Feb. 1776, in Hoffman and Molyncaux, eds., Lee Family Papers, Reel 2.

76 William Eddis, Letter 26, 16 Jan. 1776, in William Eddis, *Letters from America,* ed. Aubrey C. Land (Cambridge. Mass., 1969), 133: Edward Rutledge to Ralph Izard, 8 Dec, 1775, in *Izard Correspondence*, 165: [John Leacock]. *The Fall of British Tyranny, or. American Liberty Triumphant: The First Campaign …* (Philadelphia, 1776), 48. Cf. Gary B. Nash, *Forging Freedom: The Formation of Philadelphia's Black Community, 1720–1840* (Cambridge. Mass., 1988), 46; Quarles, *Negro in the Revolution,* p. 20, 20n.

77 James Iredell, untitled essay, June 1776, in Don Higginbotham. ed., *The Papers of James Iredell* (3 vols, to date; Raleigh, 1976–), 1:409.

78 [Leacock]. *Fall of British Tyranny,* p. 49. On British cooperation with Indians as a cause of white Americans' growing alienation from Britain, see Wood, "'Liberty Is Sweet,'" 169; Selby, *Revolution in Virginia,* p. 92: and *Virginia Gazette* (Pinkney), 3 Aug. 1775. Free colonists were also angry at Dunmore for emancipating and arming convict servants ([Leacock], *Fall of British Tyranny,* 45; *Virginia Gazette* [Dixon and Hunter), 17 Feb. 1776).

79 *Virginia Gazette* (Dixon and Hunter), 29 Apr. 1775 (supplement).

80 Quarles, *Negro in the Revolution,* 171–72: Hodges, ed., *Black Loyalist Directory,* 198 (quotation).

81 See, for example, Burk. Jones, and Girardin, *History of Virginia,* 4:134n; Eckenrode, *Revolution in Virginia,* 73; Dumas Malone, *Jefferson and His Time,* vol. 1: *Jefferson the Virginian* (Boston, 1948), 215; Billings, Selby, and Tate, *Colonial Virginia,* p. 343; Clifford Dowdey, *The Great Plantation; A Profile of Berkeley Hundred and Plantation Virginia from Jamestown to Appomattox* (New York and Toronto, 1957), 230–31: Campbell, *History of Virginia,* 634; John C. Miller, *Origins of the American Revolution* (Boston, 1943), p. 478; and Dabney, *New Dominion,* 131.

Several students of the struggle for black freedom have also asserted that the slaves helped push whites into the American Revolution. See, for example, Quarles. *Negro in the Revolution,* 19: Wood, "'Liberty Is Sweet,'" 171; and Frey, *Water from the Rock*, 78.

82 *Virginia Gazette* (Pinkney), 4 May 1775.

83 Quarles, *Negro in the Revolution,* pp. 20–22; Schwarz. *Twice Condemned,* 181.

84 For a similar argument – that enslaved Americans, through their actions, helped push Abraham Lincoln into issuing his Emancipation Proclamation – see W. E. Burghardt Du Bois. *Black Reconstruction: An Essay toward a History of the Part Which Black Folk Played in the Attempt to Reconstruct Democracy in America, 1860–1880* (New York, 1935), chap. 4; and Vincent Harding, *There Is a River: The Black Struggle for Freedom in America* (New York and London, 1981), chap. 11.

85 Unidentified letter, 30 Nov. 1775, in Force, comp., *American Archives,* 4th ser., 3:1387.

86 Mare Egnal, *A Mighty Empire: The Origins of the American Revolution* (Ithaca. N.Y., and London, 1988), 302 (quotation). In Virginia, "the classic Progressive conflict of domestic interests appears not to have taken place in the political realm" (Herbert Sloan and Peter Onuf, "Politics, Culture, and the Revolution in Virginia: A Review of Recent Work," *VMHB* 91 [1983]: 262, 264 [quotation]). "[A]lone among the thirteen provinces," Virginia "did not face armed internal dispute during the revolutionary era" (Edward Countryman, *The American Revolution* [New York, 1985], 35). Many Progressive historians implicitly acknowledged that the internal conflict thesis did not apply to Virginia, where the ruling class endorsed the independence movement. Instead, Progressive historians studying Virginia emphasized the economic motives that inspired free farmers at all income levels. See Isaac Samuel Harrell, *Loyalism in Virginia: Chapters in the Economic History of the Revolution* (Durham, N.C., 1926), v–vi, 5; and Charles A. Beard, *Economic Origins of Jeffersonian Democracy* (New York, 1949), 270. For a revision of this economic interpretation of the Revolution in Virginia, see Woody Holton, *Forced Founders: How Indians, Debtors, and Slaves Helped Turn Elite Virginians into American Revolutionaries* (Chapel Hill, forthcoming).

87 James Titus, *The Old Dominion at War: Society: Politics, and Warfare in Late Colonial Virginia,* American Military History (Columbia. S.C., 1991); Albert H. Tillson, Jr., *Gentry and Common Folk: Political Culture on a Virginia Frontier, 1740– 1789* (Lexington, Ky., 1991), 45–77; McDonnell, "Politics of Mobilization."

# 6
# TWENTY-SEVEN REASONS FOR INDEPENDENCE

*Robert G. Parkinson*

## Introduction

The Declaration of Independence both culminated and summarized a process of revolutionary protest against British rule. Here Robert G. Parkinson analyzes the Declaration, particularly its section of grievances against George III. Parkinson argues that the twenty-seven grievances have been unfairly overshadowed by the document's more famous opening lines. For contemporaries, the charges were crucial for justifying political separation from Britain and for enlisting support for the Revolutionary War.

Parkinson further contends that the order of the grievances matters. The indictment builds toward the final, five most severe charges, all of which highlight war crimes committed by George III and the British. The twenty-seventh and last grievance blames the king for exciting "domestic insurrections amongst us," a veiled reference to Virginia Governor Lord Dunmore's Proclamation offering freedom to slaves who left their American masters for the British war effort. As the previous selection by Woody Holton makes clear, few actions had more influence in motivating wavering Virginia planters to support American independence. The twenty-seventh grievance also accuses the king of mobilizing "merciless Indian savages" in war against the colonists. Although the strong rhetoric against Britain's black and Indian allies no doubt helped to secure support for independence, it came at the high cost of weaving racial prejudice into the nation's most beloved founding document.

- Are you persuaded by Parkinson's argument that the soaring opening lines to the Declaration of Independence came to mean more to later generations than to people alive at the time? If so, how do you explain this evolving interpretation of the document?
- Are you surprised by the emphasis on war in the Declaration? Does this emphasis diminish some of the loftier political ideals outlined in the document and promoted in the American revolutionary cause?
- Congress removed acerbic passages against the British people and American loyalists in Thomas Jefferson's original version of the Declaration for being too controversial and even counterproductive. Why, then, did grievances pertaining to Indians and African Americans become more strongly worded in the revision process? What, if any, risks did the new nation incur by defining potentially large numbers of nonwhites as enemies?

Americans have long interpreted, analyzed, and dissected the opening lines of the Declaration of Independence. Historians Carl Becker, Garry Wills, and others have contended that the preamble is the most important part of the Declaration and have wrestled with the meaning of its key words and phrases: "all," "men," "created," "equal," "pursuit of happiness," "inalienable rights," and "self-evident truths." Few, however, have given much attention to the twenty-seven reasons why the Second Continental Congress believed the establishment of an independent United States was justified – and necessary.[1]

Preoccupation with the preamble contrasts the reception of the Declaration by the "candid world" of 1776. British pamphleteer John Lind published *An Answer to the Declaration of the American Congress* that ran to one hundred and thirty pages. Of these, he devoted a hundred and ten to rebutting the list of complaints and grievances that the Declaration levied against Britain's King George III. A mere four pages toward the end addressed the opening paragraphs of the Declaration, only to dismiss them. "Of the preamble," Lind mocked, "I have taken little or no notice. The truth is, little or none does it deserve."[2] Sarcasm aside, he had a point: there was already a broad consensus among enlightened patriots concerning the ideas expressed in the preamble, including the consent of the governed and the right to revolution. Late in life, even Jefferson would admit that the Declaration did not aim at "originality of principle or sentiment."[3]

The list of the colonist's grievances, on the other hand, was crucial to the Declaration's immediate reception. It had to be both convincing and compelling. Long before future generations would revere it as a sacred text, in its time the Declaration was fundamentally a political document with pressing aims: it had to clarify a confusing military conflict, distinguish friends from enemies, inspire armed resistance, and garner sympathy (and aid) from European powers. Being now far removed from the turmoil,

it is hard for us to understand the treacherous situation in which Congress approved and published the Declaration. While the delegates debated, edited, and ratified the Declaration, the largest invasion fleet ever assembled was already en route to New York. Their decision to use the present tense to frame their accusation that George III "is, at this time, transporting large Armies of foreign mercenaries" surely reflected their worries about what might lie ahead. In fact, New York fell to the British commanders only a few days after independence was declared.

If the delegates expected thousands of Americans to put their lives at risk voluntarily, they knew they had to craft a manifesto that would lay out the reasons why. The twenty-seven charges leveled at George III were the heart of the matter. Originally Jefferson provided twenty-nine, but, during the editing sessions on 2–3 July, Congress cut two. The accusations were hardly assembled at random. Instead of presenting the evidences of the king's tyrannical oppressions chronologically, Jefferson grouped them thematically for maximum rhetorical effect. They begin slowly and then gain emotional speed. The first dozen detail the king's abuses of executive power, the next ten protest "pretended legislation," while the final five document acts of war and cruelty.

The twelve grievances that begin the list of facts and proof reach back a decade or more into the imperial crisis. They center on abuses of executive authority, accusing the king of multiple misdeeds, especially concerning the legitimacy of colonial assemblies and the authority of the laws they passed. Many refer to specific, local disagreements. The fourth charge, for example, reads: "He has called together legislative bodies at places unusual, uncomfortable, and distant from the depository of their public records, for the sole purpose of fatiguing them into compliance with his measures." John Adams, the powerful Massachusetts delegate who was one of the committee of five charged with drafting the Declaration, likely had Jefferson add this charge in order to voice Massachusetts's frustration with the forced removal of their assembly from Boston to Cambridge in the early 1770s. Yet, indicting the king for having caused fatigue and discomfort – or, as in the case of the seventh charge, for not encouraging British subjects to emigrate to America – could not have sufficed to inspire engagement in a bloody conflict. Furthermore, the relatively moderate tone of this section is sustained by the use of objective verbs: "obstructed," "refused," "affected." Nevertheless, toward the end of this initial group of accusations, Jefferson foreshadows his strategy of raising emotional tenor by invoking images of Old Testament plagues, accusing George III of sending "hither Swarms of Officers to harass our people, and eat out their substance."

The second group of grievances focuses on specific acts of the British Parliament and the king's willingness to enforce them. "He gave assent" to Parliament, the thirteenth charge declares, a "jurisdiction foreign to our Constitution, and unacknowledged by our laws," and supported its "pretended legislation." The following nine charges docket a menu of legislative acts that colonists deemed unfair, including each of the so-called Coercive or Intolerable Acts, the mercantile regulations that governed imperial trade, and the Quebec Act, which tolerated Catholicism and French law in the new British colony of Canada. Here we begin to see the principal American worries about encroaching British tyranny: suspending a colony's charter; keeping a standing army among the populace during peacetime; taxing without representation; and challenging trials by jury. To heighten the perception of these acts as an unceasing assault on American liberties, Jefferson abandons his device of blaming the king personally by beginning each accusation with a punctual "he has." Instead, charges fourteen through twenty-two advance in a steady cadence punctuated by colons. Rhetorically, they function as a single long sentence, embodying the sheer weight of oppression the American colonists had suffered during the previous decade.

Yet the real drama is still to come. Building toward a climax, the final five charges highlight the past year's violence. Jefferson's selection of verbs is now more evocative and stirring, and George's crimes more heinous: the king has "plundered," "ravaged," and "destroyed" his American subjects. He has forced them to become "executioners of their friends and brethren." He has recruited foreign mercenaries "to complete the works of death, desolation, and tyranny, already begun with circumstances of cruelty and perfidy, scarcely paralleled in the most barbarous Ages, and totally unworthy the Head of a Civilized Nation." These last accusations had to be decisive in their effect. Their acceptance by the "candid world," both at home and abroad, would determine whether American independence was legitimate and defensible – or not.

The delegates understood the rhetorical importance of the final set of charges. They labored over them more than all the other grievances during their editing sessions on 2–3 July. Other than rearranging a few words or slicing extraneous phrases, Congress allowed Jefferson's first twenty grievances to enter the final Declaration mostly intact. As the stakes increased, however, so did Congress's attention. In several instances, the delegates amplified the king's crimes, adding emotional phrases such as "waging war against us" and the stinging if unsupported claim that his hiring of German troops went beyond all barbarity.

They also struck out two of Jefferson's accusations entirely as too controversial or confusing. The first charged George III with inciting loyalists to fight for the promise of gaining confiscated patriot property. The second was a long passage that blamed him for the crime of "waging cruel war against human nature itself" by promoting the slave trade and then doubly damning him for manipulating "those very people to rise in arms among us, and to purchase that liberty of which he has deprived them, by murdering the people upon whom he also obtruded them, thus paying off former crimes committed against the liberties of one people, with crimes which he urges them to commit against the lives of another." Yet blaming the king wholesale for the slave trade was deemed too tenuous – and dangerous – to include as the final, climactic accusation, so Congress eliminated that part of the charge.[4] The delegates retained the second part, however, with some important modifications. Whereas Jefferson had distinguished three categories among the groups that the Crown had enlisted to help put down the colonial rebellion – namely Indians, loyalists, and slaves – Congress removed the reference to the Tories and conjoined the actions of native and enslaved peoples to create a more succinct and powerful conclusion: "He has excited domestic insurrections amongst us and has endeavoured to bring on the inhabitants of our frontiers the merciless savages, whose known rule of warfare is an undistinguished destruction of all ages, sexes, and conditions."[5] This would become the twenty-seventh and final charge against George III, the ultimate justification for breaking from British rule.

This concluding charge was the product of widespread anxiety. In the sixteen months since the battles of Lexington and Concord, one of the most highly publicized concerns had been the role slaves and frontier Indians had played in the conflict. Newspapers throughout the continent kept their readers well informed about British efforts to enlist Indian support and attempts by royal governors to encourage slaves to abandon their masters and join the fight against them. Although most Indians had remained tranquil during the first year of the Revolutionary War, many colonists worried about what influence Canadian governor Guy Carleton and Indian agent Guy Johnson would have on the future of the conflict in the north. Meanwhile, the proclamation in November 1775 by Royal Governor of Virginia Lord Dunmore, which promised freedom to those slaves who could reach his command, lent substance to the nightmares of many southerners. These two scenarios, which were widely feared in the months leading up to independence, were brought together in Congress's final grievance against the king.

The fearsome rhetoric of this ultimate accusation would have powerful consequences, casting a long shadow over the idea of who was "American," and who did not belong to the new nation. At the core of the Declaration lies a distinction between friends and enemies, Americans and Britons, patriots and King George III. The opening lines of the Declaration are the announcement of the separation of one people from another: "When in the course of human events it becomes necessary for one people to dissolve the political bonds which have connected them with another." Some who first heard the Declaration immediately understood the implication. After Colonel Arthur St. Clair read the Declaration to a cheering crowd at the already war-weary post at Fort Ticonderoga, New York, an observer commented that "it was pleasing to see the spirits of the soldiers so raised after all their calamities, the language of every man's countenance was, now we are a people!"[6] The ecstatic militia grasped the basic notion, but the underlying question was more complicated: who exactly were the American people?

The transfer of blame from Parliament to King George himself issued as a product of powerful rhetoric and argument. Tom Paine's sensational pamphlet *Common Sense* convinced thousands of Americans that they should revoke their loyalty to their formerly beloved King George. In the Declaration, Jefferson addressed the colonist's grievances directly to the king. He began most of the accusations with the phrase "he has," personally blaming the king for each injustice. George III, not his ministers nor Parliament, was America's enemy. Yet others fought on his behalf, most frighteningly rebellious slaves and Indian allies. When the Declaration connected these proxy fighters to the king, they also enlarged the definition of America's enemy to include those groups. Leaving no room for blacks or Indians who might otherwise have supported the patriot cause – and there were thousands who did – the Declaration portrayed them all as passive, mindless, bloodthirsty barbarians too naïve to realize they were being duped by a tyrant. *"We"* would never fall victim to such crimes. But who were *we*? The twenty-seventh charge implied that the *we* comprised those patriotic people who had the foresight and moral courage to resist the "repeated injuries and usurpations" of the "Present King of Great Britain." *We* – the American people – could not include the king nor his helpers, the "merciless savages" and "domestic insurrectionists."

At the crucial founding moment, therefore, the definition of an American identity was cast as a negative: not-British. But the heated language of the Declaration's twenty-seventh grievance gave it still another shape: not-black and not-Indian as well. At least one group of Americans understood this construction perfectly. At the same time that soldiers at Fort Ticonderoga brightened at the thought of now being a people, another crowd on Long Island's north shore gathered to celebrate the same announcement. They showed their approval for independence by constructing a visual representation of their multiple enemies. A newspaper report detailed the actions of the crowd that July afternoon: "An effigy of [George III] being hastily fabricated out of base materials, with its face black like *Dunmore's* Virginia regiment, its head adorned with a wooden crown, and its head stuck full of feathers, like *Carleton* and *Johnson's* savages, and its body wrapped in the Union [Jack] instead of a robe of state, and lined with *gunpowder,* which the original seems fond of." "The whole," the article concluded, "was hung on a gallows, exploded and burnt to ashes."[7] The crowd of Long Islanders simply acted out the text of the Declaration. By animating and then destroying the panoply of enemies arrayed against their new nation, they used fire instead of ink to attack and kill them. They consigned all their enemies – the king, the "merciless savages," and the "domestic insurrectionists" – to the flames, leaving the "Americans" to stand triumphantly and watch the blaze.

Exposing the king's tyranny, the twenty-seven grievances provided a negative identity against which the first semblance of a common national identity could be realized. That negative identity, however, intersected with long held prejudices against blacks and Indians that had grown up throughout the colonial period. To suit the particular political needs of independence, Jefferson and Congress played upon these fears "in the name, and by authority of the good people of the colonies." According to the logic of the Declaration, only after this ultimate, shocking breach of trust was pronounced could independence be justified fully, leaving Congress no choice but to declare the colonies free and independent states. By so doing, however, Congress fixed a devastating image at the very heart of America's founding document. The Declaration fastened racial prejudice to national identity.

We should therefore be wary of neglecting the list of grievances in our preoccupation and passion for the Declaration's more famous and familiar preamble. In its time, the core statement of grievances shouldered the burden of convincing beleaguered colonists and their allies across the Atlantic that the case for American independence was just and necessary. The final charge reflected an emerging conception of American identity, and of the new nation's enemies, that belied the soaring and optimistic phrases of Jefferson's opening paragraphs.

## Notes

1  See Garry Wills, *Inventing America; Jefferson's Declaration of Independence* (Garden City, NY, 1978), Carl L. Becker (New York, 1956 [1922]), especially 202–3, and Jack P. Greene, *Imperatives, Behaviors, and Identities: Essays in Early American Cultural History* (Charlottesville, VA, 1992), 236–67.

2  John Lind, *An Answer to the Declaration of the American Congress* (London, 1776), 119. See also Wills, *Inventing America,* 65–66.

3  Thomas Jefferson to Henry Lee, 8 May 1825, in *Jefferson: Writings,* ed. Merrill Peterson (New York, 1984), 1501.

4 Congress did not, as Carl Becker reported, omit this passage "altogether" (see his *Declaration of Independence*, 213). For more on Jefferson's slave trade accusation see Pauline Maier, *American Scripture: Making the Declaration of Independence* (New York, 1997), 120–22; Wills, *Inventing America*, 72–74; and Paul Finkelman, "Jefferson and Slavery: 'Treason Against the Hopes of the World'," in *Jeffersonian Legacies,* ed. Peter S. Onuf (Charlottesville, VA, 1993), 190–92.

5 There is some scholarly debate over whom exactly Congress meant by "domestics." Stanley Kaplan believed that it was an explicit reference to Lord Dunmore's emancipation proclamation in Virginia, hence "domestics" meant strictly slaves; see his article "The 'Domestic Insurrections' of the Declaration of Independence," *Journal of Negro History* 61 (July 1976), 243–55. Stephen Lucas disagrees, contending that "domestics" was an umbrella term that included loyalists, servants, and slaves who were all disaffected to the patriot cause; see his article "Justifying America: The Declaration of Independence as a Rhetorical Document," in *American Rhetoric: Context and Criticism,* ed. Thomas W. Benson (Carbondale, IL, 1989), 109. For at least one contemporary critic, the answer to this question was obvious. John Lind wrote: "but how did his Majesty's Governors excite domestic insurrections? Did they set father against son, or son against father, or brother against brother? No – they offered *freedom* to the *slaves* of these assertors of liberty" (Lind, *Answer to the Declaration,* 107).

6 *New York Constitutional Gazette,* 12 August 1776.

7 *New York Journal*, 8 August 1776.

# PART III

# WAR AND THE HOME FRONT

# 7
# THE MILITARY CONFLICT CONSIDERED AS A REVOLUTIONARY WAR

*John Shy*

## Introduction

Students enrolled in courses on the American Revolution are often surprised to encounter little material on the actual fighting of the war. Since the 1960s, scholarship on the Revolution has shifted decisively away from military and, to a lesser extent, political topics and toward issues of society and culture. The overriding concern has been to consider how revolutionary the Revolution was in American life rather than to determine how the United States won and Britain lost the conflict.

John Shy argues that the military and social histories of the Revolution were deeply interrelated and that, therefore, the one cannot be understood without reference to the other. In particular, he contends that British and American military fortunes hinged on convincing civilians who were apathetic, neutral, or timid, to finally take a stand. Shy finds that the British forces built a counterproductive track record of alienating civilians wherever they marched, whereas rebel militias were effective at enforcing loyalty to the United States. Thus, even though the Continental Army had a rather poor overall record in conventional battles against the British, American forces in general were much more successful in the battle for civilian hearts and minds. This achievement allowed American and French forces to maintain the cause until conditions were just right for them to strike a decisive blow against the British at Yorktown. It is not American patriotism or British bungling that explain the outcome of the war, Shy asserts, but the reciprocal influence of military events on civilian loyalties and of civilian loyalties on military fortunes.

In addition to its broad interpretation of the war, Shy's essay is a model of explaining cause and effect, or, in contemporary parlance, of historical contingency.

- In what ways did British assumptions about American loyalties shape British strategy, how did those assumptions change over time, and what factors shaped those assumptions?
- To what extent did American loyalties differ by region and how did those loyalties change over time in response to fighting in the neighborhood?
- Shy argues that the contending armies were "political teachers" for American society. What lessons did they teach?
- Given the inability of the British army or loyalist militias to enforce loyalty to the crown, what possibility was there for the British to win this war? Would defeating the Continental Army have been enough?

To ask whether the military conflict of the American Revolution was in any sense a "revolutionary war" is to bring together two distinct and troubled lines of historical inquiry. One is the line followed by military historians, who from the time of Charles Stedman have tried to explain the outcome of the war and especially to answer the question of how one of the greatest military powers in the world could have been defeated by a few million scattered, inadequately armed, and badly trained colonials. The question itself, when posed in this way, has half suggested to some military historians an answer that would necessarily go beyond conventional forms of military explanation and would emphasize revolutionary methods of fighting and revolutionary sources of military strength. But perhaps a majority of the military historians of the American Revolution have rejected any such interpretation; they explain British defeat in terms of British mistakes, without resorting to American marksmanship, Indian fighting tactics, or massive popular resistance as major factors. Between these two schools of thought, a narrowly cast, poorly focused debate has gone on for almost two centuries over whether the war demands a "revolutionary" interpretation.[1]

The other line of inquiry has concerned a greater number of historians, though for a shorter period of time. It became truly prominent less than fifty years ago when J. Franklin Jameson gave his famous lectures on the social effects of the Revolution. Since then, no question has aroused more interest and drawn more scholarly energy than the one posed by Jameson: did the Revolution change American society?[2] Although wars are notoriously effective agents of change, the war of the American Revolution has received little attention from those historians who have tried to answer Jameson's question. Perhaps most of the difficulty lies in Jameson's categories, which were not directly related to the war and its effects. Moreover, the debate among historians over the question of revolutionary change has largely been an argument with Jameson and other historians of the Progressive school, who

combined their faith that revolutionary change had indeed occurred with a deep distaste for all things military: neither they nor their critics have been much disposed to consider the possibly revolutionary effects of the war itself.[3]

It is in this dual sense, then, that we can ask about the military conflict – revolutionary in structure? revolutionary in effects? And, of course, it is likely that the answers to these two questions are related to each other.

Some risk is run by asking questions in this way. Jameson and other Progressive historians projected the social and political concerns of industrial America onto an eighteenth-century screen, thereby confusing their and our understanding of what actually happened in the Revolution.[4] Likewise, much writing on the military history of the Revolution is contaminated with the preoccupations of military theory, especially with the application and illustration of so-called principles of war, which lie near the center of what has passed for military science in the nineteenth and twentieth centuries.[5] Both lines of inquiry have thus been stunted by unhistorical thinking, and the warning to us is plain. When we ask in the 1970s about "revolutionary war" in the eighteenth century, we should admit that our own nightmares, as much as any desire to push back the frontier of historical knowledge, give rise to the question. By being candid about the reasons why "revolutionary war" seems especially interesting at this time, we may be able to avoid some of the pitfalls that our predecessors unwittingly dug for themselves. We dare not argue that the American Revolutionary War was basically like modern revolutionary wars in Indochina and elsewhere; rather, we ask only whether the doctrines, the studies, and the general experience of "revolutionary warfare" in the twentieth century provide some insight into the American Revolutionary War. The answer, with due caution and qualification, is yes.[6]

The social history and the military history of the Revolution have seldom come together in the past because military historians tend to regard the war as an instrument managed on each side with more or less skill, while social historians treat military operations, if at all, as incidental to the study of politics and public finance. But if the war is restored to the central position that it had for the Revolutionary generation, and if it is seen not merely as an instrument but as a process, which entangled large numbers of people for a long period of time in experiences of remarkable intensity, then it may be possible to bring the study of the war and the study of the Revolution more closely together, to the benefit of both.

[ … ]

British understanding of the war was often cloudy and sometimes completely wrong, but the record of British experience provides a uniquely valuable way of looking at the war; like most modern historians, British leaders were less interested in allocating praise or blame among the Americans than in grasping the nature of the phenomenon with which they had to deal. Like other leaders in more recent, comparable situations, they were slow to learn, almost blind to certain key elements of their problem, badly confused beneath a veneer of confidence and expertise, and repeatedly caught in military and political traps of their own creation. But they were not stupid, and their persistent efforts to understand in order to act effectively give us the chance to consider the Revolutionary War apart from the parochial concerns and commitments that have paralyzed so many efforts to analyze it from the inside. Moreover, our own painful experience with revolutionary war may give us an empathetic understanding, a special sensitivity needed for the extraction of meaning from the record of British frustration.

British efforts to interpret and put down rebellion in the American colonies divide into three distinct stages. For almost a decade of agitation before the war, successive British governments had defined their American problem as one of law enforcement and the maintenance of order; in general, legal measures were bound by the belief that, once legitimate grievances were redressed, trouble and resistance was the fault of a few recalcitrant individuals.

Policy based on this belief failed, most obviously because these individuals seemed to command widespread local sympathy, an attitude that crippled judicial machinery. In early 1774, after the destruction of tea at Boston, the British government adopted a new interpretation of its American problem, which was that insurgency had a center – Boston – and that this center could and ought to be isolated and punished. The new policy assumed that other colonies, and even rural Massachusetts, were disturbed by the extremity of the latest acts of Boston insurgents and could be intimidated by the example made of the Boston community. The policy was thus seen to depend upon the application of overwhelming force, within the framework of civil law, to achieve clear-cut success at a single geographical point.[7]

Of course, the assumption proved completely wrong. Coercive laws and the manifest intention to enforce them with troops gave insurgent leaders greater leverage than ever before outside Boston itself.[8] Despite their misgivings, inhabitants of rural Massachusetts and other colonies concluded that they had no choice but to support Boston, since the new policy of community isolation and punishment seemed to threaten the political and legal integrity of every other community and colony. From this support, Boston acquired sufficient force to make the first military encounters – at Lexington, Concord, and Bunker Hill – inconclusive and thus susceptible to interpretation as moral victories for the insurgents. Nothing did more to expand and consolidate rebel support throughout America.

Some aspects of the British performance in this first stage are worth noting. The outbreak of open fighting came in an attempt to break up what may be described as an insurgent base area whose existence cast doubt on the basic assumption. British intelligence of the target was good, but it failed in two other critical respects. It could not prevent the transmission of every British order and movement throughout the civilian population, and it grossly underestimated the rebel will and capability for large-scale combat: "These people show a spirit and conduct against us that they never showed against the French, and everybody has judged them from their former appearance and behavior, which has led many into great mistakes," General Gage reported after the battles of Lexington and Concord.[9] Related to this failure was the psychology of the British command. The long period of relative inaction before the outbreak and Gage's increasingly pessimistic estimates of the situation during that period finally put him in the position of having to take some action in order to redeem himself in the eyes of his own government. The first setback at Lexington in April prepared the way for the second at Bunker Hill in June, since an even more sensational success was required to redeem the initial failure. General Burgoyne explained why a tactically reckless assault was made at Bunker Hill when he wrote that "the respect and control and subordination of government depends in a great measure upon the idea that trained troops are invincible against any numbers or any position of untrained rabble; and this idea was a little in suspense since the 19th of April."[10]

With the outbreak of actual fighting, the concept of the problem as essentially a police action, however massive and extraordinary that action might be, quickly faded away and was replaced by the belief that the government faced a fairly conventional war that could be conducted along classical lines. The American rebels were hastily organizing an army on the European model, and the game now seemed to be one of maneuvering in order to bring the rebel army to decisive battle or, better still, to destroy it without costly fighting. Accordingly, the British shifted their base from Boston, a dead end in terms of classical strategy, to New York, which was a superior port with access to the best lines of communication into the American interior. An incidental consideration, but no more than that, was the greater friendliness of the civilian population in the Middle Atlantic theater of operations as compared with New England.[11]

The underlying policy assumption of this second stage, not very closely examined at the time, was that success in conventional operations against the main rebel army would more or less automatically bring a restoration of political control in the wake of military victory. The assumption proved to be not wholly wrong. A series of tactical successes through the summer and fall of 1776 not only secured the New York port area but produced a striking collapse of resistance in New Jersey as well. Without any special effort by the British command, local rebel leaders fled or went into hiding as the main rebel army withdrew. The local rebel militia, which had firmly controlled the communities of New Jersey, tended to disintegrate and to be replaced by an improvised Loyal militia. It is clear that almost every civilian in New Jersey believed that the rebellion would collapse completely and that it was not too soon to reach an accommodation with the royal authorities. The government granted free pardon to all civilians who would take an oath of allegiance, and almost three thousand Americans accepted the offer in a few weeks, including one signer of the Declaration of Independence.[12]

The failure of the British campaign in New Jersey, after such a promising start, had two major causes, one external, the other internal. The internal cause is summarized in the remarks of two British observers: one noted that the lenient policy toward the civilian population "violently offends all those who have suffered for their attachment to government"; the other noted "the licentiousness of the troops, who committed every species of rapine and plunder."[13] There is ample evidence from both sides to confirm these observations. British regulars and especially their non-English-speaking German auxiliaries – products of the hard school of European warfare – tended to regard all civilians as possible rebels and hence fair game. Even if civilians avoided the regular foragers, they were not permitted to relapse into passive loyalty if they had ever shown the slightest sympathy for the rebel cause. Loyal bands of native militia regarded retribution as their principal function and were determined that no rebel should escape, pardon or no pardon. In many cases, former neutrals or lukewarm rebels found no advantage in submission to government and came to see flight, destruction, or resistance as the only available alternatives.[14]

The other, external cause of failure stemmed from the British attempt to control and live off the central part of the state: brigade garrisons were deployed among towns, mainly for administrative convenience. Not surprisingly, the rebel main army, weak as it was, managed to achieve local superiority and exploit its excellent tactical intelligence to pick off two of these garrisons, at Trenton in late December and at Princeton in early January. The tactical effects of these small battles were modest, but the strategic and psychological effects were enormous. British forces withdrew from all exposed locations and henceforth concentrated in the area from Perth Amboy to New Brunswick. The morale of rebels, already sensitized by harsh treatment, soared; while the morale of Loyal civilians, now out of range of British regular support, dropped sharply. Almost all New Jersey quickly came under insurgent control. The international repercussions of Trenton and Princeton were likewise serious.[15]

One noteworthy point: in the only intensive study made of a single community during this period (Bergen County, New Jersey), it is apparent that the local and bloody battles between rebel and Loyal militia were related to prewar animosities between ethnic groups, political rivals, churches, and even neighbors.[16]

The campaign of 1777 was essentially a continuation of the strategy of 1776; its object was to destroy, disperse, or demoralize the rebel main army and to quarantine New England insurgency by gaining control of the Hudson valley. But the assessment of civilian attitudes became more important than it had been in 1776 and affected planning in two ways: because the unexpected continuation of the war for another year strained British military manpower, one British force would move to Philadelphia, not only luring the main rebel army to defend its capital but also permitting the recruitment of badly needed provincial troops from the supposedly friendly population. Another British force would move down the Champlain-Mohawk-Hudson corridor on the assumption that the scattered population of the area was Loyal or at least not actively hostile and that Indian auxiliaries could intimidate those who might lean toward rebellion.[17] The campaign was a disaster, in large part because the intelligence estimates, gleaned mainly from exile sources, were much too optimistic. The Canadian force simply drowned at Saratoga in a hostile sea, which its Indian allies had done something to roil and its commander had not foreseen and done little to calm. The army at Philadelphia, whose commander had assumed that the northern army could take care of itself, found that the march of his men through the countryside from Chesapeake Bay had created new rebels and that Pennsylvania "friendliness" did not go beyond selling what was needed to feed the troops penned up in the city.[18] Other factors contributed to the disaster of 1777, especially a three-way failure to agree on the basic idea of the whole operation, which was attributable only in part to the slowness of transatlantic communications. But primary was the miscalculation of objectives and of time-space factors through an erroneous conception of the civilian environment within which military operations were to be conducted.[19]

Throughout this second stage of the war, the British military and naval commanders, the brothers Howe, were empowered to negotiate with rebel leaders. These negotiations came to nothing because the rebel military situation was never truly desperate except briefly at the end of 1776 and because rebel unity so patently depended on adherence to political demands that the British government was not yet willing to concede. It has sometimes been argued that the British attempt to unify politics and warfare inhibited military operations, because the Howe brothers allegedly withheld the full force of the military stick in order to dangle the political carrot more enticingly. Little contemporary evidence supports the criticism, though the Howes were bitterly attacked once their failure was apparent. The effects that a ruthless naval blockade and the pursuit of armed rebels to utter destruction might have had on any real pacification of the troubled areas were unpredictably double-edged. The Howes knew this, and so did everyone else; awareness did not depend on having formal powers to negotiate. Only after their strategy had failed, and especially after the fiasco of 1777, did their critics become retrospectively wise about the campaign of 1776. In fact, the Howes conducted operations in that first year with great skill and smoothness; understanding between army and navy was never better. Washington's army had been shattered at minimal cost; to have expected relentless exploitation of success was to ignore the basic character of eighteenth-century armies, technology, and military doctrine. Battles were murderous, desertion rates soared whenever an army became dispersed and control relaxed, tactical fortunes often turned abruptly at just the moment when one side tried to push an advantage beyond the limits of a powerful but rigid system of fighting, and trained replacements were pure gold. All these characteristics of eighteenth-century warfare were more acute when operations occurred in a large and distant country, against a semi-skilled but numerous and enthusiastic enemy; but they were by no means peculiar to American conditions. If anything, the lessons learned from the American campaigns of the Seven Years' War, not to mention Lexington, Concord, and Bunker Hill, pointed to the need for more, not less, than the usual amount of tactical caution. The most serious criticism of the Howes' campaign in 1776 is simply that it failed to end the rebellion.[20]

The outline of the third and last stage of British strategy took a year to emerge from the confusion that followed the defeat at Saratoga. The French fished more openly and aggressively for advantage in North America, and the British response was to escalate by declaring war against France. The West Indies, where both powers had large economic and military stakes, pulled the strategic center of gravity southward and seaward. During 1778, the British army on the continent remained on the defensive, cut its commitments by evacuating Philadelphia, and used bases at New York and Rhode Island to carry out a campaign of coastal harassment, while Indian allies put pressure on the rebel frontiers. Meanwhile, a general re-evaluation of British strategy was taking place.[21]

For the first time, the civilian population came to be the major factor in planning. As never before, it was seen that Loyal and neutral civilians had to be organized and protected before any lasting results could be achieved and that the great pool of civilian manpower largely accounted for the surprising resilience of the rebel main armies. Because civilian response had so far been disappointing in New England and the Middle Atlantic states, because West Indian and mainland operations now had to be coordinated, and because earlier, small-scale operations had produced an unexpectedly favorable response from civilians in the southern colonies, it was decided to begin the new campaign in the South. Some British officials had always seen the South as the soft underbelly of the rebellion, with its scattered population, its fear of slave uprisings, strong Indian tribes at its back, and a split between tidewater and up-country societies in the Carolinas that approached a state of civil war. A heavy stream of information from Loyal Americans supported this kind of thinking. At last it was understood that the recruitment of Loyal provincial troops merely for use in conventional operations often had deprived an area of the very people who might control it; high priority would now be given to the formation of local self-defense forces. The basic concept was to regain military control of some one major colony, restore full civil government, and then expand both control and government in a step-by-step operation conducted behind a slowly advancing screen of British regulars. From a police operation, and then a classical military confrontation, British strategy had finally become a comprehensive plan of pacification directed against a revolutionary war.[22]

The new strategy was linked to the political situation in Britain itself: increasingly, the government had justified a costly and controversial war to members of the House of Commons on the grounds that Britain had an unbreakable commitment to defend Loyal Americans against rebel vengeance. The government thus staked its political life on the success of pacification in the South. The decision, however, was not seen as a gamble so much as the pursuit of a logical course, because the government, especially the king and his principal strategic planner, Lord George Germain, had always believed that most Americans, given a chance to choose freely, would support the Crown. When Lord North, nominally prime minister, but in a weak position within his own government, expressed an opinion that the war was no longer worth its cost, the king rebuked him by saying that "this is only weighing such events in the scale of a tradesman behind his counter" and that American independence would surely lead to the loss, piece by piece, of the rest of the British Empire, including Ireland. It might be said, without exaggeration, that North's cost-benefit analysis of the situation lost out to the king's domino theory.[23]

The new campaign began well. Amphibious attack captured Savannah at the end of 1778 and led to a collapse of rebel resistance in the more densely populated part of Georgia. Twenty Loyal militia companies were organized, and 1400 Georgians swore allegiance to the king. Yet certain problems appeared that would never be solved. In attempting to clear rebel remnants away from pacified areas, British regulars pushed detachments to Augusta and toward Charleston, beyond the limit where they could be permanently maintained at that time. Subsequent withdrawal of these detachments led to the deterioration of Loyal militia units left

behind in the outlying areas and to an adverse effect on the future behavior of their Loyal and neutral residents. Furthermore, regular commanders revealed themselves as unduly optimistic in deciding that any particular area had been pacified and could safely be left to defend itself. Finally, the troops, and even some of their commanders, simply could not be made to treat civilians – except those actually in arms for the Crown – as anything but suspected rebels despite explicit directives from London and headquarters to the contrary.[24]

Large reinforcements in 1780 brought about the capture of Charleston and its large rebel garrison in May; a small rebel army that entered the Carolinas in August was quickly destroyed at Camden. Now British mounted forces successfully employed irregular tactics and achieved tactical mobility equal or superior to that of the rebels themselves. Upcountry, the Loyal militia was organized district by district; men over forty were assigned to local defense, while those younger served as territorial auxiliaries. Every effort was made to meet the rebel threat by effective countermeasures at the local level. Moreover, the orders from General Clinton to the inspector of militia show the spirit in which these measures were undertaken: "You will pay particular attention to restrain the [Loyal] militia from offering violence to innocent and inoffensive people, and by all means in your power protect the aged, the infirm, the women and children from insult and outrage."[25]

In the end, the policy failed; the question is why? Small groups of rebel irregulars could not be eliminated altogether. They hid in some of the least accessible swamps and mountains or operated from unpacified pro-rebel locations on the periphery – in upper Georgia or southern North Carolina. These irregular bands made complete physical security unattainable for many pacified areas. Rebel guerrillas and militia could achieve local superiority against any particular body of Loyal self-defense militia and sometimes even against mobile detachments. In an action reminiscent of both Trenton and

Saratoga, a group of rebels quickly built up strength in October to wipe out an overextended Loyal force of a thousand men at King's Mountain, North Carolina. Thus, neither side had the capability of fully protecting its supporters among the civilian population, and a ferocious guerrilla war spread throughout South Carolina and into Georgia and North Carolina. Areas thought to have been pacified quickly slipped out of control, sometimes because Loyal forces fought their own little wars of counter-terror against rebels, rebel sympathizers, suspects, and anyone else they disliked.

Almost every British action appears to have exacerbated this situation. The chronic rough treatment of civilians by regulars simply could not be curbed to any significant extent. Moreover, the British force under Tarleton that had successfully employed irregular tactics soon acquired in the course of its operations a reputation for inhumanity that drove apathetic civilians toward the rebels for protection. A proclamation offering full rights of citizenship and pardon to all who would take the oath of allegiance, but declaring all others as rebels, drove many paroled rebel prisoners out of the neutral position that they had assumed and back into active rebellion. At the same time, the conciliatory aspect of this policy infuriated Loyal auxiliaries, militia, and irregulars, who increasingly ignored official policy and orders and took matters into their own hands. A Loyalist observer, who had defected some time before from the rebel side, described South Carolina as "a piece of patch work, the inhabitants of every settlement, when united in sentiment, being in arms for the side they liked best and making continual inroads into one another's settlements."[26] During this civil war, there was little difference between Loyalists and rebels in terms of organization, tactics, or the use of terror. Pacification had failed well before a new rebel army was organized under General Nathanael Greene in central North Carolina.

The failure of pacification, and the appearance of this large rebel force to the

northward, led General Cornwallis to return, almost with a sigh of relief, to more conventional operations. Priorities were shifted, mobile forces were concentrated, and the principal objective became the destruction of the rebel army through maneuver, battle, and pursuit.[27] This reversion to the strategy of 1776–77 ended in the disaster at Yorktown in October 1781, when the British navy momentarily lost control of sea lines of communication with its southern army. From that time on, all serious attempts to pacify the American interior were given up, and only New York and Charleston were kept as impregnable enclaves until the declaration of peace in early 1783.[28]

Certain aspects of the failure of this third stage of British strategy require emphasis. One is that neither British nor rebel leaders regarded the bloody civil war in the South as "favorable" to their side; both tried to curb it in order to gain political control and to prevent large-scale alienation of potentially friendly civilians. But it *was* beneficial to the rebels inasmuch as they could choose to operate in pro-rebel areas while the British were constrained to operate everywhere. Furthermore, the relative proximity of a large British regular army had a surprisingly unfavorable effect on civilian attitudes. Civilians tended to over-react to the army. Depending on the particular circumstances, civilians were intimidated by it and so behaved "Loyally," for which they later suffered; or they were disillusioned by its predatory conduct and lack of sympathy for the precarious position of the civilian; or they felt secure in its presence and committed violent acts under its aegis, which ultimately created pro-rebel sympathy; or they saw it as an alternative, a place of flight and refuge; or they were demoralized when it moved away and refused to protect them, their homes, and families.

This last point is most important to our subject: every major British troop movement in the American Revolution created shock waves of civilian behavior in the surrounding area. Only the scale of British operations in the

South, where the British were more aware of the problem and tried to control it, makes those shock waves especially visible in the latter stages of the conflict. But repeatedly, throughout the war, Loyal and neutral civilians had responded excessively, prematurely, and unwisely, at least in terms of their own personal security, to the appearance of British troops, only to see those troops withdraw or move elsewhere. British leaders throughout the war had assumed that civilian attitudes and behavior were more or less constant factors that could be measured by civilian actions; American behavior on any one occasion was taken not only to indicate attitudes but also to predict behavior on the next occasion. In fact, each of these occasions brought about a permanent change in the attitude and behavior of those civilians who were involved in, or even aware of, what happened: over time, these occasions had a major, cumulative effect. By 1780–81, earlier in some places, most Americans, however weary, unhappy, or apathetic toward the rebellion they might be, were fairly sure of one thing: the British government no longer could or would maintain its presence, and sooner or later the rebels would return. Under these circumstances, civilian attitudes could no longer be manipulated by British policies or actions.

British strategy may seem but distantly related to the war's impact on American society; in fact, analysis of the first illuminates the second, leading us directly back to the question of effects posed by Jameson. Reflected in the foregoing account of British operations and their difficulties is a changing pattern of American behavior. More direct kinds of evidence, generated by the American war effort itself, distort the picture by concentrating either on a committed but small minority or, in the tones of Jeremiah, on the failure of others to do all that they could or should have to support the Revolution. What the British record on the other hand reveals is something rather different: the response of the whole population to the multifarious stimuli of war. British estimates of American attitudes were frequently in error, but seldom were they completely mistaken. They were prone to exaggerate the intensity of Loyalism, they usually blurred the relationship between attitude and likely behavior, and they often mistook Loyal behavior as a sign of unshakable loyalty. But these estimates, when placed in the context of the British experience and when tested against evidence from the other side, give us a way of understanding the effect of the war on American society.

In the first place, two standard versions of the war are called into question, if not discredited altogether, by a British perspective. One is the interpretation that turns the fact of British military failure into a hymn to the American spirit, recounting how Revolutionary courage, belief, and solidarity frustrated every British design. The other interpretation would reverse the emphasis; according to it, nothing but luck, timely French aid, and a tiny group of dedicated men stood between American liberties and British repression. The British version of the war indicates that the Revolution was neither as irresistible nor as fragile, respectively, as these other versions suggest.

What emerges from the British record, especially when an effort is made to distinguish between the earlier wishful fantasies and the cold insights wrung from later disillusionment, is a picture of the great middle group of Americans.[29] Almost certainly a majority of the population, these were the people who were dubious, afraid, uncertain, indecisive, many of whom felt that there was nothing at stake that could justify involving themselves and their families in extreme hazard and suffering. These are the people lost from sight in the Revolutionary record or dismissed as "the timid." With not even poverty to redeem them, they are also passed over by historians who believe that the inert mass of people in any epoch deserve nothing better than obscurity. These people, however, did count, because they made up a large proportion of a revolutionary republic whose very existence depended on counting.

From a British perspective, it appears that a great many of these people were changed by the war. Beginning as uneasy but suggestible, manipulable, potentially loyal subjects of the Crown, they ended as knowing, skeptical, wary citizens of the United States. In this sense, the war was a political education conducted by military means, and no one learned more than the apathetic majority as they scurried to restore some measure of order and security in their disrupted lives. The British army was, of course, one of the chief political teachers; in its erratic progress from North to South over the course of seven years, the army directly touched hundreds of thousands of individuals, eliciting behavior that would identify each in political terms while teaching him something about politics. Nothing shows better the success of its instructional effort than its ever-greater difficulty in predicting and controlling the behavior of the presumably apathetic majority. And as we examine the British record for more specific clues to the impact of the war, a second institution, which also played the role of political teacher, comes into clearer focus. That institution is the militia. Earlier essays in this volume have discussed, from several viewpoints, the political and military importance of a population legally required to own and bear arms. Here that discussion can be summarized, amplified, and set in the broadest context of the Revolution.

The British and their allies were fascinated by the rebel militia.[30] Poorly trained and badly led, often without bayonets, seldom comprised of the deadly marksmen dear to American legend, the Revolutionary militia was much more than a military joke, and perhaps the British came to understand that better than did many Americans themselves. The militia enforced law and maintained order wherever the British army did not, and its presence made the movement of smaller British formations dangerous. Washington never ceased complaining about his militia – about their undependability, their indiscipline, their cowardice under fire – but from the British viewpoint, rebel militia was one of the most troublesome and predictable elements in a confusing war. The militia nullified every British attempt to impose royal authority short of using massive armed force. The militia regularly made British light infantry, German Jäger, and Tory raiders pay a price, whatever the cost to the militia itself, for their constant probing, foraging, and marauding. The militia never failed in a real emergency to provide reinforcements and even reluctant draftees for the State and Continental regular forces. From the British viewpoint, the militia was the virtually inexhaustible reservoir of rebel military manpower, and it was also the sand in the gears of the pacification machine.[31]

When we look more closely at the rebel militia, an interesting if obvious fact confronts us: the prudent, politically apathetic majority of white American males was not eager to serve actively in the militia, but many of them did nonetheless. Their wives were perhaps even less enthusiastic; in an agrarian society with a chronic labor shortage, manpower was too important to the welfare, even the survival, of the family. But the sheer busyness of British strategy in the early years of the war – from Boston to New York to Philadelphia, into Long Island and Rhode Island, across New Jersey and Delaware, along the Carolina and Connecticut coasts, up Lakes Champlain and George and down the Mohawk River – made it difficult to know how to be prudent. In the later years of the war, growing British sophistication about the nature of the war made prudence increasingly dangerous, especially from Virginia southward and in a great arc around New York City. Under the circumstances, enrollment in the militia could be a test of loyalty to one side or the other, and it could be a kind of insurance – the readiest form of personal security in a precarious world. But the militia was also a coercive instrument: it was the ultimate sanction of political authority in its own district, and in the mysterious way of all large organizations it kept its own grumbling membership in line. Of course, whole districts might go Tory, just as whole militia units crumbled under pressure, but rarely were nearby rebel forces unable to intervene, salvage, and restore these situations. A reservoir, sand in the gears, the militia also looked like a great spongy mass that could be pushed aside or maimed temporarily but that had no vital center and could not be destroyed.

Take a concrete example: in December 1776 the new State of Connecticut passed a law, not very different from old laws in Connecticut and elsewhere, establishing a military organization. It reiterated the obligation of all males between sixteen and sixty to serve in the militia, excepting only congressmen, certain members of State government, ministers of the gospel, Yale tutors and students, and Negroes, Indians, and mulattoes. Officers were to be elected, and no one over fifty could be forced to march out of the State. As in the past, it was legally possible to provide a substitute or pay a £5 fine, but only if drafted for active service.[32]

Five months after the passage of the new militia law, a committee of the Connecticut Assembly reported on the case of Nathaniel Jones and seventeen other men from Farmington.[33] Jones and his associates, imprisoned "on suspicion of their being inimical to America,"' had petitioned for pardon and release and swore that they were now "ready and willing to join with their country and to do their utmost for its defence." They found themselves in jail because, a month before, they had failed to join their militia unit in opposing Governor Tryon's destructive raid on Danbury; their negative act had identified them as suspected persons, if not outright Tories. In order to clear themselves, they were forced to undergo individual' grilling by the legislative committee, which finally reported favorably on the men from Farmington in the following terms: " ... They were indeed grossly ignorant of the true grounds of the present war with Great Britain. ... They appeared to be penitent of their former conduct, professed themselves convinced since the Danbury alarm that there was no such thing as remaining neuters. ... The destruction made there by the Tories was matter of conviction to them."

It is a simple story, repeated hundreds of times in the course of the Revolutionary War, and it makes a simple but very important point. While military historians have generally clucked over the failure of the Connecticut militia to trap and destroy Tryon's raiders, the real significance of this episode is that Nathaniel Jones and many other apathetic, apolitical men, who simply did not want to become perilously involved in a civil war, learned that trying to "remain neuter" was also perilous. In late April 1777 they had tried to evade a political choice, but in the end they had to beg, in the old language of religious conversion that spoke of "matter of conviction," for a second chance to choose. The mechanism of their political conversion was the militia. Unlike other tests of allegiance, which either applied to only a few of the most prominent or notorious, or else, like the oath, lacked both the urgency and the administrative machinery needed to make it effective, the military obligation sooner or later thrust itself directly into the lives of even the most apathetic. Mere enrollment and occasional drilling were not all that the militia demanded, because eventually almost every colonial county had its equivalent of the Danbury raid, when men actually had either to take arms in an emergency or to do something that would visibly label them as suspicious or "disloyal" persons. Popular military service was as old as the colonies, but never before had its performance or avoidance defined political categories.

Evidence from both sides records how time and again, in place after place, the movement of British forces combined with the American obligation of universal military service to politicize communities and individuals. John Davies of Charlestown, South Carolina, was able to evade the rebel oath until 1779, when he was obliged to take up arms; having refused, he spent four months on a prison ship. The same thing happened to John Pearness, Thomas Mackaness, David Lorimer, and Colonel John Philips and his two sons, who learned that refusal to serve in the militia meant trial by court-martial. Alex Chesney, on the other hand, gave in and served actively in the American forces on three separate occasions. In England after the war, Colonel Philips testified in Chesney's behalf: "He does not think the worse of him because he served in the Rebel Army," said Colonel Philips, "many good men were obliged to do it."[34] While these good men and others were suffering for their reluctance to serve in the South Carolina militia, George Grant was being hauled before the Commissioners for Detecting and Defeating Conspiracies in Albany County, New York, "as a Person of suspicious Character"; he was given the choice of jail or "enrolling himself in some Militia Company."[35] To the Albany commissioners, the militia was as much a political as a military organization; when they learned that some of the people who lived on the frontier and enrolled in Major Ezekiel Taylor's militia regiment were rumored to be "disaffected," they asked the major for a regimental roll with the "Political Character of Each Man" noted so that the "disaffected" might be "removed" from this sensitive part of the state.[36] A similar crunch had come for many Pennsylvanians in late 1776; it did not come for most Virginians until the spring of 1779.[37] But virtually everywhere, in time, it came.

The pattern of wartime politicization may be seen in dozens of minor military actions; one last example will suffice. When the British established a small post on the Penobscot River in June 1779, Brigadier General Francis McLean, an exceptionally able officer, found the local settlers terrified by their belief "that His Majesty's troops were accustom'd to plunder and treat the Country where their operations led them with the greatest inhumanity." McLean set out to correct this mistaken idea. Through promises and humane treatment, he persuaded some five hundred people to come in and take the oath to the king; "yet numbers of the young men of the country have gone westward," he reported, "and attempts have been made to raise the people tho' hitherto without success." He was sure that most of the settlers between Boston and the Penobscot were Loyal, but he also saw that "the impossibility in our present

circumstances of affording them protection from the threats of the opposite party obliges them to act with caution ..." For three weeks in July and August, McLean's force was under attack and siege by an amphibious expedition sent from Boston. The siege failed and the American fleet was driven off, but McLean had to report that "most of the inhabitants ... notwithstanding their oath of allegiance, and fidelity to His Majesty were compelled to join the enemy ..." He still had hopes and worked to recapture the popular support enjoyed by the British in June. Tories from Boston swore that a strong force of Loyal militia could be organized around the Penobscot garrison. But by October, McLean had all but given up; in spite of his gentle policy and their oaths of allegiance, he did not believe that the king could count on more than ten of the inhabitants along the whole river. Things looked a little brighter in November, but only because refugees from the rebels had begun to stream into the area around the British post. Eighteen months later, McLean's successor begged to evacuate the Penobscot post because he could not stop the local settlers from enticing his redcoats to desert.[38] As in New Jersey earlier and the Carolinas later, the dynamics of British intrusion and American reaction produced first a change, then a hardening of the local political situation. A tough or desperate few fled to the British for protection, while the rest gave at least the appearance of zeal for the American cause. But whether sham or not, their new Revolutionary commitment could rarely be reversed again, either by the tact of a McLean or the terrorism of a Tarleton.

It has always seemed slightly implausible that the American Republic was born out of a congeries of squabbling, unstable colonies, and that labor was induced by nothing more than a few routine grievances expressed in abstract if elegant prose. The Revolutionary War, considered as a political education for the masses, helps to fill the explanatory gap, provided we are willing to extrapolate a little from the evidence.

The broad popular basis of military organization forced thousands of more or less unwilling people to associate themselves openly and actively with the cause. In an age when single-shot muzzleloaders were the standard instrument of coercion, sheer numbers were most important, and naked majoritarianism could grow from the barrels of muskets. The absolute need to organize and hold a majority of gunmen had still wider implications: it required some kind of consensus, at least among the armed majority, in order to ward off incipient mutiny and dissolution. In the last years of the war, consensus probably operated to ease some of the pressure within the militia itself; derelictions of duty, once minimal loyalty to the Revolution could be taken for granted, were no longer treated as political crimes, but rather were punished as minor offenses. Likewise, the readiness shown soon after the war of the whole society to stop persecuting those Loyalists who had not actually emigrated, despite the desire of many to purge the Republic of Toryism, may be a measure of the curiously moderating effect of mass military participation.

Another effect of the war was the rapid erosion of deferential political behavior, which had characterized above all the apolitical majority; once they had seen and even taken part in hounding, humiliating, perhaps killing men known to them as social superiors, they could not easily reacquire the unthinking respect for wealth and status that underpinned the old order. And in a time of notorious duplicity and corruption, evident by 1779 in contemporary accounts from every hand, it was equally difficult to defer to new leaders, though many of them had been part of the old elite.

American laments for the decline of public virtue in the later years of the war may be read simply as so many jeremiads, but British evidence points to the sordid reality beneath the rhetoric. The British interpreted what they saw as war-weariness; what they actually were seeing was the extent to which rebellion had successfully recruited the apathetic. The continuing obsession with "virtue," so central to political discourse during the postwar years, derived as much from the depressing spectacle of the compromises forced by the irresistible demands of revolutionary warfare as it did from the logic of classical republican theory.[39] In the end, of course, military and diplomatic success colored memory. Reluctance and resentment were readily forgotten, and the bare record of participation was all that mattered. After the fortunes and pressures of war had destroyed his other alternatives, each member of a large majority could claim his tiny but concrete share in the creation of the United States.

Beyond this hothouse nationalism, whose strengths and weaknesses would baffle observers for decades, there was at least one more visible effect that the war, working through the agency of the militia, had on American politics: the sharpening of the struggle between central and local authority. The many bitter words of Washington about the militia, the public outburst between Aedanus Burke and Alexander Hamilton over the respective roles of militia and regular forces in the southern campaign, prefigure the constituencies who fought over the Constitution and later organized as political parties.[40] If the Revolutionary militia is considered in its political role, then the relative apathy of the more numerous Antifederalists in 1787–88 is less puzzling.

That a long, straggling, often disruptive and sometimes atrocious war had lasting effects on a society of three million people is not surprising. The difficulty has always been in discerning and describing those effects and in explaining them, without resort to some mystical notion of American character. The correctness in detail of my own oblique attack on this problem through the medium of British strategy and American response is less important than the concept of the Revolutionary War, not as an instrument of policy or a sequence of military operations, but as a social process of political education that can be explored, and should be analyzed.

## Notes

1. Don Higginbotham. "American Historians and the Military History of the American Revolution," *American Historical Review,* LXX (1964), 18–34, surveys the military historical writing about the Revolution and describes the recent revival of interest in the subject. But it is remarkable how little even this revival has impinged on study of the Revolution as a whole. Higginbotham's *The War of American Independence* (New York, 1971), more than any previous general account, seeks to relate the military and nonmilitary segments of the war; basic research in this direction, however, has hardly begun.

2. J. Franklin Jameson, *The American Revolution Considered as a Social Movement* (Princeton, 1926).

3. Frederick B. Tolles, "The American Revolution Considered as a Social Movement: A Re-evaluation," *American Historical Review,* LX (1954), 1–12, reprinted in the paperback edition of Jameson (Princeton, 1967), surveys the critical attack on Jameson's argument. Two unjustly neglected books that seek to relate the direct pressure of warfare to major political developments are Bernhard Knollenberg, *Washington and the Revolution* (New York, 1940), and Curtis Nettels, *George Washington and American Independence* (New York, 1951). While both Bernard Bailyn, *The Ideological Origins of the American Revolution* (Cambridge, Mass., 1967), and Gordon S. Wood, *The Creation of the American Republic, 1776–1787* (Chapel Hill, 1969), stress the intellectual and even psychological changes wrought by revolution, the former stresses prewar Whig-Tory conflict, while the latter rarely (e.g., 324) sees wartime events as agents of intellectual change. Jackson T. Main, *The Social Structure of Revolutionary America* (Princeton, 1965), finds, on the whole, relatively little perceptible change in socioeconomic structure and so is not disposed to consider the possible effects of the war.

4. Richard Hofstadter, *The Progressive Historians: Turner, Beard, Parrington* (New York, 1968).

5. On military history, see Peter Paret, "The History of War," *Daedalus,* C (1971), 376–96. On the principles of war, see Bernard Brodie, "Strategy as a Science," *World Politics,* I (1949), 467–88.

6. For another, differently directed discussion of the relevance of the twentieth century to the eighteenth, see Thomas C. Barrow, "The American Revolution as a Colonial War for Independence," *William and Mary Quarterly,* 3rd series, XXV (1968), 452–64. Of the reverse relationship – the relevance of the American Revolution to twentieth-century revolution – there is no question here, although Richard B. Morris and Clinton Rossiter, among others, have written books on the subject.

7. The final crisis, and the thinking that shaped it on the British side, can be traced in Bernard Donoughue, *British Politics and the American Revolution: The Path to War 1773–1775* (London, 1964); Benjamin W. Labaree, *The Boston Tea Party* (New York, 1964); and John Shy, *Toward Lexington: The Role of the British Army in the Coming of the American Revolution* (Princeton, 1965), chap. 9.

8. How Boston kept itself from being effectively isolated can be followed in Richard D. Brown, *Revolutionary Politics in Massachusetts: The Boston Committee of Correspondence and the Towns, 1772–1774* (Cambridge, Mass., 1970).

9. Gage to Secretary at War Barrington, "Private," June 26, 1775, Clarence E. Carter, ed., *The Correspondence of General Thomas Gage ... 1763–1775* (New Haven, 1931–33), II, 686–87..

10. Burgoyne to Germain, Aug. 20, 1775, Germain Papers, William L. Clements Library, Ann Arbor, Michigan.

11. Mackesy, *War for America,* 35, 42; Willcox, *Clinton,* 55, 58; Smith, *Loyalists,* 41. The question of strategic intentions and expectations, especially in the case of General Howe, is murky. Although he said that he expected to destroy Washington's army in battle, there is some reason to believe that he hoped to win a decisive victory in the chess-like manner idealized by Maurice de Saxe (see Jon M. White, *Marshal of France* [London, 1962], 272–73), by maneuvering Washington out of richer, more populous areas and into a tactically hopeless position, where the only rational choice would be for the rebel army to break up and flee, all without major bloodshed. This kind of strategic thinking, so characteristic of the ancien régime, would later move Clausewitz to scorn (*On War,* trans. O. J. Matthijs Jolles [Washington, D.C., 1950], 210); but

even Clausewitz elsewhere admitted mat battles unfought, like the unpaid bills of commercial credit, functioned as the nexus of strategy *(ibid.,* 27, 123). The point here is that Howe, by threatening to fight only under favorable circumstances, no doubt hoped to minimize fighting. The tension, obvious to Clausewitz and to ourselves, between the conquest of territory and the destruction of enemy armed force, was less felt in the eighteenth century, when the very objects of war tended to be territorial and the costs of major battle, even to the victor, seemed extraordinarily high.

12. Leonard Lundin, *Cockpit of the Revolution: The War for Independence in New Jersey* (Princeton, 1940), 157ff.

13. I. E. Tatum, ed., *The American Journal of Ambrose Serle, Secretary to Lord Howe, 1776–1778* (San Marino, Calif., 1940), 155; "Journals of Lieut.-Col. Stephen Kemble," *The Kemble Papers,* New York Historical Society, *Collections,* XVI (New York, 1884), I, 160.

14. W. A. Whitehead et al., eds., *Archives of the Slate of New Jersey, 1631–1800,* 2nd series (Trenton 1901), I, 276ff, contains numerous accounts of minor skirmishes and affrays, reported in newspapers on both sides. Col. Charles Stuart to his father, the Earl of Bute, Feb. 4, 1777, E. Stuart-Wortley, ed., *A Prime Minister and His Son* (London, 1925), 99, is an especially clear statement of the problem. Some British officers, like the young Lord Rawdon, had expected positive results from the brutal conduct of the army in New Jersey. While still at New York he had written: "I think we should (whenever we get further into the country) give free liberty to the soldiers to ravage it at will, that these infatuated creatures may feel what a calamity war is." To the Earl of Hastings, Sept. 25, 1776, *MSS of Hastings,* III, 185.

15. The loss of British control in New Jersey is illustrated in a letter written by James Murray, a British officer, to his sister, from Perth Amboy, Feb. 25, 1777: "As the rascals are skulking about the whole country, it is impossible to move with any degree of safety without a pretty large escort, and even then you are exposed to a dirty kind of *tiraillerie* … . Would you believe that it was looked upon as a rash attempt to go [to New Brunswick] by land accompanied by two Light

Dragoons, tho' there are not above 5 or 6 miles of the road, and these next to the shore, but what are occupied by our troops?" Eric Robson, ed., *Letters from America, 1773–1780* (Manchester, 1951), 38–42.

16. Adrian Leiby, *The Hackensack Valley in the American Revolutionary War* (New Brunswick, 1962), 20.

17. Mackesy, *War for America,* 103–24; Smith, *Loyalists,* 44–59. Although the basic strategic concept remained that of "proving the superiority of the British troops over the army of the rebels" in order to produce a collapse of American morale and a more or less automatic political settlement (Germain to Gen. Howe, Oct. 18, 1776, Germain Papers, Clements Library), there is evidence of growing British interest in the attitudes of the local population. See, for example, Burgoyne to Clinton, Quebec, Nov. 7, 1776, Clinton Papers, Clements Library; Gen. Howe to Germain, Dec. 20, 1776 (extract), and Howe to Clinton, Apr. 5, 1777, Germain Papers.

18. On the popular response to the British march from Elkton, Maryland to Philadelphia, see B. A. Uhlendorf, ed., *Revolution in America: Confidential Letters and Journals, 1776–1784, of Adjutant General Major Baurmeister of the Hessian Forces* (New Brunswick, 1957), 95–113, and Alexander Graydon, *Memoirs of His Own Time* (Philadelphia, 1846), 285, 306. In Uhlendorf, ed., *Revolution in America,* 134–39, 148, 157, 162, 169, Baurmeister gives a graphic account of guerrilla warfare around Philadelphia during the following winter and spring.

19. Mackesy, *War for America,* 121–44.

20. The special constraints on strategy imposed by eighteenth-century tactics and organization are discussed and revealed in Stanley M. Pargellis, "Braddock's Defeat," *American Historical Review,* XLI (1936), 253–69, and *Lord Loudoun in North America* (New Haven, 1933), and in C. P. Stacey, *Quebec, 1759* (New York, 1959).

21. Mackesy, *War for America,* 156–58, 252–56; Willcox, *Clinton,* 260ff.

22. Smith, *Loyalists,* 79–99; Mackesy, *War for American,* 252ff.

23. The king to Lord North, June 11, 1779, John W. Fortescue, ed., *The Correspondence of King George the Third* … (London, 1927–28), III, 351.

24. Mackesy, *War f or America,* 267–68; Smith, *Loyalists,* 100–105, 126–42.

25. Quoted from the Clinton Papers, Clements Library, in Wickwire. *Cornwallis,* 427, n. 55. On the success of British irregular tactics, see *ibid.,* 132–33, 164–65, and Bass, *Tarleton.*

26. "Colonel Robert Gray's Observations on the War in Carolina," *South Carolina Historical and Genealogical Magazine,* XI (1910), 153. This is a remarkable document, conveying a vivid sense of the chaotic situation in those areas of South Carolina not occupied in strength by British forces. On the failure of British pacification even before the appearance of Greene's army, see Lord Rawdon to Maj. Leslie, Oct. 24, 1780, *Report on the Manuscripts of Mrs. Stopford-Sackville* ... , Hist. MSS Comm., *Fifteenth Report* (London, 1910), II, 185, hereafter cited as *MSS of Stopford-Sackville,* II.

27. Wickwire, *Cornwallis,* 169–95. But see also Willcox, *Clinton,* 352–53, and Mackesy, *War for America,* 343–45.

28. Macksey, *War f or America,* 404–36, 473–77, 487–94.

29 Barrow, "American Revolution as a Colonial War for Independence," *William and Mary Quarterly,* 3rd series, XXV (1968), 459, also thinks that neutral or moderate elements were "often a majority."

30. Uhlendorf, ed., *Revolution in America,* contains the most revealing account of British and Allied day-to-day awareness of rebel militia.

31. Baron Ludwig von Closen, a member of the French expeditionary force, noted in his journal on Apr. 12, 1781: "The Americans lose 600 men in a day, and 8 days later 1200 others rejoin the army; whereas, to replace 10 men in the English army is quite an undertaking." Evelyn M. Acomb, ed. and trans., *The Revolutionary Journal of Baron Ludwig von Closen, 1780–1783* (Chapel Hill, 1958), 75. In Uhlendorf, ed., *Revolution in America* esp. 353–54, Baurmeister describes the rebel militia at its best, near the end of the war. See also the "Journal of John Charles Philip von Krafft, of the Regiment von Bose, 1776–1784," New York Historical Society, *Collections,* XV (New York, 1883), 43–142.

32 Charles J. Hoadly, ed., *The Public Records of the State of Connecticut* (Hartford, 1894), I, 91ff.

33. *Ibid.,* 259–60.

34. H. E. Egerton, ed., *The Royal Commission on the Losses and Services of American Loyalists, 1783 to 1785* (Oxford, 1915), 49; also 10, 32, 35, 41, 43–44, 48.

35. V. H. Paltsits, ed., *Minutes of the Commissioners for Detecting and Defeating Conspiracies in the State of New York: Albany County Sessions, 1778–1781* (Albany, 1909), I, 369.

36. *Ibid.,* II, 735.

37. Minutes of the Council of Safety, *Pennsylvania Archives,* 1st series, XI, 38, 54–55; 94; Edmund Pendleton to William Woodford, May 24, 1779, David J. Mays, ed., *Letters and Papers of Edmund Pendleton* (Charlottesville, 1967), I, 285–86.

38. The Penobscot episode can be followed in the reports *to* Clinton in Hist. MSS Comm., *Report on American Manuscripts in the Royal Institution of Great Britain* (London, 1904–9), I, 458–60; II, 14–18, 45, 52, 66, 83, 144, 258. Some interesting observations are in Uhlendorf, ed., *Revolution in America,* 313, to the effect that McLean "is probably the first Briton who understands the art of winning the confidence of the inhabitants. He has organized militia twenty miles inland." See also 342.

39. On virtue, see Wood, *Creation of the American Republic,* 65–70.

40. For the exchange between Hamilton and Burke, see Harold C. Syrett and Jacob E. Cooke, eds., *The Papers of Alexander Hamilton* (New York, 1961–), VI, 333–37, 357–58.

# 8
# CLASS WAR?

*Class Struggles during the American Revolution in Virginia*

## Michael A. McDonnell

## Introduction

If applied flexibly, the analytical category of class promises multiple insights for historians of the American Revolution and other fields. That is the message of this prize-winning essay by Michael A. McDonnell. In Marxist theory, class reflects a group's position within a capitalist society based on its role in economic production. The theory identifies two fixed groups, or classes, within any industrialized society: capitalists, or the bourgeoisie, who own the means of production (such as a factory) and purchase the labor power of others; and workers, or the proletariat, who, without the benefits of capital, must sell their own labor power. No one would mistake colonial Virginia for an industrialized society, but McDonnell attributes great importance to material differences and economic inequalities between different groups in any historical situation.

He uses this fluid approach to class to expose divisions within Virginia during the American Revolutionary War. Historians have long viewed the most important division in Virginia and other slave societies as that between masters and slaves. Yet, as McDonnell shows, this simple dichotomy misses important differences among whites, who composed not one but three broad economic groups: gentlemen, usually large plantation owners; the "middling sort," often small planters or otherwise self-employed individuals; and the "lower sort," generally poor wage-earners. During the Revolution, the groups all came into conflict over their expected contributions to the war effort. While gentlemen could mostly buy their way out of military service, the middling sort comprised the militia and the poor were designated for service in the Continental Army. Open resentments over these obligations, especially toward gentlemen, often paralyzed Virginia, leaving it unable to mobilize adequate military forces. Even in the face of grave threats, such as Governor Lord Dunmore's Proclamation offering freedom to slaves in November 1775 and British raids on the state starting in October 1780 (which nearly resulted in the capture of Governor Thomas Jefferson), Virginia struggled to respond. The class divisions that had become an increasingly prominent feature of Virginia's white society proved nearly fatal in war.

- Consider McDonnell's essay in relation to Woody Holton's portrait of Virginia on the eve of independence. Did the colony's decision for independence, influenced largely by Dunmore's Proclamation, reflect mostly elite sentiments? Or did race still have the broad power to trump class in moments of crisis?
- At the end of the war, Virginia legislators considered but ultimately rejected a plan to follow the British example and arm slaves (free blacks were already permitted into military forces). Instead, the state offered slaves as an optional bounty to whites who enlisted in the Continental Army. How does the decision illustrate the ways that issues of race and class intersected in Virginia? What might have been the short-term and long-term consequences of arming slaves?
- McDonnell notes that ideas based on gender interacted with race and class to influence mobilization in wartime Virginia. How did gendered notions of household independence contribute to the state's military recruiting difficulties?

After an extraordinary debate, even for an extraordinary time, legislators in the Virginia General Assembly in the fall of 1780 came up with a startling offer to needy whites in the state. For joining the Continental army, new recruits were promised not only a parcel of land large enough to enfranchise them but also an enslaved Virginian as an extra bounty. Yet this controversial offer was merely a compromise solution to conceal a more profound debate in the legislature that fall. Desperate for soldiers amid a series of British invasions, the Virginia legislature initially debated even more radical plans to redistribute property from the most wealthy in the state to the poorest in return for military service. Many legislators argued that the wealthiest slaveholders in particular, who generally had not fought in the war, ought to give up a larger share of their slaves to those who had.

Though many commentators, starting with James Madison, have remarked on the perverse logic of rewarding soldiers fighting for so-called liberty with enslaved Virginians, few have taken note of the full contours of the revealing debate that fall. In discussing this legislation, most delegates to the assembly seemed more concerned about class and labor issues and not quite so much about race and slavery as modern historians might expect. Legislators seemed to think that the only way to make military service attractive to potential recruits was to offer enslaved Virginians to nonslaveholding lower-class whites. Joseph Jones told Madison that the "Negro bounty cannot fail to procure Men for the War." On the other end of the social spectrum, Jones thought that, though the "scheme bears hard upon those wealthy in Negros," in the present political climate any opposition from wealthy slaveholders would come to naught. Jones told Madison: "You know a great part of our House are not of that Class or own so few of them as not to come within the Law shd. it pass." Indeed one representative from the western county of Botetourt, Thomas Madison, believed that the legislature introduced this scheme precisely because they wanted to make the wealthy pay their share of the war. Finally, the one major reason legislators did not do as James Madison and several others suggested and arm enslaved Virginians, Jones asserted, was because such a move would "draw off immediately such a number of the best labourers for the Culture of the Earth as to ruin individuals." What enslaved Virginians produced by their labor, Jones claimed, was "but barely sufficient to keep us joging along with the great expence of the war." Jones, though a supporter of eventual freedom for blacks, argued that it had to be done gradually so planters could find replacement laborers, "or we shall suffer exceedingly under the sudden revolution which perhaps arming them wod. produce."[1]

But if Jones worried about a revolution in labor practices, another wealthy Virginian, Theodorick Bland, was angry about a different kind of revolution he felt was brewing from below. Increasingly frustrated by Virginia's inability to defend itself in the face of repeated British invasions, Bland watched helplessly as his neighbors refused to turn out for military service and rioted against attempts to draft them into the army as his own enslaved population grew more restive. In addition to these challenges from below, Bland was also feeling the pinch of high progressive taxes laid by the legislature to pay for increasing bounties for soldiers. Bland worried that the elected legislators who supported middle-class demands for redistributive taxes – whether in slaves or any other kind of property – to pay higher bounties to lower-class soldiers were "enemies to America, or fools or knaves, or all three." He feared their actions might "bring on a revolution in this state," a consequence that he thought was actually the "wish of a majority of the assembly."[2]

What are historians to make of this revealing debate and recurring expressions of what seem to have been class divisions in a white society generally depicted as united in its opposition to Britain and in its shared social interests and coherent culture? Several interrelated issues seem to stand in the way of understanding this puzzle. Scholars have, perhaps understandably, focused a great deal of attention on race and slavery in Virginia. Most historians have, in a metaphorical sense, followed James Madison's cue and wondered about the contradictions inherent in a slaveholding society amid a war for supposed liberty. And in thinking about this paradox, historians are still under the influence of Edmund Morgan's powerful argument that the need for racial unity smoothed over class divisions in Virginia and created a shared commitment to racial slavery, which was the basis of a cohesive white culture in the eighteenth century. Moreover, whereas the imperatives of maintaining that system meant that elite literate Virginians were always reluctant to "air their dirty linen," as one scholar has put it, Morgan's persuasive argument has also meant that historians have seldom looked for divisions among whites and have not been sure what to do with, or how much weight to give to, comments such as those of Theodorick Bland when they have found them. Scholars have been too quick to accept elites' self-reassuring rhetoric about the apparent unity and harmony of the state, especially during times of stress.[3]

In an important sense, then, Morgan's thesis has helped promote a powerful image that has obscured more than it was supposed to reveal: a general image of eighteenth-century Virginia as a slave society, one divided only by masters and slaves. There is, in this image, little room for serious economic inequalities, little room for those discontented others that have been found stirring up trouble elsewhere in the early modern world: the urban poor of London, Boston, or Philadelphia, for example, or the rural and recently dispossessed laborers and tenants of the Peak District, the newly opened mines of South Wales, or even the great manors of New York.[4] In Virginia the apparent absence or insignificance of such groups, combined with the shadow of slavery, has obscured any attempts to uncover nonracial divisions within the colony.

Despite popular images of Virginia as a slave society, divided between white planters and enslaved blacks, Virginia was a more complicated place.[5] Enslaved Virginians formed only the bottom of a hierarchical edifice that included male and female convicts and indentured servants, apprentices, free wage laborers and overseers, tenant farmers and nonslaveholding smallholders, slaveholding and nonslaveholding yeoman farmers and substantial slaveholding planters, and, finally, local and cosmopolitan elites who often held hundreds of Africans in bondage and owned thousands of acres of land throughout the colony. Moreover, even within some of these apparently monolithic social blocks, many, sometimes overlapping, layers of differences helped complicate social relations within and between different classes of Virginians. Ultimately, as any self-respecting gentleman, tenant farmer, or enslaved Virginian would know, this was a deeply divided and carefully defined hierarchical society in which social and economic inequalities were on conspicuous display.[6]

Scholarship has begun to delineate these divisions, yet it still seems difficult to talk about class in early modern Virginia. If a simplified black-and-white view of Virginia's social structure has often obscured the multilayered hierarchical complexity of the colony, a more general tendency to divide colonial society between dependents and independents has given rise to what seems to be one of the biggest challenges to a class analysis of the revolutionary era: the existence of a proportionally large group of landowning middling sorts. Most critics of the concept of class and its applicability to early American studies point to the size and growth of a group of people who were neither patricians nor plebeians, or among either the few or the many, but rather were independent farmers, merchants, and artisans.[7] Even if historians ignore the large number of landless whites in Virginia (to say nothing of enslaved Virginians), including servants, laborers, and tenants, they still have to acknowledge that a majority of white men in Virginia owned and farmed land; that is, they owned the means of production. But does that mean that Virginia landholders – the bulk of the people, the middling sort – somehow, as theorists, historians, and the public alike seem to assume, "lay outside the framework of class"?[8]

This large group of property holders seems to frustrate class analysis according to a long-standing theoretical and historiographical tradition, starting with Karl Marx and articulated most forcefully by E. P. Thompson, which has generally associated class with a particular kind of space (industrial, semi-industrial, waged work), period (late eighteenth and early nineteenth century), and political activism (horizontal consciousness and a self-aware articulation of alternative social and political visions, often at a national level). The history of class formation, too, centered on the working class and the rise of the proletariat: "the economic and political transformation during which artisans and small farmers lost control of their skills and land and were increasingly required to sell their labor for wages in the market." Given these associations, scholars should not be surprised if this kind of class was not present in other spaces, times, and forms. Eighteenth-century Virginia, for one, does not seem to fit this model of class, class consciousness, and class struggle. Where do landholding planters and farmers, great and small, fit?[9]

Yet if Thompson's earlier work seemed to create a barrier to thinking about class in other contexts, his later thoughts on the subject give historians the insights needed to demolish it. In a 1978 essay, for example, Thompson talked about class as a much more fluid historical category, one "derived from the observation of social process over time." And classes, at least before the nineteenth century, did not really exist outside the struggles that, in effect, helped define them. There are no simple equations, forms, or models, Thompson notes, because "class eventuates as men and women *live* their productive relations, and as they *experience* their determinate situations, within 'the *ensemble* of

the social relations,' with their inherited culture and expectations, and as they handle these experiences in cultural ways."[10] Class, then, is a process, not a set of predetermined categories, and particular sorts of relations may or may not be based on people's relationships to the means of production, but they are at the very least based on material circumstances and economic inequalities and, as in the case of eighteenth-century Virginia, are interconnected with and shaped by other factors such as race and gender. Defined this way class can be used as a means to examine and interrogate relations between social groups, particularly where economic inequalities were marked.[11]

A more fluid definition of class and class struggles, then, frees historians to examine afresh the kinds of struggles and divisions that seemed to plague Virginia during the Revolutionary War. Indeed work that takes this broader view of class has already forced scholars to think anew. Woody Holton, among others, has persuasively argued that even the coming of the American Revolution was very much a product of class conflict, and in Virginia, no less. Yet class as a tool of historical analysis might be even more useful in studying the war itself, given the economic strains and demands it imposed on different social groups. Concerned elites began mobilizing for war in a manner that reflected a highly articulated class-based vision of society and their anxieties over the effects of possible war on the enslaved class (that is, anxieties to secure their property). But a careful reading of mobilization in the state reveals that white Virginians constantly fought among themselves about who ought to serve and on what terms: conflicts that usually manifested themselves as riots against conscription, resistance to militia callouts, threats of civil disobedience, and even legislative turnover as enfranchised white Virginians took their grievances to the polls. In the end the demands made of various groups during the war forced people from different socioeconomic backgrounds to defend their interests individually, and then often collectively, sometimes coalescing as distinct classes to protect those interests and what they perceived, at times, as their rights. If these different groups were not conscious before the war of their collective interests as classes, in relation to one another, the revolutionary conflict certainly helped make those common interests much clearer.[12]

Ultimately, too, by looking at these contests, historians might better understand why Bland believed that Virginia was on the brink of real revolution. And scholars might also complicate and enrich Morgan's findings about the interrelationship between race, class, and slavery – because race and slavery played a part in the Revolutionary War, though not quite in the way scholars expected. Rebellious enslaved Virginians, for example, helped encourage the British to focus their attention on Virginia at various times throughout the war. Yet in the face of threats from within and without, whites did not unite and rally to the cause; instead, slavery helped to cripple mobilization and divide whites in diverse ways. Throughout the war lower- and middling-class white Virginians did not hesitate to organize collective and sometimes violent resistance to ruling-class measures. Slavery was therefore central to the Revolutionary War in Virginia, but in helping to divide whites, not unite them. Such divisions forced patriot leaders in the new state to finally think about some revolutionary proposals of their own.[13]

When patriot leaders in Virginia turned to the serious business of preparing for war in 1775, their initial proposals reflected a colonial military tradition based on an idea of a white society divided into three orders: gentlemen, the middling sort, and the lower sort.[14] To try to simultaneously rouse popular enthusiasm for the cause and provide for an effective defense, they designed a hierarchy of armed services: they created sixteen battalions of better trained and disciplined elite militia called the minutemen (designed to replace the "independant companies of gentlemen Voluntiers"); they resurrected the regular militia (in which all free whites were expected to serve); and they established two regiments of regular troops who would serve as the Virginia contingent of the newly created Continental army. In creating a hierarchical military organization, patriot leaders in Virginia were gearing up for what was possibly the biggest confrontation they would ever face; they were also following a specific colonial tradition. Virginians had to worry about not only the might of the British army and navy but also the numerous threats from within. The most significant of these challenges came from their own slaves. Enslaved Virginians had panicked white Virginians on several occasions during previous wars. Blacks knew that war among whites presented opportunities for freedom. The imperial dispute only gave black Virginians further hope. Anxious patriot leaders knew that they were vulnerable should war come.[15]

Given the circumstances, most patriot leaders in Virginia wanted to send a clear and forceful message to enslaved Virginians contemplating insurrection or joining Governor Dunmore. They hoped that a semipermanent regular force combined with a reinvigorated militia and an elite group of minutemen would offer a sufficient internal as well as external line of defense. Just to be sure, though, delegates to the revolutionary convention also empowered commanding officers to appoint patrollers from among the militia as needed. Moreover, to try to smother the embers of black rebelliousness before they could ignite, the convention exempted all overseers of four tithables residing on a plantation from any militia service.[16]

In the initial flurry of enthusiasm for war, there should have been little difference between these services. But gentlemen themselves drew the first distinctions. George Mason, the chief architect of the military plan, gave strict instructions to his own son to join only the minuteman service. It was, he explained, "the true natural, and safest Defence of this, or any other free Country" and, as he told George Washington, would be composed of men "in whose Hands the Sword may be safely trusted."

Another prominent patriot, George Gilmer, hoped the new minuteman plan would be "on such footing as essentially to draw in Gent'n of the first property in the Colony" and immediately signed up. In contrast, drawing on the rhetoric of anti-standing army ideology, Mason instructed a friend to tell his son that it was "very contrary to my Inclination" that he should enter into the regular service, and he was "by all Means against it." Mason wanted to encourage the success of the minuteman service, yet he also reflected the common belief and inherited Anglo-American tradition that only the dregs of society would serve in a professional army.[17]

Such attitudes did not bode well for the success of the new military arrangements. Initial mobilization for war exposed preexisting tensions and divisions among white Virginians. Many poorer or smallholding militia members particularly resented the exemptions allowed from the militia, for example. They believed the exemption of overseers shielded wealthier slave owners from military service at the expense of nonslaveholders. Several hundred militia, mainly from the southside, complained about the exemption in petitions sent to the same revolutionary convention that was to decide on independence. Because the law stipulated that a planter could exempt one overseer for every four enslaved Virginians, the petitioners believed that many wealthy planters had "become Overseers that Otherways would not, on purpose to Screen themselves from Fighting in defence of their Country as well as their own Property." Not only were most of them "Strong healthy able bodied Men" but also "many of them [were] possessed of Considerable Property in Lands and Slaves." Class differences were clearly at the forefront of such gendered complaints, and the petitioners did not hesitate to make these explicit. "Many of your Petitioners are poor men with Families that are Incapable of Supporting themselves without our Labour & assistance," they insisted. It was therefore "extreamly hard & no ways equatable or Just that we should be obliged to leave our Families in such a Situation that if ever we

shou'd return again [we] Woud find our Wives & Children disperse'd up & down the Country abeging, or at home a Starving." Whereas the "Overseers are aliving in ease & Affluence," they complained, the petitioners forced to do military duty away from home would be "quite unable to help" their families procure "the Necessaries of life."[18]

Nor did white Virginians flock to the minuteman service. Enlistments were hampered by elites' own admission that gentlemen were not signing up in the numbers expected. Those who joined generally procured commissions as appointed officers in the minute service and were usually appointed by friends and family on presiding county committees. Smallholding farmers were loathe to spend more time than necessary in training and also were galled that appointed officers in the corps – usually gentlemen – were paid up to sixty times more than an enlisted man when they were training or on duty. Patriot leaders and officers had called for such a wide pay disparity to enforce discipline and subordination among the rank and file. But middling white Virginians, living amid a slave society, were hardly reconciled to the idea of subordination. Gilmer, in trying to rally his neighbors to join the minutemen, inadvertently pointed out the problem by using a metaphor that must have infuriated his neighbors. Since "time immemorial," he declared, "every head or chief has had marks of distinction and certain emoluments above those under him … The Custom is so prevalent with ourselves," he pointed out, "that every planter allows his Gang leader certain, indulgences and emoluments above the rest of his slaves." In comparing the new military establishment with the institution of slavery in Virginia, Gilmer in one breath infuriated his neighbors and betrayed the anxieties that many prominent planters felt about the lack of control they had over their enslaved workers and their white inferiors.[19]

Incredibly, protests about the newly resurrected militia and faltering enlistments in the minuteman service came during the crisis that Virginia Governor Dunmore had unleashed with his well-known proclamation of November 1775, declaring all servants and enslaved people belonging to patriot masters free if they would join him in fighting their traitorous masters. Such problems showed that when racial solidarity was most essential, white Virginians had difficulty surmounting class differences. It might have seemed worse to patriot leaders that Dunmore's proclamation had given rise to reports throughout the colony detailing black and white cooperation in defiance of patriot authority. At Isaac Zane's Marlborough Iron Works in Frederick County, white convict servants and enslaved black workers banded together to escape to the British. In Fincastle County in the southwestern corner of Virginia, John Hiell tried to stir up cooperation between white servants and slaves after Dunmore's proclamation. Hiell told "a Servant man" that in about a month "he and all the negroes would get their Freedom." And on Virginia's Eastern Shore, patriot leaders worried that Dunmore's plans to unite "fishermen … all the lower Class of People," and a large enslaved population against the "Committee-Men and other principal People" had worked. They feared that without protection, they would be "exposed to the fury of the People."[20]

Despite such apparent threats from below, middle-class militia showed little inclination to lay aside their own interests for the sake of protecting gentlemen who seemed little inclined to protect themselves. Even something so basic as slave patrols raised class tensions in the early years of the war. In the April 1776 elections to vote for independence, Landon Carter was disgusted to hear that one man was elected after he had exclaimed "agst the Patrolling law, because a poor man was made to pay for keeping a rich mans Slaves in order," Middling and lower-class white Virginians resented the renewed power militia officers had to force them into serving as patrollers. Such reports fueled Carter's anxiety that the coming of independence would mean a heightening of class tensions. Others expressed similar fears in revealing language. One of

Carter's neighbors, Walter Jones, described the electoral politics of late 1775 as a form of "plebeian Infamy." And an officer from Loudoun County, worried about a tenant uprising in that region that had been sparked by military mobilization in the early months of 1776, used the language of the English Revolution when he asked a colleague: "How goes on the spirit of Levelling? Is all quiet?" It was with some relief, then, that patriot leaders formed a new state government in the summer of 1776 and, shortly afterward, watched the dreaded Dunmore sail out of the Chesapeake toward New York.[21]

Resistance to these early mobilization efforts, and particularly the minuteman service – which actually suited Virginia's dispersed and vulnerable settlement patterns – forced patriot leaders to rely almost entirely on an enlarged regular force. By the end of 1776, they had completely scrapped the minuteman service and called for a much larger group of regular soldiers that would serve as a permanent wartime professional army for the protection of the state. To entice recruits they relied less and less on enthusiasm for the cause and more on offers and promises, often unfulfilled, of increasingly generous enlistment bounties and regular pay. Though it was not initially clear, the fledgling state had fallen back on a transatlantic tradition of targeting the unemployed, wage laborers, and the landless poor to fight the wars of the ruling government.

The full class-based contours of elites' military policy became clearer as the demand for soldiers increased. Though few explicitly stated it, most people believed that only the poor and the marginal would or should join the Continental army. New laws exposed and encouraged this general impression. Struggling to raise men for the new Continental regiments demanded by George Washington and Congress at the end of 1776, the new state government passed a law authorizing impressment of the increasing number of "rogues and vagabonds" that they believed besieged the state. The assembly gave justices of the peace and the governor wide powers to imprison and ultimately impress such people into the armed services. The representatives also defined vagabonds quite broadly as any able-bodied men who neglected or refused to pay their public county and parish levies and who had no visible estate. By accepting the very lowest classes, army recruiters also helped to reinforce a general impression that the Continental army was, like the British army, full of the dregs of society. In 1775 the convention had forbidden recruiters to enlist any servants at all, unless they were apprentices who had the written consent of their masters. Yet desperation drove recruiters to enlist anyone that seemed willing to serve. Indentured and convict servants took full advantage.[22]

So, too, did enslaved Virginians. The 1775 prohibition against enlisting servants also applied to them. At some point between late 1775 and early 1777, however, desperate recruiters began allowing at least free blacks into the Virginia line, leading many enslaved Virginians to present themselves to recruiters as freemen. Recruiting officers, desperate to fulfill their quotas of soldiers to gain commissions, were quick to turn a blind eye to such subterfuges and happily accepted black Virginians, free and unfree. The presence of the lowest classes of Virginians – servants and slaves – in the army only reinforced an impression that it was no place for respectable middling sorts, let alone gentlemen, unless in a position of authority.[23]

As General Washington's fortunes around New York went from bad to worse during the winter of 1776–77, he and Congress put considerable pressure on the states to coerce more citizens into the army. Attitudes about who should serve became more explicit as the demand for soldiers increased. Virginians at the continental level, at least, were clear about who ought to be targeted. Richard Henry Lee, a Virginia congressional delegate, told Thomas Jefferson that there were too many "lazy, worthless young Men" in the state who ought to be forced into service. Washington

was more explicit about who ultimately ought to fill the ranks of the army, whatever method they chose to employ. The general felt that the army could only be filled with "the lower Class of People." Though he had hoped they could hold our sufficient inducements for the lower sort to enlist voluntarily, Washington believed that they could not now avoid the "necessity of compelling them to inlist."[24]

The Virginia General Assembly complied with the request, instituting a draft in the spring of 1777. But contrary to suggestions made by Washington and Congress to draft men indiscriminately and allow conscripts a chance to find substitutes, the assembly chose specifically to target the more vulnerable in society. Draftees would not be picked by open lottery but rather picked out by field officers and the four most senior magistrates of each county. If volunteers were not forthcoming, these officials were given the power to "fix upon and draught one man" who, in their opinion, could "be best spared, and will be most serviceable." The new recruits, or picked conscripts, were to serve for a full three years. As one recruiting officer put it later in the year, the draft was designed to force the "expendables" into service or, more explicitly, according to John Chilton, the "Lazy fellows who lurk about and are pests to Society."[25]

If patriot leaders and middling Virginians were content to shift the burden of fighting, the lower sort on whom that burden fell were quick to fight back. Would-be recruits forced patriots to raise bounty money, bargained with their neighbors for their services as substitutes in the militia, and resisted and evaded the draft when coerced into service. In some places they violently resisted any and all attempts to conscript soldiers. In other places, once drafted, they simply deserted and found refuge, usually with friends and family.[26]

Lower-class resistance was so vehement that by early 1778 Virginia legislators were forced to abandon the idea of raising men by a draft altogether and turn, instead, to high bounties and short terms of service. When the assembly made economic enticements the sole inducement to join the army in 1778 and 1779, the inflation of bounty rewards accelerated. By early 1779 Robert Honyman reported that recruiting officers were paying up to $450 more than the prescribed bounty of $300 to procure recruits, By the fall of 1779, the sums given to recruits for the army had reached critical proportions. Because of rising inflation, Edmund Pendleton thought that almost every man enlisted had cost, on average, about £5,000 each.[27]

More generally, a renewed demand for workers combined with the manpower needs of the military meant that wage earners commanded a newfound power over prospective employers. Those who labored for a living could also manipulate the recruiting laws to their own advantage. Potential recruits often found ways to capitalize on the desperation of patriot leaders to raise new troops. They took advantage of the already-generous enlistment schemes to give themselves maximum benefit and return on their risk. They took advantage of spiraling inflation, and they contributed to it. Recruits were also allowed to receive any payments that other men might give to serve in their stead. The evidence suggests that many did all they could to get as much money as possible for their desperately needed services. Even before recruiting began each year, bidding for potential soldiers helped drive up prices. Some recruiting officers had to resort to offering additional incentives to potential recruits, often out of their own pocket. One officer complained that such men had "spoilt the recruiting Service" by offering up to $50 per man. Yet officers were at the mercy of the men they were trying to recruit. Raleigh Colston, the captain of the sloop *Liberty,* learned this lesson when he tried to invoke patriotism as a good reason for his crew to take lower wages. The crew made it clear on what terms they would serve. The spokesman for the crew declared: "Country here or Country there, damn my Eyes and limbs but I'll serve them that give the best wages."[28]

Wealthier Virginians were particularly angry because they had to pay out so much, seemingly for so little. David Jameson complained that, though such exorbitant sums had been paid out to hire recruits, only a temporary and inadequate army had been raised. The bounty money recruits had received, Jameson asserted, was more than enough to secure their services for the duration of the war, instead of a mere eighteen months. He grumbled that it was really "enough for-life." Many gentlemen were furious that ordinary Virginians could and would protect their own interests. In a letter to George Washington in 1778, Pendleton complained about the demands of those he felt ought to bear the burden of military service. The "demon of avarice, and spirit of extortion," he exclaimed, "seem to have expelled the pure patriotism from, the breasts of those who usually compose armies."[29]

The end result of lower-class resistance through the middle years of the war was that the war effort simply ground to a halt. Despite the pleas of continental officials, Virginia legislators failed to put teeth into their recruiting laws through the rest of 1778, 1779, and into 1780. By late May 1778, only 716 of the 8,000 men asked for the previous fall had been raised through the draft or through substitutions. Washington wrote in late May 1778 that out of the 1,500 recruits requested from the previous draft together with the 2,000 men the assembly ordered drafted in February 1778, they had only received 1,242 men. Washington lamented that this was "so horrible a deficiency." Of all the drafts and volunteers ordered raised, Patrick Henry thought that "not one half of the Number voted by the Assembly have got to Camp." One army chaplain wrote definitively, "Virginia makes the poorest figure of any State in the Recruiting way."[30]

As Virginians divided among themselves and hoped for peace, the British, believing themselves at a stalemate in the North, moved to bring the war to the South and open up a new front in the stagnating conflict. More thinly settled than the northern colonies, more vulnerable by sea, more dependent on foreign markets for imports and their exports, and arguably much more valuable to Britain than the northern colonies, the southern colonies loomed large in British thinking in late 1778 and early 1779. Moreover intelligence reports of loyalist support encouraged the British to think that they might make more progress in the southern states than they had in the northern ones. These reports, combined with the knowledge that enslaved Americans might augment British numbers, or at least keep a vulnerable people at home, encouraged the British to think they could more easily subdue the South than the North.[31] It was not until British strategy shifted southward that Virginia leaders again took the war seriously, though they only really did so after the state lost the remnants of its contingent of Continental army soldiers at the fall of Charleston in 1780. The assembly, under mounting pressure from Congress and officers such as George Washington, finally expanded their mobilization efforts. They did this by putting pressure on the middling classes: by requiring them for more extensive militia service and by reinstituting and expanding the draft, this time to include all men.

But middle-class militia members had their own agenda and, unlike their lower-class neighbors, they had the more direct political clout to force it on their elected officials in the assembly. They first demanded that calls on the militia be limited to short terms of service close to home. Most were adamant that they would not serve outside the state, particularly in what they believed to be the dangerous climate of the southern states. Yet middling militiamen were equally insistent that their taxpaying status should exempt them from fighting altogether and that the state ought to spend their tax money on raising a proper army and filling it with their lower-class neighbors. As one group of militia claimed as early as 1776, militia training was now unnecessary because Virginia had "an Army regularly trained," for which the militia were paying. Under these circumstances the

militia ought to be called out only when needed to aid in defense against an invasion and ought not to be called "so frequently from their homes" unless absolutely "necessary." In arguing that the payment of taxes was sufficient sacrifice to secure protection, the militia from Chesterfield adopted a position similar to one taken by middle-class counterparts in England during the Seven Years' War.[32]

[…]

Under a barrage of petitions, the Virginia General Assembly, when forced to reinstitute the draft in early 1780 under the pressure of the British invasion of the South, incorporated these new demands in their recruiting law. In the new law, bounty money raised by militia to hire soldiers would be paid in proportion to taxable property and would contribute toward the militia's next tax assessment. But the new law for recruiting Continental army troops stipulated that everyone with assessable wealth in the county – even those exempted from actual service – had to be included in a division and contribute toward raising bounty money and a soldier. Each division had to have roughly equal amounts of property. Thus any one division would not be composed of a disproportionate number of particularly poor or especially wealthy men.[33]

Most radically, each division was given the power to raise any amount of money – in addition to the state and continental bounties – to try to recruit soldiers to exempt themselves. The legislature did not cap the amount of money each group could raise as an added incentive to recruits. Any extra bounty money pledged to potential recruits would come out of the pockets of everyone in the division, not just the militia who were liable to be drafted. And the money would have to be paid by everyone in equal proportion to their wealth. Moreover the group as a whole was responsible for finding a recruit. The new law had shifted the burden of the draft from the individual to the community, and from people to property. Thus, in reintroducing the draft in Virginia, legislators had given all active militia members the power and means to buy themselves out of service with, in part, the wealth of the often inactive.[34]

The end result of the new law was that for the first time in the war, the loudest complaints about the new draft came from the wealthy. Many well-off Virginians, particularly those who were exempted from actually serving in the militia, were angry that their property was now at the disposal of poorer Virginians to hire recruits and escape the draft. One of the wealthiest men in the state, David Jameson, complained that the recruiting act would prove a "heavy tax" for people such as him. Few men, he believed, would take the risk of being drafted, so they would try to raise as much money within their division as they could. "Who will run the risk of being drafted," Jameson complained, "if he can by taxing his Neighbours procure a Man."[35]

Jameson was, at least in part, right. Many men with little or no taxable property ensured they did not fall prey to the draft. They pushed up the bounty money in a desperate bid to avoid a draft in their division. With the extra money raised in proportion to wealth, the bounty tax would fall heaviest on the wealthiest men. Robert Pleasants, an immensely wealthy Quaker from Henrico County, complained about the militia in his division who actually owned no property. He thought it was "highly unreasonable" that the men who were not liable to pay anything "should have it in their power, to hire a man on any terms they please at my expence, to screen themselves from a draft." Theodorick Bland Senior, another wealthy and prominent Virginian, also complained about the leveling effects of the new draft law. Bland owned property in at least two different counties and had thus been forced to pay out twice. Militia in his Amelia County division had demanded almost £525 from him alone, and his neighbors in his home county had run up a charge of £1,435. On top of this he had also paid £600 for his son's proportion toward a new recruit. With a total bill of more than £2,500, Bland was furious with the assembly's draft law. He expressed his disgust in clear class terms.

The assembly had, he asserted, given too much power to the propertyless, or lower, classes. Legislators had effectively "put the power of taxation into the hands of the very lowest class of people," he claimed. Bland believed there would be only one result in such circumstances; such laws would "reduce the most opulent fortune to a level with that of the inferior class of people."[36]

Despite the popularity of the new recruiting law, the effects were obscured by a renewed British offensive in the South, this time targeted directly at Virginia. Beginning in October 1780, the British mounted a series of devastating raids in the state, which would eventually culminate in the rendezvous of Benedict Arnold and Charles Cornwallis, the near capture of Governor Thomas Jefferson, and the almost complete breakdown of mobilization in Virginia. Throughout the yearlong ordeal, slavery cast a long shadow on events, and the paralysis Virginia experienced helps reveal the extent to which slavery affected mobilization in Virginia and intersected with class and gender.

The British came to Virginia with an eye on the rich resources of the state, which included the thousands of enslaved Virginians who could either be turned into extra plunder or used to help bring the states rebels to their knees. Many enslaved Virginians were eager to encourage the British. As in the past, when the British came calling, the lowest class of Virginians made the best of the opportunity. Though white Virginians complained that the British took enslaved Virginians as plunder, most knew that blacks sought their own freedom. Robert Honyman admitted in May that the British troops, officers and soldiers alike, had "enticed & flattered the Negroes, & prevailed on vast numbers to go along with them, but they did not compel any." Indeed, thought Honyman, enslaved Virginians "flocked to the Enemy from all quarters even from the remote parts."[37]

Though the actual number of enslaved Virginians who sought refuge with the British may have been exaggerated, wealthy Virginia slaveholders were mortified at the prospect of losing everything. Rumors and reports of great losses were rife. Honyman thought that some planters had lost "20, 30, 40, 50, 60 or 70 Negroes besides their stocks of cattle, sheep and horses." The damage the British had done and the losses inflicted on white Virginians in the Piedmont and tidewater sections of the James River, claimed Honyman, were "unspeakable." Along the Potomac and Rappahannock rivers, too, planters suffered from losses of slaves. When the British raided Mount Vernon, seventeen enslaved Virginians fled, including some of Washington's most trusted house servants and artisans. Further south John Banister lost eleven slaves in the first British raid on Petersburg; when the British suddenly returned in early May, the rest of his enslaved population vanished.[38]

Enslaved Virginians ran off in enough numbers that propertied Virginians put the protection of their valuables ahead of the common defense. Many planters began moving their stocks and enslaved population up the country and out of the way of the British. Many patriot leaders also took flight. Edmund Pendleton, Richard Henry Lee, and eventually George Mason were among the more prominent Virginians who abandoned their homes when the British were in the Piedmont. Even Thomas Nelson, who was at the head of the Virginia militia that had turned out, took time during Cornwallis's advance to return to his Hanover County plantation to pack up some of his property and his family and send them to safety. Some, like Pendleton, took as many enslaved Virginians as they could manage to convey.[39]

But many white, usually propertied, Virginians harbored a deep-seated fear that Virginia's enslaved population would not just take the opportunity to flee to the British. They had some firsthand evidence. For example Jack of Botetourt County, who had a previous history of rebellious behavior, tried to poison a Captain Madison and a Major Quick when the British invaded the state. He then set about "enlisting several negroes to raise in arms and join Lord Cornwallis." Jack was to be their captain. After

getting caught, Jack quickly escaped and helped free a number of deserters and Tories who were in chains with him, and he hid out for a number of weeks before being caught again. While in hiding Jack must have struck fear into whites in the area. One man said he was at large, "Sometimes going armed with a Gun and at other times with a Pistol" and "threatening Revenge upon those that apprehended him and those who were Witnesses against him." He was well known to neighbors as a "rebellious Servant and corrupter of other Servants."[40]

With many wealthy Virginians on the run in an effort to save their property, many militia stayed at home during the British invasions. By 1781 most state officials were resigned that militia in the immediate vicinity of British forces simply would not turn out. When the British came calling in Hampton in Elizabeth City County in the fall of 1780, for example, militia officers told their men that "every man who had a Family" could retire and "do the best for them they could." The officers later told the assembly that they had been forced to put the "Personal welfare of their wives Children and themselves with their property" first and make terms with the British. After leading the militia in the lower counties during the British invasion in the fall of 1780, James Innes could only conclude that "no aid of militia could ever be drawn from the part of the Country immediately invaded." Whether trying to protect their property or protect their families from rebellious slaves, middling Virginians were adamant about guarding their patriarchy and independence.[41]

Virginia's lowest class, then, also helped cripple mobilization in the state by keeping white fears alive. Yet the influence of slavery on the course of the Revolutionary War did not end there. Though many historians have assumed that slavery helped unify white communities in times of trouble or stress, the ownership of enslaved Virginians caused deep divisions among whites in wartime. From the start of the war, for example, militia throughout Virginia were quick to point out that slaveholding exacerbated the inequities of military service in different respects. In addition to complaints about wealthy slaveholders making themselves overseers to avoid military service, militia from Chesterfield County also pointed out as early as 1776 that even when elites did their part, military service for nonslaveholders was a much greater burden than for those who owned enslaved Virginians. Absent slave owners still had workers in their fields. In contrast, Chesterfield petitioners claimed, militia service was particularly "burthensome" for the "poorer sort who have not a slave to labour for them." Such complaints grew more common as the demands of war put a greater strain on farmers' abilities to maintain their independence in the face of numerous and intrusive callouts. Even as the British were chasing legislators out of Charlottesville, militia members from counties farther west especially claimed that the planter-dominated legislature did not understand how difficult it was for farmers without slaves to leave their farms for any length, of time. More than one hundred militia members from Pittsylvania County made their gendered worries explicit when they pledged their money, their service, and their supplies to the war effort, but only "in such a manner as would not totally ruin themselves, their Wives and Children." The present recruiting law, they claimed, would do just that, as many of the petitioners were "poor men without a single Slave, with a Wife and many small Children to maintain." Taking such men away from their families, the petitioners asserted, "would reduce them to the most indigent circumstances and hard grinding Want."[42]

Slaveholding, then, particularly toward the end of the war, increasingly became the touchstone for class divisions among white Virginians. Time and again, on different issues surrounding mobilization, militia from across the state, not just slave-poor regions, made claims based on slaveholding inequality. Sometimes their claims implicitly contrasted slaveholders with nonslaveholders. Militia from Botetourt County, for example, explained that yet another militia callout in the spring of 1781 would bring ruin to nonslaveholders especially: "The Season of the year is Such, that to Call on men, with Families, and who have no Other possible means to support themselves and Families but by their own Labour, no other alternative but inevitable Ruin, must be the Consequence, for before their Return the season for Sowing and planting will be over."[43]

At other times, however, militia were explicit about the inequalities in Virginia. In the spring of 1780, for example, Charlotte County militia members, in a petition to the legislature, rendered an explicit analysis of the problem of wartime mobilization by laying bare what they saw as the class-based injustice of military service. They told the assembly that "in the personal services expected from the Citizens of this Commonwealth, the poor among us who scarce obtain a precarious subsistence by the sweat of their brow, are call'd upon as often and bound to perform equal Military duty in defence of their little as the great & oppulent in defence of their abundance." Yet the petitioners were angry that many wealthy Virginians were able to avoid even an equal amount of service. The "great & oppulent," the petitioners asserted, "who contribute very little personal labour in support of their families, often find means to screen themselves altogether from those military services which the poor and indigent are on all occasions taken from their homes to perform in person." What was worse, they claimed, was that slaveholders benefited twice over; whereas nonslaveholding whites – the "poor and laborious," they claimed – risked their lives, their families, and their estates through their personal service in the militia, slaveholding planters exempted themselves from service and grew personally rich on the backs of their slaves' labor. They particularly resented that "the poor who bear the heat and burthen of Military duty" were taxed the same amount as owners of enslaved Virginians were for their laborers who worked, the petitioners claimed, "only to support the extravigance of a Voluptuous master."[44]

Given that slavery helped bring the British to Virginia in the first place, that slavery was at the center of divisions among whites, and that slavery helped cripple mobilization in diverse ways, patriot leaders in the state were presented with a revolutionary dilemma in the latter years of the war. Because fearful middling whites refused to serve in the armed forces and poorer farmers and laborers were resentful of slaveholders' wealth, patriot leaders were forced into thinking about some revolutionary proposals of their own.

In the fall of 1780, Joseph Jones revealed the outlines of the radical new plan to raise a more permanent army with which this article began. The plan showed not only how far the representatives were prepared to go to avoid a draft but also to what extent legislators had listened to class-based complaints that the wealthy in Virginia had not borne their fair share in paying for the war. And, in the end, even the compromise solution reflected a significant concession to poorer Virginians. New recruits who enlisted for the duration of the war – in effect to create the more permanent army George Washington had wanted from the start and that more middling Virginians had begun to demand as the war wore on – were promised a "healthy sound negro" from age ten to thirty or £60 in gold or silver (at the option of the soldier), plus three hundred acres of land to be received at the end of the war. Thus lower-class Virginians were finally able to extract a huge windfall in return for their services to the state. They would get enough land to vote and also receive money enough to establish themselves or an enslaved Virginian to make that land more productive. For their part anxious legislators may have hoped that in addition to raising a more permanent army they were also making a judicious move to create some kind of alliance between poor whites and wealthy slave owners.[45]

In the face of their desperate struggle with the British and their own population, however, some white patriots began exploring yet another, even more radical, alternative. James Madison, sitting as an observer in Congress, believed the idea of giving enslaved Virginians away as bounties was "inhuman and cruel." He thought it would be much better if patriot leaders in Virginia took the more obvious step and allowed the enslaved to serve in the army themselves. "Would it not be as well to liberate and make soldiers at once of the blacks themselves as to make them instruments for enlisting white Soldiers?" he asked Jones. Madison thought that such a move would "certainly be more consonant to the principles of liberty which ought never to be lost sight of in a contest for liberty."[46]

A few months later, a Major Alexander Dick agreed with Madison. Trying desperately to recruit men for one of the three regiments for the new state forces in the spring of 1781, Dick suggested that Virginia formalize an already informal practice of allowing enslaved Virginians to enlist in the army. Dick was having trouble recruiting a new state regiment and believed that there was "no probability of recruiting the Regiment" with white Virginians. In the circumstances Dick, echoing Madison's suggestion, argued that they should consider accepting "likely young negro fellow's" from planters who would then be given compensation. In turn the enslaved recruit would "be declared free upon inlisting for the War at the end of which, they shall be intitled to all the benefits of Conl. Soldiers." Dick believed that the plan would succeed because enslaved soldiers would make for good recruits and, apparently without a trace of irony, felt that the "the men will be equal to any."[47]

Perhaps because Dick had inadvertently pointed out the perils of such a plan, the legislature did not take up his suggestion. Yet Madison and Dick may not have been the only proponents of such a move, for Jones countered Madison's proposal with some seemingly well-rehearsed objections to arming enslaved Virginians. Significantly, Jones thought there were practical reasons for keeping slaves at home. He admitted that enslaved workers were vital to the independence of those who owned them, thus at least implicitly acknowledging the arguments of nonslaveholding militia. Though the freedom of enslaved Americans was an important object, Jones protested that it should be done gradually so the planters could find laborers to replace them, "or we shall suffer exceedingly under the sudden revolution which perhaps arming them wod. produce."[48]

But there were other objections, too. Perhaps white Virginians did not support the move in larger numbers because too many enslaved Virginians had, so far in the crisis, shown little inclination to support their patriot masters. Indeed Jones worried that arming enslaved Virginians might encourage the British to do likewise, as they had done before. No doubt with the nearly anarchic conditions of the fall of 1775 in mind, Jones thought that the British would be tempted once again to "fight us in our own way." They could probably count on full support from enslaved Virginians, unlike white patriots themselves. The consequences, Jones thought, would be disastrous. If the British armed the enslaved, "this wod. bring on the Southern States probably inevitable ruin."[49]

With such a scenario in mind, patriot leaders tried their luck with lower-class whites instead. Giving slaves as a bounty for soldiers was an ingenious response on the part of some elites to avert the kind of ruin Jones talked about and save the state. Yet the idea of taking those slaves from the wealthiest of planters in the state revealed the extent to which class conflicts, defined as conflicts that grew out of economic inequalities, had permeated the political culture of the new state. Taking enslaved Virginians from the wealthiest class was a response to middle-class complaints about having to shoulder too much of the burden of the war. Offering slaves to lower-class whites was a response, in turn, to rising demands from that class of people to be paid adequately for their service. That new recruits would be given not only an enslaved Virginian but also land and thus the vote meant that many elite whites were willing to make at least some sacrifices and concessions to their

middling and lower-class neighbors. The heaviest price for this deal would be paid by enslaved Virginians as well as Native Americans, in whose hands the land promised to new recruits almost certainly lay. Class conflict in Virginia during the Revolutionary War ultimately resulted not in radical solutions such as freeing enslaved Virginians to fight for freedom but rather in more ingenious yet conservative solutions that continued the expropriation of the labor of slaves and the land of Native Americans.

As it turned out, the debate over the new legislation was overshadowed when the British launched another series of devastating raids on Virginia beginning in January 1781. And though historians remember 1781 for George Washington's victory over Charles Cornwallis at Yorktown, it was also the year in which tensions among white Virginians reached the boiling point and the full implications of the previously simmering class divisions became clear. Perhaps the most intriguing aspect of Virginia's mobilization throughout the war, but especially in 1781, is that, despite the immediate threat posed by the British and enslaved Virginians, white Virginians failed to act in concert. Instead they divided and argued among themselves. They passively resisted and verbally protested against militia service, and some went even further. As the British roamed freely across the state in May and June, many militia throughout Virginia actually rioted in protest against military service. Several hundred militia members gathered in places including Augusta, Accomack, Hampshire, and Northampton counties to force local authorities to stop recruiting. In many other places, threats of such collective action were enough to stop worried officials from acting.[50]

Though these riots and protests originated from diverse and sometimes particular causes, several began as a result of the smoldering resentment many poorer and economically vulnerable farmers felt toward wealthy slaveholding planters who had exempted themselves from military service or were quick to flee in the face of British raids. In one of the rare court martial records extant, such economically based grievances were laid bare. Amid a British raid up the Potomac in 1781, the militia of the Northern Neck were called out to defend the region. Instead several militia organized a barbecue in Richmond County to rally support among those who were fed up and unwilling to serve any longer. The barbecue ended in armed conflict against state authorities. The leaders made class-based appeals to their friends and neighbors. One man told authorities that the ringleaders of the conspiracy declared "the Rich wanted the Poor to fight for them, to defend there property, whilst they refused to fight for themselves."[51]

Behind this revealing bravado were men living on the edge. One alleged leader of the barbecue, Edward Wright – described as a "hardworking" but "illiterate" man by authorities – had served often in the patriot militia. Yet in 1781 he found himself unwell and struggling to make ends meet in the face of constant callouts and increasing taxes. He had told another man that he would happily turn out in a few weeks' time after he could lessen his stock to free up basic food stores for his family, and after he returned to full health. In dire circumstances Wright, like others, may also have been tipped over the edge by the numbers of gentlemen in Richmond County who had used their genteel connections to get themselves declared exempt from any militia duty at all on account of their age or health. In a desperate effort to protect his patriarchy, Wright was prepared to incite civil war amid one of the more dense populations of enslaved workers in Virginia. Racial solidarity was no protection against class divisions in Virginia's Revolutionary War.[52]

The Richmond County barbecue was only the tip of the insurrectionary iceberg in 1781. It was also typical of the rampant divisions among white Virginians that crippled mobilization in the state at another key moment in the war. Virginia may have had as many as fifty thousand militia in the state in 1781, but Governors Jefferson and Nelson were unable to concentrate such

a force against Cornwallis. They were plagued by stubborn resistance to militia callouts, even to fight within the state, defending hearth and home. Lower-class and middling Virginians had simply had enough of the rich man's war. When Cornwallis made his fateful decision to move to Yorktown, General Washington made his move. Yet few of his fellow white Virginians were there at the final triumph of the Continental army. Even the best estimates of the number of militia at Yorktown show that perhaps no more than three thousand Virginia militiamen participated in some way, whereas seventy-eight hundred French troops and more than five thousand Continental army troops – mainly from states north of Virginia – played the greatest role. Ironically, even tragically, there may have been, more black Virginians with Cornwallis than white Virginians fighting with Washington.[53]

Close attention to mobilization, then, reveals that, contrary to elites' anxious rhetoric of unity, Virginia was racked by internal divisions, conflicts, and contests, often over the all-important question of who should serve. Acknowledging and identifying these wartime protests is difficult enough; explaining the roots of these divisions is even more problematic. But a careful reading of the protests reveals that these divisions were expressed in terms of the conflicting interests of different groups and the unjust or unequal effect of specific policies. Repeatedly, such divisions occurred along the lines of propertyholding and socioeconomic status. The war made tremendous economic demands on people; how one reacted to these demands was often a reflection of one's economic position.

Such divisions were not always expressed in a consistent and coherent language of class or class consciousness. But historians should not abandon the notion of class as a useful way of understanding the conflicts that clearly divided the state. The Revolution forced white men to recognize (if they had not already) that their apparently unified society was divided by deep-seated and conflicting socioeconomic interests.

As they struggled to give expression to their differences, the men of the time spoke of rich and poor, of freedom and coercion, of manly independence and abjection, of the propertied and propertyless, and of the degrees of material wealth, usually in the form of acres of productive land and numbers of enslaved workers. To interpret what they were trying to say, historians need the vocabulary of class; yet, to understand class in revolutionary Virginia, scholars need to extend and complicate that vocabulary, attending to the locally and chronologically specific, and not simply look for the ghostly antecedents of a nineteenth-century model.

In this respect scholarship on independents and dependents helps modern historians appreciate that some of these struggles at least arose around deeply entrenched gendered notions of the household and household independence in particular. As Kathleen M. Brown has written, for wealthy planters in Virginia, independence and authority emanated from the home or plantation. Elite planters at least dreamed of "hegemonic authority over compliant wives, children, and slaves and of unquestioned political leadership over less privileged men." Though political leadership may not have been so important, the dependence of household members was crucial to the independence of, as Stephanie McCurry puts it, "masters of small worlds," too. Smallholding farmers – those whom McCurry has called "self-working farmers" with few or no slaves to work for them – especially worried about their mastery over the household independence as calls for their military service increased. They protested that their own labor was essential to their household economy. What they were most fearful of, they claimed, was that should they be compelled to serve in the military for longer terms, they might lose their independence by finding on their return that their wives and children were forced to go about, as they put it, "abeging" and "aSlaving." In an important sense, then, manliness was threatened, rather than affirmed, by extended periods of military service, particularly for those who owned insufficient dependents (enslaved Virginians) to maintain white household independence.[54]

These kinds of conflicts demonstrate, too, that slavery, race, and gender are important components of any explanation of wartime disunity in Virginia. Yet they also point to the fact that such explanations are insufficient without thinking about the ways in which class and perceptions of class intersected with race and gender and powerfully shaped what were or became class struggles during the revolutionary conflict. Elite Virginians, for example, acknowledged the importance of household independence and, early in the war, tried to target the lower sort for longer terms of military service, in part because they were not seen to be tied to a household. Elites believed the lower sort had no independence to preserve and no small world to master. But when the demands of the war forced the ruling class to expand their search for soldiers to more independent Virginians, smallholding farmers protested vigorously and sometimes violently. The more that self-working Virginians' ability to protect the household was eroded, the more violent their protests.[55]

Moreover, at various times during the war, many of these poorer and vulnerable yet aspiring middle-class farmers lashed out at their wealthier, slave-owning neighbors. At other times at least some of these same people focused their wrath on those below them, accusing lower-class propertyless whites of fleecing more virtuous citizens. But such class conflict also produced indirect as well as direct changes. The militia's assertion of their own rights, for example, reaffirmed a virulent form of patriarchy in their own households that in some ways transcended class. And enslaved Virginians' active resistance throughout the war brought about a backlash from whites that slowed progress toward emancipation. Indeed postwar proslavery petitions show that white militia not only used enslaved Virginians' resistance to justify continued bondage but also claimed that their own wartime sacrifices and military service, however limited they may have been, justified their claims to keeping a tenacious hold on their property. In doing so middling slaveholding militia, for the first time, used revolutionary principles and their revolutionary participation to legitimate the continued enslavement of black Virginians.[56]

The debate over slavery suggests that if class as a tool of analysis enriches modern historians' understanding of the Revolutionary War in Virginia – and, in particular, the desperate struggles that racked the state and undermined its ability to mobilize effectively – it also enriches scholars' understanding of the immediate consequences of such a massive failing, These conflicts, and the struggles of all to understand and express them, manifested themselves in a direct manner in Virginia's postwar politics, and the deep-seated anxieties of elites about the conduct of war and those troubled postwar politics also shaped the move toward the Constitution. An examination of these events is beyond the scope of this article, but one or two examples are suggestive.

Throughout the war in Virginia, contemporaries had observed what to many seemed a disturbing phenomenon: high legislative turnover in the annual elections. At times such turnover was specifically attributed to discontent over military policies. Interest in elections in the spring of 1780 seemed to be higher than ever. Robert Honyman thought that voting Virginians were more unhappy than ever before and, accordingly, "choose those who make fair promises of altering things for the better." As a result Honyman believed that the quality of those chosen was diminished. "Many of those chosen," he reported, "are men of mean abilities & no rank." It was this same legislature that debated the plans to redistribute enslaved workers from rich Virginians to poorer ones. As Joseph Jones noted to James Madison, it was precisely because of the different composition of the legislature that such a proposal was even on the table, as it was also the same legislature

that Theodorick Bland complained about so vehemently in January 1781.[57]

The high annual legislative turnover slowed in the postwar period, yet the more conflict-ridden politics did not. As Herbert Sloan and Peter Onuf have noted, the "most striking thing about Virginia politics in the postwar period" is that, despite a return to the same leadership of the prewar years, "the harmony so characteristic of the prewar years is completely absent." Postwar politics in the Old Dominion moved away from more consensual practices and marked the "beginnings of sustained conflict between legislative factions over public policy, and of issue-oriented appeals to constituents," usually over the same kind of vital economic issues that divided Virginians during the war: taxes, paper money, and debts. In short they were conflicts over who would pay for the war and how. Increasingly, in the postwar period more legislators were more willing to jeopardize provincial, and eventually national, harmony and consensus for the sake of the interests of their constituents. And learning more about the postwar political conflicts over paper money, debts, and taxes reveals that these, too, were often class conflicts that grew out of real economic inequalities.[58]

Recognizing and acknowledging the conflicts that divided Virginians during and immediately after the war, and the extent to which these conflicts severely crippled mobilization and later the repayments of wartime debts, might also help historians to finally bridge the gap between stories of what John Shy has characterized as the destructive American War of Independence and the so-called constructive political revolution that culminated in the creation of a federal Constitution. For, in the end, the divisive and crippling experience of the war helped produce a small group of committed nationalists who emerged from the patriot leadership. These men were generally those who had occupied important positions during the Revolution, but outside their own states. Significantly, this nationalist cadre included Continental army officers, such as George Washington, who were frustrated by the conflicts at the state level that undermined a successful war effort. Almost every general in the Continental army supported moves to strengthen the powers of the federal government. Precisely because so many people defended their class interests and refused to fight the war on terms proposed by elites, many elites themselves, in turn, began thinking about new ways of organizing society and politics to protect a notion of society that some, at least, believed was increasingly under threat. These new ideas became particularly evident in elites' responses to the massive tax resistance of the 1780s, in which thousands of farmers justified their refusal to pay taxes on the basis of their wartime military service and material sacrifices. Just as the anxiety of some elites found expression in a heightening of postwar political tensions among state legislators, it also pushed some to radically rethink the nature and structure of the fledgling union. The political settlement of 1787 thus reflected the class-based conflict that had been endemic throughout the war.[59]

At the very least, the divisive experience of the war and postwar period – the harsh realities of such a long and protracted war that clearly revealed divisions and internal conflict far more than consensus and shared values – goes far in explaining the change of mood "between the euphoria at Philadelphia in 1776," as Shy has written, "and the hard-headedness of many of the same men, when, eleven years later, in the same city, they hammered out a federal constitution." Class conflicts, then, helped produce a "new realism, almost a cynicism, about human nature that is one key to American political survival after 1783." Clearly, state and national leaders, the most self-conscious class of all, were affected not just by the arguments and debates of their colleagues in the legislative chambers but more fundamentally by the many voices and actions of those they lived with, listened to, and often struggled against. Further recovery of the complex nuances of those debates, dialogues, and struggles throughout this period would not

only enrich but also irrevocably alter modern history's understanding of the founding period.[60]

## Notes

Michael A. McDonnell is a lecturer at the University of Sydney, Australia. He owes many thanks to the diverse people who commented on earlier versions of this article, including conference participants in three different countries, but particularly Terry Bouton, Seth Cotlar, Matthew Dennis, Dallete Hemphill, Katherine Hermes, Ron Hoffman, Woody Holton, Rhys Isaac, Marjoleine Kars, Allan Kulikoff, Simon Middleton, Marcus Rediker, David Rollison, Steve Sarson, Billy Smith, Robert Sweeny, Alan Taylor, Fredrika Teute, Frances Thomas, Peter Thompson, Peter Way, Andy Wood, and Al Young. More recently, new colleagues in the American History reading group in Sydney, and especially Frances Clarke, Clare Corbould, Stephen Robertson, Ian Tyrrell, and Shane White, have helped shape and sharpen this analysis, as have Australianists Kirsten McKenzie and Penny Russell, and students in his seminar class this past semester, titled "Class Struggles in the Atlantic World." He also wishes to thank Richard Waterhouse and the School of Philosophical and Historical Inquiry and the University of Sydney for their generous support of his research.

1  Edmund Pendleton to James Madison, Jan. 1, 1781, Joseph Jones to Madison, Nov. 18, Dec. 1, Dec. 8, 1780, in William T. Hutchinson and William M. E. Rachal, eds., *The Papers of James Madison* (Chicago, 1962), 2: 268, 183, 219, 232–33; Thomas Madison to William Preston, Nov. 30, 1780, in Preston Papers, Virginia Historical Society, Richmond.

2  Theodorick Bland Sr. to Theodorick Bland Jr., Jan. 8, 1781, in Charles Campbell, ed., *The Bland Papers: Being a Selection from the Manuscripts of Colonel Theodorick Bland, Jr.* (Petersburg, Va., 1843), 2: 51. See also A. Drummond to John Coles, Mar. 13, [1781], in Carter-Smith Papers, Alderman Library, University of Virginia, Charlottesville.

3  Ironically, Edmund Morgan's analysis of seventeenth-century Virginia gave historians one of the most powerful and explicit class-based analyses of colonial society ever written

(Morgan, *American Slavery, American Freedom: The Ordeal of Colonial Virginia* [New York, 1975]); see also T.H. Breen, "A Changing Labor Force and Race Relations in Virginia, 1660–1710," in *Puritans and Adventurers: Change and Persistence in Early America* (New York, 1993), 127–47. For gentlemen's reluctance to talk about problems, see Emory G. Evans, "Trouble in the Backcountry: Disaffection in Southwest Virginia during the American Revolution," in *An Uncivil War: The Southern Backcountry during the American Revolution,* ed. Ronald Hoffman, Thad W. Tate, and Peter J. Albert (Charlottesville, Va., 1985), 180 ("dirty linen"). When whites uncovered a conspiracy of enslaved Virginians who were plotting their escape in the event of open hostilities between the British and the Virginians on the eve of the Revolutionary War, James Madison thought it "prudent [that] such attempts should be concealed as well as suppressed [to] prevent the Infection" (Madison to William Bradford, Nov. 26, 1774, in Hutchinson and Rachat, *Papers of James Madison,* 1: 129–30).

4  See, for example, Gary B. Nash, *The Urban Crucible: Social Change, Political Consciousness, and the Origins of the American Revolution* (Cambridge, Mass., 1979); Edward Countryman, *A People in Revolution: The American Revolution and Political Society in New York, 1760–1700* (Baltimore, 1981); Billy G. Smith, *The "Lower Sort": Philadelphia's Laboring People, 1750–1800* (Ithaca, N.Y., 1990); Peter Linebaugh, *The London Hanged: Crime and Civil Society in the Eighteenth Century* (London, 1991); Andy Wood, *The Polities of Social Conflict: The Peak Country, 1520–1770* (Cambridge, 1999); Peter Linebaugh and Marcus Rediker, *The Many-Headed Hydra: Sailors, Slaves, Commoners, and the Hidden History of the Revolutionary Atlantic* (Boston, 2000); Thomas J. Humphrey, *Land and Liberty: Hudson Valley Riots in the Age of Revolution* (DeKalb, Ill., 2004). Important exceptions to the idea of an untroubled or undivided Virginia can be found in Rhys Isaac, *The Transformation of Virginia, 1740–1790* (Chapel Hill, N.C., 1982); Albert H. Tillson Jr., *Gentry and Common Folk: Political Culture on a Virginia Frontier, 1740–1780* (Lexington, Ky., 1991); Woody Holton, *Forced Founders: Indians, Debtors, Slaves, and the Making of the American Revolution* (Chapel Hill, N.C., 1999). In. a similar vein, Stephanie McCurry

writes about the powerful images that have obscured modem readers' view of lower and middling-class farmers in antebellum South Carolina (McCurry, *Masters of Small Worlds: Yeoman Households, Gender Relations, and the Political Culture of the Antebellum South Carolina Low Country* [New York, 1995], esp. 37–45).

5  Even among African American communities, divisions were sometimes pronounced. See Ira Berlin, *Many Thousands Gone: The First Two Centuries of Slavery in North America* (Cambridge, Mass., 1998).

6  Isaac, *Transformation of Virginia;* Philip D. Morgan, *Slave Counterpoint: Black Culture in the Eighteenth-Century Chesapeake and Lowcountry* (Chapel Hill, N.C, 1998). See also Steven Sarson, "Landlessness and Tenancy in Early National Prince George's County, Maryland," *William and Mary Quarterly,* 3d ser., 57, no. 3 (July 2000): 585–94; Sarson, "Similarities and Continuities: Free Society in the Tobacco South before and after the American Revolution," in *Empire and Nation: The American Revolution in the Atlantic World,* ed. Eliga H. Gould and Peter S. Onuf (Baltimore, 2005).

7  See esp. Jack P. Greene, *Pursuits of Happiness: The Social Development of Early Modern British Colonies and the Formation of American Culture* (Chapel Hill, NC., 1988); Greene, "Convergence: Development of an American Society, 1720–1780," in *Diversity and Unity in Early North America,* ed. Philip D. Morgan (London, 1993), 43–72.

8  Allan Kulikoff, "Whither the Progress of Inequality," *WMQ* 57, no. 4 (October 2000): 832 (quotation). Significantly, historians of early America have long been comfortable with acknowledging elite perceptions of class and have spent a great deal of time of late demonstrating the various ways in which elites consciously strove to distance and distinguish themselves from other classes. Despite this literature, however, historians have much more trouble acknowledging lower- and middling-class consciousness. Surely, elites' constant striving to distance themselves from the rest of colonial society did not go unnoticed?

9  E. P. Thompson, *The Making of the English Working Class* (New York, 1963); Simon Middleton, "Rethinking Class in Early America:

The Struggle for Rights and Privileges in Seventeenth-Century New York" (paper presented at the Seventh Annual Omohundro Institute of Early American History and Culture Conference, Glasgow, Scotland, July 12, 2001), 2, wherein Middleton argues that class is tied too forcefully and exclusively to the emergence of what he calls the "immiserating effects of early industrialization" in the nineteenth century and the emergence of a clear and coherent "working class." See also Simon Middleton and Billy G. Smith, introduction to unpublished paper.

10 E. P. Thompson, "Eighteenth-Century English Society: Class Struggle without Class?" *Social History* 3, no. 2 (May 1578): 147–50 (quotations, 147, 150).

11 Eschewing the "proletarianization paradigm," several new Anglo-American scholars, focusing particularly on the middling sort, have drawn on Marxist-feminist theories of standpoint and, in Simon Middleton's words, begun to think about class "in terms of its effects – rather than as a condition embedded in social structures or as a self-consciousness arising (mystically) out of subjective experiences." Thus historians can begin to focus on the "endless variability in the conditions within which classes form and the volatility of interests and struggles that develop with classes" (Middleton, "Rethinking Class in Early America," 3 [quotation]. See also Wood, *Politics of Social Conflict,* chap. 1; Peter Way, "Rebellion of the Regulars: Working Soldiers and the Mutiny of 1763–1764," *WMQ* 57, no. 4 [October 2000]: 765; C. Dallett Hemphill, "Manners and Class in the Revolutionary Era: A Transatlantic Comparison," *WMQ* 63, no. 2 [April 2006]: 345–72).

12 Holton, *Forced Founders.* See also the large corpus of work of Rhys Isaac, who made historians rethink many commonly held assumptions about Virginia society and the Revolution, esp, Isaac, *Transformation of Virginia.* See also Kulikoff, "Death and Rebirth of Class Analysis," 32. My debt to Allan Kulikoff, in particular, for his theoretical work and long-term, perspective is great. In addition to the other works cited in this article, see also Kulikoff, *The Agrarian Origins of American Capitalism* (Charlottesville, Va., 1992), esp. chaps. 1–2; Kulikoff, "Was the American Revolution a Bourgeois Revolution?" in *The*

*Transforming Hand of Revolution: Reconsidering the American Revolution as a Social Movement,* ed. Ronald Hoffman and Peter J, Albert (Charlottesville, Va., 1996), 58–89; Kulikoff, "Revolutionary Violence and the Origins of American Democracy," *Journal of the Historical Society* 1, no. 1 (April 2002): 229–60.

13 To appreciate these challenges, historians must first acknowledge elite denials of divisions for what they were – a self-reassuring rhetoric designed to try to isolate the disaffected and promote unity in an otherwise disunited society – and begin to pay much more attention to the grievances of those who protested against elite attempts to mobilize for war. When they discussed it, most gentlemen dismissed protests as self-interested and unpatriotic, merely the actions of a small but vocal group of the disaffected, or a few disgruntled Tories who could and should be ignored. A more subtle reading of the conflicts that racked Virginia reveals, however, that if many of the men labeled as Tories were not prepared to fight for the patriots, neither were they prepared to die for the British. In times of war, as scholars have learned again only too recently, the first casualty is usually a fair and adequate airing and representation of dissenting opinions and views. For a look at the language of loyalty, see Michael A. McDonnell, "A World Turned 'Topsy Turvy': Robert Munford, *The Patriots,* and the Crisis of the Revolution in Virginia," *WMQ* 61, no, 2 (April 2004); 235–70. For a look at the extent of so-called loyalism in Virginia, see esp. Adele Hast, *Loyalism in Revolutionary Virginia: The Norfolk Area and the Eastern Shore* (Ann Arbor, Mich., 1982); Evans, "Trouble in the Backcountry."

14 Elites and others in Virginia did not always use a specific language of class. But as Keith Wrightson, David Cannadine, and others have shown, the early modern era was a period of transition in the kinds of language used by contemporaries to describe their views of society. At least three kinds of descriptions were in use and would gradually merge into a "discourse of class" by the mid- to the end of the eighteenth century. These characterizations included an idea of society as finely graded hierarchies or ranks (that had evolved from the medieval notion of the three estates) comprised of "sorts of people": usually the "better sort" versus the "meaner

sort" or "poorer sort" and, at least since the mid-seventeenth century, the "middling sort." Such language choices overlapped in their use, were "conceptually muddled, but … admirably flexible," and each was used to characterize social relations and inequalities even as a more specific class discourse was emerging in the eighteenth century (see esp. Wrightson, "Class," in *The British Atlantic World, 1500–1800,* ed. David Armitage and Michael J. Braddick [Basingstoke, Eng., 2002], 131–38 [quotations, 134–36]; see also Cannadine, *The Rise and Fall of Class in Britain* [New York, 1999], esp. chap. 1).

15  Fairfax County Militia Association, (Sept. 21, 1774], in Rutland, *Papers of George Mason,* 1:2 11 ("gentlemen Voluntiers"). See esp. William Lee to R. C. Nicholas, Mar. 6, 1775, in Worthington Chauncey Ford, ed., *Letters of William Lee, 1766–1783* (Brooklyn, N.Y., 1851), 1: 144; James Madison to William Bradford, Nov. 26, 1774, in Hutchinson and Rachal, *Papers of James Madison,* 1: 129–30; Gerald W. Mullin, *Flight and Rebellion: Slave Resistance in Eighteenth-Century Virginia* (New York, 1971); Peter H. Wood, "The Changing Population of the Colonial South: An Overview by Race and Region, 1685–1790," in *Powhatan's Mantle: Indians in. the Colonial Southeast,* ed. Wood, Gregory A. Waselkov, and M. Thomas Hatley (Lincoln, Neb., 1989), 38; Sylvia R. Frey, *Water from the Rock: Black Resistance in a Revolutionary Age* (Princeton, N.J., 1991); James Titus, *The Old Dominion at War: Society, Politics, and Warfare in Late Colonial Virginia* (Columbia, S.C., 1991), 75–76; Wood, "'Liberty is Sweet': African-American Freedom Struggles in the Years before White Independence," in Young, *Beyond the American Revolution,* 154, 160; Holton, *Forced Founders,* 141, 248.

16  Robert L. Scribner and Brent Tarter, eds., *Revolutionary Virginia: The Road to Independence* (Charlottesville, Va., 1977), 3: 406, 463, 466, 471, 476; William Waller Hening, ed., *The Statutes at Large; Being a Collection of all the Laws of Virginia* … (1821; repr., Charlottesville, Va., 1969), 9: 27–35.

17  George Mason to Martin Cockburn, Aug. 5, 1775, in Rutland, *Papers of George Mason,* 1: 145–46 (quotations, 245); Mason to George Washington, Oct, 14, 1775, ibid., 1: 255–56; George Gilmer to Charles Carter, July 15, 1775,

in R. A. Brock, ed., *Miscellaneous Papers, 1672–1865 … in the Collections of the Virginia Historical Society* … (Richmond, Va., 1887), 91; Gilmer, Commonplace Book entry (summer 1775), ibid., 90. See also Gilmer to Thomas Jefferson, [July 26 or 17, 1775], in Julian P. Boyd, ed., *The Papers of Thomas Jefferson* (Princeton, N.J., 1950), 1: 238. For studies of this martial tradition, see Morgan, *American Slavery, American Freedom.,* 340; E. Wayne Carp, "Early American Military History; A Review of Recent Work," *VMHB* 94, no. 3 (July 1986); 272; Don Higginbotham, "The Military Institutions of Colonial America: The Rhetoric and the Reality," in *War and Society in Revolutionary America: The Wider Dimensions of Conflict* (Columbia, S.C., 1988), 19; Titus, *The Old Dominion at War,* 4, 59, 80, 98–99.

18  "Petition of Amelia County Militiamen," [May 23, 1776], in Scribner and Tarter, *Revolutionary Virginia,* 7: 236–39; Proceedings of the Fifth Virginia Convention, June 4, 1776, ibid., 7; 349; "Petition of Inhabitants of Lunenburg County," [Apr. 26, 1776], ibid., 6: 474–77 ("Overseers that Otherways," 475). See also Mecklenburg County Petition, May 13, 1776, ibid., 7: 114–15; see also Proceedings of the Fifth Virginia Convention, May 10, 177 (3, ibid., 7: 87, for a similar petition from Chesterfield County (the actual petition has never been found); Hening, *Statutes at Large,* 9: 89, 18, 31. Allan Kulikoff discusses the struggle over exemptions of overseers and its significance in Kulikoff, "American Revolution, Capitalism, and Formation of the Yeoman Classes," 80–119.

19  Charles Lee and George Washington later noted that a wide pay gap was essential to military discipline and subordination in the ranks. If an officer was in no way distinguished, Washington argued, his men would "consider, and treat him as an equal; and … regard him no more than a broomstick" (Washington to the President of Congress, Sept. 24, 1776, in, John C. Fitzpatrick, ed., *The Writings of George Washington from the Original Manuscript Sources, 1745–1799* [Washington, D.C., 1932], 6: 108–9 (quotation, 110); Lee to Benjamin Rush, Oct. 10, [1775], in *The Lee Papers, Vol, 1:1754–1776,* in *Collections of the New-York Historical Society for the Year 1871* [New York, 1871], 212; General Orders, Apr, 3, 1776, in "Orderly Book of the Company of Captain George Stubblefield, Fifth Virginia

Regiment, from March 3, 1776, to July 10, 1776, Inclusive," in Brock, *Miscellaneous Papers, 1672–1865,* 159; "Address of George Gilmer to the Inhabitants of Albemarle," ibid., 126, 128). For a full account of the minuteman failure, see Michael A. McDonnell, "Popular Mobilization and Political Culture in Revolutionary Virginia: The Failure of the Minutemen and the Revolution from Below," *Journal of American History* 85, no. 3 (December 1998): 946–81.

20 "Dunmore, Proclamation, Nov. 7, 1775," in Scribner and Tarter, *Revolutionary Virginia,* 4: 334–35; "To the Public," "Thirty Dollars Reward," [Williamsburg] *Virginia Gazette* (Dixon and Hunter), June 15, Nov. 22, 1776. See also "Norfolk, September 20," notice for Plìm, *Va. Gaz.* (Dixon and Hunter), Sept, 23, 1775; Thomas Parramore and John Bowdoin Jr. to the Committee of Safety, Apt. 23, 1776, in Scribner and Tarter, *Revolutionary Virginia,* 6: 449; Fincastle County Committee Proceedings, Jan. 10, 1776, ibid., 5: 376, 382 n, 28; Memorial of John Hiell, May 11, Nov. 23, 1785, in Audit Office 13/31, Public Records Office, London. White Virginians were besieged on all sides by reports of cooperation between rebellious slaves and disgruntled whites. Reports emanating from Maryland were particularly worrying. See, in particular, Ronald Hoffman, *A Spirit of Dissension: Economics, Politics, and the Revolution in Maryland* (Baltimore, 1973), 147–48; Committee of Northampton County to the President of the Continental Congress, Nov. 25, 1775, in Scribner and Tarter, *Revolutionary Virginia,* 4: 468–69. See also Accomack County Committee to the Delegates of the Proceedings of the Fourth Virginia Convention, Nov. 30, 1775, ibid., 4: 498; John Gollete to Lord Dunmore, Dec 20, 1775, ibid., 5: 198, 204 n. 3; Patrick Henry to Edmund Pendleton, Dec. 13, 1775, ibid., 5: 117; Petition of Inhabitants of Norfolk and Princess Anne Counties, [Jan. 8, 1776], ibid., 5: 362–63, Proceedings of the Fourth Virginia. Convention, Jan. 13, 1776, ibid., 5: 396–97.

21 Walter Jones to Landon Carter, Oct. 14, 1775, in Sabine Hall Collection, University of Virginia. For an account of the circumstances surrounding this episode, see Michael A. McDonnell, *The Politics of War: Race, Class, and Conflict in Revolutionary Virginia,* chap. 5, forthcoming. James Hendricks

to Leven Powell, [June] 5, 1776, in Robert C. Powell, ed., *A Biographical Sketch of Col. Leven Powell* (Alexandria, Va., 1877), 85. For a full account of the Loudoun Country uprising, see Woody Holton and Michael A. McDonnell, "Patriot vs. Patriot: Social Conflict in Virginia and the Origins of the American Revolution," *Journal of American Studies* 34, no. 2 (August 2000): 231–56. Landon Carter to George Washington, May 9, 1776, in W. W. Abbot and Dorothy Twohig, eds., *The Papers of George Washington, Revolutionary War Series* (Charlottesville, Va., 1991), 4: 236–37, 140, 240 n. 5. For the coming of independence and the reestablishment of government as a relief to patriot leaders, see Holton, *Forced Founders;* McDonnell, *Politics of War,* esp. chap. 7. Scholars have been influenced by an older, more patriotic scholarship, reinforced by Charles Royster's powerful image of the *rage militaire* that gripped the colonies in 1775–76, in Royster, *A Revolutionary People at War: The Continental Army and American Character, 1775–1783* (Chapel Hill, N.C., 1979), and backed up by detailed New England studies such as Robert A. Gross, *The Minutemen and Their World* (New York, 1976). The extent of the *rage militaire* in places such as Virginia remains suspect. See McDonnell, *Journal of American History* 85: 946–81.

22 By mid-1777 George Washington believed that the Virginia line of the Continental army was full of convict servants purchased from their masters by recruiting officers, "Convict Servants," he explained to Congress, "compose no small proportion of the Men from the Upper and more interior Part of that State" (Washington to the President of Congress, May 13, 1777, in Fitzpatrick, *Writings of George Washington,* 8: 56; Nicholas Cresswell, *The Journal of Nicholas Cresswell* [London, 1925], 176, 180, 186–87 [Dec. 14, 1776, Jan. 7, Mar. 3, Mar. 10, 1777]). The assembly formalized the practice of enlisting servants in May 1777 when it allowed recruiting officers to enlist servants and apprentices, apparently without their masters' consent (see Hening, *Statutes at Large,* 9: 12, 216–17, 175–76).

23 Hening, *Statutes at Large,* 9: 280. By May 1777 enough enslaved Virginians had run away and joined the army to alarm the assembly. Legislators complained that "several negro slaves" had deserted their masters and enlisted,

and they tried to close the loophole by declaring the practice of enrolling black or mulatto Virginians unlawful unless they produced a certificate affirming their free status from a local justice of the peace. In doing so they gave official sanction to the practice of enrolling free blacks into the army, a practice not adopted in Maryland until 1780 and not adopted at all south of Virginia. They also opened the door for enslaved Virginians to gain their freedom from their masters by offering to serve as substitutes for them if they were drafted (see Benjamin Quarles, *The Negro in the American Revolution* [Chapel Hill, N.C., 1961], 56–57).

24 Richard Henry Lee to Thomas Jefferson, Apr. 29, 1777, in Boyd, *Papers of Thomas Jefferson,* 2: 13–14; George Washington to Patrick Henry, May 17, 1777, in Fitzpatrick, *Writings of George Washington,* 8: 77–78.

25 Hening, *Statutes at Large,* 9: 275–80; Diary of Robert Honyman, Jan. 2, 1776–Mar. 11, 1782 (see esp. Aug. 29, 1777), Alderman Library, University of Virginia (on microfilm); Edmund Pendleton to William Woodford, June 28, 1777, in David John Mays, ed., *The Letters and Papers of Edmund Pendleton, 1734–1803* (Charlottesville, Va., 1967), 1: 215; John Chilton to his brother [Charles Chilton?], Aug. 11, 1777, in Keith Family of Woodburn, Fauquier Co., Papers, Virginia Historical Society. The field officers and justices were also responsible for pooling their own money and raising a man themselves. Ironically, advertisements for deserters may have also contributed to faltering voluntary enlistments in the army, since they were very similar in tone to advertisements for runaway servants and slaves and painted a graphic picture of the motley crew who were compelled and coerced into the army.

26 For details of lower-class resistance in 1777 and 1778, see McDonnell, *Politics of War,* chaps. 8–9. See also McDonnell, "Fit for Common Service? Class, Race and Recruitment in Revolutionary Virginia," in *Revolutionary War and Society,* ed. John P. Resch and Walter Sargent (DeKalb, Ill., 2006).

27 Diary of Robert Honyman, Mar. 12, 1779, Alderman Library, University of Virginia; Arthur Campbell to Patrick Henry, Mar. 15, 1779, in Wm. P. Palmer, ed., *Calendar of Virginia State Papers and other Manuscripts, 1652–1781, Preserved in*

*the Capital at Richmond* (Richmond, Va., 1875) 1: 317; Edmund Pendleton to James Madison, Sept. 25, 1779, in Mays, *Letters and Papers of Edmund Pendleton,* 1: 308–9.

28 Col. Digges to Theodotick Bland, Sept. 16, 1777, in Campbell, *Bland Papers,* 1; 69; Granville Smith to Leven Powell, Aug. 18, 1777, in "The Leven Powell Correspondence, 1775–1787," *John P. Brunch Historical Papers of Randolph-Macan College* 2 (June 1902): 125; Raleigh Colston to William Aylett, Oct. 24, 1777, in Selby, *Revolution in Virginia,* 172. The aggrieved captain thought the crew were "a sett of unfeeling animals." As the Virginia legislature continued to print money to pay the large bounties it promised and other wartime costs, prices for goods and also for military labor rose quickly. As early as January 1777, Robert Honyman reported that "every thing rises exceedingly in price, owing to the immense quantity of paper money, & likewise to the precariousness of its credit" (Diary of Robert Honyman, Jan, 16, 1777, Alderman Library, University of Virginia. See also Apr. 10, 1777). In 1778 Lund Washington also noted that it was difficult to find seamen to outfit a privateer in his possession because they were in such high demand. He was furious that he had to negotiate so much with a local carpenter (ibid., June 6, 1778; L. Washington to George Washington, Mat. 18, Apr. 1, 1778, Library of Virginia, see also Sept. 2, 1778; H. R. McIlwaine, ed., *Legislative Journals of the Council of Colonial Virginia* [Richmond, Va., 1918], 2: 99, 112–13 [Mar. 7, Mar. 30, 1778]). On labor shortages in the mid-Atlantic region during the war, see esp. Michael V. Kennedy, "The Home Front during the War for Independence: The Effect of Labor Shortages on Commercial Production in the Mid-Atlantic," in *A Companion to the American Revolution,* ed. Jack P. Greene and J. R. Pole (Maiden, Mass., 2000), 332–41.

29 David Jameson to James Madison, Sept. 20, 1780, in Hutchinson and Rachal, *Papers of James Madison,* 2: 94; Edmund Pendleton to Madison, Sept. 25, 1780, Pendleton to George Washington, Dec. 22, 1778, in Mays, *Letters and Papers of Edmund Pendleton,* 1: 309, 276–77. For "demon of avarice," see Pendleton to Washington, May 21, 1778, in John Robert Sellers, "The Virginia Continental Line, 1775–1780" (Ph.D. diss., Tulane University, 1968), 289. See also Diary of

Robert Honyman, June 6, 1778, Feb. 15, 1779, Alderman Library, University of Virginia.

30 George Washington to Richard Henry Lee, May 25, 1778, in Fitzpatrick, *Writings of George Washington,* 11: 451. See also ibid., 11: 438 n. 43; Patrick Henry to Henry Laurens, June 18, 1778, in Hutchinson and Rachal, *Papers of James Madison,* 1: 245; David Griffith to Leven Powell, June 3, 1778, in Powell, *Biographical Sketch of Col. Leven Powell,* 79; Lee to Thomas Jefferson, May 2, May 3, 1778, in Boyd, *Papers of Thomas Jefferson,* 2: 176–77. See also Baylor Hill to Theodorick Bland, May 5, 1778, in Bland Family Papers, Virginia Historical Society. The draft also short-circuited the volunteer scheme. In particular the high prices paid by many counties and individuals to induce men to serve in their stead or as part of the county quota drove up bounties generally. Potential recruits simply refused to volunteer for the armed forces when they could sell their services to their neighbors for much higher prices. Robert Honyman noted in mid-March 1778 that recruiting for the volunteer scheme "scarce advances at all." There were "none at all offering for that service" (Diary of Robert Honyman, Mar. 15, 1778, Alderman Library, University of Virginia).

31 Don Higginbotham, *The War of American Independence: Military Attitudes, Policies, and Practice, 1763–1789* (New York, 1971), 352–54.

32 Proceedings of the Fifth Virginia Convention, May 7, 1776, in Scribnet and Tarter, *Revolutionary Virginia,* 7: 47; Hening, *Statutes at Large,* 9: 140; Eliga H. Gould, "To Strengthen the King's Hands: Dynastic Legitimacy, Militia Reform, and Ideas of National Unity in England, 1745–1760," *Historical Journal* 34, no. 2 (June 1991): 329–48; Gould, *The Persistence of Empire: British Political Culture in the Age of the American Revolution* (Chapel Hill, N.C., 2000), esp. 72–105.

33 Hening, *Statutes at Large,* 10: 257–62.

34 Ibid. The legislature also targeted pacifists, including Quakers and Mennonites, who were now expected to carry the full costs of finding substitutes.

35 David Jameson to James Madison, Aug. 13, 1780, in Hutchinson and Rachal, *Papers of James Madison,* 2; 58.

36 Robert Pleasants thought that when his neighbors believed themselves safe from a draft, they "don't

... feel for others." He had heard that one of the men in his division had announced he would give £50,000 for a recruit "rather than submit to a draft" (Pleasants to Col. Turner Southall, Sept. 3, 1780, in Robert Pleasants of Curles, Henrico County, Letterbook, Library of Virginia). Theodorick Bland Sr. to Theodorick Bland Jr., Oct. 21, 1780, in Campbell, *Bland Papers,* 2: 37–38.

37 Extract of Court Records, Prince William County, [June 7, 1781], Virginia Legislative Pendons, Library of Virginia; Diary of Robert Honyman, May 11, June 1, June 5, July 22, 1781, Alderman Library, University of Virginia. See also *Journal of the House of Delegates of Virginia* (Charlottesville, Va., 1781), 14; H. J. Eckenrode, *The Revolution in Virginia* (1916; repr., Hamden, Conn., 1964), 259; Edmund Pendleton to James Madison, May 7, 1781, in Mays, *Letters and Papers of Edmund Pendleton,* 1: 354; Selby, *Revolution in Virginia.,* 274; Frey, *Water from the Rock,* 156–57.

38 Diary of Robert Honyman, May 11, May 27, 1781, Alderman Library, University of Virginia; John Banister to Theodorick Bland, May 16, 1781, in Campbell, *Bland Papers,* 2: 68–70; Richard Henry Lee to William Lee, July 15, 1781, in James Curtis Ballagh, ed., *The Letters of Richard Henry Lee* (1914; repr., New York, 1970), 2: 242; R. H. Lee to [George Washington], Sept. 17, 1781, ibid., 2: 256; Selby, *Revolution in Virginia,* 175; Frey, *Water from the Rock,* 159, 167; Berlin, *Many Thousands Gone,* 259. Cassandra Pybus does a good job separating rhetoric from reality regarding the number of enslaved Virginians who fled to the British in Pybus, "Jefferson's Faulty Math: The Question of Slave Defections in the American Revolution," *WMQ* 62, no. 1 (April 2005): 243–64. The exaggerated accounts given by contemporaries, however, raise intriguing questions about the perceptions and magnified fears of planters during the crisis.

39 Diary of Robert Honyman, May 27, May 30, 1781, Alderman Library, University of Virginia; Richard Henry Lee to Arthur Lee, June 4, 1781, in Ballagh, *Letters of Richard Henry Lee,* 2: 230; Edmund Pendleton to James Madison, July 6, July 23, 1781, in Mays, *Letters and Papers of Edmund Pendleton,* 1: 365, 367; George Mason to Pearson Chapman, May 31, 1781, in Rutland, *Papers of George Mason,* 2: 688; Emory G. Evans, *Thomas Nelson and the Revolution in Virginia* (Williamsburg,

Va., 1978), 100–101; Selby, *Revolution in Virginia-,* 271–72.; Frey, *Water from the Rock,* 166.

40 Contrary to usual practice, locals demanded that the court execute Jack and make him "an example of Justice and not of Mercy" (Palmer, *Calendar of Virginia State Papers,* 1: 477–78; Patrick Lockhart to Governor Nelson, Nov. 16, 1781, ibid., a: 604–5).

41 Elizabeth City County Petition, [Mar. 8, 1781], Virginia Legislative Petitions, Library of Virginia; James Innes to Thomas Jefferson, Oct. [21?], 1780, in Boyd, *Papers of Thomas Jefferson,* 4: 55. The problem seems to have been widespread. See, for example, the General Assembly of North Carolina to Jefferson, Feb. 14, 1781, ibid., 4: 610–11.

42 Proceedings of the Fifth Virginia Convention, May 7, 1776, in Scribner and Tarter, *Revolutionary Virginia,* 7: 47; Hening, *Statutes at Large,* 9: 140; Gould, *Persistence of Empire,* esp. 72–105; Gould, *Historical Journal* 34; 329–48. For "most indigent circumstances," see Pittsylvania County Petition, [June 19, 1781], Virginia Legislative Petitions, Library of Virginia. See also Amherst County Petitions, [May 19, 1781], ibid.

43 George Skillern to Jefferson, Apr. 14, 1781, in Boyd, *Papers of Thomas Jefferson,* 5: 449–50.

44 Charlotte County Petition, [May 26, 1780], Virginia Legislative Petitions, Library of Virginia.

45 See Joseph Jones to James Madison, Nov. 18, 1780, in Hutchinson and Radial, *Papers of James Madison,* 2: 182–83; undated bill, Legislative Department, Rough Bills, Library of Virginia (brought to my attention by Brent Tarter at the Library of Virginia). Hening, *Statutes at Large,* 10: 326–37.

46 James Madison to Joseph Jones, Nov. 28, 1780, Jones to Madison, Dec. 8, 1780, in Hutchinson and Rachal, *Papers of James Madison,* 2: 209, 233. The editors note that Madison intended this part of his letter for publication. Maryland leaders authorized the enlistment of enslaved men into the army in their legislative session in the fall of 1780. The following year, however, they stopped short of raising an entire regiment of enslaved Marylanders (ibid., 2: 210 n. 1; Quarks, *Negro in the American Revolution,* 56–57).

47 Alexander Dick to the Speaker of the House, May 11, 1781, box 2, Executive Communications, Library of Virginia.

48 Edmund Pendleton to James Madison, Jan. 1, 1781, Joseph Jones to Madison, Dec. 8, 1780, in Hutchinson and Rachal, *Papers of James Madison,* 2: 268, 232–33.

49 Joseph Jones to James Madison, Dec. 8, 1780, in Hutchinson and Rachal, *Papers of James Madison,* 2: 23–33.

50 For a full account of the riots and protests of 1781, see McDonnell, *Politics of War,* chap. 13.

51 Testimony of Vincent Redman and others, "Proceedings of a General Court Martial," June 18, 1781, in Executive Papers, Library of Virginia.

52 Testimony of William Bernard and others, "Proceedings of a General Court Martial," June 19, 1781, ibid. For a full account of the insurrections and problems of mobilization in 1781, see McDonnell, *Politics of War,* chap. 12.

53 Robert Honyman, who raced to Yorktown to see the showdown between George Washington and Charles Cornwallis, was disappointed with the small number of Virginia troops he found there. He believed that there were "but few" in the camp before York and no more than about fifteen hundred of the estimated fifteen thousand troops he saw there were militia members. Most, he reckoned, were French troops (Diary of Robert Honyman, Sept. 3, Sept. 5, Sept. 15, Oct. 7, Oct. 15, 1781, Alderman Library, University of Virginia). William Davies made the estimate of the total number of militia members available based on returns available to him at the war office in July 1781. He included all militiamen east of the Allegheny Mountains (see Davies to David Jameson, July 14, 1781, in Palmer, *Calendar of Virginia State Papers,* 2: 219). For militia members not staying the course, see Evans, *Thomas Nelson,* 117–18; Davies to Thomas Nelson, Sept, 15, Oct. 10, 1781, in War Office Orders [Letters], Aug. 15–Nov. 1, 1781, Library of Virginia; Nelson to Davies, Sept. 19, 1781, in H. R. McIlwaine, ed., *Official Letters of the Governors of the State of Virginia* (Richmond, Va., 1929), 3: 59; James Clay to Nelson, Sept. 13, 1781, in Executive Papers, Library of Virginia. For the number of enslaved Virginians with Cornwallis and the British, see Pybus, *WMQ 62;* 256–57.

54 Kathleen M. Brown, *Good Wives, Nasty Wenches, and Anxious Patriarchs: Gender, Race, and Power in Colonial Virginia* (Chapel Hill, N.C., 1996), 321. Brown noted that Virginia gentlemen secured their power through five sources: land ownership, control over sexual access to women,

rights to the labor of slaves and servants, formal access to political life, and the ability to create and manipulate symbols signifying these other sources of power (323–27, 347). For enslaved Virginians and early royal efforts to subdue the patriots, see Holton, *Forced Founders,* esp. chap. 5; McCurry, *Masters of Small Worlds,* 50.

55  For the importance and centrality of patriarchy and the household economy, see esp, McCurry, *Masters of Small Worlds,* as well as Alice Kessler-Harris, "Treating the Male as Other': Redefining the Parameters of Labor History," *Labor History* 34, nos. 2–3 (Spring–Summer 1993): 202. Patriarchy is key. Elites' acknowledgment of patriarchy's being almost as important as property in creating, and co-opting, a citizenry of virtuous republicans can be seen in George Mason's constitutional proposal to enfranchise fathers with three children to support (see Rutland, *Papers of George Mason,* 1: 303).

56  Some middle-class demands were transatlantic in scope. As Peter Way has shown, the British army was very much a protocapitalist organization (Way, *WMQ* 57). And, as Eliga Gould has discovered in Britain, middle-class taxpayers there demanded the right to be armchair citizens and exempted themselves from military service (Gould, *Persistence of Empire*). As Allan Kulikoff notes, farmers and artisans not only struggled with great planters and land speculators for control over their land and property but also supplied essential support for slavery and the regulation of laborers and servants. Drawing on Eric Olin Wright's work, Kulikoff notes that the middle classes "can be dominant and subordinate, exploited and exploiting. To maintain their grip on property, they make complex interclass alliances, tying themselves to rulers or – less often – to classes beneath them" (Kulikoff, *WMQ* 57: 832). For postwar, proslavery petitions, see Fredrika Teute Schmidt and Barbara Ripel Wilhelm, "Early Proslavery Petitions in Virginia," *WMQ* 30, no. 1 (January 1973): 133–46.

57  Diary of Robert Honyman, Dec 20, 1779, Apr. 15, 1780, Alderman Library, University of Virginia (see also July 4, 1780). Edmund Pendleton to James Madison, Jan. 1, 1781, Joseph Jones to Madison., Nov. 18, Dec. 2, Dec. 8, 1780, in Hutchinson and Rachal, *Papers of James Madison,* 2: 268, 183, 219, 232–33; Thomas Madison to William Preston, Nov. 30, 1780, in Preston Papers, Virginia Historical Society.

58  See Herbert Sloan and Peter Onuf, "Politics, Culture, and the Revolution in Virginia: A Review of Recent Work," *VMHB* 91, no. 3 (July 1983): 280, 279. See also Norman K. Risjord, *Chesapeake Politics, 1781–1800* (New York, 1978), and more generally, the revealing findings of Woody Holten, "'Divide et Impera': *Federalist 10* in a Wider Sphere," *WMQ* 62, no. 2 (April 2005): 175–212, and esp. Holton, "'From the Labours of Others': The War Bonds Controversy and the Origins of the Constitution in New England," *WMQ* 61, no. 2 (April 2004): 271–316.

59  The link between army officers and Federalists is an old one, but the reasons for this connection have been less well explored. See Stanley Elkins and Eric McKitrick, *The Founding Fathers: Young Men of the Revolution* (Washington, D.C., 1962), but for a more recent take on this idea, see Don Higginbotham, "War and State Formation in Revolutionary America," in Gould and Onuf, *Empire and Nation.*

60  For John Shy's comments, see Shy, "American Society and Its War for Independence," in *A People Numerous and Armed: Reflections on the Military Struggle for American Independence* (New York, 1976), 119, 131–32. For an extended rumination on this theme, see Michael A. McDonnell, "National Identity and the American War for Independence Reconsidered," *Australasian Journal of American Studies* 20, no. 1 (July 2001): 3–17. That article owes a great deal to the suggestive insights of John Murrin, "Roof without Walls: The Dilemma of American National Identity," in *Beyond Confederation: Origins of the Constitution and American National Identity,* ed. Richard Beeman, Stephen Botein, and Edward C. Carter (Chapel Hill, N.C., 1987). For two other suggestive outcomes of tying the war years together with the postwar years, see Saul Cornell's nuanced and class-based evaluation of Anti-Federalism, in Cornell, *The Other Founders: Anti-Federalism and the Dissenting Tradition in America, 1788–1828* (Chapel Hill, N.C., 1999); and Terry Bouton's superb piece, Bouton, "A Road Closed: Rural Insurgency in Post-Independence Pennsylvania," *Journal of American History* 87, no. 3 (December 2000): 855–87.

# 9

# EIGHTEENTH-CENTURY AMERICAN WOMEN IN PEACE AND WAR

*The Case of the Loyalists*

## Mary Beth Norton

## Introduction

Mary Beth Norton's study of loyalist women cuts across the grain of recent scholarship emphasizing white women as important agents in Revolutionary America. A number of scholars have focused on Revolutionary women boycotting British goods, leading bread riots, or even disguising themselves as men to fight in the Continental Army. Norton offers a different perspective. She argues, first, that most women experienced the war in the context of home and family, second, that they exercised less control over their lives than their male counterparts, and third, that they were culturally conditioned to view themselves as "helpless" amid the vagaries of war. Additionally, Norton suggests that her subjects' lives were structured by rigid separate spheres for women and men, which some historians associate more with the nineteenth century than the eighteenth.

Norton bases her study on 468 cases of loyalist women applying for compensation from the British government for their wartime losses of property. She finds the documents these women left behind to be useful in a number of respects. They enable us to see how little most of these women knew about their family's financial matters – the farm's acreage, the value of its equipment, the amount of money owed to and by the family. At the same time, loyalist women were much more knowledgeable than men about household furnishings, and more emotionally concerned about the condition of family and friends. Few of the women mentioned ever having earned their own money. They often lacked the skills, contacts, and knowledge to pursue their claims as effectively as men did. Combined with the stress of caring for children, their petitions show signs of considerable psychological anguish. Not surprisingly, they tended to receive less compensation than their male counterparts.

Norton's study raises questions about the condition of white women generally in Revolutionary America:

- The loyalist women Norton studies came from a wide variety of social backgrounds. To what extent are Norton's findings applicable to a variety of white American women, loyalist, patriot, rural and urban? Would the women of patriot families have felt more empowered than those of loyalist families given that their side won?
- If Norton is correct that most women were relatively uninvolved in business and politics, and that they viewed themselves as "helpless" in the face of wartime upheavals, what should we make of the women who played such a pivotal roles in colonial boycotts of British goods during the imperial crises, as discussed in the essay by T.H. Breen?
- How did gender expectations shape the language of the petitioners treated in this essay? Does the influence of those expectations on women's language qualify Norton's findings about how women expressed their feelings about the war and its aftermath?
- In another essay in this volume, Maya Jasanoff takes a broader, global view of the loyalist experience drawing on a wider body of sources than Norton does here. How do Jasanoff's findings compare with those of Norton?

In recent years historians have come to recognize the central role of the family in the shaping of American society. Especially in the eighteenth century, when "household" and "family" were synonymous terms, and when household manufactures constituted a major contribution to the economy, the person who ran the household – the wife and mother – occupied a position of crucial significance. Yet those who have studied eighteenth-century women have usually chosen to focus on a few outstanding, perhaps unrepresentative individuals, such as Eliza Lucas Pinckney, Abigail Smith Adams, and Mercy Otis Warren. They have also emphasized the activities of women outside the home and have concentrated on the prescriptive literature of the day. Little has been done to examine in depth the lives actually led by the majority of colonial women or to assess the impact of the Revolution upon them.[1]

Such a study can illuminate a number of important topics. Demographic scholars are beginning to discover the dimensions of eighteenth-century households, but a knowledge of size alone means little without a delineation of roles filled by husband and wife within those households.[2] Historians of nineteenth-century American women have analyzed the ideology which has been termed the "cult of true womanhood" or the "cult of domesticity," but the relationship of these ideas to the lives of women in the preceding century remains largely unexplored.[3] And although some historians of the Revolution now view the war as a socially disruptive phenomenon, they have not yet applied that insight specifically to the study of the family.[4]

Fortunately, at least one set of documents contains material relevant to an investigation of all these aspects of late eighteenth-century American family life: the 281 volumes of the loyalist claims, housed at the Public Record Office in London. Although these manuscripts have been used extensively for political and economic studies of loyalism, they have only once before been utilized for an examination of colonial society.[5] What makes the loyalist claims uniquely useful is the fact that they contain information not only about the personal wartime experiences of thousands of Americans but also about the modes of life the war disrupted.

Among the 3,225 loyalists who presented claims to the British government after the war were 468 American refugee women. The analysis that follows is based upon an examination of the documents – formal memorials, loss schedules, and private letters – submitted by these women to the loyalist claims commission, and on the commission's nearly verbatim records of the women's personal appearances before them.[6] These women cannot be said to compose a statistically reliable sample of American womanhood. It is entirely possible that loyalist families differed demographically and economically, as well as politically, from their revolutionary neighbors, and it is highly probable that the refugee claimants did not accurately represent even the loyalist population, much less that of the colonies as a whole.[7] Nonetheless, the 468 claimants included white women of all descriptions, from every colony and all social and economic levels: they were educated and illiterate; married, widowed, single, and deserted; rural and urban; wealthy, middling, and poverty-stricken. Accordingly, used with care, the loyalist claims can tell us much about the varieties of female experience in America in the third quarter of the eighteenth century.[8]

One aspect of prewar family life that is systematically revealed in the claims documents is the economic relationship of husband and wife within the household. All claimants, male and female alike, had to supply the commission with detailed estimates of property losses. Given the circumstances of the war, documentary evidence such as deeds, bills of sale, and wills was rarely available in complete form, and the commission therefore relied extensively upon the sworn testimony of the claimants and their witnesses in assessing losses. The claimants had nothing to gain by withholding information, because the amount of compensation they received depended in large part on their ability to describe their losses. Consequently, it may be assumed that what the loyalists told the commission, both orally and in writing, represented the full extent of their knowledge of their families' income and property.[9] The women's claims thus make it possible to determine the nature of their participation in the financial affairs of their households.

Strikingly, although male loyalists consistently supplied detailed assessments of the worth of their holdings, many women were unable to place precise valuations on the property for which they claimed compensation. Time after time similar phrases appear in the records of oral testimony before the commission: "She cant say what the Houses cost or what they woud have sold for" (the widow of a Norfolk merchant); "Says she is much a Stranger to the state of Her Husband's Concerns" (the widow of a storekeeper from Ninety-Six, South Carolina); "It was meadow Land, she cannot speak of the Value" (a New Jersey farmer's widow); "Her husband was a Trader and had many Debts owing to him She does not know how much they amounted to" (a widow from Ninety-Six); "She can't speak to the Value of the Stock in Trade" (a Rhode Island merchant's widow); "It was a good Tract but does not know how to value it" (the widow of a Crown Point farmer).[10]

Even when women submitted detailed loss schedules in writing, they frequently revealed at their oral examinations that they had relied on male relatives or friends, or even on vaguely recalled statements made by their dead husbands, in arriving at the apparently knowledgeable estimates they had initially given to the commission. For example, a New Jersey woman, questioned about her husband's annual income, referred the commissioners to her father and other male witnesses, admitting that she did not know the amount he had earned. Similarly, the widow of a Charleston saddler told the commissioners that "she does not know the Amount of Her husband's Property, but she remembers to have heard him say in the year

1777 that he was worth £2,000 sterling clear of all Debts." Such statements abound in the claims records: "She is unable to speak to the value of the Plantn herself, but refers to Mr. Cassills"; "Says she cannot speak to the Value – the Valuatn was made by Capt McDonald and Major Munro"; "Says her Son in Law Capt Douglas is better acquainted with the particulars of her property than herself and she refers to him for an Account thereof."[11]

Although many female claimants thus lacked specific knowledge of their families' finances, there were substantial variations within the general pattern. The very wealthiest women – like Isabella Logan of Virginia (who could say only that she and her husband had lived in "a new Elegant, large double Brick House with two wings all finish'd in the best taste with Articles from London") and Mrs. Egerton Leigh of South Carolina (who gave it as her opinion that her husband had "a considerable real Estate as well as personal property … worth more than £10,000 … tho' she cannot herself speak to it with accuracy") – also tended to be the ones most incapable of describing their husbands' business affairs.[12] Yet some wealthy, well-educated women were conversant with nearly every detail of the family finances. For the most part, this latter group was composed of women who had brought the property they described to their husbands at marriage or who had been widowed before the war and had served as executrixes of the estates in question for some time. A case in point is that of Sarah Gould Troutbeck, daughter, executrix, and primary heir of John Gould, a prosperous Boston merchant. Her husband John, an Anglican clergyman, died in 1778, and so she carried the full burden of presenting the family's claim to the commission. Although she deprecatingly described herself to the board as "a poor weak Woman unused to business," she supplied the commissioners with detailed evidence of her losses and unrelentingly pursued her debtors. "Your not hearing from me for so long a time may induce you to think I have relinquishd my claim to the intrest due on your note," she informed one man in 1788. "If you realy entertain any such thoughts I must beg leave to undeceive you." In addition, she did what few loyalists of either sex had the courage to attempt – return to the United States to try to recover her property. When she arrived in 1785, she found her estates "in the greatest confusion" but nevertheless managed within several months to repossess one house and to collect some debts. In the end she apparently won restoration of most of her holdings.[13]

Yet not all the female loyalists who had inherited property in their own right were as familiar with it as was Sarah Troutbeck. Another Massachusetts woman admitted to the commissioners that she did not know the value of the 550 acres left her by a relative, or even how much of the land was cultivated. "Her Brother managed everything for her and gave her what Money she wanted," she explained. In the same vein, a New Yorker was aware that her father had left her some property in his will, but "she does not know what property." A Charleston resident who had owned a house jointly with her brother commented that "it was a good House," but the commission noted, "she does not know the Value of it." And twice-widowed Jane Gibbes, claiming for the farms owned by her back-country South Carolina husbands, told the commission that she had relied on neighbors to assess the worth of the property, for "she can't speak positively to the value of her Lands herself."[14]

But if Jane Gibbes could not precisely evaluate the farms she had lived on, she still knew a good deal about them. She described the total acreage, the amount of land under cultivation, the crops planted, and the livestock that had been lost. In this she was representative of most rural female loyalists with claims that were not complicated by the existence of mortgages or outstanding debts. Although they did not always know the exact value of the land for which they requested reimbursement, they could supply the commission with many important details about the family property: the number of cattle, horses, sheep, and hogs; the

types of tools used; the acreage planted, and with what crops; the amounts of grain and other foodstuffs stored for the winter; and the value of such unusual possessions as beehives or a "Covering Horse." It was when they were asked about property on which they had not lived, about debts owed by their husbands, or about details of wills or mortgages that they most often admitted ignorance.[15]

A good example is Mary McAlpin, who had settled with her husband on a farm near Saratoga, New York, in 1767. She did not know what her husband had paid for some unimproved lands, or the acreage of another farm he had purchased, but she was well acquainted with the property on which they had lived. The farm, she told the commissioners, "had been wholly cleared and Improved and was in the most perfect State of Cultivation." There were two "Log Houses plaistered and floored," one for them and one for their hired laborers, and sufficient materials on hand to build "a large and Commodious Brick House." Her husband had planted wheat, rye, peas, oats, barley, corn, turnips, potatoes, and melons; and "the Meadows had been laid down or sown with Clover and Timothy Grass, the two kind of Grass Seeds most Valued in that Country." The McAlpins had had a kitchen garden that produced "in great abundance every Vegitable usually cultivated in that part of America." Moreover, the farm was "well Provided" with such utensils as "a Team waggon, Carts sledges Carwls [sic] Wheels for Waggons, Wheels for Carts, Wheelbarrows, drags for Timber Ploughs, Harrows Hay Sythes Brush Sythes Grubbling Harrows, and all sorts of Carpenters Tools Shoemakers Tools Shovels, Spades, Axes Iron Crow Barrs etc."

After offering all these details, however, Mrs. McAlpin proved unable to assess the value of the property accurately. She gave the commission a total claim of £6,000, clearly an estimate, and when asked to break down a particular item on her schedule into its component parts she could not do so, saying that "She valued the Whole in the Lump in that Sum." Moreover, she proved ignorant of the terms of her husband's will, confusedly telling the commissioners that he had "left his real personal Estate to his Son – This she supposes was his Lands" (the board's secretary noted carefully, "This is her own Expression"), when in fact she had been left a life interest in the real estate plus half the personal estate.[16] In short, Mary McAlpin typifies the rural female claimant, though her husband's property was substantially larger than average. She knew what he had owned, but she did not know exactly how much it was worth. She was well acquainted with the day-to-day operations of the farm but understood very little about the general family finances. And she knew nothing at all about legal or business terminology.

The pattern for urban dwellers was more varied. In the first place, included in their number were most of the wealthy women mentioned earlier, both those who knew little or nothing about their husbands' estates and those who, like Sarah Troutbeck, were conversant with the family holdings. Secondly, a higher percentage of urban women engaged directly in business. Among the 468 female claimants there were forty-three who declared either that they had earned money on their own or that they had assisted their husbands in some way. Only three of these forty-three can be described as rural: a tavernkeeper's wife from Ticonderoga, a small shopkeeper from Niagara, and the housekeeper for the family of Col. Guy Johnson. All the other working women came from cities such as Boston, Philadelphia, Charleston, and New York, or from smaller but substantial towns like Williamsburg, Wilmington, N.C., and Baltimore. The urban women's occupations were as varied as the urban centers in which they resided. There were ten who took lodgers, eighteen shopkeepers and merchants of various sorts, five tavernkeepers, four milliners, two mantua makers, a seamstress, a midwife, an owner of a coffeehouse, a schoolteacher, a printer, one who did not specify an occupation, and two prostitutes who described themselves as owners of a small shop and declared that their

house had been "always open" to British officers needing "aid and attention."[17]

As might be expected, the women who had managed businesses or assisted their husbands (one wrote that she was "truly his Partner" in a "steady Course of painfull Industry") were best informed about the value of their property. Those who had been grocers or milliners could usually list in detail the stock they had lost; the midwife had witnesses to support her claim to a high annual income from her profession; the boardinghouse keepers knew what they had spent for furniture and supplies; and the printer could readily value her shop's equipment.[18] But even these working women could not give a full report on all aspects of their husbands' holdings: the widow of a Boston storekeeper, for example, could accurately list their stock in trade but admitted ignorance of the value of the property her husband had inherited from his father, and although the widow of another Boston merchant had carried on the business after her husband was wounded at Bunker Hill, she was not familiar with the overall value of their property.[19]

It is therefore not surprising that women claimants on the average received a smaller return on their claims than did their male counterparts. Since the commissioners reimbursed only for fully proven losses, the amounts awarded are a crude indicator of the relative ability of individual refugees to describe their losses and to muster written and oral evidence on their own behalf. If women had known as much as their husbands about the family estates, there would have been little or no difference between the average amounts granted to each sex. But of the claims heard in England for which complete information is available, 660 loyalist men received an average return of 39.5 percent, while for 71 women the figure was 34.1 percent. And this calculation does not take into account the large number of women's claims, including some submitted by businesswomen, which were entirely disallowed for lack of proof.[20]

In the absence of data for other time periods and populations, it is difficult to assess the significance of the figures that show that slightly less than 10 percent (9.2 percent, to be exact) of the loyalist refugee women worked outside the home. Historians have tended to stress the widespread participation of colonial women in economic enterprise, usually as a means of distinguishing them from their reputedly more confined nineteenth-century counterparts.[21] The claims documents demonstrate that some women engaged in business, either alone or with their husbands, but 9.2 percent may be either a large or a small proportion of the total female population, depending on how one looks at it. The figures themselves must remain somewhat ambiguous, at least until additional data are obtained.[22] What is not at all ambiguous, however, is the distinctive pattern of the female claimants' knowledge.

For regardless of whether they came from rural or urban areas, and regardless of their background or degree of participation in business, the loyalist women testified almost exclusively on the basis of their knowledge of those parts of the family property with which their own lives brought them into regular contact. What they uniformly lacked were those pieces of information about business matters that could have been supplied only by their husbands. Evidently, late eighteenth-century American men, at least those who became loyalists, did not systematically discuss matters of family finances with their wives. From that fact it may be inferred that the men – and their wives as well, perhaps – accepted the dictum that woman's place was in the home. After all, that was where more than 90 percent of the loyalist women stayed, and their ignorance of the broader aspects of their families' economic circumstances indicates that their interest in such affairs was either minimal or else deliberately thwarted by their husbands.[23]

It would therefore appear that the 9 percent figure for working women is evidence not of a climate favorable to feminine enterprise but rather of the opposite: women were expected to remain largely within the home unless forced by necessity, such as the illness or death of their husbands, to do otherwise. The fact that fewer than one-half (seventeen, to be precise) of the working women enumerated earlier had healthy, living husbands at the time they engaged in business leads toward the same conclusion. The implication is that in mid-eighteenth-century America woman's sphere was rigidly defined at all levels of society, not merely in the wealthy households in which this phenomenon has been recognized.[24]

This tentative conclusion is supported by evidence drawn from another aspect of the claims, for a concomitant of the contention that colonial women often engaged in business endeavors has been the assertion that colonial men, as the theoretical and legal heads of household, frequently assumed a large share of domestic responsibilities.[25] Yet if men had been deeply involved in running their households – in keeping accounts and making purchases, even if not in doing day-to-day chores – they should have described household furnishings in much the same detail as their wives used. But just as female claimants were unable to delineate their husbands' business dealings accurately, so men separated from their wives – regardless of their social status – failed to submit specific lists of lost household items like furniture, dishes, or kitchen utensils. One such refugee observed to the commission in 1788, "As Household Furniture consists of a Variety of Articles, at this distance of time I cannot sufficiently recollect them so as to fix a Value on them to the Satisfaction of my mind."[26] It is impossible to imagine a loyalist woman making a comparable statement. For her, what to a man was simply "a Variety of Articles" resolved itself into such familiar and cherished objects as "1 Compleat set blue and white Tea and Table China," "a Large new Goose feather Bed, bolster Pillows and Bedstead," "a Small painted Book Case and Desk," "1 Japan Tea Board," "2 smoothing Irons," and "1 old brass Coffee Pott." Moreover, although men usually noted losses of clothing in a general way, by listing a single undifferentiated sum, women frequently claimed for specific articles of jewelry and apparel. For example, Mary Swords of Saratoga disclosed that she had lost to rebel plunderers a "Long Scarlet Cloak" and a "Velvet Muff and Tippett," in addition to "One pair of Ear Rings French paste set in Gold," "One small pair of Ear Rings Garnets," and "one Gold Broatch with a small diamond Top."[27]

The significance of such lists lies not only in the fact that they indicate what kinds of property the claimants knew well enough to describe accurately and in detail, but also in the insight they provide into the possessions which claimants thought were sufficiently important to mention individually. For example, a rural New York woman left no doubt about her pride in "a fine large new stove"; a resident of Manhattan carefully noted that one of her lost beds was covered in "Red Damask"; and a Rhode Islander called attention to the closets in her "large new dwelling house."[28] The differentiated contents of men's and women's claims thus take on more importance, since the contrasting lists not only suggest the extent of the claimants' knowledge but also reveal their assessments of the relative importance of their possessions. To men, furniture, dishes, and clothing could easily be lumped together under general headings; to women, such possessions had to be carefully enumerated and described.

In the end, all of the evidence that can be drawn from the loyalist claims points to the conclusion that the lives of the vast majority of women in the Revolutionary era revolved around their immediate households to a notable degree. The economic function of those households in relation to the family property largely determined the extent of their knowledge of that property. In rural areas, where women's household chores included caring for the stock and perhaps occasionally working in the fields, women were conversant with a greater proportion of the family estates than were urban women, whose knowledge was for the most part confined to the furnishings of the houses in which they lived, unless they had been widowed before the war or had worked outside

the home. The wealth of the family was thus a less significant determinant of the woman's role than was the nature of the household. To be sure, at the extreme ends of the economic scale, wealth and education, or the lack of them, affected a woman's comprehension of her family's property, but what the women displayed were relative degrees of ignorance. If the loyalist claimants are at all representative, very few married colonial women were familiar with the broader aspects of their families' financial affairs. Regardless of where they lived, they were largely insulated from the agricultural and business worlds in which their husbands engaged daily. As a result, the Revolutionary War, which deprived female loyalists of the households in which they had lived and worked, and which at the same time forced them to confront directly the wider worlds of which they had had little previous knowledge, was for them an undeniably traumatic experience.

At the outbreak of the war, loyalist women expected that "their Sex and the Humanity of a civilized People" would protect them from "disrespectfull Indignities." Most of them soon learned otherwise. Rebel men may have paid lip service to the ideal that women and children should be treated as noncombatants, but in practice they consigned female loyalists to much the same fate as their male relatives. Left behind by their fleeing husbands (either because of the anticipated difficulties of a journey to the British lines or in the hope that the family property might thereby be preserved), loyalist wives, with their children, frequently found themselves "stripped of every Thing" by American troops who, as one woman put it, "not contented with possessing themselves of her property were disposed to visit severity upon her person and Those of her friends."[29] Female loyalists were often verbally abused, imprisoned, and threatened with bodily harm even when they had not taken an active role in opposing the rebel cause.[30]

When they had assisted the British – and many aided prisoners or gathered intelligence – their fate was far worse. For example, the New

Yorker Lorenda Holmes, who carried letters through the lines in 1776, was stripped by an angry band of committeemen and dragged "to the Drawing Room Window … exposing her to many Thousands of People Naked." On this occasion Mrs. Holmes admitted that she "received no wounds or bruises from them only shame and horror of the Mind," but a few months later, after she had shown some refugees the way to the British camp, an American officer came to her house and held her "right foot upon the Coals until he had burnt it in a most shocking manner," telling her "he would learn her to carry off Loyalists to the British Army."[31]

As can readily be imagined, the women did not come through such experiences emotionally unscathed. One Massachusetts mother reported that her twelve-year-old daughter suffered from "nervous Fits" as a result of "the usage she met with from the Mobs"; and another New England woman, the wife of a merchant who was an early target of the local committee because he resisted the nonimportation movement, described to a female friend her reaction to a threatening letter they had received: "I have never injoyed one hours real Sattisfaction since the receipt of that Dreadfull Letter my mind is in continual agitation and the very rustling of the Trees alarms me." Some time later the same woman was unfortunate enough to be abused by a rebel militiaman. After that incident, she reported, "I did not recover from my fright for several days. The sound of drum or the sight of a gun put me into such a tremor that I could not command myself."[32] It was only natural for these women to look forward with longing to the day when they could escape to Canada or, better still, to England, "a land of peace, liberty and plenty." It seemed to them that their troubles would end when they finally left America. But, as one wrote later with the benefit of hindsight, their "severest trials were just begun."[33]

Male and female refugees alike confronted difficult problems in England and Canada – finding housing, obtaining financial support, settling into a new environment. For women,

especially widows with families, the difficulties were compounded. The Bostonian Hannah Winslow found the right words: it was a "cruell" truth, she told her sister-in-law, that "when a woman with a family, and Particularly a large one, looses her Husband and Protector People are afraid to keep up the Acquaintance least they may ask favrs."[34] Many of the men quickly reestablished their American friendship networks through the coffeehouses and refugee organizations; the women were deprived not only of the companionship such associations provided but also of the information about pensions and claims that was transmitted along the male networks. As a result, a higher proportion of female than male loyalists made errors in their applications for government assistance, by directing the memorials to the wrong officials and failing to meet deadlines, often because they learned too late about compensation programs. Their standard excuses – that they "had nobody to advise with" and that they "did not know how to do it" – were greeted with skepticism by the claims commission, but they were undoubtedly true.[35]

On the whole, female loyalists appear to have fared worse in England than their male counterparts, and for two major reasons. In the first place, the commissioners usually gave women annual pensions that were from £10 to £20 lower than those received by men, apparently because they believed that the women had fewer expenses, but also because in most cases the women could not claim the extra merit of having actively served the royal cause.[36] Second, fewer women than men found work to supplement the sums they received from the government. To the wealthier female refugees work seemed so automatically foreclosed as an option that only a small number thought it necessary to explain to the commission why they could not contribute to their own support. Mary Serjeant, the widow of a Massachusetts clergyman, even regarded her former affluence as a sufficient reason in itself for her failure to seek employment. In

1782 she told the commissioners, "Educated as a Gentlewoman myself and brought up to no business I submit it to your [torn], Gentlemen, how very scanty must be the Subsistence which my Own Industry [can] procure us." Those who did try to earn additional income (many of whom had also worked outside the home in America) usually took in needlework or hired out as servants or housekeepers, but even they had trouble making ends meet. One orphaned young woman reported, "I can support myself with my needle: but not my two Sisters and infant Brother"; and another, who had learned the trade of mantua making, commented, "I now got Work for my self [*sic*] – but being oblidged to give long credit and haveing no Money of my one [*sic*] to go on with, I lived Cheifly upon tea which with night working brought me almost into the last stadge of a Consumtion so that when I rec'd my Money for work it went almost [all] to dockters."[37]

Many of the loyalist women displayed a good deal of resilience. Some managed to support themselves, among them the Wells sisters of Charleston, who in 1789 opened a London boardinghouse for young ladies whose parents wished them to have a "suitable" introduction to society. Others survived what might seem an overwhelming series of setbacks – for example, Susannah Marshall of Maryland, who, after running taverns in Baltimore and Head of Elk and trying but failing to join Lord Dunmore off Norfolk in 1776, finally left the United States by sea the following year, only to have her chartered ship captured first by the Americans and then by the British. In the process she lost all the goods she had managed to salvage from her earlier moves, and when she arrived in England she not only learned of her husband's death but was unsuccessful in her application for a subsistence pension. Refusing to give up, she went to work as a nurse to support her children, and although she described herself to the commission in 1785 as "very Old and feeble," she lived long enough to be granted a permanent annual allowance of £20 in 1789.[38]

Susannah Marshall, though, had years of experience as a tavernkeeper behind her and was thus more capable of coping with her myriad difficulties than were women whose prewar experience had been restricted to their households. Such women recognized that they were "less able than many who never knew happier days to bear hardships and struggle with adversity." These women, especially those who had been, as one of them put it, *"born to better expectations"* in America, spoke despairingly of encounters with "difficultys of which she had no experience in her former life," of "Adversities which not many years before she scarcely thought it possible, that in any situation, she should ever experience."[39]

For women like these, exile in England or Canada was one long nightmare. Their relief requests have a desperate, supplicating tone that is largely absent from those submitted by men. One bewailed the impending birth of her third child, asking, "What can I do in my Condishtion deprived of helth with out Friends or mony with a helpless family to suffer with me?" Another begged the commission's secretary for assistance "with all humility" because "the merciless man I lodge with, threatens to sell the two or three trifling articles I have and put a Padlock on the Room unless I pay him the Rent amounting to near a Pound." By contrast, when a man prepared a memorial for the exceptionally distressed Mrs. Sarah Baker, he coolly told the commissioners that they should assist her because her children "as Soldiers or Sailors in his Majesty's Service may in future compensate the present Expence of saving them."[40]

The straits to which some of the female refugees were driven were dramatically illustrated in early 1783 when a South Carolina woman appeared before the commission "in Rags," explaining that she had been "obliged to pawn her Goods." It was but the first incident of many. Time and again women revealed that they had sold or pawned their clothes – which were usually their most valuable possessions – to buy food for themselves and their children.

One was literally "reduced to the last shift" when she testified before the commission; another, the New Yorker Alicia Young, pawned so much that "the want of our apparel made our situation very deplorable" until friends helped her to redeem some of her possessions. Strikingly, no man ever told the commission stories like these. Either male refugees were able to find alternatives to pawning their clothes, or, if they did not, they were too ashamed to admit it.[41]

Such hardships took a terrible mental as well as physical toll. Evidence of extreme mental stress permeates the female loyalists' petitions and letters, while it is largely absent from the memorials of male exiles. The women speak constantly of their "Fear, Fatigue and Anxiety of Mind," their "lowness of Spirit," their "inexpressable" distress, their "accumulated anguish." They repeatedly describe themselves as "desolate and distressed," as "disconsolate, Distressed and helpless … with a broken Spirit Ruined health and Constitution," as "Oppressed in body and distressed in mind."[42] "I am overwhelm'd with misfortunes," wrote one. Poverty "distracts and terrifies me," said another; and a third begged "that she may not be left a Prey to Poverty, and her constant companons [*sic*], Calamity and Sorrow." "My pen is unable to describe the horrors of My Mind – or the deploreable Situation of Myself and Infant family," Alicia Young told a member of the commission. "Judge then Dr Sir what is to become of me, or what we are to exist upon – I have no kind of resource … . oh Sir the horrors of my Situation is almost too much for me to bear." Most revealing of all was the wife of a Connecticut refugee: "Nature it self languishes," Mary Taylor wrote, "the hours that I should rest, I awake in such an aggitation of mind, as though I had to suffer for sins, that I neaver committed, I allmost shudder when I approache the Doone [doom?] – as every thing appears to be conspired against me, the Baker, and Bucher, seams to be weary of serving me oh porvity what is its Crime, may some have Compassion on those who feeals its power – for

I can doo nothing – but baith my infant with my tears – while seeing my Husbands sinking under the waight of his misfortuens, unable to afford me any release."[43]

Even taking into account the likelihood that it was more socially acceptable for women to reveal their emotions, the divergence between men's and women's memorials is too marked to be explained by that factor alone. It is necessary to probe more deeply and to examine men's and women's varying uses of language in order to delineate the full dimensions of the difference.[44] As C. Wright Mills pointed out in an influential article some years ago, actions or motives and the vocabularies utilized to describe them cannot be wholly separated, and commonly used adjectives can therefore reveal the limitations placed on one's actions by one's social role. Mills asserted that "the 'Real Attitude or Motive' is not something different in kind from the verbalization or the 'opinion,'" and that "the long acting out of a role, with its appropriate motives, will often induce a man [or, one is compelled to add, a woman] to become what at first he merely sought to appear." Furthermore, Mills noted, people perceive situations in terms of specific, "delimited" vocabularies, and thus adjectives can themselves promote or deter certain actions. When adjectives are "typical and relatively unquestioned accompaniments of typical situations," he concluded, "such words often function as directives and incentives by virtue of their being the judgements of others as anticipated by the actor."[45]

In this theoretical context the specific words used by female loyalists may be analyzed as a means of understanding the ways in which they perceived themselves and their circumstances. Their very phraseology – and the manner in which it differs from that of their male counterparts – can provide insights into the matrix of attitudes that helped to shape the way they thought and acted. If Mills is correct, the question whether the women were deliberately telling the commission what they thought it wanted to hear becomes irrelevant: it is enough to say that they were acting in accordance with a prescribed role, and that that role helped to determine how they acted.[46]

With these observations in mind, the fact that the women refugees displayed an intense awareness of their own femininity assumes a crucial significance. The phrases permeate the pages of the petitions from rich and poor alike: "Though a Woman"; "perhaps no Woman in America in equal Circumstances"; "being done by a Woman"; "being a poor lame and infirm Woman." In short, in the female loyalists' minds their actions and abilities were to a certain extent defined by their sex. Femininity was the constant point of reference in measuring their achievements and making their self-assessments. Moreover, the fact of their womanhood was used in a deprecating sense. In their own eyes, they gained merit by not acting like women. Her services were "allmost Matchless, (being done by a Woman)," wrote one; "tho' a Woman, she was the first that went out of the Gates to welcome the Royal Army," declared another. Femininity also provided a ready and plausible excuse for failures of action or of knowledge. A South Carolinian said she had not signed the address to the king in Charleston in 1780 because "it was not posable for a woman to come near the office." A Pennsylvanian apologized for any errors in her loss estimate with the comment, "as far as a Woman can know, she believes the contents to be true." A Nova Scotian said she had not submitted a claim by the deadline because of "being a lone Woman in her Husband's Absence and not having any person to Advise with." A Vermonter made the ultimate argument: "had she been a man, Instead, of a poor helpless woman – should not have faild of being in the British Servace."[47]

The pervasive implication is one of perceived inferiority, and this implication is enhanced by the word women used most often to describe themselves: "helpless." "Being a Poor helpless Widow"; "she is left a helpless Widow"; "a helpless woman advanced in life"; "being a helpless woman": such phrases appear again and again in the claims memorials.[48]

Male loyalists might term themselves "very unhappy," "wretched," "extremely distressed," or "exceedingly embarrassed," but *never* were they "helpless." For them, the most characteristic self-description was "unfortunate," a word that carried entirely different, even contrary, connotations.[49] Male loyalists can be said to have seen their circumstances as not of their own making, as even being reversible with luck. The condition of women, however, was inherent in themselves; nothing they could do could change their circumstances. By definition, indeed, they were incapable of helping themselves.

It should be stressed here that, although women commonly described themselves as "helpless," their use of that word did not necessarily mean that they were in fact helpless. It indicates rather that they perceived themselves thus, and that that perception in turn perhaps affected the way they acted (for example, in seeking charitable support instead of looking for work). Similarly, the fact that men failed to utilize the adjective "helpless" to refer to themselves does not mean that they were not helpless, for some of them surely were; it merely shows that – however incorrectly – they did think that they could change their circumstances. These two words, with all their connotations, encapsulate much of the divergence between male and female self-perceptions in late eighteenth-century America, even if they do not necessarily indicate much about the realities of male-female relationships in the colonies.[50]

There was, of course, more to the difference in sex roles than the sex-related ways in which colonial Americans looked at themselves. The claims documents also suggest that women and men placed varying emphases on familial ties. For women, such relationships seemed to take on a special order of magnitude. Specifically, men never said, as several women did, that after their spouses' deaths they were so "inconsolable" that they were unable to function. One woman declared that after her husband's execution by the rebels she was "bereft of her reason for near three months," and another described herself as "rendred almost totally incapable of Even writing my own Name or any assistance in any Shape that Could have the least Tendency to getting my Bread."[51] Furthermore, although loyalist men expressed concern over the plight of the children they could not support adequately, women were much more emotionally involved in the fate of their offspring. "Your goodness will easily conceive, what I must feel for My *Children,*" Alicia Young told a claims commissioner; "for myself – I care not – Misfortunes and distress have long since made me totally indifferent to everything in the World but *Them* – they have no provision – no provider – no protector – but God – and me." Women noted that their "Sorrows" were increased by the knowledge that their children were "Partners in this Scene of Indigence." Margaret Draper, widow of a Boston printer, explained that although she had been ill and suffering from a "disorderd Mind," "what adds to my affliction is, my fears for my Daughter, who may soon be left a Stranger and friendless." In the same vein, a New Jersey woman commented that she had "the inexpressible mortification of seeing my Children in want of many necessaries and conveniencies ... . and what still more distresses me, is to think that I am obliged by partaking of it, to lessen even the small portion they have."[52]

The women's emphasis on their families is entirely compatible with the earlier observation concerning the importance of their households in their lives. If their menfolk were preoccupied with the monetary consequences of adhering to the crown, the women were more aware of the human tragedy brought about by the war. They saw their plight and that of their children in much more personal terms than did their husbands. Likewise, they personalized the fact of their exile in a way that male loyalists did not, by almost invariably commenting that they were "left friendless in a strange Country." Refugee men, though they might call themselves "strangers," rarely noted a lack of friends, perhaps because of the coffeehouse networks. To women, by contrast, the fact that they were not surrounded by friends and neighbors seemed calamitous. "I

am without Friends or Money," declared one; I am "a friendless, forlorn Woman ... a Stranger to this Country, and surrounded by evils," said another. She is "far from her native Country, and numerous Friends and Relations where she formerly lived, much respected," wrote a third of her own condition.[53]

When the female refugees talked of settling elsewhere or of returning to the United States, they spoke chiefly of the friends and relatives they would find at their intended destinations. Indeed, it appears from the claims that at least six women went into exile solely because their friends and relatives did. A loyalist woman who remained in the United States after the war explained that she did so because she chose "to reside near my relations [rather] than to carry my family to a strange Country where in case of my death they would be at the mercy of strangers." And Mary Serjeant's description of her situation in America as it would have been had her husband not been a loyalist carried the implication that she wished she too had stayed at home: "His poor Children and disconsolate Widow would now have had a House of their own and some Land adjoining to it And instead of being almost destitute in a Land of Strangers would have remained among some Relatives."[54]

In sum, evidence drawn from the loyalist claims strongly suggests that late-eighteenth-century women had fully internalized the roles laid out for them in the polite literature of the day. Their experience was largely confined to their households, either because they chose that course or because they were forced into it. They perceived themselves as "helpless" – even if at times their actions showed that they were not – and they strongly valued ties with family and friends. When the Revolution tore them from the familiar patterns of their lives in America, they felt abandoned and adrift, far more so than did their male relatives, for whom the human contacts cherished by the women seemed to mean less or at least were more easily replaced by those friendships that persisted into exile.

The picture of the late-eighteenth-century woman that emerges from the loyalist claims, therefore, is of one who was almost wholly domestic, in the sense that that word would be used in the nineteenth-century United States. But at the same time the colonial woman's image of herself lacked the positive attributes with which her nineteenth-century counterpart could presumably console herself. The eighteenth-century American woman was primarily a wife and a mother, but America had not yet developed an ideology that would proclaim the social value of motherhood. That was to come with republicanism – and loyalist women, by a final irony, were excluded by their political allegiance from that republican assurance.[55]

## Notes

Ms. Norton is a member of the Department of History, Cornell University. She wishes to thank Carol Berkin, Carl Kaestle, Pauline Maier, Robert Wells, and Peter Wood for their comments on an earlier version of this article. A portion of it was read at the Second Berkshire Conference on the History of Women, held at Radcliffe College, Oct. 1974.

1   See, for example, such works as Mary Sumner Benson, *Women in Eighteenth-Century America: A Study of Opinion and Social Usage* (New York, 1935); Elisabeth Anthony Dexter, *Colonial Women of Affairs,* 2d ed. (New York, 1931); and Joan Hoff Wilson, "Dancing Dogs of the Colonial Period: Women Scientists," *Early American Literature,* VII (1973), 225–235. Notable exceptions are Julia Cherry Spruill, *Women's Life and Work in the Southern Colonies* (Chapel Hill, N.C., 1938), and Eugenie Andruss Leonard, *The Dear-Bought Heritage* (Philadelphia, 1965). On the importance of the early American family see David Rothman, "A Note on the Study of the Colonial Family," *William and Mary Quarterly,* 3d Ser., XXIII (1966), 627–634.

2   Two recent works that deal with family size, among other topics, are Robert V. Wells, "Household Size and Composition in the British Colonies in America, 1675–1775," *Journal of Interdisciplinary History,* IV (1974), 543–570, and

Daniel Scott Smith, "Population, Family and Society in Hingham, Massachusetts, 1635–1880" (Ph.D. diss., University of California, Berkeley, 1973). Internal household relationships in 17th-century New England have been analyzed by Edmund S. Morgan, *The Puritan Family: Religion & Domestic Relations in Seventeenth-Century New England* (Boston, 1944), and John Demos, *A Little Commonwealth: Family Life in Plymouth Colony* (New York, 1970).

3   Barbara Welter, "The Cult of True Womanhood, 1820–1860," *American Quarterly,* XVII (1966), 151–174, was the first to outline the dimensions of this ideology. For writings dealing with some of the implications of the "cult of domesticity" see Carroll Smith-Rosenberg, "The Historical Woman: Sex Roles and Role Conflict in 19th-century America," *Social Research,* XXXIX (1972), 652–678; Ann Douglas Wood, "Mrs. Sigourney and the Sensibility of the Inner Space," *New England Quarterly,* XLV (1972), 163–181; Kathryn Kish Sklar, *Catharine Beecher: A Study in American Domesticity* (New Haven, Conn., 1973); and Nancy Falik Cott, "In the Bonds of Womanhood: Perspectives on Female Experience and Consciousness in New England, 1780–1830" (Ph.D. diss., Brandeis University, 1974), esp. chap. 6. An explicit assertion that women were better off in 18th-century America than they were later is found in Dexter, *Colonial Women of Affairs,* vii, 189–192, and in Page Smith, *Daughters of the Promised Land* (Boston, 1970), 37–76. But two European historians have appropriately warned that it may be dangerous to assume the existence of a "golden, preindustrial age" for women, noting that the "goldenness is seen almost exclusively in terms of women's work and its presumed relationship to family power, not in terms of other vital aspects of their lives, including the physical burdens of work and child bearing." Patricia Branca and Peter N. Stearns, "On the History of Modern Women, a Research Note," *AHA Newsletter,* XII (Sept. 1974), 6.

4   For example, John Shy, "The American Revolution: The Military Conflict Considered as a Revolutionary War," in Stephen G. Kurtz and James H. Hutson, eds., *Essays on the American Revolution* (Chapel Hill, N.C., 1973), 121–156; John Shy, "The Loyalist Problem in the Lower

Hudson Valley: The British Perspective," in Robert A. East and Jacob Judd, eds., *The Loyalist Americans: A Focus on Greater New York* (Tarrytown, N.Y., 1975), 3–13; and Ronald Hoffman, *A Spirit of Dissension: Economics, Politics, and the Revolution in Maryland* (Baltimore, 1973), esp. chaps. 6, 8.

5 Catherine S. Crary, "The Humble Immigrant and the American Dream: Some Case Histories, 1746–1776," *Mississippi Valley Historical Review,* XLVI (1959), 46–66.

6 For a detailed examination of the claims process see Mary Beth Norton, *The British-Americans: The Loyalist Exiles in England,* 1774–1789 (Boston, 1972), 185–222. More than 468 women appear in the claims documents; excluded from the sample selected for this article are all female children, all English women who never lived in America (but who were eligible for compensation as heirs of loyalists), and all American women who did not personally pursue a claim (that is, whose husbands took the entire responsibility for presenting the family's claims). In addition to those requesting reimbursement for property losses, the sample includes a number of women – mostly the very poor, who had lost only a small amount of property, if any – who applied solely for the subsistence pensions which were also awarded by the claims commissioners. On the allowance system see *ibid.,* 52–61, 111–121, and 225–229.

7 On the statistical biases of the loyalist claims see Eugene Fingerhut, "Uses and Abuses of the American Loyalists Claims: A Critique of Quantitative Analyses," *WMQ,* 3d Ser., XXV (1968), 245–258.

8 This approach to women in the Revolutionary era differs from the traditional focus on their public contributions to the war effort. See, for example, Elizabeth F. Ellet, *The Women of the American Revolution* (New York, 1848–1850); Walter Hart Blumenthal, *Women Camp Followers of the American Revolution* (Philadelphia, 1952); Elizabeth Cornetti, "Women in the American Revolution," *NEQ,* XX (1947), 329–346; and Linda Grant DePauw, *Four Traditions: Women of New York during the American Revolution* (Albany, 1974).

9 Only if they intended to commit fraud could loyalists gain by withholding information from the commission; two refugees, for example, requested compensation for property they had already sold during the war. But the commissioners found deliberately fraudulent only 10 of the claims submitted to them, and although they disallowed others for "gross prevarication," none of the claims falling into either category were submitted by women. See Norton, *British-Americans,* 217–219, on the incidence of fraud, and 203–205, 216–217, on the importance of accurate testimony.

10 Joyce Dawson, testimony, May 5, 1787, A.O. 12/56, 330, Public Record Office; Isabella McLaurin, testimony, Nov. 27, 1784, A.O. 12/47, 233; Margaret Hutchinson, testimony, Aug. 10, 1786, A.O. 12/16, 34; Margaret Reynolds, testimony, Dec. 9, 1783, A.O. 12/46, 168; case of Mrs. Bowers, Feb. 24, 1783, A.O. 12/99, 48; Elizabeth Campbell, testimony, n.d., A.O. 12/26, 267. For other similar statements see A.O. 12/10, 254, A.O. 12/48, 233, A.O. 12/50, 390–391, and A.O. 13/68, pt. 1, 183.

11 Frances Dongan, testimony, Dec. 6, 1784, A.O. 12/13, 267–272; case of Charlotte Pollock, June 27, 1783, A.O. 12/99, 336; Mary Ann Balfour, testimony, Mar. 13, 1786, A.O. 12/48, 242; Janet Murchison, testimony, July 26, 1786, A.O. 12/34, 405; Mary Kearsley, testimony, Apr. 28, 1785, A.O. 12/38, 282. Cf. Mrs. Kearsley's testimony with her written memorial, A.O. 13/102, 324–329. And see, for other examples, A.O. 12/4, 220, A.O. 12/14, 265, A.O. 12/47, 239, A.O. 13/63, 342, and A.O. 13/94, 318–326.

12 Isabella Logan, loss schedule, Feb. 17, 1784, A.O. 13/32, 129; case of Lady Leigh, July 1, 1783, A.O. 12/99, 313. See also the claim of Mary Auchmuty, A.O. 12/24, 114–117, 264–266, and A.O. 13/63, 133–140.

13 Sarah Troutbeck to commissioners, June 5, 1787, A.O. 13/49, pt. 2, 565; Troutbeck to Samuel Peters, May 22, 1788, Peters Papers, III, fol. 83 (microfilm), New-York Historical Society, New York City; Troutbeck to commissioners, Jan. 3, 1785, A.O. 13/137, 609. Her total claim covers fols. 539–590 in A.O. 13/49, Pt. 2, and fols. 726–740 in A.O. 13/74. On the recovery of her property see A.O. 12/81, 47. For other examples of well-to-do women with a good knowledge of the family property see A.O. 13/134, 571–574, and A.O. 12/54, 61–71 (Mary

Rothery), A.O. 13/64, 81–99, and A.O. 13/97, 344–348 (Henrietta Colden), and A.O. 12/13, 311–314 (Mary Poynton). Mary Winslow knew her own property in detail but was not so familiar with her husband's (A.O. 13/79, 757–758).

14  Case of Mrs. Dumaresq, Mar. 31, 1783, A.O. 12/99, 134; case of Margaret Smithies, Nov. 13, 1783, A.O. 12/100, 66; case of Barbara Mergath, May 8, 1783, A.O. 12/99, 234; Jane Gibbes, testimony, Dec. 15, 1783, A.O. 12/46, 245–247.

15  Jane Gibbes, testimony, Dec. 16, 1783, A.O. 12/46, 247–249; Widow Boyce, loss schedule, Oct. 16, 1783, A.O. 13/90, 181; Elizabeth Hogal, loss schedule, n.d., A.O. 12/27, 37. Typical examples of claims submitted by rural women may be found in A.O. 13/56, 91–93, A.O. 13/138, 475, A.O. 12/4, 72–74, A.O. 12/20, 270–271, A.O. 12/26, 14–16, and A.O. 12/29, 79. Cf. claims from rural men in A.O. 13/79, 73–77, 211–216. For a claim involving property owned elsewhere see that of Elinor Maybee, A.O. 12/28, 343–346, and A.O. 12/64, 1; for one involving both a mortgage and a misread will see that of Margaret Hutchinson, A.O. 12/16, 33–37, and A.O. 12/63, 61.

16  Mary McAlpin, loss schedule, n.d., A.O. 13/131, 10–11, and testimony, Nov. 14, 1785, A.O. 12/21, 51–65.

17  The list totals more than 40 because some women listed two enterprises. The women divided as follows: 10 each from New York City and Charleston, 7 each from Boston and Philadelphia, 2 from Baltimore, and 1 each from Savannah, Williamsburg, Wilmington, N.C., and St. Augustine. Twenty-eight were long-time widows or single, or were married but operated businesses independently of their husbands; 8 assisted their husbands; and 7 took over businesses after the death or incapacitation of their husbands.

18  The quotation is from Rachel Wetmore, claims memorial, Mar. 25, 1786, A.O. 13/16, 271. For a milliner's claim see Margaret Hutchinson's, A.O. 13/96, 601–602; for a grocer and boardinghouse keeper's see Sarah Simpson's, A.O. 12/25, 25–28. The midwife, Janet Cumming, claimed to have made £400 sterling annually, and her witnesses confirmed that estimate (A.O. 12/50, 347–348). See also Margaret Draper's original and revised loss estimates, A.O. 13/44, 342–344, 387, and Mary Airey's schedule, A.O. 12/24, 79.

19  Hannah Pollard, claims memorial and testimony, A.O. 13/49, Pt. 1, 158–159, 166; testimony re: claim of Mary Campbell, Oct. 24, 1786, A.O. 12/50, 103–105. The detailed schedule presented by the tavernkeeper Rachel Brain had been prepared by her husband before his death; see A.O. 12/26, 308–310.

20  For a general discussion of claims receipts see Norton, *British-Americans,* 216–220. Property claims submitted by 10 of the businesswomen were disallowed, and at least another 10 of them apparently did not pursue a claim for lost property. (Because of the destruction and disappearance of some of the claims records it is impossible to be more precise.)

21  This emphasis appears to have resulted from the influence of Dexter's *Colonial Women of Affairs.* Although she was careful to explain that she had searched only for examples of women who worked outside the home, and although she did not attempt to estimate the percentage of such women in the female population as a whole, historians who draw upon her book invariably stress the wide-ranging economic interests of colonial women. See, for example, Gerda Lerner, *The Woman in American History* (Reading, Mass., 1971), 15–19, and Carol Ruth Berkin, *Within the Conjuror's Circle: Women in Colonial America* (Morristown, N.J., 1974), 8–10.

22  If anything, the loyalist claimants tended to be more urban than other loyalists and the rest of the American population, and therefore would presumably over-represent working women. See the analysis in Norton, *British-Americans,* 37–39, and Fingerhut, "Uses and Abuses of Loyalists' Claims," *WMQ,* 3d Ser., XXV (1968), 245–258. Further, the method of choosing the sample – including only those women who themselves submitted claims and pension applications – would also tend to bias the result in favor of working women, since they would be the most likely to act on their own.

23  The failure of 18th-century men to discuss finances with their wives is also revealed in such letters as that of Jane Robbins to her daughter Hannah Gilman, Sept. 1799, Gilman Papers, Massachusetts Historical Society, Boston. Mrs. Robbins declared that, although her husband had made his will some years before, "I never saw it till after his death." Further, she informed her daughter, on his

deathbed he told her, "I should have many debts to pay that I knew nothing about."

24 Berkin, *Conjuror's Circle,* 12–14, and Nancy F. Cott, ed., *Root of Bitterness: Documents of the Social History of American Women* (New York, 1972), 8–10, link sex role differentiation specifically to the upper classes that were emerging in the process which has been called "Europeanization" or "Anglicization."

25 See, for example, Spruill, *Women's Life and Work,* 78–79.

26 David Ingersoll to commissioners, July 30, 1788, A.O. 13/74, 288. For rare cases of men who did list household furnishings see A.O. 13/98, 431–432, and A.O. 13/73. 140–155.

27 Martha Leslie, loss schedule, Mar. 25, 1784, A.O. 13/91, 2–3; Frances Dongan, inventory, [Nov. 1, 1783], A.O. 13/109, 45; Catherine Bowles, loss schedule, May 10, 1783, A.O. 13/90, 175–176; Mary Swords, "Things Plundered from me by the Rebels," n.d., A.O. 13/67, 311.

28 Mary Gibbins, loss schedule, n.d., A.O. 13/80, 167; "Estimate of Losses sustained at New York by Hannah Foy in the year 1775" [1782], A.O. 13/54, 431; Elizabeth Bowers, loss schedule, n.d., A.O. 13/68, pt. 1, 64.

29 Sarah Stuart, memorial to Lords of Treasury, Jan. 22, 1786, A.O. 13/135, 702; Elizabeth Phillips, affidavit, Oct. 9, 1788, A.O. 13/67, 303; Phebe Stevens, claims memorial, Mar. 23, 1784, A.O. 13/83, 580. For accounts of rebel looting see, for example, A.O. 12/56, 326–327, A.O. 13/73, 485, A.O. 13/91, 190, A.O. 13/93, 556, A.O. 13/102, 1278, A.O. 13/109, 43, A.O. 13/121, 478, and A.O. 13/126, 589.

30 See, for example, A.O. 12/21, 53–54, A.O. 13/110, 351, A.O. 13/112, 55, A.O. 13/123, 240–241, A.O. 13/128, 7, and A.O. 13/135, 698. Two women said they suffered miscarriages as a result of scuffles with Revolutionary troops (A.O. 13/81, 59, and A.O. 13/64, 76–77), and a third was raped by a rebel soldier. The latter incident is discussed in Thomas Goldthwait to his daughter Catherine, Aug. 20, 1779, J. M. Robbins Papers, Mass. Hist. Soc.

31 Lorenda Holmes, claims memorial, n.d., A.O. 13/65, 529–530. Similar though less graphic tales were recounted by other women whose assistance to the British was also discovered by the Revolutionaries. See A.O. 12/49, 56–58,

A.O. 12/102, 80, A.O. 13/45, 530, A.O. 13/67, 192, A.O. 13/68, 125, A.O. 13/96, 263, and A.O. 13/102, 1107.

32 Mary Serjeant, loss schedule, Feb. 19, 1783, A.O. 13/49, pt. 1, 285; Christian Barnes to Elizabeth Smith, July 13–28, 1770, Christian Barnes Letterbook, Library of Congress; Barnes to Elizabeth Smith Inman, Apr. [2]9, [1775], in Nina Moore Tiffany, ed., *Letters of James Murray, Loyalist* (Boston, 1901), 187–188.

33 Louisa Susannah Wells Aikman, *The Journal of a Voyage from Charlestown, S.C., to London undertaken during the American Revolution …* (New York, 1906), 52; Catherine Goldthwait to Elizabeth [Inman], Mar. 27, 1780, Robbins Papers, Mass. Hist. Soc. For a discussion of the loyalists' initial optimism and subsequent disillusionment see Mary Beth Norton, "The Loyalists' Image of England: Ideal and Reality," *Albion,* 111 (1971), 62–71.

34 Hannah Winslow to [a sister-in-law], June 27, 1779, Winslow Papers, Mass. Hist. Soc. See also Rebecca Dolbeare to John Dolbeare, Aug. 30, 1780, Dolbeare Papers, Mass. Hist. Soc; Polly Dibblee to William Jarvis, Nov. 1787, A.O. 13/41, 248. For a general discussion of the exiles' financial problems see Norton, *British-Americans,* 49–61. For another similar observation by a single woman see Louisa Oliver to Andrew Spooner, Mar. 1, 1788, Hutchinson-Oliver Papers, Mass. Hist. Soc.

35 The quotation is from the case of Mary Hind, Feb. 1783, A.O. 12/99, 35· For examples of other women who claimed ignorance of proper forms and application procedures see A.O. 12/46, 165, A.O. 12/99, 238, A.O. 13/24, 284, A.O. 13/26, 63, 199, 282, 360, A.O. 13/113, 88, A.O. 13/131, 65, and A.O. 13/137, 150. Of course, a few men also made similar claims; see, for example, A.O. 12/43, 322–325, 328–331, and A.O. 12/46, 63. On the male networks see Norton, *British Americans,* 63–79, 162–164, 186–196, 206–216. The memorials submitted by women were not only more prone to error but also more informal, less likely to be written in the third person, less likely to contain the sorts of ritualistic phrases and arguments used by the men, and consequently more likely to be personally revealing.

36 Norton, *British-Americans,* 52–61, 111–121, discusses the bases for pension decisions. It was

standard practice for the commission to lower a family's allotment immediately after the death of the husband, regardless of the fact that the widow usually had to meet medical and funeral expenses at exactly that time. The pension records (A.O. 12/99–105, and T. 50/11ff, Public Record Office) show that women's pensions were normally smaller than men's. In addition, T. 50/11 reveals a clear case of discrimination: in 1789 the Charleston midwife Janet Cumming (see note 18 above) was, under the commission's rules, entitled to an annual pension of £200 for loss of profession (she was the only woman to qualify for one in her own right); instead, she was granted only a £50 widow's allowance.

37  Mary Serjeant to John Wilmot and Daniel P. Coke, Dec. 1, 1782, A.O. 13/49, pt. 1, 283; Ann Asby to commissioners, Apr. 14, 1788, A.O. 13/43, 147; Susanna Sandys, memorial, n.d., A.O. 13/84, 613. (Sandys was English, though the daughter of a refugee, and is quoted here because of the detailed nature of her comments.) For a statement similar to Mrs. Serjeant's see Margaret Smythies to Lords of Treasury, Jan. 23, 1782, A.O. 13/67, 230. For two women who did explain why they could not work see A.O. 13/75, 627, and A.O. 13/53, 193. Information about nearly all the loyalist women who worked in England may be located in the following documents: A.O. 12/30, 230, A.O. 12/90, 50, 244, 264, A.O. 12/101, 137, A.O. 12/102, 87, 136, 164, 165, 175, 187, A.O. 13/43, 661, A.O. 13/44, 427, A.O. 13/71, 156, and A.O. 13/131. 359.

38  On the Wells sisters' enterprise see Steuart Papers, 5041, fol. 123, National Library of Scotland, Edinburgh; Ann Elmsley to James Parker [1789?], Parker Papers, Pt, IV, no. 15, Liverpool Record Office, England; and Aikman, *Journal of a Voyage*, 71. Susannah Marshall's story may be traced in A.O. 13/62, 4, 7, A.O. 12/6, 257–263, and A.O. 12/99, 244.

39  Harriet, Mary, Sarah, and Elizabeth Dawson and Ann Dawson Murray to commissioners, n.d., A. O. 13/113, 195; Mary Muirson to Lords of Treasury, May 28, 1784, A.O. 13/56, 342; Isabella Logan, claims memorial, Feb. 17, 1784, A.O. 13/32, 126; Patience Johnston, claims memorial, Dec. 21, 1785, A.O. 13/26, 196. For similar statements see A.O. 13/40, 93, A.O. 13/75, 354, 603, A.O. 13/132, 257, and A.O. 13/134, 504.

40  Mary Lowry to [Samuel Remnant], n.d., A.O. 13/31, 202; Mary Curtain to Charles Monro, July 7, 1789, A.O. 13/137, 98; Samuel Peters to Daniel P. Coke, Nov. 20, 1784, A.O. 13/43, 352. Cf. the statements in the text with those of men; for example, Samuel Porter to Lords of Treasury, Feb. 23, 1776, T. 1/520, 27; Thomas Banks to Lords of Treasury, Feb. 9, 1779, T. 1/552, 3; John Saunders to Lords of Treasury, Mar. 31, 1785, F.O. 4/1, 248, Public Record Office.

41  Case of Margaret Reynolds, Mar. 26, 1783, A.O. 12/99, 116; Charlotte Mayne to – [Aug. 1783], H.O. 42/3, Public Record Office; Alicia Young to Robert Mackenzie, June 3, 1789, A.O. 13/67, 641. Mrs. Young gave the commissioners a detailed list of the items she had pawned (A.O. 13/67, 646). For other similar accounts of women pawning or selling their goods see A.O. 12/99, 13, 56, 60, A.O. 12/101, 196, 364, A.O. 13/43, 350, A.O. 13/64, 76, and A.O. 13/135, 81, 426.

42  "Mrs Derbage's Narrative," Mar. 1789, A.O. 13/34, 298; Penelope Nicoll, deposition, July 6, 1787, A.O. 13/68, 267; Mary Broadhead to commissioners, Nov. 12, 1788, A.O. 13/125, 626; Margaret Draper to John Robinson, June 27, 1777, A.O. 13/44, 345; Rose Brailsford to Lords of Treasury, Dec. 29, 1779, A.O. 13/125, 580; Joyce Dawson to Lord Dunmore, July 24, 1781, A.O. 13/28, 220; Charlotte Pollock to Lords of Treasury, n.d., A.O. 13/133, 442.

43  Lucy Necks to Lady North, Aug. 14, 1781, A.O. 13/32, 155; Elizabeth Barkesdale to commissioners, Nov. 24, 1786, A.O. 13/125, 402; Lydia Doty to Lords of Treasury, May 8, 1782, A.O. 13/113, 328; Alicia Young to Robert Mackenzie, June 6, 1789, A.O. 13/67, 643; Mary Taylor to commissioners, Apr. 12, 1783, A.O. 13/42, 590. In sharp contrast to such statements, Andrew Allen, a male refugee, wrote in Feb. 1783, "Notwithstanding what has happened I have the Satisfaction to feel my Spirits unbroken and my Mind prepared to look forwards without Despondency." Allen to James Hamilton, Feb. 3, 1783, Dreer Collection, Historical Society of Pennsylvania, Philadelphia.

44  Recent articles by linguists raise provocative questions about sex differences in speech. Most of them are concerned with 20th-century oral expression, however, and it is difficult to determine how accurately they apply to 18th-

century documents. Among the most interesting are Nancy Faires Conklin, "Toward a Feminist Analysis of Linguistic Behavior," *University of Michigan Papers in Women's Studies,* I (1974), 51–73; Mary Ritchie Key, "Linguistic Behavior of Male and Female," *Linguistics: An International Review,* LXXXVIII (1972), 15–31; Cheris Kramer, "Women's Speech: Separate but Unequal?," *The Quarterly Journal of Speech,* LX (1974), 14–24; and Robin Lakoff, "Language and Woman's Place," *Language in Society,* II (1974), 45–79.

45　C. Wright Mills, "Situated Actions and Vocabularies of Motive," *American Sociological Review,* V (1940), 904–913, esp. 906–909.

46　The only woman claimant who appears to have manipulatively assumed a "feminine" role was Sarah Troutbeck. It is also difficult to determine, first, what it was that the commission "wanted" to hear from female loyalists and, second, how the women would know what the commission wanted, given their isolation from the male information networks. It could perhaps be argued that every 18th-century woman "knew" what every 18th-century man expected of her, but the fact is that the women claimants had a great deal to gain by displaying a very "unfeminine" knowledge of their husband's estates and by demonstrating their competence to the commission. See, for example, A.O. 12/101, 186, A.O. 12/40, 40–44, and A.O. 12/66, 6.

47　The long quotations: Margaret Hutchinson, claims memorial, Feb. 23, 1784, A.O. 13/96, 601; Eleanor Lestor, claims memorial, n.d., A.O. 12/48, 359; Elizabeth Thompson to John Forster, Dec. 21, 1785, A.O. 13/136, 8; Mary Kearsley, testimony, Apr. 28, 1785, A.O. 12/38, 282; Mary Williams, affidavit, Dec. 21, 1785, A.O. 13/26, 535; Catherine Chilsom, claims memorial, Mar. 11, 1786, A.O. 13/24, 90. The shorter phrases: A.O. 13/16, 271, A.O. 13/24, 357, A.O. 13/26, 357.

48　A.O. 13/118, 488, A.O. 13/67, 234, A.O. 13/73, 586, A.O. 13/81, 59. Men also described women in the same terms; for examples see A.O. 13/28, 215, and A.O. 12/101, 235. The widows of Revolutionary soldiers also called themselves "helpless"; see, for example, Papers of the Continental Congress, V, 16 (M–41), Roll 50, V, 37, 122 (M–42), Roll 55, National Archives.

49　T. 1/612, 157, A.O. 13/53, 62, A.O. 13/137, 574, A.O. 12/8, 124. For a few "unfortunate" men see

A.O. 12/46, 104, A.O. 12/51, 208, A.O. 12/13, 188, and A.O. 12/42, 132.

50　The women who were most definitely not helpless (for example, Susannah Marshall, Janet Cumming, and Sarah Troutbeck) did not use that word to describe themselves. Consequently, it appears that the term was not simply a formulaic one utilized by all women indiscriminately, but rather that it represented a real self-perception of those who did use it. At least one 18th-century woman recognized the sex-typed usage of the word "helpless." In her book of essays, Judith Sargent Murray noted that she hoped that "the term, *helpless widow,* might be rendered as unfrequent and inapplicable as that of *helpless widower.*" See Judith Sargent Murray, *The Gleaner,* III (Boston, 1789), 223.

51　Isabella Logan, claims memorial, Feb. 17, 1784, A.O. 13/32, 126; Jane Hilding, claims memorial, July 30, 1788, A.O. 13/46, 315; Joyce Dawson to Lord Dunmore, July 24, 1781, A.O. 13/28, 220. Also of interest is Jane Constable to Lords of Treasury, n.d., A.O. 13/73, 374.

52　Alicia Young to Robert Mackenzie, June 6, 1789, A.O. 13/67, 643; Jane Roberts, claims memorial, Mar. 17, 1784, A.O. 13/71, 245; Margaret Draper to Lord – –, Oct. 15, 1782, A.O. 13/44, 349; Elizabeth Skinner to commissioners, Aug. 28, 1786, A.O. 13/112, 61. Mrs. Draper lived to see her daughter well married (Margaret Draper to the Misses Byles, June 21, 1784, Byles Papers, 1, 134, Mass. Hist. Soc.). Cf. men's attitudes toward their children and other dependents in A.O. 13/75, 556, A.O. 12/105, 115, A.O. 13/131, 399, and A.O. 13/137, 2.

53　Elizabeth Putnam to Thomas Dundas, Nov. 7, 1789, A.O. 13/75, 309; Elizabeth Dumaresq to Lord Shelburne, Sept. 14, 1782, A.O. 13/44, 429; Elizabeth Barkesdale to commissioners, Nov. 24, 1786, A.O. 13/125, 402, Rachel Wetmore, claims memorial, Mar. 25, 1786, A.O. 13/16, 272. Other comments on neighbors and relatives may be found in A.O. 12/3, 231, A.O. 12/56, 339, A.O. 13/25, 275, A.O. 13/32, 595, A.O. 13/44, 345, A.O. 13/75, 544, 641, and A.O. 13/107, 271. Mr. and Mrs. James Parker had an interesting exchange of letters on the subject of whether she would join him in England, in which her ties to her American friends figured strongly. "Tho I would not hesitate one moment to go with you my Dearest friend to any place on earth, yet I cannot think of parting forever with my Dear and valuable friends on this side the atlantick, without many a heart felt sigh," she wrote on July 24, 1783. His response (Mar. 5, 1784) recognized her concern: "I realy sympathize with you on this trying scene of leaving of your Country and all our friends." Parker Papers, Pt. VIII, nos. 26, 31, Liverpool Record Office.

54  Elizabeth Macnair to John Hamilton, Dec. 27, 1789, A.O. 13/131, 400; Mary Serjeant to John Wilmot and Daniel P. Coke, Dec. 1, 1782, A.O. 13/49, Pt. 1, 283. See also A.O. 13/34, 471, and A.O. 13/70B, 145, on resettlement. For women who followed friends and relatives into exile see A.O. 13/116, 468, A.O. 13/114, 662, A.O. 12/102, 24, and A.O. 13/37, 3.

55  On the development of republican ideology pertaining to women see Linda K. Kerber, "Daughters of Columbia: Educating Women for the Republic, 1787–1805," in Stanley Elkins and Eric McKitrick, eds., *The Hofstadter Aegis* (New York, 1974), 36–59.

# 10

# RESTRAINT AND RETALIATION

*The North Carolina Militias and the Backcountry War of 1780–1782*

## Wayne E. Lee

## Introduction

One could make a strong argument that North Carolina was as central to America's victory in the Revolutionary War as any other state. By the spring of 1780, the British war effort had gained a second life by shifting its emphasis from the northern to southern colonies. In May, General Henry Clinton built on British gains in Georgia by conquering Charleston, after which he dispatched the regular British army under General Charles Cornwallis and loyalist units under British officers, such as Banastre Tarleton and Patrick Ferguson, to pacify the Carolinas. American forces, particularly North and South Carolina militiamen, stopped the British momentum in a series of battles in and near North Carolina: King's Mountain, October 7, 1780; Cowpens, January 17, 1781; and Guilford Court House, March 15, 1781. Guilford Court House, though technically a British victory, so weakened General Cornwallis's army that he gave up on retaking the Carolinas and turned his efforts to Virginia. There his army suffered a resounding defeat at Yorktown in October 1781 that secured American victory in the war.

In this selection, Wayne E. Lee focuses on the backcountry partisan war that took place between the large battles in Britain's southern campaign. The region witnessed some of the most horrific violence of the war, a phenomenon that Lee attempts to understand and put into historical context. He argues that backcountry fighting, though certainly gruesome, was not completely devoid of principles. American soldiers were well aware of the European rules of war and also aspired to republican notions of virtuous war. The Continental Army was particularly restrained, mostly abiding by its own strict articles of war. In addition, although the Americans forced significant numbers of loyalist prisoners into the Continental service, they paroled the vast majority of British prisoners or exchanged them for American prisoners; few loyalist or British prisoners were killed.

According to Lee, many violent transgressions on the American side occurred because of the institutionally weak nature of militias. They had minimal government oversight. Moreover, the frequent turnover of men and officers in militias limited the role of peers and leaders in stopping unjust acts of violence. Finally, both American and European law allowed for some retaliation by victims of violence. This helped to create a vicious circle in which the Americans and the British, along with their loyalist supporters, traded one act of atrocity after another. Despite legitimate hopes for restraint, therefore, combatants in the southern partisan war fell into patterns of escalating violence.

- Lee's portrayal of militias is much less triumphal than John Shy's depiction in the opening of this section. Are their interpretations mutually exclusive, or was it possible for militias to advance the American cause even while committing acts that violated the standard of conduct expected by George Washington and high-ranking officers?
- Although recruiting soldiers was not easy anywhere in the new United States, North Carolina did not have the same amount of difficulty as its neighbor Virginia experienced (as explained in the essay by Michael A. McDonnell). What are some factors in both states that help to explain the difference?

- Consider the advantages and disadvantages of excessive violence in the American Revolutionary War. If, on at least one level, the purpose of war is to destroy one's opponent, why did Washington and other American military leaders so disapprove of the tactics used in the southern backcountry war?

The worst of the American Revolutionary War came late to North Carolina. North Carolina's rebels had quickly gained control of the colony at the outset of the war, defeated the most dramatic loyalist counterstroke at Moore's Creek Bridge in 1776, devastated the Cherokees' country for their attempt to join the British war effort, and then more or less contained any serious intrastate resistance for the next three years. The Tories never entirely ceased their efforts to organize and resist but, by and large, a kind of seething calm held the countryside until 1780 and the British capture of Charleston.

The fall of Charleston brought war back to North Carolina with a fury unallayed by the delay. The fratricidal nature of that war has become something of a truism, and many stories attest to its ugliness. In 1781, a volunteer militia company commanded by Colonel John Moffitt captured the "grayheaded" father of a known Tory clan and questioned him severely as to the whereabouts of his sons, repeatedly threatening him with death. At one point, a fellow soldier handed an improvised spear to our witness for this story, one James Collins, and suggested that he run the old man through.[1] On the loyalist side, the notorious David Fanning recounted how in May of 1781 he and a small party of his men were surprised and surrounded in a friend's house. They rushed out to overwhelm the ambushers and successfully reached the woods. Two of his men were taken, however, "one of which the Rebels shot in cold Blood, and the other they hanged on the spot where we had Killed the man a few Days before." "Exasperated," Fanning retaliated on a party of rebels plundering a house. In a half-hour skirmish Fanning and his men killed two, wounded three, and captured two more. Following up on his success, over the next few days he attacked several other rebel parties, killing seven, wounding ten and capturing eight.[2]

In a yet more brutal example of the internecine struggle during those years, in February 1781, a combined force of Continental cavalry and North Carolina militia used confusion over uniforms to surprise and decimate a loyalist column. The next day prodded by his comrades, militiaman Moses Hall wandered over to see some of the prisoners. "We went to where six were standing together. Some discussion taking place, I heard some of our men cry out, 'Remember Buford,' and the prisoners were immediately hewed to pieces with broadswords."[3]

These and similar tales of murder, mistreatment, and plunder litter the records of the Southern war in its later years. But in examining such stories, we must be careful to consider contemporary values and understandings of violence. Careful analysis will show that these are stories of both restraint and of escalation. Values and hopes for a virtuous way of war did not always hold together, but often they did. A careful look at the nature of the war in North Carolina from 1780 to 1782 reveals a complex story of a society struggling with the strains of war, hoping for restraint, fearing escalation, all while trying to bring their cause to a successful conclusion.

## Values and Restraint

Violence is always judged. Observers and participants evaluate its legitimacy or criminality, but they do so from within their own cultural framework. The battlefield and nonbattlefield quasi-military violence of the War of Independence can only be understood within that era's cultural understanding of what war was and how it should be conducted. Those values and understandings in turn shaped individual reactions to the war they saw, and their reactions then formed part of the landscape of the war.

Precedents and preconceptions shape decisions about wielding violence, in part by creating communal standards that individuals hesitate to violate for fear of social censure. Preconceptions also shape reactions to violence, whether outrage at violations of precedent or grudging acceptance of certain inevitabilities. The social and political environment in turn sets other conditions: the speed and reliability of reports of violence, the level of sensitivity to certain types of violence (for example, racial dynamics in response to reports of violence by Indians or slaves); and, the probability of censure. To precedent and environment, one must add contingency. Individuals pursue their own purposes, ignore social convention, or might, to use one historian's phrase, have a "sadistic predisposition to violence."[4] Such individually contingent acts then feed back into the wider social expectations and environment of war, shaping more collective responses. The norms of war alone, therefore, did not determine behavior, but they did condition it. Individual decisions about violence were pressured by concern for what others would think, and thus a substantial part of explaining the war's escalation lies in examining the ways in which individual and small-group decisions made under the stresses of war had become separated from prewar communal values and pressures.

To see the peculiar nature of the backcountry war, we must first understand the general conventions and prevailing values that governed the conduct of war during the American Revolution. We must then analyze the incarnation of those values in the militia. The values and expectations can be reduced to four groups. The first group includes the traditional limits on military violence rooted in popular morality, European military formalism (the "rules" of war), and the cult of honor. These conventions limited gratuitous violence. They prescribed treatment of enemy troops and civilians that was considered to be lawful and fair. Revolutionary Americans had developed a second group of values revolving around republican notions of virtuous war waged by citizens. Historians have long noted how republican ideology incorporated a belief in the military efficiency and political safety of an armed citizenry.[5] But also imbedded in the idea of a virtuous republican army was the expectation that its use of violence would be restrained, avoiding the wanton destruction of innocent life and property. This belief generated frequent comparisons of restrained American behavior to the excessive violence of the British.[6] A third set of beliefs recognized that war brought sacrifices. A certain amount of loss brought about by the need for armies to eat, and the normal killing and dying in battle, were only to be expected. Finally, although military convention and the republican notion of virtue acted as restraints on warfare, their effect on violence in North Carolina was diminished by the cultural legitimacy of retaliation or retribution. Behavior that exceeded normative limits on violence merited retaliation in kind. Just what those limits were and what kind of retaliation was meted out resulted from individual decisions and from the norms established by communities and institutions. Thus, the type and level of violence would be varied and dynamic, but not necessarily chaotic. Between 1780 and 1782, military conventions and republican ideals that restrained violence weakened as boundaries on retribution and retaliation expanded. Furthermore, embedded in that process of weakening restraints and expanding retaliation was another process whereby both individuals and the Revolutionary government justified the legitimacy of new levels of violence. They knew they were rewriting the rules, and in rewriting them they sought not only to "cover" their actions, but also to find ways to impose a modicum of order even on this more violent vision of war.

The extent to which the limits on military violence continued to function, even within these worst years of the war, is illustrated in Collins's experience of interrogating the "grayheaded" old Tory. While Colonel Moffitt questioned the old man and he pleaded ignorance of his sons' whereabouts and begged for his life, another member of the militia company pulled Collins aside, handed him a spear, and asked him to quickly run the old man through. Collins's horrified refusal and his reasons reveal not only the values in play, but also the structures reinforcing them. Collins said, "He is too old; besides the colonel would never forgive me; he is a prisoner and he don't intend to kill him." Both traditional morality and European military formalism suggested that the old were not proper targets of war, and the colonel's adherence to that formal code put a protective shield around the prisoner. Furthermore, Collins's respect for Colonel Moffitt, which his memoir makes clear, prevented him from going against Moffitt's presumed wishes. Note also how his statement implies Moffitt's past history of restrained treatment of prisoners. Collins continued his account, recalling that the other militiaman then offered him money to kill the old man. Collins persisted in his refusal, scorning the instigator who "would bribe me to do a deed that he himself would be ashamed of." Here we see the judgment of the community of soldiery, particularly that of a respected officer, restraining each other from "shameful" acts. Collins ceased to respect the other man, avoided that soldier thereafter, and believed him "rotten at the core." Collins even suspected that the man later "ran distracted and died so" from a "remorse [which] had overtaken him." As for the old man, he was set free.

This is merely one anecdote, but other evidence reveals both the nature of restraints on war and their continued, though weakening, function in North Carolina from 1780 to 1782.[7] One way to see how those values continued to function was in the judgments the combatants made of each other on the basis of their conscious gradation of violent acts. The basic distinction appeared simple enough: in an oft-repeated phrase, there were Tories who were proper soldiers or were noncombatants, and then there were Tories "who have been guilty of murder, robbery, house-burning and offences

out of the military line."[8] Murder and house burning were in a clear-cut category of their own, and men guilty of such acts repeatedly were excluded from late-war truces or pardons, or became the specific targets of retribution.[9] Collins, for example, noted that "those we called the 'pet Tories,' or neutrals, we never disturbed," but with the war in the rebels' hands in 1782, his company "commenced ferreting out the Tories … such as had been in the habit of plundering, burning, and murdering."[10] A similarly clear-cut category was desertion and fighting for the other side. Elijah Alexander, a militiaman in company with Continental Army troops in 1781, recalled taking a group of prisoners, five of whom proved to be deserters. They were "all hung on one gallows." It is important to point out, however, that Alexander continued on to record how the other Tories were guarded, some court-martialed and whipped, and others "sent to jail or headquarters."[11]

If murder, house burning, and desertion were clearly unacceptable, the question of robbery was somewhat thornier. After all, violence in the "military line" was to be excused, but the exact moment when provisioning became plundering was a fine line. The Reverend Samuel McCorkle laid out the ideological basis in a sermon against plundering, noting that it had "degrees of aggravation." Where "taking … victualls from their foes" was one thing, "the taking of money to a considerable amount … . The taking of horses and cattle, and slaves, and furniture" aggravated the offense to a felony.[12] Whig soldiers and politicians made similar distinctions. William Davie, a partisan leader sometimes accused of excesses, turned some of his prisoners over to Continental control and, when asked about them, said they were guilty "of no particular crime, but the general one of their being Kings Militia."[13] Witnesses in the 1782 treason trial of Samuel Bryant, a leading Tory officer, acknowledged that he had not "committed any violences more than any other Army would have done in similar circumstances, in supplying themselves with Arms, ammunitions, provisions, horses, &c., there being no proof of [him] having been guilty of any murders, house-burning or plundering except as above mentioned for the support of their Army." In light of this testimony, the governor reprieved Bryant, changing his status from a criminal punishable by death to an exchangeable prisoner.[14]

In short, some kinds of plundering were worse than others. Official impressment of needed provisions was more or less accepted, provided it was done with the appropriate formality (by officers, preferably with advance notice), and some attempt was made to pay or at least provide receipts.[15] Soldiers "carving for themselves" for subsistence was considered an offense, but not so much as soldiers taking nonmilitary necessities.[16] Finally, and most egregious, were the situations in which officers were seen to direct soldiers in the taking of nonmilitary necessities.[17] This sense of gradation, often ignored by historians, was of great concern to the populace and to the soldiers themselves, who can be found avoiding stepping over certain lines within this "hierarchy" of plunder. A number of examples from the Moravian communities are particularly vivid in this respect. Members of one militia company tried to take blankets but, when asked, were unable to show their "press warrant" authorizing such impressment and so left with nothing. Another group accosted a rider named Graeter on the road, threatening to shoot him if he did not give up his horse. "He risked that and they let him alone." Some militiamen expressed remorse at their previous behavior in the Moravian towns and were more restrained in later visits, whereas some stepped in to prevent the depredations of other militiamen. One militia company even took the time to repay the Moravians with provisions when their own official supplies caught up with them.[18] These distinctions of plunder and the consequent judgments of plunderers, however fine, continued to be made, and were even applied in the courts-martial of Tory prisoners.

The treatment of prisoners provided the clearest view of the Whig government's struggle to restrain itself and its military arm under traditional norms of war. In the main they succeeded, but with notable lapses. Most prisoners faced three decisions about their fate. The first came as they tried to surrender. Soldiers or militiamen in the heat of battle were known to refuse requests for quarter, and, though such "hot-blooded" killings were condemned by eighteenth-century military ethics, it was considered less of a crime than killing them in cold blood later. Being a captive was the second decision point. What would the leaders and men of the capturing unit decide to do with their prisoners? Most tales of mistreatment and murder occur at this point in a prisoner's transition from freedom to captivity, perhaps because such treatment at this stage was the most illegitimate – and therefore remembered and recorded. The leaders and men of militia units might seek vengeance, and sometimes exact it from their prisoners, but when doing so they sought to clothe their behavior in as much judicial legitimacy as possible, perhaps to assuage their consciences and perhaps to provide a legal shield. Whigs used courts-martial (formal and informal) to decide the fate of many loyalist prisoners. When William Gipson's company captured two Tories in 1779 they took the trouble to escort them a full fifteen miles to the Guilford County courthouse and there held a court-martial. The Whig company condemned Hugh McPherson, a "notorious" Tory, and shot him. They sentenced the other to "be spicketed," that is, suspended over a sharp pin, with his bare foot tenuously perched on the point. This was nominally a traditional disciplinary punishment for cavalrymen, but in this instance they went beyond the norm and actually slowly drove the pin through his foot.[19] There are many similar reports of Whig militias bringing in Tories and sentencing them to be whipped, and even occasionally to be hanged or shot, after a quick court-martial.[20] In one extended example, around a hundred Tory prisoners trickled into the Moravian towns in August and September of 1780. The militia held a series of trials, whipped some of the prisoners – a few more severely than others – hanged one on his own confession, enlisted many in the rebel forces, and released others on "certain conditions."[21]

The most famous incident was that of the prisoners from British Colonel Patrick Ferguson's loyalist corps taken at King's Mountain. In the week following the battle, several loyalists were tried and hanged, but the process also tells a tale of restraint and a desire for legitimacy. The Whig field officers convened a court-martial, supposedly motivated by reports of hangings of rebels by loyalists in South Carolina, and convicted thirty-six Tories (out of hundreds of prisoners) of "breaking open houses, killing the men, turning the women and children out of doors, and burning the houses." Determined to inject an air of legality into the proceedings, someone retrieved a copy of the North Carolina law that authorized two magistrates to summon a jury, and, because several militia officers present were in fact also magistrates, it was cited as the basis for the trial. Three men at a time were hanged until nine were dead, and then the officers ended it.[22] Even the manner of execution is significant. In the case of the King's Mountain prisoners, and in many of the more "informal" and illegal executions, the method of choice was hanging.[23] Hanging as a method of execution not only lent a judicial aspect to the killing, but also emphasized the supposed criminality of the victim.

A loyalist prisoner who survived his initial period of capture, as the evidence suggests the vast majority did, then faced the judgment of the North Carolina state government. They were even more likely to survive this judgment, though the Whigs continued until the end of the war to debate how to define the status of prisoners and thus how to treat them. For the most part, however, they fell back on the standard eighteenth-century utilitarian solution of treating them as exchangeable prisoners of war.[24] The process of exchange was never perfectly formalized between the American and British militaries during the war (especially

for loyalist prisoners), but it achieved a kind of regularity that made preserving the lives of loyalist prisoners worthwhile.[25] There were exceptions. Public pressure operated to exact vengeance, and the government's consequent wavering over whether to treat a loyalist as a civil prisoner or as an exchangeable prisoner of war resulted in what were probably somewhat random decisions. Typically, however, the government tried to distinguish between "types" of Tories by relying on definitions of violent acts to decide the issue. Those Tories who could be shown to have "been guilty of murder, robbery, house-burning, and offences out of the Military Line" were likely to be treated as civil criminals under the treason law.[26] Persons who had not committed such crimes could be exchanged. There was also a temptation among some Whig leaders to forcibly enlist captured loyalists into the Continental Army or active militia service. For example, several hundred of the nearly 600 prisoners taken at King's Mountain were paroled on the condition that they enlist for a three-month tour in the militia.[27] Such service would not only earn the loyalist a pardon, but would also help the Whigs fill the ranks.[28]

In the end, it is critical to emphasize that dramatic stories notwithstanding, the vast majority of prisoners taken on both sides were either paroled or held until exchanged, with a significant percentage of loyalist prisoners being forcibly enrolled into Continental service.[29] Perhaps the clearest evidence for this effort to restrain the spiral of wartime violence can be found in the fate of the leading men of Colonel David Fanning's loyalist militia. David Fanning was easily the most notorious, and probably the most successful, of the North Carolina loyalist leaders. His success and his violence made him and his men the most feared and hated partisans in North Carolina. Despite that fact, when Fanning sat down in New Brunswick in 1790 to write his memoir of the war, he was able to report that a startling number of his officers were alive and living in North Carolina. Of fifty-six officers whose fates he knew (seven were either unknown or in Charleston at the time of the British evacuation), he reported that twenty-two were living in North or South Carolina (plus one more in Pennsylvania). Six had been "killed," apparently in battle, five had been executed more or less judicially, and only five had been, in his words, "murdered." The remainder had either died, fled to other British possessions, or joined the rebels (three men).[30] That a full 41 percent of the *officers* of the *most notorious* loyalist unit in North Carolina would still be living in the American states – the majority still in North Carolina – speaks volumes for the survival rate, if not the pleasantries, of being a prisoner.

## The Breakdown of Restraint

One historian has characterized the war in the South as creating a "society altogether lacking a sense of civic polity."[31] In fact, the story is more complex than that. This was a society struggling to contain the savagery of war, sometimes succeeding and sometimes failing. Between 1780 and 1782 the failure of restraint became more marked, but never disappeared. So how and why did restraint break down?

Fundamentally the war outside Continental or British lines was a "people's war," waged by transient and institutionally weak militias, using operational techniques that undermined traditional restraints on military violence.[32] Furthermore, the militias' failures of restraint played out in an environment that by 1780 was charged by the Whig government's demands for men and material to support the war effort, and especially by the government's confiscations of loyalist property.[33] The Whig control of the countryside since 1776 had not kept tensions from escalating, and when the British army arrived in the area after the capture of Charleston, it catalyzed loyalist resistance. Throughout the war, wherever the British army could project its power, loyalists surfaced.[34] Added to this environment were the true "Banditti," small groups of individuals determined to take advantage of the war for purely personal gain.[35]

Finally, and perhaps most often cited as the cause of the Southern war's violence, the British army struggled internally over whether to treat the Americans as rebels deserving only fire and the sword or to try and win back their allegiance with an eye to postwar reconciliation. The British never fully committed to either path, and individual officers followed the course of their personal preference. Those who chose the fire and sword policy quickly became notorious, and their activities rapidly led to retaliation in kind.[36] Pointing to the British army's presence or their atrocities, however, does not suffice to explain the escalation of violence by the militias, largely because the Continental Army also operated in the same area and, in general, did not respond with greater violence.[37] For similar reasons, it is not enough merely to say that war naturally engenders such violence. It is also inaccurate to call this a "backcountry" war and then explain it on the basis of the particularities of the backcountry – its less-developed political institutions or its rougher breed of men.[38] Among other factors, the "backcountry" war was not confined to the backcountry, at least not in North Carolina. The militias scourged each other right up to the edge of Wilmington and New Bern.[39] A better explanation lies in the weakness of the new state, the cultural value placed on retaliation, and the nature and history of the militia.

With the reigniting of war in the South, one finds not only a continued struggle to maintain traditional restraints on violence, but also a process of rewriting the rules of warfare to effectively legitimize a greater latitude of violence. At the outset of the war, North Carolina's Whigs struggled to fight the virtuous war demanded by republicanism and as defined by the traditional mores supporting restraint in war – morality, military formalism, and honor. As the war progressed, however, three factors combined to undermine their efforts. First, the new state lacked the political coherence to regularly supply its troops or to make consistent judgments about prisoners. In essence, war making was decentralized, and it was left to local communities and militiamen to set the standards of permissible violence. The second factor was the basic cultural legitimacy of retaliation. One violation of norms led to another. The third factor was inability of the militias to contain the plague like spread of the desire for revenge. This inability was rooted in the militia structure itself. Its basic organization undermined preexisting community restraints because, when mobilized, the militias came to resemble mercenaries seeking plunder and revenge in contrast to the more disciplined and professional Continental Army. Furthermore, its enforcement missions and operational techniques were ill suited to restraint. Rather than containing the plague of revenge, the militia structure often spread it.

## The Infant State

The weak administrative power of the new state meant that the local militias acted with a minimum of centralized oversight. Militia units were largely local and on their own. They mobilized and demobilized in rapid succession and, because they lacked a reliable source of supplies from a financially prostrate state, militiamen often ravaged the countryside for their needs. By contrast, even though it too was desperate for supplies, the Continental Army attempted to maintain at least the pretense of reimbursement (providing receipts or certificates) and was committed to restraining the troops.[40] The Moravian Frederick Marshall admitted that one "must say for the regular troops … that their officers kept good order among them." He blamed the excesses on "camp followers, single soldiers, and especially by the militia."[41] The Continental officers also helped prevent abuses by their more consistent practice in sending quartering officers ahead of troops to systematize the collection of supplies.[42]

The militias lacked this sort of institutional regularity and were even less likely to come equipped with a method of payment. State officials recognized the problem and created a Board of War in an effort to streamline the provisioning system. Among other emergency measures, they shifted to a tax "in kind" in response to the extraordinary depreciation of the currency which had dramatically accelerated in 1779.[43] Their fears were clear. The board wrote to Thomas Polk in 1780 that "if we do not feed the soldiers they must take care of themselves, and will do it at the point of the Bayonet," or, employing the more common phrase, they "will carve for themselves."[44] Residents too recognized that many of the unpleasant confrontations with soldiers arose from their unexpected arrival and peremptory demands for supply.[45] Militia soldiers put to the necessity of supplying themselves found it all too easy to take more than necessities. As one militia officer summed up, the militia was "without regular supplies of provisions or forage," and so each man, when out of food, would supply himself from local homes, "which all considered they had a right to do at the house of friend or foe." The officer grimly concluded that this system provided "men of dishonest propensities an opportunity of taking many things which necessity did not require."[46]

The second problem created by the lack of state oversight was the absence of a consistent policy for defining who was a prisoner of war and the conventions for treating prisoners. As discussed previously, militia units often were free to contrive their own definitions and methods of treatment. The temptation of both rebel and loyalist militias was to treat prisoners as traitors. The proximity of regular troops, however, could restrain militias from executing captives. In the case of loyalist David Fanning, for example, as long as the British army maintained its base in Wilmington, he regularly turned over prisoners to the British commander who would either hold or parole them. When the British evacuated Wilmington in November 1781, we find Fanning more regularly killing prisoners, though he continued to parole some on his own authority until the very end.[47]

## Legitimizing Retaliation

More important than weak state authority, the cultural legitimacy of retaliation that had existed prior to the war took on a new and frightful dimension for both rebels and loyalists. Both expanded retaliation to include retribution against groups of people who were, or were believed to be, sympathetic to opponents. The customary right of retaliation had been explicitly codified in European notions of war. The legal theorist Emmerich Vattel wrote in 1758 that retaliation should be avoided, but a sovereign who "is dealing with an inhuman enemy who frequently commits atrocities such as … [hanging prisoners without cause] may refuse to spare the lives of certain prisoners whom he captures."[48] Vattel thus acknowledged a "Law of Retaliation," a phrase frequently used by combatants in North Carolina. In their minds, retaliation was not only a human urge but a quasi-legal right. Even colonial religious leaders admitted the right to retaliate, emphasizing only that it should be a carried out by the state, not indulged in privately.[49] This legalistic view of retaliation blended with the more generalized popular ideology of an individual's right of self-redress – the right "to make themselves whole" in response to injury or affront.[50] This expansive and quasi-legal vision of retaliation played the crucial role of making previously immoral acts into legitimate acts of war, thereby clearing consciences.[51]

Consider the issue of conscience in militiaman Moses Hall's tale of the killing of six prisoners. We have already seen how the men who "hewed to pieces" the prisoners did so after some discussion among themselves, followed by their shouts referring to the treatment of Buford's command at the Waxhaws – their justification for retaliating. Hall, not privy to the discussion, was initially horrified. The next day, however, Hall "discovered lying upon the ground … [what] proved to be a youth of about sixteen who, having come out to view the British troops through curiosity, for fear he might give information to our troops, they had run him

through with a bayonet … . The sight of this unoffending boy, butchered … relieved me of my distressful feelings for the slaughter of the Tories, and I desired nothing so much as the opportunity of participating in their destruction."[52] Hall's conscience, through *eight* previous tours of duty as a militiaman, had survived intact. This incident cleared it.

Hall was not alone in his reaction to atrocity. Numerous militiamen from both sides explained how atrocities motivated them to retaliate. Such accounts repeat phrases like "excusable and justifiable retaliation," or "just retaliation."[53] Furthermore, certain aspects of the British war effort were seen to violate expectations of war, stimulating rebel responses. Most notable in this category was the use of Indians as allies – a people seen as adhering to no limits and whose use in and of itself therefore constituted an atrocity. North Carolina militia general Griffith Rutherford described Tories who worked in concert with the Indians as "inhuman hostile wretches" and "unchristian foes in strong alliance with [a] savage enemy."[54]

Rumor and propaganda of atrocities reduced restraints on violence by justifying retaliation against men whose crimes were merely alleged. The formulaic nature of atrocity accusations heightened real tensions over violence, which were further aggravated in the Southern backcountry by rumor spread through a diffusely settled countryside. News arrived by word of mouth, which usually told only one side of the story. Militiamen fed on these kinds of stories. They entered the fray prepared to believe the very worst of their opponents and, even if they were not retaliating for personal injury could do so for atrocities that had no basis other than rumor.

In North Carolina and elsewhere, Continental Army officers and Whig leadership recognized the political benefits of withholding retaliation and thereby winning the hearts and minds of the countryside. Washington himself admitted to being tempted "to retaliation," but both "humanity and policy forbid the measure."

He believed that "their wanton cruelty injures rather than benefits their cause; that with our forbearance, justly secured to us the attachment of all good men."[55]

Unfortunately, the militias frequently proved incapable of such restraint. The cultural and quasi-legal legitimacy of retaliation not only "cleared consciences." Collective agreement within a militia unit to commit acts of retribution could neutralize both individual reservations and opposing communal social norms. If at least some collective agreement existed that retaliation was justified, neither the individual's conscience nor the community would object. Lacking communal support for retaliation, an individual who feared social or judicial censure might withhold violence. The crucial, unstated issue here is the definition of "community." In republican theory, a militia was a group of armed citizens who carried the community's republican values with them into military service. The "military community" and civilian society were supposed to be congruent. In fact, North Carolina developed two different kinds of militia units – the regular enrolled militia and the volunteer militia – neither of which proved to be congruent to civilian society. For both types, their wartime structure and mission weakened powers of judicial censure. The structure of the regular militia undermined community-based social censure, whereas the volunteer militia tended to create a new community altogether, obeying a different set of values. In whatever form, the militias failed their revolutionary purpose to demonstrate the power of virtue in a righteous cause. Instead of functioning as the arm of controlled state justice and defense, the militias all too often became instruments of private retaliation.

## Militia Organization and the Breakdown of Community Restraint

Within a military, or even a paramilitary organization, there are two sets of outside pressures on individual behavior: the formal threat of punishment by a military hierarchy and the informal, internal threat of communal disapproval by one's peers.[56] As seen above, the state had little or no control over its militias. Moreover, regular troops were a source of restraint only if they were nearby or acting in concert with the militias. The structures and practices of North Carolina's regular enrolled militia tended to weaken both formal and informal censure that could restrain wanton violence. Militia officers were ill equipped to punish their soldiers, and the units themselves were usually all-too-temporary fraternities, lacking either a wide cross section of their home communities or sufficient permanence to develop their own sense of community.

One way for a military organization to maintain a sense of community and the consequent power to exert peer pressure is to recruit units from an existing community and from a relatively wide cross section of that community's social structure. The other is to take a diverse assortment of recruits and inculcate a sense of community first through training and then through sustained service together. The wartime militia laws in North Carolina undercut both possibilities. Before the war, the peacetime militia law required nearly universal male service. Some exemptions existed for various professions, but North Carolina's militia system included the vast majority of white men within its umbrella, including even servants after 1746.[57] Although most settlers in the North Carolina Piedmont had not settled in towns, and each farm could be quite distant from the next, they were nevertheless perceived as neighborhoods, usually ethnically cohesive, and often defined by the creek lines upon which all their homes lay.[58] Companies were formed from such neighborhoods, and regiments from counties. "Private" musters for companies were supposed to be held three to five times per year, whereas "general" musters for the full regiment were held annually. All officers were nominally appointed by the governor, but the governor usually appointed captains and below on the basis of recommendations by the counties' senior officers. In essence, a peacetime militia company was very likely to closely reflect the inhabitants of a given district, up and down the social scale, without including slaves. James Bartholomees has reconstructed the membership and homestead locations of a representative peacetime militia company, demonstrating its neighborhood coherence.[59] With the outbreak of war, however, the new North Carolina government divided each company into five divisions: four for active service and the fifth as a reserve composed of the old and infirm. The idea was that each company when called up for service would send one-quarter of its strength (one division) for a three-month tour. That division would join with other company "quarters" to form a composite company.[60]

This divisional structure had a variety of negative effects on the enrolled militia's ability to contain violence. First, actively serving companies were composites of a variety of neighborhoods, breaking down the sense of community that might have existed in a neighborhood company. This reduced the concern members had for condemnation by their peers: these were men with whom they had had no dealings in the past and might not again in the future. Their judgments of each other did not have a lasting impact. At the same time, the system's standard three-month tour not only prevented the building of a strong military community, but also tended to shift officers around frequently or even randomly.[61] The Wilkes County militia was drafted twice in 1778: once for men and once for officers.[62] This shifting of officers and soldiers undercut the mutual personal respect between the leaders and the led that formed the theoretical keystone of a militia system. Robert Kincaid, recounting his tour of militia service in 1781, had difficulty remembering all of the different officers under whom he had served in just a three-month stint.[63] Jesse Ausley, a resident of Wake County, recalled being commanded

by officers from Orange County and for one tour simply noted that "there was very little Regularity as to officers."[64] Nathan Grantham's experience might be extreme, but he recalled serving five successive three to four-month tours, under different captains, and usually in a different regiment.[65] Consider again James Collins's story. In this case, his is the exception that proves the rule. Collins's company was a cohesive and stable volunteer company that had already served together around eight months, under the command of Colonel Moffitt, who had been elected to the position. Collins served in a military community where his respect for Moffitt and the unnamed instigator's fear of condemnation by his military peers helped save a prisoner's life.

Collins's story brings up the distinction between regularly called-up militia and "volunteer" militia units. Moffitt's volunteer unit appears to have been fairly restrained, in this case relying on a sense of community and a respected leader's observance of the formalities of war. Being volunteer units, however, did not guarantee adherence to conventional rules of war because the men who joined them were often those motivated to fight either for personal revenge or for personal profit.[66] Once in service with other such men, and serving for longer periods of time, they developed divergent community standards of behavior that condoned plunder as their own just reward or revenge. It comes as no surprise that volunteer units were the ones most often blamed for plundering.[67] William Gipson, the militiaman who recalled "spicketing" a Tory prisoner, had joined that volunteer unit in 1779 after his mother had been "tied up and whipped by the Tories" and his own home "almost entirely destroyed."[68] British outrages could also precipitate rebel volunteer retaliation on the more vulnerable Tories. The British expeditionary force from Wilmington to New Bern in August 1781 stopped to burn the homes of General Bryan, William Herritage, William Coxe, and Longfield Coxe. Almost immediately thereafter, Bryan, Herritage, and the Coxes "raised a party & burnt up all the Houses of the Tories near them."[69] The North Carolina Board of War feared the uncontrolled behavior of these units and sought to place them under regular command.[70]

In addition to the separate structural problems inherent to the "regular" militia and the volunteer militia, the substitute system also may have weakened the military sense of community. When a call went out to raise the militia for a given period, the usual procedure was first to prescribe a quota for a specific locale and then call for volunteers (individual volunteers to such a call-up were distinctly different from "volunteer units"). Usually there were insufficient volunteers to meet the quota, so a draft was needed.[71] Persons drafted could hire a substitute. Many veterans recalled serving as substitutes, but they rarely made clear in their pension claims whether they did so within their communities – substituting for family members or friends – or were doing so on a more "professional" traveling basis.[72] In the one case – substituting one neighborhood man for another – the substitute system would have had little effect on the cohesion of neighborhood units about to be split up anyway. In the case of the "professional" substitute, they might be thought to have contributed to a new military community, but the militia tours in which they served were too brief. In short, the substitute system may not have further hurt the system's ability to sponsor community and restrain violence, but it certainly did not help.

In summary, the divisional system, the short tours, the frequent change of officers, and possibly the substitute system all interfered with the capacity of soldiers in the regular enrolled rebel militia to influence and restrain each other's violent behavior in the field. The normal mechanisms of worrying about one's reputation in the eyes of one's community did not function in this environment. Volunteer units, in contrast, developed a peer community based on longer service, but – with the exception of units such as Moffitt's – their initial motivations to serve

actually encouraged a more violent standard of behavior.

Both volunteer and regular militia units were unable to rely on the authority of officers alone to control violence. To borrow an eighteenth-century term, the militia in North Carolina had long been "democratical."[73] General Nathanael Greene's comment on the subject remains the most famous: "With the militia everybody is a general, and the powers of government are so feeble, that it is with the utmost difficulty you can restrain them from plundering one another."[74] In practice, many of the junior officers were elected, and, when the officers were not of their choosing, the militia might refuse to serve. Sixty men from Cumberland County voluntarily turned out and found themselves put under the command of Captain John Matthews. Because they had not been consulted on Matthews' appointment, the soldiers at muster refused to act under him, citing his previous cowardice, and they demanded the "liberty to choose their officer."[75] A man's reputation was critical to his suitability to serve as a militia officer, and part of that reputation was that he not be too strict and "disgust the militia."[76] Thus, militiamen tended to select officers who reflected their values and wishes.[77] This became a serious problem for military order when men volunteered intent on revenge or plunder. In their minds, officers were to aid them, not deter their lust for violence.

Many soldiers, particularly in volunteer units, entered service with the expectation of plunder, either from purely profit-seeking motives, as a substitute for pay, or to "make themselves whole" in retaliation for having been plundered themselves.[78] The Whig leadership did not always help matters in this regard. In their desperation to find ways to encourage the enlistment of soldiers whom they could neither supply nor adequately pay, they often resorted to the promise of plunder instead. Most notoriously, South Carolina militia general Thomas Sumter promised enlistees a captured slave.[79] Further south, the Georgia Council offered commissions and the right to keep plunder to any man who would raise fifteen other men to raid British Florida.[80] North Carolina Whig Whitmel Hill regretted using plunder as an incentive: "Our distrest Militia … will claim to themselves some compensation for their services … . This plundering I should not generally encourage, but in the present instance I think it justifiable."[81]

This hope to profit from soldiering within a "democratical" officer-soldier relationship meant that even officers who wanted to prevent plundering often had to give in to their soldiers' preferences. The Moravians recorded one officer's internal struggle to find "pluck enough" to order the restoration of plundered property, but only after he had been confronted by the victims of his soldiers' greed.[82] British Major Patrick Ferguson acknowledged the problems of controlling loyalist troops, advising that "some latitude" should be allowed for the lesser acts of plundering, so as to contribute to greater overall discipline.[83] Similarly, rebel militias in southwest Virginia plundered, divided, and sold loyalist property "to which the officers have submitted, otherwise it would be impossible to get men on these pressing occasions."[84]

Besides the hopes for plunder, militia units often set their own standards for the treatment of prisoners. In some instances, soldiers demanded harsher treatment than that preferred by officers; in others, they were the restraining influence on more bloody-minded officers. Such incidents rarely appear in the official records of the war but are common in the early oral history and folklore compilations and occasionally surface in the usually laconic pension records. Two examples will suffice here. In late 1781, some of loyalist Colonel David Fanning's men captured rebel militia colonel Thomas Dugan and brought him to Fanning. Fanning determined to execute him, "but some of Fanning's men being his intimate acquaintances, and personal friends, wished to save him … . One man particularly, … interested himself so warmly that he got a decided majority opposed to his execution, and Fanning was compelled, much against his will to revoke the sentence." Instead, leaning

on the continued presence of the British army in Wilmington, Fanning turned Dugan over to British control.[85] The British commander in Wilmington sentenced Dugan to be executed, and on the day he was to be hanged Major John Elrod spared his life. Ironically, a few months later a released Dugan found himself leading a band of militia that captured Elrod in a nighttime retaliatory raid. According to the oral history of the area, Dugan, obliged to Elrod for saving his life, was nevertheless unable to deflect his soldiers' desire to execute Elrod for Elrod's earlier killing of another Whig. After a "kind of court martial or consultation" he was tied to a tree and shot.[86]

Neither the officers themselves, nor even the more distant authorities of the state, seemed to possess the willingness or the capacity to punish militiamen for their misdeeds. There are virtually no records of courts-martial being held to discipline militiamen for civilian or military offenses.[87] Furthermore, the North Carolina militia law was quite lenient, specifying only a ten-pound fine for desertion, mutiny, or quitting one's post. The old colonial corporal punishments that had been retained under the 1774 militia law were absent from the 1777 version.[88] Fines seem to have been preferred, though militia officers were allowed discretion to administer punishments other than death. The initial militia law of 1776 specified that "each and every Company make such regulations as to them shall seem best, for non-attendance, disobedience, and misbehavior, at Musters by Companies."[89] Flaws within the militia law made it difficult to hold punitive courts at all. Governor Burke pointed out that the law required all of the officers making up the court be from the same regiment as the offender, but too often the officers themselves were the offenders.[90] Near the end of the war, Burke complained that the militia law contained "no adequate provisions … for restraining or governing either men or officers when in actual service."[91] There are reports of unofficial punishment being meted out in cases of disorder; one such convict received seventeen lashes. But there are as many examples of plunderers being slapped on the wrist; several such men were merely made to return the stolen items and promise not to steal again.[92] Lieutenant Colonel Thomas Taylor of Orange County, accused of permitting "the men under his command to plunder and maraud in a most offensive and disgraceful manner," was suspended, but only after a special act of the North Carolina Senate.[93]

In contrast to the weakness of state law and the tenuous authority of militia officers, the Continental Army followed strikingly different rules. It adopted fairly stringent articles of war from the outset, and they became more severe over the course of the war, especially in the punishment of plunderers.[94] Continental Army order books are filled with warnings to soldiers not to plunder, with dire threats of punishment and even death. Those same order books often record infliction of such punishment, to include flogging and execution. One historian has argued that, although George Washington often commuted sentences for various offenses, he very rarely showed mercy to plunderers.[95] Unlike the militias, courts-martial were exceedingly common and punishment for plundering was severe.[96]

The state's and the militia officers' weaknesses undermined both types of militias' efforts to live up to societal expectations of restrained virtuous war. The regularly raised, "official" militia lacked the communal coherence necessary for internal systems of censure. The volunteer militia took the field fired by motives that legitimated more extreme visions of acceptable violence – they had "communal coherence," but of a different quality than the wider society. Even when not simply self-interested bandits, they felt their violence legitimated by the law of retaliation. Finally, both the regular and the volunteer militias lacked the social distance between officers and men necessary for authoritarian control of excessive violence. All of these weaknesses were exposed and accentuated by the missions required of militias and by the tactics they adopted to fulfill them.

From the very beginning of the war, one of the most important of the rebel militias' roles was the maintenance of loyalty to the Whig cause. Militias became the investigative arm, the police force, and the enforcers of a partisan government.[97] This mission grew naturally out of the extralegal activities of the committees of safety as the state moved from resistance to rebellion in 1775. In November 1775, militia units were found tarring and feathering loyalist Cullen Pollock in Chowan County, whereas in New Hanover County the militia went from door to door confiscating loyalists' weapons, leaving one per white man in each house.[98]

As the war progressed, the Whig government continued to use militias as political enforcers, to make arrests, administer loyalty oaths, confiscate arms, and eventually confiscate loyalist property. Such practices put the militiamen in the very awkward position of making individuals and individuals' homes the focus for their activity. Eighteenth-century Euro-American notions of war did not include warring against specific individuals. Military activity was supposed to be conducted between armies, the formally constituted bodies representing opposing states. Although individual houses could be the targets of foraging or even quartering, the individuals within those houses were not supposed to be harmed or carried away. The reality of European warfare often belied this expectation – particularly if an army was ordered to devastate the countryside for military reasons. Nevertheless, the expectation of restraint remained.

Unfortunately, the service experiences of many militiamen broke down this restraint against war on individuals, and, because most militiamen served a number of tours, they brought that experience with them in each succeeding tour.[99] As the war dragged on, there was a logical devolution of the militias from enforcement of provincial law to the more violent late-war "scour." The rebel militias took it upon themselves to "scour" the countryside for Tories. Restraint on militia enforcement diminished when the North Carolina Senate officially authorized such scouring in August 1778. The law empowered the county court or any three justices of the peace to call out the militia to "compel tories or other disorderly people of their county to a due observance of the law."[100]

Where scourings may have begun as missions to enforce the law, they quickly deteriorated into punitive expeditions. William Lenoir's account highlights this deterioration. In 1778 he went on three expeditions, ostensibly to enforce the loyalty oath. In the first, he and his companions found no Tories in three days of searching. In the spring, however, while pursuing some Tories into the Blue Ridge Mountains, they captured some who "were mostly permitted to go at large, after an examination, in which they generally made recantation, and [illegible] promises of loyalty to the cause of independence and in some instances … [took] the oath." Immediately after returning home, however, Lenoir and his company set out again in pursuit of yet more Tories. On capturing one, they tried to get information from the prisoner about other Tories. When the man refused, "Colonel [Benjamin] Cleveland adopted the expedient of Hanging him for a while to the limb of a tree or a bent down sapling, but which did not produce the desired effect until the dose was repeated a second time with more severity then the first."[101] Later in the war, Frederick Smith crossed the path of a party of Whig militia, who questioned him as to his loyalties. Unsure who was asking, he guessed wrong, and they proceeded to hang him briefly from a tree, cutting him down before he died. Not to be outdone, a loyalist militia unit that later crossed paths with Smith asked him the same question. Again Smith guessed wrong as to the identity of those asking and again was "half-hanged" for his trouble.[102]

The deterioration was even more marked as militiamen on a scouring expedition deliberately sought out those they "knew" were Tories. Scouring became a means to intimidate suspected Tories. The experience of John Evans is instructive.[103] Sometime in 1780, the light horse militia company of Nash County arrived at his house, arrested him, carried him to the courthouse, and "threatened [him] … with hanging, a Gallows being erected on the spot." Terrified, he agreed to enlist for eighteen months. When he asked the reasons for his arrest, the militia told him that they had heard that he wanted to take up arms and join a Tory band in Edgecombe County and that he had asked someone else's advice on the matter. Although the determination of Evans's loyalties may have been a little cavalier, others' loyalties were often accurately known, leading to nighttime expeditions to surprise partisans of the other side in their homes. The victims of many such raids did not survive.[104] Many did, however, and James Collins's account of his units' methods of scouring testifies to the continued functioning of some restraints. He claimed that they would surprise a Tory house, force the doors, extinguish the lights, back the man of the house into a corner, and swing away with swords, "but taking care to strike the wall or some object that was in the way." They would then pull down the house to the roof joists, and spare the Tory himself, provided he left. Collins further claimed that the only property disturbed was the house itself.[105]

The militiamen's experience with Indian warfare also weakened restraints on the use of force. The history of Indian wars in the colonies had led the militia to develop tactics that included a preference for night or dawn attacks, ambushes, and harassing parties.[106] Gregory Knouff has argued that this preference was reinforced by the backcountry men's investment of their masculine identity in a frontier style of war. They wanted to be seen as tough, independent, even violent men who fought Indians while using an Indian style of war.[107]

There were consequences to this style of warfare. Ambushes and night attacks were notoriously difficult to control once begun.[108] In situations like these, quarter was often refused.[109]

In his pension statement, Thomas Cummings simply noted of one of his militia tours that, although no engagement was entered into, "a number of Tories were shot and cut to pieces" in the swamps.[110] For many militiamen, their only knowledge of war had been of the particularly unrestrained kind practiced against Indians. The most-common technique of waging war against elusive Indians was to burn their fields and towns, depriving them of sustenance; this was known in the seventeenth century as the "feed fight."[111] Frustrated militiamen could easily turn such a strategy against a white enemy. Stephen Cobb complained to the governor in July 1779 that he had been repeatedly threatened by a Tory band led by "the Basses." He pointed out that he had tried everything in his power "to take them without killing them." He had failed, and, if he did not get state help soon, he wanted a warrant to "take them dead or alive, and to destroy what they have if they will not surrender themselves."[112] This combination of using an Indian style of war that was difficult to control with an experience of scorched earth war *against* Indians helped pave the descent into retaliatory war.

Militia violence in the latter years of the war in North Carolina was neither unadulterated carnage nor the virtuous war that many had hoped for. The violence of the war was shaped more by collective values *about* war and the past and present experience *of* war. Honor and morality restrained violence, while the right of self-redress unleashed it. Past experience of war both demanded restraint according to the "customs and usages of war" and bore witness to unlimited destruction previously waged against Indians. Historians' explanations for the devolution of the war's violence into savagery have emphasized either preexisting social tensions or simple lashing back at British misbehavior. Those explanations account for neither North Carolinians' values about war nor the nature of the militia as an institution. Communal values about violence in war not only attempted to moderate behavior, but

also set the conditions under which retaliation became "necessary." People lashed out with violence because they were angry about violence. They soon discovered that, when they did lash out, censure from within or from without the military community did not exist. In part censure did not exist because the culture authorized retaliation and because the infant state lacked the bureaucratic mechanisms necessary to enforce military conventions. And finally, censure did not exist because some militia units had redefined their values to include actions formerly beyond the pale, such as plundering and vengeance.

Two final anecdotes can best capture the complexity of violence. Both incidents are found in the pension claims of militiamen, whose memories were sometimes dimmed by time, but also sometimes freed from constraint by their age. In November 1781, Bryan McCullen avoided a draft by volunteering to serve a three-month tour under Captain John Grantham. His company went scouring for Tories in Dobbs County, found some, and a skirmish ensued. Then, in McCullen's extraordinarily blasé phrasing, "one of the Tories viz. Absalom Davis was taken prisoner and afterwards killed."[113]

In contrast, Robert Knox's group, during a tour at about the same time, went in pursuit of the notorious Tory Colonel John Moore. Unable to find him, they instead went to the home of his father, Moses Moore. There the soldiers took a rather simple revenge: "destroy[ing] his oats by throwing them over to the horses." This "the officers prevent[ed] when they came up."[114] These two simple stories actually tell a complex tale. In them we find short militia tours, Tory "scourings," the use of local knowledge to target the homes of "known" individuals, the "feed fight" tactic, and the casual killing of a prisoner contrasted with the intervention of officers at a more trifling offense. Many other such complex tales could be told, and in each of them we would find a struggle between the desire for a virtuous war and the urge for personal retribution.

# Notes

I am indebted to many people for their help with this essay. In particular I would like to thank the members of the Kentucky Early Americanist seminar, Glenn Crothers, Brad Wood, Debra Meyers, and Ken Williams. I also appreciate the close readings provided by John Resch and Rhonda Lee and the research assistance of George Stevenson at the North Carolina Archives. Although there is new evidence and argumentation here, portions of this essay appeared in Wayne E. Lee, *Crowds and Soldiers in Revolutionary North Carolina: The Culture of Violence in Riot and War* (Gainesville: University Press of Florida, 2001), chaps. 5–7, and are reprinted here by permission of that press.

1 James Collins, *Autobiography of a Revolutionary Soldier,* ed. John M. Roberts (Clinton, La.: Feliciana Democrat, 1859; repr., New York: Arno Press, 1979), pp. 55–56. Bobby Gilmer Moss, *The Patriots at King's Mountain* (Blacksburg, S.C: Scotia-Hibernia Press, 1990), pp. 51–52, 186; Lyman C. Draper, *King's Mountain and Its Heroes* (Cincinnati: Peter G. Thomson, 1881; repr., Baltimore: Genealogical Publishing Co., 1997), p. 465.

2 David Fanning, *The Narrative of Col. David Fanning,* ed. Lindley S. Butler (Davidson, N.C.: Briarpatch Press, 1981), pp. 35–36 (hereafter *DFN*).

3 John C. Dann, ed., *The Revolution Remembered: Eyewitness Accounts of the War for Independence* (Chicago: University of Chicago Press, 1980), p. 202. "Remember Buford" was a reference to the massacre of surrendering Continentals under Abraham Buford's command at Waxhaws, S.C., by Colonel Banastre Tarleton in 1780.

4 David J. Fowler, "Egregious Villains, Wood Rangers, and London Traders: The Pine Robber Phenomenon in New Jersey during the Revolutionary War" (Ph.D. diss., Rutgers University, 1987), p. 21.

5 Charles Royster, *A Revolutionary People at War: The Continental Army and American Character, 1775–1783* (New York: W. W. Norton, 1979), pp. 25–53; James Kirby Martin and Mark Edward Lender, *A Respectable Army: The Military Origins of the Republic, 1763–1789* (Arlington Heights, 111: Harlan Davidson, 1982), pp. 30–34; John Morgan Dederer, *War in America to 1775: Before Yankee Doodle* (New York: New York University Press, 1990), pp. 196–97, 208–9; Lawrence Delbert Cress, *Citizens in Arms: The Army and Militia in American Society to the War of 1812* (Chapel Hill: University of North Carolina Press, 1982), p. 26.

6 James Kirby Martin, ed., *Ordinary Courage: The Revolutionary War Adventures of Joseph Plumb Martin,* 2nd ed. (New York: Brandywine Press, 1999), p. 120; James Thacher, *Military Journal of the American Revolution, 1775–1783* (Gansevoort, N.Y.: Corner House Publications, 1998), pp. 107–12. The same ideology of virtuous restraint can be found in John Adams's prewar tract, "On Private Revenge, no. 1," in C. Bradley Thompson, ed., *The Revolutionary Writings of John Adams* (Indianapolis, Ind.: Liberty Fund, 2000), pp. 6–7; and the sermon of the Reverend William Emerson, cited in Robert A. Gross, *The Minutemen and Their World* (New York: Hill and Wang, 1976), p. 73.

7 Wayne E. Lee, *Crowds and Soldiers in Revolutionary North Carolina: The Culture of Violence in Riot and War* (Gainesville: University Press of Florida, 2001), pp. 179–94.

8 Walter Clark, ed., *The State Records of North Carolina,* 26 vols. (Winston and Goldsboro, N.C.: various publishers, 1895–1907), 16:416–18 (hereafter *NCSR*).

9 *NCSR,* 17:1049, 16:566.

10 Collins, *Autobiography,* p. 66.

11 Elijah Alexander (W5201), Revolutionary War Pension and Bounty-Land-Warrant Application Files, National Archives, Washington (hereafter PenRec with claim number).

12 "Sermon against Plundering," Samuel E. McCorkle Papers, Duke University Special Collections, Durham, N.C.

13 Davie to Sumner, October 7, 1780, Horatio Gates Papers, Microfilm edition prepared by the New York Historical Society and the National Historical Records and Publications Commission (hereafter HGP).

14 *NCSR,* 16:268–69, 22:610–11.

15 Petition of Sundry Inhabitants of Salisbury and Parts Adjacent, April–May, 1782, Joint Standing Committees, Propositions & Grievances – Report and papers, General Assembly Session Records, North Carolina Department of Archives and History, Raleigh, N.C. (hereafter NCA); *NCSR,* 15:503–4; Martin, *Ordinary Courage,* p. 69;

Samuel McCorkle, "Sermon against Plundering"; Adelaide L. Fries, ed., *Records of the Moravians in North Carolina,* 11 vols. (Raleigh, N.C: North Carolina Historical Commission, 1922–1969), 3:1409 (hereafter *MR); William Henry Foote, Sketches of North Carolina: Historical and Biographical* (New York: Robert Carter, 1846), p. 417; Nathanael Greene, *The Papers of General Nathanael Greene,* 13 vols., ed. Richard K. Showman, et al. (Chapel Hill: University of North Carolina Press, 1976–2005), 6:589–90 (hereafter *NGP).*

16  *NCSR,* 14:392. The "carving" phrase was a common one.

17  *New Jersey Gazette,* August 5, 1778; *MR,* 4:1622, 1910; *NCSR,* 16:527–28; Thacher, *Military Journal,* p. 77.

18  *MR,* 3:1253–54; 4:1549; 3:1277–78; 4:1644, 1666, 1678–80, 1701–1702; 4:1759. All of these examples are taken from situations where officer intervention is either absent or not directly mentioned in the source. There are many more examples of restraint imposed or attempted by officers.

19  Dann, *Revolution Remembered,* pp. 188–89. For the traditional use of spicketing, or picqueting, see R. E. Scouller, *The Armies of Queen Anne* (Oxford: Clarendon Press, 1966), pp. 268, 390; Scott Claver, *Under the Lash: A History of Corporal Punishment in the British Armed Forces* (London: Torchstream Books, 1954), pp. 12–13. "Picqueting" was still listed as a punishment in the North Carolina militia law in 1774. *NCSR,* 23:943. Such a punishment was also described as appropriate for slaves in Hunter Dickinson Farish, ed., *The Journal and Letters of Philip Vickers Fithian: A Plantation Tutor of the Old Dominion, 1773–1774* (Charlottesville: University Press of Virginia, 1968), pp. 38–39.

20  Elijah Alexander Papers, NCA. Other incidents in E. W. Caruthers, *The Old North State* (originally published as *Revolutionary Incidents and Sketches of Character Chiefly in the "Old North State"* [Philadelphia: Hayes & Zell, 1854–1856; repr., Greensboro, N.C: Guilford County Genealogical Society, 1994], pp. 87–88); Pension Record of Robert Love, transcribed in The David Schenk Papers, NCA; Pension Record of Peter Banks in Betty J. Camin, ed., *North Carolina Revolutionary War Pension Applications,* 3 vols. (Raleigh, N.C:

privately published, 1983) (Camin's volume is a typescript of pension documents found in county courthouses, which may or may not also be in the National Archives), 1:18.

21  *MR,* 4:1625–28.

22  *NCSR,* 15:109. Draper, *King's Mountain,* 332.

23  John H. Wheeler, *Historical Sketches of North Carolina, from 1584 to 1851,* 2 vols. (Philadelphia: Lippincott, Grambo and Co., 1851), 2:444; fn.35.

24  *NCSR,* 14:462–64; 17:668; 16:269, 318, 565–69, 685–86.

25  British prisoners, once taken, were usually treated according to the customs of war. Charles H. Metzger, *The Prisoner in the American Revolution* (Chicago: Loyola University Press, 1971), pp. 1–2; Betsy Knight, "Prisoner Exchange and Parole in the American Revolution," *William and Mary Quarterly,* 3rd ser., 48 (April 1991): 202, 210ff.

26  *NCSR,* 16:416–18. See also *NCSR,* 16:684.

27  Exact numbers are elusive; Greene repeatedly struggled and failed to get returns of prisoners taken, paroled, or held. *NGP,* 6:544, 7:48, 67; *NCSR,* 14:727, 15:xiv, 17:668; *MR,* 4:1574, 1576, 1633; Draper, *King's Mountain,* pp. 357–60. Emory G. Evans, "Trouble in the Backcountry: Disaffection in Southwest Virginia during the American Revolution," in Ronald Hoffman, Thad W. Tate, and Peter J. Albert, eds., *An Uncivil War: The Southern Backcountry during the American Revolution* (Charlottesville: University of Virginia Press, 1985), pp. 199–200, 205; *MR,* 4:1626–28; Harry M. Ward, *Between the Lines: Banditti of the American Revolution* (Westport, Conn.: Praeger, 2002), p. 88.

28  General Gates to the Board of War, November 15, 1780; Colonel Thomas Wade to General Gates, November, 23, 1780, both HGP; *NCSR,* 17:668, 1049; 16:229–31, 511, 522, 689–90. *NCSR,* 15:151–52. South Carolina instituted a similar system in the summer of 1781. Jerome J. Nadelhaft, *The Disorders of War: The Revolution in South Carolina* (Orono: University of Maine at Orono Press, 1981), p. 71.

29  To attempt to quantify the survival rate of prisoners is impossible, because the records simply do not exist. Examining the pension records of North Carolina militiamen, however, one finds the experience of taking, delivering, and/or guarding prisoners to be extraordinarily

common, far more common than accounts of killing them, even of killing them after a court-martial. Of 110 randomly selected pension records of North Carolina militiamen, ten (9 percent) specifically recalled an entire tour spent guarding or escorting prisoners. In Camin's collection of the pension statements of sixty-two militiamen, twelve (19 percent) recalled such tours. Although these numbers may seem small, when one considers how laconic most pension records are, the survival of this detail in 9 percent and 19 percent of them is significant.

30  *DFN*, pp. 39–43.

31  Richard R. Beeman, "The Political Response to Social Conflict in the Southern Backcountry: A Comparative View of Virginia and the Carolinas during the Revolution," in Hoffman, Tate, and Albert, *An Uncivil War*, p. 232; Ward, *Between the Lines*, pp. 221–27.

32  For the "people's war" characterization, see Stephen Conway, *The War of American Independence, 1775–1783* (London: Edward Arnold, 1995), pp. 245–47; John Resch, *Suffering Soldiers: Revolutionary War Veterans, Moral Sentiment, and Political Culture in the Early Republic* (Amherst: University of Massachusetts Press, 1999), pp. 1–46.

33  Lee, *Crowds and Soldiers*, pp. 164–75; Robert O. DeMond, *The Loyalists in North Carolina during the Revolution* (Durham, N.C.: Duke University Press, 1940), pp. 153–80.

34  John Shy, "Hearts and Minds in the American Revolution: The Case of 'Long Bill' Scott and Peterborough, New Hampshire," in *A People Numerous and Aimed*, rev. ed. (Ann Arbor: University of Michigan Press, 1990), p. 178; Fowler, "Egregious Villains," p. 38ff; Wallace Brown, *The King's Friends: The Composition and Motives of the American Loyalist Claimants* (Providence, R.I.: Brown University Press, 1965), pp. 58–61.

35  Martha Condray Searcy, *The Georgia-Florida Contest in the American Revolution, 1776–1778* (Tuscaloosa: University of Alabama Press, 1985), p. 128; Ward, *Between the Lines*.

36  Armstrong Starkey, "War and Culture, A Case Study: The Enlightenment and the Conduct of the British Army in America, 1755–1781," *War and Society* 8 (1990): 1–28; Stephen Conway, "To Subdue America: British Army Officers and the Conduct of the Revolutionary War," *William and Mary Quarterly*, 3rd ser., 43 (July 1986): 381–407, and "'The Great Mischief Complain'd of:' Reflections on the Misconduct of British Soldiers in the Revolutionary War," *William and Mary Quarterly*, 3rd ser., 47 (July 1990): 370–90; Paul H. Smith, *Loyalists and Redcoats: A Study in British Revolutionary Policy* (New York: W. W. Norton, 1972); Shy, "Hearts and Minds," pp. 163–80; Nadelhaft, *Disorders*, pp. 55–58; Louis D. F. Frasche, "Problems of Command: Cornwallis, Partisans and Militia, 1780," *Military Review* 57 (1977): 62; Jac Weller, "The Irregular War in the South," *Military Affairs* 24 (1960): 133; Russell F. Weigley *The Partisan War: The South Carolina Campaigns of 1780–82* (Columbia: University of South Carolina Press, 1970), pp. 12–13.

37  Don Higginbotham, "The American Militia: A Traditional Institution with Revolutionary Responsibilities," in Don Higginbotham, ed., *Reconsiderations on the Revolutionary War* (Westport, Conn.: Greenwood Press, 1978), p. 100.

38  Jack Greene, "Independence, Improvement and Authority," in Hoffman, Tate, and Albert, *An Uncivil War*, pp. 3–36.

39  Ward, *Between the Lines*, pp. 153–68, 222; Nadelhaft, *Disorders*, pp. 64–66; Weigley, *Partisan War*, pp. 22–23; Searcy, *Georgia–Florida*.

40  Lee, *Crowds and Soldiers*, pp. 212–19.

41  MR, 4:1910.

42  *MR*, 4:1573.

43  *NCSR*, 24:344–47, 390–94. MR, 4:1623, 1629–30.

44  *NCSR*, 14:392, 405. See also *NCSR*, 15:329; William A. Graham, *General Joseph Graham and His Papers on North Carolina Revolutionary History* (Raleigh, N.C.: Edwards & Broughton, 1904), p. 312.

45  The Moravians made this problem explicit, complaining that the real blame for the impromptu demands made on them for provisions was that the "Commissary does not look after the soldiers and does not provide for them." *MR*, 4:1758. Two weeks after that comment, another militia company repaid the Moravians in food once their own supplies came up with them. *MR*, 4:1759.

46  Graham, *Graham's Papers*, p. 348.

47  *DFN*, pp. 35, 36, 45, 48, 51, 53, 55–56, 60, 68, 72, 76. The details of Fanning's admittedly self-

serving account are usually confirmed by pro-Whig sources.

48  Emmerich de Vattel, *The Law of Nations,* trans. Charles G. Fenwick. The Classics of International Law (New York: Oceana Publications, 1964), pp. 280–81.

49  Reginald C. Stuart, "'For the Lord is a Man of Warr': The Colonial New England View of War and the American Revolution," *Journal of Church & State* 23 (1981): 523; McCorkle, "Sermon against Plunderers."

50  Bertram Wyatt-Brown, *Southern Horror: Ethics and Behavior in the Old South* (New York: Oxford University Press, 1982), pp. xv, 34; Richard Maxwell Brown, *No Duty to Retreat: Violence and Values in American History and Society* (Oxford: Oxford University Press, 1991), and *Strain of Violence: Historical Studies of American Violence and Vigilantism* (New York: Oxford University Press, 1975); David H. Fischer, *Albion's Seed* (Oxford: Oxford University Press, 1989), pp. 765–68. Quote is from McCorkle, "Sermon against Plunderers."

51  Ward, *Between the Lines,* pp. 78, 126; *DFN,* p. 106; Metzger, *The Prisoner,* pp. 154–58; Knight, "Prisoner Exchange."

52  Dann, *Revolution Remembered,* pp. 202–3.

53  Quotations are from Petition of William Linton to General Assembly, October 3, 1783, April 20–May 18, Reports and Papers, Joint Select Committees, General Assembly Session Records, NCA; Petition of Henry Reed and others, (January 3, 1787] Gen. Assy. Sess. Recs., Nov. 1786–Jan. 1787, Senate Joint Resolutions, Jan. 1–7, NCA.

54  *NCSR,* 13:283.

55  George Washington, *The Papers of George Washington,* 14 vols. Revolutionary War Series, Philander D. Chase, ed. (Charlottesville: University Press of Virginia, 1985–2004), 9:223.

56  A third force would be individual conscience, but it is less visible in the records and is frankly almost inseparably tied to the second; however, it can occasionally be observed in the sources. For example, Frederick Smith, a would-be neutral in the war, was left hanging by a group of militiamen (of which side is unclear). One individual from the group doubled back and cut him down before he strangled. Caruthers, *Old North State,* p. 171. In a more striking example,

militia captain James Devane refused orders to round up Tory women and children and carry them into Wilmington, describing it as "repulsive to his feelings." Camin, *Pension Applications,* 1:87.

57  *NCSR,* 23:29; 244–47; 25:334–37; 13:518–22; James W. Titus, *The Old Dominion at War: Society, Politics, and Warfare in Late Colonial Virginia* (Columbia, S.C.: University of South Carolina Press, 1991), p. 2.

58  Robert W. Ramsey, *Carolina Cradle: Settlement of the Northwest Carolina Frontier, 1747–1776* (Chapel Hill: University of North Carolina Press, 1964); S. Scott Rohrer, "Searching for Land and God: The Pietist Migration to North Carolina in the Late Colonial Period," *North Carolina Historical Review* 79 (2002): 432–35; Rachel N. Klein, "Frontier Planters and the American Revolution," in Hoffman, Tate, and Albert, *An Uncivil War,* p. 46.

59  James Boone Bartholomees, Jr., "Fight or Flee: The Combat Performance of the North Carolina Militia in the Cowpens-Guilford Courthouse Campaign, January to March 1781" (Ph.D. diss., Duke University, 1978), pp. 214–34. These peacetime structures during the colonial era were rarely mobilized intact. The militia served as a pool of manpower from which volunteers were preferred, but drafts would be made when necessary.

60  NCCR, 10:196–201.

61  This was not only true in law, but is borne out by virtually every pension application that refers to militia service.

62  Pension Record of Richard Allen, Sr., in Camin, *Pension Applications,* p. 98.

63  Robert Kincaid, PenRec (W26186).

64  Jesse Ausley, PenRec (W27520); Sterling Cooper, PenRec (S6776).

65  Nathan Grantham, PenRec (S31716).

66  *NGP,* 6:546 n.9; Foote, *Sketches,* pp. 315, 326; *NCSR,* 15:105.

67  Smallwood to Gates, October 31, 1780, HGP.

68  Dann, *Revolution Remembered,* pp. 186–87.

69  *NCSR,* 15:626–27.

70  *NCSR,* 14:451.

71  *NCSR,* 24:154–55; *MR,* 3:1113, 1250; *NCSR,* 12:iii–iv.

72  Of ninety-nine randomly sampled pensioners who served in the North Carolina militia, twenty-four (24 percent) had either served as or hired substitutes. If one counts the number

of tours as a substitute versus the total number of tours served by those same men (340 total tours versus 30 tours as substitutes), it is only 8 percent. These numbers cannot be precise. Most pensioners tried to be clear on what basis they served, whether as volunteer, draftee, or substitute, but their petitions clearly do not reflect perfectly their service. The ninety-nine men sampled here are only those whose pension records were sufficiently clear to distinguish tours, but that only excluded a very few.

73  Lee, *Crowds and Soldiers,* pp. 130–31; Fred Anderson, *A People's Army: Massachusetts Soldiers and Society in the Seven Years' War* (Chapel Hill: University of North Carolina Press, 1984), pp. 48, 167–95; Harold E. Selesky, *War and Society in Colonial Connecticut* (New Haven, Conn.: Yale University Press, 1990), p. 187; Titus, *Old Dominion at War,* pp. 33–41.

74  *NGP,* 6:547.

75  *NCSR,* 11:628, 658; 13:4; James Shipman, PenRec (W17810); William Lenoir, PenRec (S7137); Wheeler, *Historical Sketches,* 2:385.

76  *NCSR,* 17:679.

77  William R. Davie, *The Revolutionary War Sketches of William R. Davie* (Raleigh, N.C.: Division of Archives and History, 1976), p. 16.

78  Graham, *Graham's Papers,* p. 312. Graham had interrupted a group of plunderers in the Moravian towns, who claimed that the Moravians were loyalists and "remonstrated that they had been plundered by Tories and had a right to make themselves whole."

79  Hugh F. Rankin, *The North Carolina Continentals* (Chapel Hill: University of North Carolina Press, 1971), p. 353.

80  Searcy, *Georgia-Florida,* p. 128

81  *NCSR,* 15:56.

82  *MR,* 4:1565.

83  Hugh F. Rankin, "Ferguson's 'Proposed Plan for Bringing the Army under strict discipline,'" in Howard H. Peckham, ed., *Sources of American Independence: Selected Manuscripts From the Collections of the William L. Clements Library* (Chicago: University of Chicago Press, 1978), 2:337.

84  Preston to Jefferson, August 8, 1780, Preston Papers, Draper Manuscript Collection, State Historical Society of Wisconsin, 5QQ50, cited in Evans, "Trouble in the Backcountry, " p. 200.

85  Caruthers, *Old North State,* p. 86; *DFN,* p. 73.

86  Caruthers, *Old North State,* pp. 87–88.

87  Court-Martial of Captain Aaron Hill, Miscellaneous Papers, Military Collection, NCA; *NCSR,* 14:468–69; Charles McDowell Papers, NCA (the entire collection is a record of his court-martial for "countenancing Tories"); *NCSR,* 22:956. See also *NCSR,* 12:712–13; 14:17; 15:431–32; NCCR, 10:560–63. The long-established system for militia courts-martial, primarily used to regulate absences from muster or inadequate equipment, does not seem to have been used as a disciplinary tool. There are few surviving examples of these regular muster courts-martial from the Revolutionary period. That they continued to occur, however, is clear. There are, for example, numerous references to them in petitions referring to irregularities in the draft process. See, for example, Petition of the Freeholders and Freemen of the District of Salisbury, December 1781, April–May 1782, Joint Standing Committees, Propositions & Grievances, General Assembly Session Records, NCA.

88  *NCSR,* 23:943; *NCSR,* 24:1–5.

89  *NCCR,* 10:199.

90  *NCSR,* 22:1039–40.

91  *NCSR,* 16:10. In South Carolina, it was not until 1782 that a law mandating severe punishment for plundering by militia men and officers was passed. S.C. Senate Journal, February 10, 1782, cited in Klein, "Frontier Planters," p. 65.

92  *MR,* 4:1681, 1683, 1776.

93  *NCSR,* 17:689.

94  Robert H. Berlin, "The Administration of Military Justice in the Continental Army during the American Revolution, 1775–1783" (Ph.D. diss., University of California at Santa Barbara, 1976).

95  Holly A. Mayer, *Belonging to the Army: Camp Followers and Community during the American Revolution* (Columbia: University of South Carolina Press, 1996), p. 41.

96  James Neagles's extensive survey of courts-martial recorded in order books found 194 examples of soldiers charged with plunder or theft from civilians (7.3 percent of the total number of courts-martial). There were undoubtedly more, but the order books often did not include enough details to determine whether certain offenses such as stealing were

committed against civilians or other soldiers. James Neagles, *Summer Soldiers: A Survey & Index of Revolutionary War Courts-Martial* (Salt Lake City: Ancestry Incorporated, 1986), p. 34.

97   The Journal of the Committee of Safety for Rowan County, July 18, 1775, Wheeler, *Historical Sketches*, 2:365, 368–69; NCCR, 10:48, 125–29, 363.

98   NCCR, 10:1027–33; Samuel Johnston to Joseph Hewes, November 26, 1775, enclosed in the letter of Vice Admiral Graves, January 29, 1776, PRO CO 5/123 transcript in English Records 13–2, NCA; *North Carolina Gazette*, December 22, 1775.

99   There was a very strong trend of individuals having multiple tours of duty in the North Carolina rebel militias. Thus, the "experience of the institution" was the multiple repeat service of individuals within it. Ninety-nine randomly selected militia pensioners served an average of 3.4 tours in the North Carolina rebel militias. The fifty-one pensioners with militia service (and distinguishable tours) transcribed in Camin averaged 2.7 tours each. In reality, both averages should be higher, because many of those pensioners lost count of their tours, and others combined one or two short militia tours with a long enlistment in the Continentals. (Continental tours are not figured into the average and militia tours are not weighted for length of service.)

100  *NCSR*, 12:775, 811.

101  William Lenoir, PenRec (S7137).

102  Caruthers, *Old North State*, pp. 171–72.

103  Petition of John Evans, *NCSR*, 15:236. See also *MR*, 4:1561, 1613.

104  Caruthers in *Old North State* and in *DFN*.

105  Collins, *Autobiography*, p. 66.

106  Higginbotham, "The American Militia," p. 99; Weigley *Partisan War*, p. 15 and passim. Although it is true that North Carolina had escaped relatively lightly from the Indian attacks of the mid-eighteenth century, many North Carolinians had arrived there from more northerly colonies. Of 114 North Carolina pensioners (militia and Continental), 32 percent had been born in Virginia, Pennsylvania, or Maryland (25 percent in North Carolina and 36 percent unknown). And, in view of the age of pensioners, these figures are weighted toward those born in North Carolina, perhaps after their parents had migrated there from the north.

107  Gregory T. Knouff, *The Soldiers' Revolution: Pennsylvania in Arms and the Forging of Early American Identity* (University Park: Pennsylvania State University Press, 2004), pp. 155–93.

108  Armstrong Starkey, "Paoli to Stony Point: Military Ethics and Weaponry during the American Revolution," *Journal of Military History* 58 (1994): 7–27

109  Davie, *Revolutionary War Sketches*, p. 12.

110  Thomas Cummings, PenRec (S6780).

111  William L. Shea, *The Virginia Militia in the Seventeenth Century* (Baton Rouge: Louisiana State University Press, 1983), pp. 20, 33.

112  *NCSR*, 14:176–77, 185–86, 15:212; Caruthers, *Old North State*, p. 64.

113  Bryan McCullen, PenRec (S9018).

114  Robert Knox, PenRec (S8803).

# PART IV

# AMERICAN CONSTITUTIONALISM AND NATION-BUILDING

# 11
# WRITING ON A CLEAN SLATE
*The Struggle to Craft State Constitutions, 1776–1780*

## Gary B. Nash

### Introduction

Histories of revolutionary America place so much emphasis on the federal Constitution that it is easy to overlook the drafting of state constitutions. State constitution-making began well before the Constitutional Convention; in some cases, states began the process even before the Continental Congress approved the Declaration of Independence. With fourteen different examples on which to draw (including Vermont), the Constitutional Convention turned to the states for lessons on framing the new United States government.

Gary B. Nash illustrates that the states provided a variety of answers to the question of how to balance liberty and order. Some states, such as Pennsylvania and Vermont, adopted constitutions that were decidedly radical for their day. For instance, these constitutions extended the franchise to white men of little or even no property; they created unicameral, popularly-elected legislatures and granted those bodies broad powers; they hemmed in the power of the executive, instituted frequent elections, and made government as transparent as possible. The idea was to broaden participation and weaken centralized power, which drafters in Pennsylvania and Vermont viewed as a crystallization of the Revolution's ideals. By contrast, the constitutions of states such as Maryland and, to a lesser extent, Massachusetts, were drawn up by wealthy, conservative interests frightened by the egalitarian impulses of the Revolution. These elites empowered the executive branch, instituted stiff property qualifications for office-holding and voting, and divided the powers of government to prevent popular movements from dictating policy. The drafters of these constitutions believed the Revolution was about independence from Britain, not the creation of a new social order.

- In the context of state constitution-making, what was the range of ways in which revolutionary Americans interpreted their own revolutionary rhetoric?
- In what ways did fighting the Revolution shape state constitutions, as, for instance, when it came to deciding whether penniless militiamen should be allowed to vote?
- Within the context of revolutionary America, just how radical or conservative were the constitutions of Pennsylvania and Maryland, respectively? How might your answer change when taking black Americans and white women into account?
- Does your perspective on the drafting of the federal Constitution change with knowledge of state constitution-making? In what ways?

By 1776, colonists were practiced at overthrowing government, but not at constructing it. In one colony after another they had closed courts, driven royal agents to cover, evicted king-appointed governors from their residences, and, at the urging of the Continental Congress, elected new men to sit in extralegal provincial legislatures and conventions. But creating new constitutionally sanctioned governments was infinitely more difficult, akin to instantly growing a new, fully formed tree after chopping down a venerable old oak. And the work of constitution making was all the more tricky because it had to be accomplished, state by state, in the vortex of a war for national liberation that was going badly.

Composing his autobiography two years after yielding the presidency to Thomas Jefferson in 1801, John Adams remembered how he urged the Second Continental Congress on October 18, 1775, "to resolve on a general recommendation to all the states to call conventions and institute regular governments." This was the beginning of "our desire of revolutionizing all the governments" – governments that had already formed outside England's authority, but only as conventions or temporary bodies, after royal governors had disbanded their legislatures.[1]

Adams was pleased in 1775 that most members of Congress agreed with him about constructing new state governments (at a time when Congress was still deeply divided on declaring independence), but he was mortified at the kind of government most of his friends desired. Pressed to come up with a model plan of government that might serve the states, he began penning "Thoughts on Government." But Adams chose not to suggest the form of government he had in mind on the congressional floor. In fact, he was chary of having Congress take a stand on *any* kind of government. "I dared not make such a motion," he recalled, "because I knew that if such a plan was adopted, it would be if not permanent yet of long duration, and it would be extremely difficult to get rid of it."

Adams would have been thrilled to see state constitutions constructed that conformed to his idea of a wisely structured government. The raw country lawyer of a decade before had now emerged as a diamond-edged intellectual deeply immersed in the science of politics. He had gained great respect in Massachusetts and in the Continental Congress for poring over the works of political theorists all the way back to classical authors, but especially those of the main English political thinkers of the last century: Hobbes, Harrington, Sydney, and Locke. "I had in my head and at my tongue's end as many projects of government as Mr. [Edmund] Burke says the Abbe Sieyes [noted French political philosopher] had in his pigeon holes." However, Adams knew that many others had been reading the same political theorists but had reached different conclusions about what constituted balanced government.

In fact, Adams had to remain mute because, for all the respect he had garnered, he was out of step with most members of Congress. Later he wrote, "I knew that every one of my friends, and all those who were the most zealous for assuming government, had at that time no idea of any other government but a contemptible legislature in one assembly, with committees for executive magistrates and judges." Even his cousin Sam Adams, fellow Massachusetts delegate to the Continental Congress, was enamored of a single-house legislature, as was his friend Thomas Cushing, a wealthy merchant and another of the Massachusetts delegates. For Adams, the idea of a unicameral legislature with a weak executive branch was naive, almost juvenile, and certainly dangerous. "The child was not yet weaned," he sputtered, and "I took care, however, always to bear my testimony against every plan of an unbalanced government."

Thus in 1776 the epochal work of making government began with sharply divided views among the leading statesmen of the revolutionary movement. On one point, consensus had developed – that the consent of the governed was the only true source or political authority. But that was a vague and elastic notion. From that one powerful idea emerged intense debate, fierce passion, and bitter controversy, in many cases so rancorous that it interfered with the armed struggle for independence. Thirteen states had to create thirteen constitutions, all to be made in the midst of war. More than five years elapsed before all thirteen were in place.

## First Attempts

The necessity to create new law began months before July 4, 1776. New Hampshire crafted a constitution six months before the Second Continental Congress declared independence. Then on May 10 and 15, 1776, Congress voted for what amounted to a virtual declaration of independence: that "the exercise of every kind of authority under the said crown should be totally suppressed, and all the powers of government, exerted under the authority of the people" be put into place. Three other states – South Carolina, New Jersey, and Virginia – had their constitutions up and running before July 4. Thereafter, delegates to constitutional conventions in seven other states rushed to construct a framework for self-governance and create fundamental laws to protect the people's basic liberties.

Constitution making absorbed people's interest, energy, and passion as never before. Heightening popular interest in making, rather than obeying, law was a flood of printed material issuing from printing presses up and down the seaboard. Cascading newspaper dialogues and political pamphlets fanned political debates. It was "a spectacle … without parallel on earth," remembered Samuel Miller, a clergyman, many years later. "Even a large portion of that class of the community which is destined to daily labor have free and constant access to public prints, receive regular information of every occurrence [and] attend to the course of political affairs … . Never were [political writings] so cheap, so universally diffused, and so easy of access."[2]

The need for a unified story of the nation's birth – a founding mythology that would underpin a national identity – has obscured the fact that Americans were deeply divided when the time came to construct these state constitutions. From a great distance, we imagine that nearly everyone involved in the call to arms would unite in creating new governments. This was hardly the case, because the opportunity to create fundamental law was an invitation to experiment, all the more so since no blueprint of a model state constitution existed, either in North America, Europe, or anywhere else. The prospect was exhilarating, but the gritty work of hammering out a constitution was divisive and exhausting. John Adams enthused over the opportunity: "How few of the human race have ever enjoyed an opportunity of making an election of government, more than of air, soil, or climate, for themselves or their children? When, before the present epocha, had three millions of people full power and a fair opportunity to form and establish the wisest and happiest government that human wisdom can contrive?"[3]

But whose wisdom? That of a few, the many, or *all* the people? Who might participate in the process of drafting a constitution, and how would they acquire that right? Who could look at the draft and decide whether it established "the wisest and happiest government that human wisdom can contrive"? Would the old property restrictions on the right to vote and hold office remain in place? Would there be a governor with veto power over laws passed by the legislature? Would the governor be elected or appointed by the legislature? How would the natural rights of life and liberty be reconciled with slavery, which ensnared one-fifth of the population and promised their offspring only a life of perpetual servitude? These and a host of other questions faced constitution drafters, whoever they were and however they were selected.

That the constitutions varied from state to state is not surprising because no state's history, economy, labor system, religion, and social composition was a replica of another's. Each had experienced its own turmoil and internal disputes, conditioning people to think in various ways about reforming government.

Also, the people of each state sent a unique set of constitution writers to the table. Neighboring Maryland and Pennsylvania, for example, had grown into very different societies by 1776. Thirty percent of Maryland's population was enslaved, but only 4 percent of Pennsylvania's. Maryland's established Anglican Church contrasted with Pennsylvania's religious diversity. Quaker pacifist tradition in Pennsylvania had no counterpart in Maryland, and Maryland's mostly Anglican tidewater aristocracy had no parallel in Pennsylvania. Hence, Maryland's constitution writers were predominantly slave-owning planters experienced in holding office and making law; Pennsylvania's constitution drafters were mostly farmers and middling urban artisans or struggling doctors and teachers with scant experience as officeholders, lawmakers, or legal experts. Out of these differences came sharply different constitutions. They shared some elements but contrasted in crucial ways: Pennsylvania's constitution shifted the center of political gravity downward in the ranks of society, while in Maryland political power remained in the hands of an elite that strictly hedged in popular sentiment.

Not every state thought it necessary to write a constitution *de novo*. Connecticut and Rhode Island amended their English charters simply by deleting all reference to the English Crown. Letting it go at that, they continued to govern themselves as before. By itself, this decision *not* to change was a slap in the face of those who wanted to write afresh on a clean slate. But in all other states, the view prevailed that "we have it in our power to begin the world over again," as Thomas Paine expressed it, and therefore the people needed a fresh beginning with a body of fundamental law to live under as free people. Rather than have their existing legislatures draft a constitution, most states called for a freshly elected convention specifically charged with the task. Many subscribed to the idea expressed by Boston's town meeting that such a body should exist "no longer than the Constitution is forming."[4]

Never before had the people dared to think of themselves as the source of authority for constructing fundamental law. This was radical, breathtaking, and inspiring. "Divine providence is about to grant you a favor," wrote Pennsylvania's provincial congress, "which few people have ever enjoyed before, the privilege of choosing Deputies to form a government under which you are to live." Far to the south, two young Charleston, South Carolina, men watching the procession of those charged with writing that state's constitution reported that the spectacle was "beheld by the people with transports and tears of joy. The people gazed at them with a kind of rapture."[5] In other states, people were similarly awestruck with what they were themselves creating: specially elected groups of constitution writers who understood that, having done their best, they must return home with no further power vested in them. Among the eleven states that wrote new constitutions, nine followed this radical innovation, with only South Carolina and Virginia allowing their sitting legislatures to assume the responsibility of drafting a constitution.

## A Militiaman's Constitution

If only an extraordinary, task-specific political body could be entrusted with the creation of fundamental law, who could vote for these special, almost godlike delegates? In this matter, Pennsylvania first strode onto radical ground. In a sharp break from nearly a century of elections in England and its far-flung colonies, Pennsylvania's lawmakers opened up the vote on the belief that all taxpaying men, rather than only property-owning men, were entitled to it. All "associators" – that is, men who had agreed to associate in the militia units as bands of brothers – were permitted to vote if they were at least twenty-one years of age, residents of Pennsylvania for at least one year, and had paid even the smallest tax. This broadening of the suffrage potentially brought about nine of every ten free adult males into the political community.

But it had one important qualification: It applied only to those ready to swear allegiance to the independence movement. Deprived of the vote were those unwilling to vow that they would not "by any means, directly or indirectly, oppose the establishment of a free government in this province by the convention now to be chosen, nor the measures adopted by the congress against the tyranny attempted to be established in these colonies by the court of Great Britain." This test of loyalty, along with the widened suffrage, proved crucial in the composition of the convention's delegates.[6] By neatly disenfranchising Tories and "Moderates," those still opposed to an outright declaration of independence, the provincial conference calling the convention paved the road for a lawmaking body that was not representative of Pennsylvania's people in their entirety but of those committed to independence and internal change. Yet a crucial step had been taken – moving from property-owner suffrage to taxpayer suffrage, which included everyone but slaves, indentured servants, and those too poor to pay even a small "head tax."

Twelve days before the election to choose constitutional convention delegates, James Cannon's broadside, addressed to the "Several Battalions of Military Associators in the Province of Pennsylvania," gave a foretaste of what was to come. Reminding the men who were shouldering arms and preparing for battle with the British that the "judiciousness of the choice which you make" will effect "the happiness of millions unborn," Cannon pinpointed the "qualifications which we think most essential to constitute a member of the approaching Convention," A teacher of mathematics at the College of Philadelphia, Cannon urged the soldiers to reject the upper-class view that in order to write a constitution, men needed "great learning, knowledge in our history, law, mathematics, etc., and a perfect acquaintance with the laws, manners, trade, constitution and policy of all nations."[7] Such men were exactly those to be distrusted if the great work to be accomplished must serve "the common interests of mankind." Reminding the militiamen of decades of simmering class hostility, Cannon warned that "Great and overgrown rich men will be improper to be trusted … . They will be too apt to be framing distinctions in society, because they will reap the benefits of all such distinctions – gentlemen of the learned professions are generally filled with quirks and quibbles of the schools; and, though we have several worthy men of great learning among us, yet, as they are very apt to indulge their disposition to refinement to a culpable degree, we would think it prudent not to have too great a proportion of such in the Convention."

What should be preferred to deep learning and professional status? "Honesty, common sense, and a plain understanding, when unbiased by sinister motives," counseled Cannon. These qualities "are fully equal to the task." Men like the voters themselves "are the most likely to frame us a good Constitution," he told the militiamen for "we are contending for the liberty which God has made our birthright: All men are entitled to it, and no set of men have a right to anything higher." At all costs, he concluded, do not vote for any delegate "who would be disposed to form any rank above that of Freemen."

Here was an argument that divided the elite from the common in every region and would continue to do so for many generations. William Henry Drayton, a South Carolina grandee, had fumed in 1769 that popular leaders had given credence to "men who were never in a way of study, or to advise on any points but rules how to cut up a beast in the market to the best advantage, to cobble an old shoe in the neatest manner, or to build a necessary house." From the other end of the coast came the rejoinder of the anonymous New Hampshire author of "The People the Best Governors," who pledged that "God … made every man equal to his neighbor and has virtually enjoined them to govern themselves by their own laws … . The people best know their own wants and necessities and therefore are best able to rule themselves.

Tent-makers, cobblers, and common tradesmen composed the legislature at Athens."[8]

The voters listened all too well so far as conservative Pennsylvania leaders and other politicos at the Continental Congress were concerned. For John Adams, who believed the *sine qua non* of a republican government was "a decency, and respect, and veneration introduced for persons in authority," this was social dynamite, in fact a perversion of good republican government. Would Pennsylvania voters, their numbers swelled by men who never before had cast a ballot, choose men of humble status and limited education simply because they seemed to be individuals of "honesty, common sense, and a plain understanding"?

It was just this prospect, that a broad suffrage would make lawmakers out of ordinary men, that made the franchise the key to the democratization of politics. In the radical view, political rights traditionally rooted in property must now be vested in the people. "The Great Secret of Government," wrote one Massachusetts town in the midst of its constitutional debate, "is governing all by all." This was the principle that now emerged in Pennsylvania. Colonies varied only modestly on how much property conferred voting rights on men. English election laws going back to 1429 limited the vote to landowners whose property yielded an annual rent of forty shillings (about one month's wages for an ordinary worker). For more than three centuries this figure "recurs like a mystic number in English and American suffrage laws," writes historian Willi Adams.[9]

Other colonies were far less radical in stipulating who could vote for the constitution-writing delegates. Propertied freemen in Maryland's Anne Arundel County, which contained the colony's capital town of Annapolis, called for the suffrage of all free adult men, but wealthy and politically experienced men such as the grandee Charles Carroll thought this "impudent and destructive of all government." This conservative view prevailed, and thus Maryland followed the old suffrage requirement

with some modification. The Committee of Mechanics of New York City argued that if every artisan was not capable of writing a constitution, every citizen could *judge* one, and ought to be consulted in a referendum of a draft constitution. "That share of common sense, which the Almighty has bountifully distributed amongst mankind in general," they reasoned, "is sufficient to quicken every one's feeling, and enable him to judge rightly, what advantages he is likely to enjoy or be deprived of, under any Constitution proposed to him." The craftsmen did not prevail in this case, and neither did their counterparts in most other states. Yet the old maxim that men without property possessed no independent judgment and therefore had no right to vote was under attack. Of all the radical steps taken in the bright light of early revolutionary enthusiasm, this was the most significant: the insistence, in the face of received wisdom dispensed by the upper class, that ordinary men struggling for a foothold on the ladder of property-owning status had just as much right to inclusion in the political community as the wealthiest shipowners, plantation proprietors, money lenders, and slaveholders.[10]

Sitting in the East Room of the Pennsylvania Statehouse with other members of the Continental Congress, Adams must have shaken his head at seeing the delegates filing into the West Room across the hall on July 15, 1776. These were the men just elected for the weightiest political task assigned in Pennsylvania since William Penn had drafted a Frame of Government for his colony in 1681. A month before, Adams had worried that new constitutions would be influenced by a "spirit of leveling, as well as that of innovation." Now, his fears materialized. The delegates numbered ninety-six. Most were farmers, a few were merchants and lawyers, others were artisans, shopkeepers, and schoolteachers. It was not unusual for an ironmonger born in Upper Silesia to be flanked by an Ulster-born farmer and an Alsatian-born shopkeeper as the deliberations went forward. A majority were immigrants or sons of immigrants from Ireland, Scotland, and Germany, and many were in their midtwenties. All but eight represented the rural counties outside Philadelphia. About half had joined up as militiamen, and most of them had been elected officers by the rank and file. Francis Alison, Philadelphia's Presbyterian minister, called them "mostly honest well meaning country men, who are employed; but entirely unacquainted with such high matters [and] hardly equal to the task to form a new plan of government."[11]

It is unlikely that more than a few of the delegates had read John Adams's advice in "Thoughts on Government," the pamphlet the Sage of Braintree had published in Philadelphia three months before. Adams had tried to neutralize Paine's most radical notions in the wildly popular *Common Sense*. But even if they had consulted Adams's "Thoughts on Government," which stressed the need for a balanced government where popular interests would be offset by conservative ones, the assembled delegates had something much different in mind.[12]

As they met in the midst of great apprehension over the British demonstration of military superiority in the summer of 1776, seven men emerged to guide and shape the debates. Four were from Philadelphia: clock maker David Rittenhouse, doctor Thomas Young, mathematics tutor James Cannon, and brewer Timothy Matlack. These were just the kind of men celebrated by Benjamin Franklin, who three decades before had gathered such artisan-citizens in the Junto, where they could improve their minds through collective reading and discuss issues of the day. Lawyers George Ross of Lancaster County and James Smith of York County, and Robert Whitehill, a farmer with legal training from Carlisle, completed the cadre. Franklin himself sat impassively as president, much of the time asleep (though sometimes he stepped across the hall to sit at sessions of the Continental Congress). Thomas Paine was absent, but his ideas were much in the heads of many delegates.

Working for eight weeks, the constitution drafters considered and then rejected three of the most honored elements of English republican thought. First they scrapped the idea of a two-house legislature with the upper house reflecting men of wealth and the lower house mirroring the common people – a replica of the British government where the House of Lords represented the aristocracy and the House of Commons represented the people at large. The case for unicameralism rested primarily on long historical experience showing that upper houses in the colonies had generally reflected the interests of the wealthy and gave institutional form to a contest of interests that did not, at least in the minds of ordinary people, serve the common good. Other historical experiences fortified the unicameralist argument: that town meetings, the Continental Congress itself, and almost a century of one-house rule in Pennsylvania had proved that dispensing with an upper house could well serve the interests of all.

Second, the drafters abandoned the idea of an independent executive branch with extensive power, especially to veto legislative bills – a governor's power commonly found in British colonies. Instead, the convention provided for an elected weak plural executive branch, composed of a president and council. It was empowered to appoint important officers, including the attorney general and judges, but given no legislative veto power. Its duty was to implement the laws passed by the legislature, not to amend or veto them.

Finally, the constitution drafters scuttled the old franchise that allowed the vote only to free, white, property-owning males, and created the most liberal franchise known in the Western world to that date. Only apprentices and the deeply impoverished, excused from paying any tax, were excluded. This was a flat-out rejection of the hoary idea that only a man with "a stake in society" would use the vote judiciously. After all, was not risking one's life on the battlefield evidence of a stake in society? How then could those risking their lives to protect the property of voting citizens be denied the vote?

Other provisions of the Pennsylvania Constitution erected hedges to prevent concentrated political power. Annual elections by ballot, used in the colonial period, were continued. "Instruct your deputies, when chosen," advised James Cannon, "to reserve an annual return of" all power into your hands." Also, the constitution guaranteed that the doors of the legislative house remain open to "all persons who behave decently," so the people from whom government derived its authority could monitor their elected legislators. Also to this end, the legislative debates and votes were to be printed weekly, in English and German, for all to see. Reflecting the fear of corrupt politicians and the determination to hold lawmakers accountable to their constituents, these measures were followed by all other states except South Carolina. Even conservative patriots endorsed these innovations promoting transparency in the decisions reached by the people's representatives.

The Pennsylvania constitution writers provided a final check against corrupt or unresponsive legislators. Having drafted, debated, and passed a law, the legislature must print and distribute it "for consideration of the people." This allowed time for public discussion of each law before the next annual election of representatives. This next legislature would then finally vote on the law passed by its predecessor. Vermont was the only state to follow Pennsylvania on this. For some conservatives, such as William Hooper of North Carolina (to whom John Adams sent his first draft of "Thoughts on Government"), this was an especially offensive constitutional requirement. "The mob," he sputtered, "made a second branch of legislature – laws subjected to their revision in order to refine them, a washing in ordure by way of purification. Taverns and dram shops are the councils to which the laws of the state are to be referred before they possess a binding influence." "K," writing anonymously

in the *Pennsylvania Packet,* agreed that this amounted to a veto power on legislation by "a part of the people, particularly such as frequent public houses where the laws are to be always posted up for consultation."[13]

Three final provisions nailed down the radical democracy desired by the Pennsylvania delegates. First, they imposed term limits that restricted a man from serving more than four one-year legislative terms every seven years – a term limit provision adopted in no other state for the lower house. This rotation of legislative power jibed with the idea that many citizens were capable of performing well in public office. Second, they specified the popular election of a "Council of Censors" once every seven years to review the constitution to ensure that it had "been preserved inviolate in every part; and whether the legislative and executive branches of government have performed their duty as guardians of the people."[14] Only Vermont mimicked this provision for monitoring the constitution's effectiveness. Third, the convention stipulated the reapportionment of the legislative assembly every seven years on the basis of census returns. This commitment to proportional representation was followed by no other state and achieved by the U.S. Congress only in 1962, when the Supreme Court ruled in the "one man-one vote" *Baker v. Carr* case.

In one proposed feature of the constitution, the Pennsylvania draftsmen went beyond the wishes of the full convention. Radical leaders Cannon and Young proposed a clause giving the state the power to limit private ownership of large tracts of land. The rationale was that "an enormous proportion of property vested in a few individuals is dangerous to the rights and destructive of the common happiness of mankind; and therefore every free state hath a right by its laws to discourage the possession of such property." This clause, a so-called agrarian law to redistribute wealth, marked the outermost boundary of radical thought. It was not a homegrown idea but one harking back to England's seventeenth-century civil war era, later to be proposed by James Burgh in his *Political Disquisitions* (1774), a treatise on politics widely read in the colonies. The *Providence Gazette* had published an excerpt of it in December 1775, arguing the need for putting a limit on the accumulation of wealth.[15]

Imbedded in this tenet was the notion that inequality was not the result of different degrees of talent or ambitiousness or the product of impersonal economic forces – the argument of conservatives. Rather, gross inequality resulted from avarice and oppression by those who, for whatever reason, had risen to the top. But the convention did not pass this agrarian law, perhaps because of its vagueness about how the state could limit the accumulation of wealth without actually confiscating private property, and partly because the delegates were unwilling to tamper with the bourgeois inclinations of most Pennsylvanians. Yet in agreeing on a clause abolishing imprisonment for debt, and on another providing for public education supported by taxes on property holdings, the constitution drafters took important steps toward achieving a more equitable society.

The constitution was a victory for small farmers, especially Scots-Irish frontiersmen with small holdings of land; for urban artisans, many of whom could not vote; and for radical intellectual reformers. It was a heavy blow to wealthy merchants, large property owners, and assorted conservatives who wanted to hold on to the old political system, which, they feared, was already slipping from their grasp. It was the culmination of a move toward a democratized polity that had been occurring piecemeal for several generations and had gained momentum as revolutionary leaders saw the necessity to mobilize the bottom as well as the middle of society. Here was the idea that the producing classes were to be valued most in a republic, and that the wealthy nonproducers, who lived by manipulating money and land, were to be valued least.

After completing its work in September 1776, as Washington's army was abandoning New York City and retreating precipitously across New Jersey at the time, the Pennsylvania Convention ordered the distribution of four hundred copies of the constitution for public consideration and debate. This in itself was a further radical innovation – to send back to the people the fruit of their elected delegates so they could endorse or reject it. The process was left vague, however, so the invitation to the public was more of an informal public-opinion poll than a formal ratification. The constitutional convention proclaimed that the document was adopted on September 28, 1776.

For Pennsylvania's militiamen, the constitution was all they hoped for. While the convention delegates were drafting the document, they had been honing their own democratic skills. Under Cannon's tutelage, privates formed their own committee to debate the selection of two brigadier generals for the Pennsylvania militia. Should the Pennsylvania assembly make the choice, as the Continental Congress recommended on June 3? Or should the militia officers make the choice? Or, should the enlisted militiamen be included in the choice of the colony's two most senior military officers? In a decision unimaginable today – perhaps equivalent to the election of the two highest officers for the National Guard of Texas – a meeting of the Committee of Privates and the board of officers decided that each battalion should send two privates and two officers to Lancaster on July 4, 1776, to elect the brigadier generals. Before ever taking the field, the Committee of Privates had won a political victory – "the right of appointing officers to command them," as they put it, and not only junior officers, but all officers up to the brigadier generals. When most of the militiamen returned to Philadelphia in late August 1776 after a six-week enlistment, they became part of the debate on the newly instituted Pennsylvania constitution.

## The Frightened Response

The militiamen for whom James Cannon had become spokesman found plenty of reasons to applaud the constitution put before

Pennsylvanians in September 1776. For them, it was like a fresh wind blowing down the corridors of established power. But for moderates and conservatives, both inside and outside Pennsylvania, the constitution was more like a gathering storm poised to wreak havoc in the Keystone State. Pennsylvania's constitution departed so radically from conventional political thought that it shocked and dismayed some patriot leaders, including Pennsylvanians Benjamin Rush, John Dickinson, James Wilson, and Robert Morris. A firestorm of criticism took only days to develop after the *Pennsylvania Evening Post* published the draft on September 10. The ensuing public debate in the Philadelphia newspapers continued far beyond the adoption of the constitution. Benjamin Rush called it "our rascally constitution" and "our state dung cart with all its dirty contents" that made the state government as dreaded as "the government of Turkey." Though he had grown up under a unicameral legislature, Rush now complained that "a single legislature is big with tyranny" and that the constitution "substituted a mob government to one of the happiest governments of the world." "Good god!" gasped John Adams after seeing the full constitution. "The people of Pennsylvania in two years will be glad to petition the crown of Britain for reconciliation in order to be delivered from the tyranny of their Constitution."[16]

Many elements of the constitution appalled conservatives and some moderates, but none more than the enlargement of the electorate. "The most flourishing commonwealths that ever existed, Athens and Rome," wrote an anonymous Philadelphian in the *Evening Post,* "were RUINED by allowing this right to people without property." The prospect of taxpayer suffrage deeply troubled John Adams. With Abigail pressing him on the right of women to vote and even conservative friends in Massachusetts advocating that the franchise should be opened to all free men, Adams upheld the traditional view on limiting suffrage to the propertied. His friend and fellow jurist James

Sullivan shocked Adams by arguing that "every member of society has a right to give his consent to the laws of the community or he owes no obedience to them." Sullivan explained further that "a very great number of the people of the colony" were disfranchised for lack of an "estate worth 40 shillings per annum" – that is, property that would produce a rent of forty shillings per year. Sullivan called the traditional practice feudal, one based on the false premise that "men [without property] are unable to account for the principles of their own actions." "The poor and the rich," he insisted, "are alike interested in that important part of government called legislation."[17]

Adams responded with a tortured defense of the age-old definition of political competency. Thinking back to his wife's ministrations, he fumed rhetorically, "Whence arises the right of the men to govern women, without their consent?" And "whence the right of the old to bind the young without theirs?" Because women's "delicacy renders them unfit for practice and experience in the great business of life … as well as the arduous cares of state," he explained. Adams knew very well that his wife, from her management of the Adams farm, her arduous care in the smallpox inoculation of their children, and her sage comments on the political scene, was far from "unfit for practice and experience in the great business of life." But he pressed on. "Children have not judgment or will of their own," he reasoned, but this was off the point since not even the most Utopian reformer suggested that children should vote or hold office. Back on point – the competency of propertyless males to exercise the vote responsibly – Adams argued that "Men in general in every society, who are wholly destitute of property, are also too little acquainted with public affairs to form a right judgment, and too dependent upon other men to have a will of their own." Only three years before, Adams had voiced no objections; indeed he applauded the political savvy of the mass of Bostonians, some five thousand strong, who thronged the public meeting that preceded the Tea Party. This, he noted in his journal, was an "exertion of popular power." Adams saw the Revolution as a "people's war," but he was unwilling to have a people's war produce a people's polity. Adams loved liberty but not equality, and from this position he would not budge through the entire course of the long Revolution.[18]

But in other states people *were* budging. In only two states – Virginia and Delaware – did state constitution writers retain the existing property qualifications (and even in Virginia some, including Thomas Jefferson, favored widening the suffrage). In New York, New Jersey, Maryland, and Georgia, constitution writers lowered the property qualifications substantially, thus broadening the electorate. North Carolina, South Carolina, and New Hampshire followed Pennsylvania's taxpayer suffrage, and Vermont enfranchised all adult males, even those who paid no tax at all. Rhode Island kept its ancient charter but enlarged the franchise to include almost all white men. In Maryland and Massachusetts, taxpayer suffrage came close to taking effect, thwarted only by close votes that favored scaled-down property qualifications.

Pennsylvania conservatives regarded the new unicameral legislature, unfettered by a governor armed with the power to veto its bills, as the second most disturbing and dangerous element of the constitution. Timothy Dwight, to become president of Yale in 1795, sputtered that "a legislature by a single house is of course no other than an organized mob. Its deliberations are necessarily tumultuous, violent and indecent." North Carolina's William Hooper called it "a beast without a head." In his "Thoughts on Government," Adams had listed six reasons for treating a one-house legislature like poison. He predicted that "A people cannot be long free, and never can be happy whose laws are made, executed and interpreted by one assembly." Fear lurked behind all his reasons, rooted especially in the pessimistic view that legislators left to themselves would "make arbitrary laws for their own interest, and adjudge all controversies in

their own favor." Adams wrote this before seeing how Pennsylvania's constitution drafters carefully hemmed in the legislators with provisions for open legislative hearings, published arguments and votes, annual elections, turnover in offices, rules against plural office-holding, and review of laws by the electorate before final endorsement or amendment by the next elected assembly. But these safeguards changed Adams's mind not one bit. Both his cousin Samuel Adams and his friend Thomas Cushing favored a unicameral legislature in 1776, but Adams was adamantly opposed.[19]

From the fall of 1776 through the fall of 1777, Pennsylvania conservatives, led by Robert Morris and John Dickinson, fought to defeat or cripple the 1776 constitution. One tactic was to argue that the next elected assembly should amend or rewrite the constitution. This mustered little support. The next tactic was for conservatives to withdraw from the legislature elected in November 1776 so that the majority supporting the constitution would be unable to obtain quorums for other legislative business. Another ploy was to refuse to serve as justices of the peace, sheriffs, and militia officers, even when popularly elected. Accusations flew in the pages of the Philadelphia press for months. Radicals charged that the conservatives' problem was that they could not "stand to be governed by leather aprons." Conservatives returned fire with charges that the radicals were "coffee-house demagogues," who would bring anarchy to William Penn's peaceable kingdom. The arguments continued in the press, in the streets, and in the taverns well into 1777. Only when the British army drove northward from the Chesapeake Bay region to capture Philadelphia in September 1777 did the anti-Constitutionalists, as opponents of the constitution called themselves, temporarily quit their attempts to scuttle the constitution. The argument was far from over, but with the British army occupying Philadelphia from September 1777 to June 1778, the Constitutionalists held their ground.

## Vermont and Maryland

To the north and south of Pennsylvania, Vermont and Maryland devised constitutions that showed how differently delegates imagined the societies they wanted to live in if the Americans succeeded in casting off the British yoke. In early 1777, the New York area known as the Grants, where so much pre-revolutionary populist activism had surfaced, finally declared itself independent. Ethan Allen, their swaggering leader, was rotting in a wretched English prison, but the Green Mountain Boys saw the war for independence as the perfect opportunity to realize their separatist dreams. Six conventions of hill town delegates met between April 1775 and January 1777 as British forces threatened to sweep all northern American combatants from the field. Led by Heman Allen, Ethan's brother, the delegates voted in January 1777 to "be a new and separate state; and for the future conduct themselves as such."[20] New York leaders regarded this as outrageous and illegal, but their governor, George Clinton, could hardly afford to send provincial troops against fellow Americans also involved in the war against England.

Calling themselves the Republic of Vermont (the name was suggested by Philadelphia's Thomas Young), the Grants residents petitioned Congress for admission as an independent state. Strenuous New York opposition convinced Congress to deny admission and admonish the Vermonters in July 1777. But that did not deter Grants residents, most of them small landowners and most of them resolutely democratic. While waiting for Congress to recognize their legitimacy, they set about constructing a constitution. Thomas Young, peripatetic ideologue, spurred them on, arguing that "you have as good a right to choose how you will be governed" as any other state, and urging them to form a government where "the people at large [are] the true proprietors of governmental power." A few years later, back in the country, Ethan Allen wrote that "They were a people between the heavens and the earth, as free as is possible to conceive any people to be; and in this condition they formed government upon the true principles of liberty and natural right."[21]

"Liberty and natural right" indeed captured the essence of the Vermont plan of government. The constitutional convention met in early July 1777 as General John Burgoyne's British forces overwhelmed the Americans at Fort Ticonderoga and rampaged through the towns where many of the delegates lived. Out of this unpromising situation emerged a constitution that in most respects followed the Pennsylvania model: a unicameral legislature; a public review of each law drafted before the next elected assembly amended or ratified it; a governor with no veto power over laws passed by an annually elected legislature; and a Council of Censors meeting once every seven years to monitor the faithful execution of constitutional principles. If the council believed the constitution was functioning improperly, it could call a popularly elected new convention to amend the constitution so that future generations would have "the same privileges of choosing how they would be governed." Whiffs of the limitation on the concentration of wealth proposed in Pennsylvania appeared in the Vermont constitution where the preamble – a "Declaration of Rights" – declared "that private property ought to be subservient to public uses" and that the state had the right of eminent domain and therefore could appropriate private property for public use if the owner was fairly compensated. Vermont was more conservative, however, in allowing multiple office-holding (such as a legislator serving simultaneously as a justice of the peace).

Vermont's constitution went further than Pennsylvania's in several respects: It provided for unrestricted manhood suffrage without even a taxpayer qualification; made all judges elective; gave special protection to debtors; and declared all slaves free, without compensation to their owners, as soon as they reached the ages of twenty-one, if male, and eighteen, if female. To be sure, few slaves resided in Vermont. Yet the state was the first to say constitutionally that slavery was illegal as a violation of "natural, inherent, and unalienable rights." The abolitionist principle received real application when Yale-trained David Avery arrived in Bennington to assume the pulpit of the Congregational church in 1779. There he found that his congregation refused to commune with him because he owned a female slave. Encouraged by Ethan Allen, the woman sued for her freedom. In another instance, a judge in 1784 ruled in favor of a runaway slave whose master produced a bill of sale proving his ownership, only to be admonished that to retain his slave property he would have to provide a bill of sale from "God Almighty."[22]

With a constitution in hand, Vermonters still had to gain legitimacy for their self-proclaimed state. Here, the old warrior Ethan Allen reentered the stage. After he was released from England in a prisoner exchange, he became Vermont's state attorney in 1778. Using what Thomas Jefferson called "the Vermont logic," that is, the right of people to create their own state, Vermonters set up courts to adjudicate the laws that their elected legislature passed. From his pivotal position as Vermont's prosecutor, Allen helped protect the land grants of Green Mountain farmers. Meanwhile, the New Yorkers still remaining in the Grants region, many of whom had become Loyalists, had to be confronted one last time. The New Yorkers regarded the self-created state of Vermont as the "offspring of anarchy," and they had resolutions from the Continental Congress to back them up. But neither they nor Congress could make the words stick. New York's legislature went so far as to threaten to withdraw from the war against England unless Congress took "speedy and vigorous measures for reducing them [the Vermonters] to an obedience."[23] This, too, was a toothless threat.

New York's passage of a conservative constitution in 1777 ended any chance that Vermonters would recognize New York's old colonial claims to the Grants region. In many respects, the New York constitution was the most conservative passed by the states, contrasting sharply with those of Vermont and Pennsylvania. It lacked a bill of rights; installed a powerful executive branch that could disband the elected legislature; created a Council of Revision of appointed supreme court judges and the elected governor with veto power over legislative bills; maintained the hefty colonial property qualification that narrowed the electorate more than in all but a few states; made most officials – from the local level to the highest state offices (except that of governor) – appointive rather than elective; and upheld all land grants issued in the colonial period (which would have invalidated the deeds of most Vermonters). Ira Allen, Ethan's youngest brother, carried the constitutions of New York and Vermont from town to town in the Green Mountain region in 1777, inviting the citizens to compare them carefully. This worked well. Most Vermonters saw in the New York document a blueprint for preserving the power of New York's elite (minus those who remained loyal to Great Britain). By one estimate, only 10 percent of Vermont's adult males would have been able to vote for the Senate and governor.[24] Forty towns in the region endorsed the Vermont constitution while rejecting New York's as perversely undemocratic.

Politically empowered as first-class citizens, men of the Grants region joined the Vermont militia, commanded by Ethan Allen after 1778, in impressive numbers. This was virtually unique among the states. Elsewhere, the war had become a poor man's fight; in Vermont it became every man's fight. Within a society filled with farmers struggling for economic security, radical politics merged with radical militarism. They fought under elected officers and were as willing to fight New Yorkers to uphold Vermont's claim to independence as they were to defend the northern frontier against the British.

Radicalism also tinctured the creation of Vermont courts. Presided over by elected judges with little formal legal training, the courts confiscated the land of Loyalists, put the land up for public auction with preference to veterans, protected the land titles of small farmers, and shunned the legal technicalities employed by trained lawyers in other states that prolonged legal proceedings and made the system of justice expensive to administer. "New York used its courts as instruments of the central state government and the interest that ran it," writes historian Michael Bellisles. But Vermonters, while they "also saw courts as a means of social control," used them especially to protect "the well-being of the immediate community rather than the success of a distant elite."[25] Created from the bottom up by the populace of the Grants region, the courts stood prepared for a final day of reckoning in the long-standing New York-Vermont dispute.

Far to the south of Vermont, other delegates were at work on their own constitutions in the spring and summer of 1776. Among the southern states, the sharpest contest took place in Maryland. Ordinary Marylanders had been gaining voice in the turmoil of revolutionary protests against English policies, and this surging populism quickly infused the debates on creating a state constitution. As in other states, the first question became: Who was entitled to vote for the delegates who would write the fundamental laws under which generations would live? In Maryland, the propertyless *seized* the vote, not waiting for radical leaders to legislate taxpayer suffrage for the purpose of electing constitution-writing delegates, as happened in Pennsylvania and Vermont. After Maryland's provincial convention in August 1776 called for the election of delegates to write a constitution, people in five counties who did not meet the property qualifications thronged the polls, threw out the election judges, and insisted that anyone who bore arms was entitled to vote. In Prince Georges County, "the inhabitants … agreed, that every taxable [man] bearing arms … had an undoubted right to vote for representatives at this time of public calamity." When the election judges resigned in protest, the people at large elected judges of their own, who then submitted the election results to the constitutional convention. In Frederick County, the Committee

of Safety chose new election judges who then ratified the vote of a mass of voters, the majority of whom "had armed in defense of the country." Also, in Kent, Worcester, and Queen Anne's counties, election judges counted the votes of propertyless militiamen.[26]

The suffrage rebels also struck in Anne Arundel County, where the Carroll family had built an immense fortune. After election judges opened the polls, a knot of men "insisted on every man having a vote that bore arms. When the judges closed the polls and ordered James Disney, an election clerk, to read the election regulations that restricted the franchise, infuriated militiamen shouted "pull him down, he shall not read, we will not hear it, and if you do not stop and let every free man vote that carries arms, we will pull the house down from under the judges." The militiamen finally backed down, but one of the men standing for election, Rezin Hammond, "advised the people to lay down their arms if they were denied the privilege of voting, for it was their right and they ought not to be deprived of it."[27]

The entrenched elite from other Maryland counties moved to stem this radical tide. Elected to the constitutional convention under the restricted franchise rules, they quickly ordered new elections in the five insurgent counties where militiamen and other propertyless men had seized the vote. But even after militiamen were turned away from the polls, the propertied voters elected radical leaders John Hall and Rezin Hammond from Anne Arundel County. It was Hammond and Hall who now carried the banner for a liberal, if not radical, constitution.

Months before the constitutional convention met, even before Congress declared independence, Hall, Hammond, and other radical reformers hammered out the equivalent of a Maryland militiamen's constitution. Meeting in June 1776 in Annapolis, where representatives of the Anne Arundel militia battalions met, they had their document ready for publication in the *Maryland Gazette* by July 18, just days after word of the Declaration of Independence reached

Maryland. Their draft was not as democratic as those constructed in Pennsylvania and Vermont, but it called for reforms that were radical compared to neighboring Virginia's constitution. A bicameral legislature would be elected annually by the people. This legislature would choose a governor with no legislative veto power and appoint all state judges. The legislature would publish its proceedings and votes annually so that the electorate could judge the responsiveness of their representatives. At the county level, the people would choose all officials, including tax assessors and sheriffs. More radical, the constitution would abolish "the unjust mode of taxation heretofore used," replacing it with taxes paid "in proportion to every person's estate." Also to serve those injured by a disordered economy, the constitution proposed to restrict all debt proceedings in court until "this time of public calamity" had ended.[28]

Armed with this reform constitution, signed by 885 Anne Arundel freemen, Rezin Hammond arrived at the constitutional convention in August 1776. The convention received even more radical proposals from Anne Arundel freeholders. Key provisions allowed the election of militia officers by militiamen themselves. Most radical was broadening the franchise to include all freemen of the state who were at least twenty-one years of age and "well affected to the present glorious cause."[29]

The gulf separating the militiamen's constitution and the gentry's notion of good government led to inflamed rhetoric and bitter disputes. Charles Carroll of Carrollton, the eldest son of the immensely wealthy Charles Carroll of Annapolis, saw no merit in framing a more democratic society and a more equitable economic system. Hammond and Hall's advocacy of the militiamen was class betrayal. They were not honest men promoting a constitution responsive to Anne Arundel citizens, who at this moment were marching north in "flying camps" to serve with Washington and his Continental army. Rather, Hammond and Hall were "evil and designing men." "Should

their schemes take place, and it is probable they will, unless vigorously counteracted by all honest men," Carroll wrote to his father, "anarchy will follow as a certain consequence; injustice, rapine and corruption in the seats of justice will prevail, and this province in a short time will be involved in all the horrors of an ungovernable and revengeful democracy, and will be dyed with the blood of its best citizens." To allow broader suffrage, to give an elected legislature more power than the governor, and to provide for debtor relief was the work of "selfish men, who are everywhere striving to throw all power into the hands of the very lowest of people, in order that they may be their masters from the abused confidence which the people have placed in them."[30]

In this view, the propertyless were incapable of voting intelligently, always tethered to their landlords, employers, and creditors, whose bidding they would promptly do as soon as they filled out a ballot. "A Watchman" in Maryland, probably Rezin Hammond, responded that "Every poor man has a life, a personal liberty, and a right to his earnings; and is in danger of being injured by government in a variety of ways" and therefore "should enjoy the right of voting for representatives, to be protectors of their lives, personal liberty, and their little property, which, though small, is yet, upon the whole, a very great object to them." Claiming that the old property qualifications in Maryland stripped the right to vote from half the state's freemen, who paid a very heavy share in the support of government" through poll taxes that fell disproportionately on the propertyless, "Watchman" insisted that taxpayer suffrage was a natural right and "the ultimate end of all freedom."[31]

For all his dyspeptic exclamations, Carroll of Carrollton need not have feared that Maryland's emerging constitution would overturn the interests of the ruling elite. The composition of the constitutional convention almost guaranteed a conservative outcome. Three-quarters of the Maryland delegates, who had to own at least fifty acres of land to stand for election, claimed more than five hundred acres. Half of them owned more than twenty enslaved Africans, and only a handful had no slaves at all. About four of every five delegates had fortunes of at least one thousand pounds (equivalent to $200,000 today). Four immensely wealthy planter lawyers became key figures writing the constitution: Charles Carroll of Carrollton, Samuel Chase, Thomas Johnson, and William Paca. They owned on average 17,500 acres and one hundred slaves each. Rivaled only by New York's constitution writers the Maryland delegates represented the most entrenched political and economic elite in North America.

"Connected by ties of kinship and interest," as Charles Carroll aptly put it, conservatives fought off the minority of delegates who wanted a democratic constitution. The result was a constitution designed to perpetuate a deeply conservative aristocratic government. This was clear from its key provisions: limited suffrage as under the old colonial qualifications; officeholding restricted as in the past to those owning extensive property; elections for lower-house representatives once in three years for candidates possessing an estate of at least five hundred pounds; voting *viva voce* as in the past, ensuring that the old patronage and clientage system remained in place; an electoral college, elected to seven-year terms by enfranchised Marylanders, consisting of upper-house delegates who must have an estate of at least one thousand pounds; election of a governor, who must have an estate of at least five thousand pounds, by the two legislative houses; and election of county and local sheriffs qualified by possession of an estate worth one thousand pounds or more. Recent research shows that the constitution, as proposed, would have limited those eligible for office in the lower house of the legislature to the top tenth of free white males and those eligible for the upper house to the wealthiest fourteenth.[32]

By the time Maryland's full constitutional convention took up the drafting committee's plan of government in October 1776, the war was going badly for the poorly clothed, armed, and provisioned American army. When radical opposition to the ultraconservative constitution surfaced, Charles Carroll of Carrollton despaired. "We are miserably divided," he wrote his father, "not only colony against colony, but in each colony there begins to appear such a spirit of disunion and discord that I am apprehensive, should we succeed against Great Britain (which I think very improbably under our circumstances), we shall be rent to pieces by civil wars and factions." It might be better, he thought, rather than "hazard civil wars amongst ourselves," to abandon the quest for independence and sue for peace with Great Britain.[33] Carroll's pessimism deepened as the convention delegates deliberated. But in fact conservatives had to make only small concessions to the radicals. They reduced the terms of office for upper-house legislators from seven to five years and lower-house legislators from three years to one year. The convention's radical minority pushed hard for broadening the electorate but lost by narrow votes on proposals to eliminate all property qualifications or reduce them to five pounds Maryland money. Instead, the convention agreed to lower the property qualification to fifty acres of land or property worth thirty pounds Maryland money. This became the threshold for membership in the political community, still denying suffrage to about half the white adult male population.

In one progressive move, the convention restored political and civil liberties to Catholics and disestablished the Church of England. Finally, the delegates signed the constitution without public review. Compared to other state constitutions, perhaps excepting that of neighboring Virginia, where aristocratic planters also controlled the constitutional convention, Maryland had shaped its political future according to the wishes of a minority of wealthy citizens. In the preamble the delegates affirmed that "All government of right originates from the people."[34] But in Maryland's case "the people" were actually only half of the white male citizens.

[…]

## Betrayal in Massachusetts

Nowhere was the debate over a constitution more protracted than in Massachusetts. Many years ago, John C. Miller, a biographer of Sam Adams, put the matter straight: "After the outbreak of war between the mother country and colonies, Massachusetts failed lamentably to take the lead in framing a new rate constitution."[35] In no other state did ideas about the people as the fountain of all political authority ebb away so quickly in the face of a resurgent conservative view that favored strict limits on popular power. This regressive movement in Massachusetts constitution making is all the more intriguing because of the particularly vibrant quality of involvement of ordinary citizens who were repeatedly asked for comment and advice on several drafts of the constitution. Brought to action, the state's town meetings produced an outpouring of down-to-earth political thinking, spawned not out of arguments among political theorists and educated lawyers, clergymen, and leisured men but mostly out of the local political experiences of men who worked with their hands.

Historians are still coming to grips with the peculiar difficulties that Massachusetts had in agreeing on a constitution. At first blush, it seems that many factors favored reaching an early settlement. Leading up to revolution, after reining in radicals such as Ebenezer Macintosh, popular leaders had fashioned an interclass alliance that set an example for other colonies resisting abhorrent British policies. Also, they had in John Adams a student of political science to whom many other colonial leaders turned for advice in forming state constitutions. Further, by the spring of 1776, the British army had evacuated eastern Massachusetts, never to reoccupy the state and tear up the countryside, as occurred in most other states. Most Loyalists left with the British, removing many of Massachusetts' ultraconservatives, thus sparing the state the civil war between patriots and Loyalists that shredded the social fabric in New York, New Jersey, and most southern states. Yet for all the conditions conducive to constitution making, Massachusetts failed repeatedly in devising a consensus constitution. Why?

Pennsylvania, Maryland, and several other states were already working on their constitutions when the Massachusetts legislature, at the beginning of June 1776, chose a drafting committee. But the legislators were unsure that they were entitled to clothe themselves with this grave responsibility. Nonetheless, they agreed to proceed. Yet nearly four months later, with the war going badly, the legislature had no draft to show. The problem was not the lack of ideas, but a fear among conservative leaders of the radical political innovations put forward by some legislators, especially those representing the hill towns of western Massachusetts. Sitting with the Continental Congress in Philadelphia, Adams sickened at what his friends reported to him. John Winthrop, distinguished scientist at Harvard and member of the legislative council, sent a distressing account of how thirty to forty men, brandishing large sticks, kept the justices from entering the Bristol County Courthouse in Taunton. Similar uprisings staged by those who opposed courts dispensing justice under commissions running in the name of George III convinced the legislature to suspend most county courts, though there was suspicion that debtors were trying to escape their creditors. For Winthrop, "these commotions" were part of "a spirit of innovation." "It seems as if everything was to be altered," he reported. "Scarce a newspaper but teems with new projects." Among these innovations were county assemblies to make local rules, and the election in each town for committees to probate wills. All of this would place authority closer to the people and reduce the high court fees detested by people of modest means. "Tis like repairing a house that is on fire," Winthrop moaned.[36]

The new mood of ordinary people in Massachusetts, it seemed, could not be ignored, swept away, or even steered in conservative directions. Or could it? Responding to Winthrop's alarmed description of populist schemes, John

Adams confided that he was "grieved to hear, as I do from various quarters, of that rage for innovation, which appears in so many wild shapes in our province." Adams's greatest fear was coming to pass: a government of ordinary people. A decade of plebeian involvement in the fracas with England had unnerved him. Adams was keenly aware that to bring the colonies into a state of open rebellion, moderate and conservative patriots had energized ordinary citizens, and in some cases, as chapter 4 relates, ordinary farmers and artisans had themselves taken the lead before beckoned to the fracas from above. In either case, ordinary citizens had become alarmingly unwilling to content themselves with the *status quo antebellum*. Reflecting his pessimistic view of ordinary people in the Bay State, Adams frowned on "ridiculous projects" such as "county assemblies, town registers, and town probates of wills, and sputtered that these projects aimed at putting authority in the hands or locally elected officials "are founded in narrow notions, sordid stinginess and profound ignorance and tend directly to barbarism." Adams would not have dared say this in front of the Boston town meeting, or in the town meeting in Braintree, where Abigail knew every attendee. But he expressed these innermost thoughts privately to Harvard's John Winthrop two weeks before he signed the Declaration of Independence.[37]

For moderates and conservatives in the legislature, the best course was to slow down on writing a constitution in the hope that the fever of the ordinary people would eventually subside. On September 17, the legislature asked the town whether they wished them to draft a constitution. Bowing to the current understanding that creating fundamental law required special approval of those who would live under it, they promised, if sanctioned to proceed, to publish their handiwork "for the inspection and perusal of the inhabitants."[38]

Responses to this canvass were varied, and the legislature, already deeply divided, took eight months to act on the town meeting responses.

This in itself was evidence of the conservatives' hope that democratic sentiment would exhaust itself. It was not to happen. Some towns, such as Concord, advised that the people should elect special delegates to perform this epochal task, drawing a clear line between lawmaking and constitution making. In neighboring Lexington, and in Pittsfield in western Massachusetts, the people wanted guarantees that town meetings across the state would have the opportunity to ratify or reject the constitution rather than simply to "inspect and peruse" it. Other towns, such as Concord and Boston, held that the suffrage must be broadened so that delegates elected for the weighty business now at hand should mirror all of the people asked to commit their lives and property to the Revolution, not just the propertied part. Consistent with the way the city had acted "as a body of the people" in the years of protest against the British, "every individual," insisted Boston's town meeting, "ought to be consulting, acting, and assisting." The towns of Worcester County, always a hotbed of radicalism, assembled in a convention in November 1776 to present a united front. Rankled by the recent redistribution of legislative seats as unfair to western parts of the state, most of the towns opposed the present legislature writing a constitution. Many of them wanted a special election for delegates to an assembly with only one task: to write a constitution that people of the commonwealth would live under for untold generations.[39]

On May 5, 1777, the upper and lower legislative houses finally reached a compromise on the most important points raised by the towns: that in the upcoming general election voters who met the old property requirement would choose delegates specifically empowered to draft a constitution, then to continue as a legislative body; that the draft would be published in Boston newspapers and sent to all towns where all males "free and twenty-one years of age" would be asked to vote up or down on the draft; and that if two-thirds of the voters approved, the constitution would be final. Seemingly, it was an adroit compromise. Conservatives had avoided a specially elected convention chosen by all free white men, the formula already adopted in other states, and in this way could screen out those most likely to represent the state's lower ranks. But they conceded that *all* adult male citizens should participate in rejecting or ratifying the constitution.

Boston's town meeting was not pleased with the compromise. By "a unanimous vote of a full meeting," Bostonians denied that it was proper for a legislative body to form a constitution. They called for an election by "the people at large," not just the propertied, to choose men specially elected to write the august document. Bostonians had zeroed in on precisely the two hedges that conservatives had erected to block a constitution resembling Pennsylvania's or Vermont's. But the election went ahead. Convening on June 15, 1777, the delegates rolled up their sleeves to begin work. They quickly agreed that one man from each county and five chosen at large should sit on a drafting committee. Thirteen came from the lower house of the legislature and four from the upper house. Boston merchant Thomas Cushing was chosen to chair the committee.

Through the summer and fall of 1777, and into early winter, the committee struggled to agree on a draft. Sometimes deadlock seemed to seize the committee. But one important breakthrough for reformers came early: It was agreed that the franchise should be broadened to include all adult freemen who paid taxes. James Warren, sitting on the drafting committee, reported to John Adams that he wanted to retain the old property requirements but "as it [the constitution] is to have the sanction of the people at large" it was best to concede this point. Conservatives on the drafting committee then dug in their heels, knowing that reform-minded committeemen wanted to bring government closer to the people through a unicameral legislature and a weak executive branch. "The Council are almost to a man against the new constitution, Warren wrote to John Adams

"and are forced to come to it with the greatest reluctance." So the committee labored through six months, searching for compromises.[40]

The deliberations of the drafting committee went unrecorded or have not survived; but Boston newspapers were filled with commentaries on the raging arguments, and these accounts help us understand why the deliberations were so protracted. Essayists showered readers with arguments over the constitution, echoing the barrage of viewpoints expressed in Pennsylvania when that state formed its constitution a year earlier. "My idea of government, wrote "Clitus," is that it is easy, simple, and cheap." A unicameral legislature elected by free manhood suffrage and a strict avoidance of an upper house and a powerful governor were the alpha and omega of democratic government. "We debase ourselves in reintroducing the worst parts of British rule. The plain question is, are we fighting and lavishing our blood and treasure to establish the freest and best government on earth, or are we about to set up a formidable court interest?" From the opposite side, "Faithful Friend" contended that "the stuff of power never was, nor never can be, in the nature of things, in the people's hands." Displaying his pessimism, shared by most conservatives and most of the wealthy, "Faithful Friend" lectured that "Man, considered abstractly and individually, is perhaps the most selfish, fierce and cruel animal in the whole creation of God." Give the people power, and "anarchy and confusion" would result. Splitting the difference was the Salem minister William Gordon. "A restricted suffrage is not fit for a free society," he argued, but he feared a unicameral legislature because "ambitious men will have more than a little ground for building up their own particular greatness upon their country's ruin."[41]

Most scholars who have scrutinized the protracted debate over the Massachusetts constitution of 1778 have considered it as an abstract document reflecting various political theories and differing assessments of the capabilities of the ordinary citizen. That was truly the case. But it needs remembering that the debate was conducted in the midst of deteriorating economic conditions in Massachusetts, amid a war that was going disastrously, and in the context of a growing clamor over war profiteering and the desirability of price controls, tension between seaboard towns and interior villages, and sinking hearts that the virtuous people counted on to make the republican ship float were becoming as scarce as hard money.

Amid these uncertainties, the drafting committee veered toward the conservative position. John Adams's return to Massachusetts in late November 1777 possibly convinced some of the committeemen to hold to the conservative line. Whatever the case, the draft was finally ready on December 11. Now the full legislature must approve it before sending it to the people.

The constitution put before the full legislature in December contained the two most important elements the conservatives wanted: a two-house legislature and a powerful executive branch. The governor would have powers greater than in almost any other state: to adjourn, prorogue, or recess the legislature with the advice of the upper chamber; to lay embargoes on any commodities for up to forty days; to appoint (with the upper house) all general, field, and staff officers of the militia; to appoint judges and justices of the peace; and, most important, to have the legislative veto power so much favored by John Adams and most conservatives. Conservatives also squelched the reformers' effort to prohibit multiple officeholding; fought off attempts to allow Catholics and other non-Protestants free exercise of religion and the right to hold office; disenfranchised free blacks and Indians; overrode a provision to end slavery in Massachusetts; and rebuffed efforts to end mandatory taxpayer support for the Congregational Church.

When the legislature met in January 1778, calling itself the convention to distinguish its constitution-writing responsibilities from its legislative tasks, it found itself no less divided

than when it had first selected a committee to do the drafting. With Boston's Thomas Cushing and Salem's John Pickering acting as the principal negotiators, three changes were made. Bending to the reformist delegates, who mostly represented western towns, the legislators stripped the governor of his veto power, giving him only one vote with the upper house on laws proposed by the lower house. Also, they increased slightly government representation of western towns. Offsetting these concessions to reformers, conservatives got much of what they wanted: graduated property requirements to vote for candidates and run for office. All free white men could vote for lower-house candidates, but the candidates themselves must have personal estates of two hundred pounds, including real estate worth half of that. Only men with sixty pounds of personal estate (actually more than had been required in the colonial period) could vote for upper-house and gubernatorial candidates. The candidates themselves were to be chosen from the upper ranks of Massachusetts society. Only men with personal estates of four hundred pounds and real estate worth half of that could stand for an upper-house seat. And only the very wealthy could run for governor – those worth one thousand pounds, including real estate of five hundred pounds. One historian characterizes the constitution as a blueprint for "a government dominated by the Whig aristocracy."[42] Even this is too mild. The draft of 1778 was by far the most conservative in the North and in its restricted suffrage and candidate property qualifications were exceeded in the South only by Maryland and South Carolina.

On March 4, 1778, the general court ordered the constitution printed and sent it to the towns with a request that they vote for or against the draft by June 15. Nearly four of every five towns rejected the constitution. Those that voted unanimously against it, or had only a handful of votes in favor, testify to how far the document's drafters had turned their backs on the democratic sentiment that had been indispensable in committing Massachusetts to revolution and supporting the war. In Boston, the center of revolutionary mobilization, 968 citizens gathered at a town meeting and renounced the constitution unanimously. Just outside Boston, Cambridge, Newton, and Brookline registered their opposition with votes of 79–0, 75–5, and 45–0, respectively. On the seacoast north of Boston, the vote was 108–0, 147–0, 109–0, 64–0, and, 46–0, respectively, against the constitution in Salem, York, Gloucester, Kittery, and Halifax. To the south of the state's capital, Scituate, Plymouth, Ipswich, and Methuen voted against the constitution by votes of 134–2, 122–8, 190–1, and 80–0. In Concord and Lexington, where the war had first erupted, townsmen were unanimously opposed. Farther west, in the hill country populated mostly by middling farmers and village artisans, opposition to the constitution was also widespread. Among the small towns opposed were South Hadley (58–4), Amherst (53–0), Sturbridge (52–0), West Springfield (52–3), Worcester (49–9), Greenwich (111–0), Sutton (220–0), and Petersham (77–0). Other towns voted narrowly for the constitution, and a few small towns voted unanimously for it. But the weight of public opinion was massively against it.[43]

Certain elements of the document were particularly offensive. The brunt of criticism – in many cases overflowing into indignation – boiled down to what voters saw as an attempt to deny political rights to ordinary men, to shield the state government from popular control, and to concentrate power in the hands of the few. For many townsmen, this smacked of the British assault on liberty. Many townsmen decried the conservatives' disfranchisement of those without sufficient property and the erection of a political color bar. From the small farming community of Lenox, in western Berkshire County, came strong language: The clause limiting the suffrage to those with sixty pounds of property "declares honest poverty a crime for which a large number of the true and faithful subjects of the state, who perhaps have fought and bled in their country's

cause, are deprived" of the right to vote. Why, asked another town, should a man "born in Africa, India, or ancient America or even being much sunburnt" be stripped of a vote? William Gordon, Salem's Congregational minister and hardly a radical, predicted that any advocate of the Enlightenment would look askance after seeing that the constitution's drafters "mean their own rights only and not those of mankind."[44]

The abiding worry over concentrated political power led many towns to deplore the rejection of a unicameral legislature while creating a powerful governor – precisely the "balanced government" that John Adams wanted. Little Boothbay, on the eastern frontier of what would become Maine, insisted that the governor and lieutenant governor were "needless in a free state," as was the upper house. All were programmed to be chosen from the wealthy, who would therefore "control the people's representatives" congregated in the lower house. Related to this complaint was fear over the appointive power handed to the upper house and governor. This was a constitution that reminded townsmen of why they had been willing to risk all in treasonous acts against their king. Like many towns, the rural village of Westminster, in Worcester County, expressed its dismay at a constitution that "deprives the people at large of appointing their own rulers and officers and places the power where it may (and no doubt will) be greatly abused" – that is, the power of judicial and militia appointments in the hands of a "selected number of men." "No officer whatsoever," the town maintained, "from the highest to the lowest ought to be put in trust but by the suffrages of the people." The lessons of the 1760s and early 1770s had taught Massachusetts this. "Who has the boldness – without blushing – to say the people are not suitable to put in their own officers?" they asked. "If so, why do we waste our blood and treasure to obtain that which, when obtained, we are not fit to enjoy – if but a selected few only are fit to appoint our rulers?" Other towns scorched the drafting convention for turning a deaf ear on widespread sentiment to prevent plural officeholding, one of the main bugbears of the late colonial system under British rule. By a unanimous vote of 111–0, the townsmen of Greenwich, in Hampshire County, admonished the convention for divesting "the good people of this state of many of the privileges which God and Nature has given them," while giving power "to a few individuals." With one voice, they called for a unicameral legislature and the election by all free males of all offices, including the state's militia general and all judges.[45]

If most towns opposed a constitution designed to minimize the power of the people at large, a small number thought it did not go far enough to ensure the rule of the well born and wealthy. A gathering of towns in Essex County, center of seaboard mercantile interests north of Boston, submitted the most pointed criticism from the conservative point of view. Their spokesman was Theophilus Parsons, a rising young Harvard-educated lawyer whose essay, "The Essex Result," argued that the constitution left propertied men insufficiently protected and open to predation from the unpropertied. Parsons reflected the views of many of the wealthy who believed that a leveling spirit had coursed through Massachusetts during the last decade, a situation exacerbated by the erosion of public virtue – the selflessness and commitment to the public good – that Adams and others had always thought necessary to sustain a republic. Parsons departed from most conservatives in believing that "all the members of the state" were entitled to the vote unless, like women, "they have not sufficient discretion or are so situated as to have no wills of their own." But their representatives, sitting in the lower house, must be strictly checked by the upper chamber, which should be the preserve of "gentlemen of education, fortune, and leisure" who made up the vast majority of those "possessed of wisdom, learning, and firmness and consistency of character." With the governor, these men must have an absolute veto power over laws passed by the lower house. "The holders of property

must be in the majority in any question affecting property," he argued. In this line of thought, Parsons and the Essex County elite had John Adams's concurrence, though Adams hoped for the political domination of the wise and virtuous rather than that of the wealthy minority whose status was based on property.[46]

Why did the Massachusetts constitution writers ignore the widespread desire for taxpayer suffrage and offices open to any free adult male citizen? And why did they dismiss the popular concern about concentrated power and the fear that men of great fortune would checkmate the lower house from their upper-house positions? One explanation is the gnawing fear of constitution writers that Massachusetts would fall into the internecine warfare that erupted in Pennsylvania after the adoption of its radical constitution. Another explanation is the absence of popular leaders who in other states – Pennsylvania is a notable example – were able to channel debate and argue forcefully for a broad-based electorate, offices open to talent, and curbs on concentrating political power in the executive branch and the upper house of a bicameral legislature. No such popular leader emerged in Massachusetts during the protracted years of constitution making. Urban radicals who might have served as the people's tribune – Boston's Sam Adams or William Molineux – were in eclipse. From the western towns, where sentiment was strongest for a constitution empowering common people, nobody emerged to promote their cause. In 1778, Northampton's Joseph Hawley, who for years had carried the radical banner, was so ill that he could not serve as a delegate to the convention. Absent such radical leaders, conservative men such as Thomas Cushing, James Warren, and John Pickering, all friends and ideological compatriots of John Adams, became effective floor leaders.

Rebuffed by a large majority of the people who had elected them to write the fundamental law, the constitution drafters of the general court stalled, waiting eight months after receiving a storm of negative votes and arguments before asking the towns in February 1779 whether they wanted to elect delegates to a new constitutional convention. The answer to that was obvious; of course there had to be a constitution. The legal system was in disarray, with courts lacking legitimacy even to function. The economy was on the edge of collapse, with problems of depreciated currency and volatile prices for basic commodities and calls for the confiscation of Loyalists' property creating a reservoir of uncertainty and disgruntlement. Even those favoring a conservative constitution were worried that merchants who had been lukewarm toward the Revolution were plundering the economy. Finally in mid-June 1779 the newly elected general court directed the towns to choose delegates for the sole purpose of writing a constitution, and enfranchised all free adult males for doing so. The convention met in Cambridge on September 1, 1779, to deal with a badly fractured, frustrated, and philosophically broken state.

This was the moment John Adams had been waiting for. Adams had returned to Massachusetts in August 1779 after a year in Paris, where he and his fellow commissioners appointed by Congress had negotiated a treaty of alliance that greatly strengthened the American cause. Chosen to represent Braintree, he was ready to restore virtue to his beloved Massachusetts, which seemed almost hopelessly ensnared in trying to agree on a constitution. He was not only chosen to be among the thirty members on the drafting committee but asked by that committee to serve as a subcommittee of one. He "had the honor to be principal engineer," he later recalled with satisfaction.[47]

The engineer now charged with rescuing Massachusetts from its constitutional morass had changed greatly during four years of war. The people in whom he had such faith in his early years as a lawyer had disappointed him. He could not have agreed more when he read a plaintive *cri de coeur* from Mercy Otis Warren just after returning from France. "The spirit of party had overtaken Massachusetts, she wrote,

and the wealthy would not involve themselves in public affairs or only "worship at the shrine of *Plutus,*" while only "a solitary few" of the "old republicans … still persevere, their hands untainted by bribes – though poverty stares them in the face – and their hearts unshaken by the levity, the luxury, the caprice or whim, the folly or ingratitude of the times."[48] Adams assuredly considered himself one of the "old re-publicans," and now he meant to show that a proper constitution would reestablish stability and restore virtue, the indispensable qualities of a true republic. As we will see, his plan did not offend those who worshiped at the shrine of Plutus but those who stared at poverty.

Adams knew that four years of war had frayed the Bay State's social fabric and deranged the economy in ways that had set farmer against merchant and urban consumer and pitted western and eastern Massachusetts communities against each other. To harness these divisions, he proposed what he had plotted out almost four years before in his "Thoughts on Government." The answer was to balance interest groups by giving the generality of people and those of wealth and status each a place in government. The people at large – Adams did not include free but unpropertied men – would elect legislators to the lower house of the legislature. Those of greater amounts of property would elect an upper house. Both houses together would elect a governor, who would have veto power over laws passed by the two-house legislature. The governor would also have great appointive power: to choose judges and justices of the peace, all militia officers, the attorney general, and even lesser state officials such as town sheriffs with the consent of a governor's council elected by the upper house. Adams called this "mixed government." In the main, this was the form of government Massachusetts had lived under since the Charter of 1691 and different only in detail from the failed constitution of 1778. The largest change from that document was to make the franchise more restrictive. Ignoring the outpouring of town criticisms of the narrowly drawn franchise in the draft constitution of 1778, Adams imposed a property requirement for voting for lower-house delegates, hence disenfranchising a large part of the adult males, and increased the amount of property the 1778 constitution required to run for the upper house and governor. Only those owning one thousand pounds of property (about $200,000 today) could run for governor, making the office more restrictive than in any other state besides Maryland and South Carolina.

In the more innovative parts of his draft, Adams made his case for moral rejuvenation. He proposed that the state actively promote Harvard College, the common schools, and both public and private institutions for disseminating knowledge about manufacturing, commerce, the arts and sciences, agriculture, and natural history. Without knowledge, there would be no virtue; without virtue, a republic could not survive. By the same token, the state should sponsor religion, specifically to ensure that the towns provided support for "the public worship of God, and of the teachers of religion and morals."

When the full convention met in late October 1779 to consider Adams's draft, which the larger drafting committee accepted, Adams and his committee made a few concessions to alarmed democratic reformers. Conservatives beat back the reformers' desire for fixed terms for supreme court justices rather than life terms, but they got the governor's absolute veto power reduced to a veto that could be overturned by a two-thirds majority in both houses of the legislature. Other matters of contention were postponed to a winter session. This was the undoing of the reformers, mostly from western towns, because severe winter weather prevented most of them from reaching Cambridge. Now in command, the conservatives yielded only in allowing militiamen to choose their officers up to the rank of captain, but this simply restored the militia election system that had been in place for the entire war.

On March 2, 1779, the constitutional convention concluded its revisions, ordered the constitution printed and sent to the towns,

asked the towns to indicate their approval or disapproval by June 1, and specified that the constitution would take effect if two-thirds of the people voting indicated their consent. Five years into a wearying war, Massachusetts adult males were asked to vote for a constitution that was no closer to the people than the rejected constitution of 1778, in fact one that ignored almost all of the reformers' objections to that document. It was one of the most conservative constitutions created among the states.

Reconvening to count the votes in early June 1780, the convention declared that the requisite two-thirds of the voters had given their approval. Massachusetts citizens were told that after a prolonged struggle, they had a constitution. But it was not a constitution that they had actually approved. Of 290 towns returning votes (only 207 have survived), only 42 accepted it without amendment. According to Stephen E. Patterson, the historian who has examined the returns most closely, nearly half of them rejected the constitution because it strangled the voice of the people at large in favor of a government controlled by the elite. Seventy-eight of these 101 towns were from the three western counties – Hampshire, Worcester, and Berkshire – where only nineteen towns approved the constitution. Eight towns in eastern Bristol County and a smaller number of towns in eastern Massachusetts also demanded democratic changes. As against these 101 dissatisfied towns, 86 endorsed the constitution in the main, and a handful wanted amendments that would have concentrated power even more narrowly. Twenty towns, as analyzed by Patterson, were so mixed in their responses as to defy categorization.[49]

The objections of Northampton were typical of the anger of many towns at the constitution put before them. In the valley town of the Berkshires, where Jonathan Edwards had long ago roused the people to worship in the Great Awakening, the sick revolutionary radical leader Joseph Hawley girded his loins for one last battle. Agreeing to moderate the town meeting convened to ratify or reject Adams's constitution, he penned a scorching critique. After a meeting that lasted until sundown, the townsmen adopted his report on May 22, 1780. The constitution, wrote Hawley, violated "the natural, essential and inalienable right" of every freeman to vote and hold office. Why should the disfranchised agree to be governed by laws in which they had no voice? The constitution would impose taxes on them and obliged them to perform public service; but they were not to vote. "Shall these poor polls," the Northampton report asked, "who have gone for us into the greatest perils, and undergone infinite fatigues in the present war to rescue us from slavery … some of them leaving at home their poor families, to endure the sufferings of hunger and nakedness, shall they now be treated by us like villains or African slaves? God forbid!" "Shall we who hold property," continued Hawley's report, "be content to see our brethren, who have done their full share in procuring that security … ; on election days, standing aloof and sneaking into corners and ashamed to show their heads, in the meetings of freemen?"[50]

Historians and political scientists have lauded constitution making in Massachusetts, pointing especially to two elements: a broadly elected constitution-writing convention and the popular ratification of its work. Three other states had already adopted constitutions written by specially elected delegates, so in this regard Massachusetts was not a pioneer. As for popular ratification, where Massachusetts was indeed unique, the process may have been followed, but the results were overturned. Only by manipulating the town votes did the convention decide that the constitution had been endorsed by a two-thirds majority. "The counting of votes," writes Patterson, "was neither mechanically nor honestly conducted, for the committee fixed upon a method of counting that would almost inevitably result in the acceptance of the constitution."[51] The people of the Commonwealth of Massachusetts would now live under a constitution they had rejected.

Most of the convention delegates probably feared that another failure to pass a constitution would fuel the conflict of interest groups that had become endemic. With legal cases piling up for lack of courts sanctioned by a constitution, creditors were especially frantic to restore the legal system. But if the convention was mainly hoping to restore stability, they did so at the price of honesty.

Objections to the constitution were not long in coming. Particularly offensive was the imposition of property qualifications for voting and officeholding. The town of Stoughton, outside Boston, expressed a common view that "taxation and representation are reciprocal and inseparably connected." On this issue, the Revolution began. But why would the constitution annul what was "not only a civil but … a natural right"? Belcherstown, at the opposite end of the state in Hampshire County, objected that the constitution denied that "liberty and freedom which we are at this day contending for." Many towns pointed out that the suffrage requirements would take away the vote from those who had elected delegates to the constitutional convention. "How many sensible, honest, and naturally industrious men, by numberless misfortunes, never acquire and possess property of the value of sixty pounds?" asked the townsmen of Mansfield, in eastern Bristol County. The town of Tyringham agreed: "We are very sensible that a very large number of the good inhabitants of this state that pay a very considerable part of the taxes of the same are by the frame of the constitution debarred of the privilege of freemen."[52]

After the constitutional convention declared its document upheld, the restricted Massachusetts electorate made John Hancock their first governor. Within days, he heard how bitter it was for men who had put their lives on the line to find that they were voteless and ineligible to hold office. It was not militiamen, but two militia captains who first protested. Captain Samuel Talbot and Lieutenant Lemuel Gay, both from Stoughton, wrote of how they, like many soldiers under them, had been "by the Constitution disfranchised, for want of property lost by many in their struggle for freedom." These were men who had previously owned property but saw their small farms or artisan's shops dwindle in value as they fought in the war. What was the point or fighting for freedom? they asked. "We can no longer with truth encourage our fellow soldiers, who are so poor as to be thus deprived of their fundamental rights, that they are fighting for their own freedom; and how can an officer possessed of the generous feelings of humanity detach any of them into a service in which they are not interested?"[53] Declining to act "under such a form of government … that appears repugnant to the principles of freedom," Captain Talbot and Lieutenant Gay resigned their commissions.

Constitution writing was over for now in Massachusetts. It had produced the lengthiest and most thoughtful discussions about government arising from the people themselves in the nineteen decades since European immigrants had settled in North America. And it had involved common people in making government, not simply living under government. In tiny hamlets with hardly more than a cluster of families as well as in large towns, men confirmed John Adams's judgment years before when he boasted that it was "as rare as a comet or an earthquake" to find a Massachusetts citizen who was not literate and capable of clear thinking.[54] But the constitution they would now live under, heavy with the fingerprints of John Adams, was not the one they wanted.

## Notes

1. L. H. Butterfield, ed., *Diary and Autobiography of John Adams,* 4 vols. (New York, 1964), 3:355–58 for Adams's ruminations on making government.
2. Samuel Miller, *A Brief Retrospect of the Eighteenth Century,* 2 vols. (New York, 1803), 2:251–52.
3. Quoted in Willi Paul Adams, *The First American Constitutions: Republican Ideology and the Making of the State Constitutions in the Revolutionary Era* (Chapel Hill, 1980), 23–24.
4. Philip S. Foner, ed., *The Complete Writings of Thomas Paine,* 2 vols. (New York, 1969), 1:6–7,

45; Marc W. Kruman, *Between Authority and Liberty: State Constitution Making in Revolutionary America* (Chapel Hill, 1997), 32.
5. Kruman, *Between Authority and Liberty,* 17–18.
6. J. Paul Selsam, *The Pennsylvania Constitution of 1776: A Study in Revolutionary Democracy* (New York, 1971), 139.
7. "To the Privates of Several Battalions of Military Associators in the Province of Pennsylvania," broadside (Philadelphia, 1776), Historical Society of Pennsylvania.
8. Clinton Lawrence Rossiter, *The Political Thought of the American Revolution* (New York, 1963), 120–21.
9. Kruman, *Between Authority and Liberty,* 88; Adams, *First American Constitutions,* 179.
10. Ronald Hoffman, *A Spirit of Dissension: Economics, Politics, and Revolution in Maryland* (Baltimore, 1973), 170–72; The Committee of Mechanics of New York City, quoted in Adams, *First American Constitutions,* 179.
11. Selsam, *Pennsylvania Constitution of 1776,* 148–49.
12. "Thoughts on Government," in *Papers of John Adams,* 11 vols., ed., Robert Joseph Taylor (Cambridge, MA, 1979), 4:86–93.
13. William Hooper, quoted in Kruman, *Between Authority and Liberty,* 150; "K," "Remarks on the Constitution of Pennsylvania," *Pennsylvania Packet,* 15 October 1776.
14. Selsam, *Pennsylvania Constitution of 1776,* 199.
15. This account follows Steven Rosswurm, *Arms, Country, and Class: The Philadelphia Militia and "Lower Sort" during the American Revolution, 1775–1783* (New Brunswick, NJ, 1987), 93–108.
16. Benjamin Rush to Anthony Wayne, *Pennsylvania Magazine of History and Biography* 70 (1946): 91; Benjamin Rush to Anthony Wayne, 24 September 1776, *Letters of Benjamin Rush,* ed., L. H. Butterfield (Philadelphia, 1951), 1:114–15, 137, 148; John Adams quoted by Benjamin Rush in Rush to Adams, 12 October 1779, *Letters of Benjamin Rush,* 1:240.
17. Kruman, *Between Authority and Liberty,* 88–89; James Sullivan to [Elbridge] Gerry, 6 May 1776, in *Papers of John Adams,* 4:212 n. 2.
18. John Adams to James Sullivan, 26 May 1776, *Papers of John Adams,* 4:210; Adams, *First American Constitutions,* 31; "people's war" quoted in John E. Ferling, "'Oh That I Was a Soldier': John Adams and the Anguish of War," *American Quarterly* 36 (1984): 264.

19. Timothy Dwight, *Travels in New England and New York,* 4 vols., ed., Barbara Miller Solomon (Cambridge, MA, 1969), 2:405; William Hooper, quoted in Gordon S. Wood, *The Creation of the American Republic, 1776–1787* (Chapel Hill, 1969), 233; Robert J. Taylor, ed., *Papers of John Adams,* 4:81, 88.

20. Michael A. Bellisles, *Revolutionary Outlaws: Ethan Allen and the Struggle for Independence on the Early American Frontier* (Charlottesville, 1993). 135.

21. Ibid., 131, 136.

22. Allen Soule and John A. Williams, eds., *Laws of Vermont* (Montpelier, VT, 1964), 5–8; Bellisles, *Revolutionary Outlaws,* 172, 235.

23. Bellisles, *Revolutionary Outlaws,* 159, 160.

24. Ibid., 341 n. 12.

25. Ibid., 178.

26. Hoffman, *A Spirit of Dissension,* 169–70; Edward C. Papenfuse and Gregory A. Stiverson, eds., *The Decisive Blow Is Struck,: A Facsimile Edition of the Proceedings of the Constitutional Convention of 1776 and the First Maryland Constitution* (1787; reprint, Annapolis, 1977), np; Kruman, *Between Authority and Liberty,* 99.

27. Hoffman, *A Spirit of Dissension,* 171.

28. Ibid.

29. Charles Carroll of Carrollton and Charles Carroll of Annapolis, *Dear Papa, Dear Charley: The Peregrinations of a Revolutionary Aristocrat,* 4 vols., ed. Ronald Hoffman (Chapel Hill, 2001), 2:940 n. 5.

30. Carroll and Carroll, *Dear Papa,* 2:941.

31. *Maryland Gazette,* 15 August 1776, quoted in Kruman, *Between Authority and Liberty,* 95.

32. Paperfuse and Stiverson, *The Decisive Blow Is Struck,* np.

33. *Hoffman, Spirit of Dissension,* 181.

34. Kruman, *Between Authority and Liberty,* 40.

35. John Chester Miller, *Sam Adams: Pioneer in Propaganda* (Boston, 1936), 355.

36. John Winthrop to John Adams, 1 June 1776, *Papers of John Adams,* 4:223–24.

37. John Winthrop to John Adams, 23 June 1776, ibid., 4:332–33.

38. Kruman, *Between Authority and Liberty,* 30.

39. For constitution making in Massachusetts, I have followed Stephen E. Patterson, *Political Parties in Revolutionary Massachusetts* (Madison, 1973), and the documents in Robert J. Taylor, ed., *Massachusetts: Colony to Commonwealth:* *Documents on the Formation of Its Constitution, 1775–1780* (Chapel Hill, 1961).

40. James Warren to John Adams, 22 June 1777, in *Warren-Adams Letters.* 2 vols. (Boston: Massachusetts Historical Society, 1917–1925), 1:334–35; 22 June 1777, in *Papers of John Adams,* 5:230 and 10 July 1777, 5:244–45.

41. *Independent Chronicle and the Universal Advertiser,* 10 July 1777, quoted in Elisha P. Douglass, *Rebels and Democrats: The Struggle for Equal Political Rights and Majority Rule During the American Revolution* (Chapel Hill, 1955), 172–73.

42. Douglass, *Rebels and Democrats,* 175.

43. Many of the town votes and criticisms are printed in Handlin and Handlin, *Popular Sources of Political Authority.*

44. Robert Joseph Taylor, *Western Massachusetts in the Revolution* (Providence, 1954), 59; *Continental journal and Weekly Advertiser,* 9 April 1778, in Douglass, *Rebels and Democrats,* 179 n. 52.

45. Douglass, *Rebels and Democrats,* 177; Taylor, *Massachusetts: Colony to Commonwealth,* 69.

46. Theophilus Parsons, quoted in Kruman, *Between Authority and Liberty,* 104; and Douglass, *Rebels and Democrats,* 182.

47. Quoted in John R. Howe, *The Changing Political Thought of John Adams* (Princeton, NJ, 1966), 82.

48. Mercy Otis Warren, 29 July 1779, in *Papers of John Adams,* 7:102.

49. Patterson, *Political Parties,* 234–37.

50. E. Francis Brown, *Joseph Hawley: Colonial Radical* (New York, 1931), 176–84; Hawley, quoted in Adams, *First Constitutions,* 211.

51. Patterson, *Political Parties,* 245.

52. Kruman, *Between Authority and Liberty,* 94; Patterson, *Political Parties,* 240–41.

53. Quoted in Gregory H. Nobles, "'Yet the Old Republicans Still Persevere': Samuel Adams, John Hancock, and the Crisis of Popular Leadership in Revolutionary Massachusetts, 1775–1790," in *The Transforming Hand of Revolution: Reconsidering the American Revolution as a Social Movement,* eds. Ronald Hoffman and Peter J. Albert (Charlottesville, 1995), 276.

54. Quoted in Richard D. Brown, *The Strength of a People: The Idea of an Informed Citizenry in America, 1650–1870* (Chapel Hill, 1996), 52; Brown examines "the recognition of the informed citizen" as the "bulwark of revolutionary liberty" in chapter 3.

# 12
# INTERESTS AND DISINTERESTEDNESS IN THE MAKING OF THE CONSTITUTION

*Gordon S. Wood*

## Introduction

It is a truism of most U.S. history textbooks that America's founders scrapped the Articles of Confederation because it was too weak. That is, it did not provide for a national government that could fulfill even some of the most basic of governing functions, including raising revenue through taxes and regulating commerce. In this penetrating analysis, Gordon S. Wood contends that our textbooks have it all wrong. The true motivation behind the Constitution was not fixing the Articles – which a broad spectrum of leaders agreed had to be done – but stemming the supposed excess of democracy taking place at the state level. Under the revolutionary state constitutions, the subject of the previous essay by Gary B. Nash, state legislatures had become far more democratic than their colonial predecessors. They were too democratic for the likes of some elites, including James Madison and Alexander Hamilton. Common people became legislators and governed according to the interests of ordinary citizens in light of the country's postwar debt and inflation crisis. They passed paper money acts, tax holidays, stay laws (extensions on debt), and other forms of relief to debtors.

This explosion of what we identify today as interest-based politics horrified the nation's elites, who still adhered to classical republican ideals. Politics for men like Madison, Hamilton, Thomas Jefferson, and George Washington was not a means to advance group interests, but rather an arena for exercising moral virtue, which they characterized as "disinterestedness." One goal of the Constitution was to claim power from the states to grant disinterested gentlemen the authority to govern according to the country's broad national interest. Yet, by the adoption of the Constitution in 1787, these elite notions of virtuous political behavior were already rapidly disappearing. Ironically, the group that best anticipated the new direction of American politics was the Antifederalists, those who are often condemned as backward for opposing the Constitution. They practiced the style of popular, interest-based politics at the state level that has become the hallmark of American political culture. Thus, while Americans today may still live under the Federalist Constitution, they practice politics according to the Antifederalist model.

- Antifederalists commonly accused Federalists of violating the principle of disinterested leadership by pursuing their own economic interests. Do you agree? How close did Federalists come to realizing the ideal of disinterestedness?
- In Wood's telling, the American Revolution proved to create a more democratic society than elite revolutionaries had even intended. What role does he ascribe to the war in transforming American society? Based on other essays in the volume, particularly those by T.H. Breen, John Shy, Gary B. Nash, Alan Taylor, Ira Berlin, and Aaron S. Fogleman, what other factors contributed to the expansion of democracy in the revolutionary era?
- Americans today revere the founders, sometimes to the point of nearly deifying them. Yet, if Wood is correct, as elites, the founders were increasingly out of touch with the democratic

impulses of their time and certainly did not share many of the same democratic values treasured by present-day Americans. How, then, might we account for the ongoing, widespread veneration of the founders?

# I

During our bicentennial celebrations of the Constitution we will gather many times to honor the makers of that Constitution, the Federalists of 1787–1788. We have certainly done so many times in the past. We have repeatedly pictured the founders, as we call them, as men of vision—bold, original, open-minded, enlightened men who deliberately created what William Gladstone once called "the most wonderful work ever struck off at a given time by the hand and purpose of man."[1] We have described them as men who knew where the future lay and went for it. Even those like Charles Beard who have denigrated their motives have seen the founders as masters of events, realistic pragmatists who knew human nature when they saw it, farsighted, economically advanced, modern men in step with the movement of history.

In contrast, we have usually viewed the opponents of the Constitution, the Antifederalists, as very tame and timid, narrow-minded and parochial men of no imagination and little faith, caught up in the ideological rigidities of the past—inflexible, suspicious men unable to look ahead and see where the United States was going. The Antifederalists seem forever doomed to be losers, bypassed by history and eternally disgraced by their opposition to the greatest constitutional achievement in our nation's history.

But maybe we have got it all wrong. Maybe the Federalists were not men of the future after all. Maybe it was the Antifederalists who really saw best and farthest. Is it possible that all those original, bold, and farsighted Federalists had their eyes not on what was coming, but on what was passing? Perhaps the roles of the participants in the contest over the Constitution in 1787–1788 ought to be reversed. If either side

in the conflict over the Constitution stood for modernity, perhaps it was the Antifederalists. They, and not the Federalists, may have been the real harbingers of the moral and political world we know—the liberal, democratic, commercially advanced world of individual pursuits of happiness.

If this is true—if indeed the founders did not stand for modernity—then it should not be surprising that they are now so lost to us, that they should have become, as we continually lament, "a galaxy of public leaders we have never been able remotely to duplicate since."[2] Instead of being the masters, were they really the victims of events? Is it possible that their Constitution failed, and failed miserably, in what they wanted it to do?

Naturally, we are reluctant to admit that the Constitution may have failed in what it set out to do, and consequently we have difficulty in fully understanding its origins. To be sure, we readily accept the necessity for a new central government in 1787. Unable to imagine the United States as ever existing without a strong national government, we regard the creation of the new structure in 1787 as inevitable. (For us it is the Articles of Confederation that cannot be taken seriously.) But the new central government seems inevitable to us only for reasons that fit our modern preconceptions. As long as people in the 1780s explain the movement for the Constitution in terms of the weaknesses of the Confederation, we can easily understand and accept their explanations. But when people in the 1780s explain the movement for the Constitution in terms other than the palpable weaknesses of the central government—in terms of a crisis in the society—we become puzzled and skeptical. A real crisis? It hardly seems believable. The 1780s were, after all, a time of great release and expansion: the population grew as never before, or since, and more Americans than ever before were off in pursuit of prosperity and happiness. "There is not upon the face of the earth a body of people more happy or rising into consequence with more rapid stride, than the Inhabitants of the United States of America," Charles Thomson told Jefferson in 1786. "Population is encreasing, new houses building, new lands clearing, new settlements forming, and new manufactures establishing with a rapidity beyond conception."[3] The general mood was high, expectant, and far from bleak. No wonder then that historians of very different persuasions have doubted that there was anything really critical happening in the society.[4]

Yet, of course, we have all those statements by people in the 1780s warning that "our situation is critical and dangerous" and that "our vices" were plunging us into "national ruin." Benjamin Rush even thought that the American people were on the verge of "degenerating into savages or devouring each other like beasts of prey." But if we think that Rush is someone with a hyperactive imagination, here is the 1786 voice of the much more sober and restrained George Washington: "What astonishing changes a few years are capable of producing... . From the high ground we stood upon, from the plain path which invited our footsteps, to be so fallen! so lost! it is really mortifying."[5]

What are we to make of such despairing and excited statements—statements that can be multiplied over and over and that were often made not in the frenzy of public debate, but in the privacy of letters to friends? Many of those historians who, like Charles Beard, believe that such statements are a gross exaggeration can conclude only that the sense of crisis was "conjured up" by the Federalists, since "actually the country faced no such emergency." But such a conspiratorial interpretation of the Constitution is hardly satisfying and tells us nothing of what such statements of alarm and foreboding meant. Why did some men, members of the elite— those who saved their letters for us to read— think America was in a crisis?[6]

Certainly it was not the defects of the Articles of Confederation that were causing this sense of crisis. These defects of the Confederation were remediable and were scarcely capable of eliciting horror and despair. To be sure, these defects did make possible the calling of the Philadelphia Convention to amend the Articles. By 1787 almost every political leader in the country, including most of the later Antifederalists, wanted something done to strengthen the Articles of Confederation. The Confederation had no power to pay its debts, no power to tax, and no power to regulate commerce, and it was daily being humiliated in its international relationships. Reform of the Articles in some way or other—particularly by granting the Congress a limited authority to tax and the power to regulate commerce—was in the air. This desire to do something about the central government was the Federalists' opportunity: it explains the willingness of people to accede to the meeting at Annapolis and the subsequent convening of delegates at Philadelphia. In fact, so acceptable and necessary seemed some sort of change in the Confederation that later Antifederalists were remarkably casual about the meeting at Philadelphia. William Findley of western Pennsylvania, for example, later claimed he was selected to go to the convention but declined when he learned that "the delegates would have no wages." Thus the seven delegates Pennsylvania sent to the convention were all residents of the city of Philadelphia (including even one, Gouverneur Morris, who was really a New Yorker), and no one at the time complained.[7]

Thus the defects of the Confederation were widely acknowledged, and many looked to the Philadelphia Convention for a remedy. But these defects do not account for the elite's expression of crisis, nor do they explain the ambitious nature of the nationalists' Virginia Plan that formed the working model for the convention's deliberations. The nationalists' aims and the Virginia Plan went way beyond what the weaknesses of the Articles demanded. Granting Congress the authority to raise revenue, to regulate trade, to pay off its debts, and to deal effectively in international affairs did not require the total scrapping of the Articles and the creation of an extraordinarily powerful and distant national government, the like of which was virtually inconceivable to Americans a decade earlier. The Virginia Plan was the remedy for more than the obvious impotence of the Confederation; it was a remedy—and an aristocratic remedy—for what were often referred to as the excesses of American democracy. It was these excesses of democracy that lay behind the elite's sense of crisis.

What excesses of democracy? What on earth could have been happening to provoke fear and horror? Not Shays's Rebellion that broke out in the winter of 1786–1787. That was an alarming clincher for many Federalists, especially in Massachusetts, but it was scarcely the cause of the Federalists' pervasive sense of crisis, which existed well before they learned of Shays's Rebellion.[8] No, it was not mobs and overt disorder that really frightened the founders. They knew about popular rioting, and had taken such occurrences more or less in stride for years. What bothered them, what they meant by the excesses of democracy, was something more insidious than mobs. It was something that we today accept as familiar, ordinary, and innocuous, but the founders did not—good old American popular politics. It was popular politics, especially as practiced in the state legislatures, that lay behind the founders' sense of crisis. The legislatures were unwilling to do "justice," and this, said Washington, is "the origin of the evils we now feel." The abuses of the state legislatures, said Madison, were "so frequent and so flagrant as to alarm the most stedfast friends of Republicanism," and these abuses, he told Jefferson in the fall of 1787, "contributed more to that uneasiness which produced the Convention, and prepared the public mind for a general reform, than those which accrued to our national character and interest from the inadequacy of the Confederation to its immediate objects."[9] Hard as it may be for us today to accept, the weaknesses of the Articles of Confederation were not the most important reasons for the making of the Constitution.

Throughout the whole period of crisis, Madison, the father of the Constitution if there ever was one, never had any doubt where the main source of the troubles lay. In his working paper drafted in the late winter of 1787 entitled "Vices of the Political System of the United States," Madison spent very little time on the impotence of the Confederation. What was really on his mind was the deficiencies of the state governments: he devoted more than half his paper to the "multiplicity," "mutability," and "injustice" of the laws passed by the states.[10] Particularly alarming and unjust in his eyes were the paper money acts, stay laws, and other forms of debtor-relief legislation that hurt creditors and violated individual property rights. And he knew personally what he was talking about. Although we usually think of Madison as a bookish scholar who got all his thoughts from his wide reading, he did not develop his ideas about the democratic excesses of the state governments by poring through the bundles of books that Jefferson was sending him from Europe. He learned about popular politics and legislative abuses firsthand—by being a member of the Virginia Assembly.

During the years 1784 through 1787 Madison attended four sessions of the Virginia legislature. They were perhaps the most frustrating and disillusioning years of his life, but also the most important years of his life, for his experience as a Virginia legislator in the 1780s was fundamental in shaping his thinking as a constitutional reformer.

Although Madison in these years had some notable legislative achievements, particularly with his shepherding into enactment Jefferson's famous bill for religious freedom, he was continually exasperated by what Jefferson years later (no doubt following Madison's own account) referred to as "the endless quibbles, chicaneries, perversions, vexations, and delays of lawyers and demi-lawyers" in the assembly. Really for the first time, Madison found out what democracy in America might mean. Not all the legislators were going to be like him or Jefferson; many of them did not even appear to be gentlemen. The Virginia legislators seemed so parochial, so illiberal, so small-minded, and most of them seemed to have only "a particular interest to serve." They had no regard for public honor or honesty. They too often made a travesty of the legislative process and were reluctant to *do* anything that might appear unpopular. They postponed taxes, subverted debts owed to the subjects of Great Britain, and passed, defeated, and repassed bills in the most haphazard ways. Madison had enlightened expectations for Virginia's port bill in 1784, but the other legislators got their self-serving hands on it and perverted it. It was the same with nearly all the legislative proposals he sought to introduce, especially those involving reform of the legal code and court system. "Important bills prepared at leisure by skilful hands," he complained, were vitiated by "crudeness and tedious discussion." What could he do with such clods? "It will little elevate your idea of our Senate," he wrote in weary disgust to Washington in 1786, to learn that the senators actually defeated a bill defining the privileges of foreign ambassadors in Virginia "on the principle … that an Alien ought not to be put on better ground than a Citizen."[11] This was carrying localism to absurdity.

It was not what republican lawmaking was supposed to be. Madison continually had to make concessions to the "prevailing sentiments," whether or not such sentiments promoted the good of the state or nation. He had to agree to bad laws for fear of getting worse ones, or give up good bills "rather than pay such a price" as opponents wanted. Today legislators are used to this sort of political horse-trading. But Madison simply was not yet ready for the logrolling and the pork-barreling that would eventually become the staples of American legislative politics. By 1786 he had "strong apprehensions" that his and Jefferson's hope for reforming the legal code

"may never be systematically perfected." The legislature was simply too popular, and appealing to the people had none of the beneficial effects good republicans had expected. A bill having to do with court reform was, for example, "to be printed for consideration of the public"; but "instead of calling forth the sanction of the wise and virtuous," this action, Madison, feared, would only "be a signal to interested men to redouble their efforts to get into the Legislature." Democracy was no solution to the problem; democracy was the problem. Madison repeatedly found himself having to beat back the "itch for paper money" and other measures "of a popular cast." Too often Madison had to admit that the only hope he had was "of moderating the fury," not defeating it.[12]

Madison, like other enthusiastic Revolutionary idealists, emerged from his experience with democratic politics in the mid-1780s a very chastened republican. It was bad enough, he wrote in his "Vices of the Political System of the United States," that legislators were often interested men or dupes of the sophistry of "a favorite leader" (like Patrick Henry). Even more alarming for the fate of republican government, however, was the fact that such legislators were only reflecting the partial interests and parochial outlooks of their constituents. Too many of the American people could not see beyond their own pocketbooks or their own neighborhoods. "Individuals of extended views, and of national pride," said Madison (and he knew whom he meant), might be able to bring public proceedings to an enlightened cosmopolitan standard, but their example could never be followed by "the multitude." "Is it to be imagined that an ordinary citizen or even an assemblyman of R. Island in estimating the policy of paper money, ever considered or cared in what light the measure would be viewed in France or Holland; or even in Massts or Connect.? It was a sufficient temptation to both that it was for their interest."[13]

Madison's experience with the populist politics of the state legislatures was especially important because of his extraordinary influence in the writing of the Federal Constitution. But his experience was not unusual; indeed, the Federalists could never have done what they did if Madison's experience was not widely shared. By the mid-1780s gentlemen up and down the continent were shaking their heads in disbelief and anger at the "private views and selfish principles" of the men they saw in the state assemblies, "men of narrow souls and no natural interest in the society." Selfish, ignorant, illiberal state legislators—"Characters too full of Local attachments and Views to permit sufficient attention to the general interest"—were bringing discredit upon popular government. They were promoting their own or their locality's particular interest, pandering "to the vulgar and sordid notions of the populace," and acting as judges in their own causes. "Private convenience, paper money, and ex post facto laws" were the "main springs" of these state lawmakers. Many of the delegates to the Philadelphia Convention were so ready to accept Madison's radical Virginia Plan and its proposed national authority to veto all state laws precisely because they shared his deep disgust with the localist and interest-ridden politics of the state legislatures. "The vile State governments are sources of pollution which will contaminate the American name for ages... Smite them," Henry Knox urged Rufus King sitting in the Philadelphia Convention, "smite them, in the name of God and the people."[14]

We today can easily appreciate the concerns of the founders with the weaknesses of the Confederation government: these seem real and tangible to us, especially in light of what we know our national government has become. But we have more difficulty in appreciating the fears the founders expressed over the democratic politics of the state legislatures—the scrambling of different interest groups, the narrow self-promoting nature of much of the lawmaking, the incessant catering to popular demands. Surely, this behavior cannot be accurately described as the "wilderness of anarchy and vice." This "excess of democracy" is, after all, what popular politics is about, and it is not different from what Americans in time came to be very used to.[15]

It may not have been different from what Americans came to be used to, and it may not even have been different from what some of the Revolutionary leaders had occasionally experienced in their colonial assemblies. But for most of the founding fathers, popular political behavior in the states during the 1780s was very different from what they expected from their republican Revolution, and for them that difference was what made the 1780s a genuine critical period.

## II

Republicanism was not supposed to stimulate selfishness and private interests, but was to divert and control them. But in states up and down the continent various narrow factional interests, especially economic, were flourishing as never before, and, more alarming still, were demanding and getting protection and satisfaction from the democratically elected state legislatures. Although interest groups and factionalism had been common in the colonial legislatures, the interests and factions of post-Revolutionary politics were different: more numerous, less personal and family-oriented, and more democratically expressive of new, widespread economic elements in the society. The Revolution, it appeared, had unleashed acquisitive and commercial forces that no one had quite realized existed.

We are only beginning to appreciate the immense consequences that the Revolution and, especially, wartime mobilization had on American society. When all the articles and monographs are in, however, I think that we will find that the Revolutionary war, like the Civil War and the two world wars, radically transformed America's society and economy. The war effort was enormous. The war went on for eight years (the longest in American history until that of Vietnam); it eventually saw one hundred thousand or more men under arms, and it touched the whole of American society to a degree that no previous event ever had. The inexhaustible needs of the army—for everything from blankets and wagons to meat and rum—brought into being a host of new manufacturing and entrepreneurial interests and made market farmers out of husbandmen who before had scarcely ever traded out of their neighborhoods. To pay for all these new war goods the Revolutionary governments issued huge sums—four hundred million to five hundred million dollars—of paper money that made its way into the hands of many people who had hitherto dealt only in a personal and bookkeeping barter economy.[16] Under the stimulus of this wartime purchasing, speculative farmers, inland traders, and profiteers of all sorts sprang up by the thousands to circulate these goods and paper money throughout the interior areas of America. By 1778, wrote Henry Laurens, "the demand for money" was no longer "confined to the capital towns and cities within a small circle of trading merchants, but spread over a surface of 1,600 miles in length, and 300 broad." The war and rapidly rising prices were creating a society in which, as one bitter commissary agent complained, "Every Man buys in order to sell again."[17] No event in the eighteenth century accelerated the capitalistic development of America more than did the Revolutionary war. It brought new producers and consumers into the market economy, it aroused latent acquisitive instincts everywhere, it stimulated inland trade as never before, and it prepared the way for the eventual momentous shift of the basis of American prosperity from external to internal commerce.

The paper money and the enormous amounts of debts that all these inland entrepreneurs, traders, shopkeepers, and market farmers thrived on were the consequences neither of poverty nor of anticommercial behavior. Debt, as we of all generations in American history ought to know, was already emerging as a symptom of expansion and enterprise. Farmers, traders, and others in these Revolutionary years

borrowed money, just as they married earlier and had more children than ever before, because they thought the future was going to be even better than the present. Common people had been increasingly buying consumer goods since at least the middle of the eighteenth century, but the Revolutionary war now gave many more ordinary farmers, often for the first time in their lives, the financial ability to purchase luxury goods that previously had been the preserve of the gentry—everything from lace finery to china dishware. It was this prospect of raising their standard of living and increasing their "pleasures and diversions" that got farmers to work harder and produce "surpluses" during the war, and there is evidence that when the availability of these "luxury" goods diminished during the war the farmers' productivity and their "surpluses" diminished too.[18] For ages men had thought that industry and frugality among the common people went together. Now suddenly in America the industriousness of ordinary people seemed dependent not on the fear of poverty, but on the prospect of luxury.[19]

The economic troubles of the 1780s came from the ending of the war and government purchasing. Too many people had too many heightened expectations and were into the market and the consumption of luxuries too deeply to make any easy adjustments to peace. The collapse of internal markets and the drying up of paper money meant diminished incomes, overextended businesses, swollen inventories of imported manufactures, and debt-laden farmers and traders. The responses of people hurt by these developments were very comprehensible: they simply wanted to continue what they had done during the war. The stay laws and other debtor-relief legislation and the printing of paper money were not the demands of backward-looking and uncommercial people. They were the demands of people who had enjoyed buying, selling, and consuming and desired to do more of it. In order to have prosperity, argued one defender of paper money in 1786, it was not enough to have an industrious people and a fertile territory; money was essential too. And for many ordinary people in the 1780s money—in the absence of gold and silver coin—meant paper money issued by governments or government loan offices. "By anticipating the products of several years labor," farmers were able to borrow loan office certificates based on land in order "to accelerate improvements" and "so to augment industry and multiply the means of carrying it on" and thereby "enrich" both themselves and the state.[20]

These calls for paper money in the 1780s were the calls of American business. The future of America's entrepreneurial activity and prosperity lay not with the hundreds of well-to-do creditor-merchants who dominated the overseas trade of the several ports along the Atlantic seaboard. Rather, it lay with the thousands upon thousands of ordinary traders, petty businessmen, aspiring artisans, and market farmers who were deep in debt and were buying and selling with each other all over America. For these people, unlike the overseas merchants who had their private bills of exchange, publicly created paper money was the only means "capable of answering all the *domestic* and *internal* purposes of a *circulating medium* in a nation" that lacked specie. The prosperity of a country, it was now argued, involved more than external commerce, more than having a surplus of exports over imports. "The *internal* commerce of the country must be promoted, by increasing its *real riches,*" which were now rightly equated with the acquisitions, improvements, and entrepreneurial activity of ordinary people.[21]

There is no exaggerating the radical significance of this heightened awareness among Americans of the importance of domestic trade. Hitherto most Americans had thought of internal trade, as William Smith of New York put it in the 1750s, as publicly worthless—a mere passing of wealth around the community from hand to hand. Such exchanging, said Smith, "tho' it may enrich an Individual," meant that "others must be poorer, in an exact proportion to his Gains; but the collective Body of the People not at all."[22]

Such was the traditional zero-sum mercantilist mentality that was now being challenged by the increased entrepreneurial activity of thousands of ordinary people. Farmers "in a new and unimproved country," it was now said, "have continual uses for money, to stock and improve their farms" or, as Madison noted, to "extend their consumption as far as credit can be obtained." And they now wanted more money than could be gotten by the old-fashioned means of applying "to a monied man for a loan from his private fortune." Consequently these farmers and other small-time entrepreneurs in state after state up and down the continent were electing representatives to their legislatures who could supply them with paper money, paper money which, as the preamble to a 1785 Pennsylvania statute establishing a loan office stated, was designed "to promote and establish the interests of internal commerce, agriculture and mechanc arts."[23] Not the defects of the Articles of Confederation, but this promotion of entrepreneurial interests by ordinary people—their endless buying and selling, their bottomless passion for luxurious consumption—was what really frightened the Federalists.

The Federalists in the 1780s had a glimpse of what America was to become—a scrambling business society dominated by the pecuniary interests of ordinary people—and they did not like what they saw. This premonition of America's future lay behind their sense of crisis and their horrified hyperbolic rhetoric. The wholesale pursuits of private interest and private luxury were, they thought, undermining America's capacity for republican government. They designed the Constitution in order to save American republicanism from the deadly effects of these private pursuits of happiness.

## III

The founders did not intend the new Constitution to change the character of the American people. They were not naive utopians; they were, as we have often noted, realistic about human nature. They had little or no faith in the power of religion or of sumptuary or other such laws to get people to behave differently. To be sure, they believed in education, and some of them put great stock in what it might do in reforming and enlightening American people. But still they generally approached their task in the 1780s with a practical, unsentimental appreciation of the givenness of human beings. They knew they lived in an age of commerce and interests. Although some of the landed gentry like Jefferson might yearn wistfully at times for America to emulate China and "abandon the ocean altogether," most of the founders welcomed America's involvement in commerce, by which, however, they commonly meant overseas trade.[24] They believed in the importance of such commerce, saw it as a major agent in the refining and civilizing of people, and were generally eager to use the power of government to promote its growth. They knew too all about "interest," which Madison defined "in the popular sense" as the "immediate augmentation of property and wealth." They accepted the inevitability and the prevalence of "interest" and respected its power. "Interest," many of them said, "is the greatest tie one man can have on another." It was, they said, "the only binding cement" for states and peoples. Hamilton put it more bluntly: "He who pays is the master."[25]

Since 1776 they had learned that it was foolish to expect most people to sacrifice their private interests for the sake of the public welfare. For the Federalists there was little left of the revolutionary utopianism of Samuel Adams. Already by the 1780s, Adams's brand of republicanism seemed archaic and Adams himself a figure from another time and place. Soon people would be shaking their heads in wonderment that such a person as Adams should have ever existed in America. "Modern times," it was said, "have produced no character like his." He was "one of Plutarch's men," a character out of the classical past. He was a Harvard-educated gentleman who devoted himself to the public. He had neither personal

ambition nor the desire for wealth. He refused to help his children and gloried in his poverty. He was without interests or even private passions. Among the Revolutionary leaders he was unique. No other leader took classical republican values quite as seriously as Adams did.[26]

In fact, the other Revolutionary leaders were very quick to expose the unreality and impracticality of Adams's kind of republican idealism. As early as 1778 Washington realized that the Revolution would never succeed if it depended on patriotism alone. "It must be aided by a prospect of interest or some reward."[27] All men could not be like Samuel Adams. It was too bad, but that was the way it was. Human beings were like that, and by the 1780s many of the younger Revolutionary leaders like Madison were willing to look at the reality of interests with a very cold eye. Madison's *Federalist* No. 10 was only the most famous and frank acknowledgment of the degree to which interests of various sorts had come to dominate American politics.

The founders thus were not dreamers who expected more from the people than they were capable of. We in fact honor the founding fathers for their realism, their down-to-earth acceptance of human nature. Perhaps this is part of our despairing effort to make them one with us, to close that terrifying gap that always seems to exist between them and us. Nevertheless, in our hearts we know that they are not one with us, that they are separated from us, as they were separated from every subsequent generation of Americans, by an immense cultural chasm. They stood for a classical world that was rapidly dying, a world so different from what followed—and from our own—that an act of imagination is required to recover it in all its fullness. They believed in democracy, to be sure, but not our modern democracy; rather, they believed in a patrician-led classical democracy in which "virtue exemplified in government will diffuse its salutary influence through the society." For them government was not an arena for furthering the interests of groups and individuals, but a means of moral betterment. What modern American politician would say, as James Wilson said in the Philadelphia Convention, that "the cultivation and improvement of the human mind was the most noble object" of government? Even Jefferson, who of all the founders most forcefully led the way, though inadvertently, to a popular liberal future, could in 1787 urge a Virginia colleague: "Cherish … the spirit of our people, and keep alive their attention. Do not be too severe upon their errors, but reclaim them by enlightening them." All the founding fathers saw themselves as moral teachers.[28] However latently utilitarian, however potentially liberal, and however enthusiastically democratic the founders may have been, they were not modern men.

Despite their acceptance of the reality of interests and commerce, the Federalists had not yet abandoned what has been called the tradition of civic humanism—that host of values transmitted from antiquity that dominated the thinking of nearly all members of the elite in the eighteenth-century Anglo-American world. By the late eighteenth century this classical tradition was much attenuated and domesticated, tamed and eaten away by modern financial and commercial developments. But something remained, and the Federalists clung to it. Despite their disillusionment with political leadership in the states, the Federalists in 1787 had not yet lost hope that at least some individuals in the society might be worthy and virtuous enough to transcend their immediate material interests and devote themselves to the public good. They remained committed to the classical idea that political leadership was essentially one of character: "The whole art of government," said Jefferson, "consists of being honest."[29] Central to this ideal of leadership was the quality of *disinterestedness*—the term the Federalists most used as a synonym for the classic conception of civic virtue: it better conveyed the increasing threats from interests that virtue now faced.

Dr. Johnson defined *disinterested* as being "superior to regard of private advantage; not influenced by private profit"; and that was what the founding fathers meant by the term.[30] We today have lost most of this older meaning. Even educated people now use *disinterested* as a synonym for *uninterested,* meaning indifferent or unconcerned. It is almost as if we cannot quite conceive of the characteristic that disinterestedness describes: we cannot quite imagine someone who is capable of rising above a pecuniary interest and being unselfish and unbiased where an interest might be present. This is simply another measure of how far we have traveled from the eighteenth century.

This eighteenth-century concept of disinterestedness was not confined either to Commonwealthmen or to the country tradition (which makes our current preoccupation with these strains of thought misleading). Nor did one have to be an American or a republican to believe in disinterestedness and the other classical values that accompanied it. Virtue or disinterestedness, like the concept of honor, lay at the heart of all prescriptions for political leadership in the eighteenth-century Anglo-American world. Throughout the century Englishmen of all political persuasions—Whigs and Tories both—struggled to find the ideal disinterested political leader amid the rising and swirling currents of financial and commercial interests that threatened to engulf their societies. Nothing more enhanced William Pitt's reputation as the great patriot than his pointed refusal in 1746 to profit from the perquisites of the traditionally lucrative office of paymaster of the forces. Pitt was living proof for the English-speaking world of the possibility of disinterestedness—that a man could be a governmental leader and yet remain free of corruption.[31]

This classical ideal of disinterestedness was based on independence and liberty. Only autonomous individuals, free of interested ties and paid by no masters, were capable of such virtue. Jefferson and other republican idealists might continue to hope that ordinary yeoman farmers in America might be independent and free enough of pecuniary temptations and interests to be virtuous. But others knew better, and if they did not, then the experience of the Revolutionary war soon opened their eyes. Washington realized almost at the outset that no common soldier could be expected to be "influenced by any other principles than those of Interest." And even among the officer corps there were only a "few … who act upon Principles of disinterestedness," and they were "comparatively speaking, no more than a drop in the Ocean."[32]

Perhaps it was as Adam Smith warned as society became more commercialized and civilized and labor more divided, ordinary people gradually lost their ability to make any just judgments about the varied interests and occupations of their country; and only "those few, who, being attached to no particular occupation themselves, have leisure and inclination to examine the occupations of other people." Perhaps then in America, as well as in Britain, only a few were free and independent enough to stand above the scramblings of the marketplace. As "Cato" had written, only "a very small Part of Mankind have Capacities large enough to judge of the Whole of Things." Only a few were liberally educated and cosmopolitan enough to have the breadth of perspective to comprehend all the different interests, and only a *few* were dispassionate and unbiased enough to adjudicate among these different interests and promote the public rather than a private good. Virtue, it was said as early as 1778, "can only dwell in superior minds, elevated above private interest and selfish views." Even Jefferson at one point admitted that only those few "whom nature has endowed with genius and virtue" could "be rendered by liberal education worthy to receive, and able to guard the sacred rights and liberties of their fellow citizens."[33] In other words, the Federalists were saying that perhaps only from among the tiny proportion of the society the eighteenth century designated as "gentlemen" could be found men capable of disinterested political leadership.

This age-old distinction between gentlemen and others in the society had a vital meaning for the Revolutionary generation that we have totally lost. It was a horizontal cleavage that divided the social hierarchy into two unequal parts almost as sharply as the distinction between officers and soldiers divided the army; indeed, the military division was related to the larger social one. Ideally the liberality for which gentlemen were known connoted freedom—freedom from material want, freedom from the caprice of others, freedom from ignorance, and freedom from manual labor. The gentleman's distinctiveness came from being independent in a world of dependencies, learned in a world only partially literate, and leisured in a world of workers.[34] Just as gentlemen were expected to staff the officer corps of the Continental army (and expected also to provide for their own rations, clothing, and equipment on salaries that were less than half those of their British counterparts), so were independent gentlemen of leisure and education expected to supply the necessary disinterested leadership for government.[35] Since such well-to-do gentry were "exempted from the lower and less honourable employments," wrote the philosopher Francis Hutcheson, they were "rather more than others obliged to an active life in some service to mankind. The publick has this claim upon them." Governmental service, in other words, was thought to be a personal sacrifice, required of certain gentlemen because of their talents, independence, and social preeminence.[36]

In eighteenth-century America it had never been easy for gentlemen to make this personal sacrifice for the public, and it became especially difficult during the Revolution. Which is why many of the Revolutionary leaders, especially those of "small fortunes" who served in the Congress, continually complained of the burdens of office and repeatedly begged to be relieved from these burdens in order to pursue their private interests. Periodic temporary retirement from the cares and commotions of office to one's country estate for refuge and rest was acceptable classical behavior. But too often America's political leaders, especially in the North, had to retire not to relaxation in the solitude and leisure of a rural retreat, but to the making of money in the busyness and bustle of a city law practice.[37]

In short, America's would-be gentlemen had a great deal of trouble in maintaining the desired classical independence and freedom from the marketplace. There were not many American gentry who were capable of living idly off the rents of tenants as the English landed aristocracy did. Of course, there were large numbers of the southern planter gentry whose leisure was based on the labor of their slaves, and these planters obviously came closest in America to fitting the classical ideal of the free and independent gentleman. But some southern planters kept taverns on the side, and many others were not as removed from the day-to-day management of their estates as their counterparts among the English landed gentry. Their overseers were not comparable to the stewards of the English gentry; thus the planters, despite their aristocratic poses, were often very busy, commercially involved men. Their livelihoods were tied directly to the vicissitudes of international trade, and they had always had an uneasy sense of being dependent on the market to an extent that the English landed aristocracy, despite its commitment to enterprising projects and improvements, never really felt. Still, the great southern planters at least approached the classical image of disinterested gentlemanly leadership, and they knew it and made the most of it throughout their history.[38]

In northern American society such independent gentlemen standing above the interests of the marketplace were harder to find, but the ideal remained strong. In ancient Rome, wrote James Wilson, magistrates and army officers were always gentleman farmers, always willing to step down "from the elevation of office" and reassume "with contentment and with pleasure, the peaceful labours of a rural and independent life." John Dickinson's pose in 1767

as a "Pennsylvania Farmer" is incomprehensible except within this classical tradition. Dickinson, the wealthy Philadelphia lawyer, wanted to assure his readers of his gentlemanly disinterestedness by informing them at the outset that he was a farmer "contented" and "undisturbed by wordly hopes or fears."[39] Prominent merchants dealing in international trade brought wealth into the society and were thus valuable members of the community, but their status as independent gentlemen was always tainted by their concern for personal profit.[40] Perhaps only a classical education that made "ancient manners familiar," as Richard Jackson once told Benjamin Franklin, could "produce a reconciliation between disinterestedness and commerce; a thing we often see, but almost always in men of a liberal education." Yet no matter how educated merchants were or how much leisure they managed for themselves, while they remained merchants they could never quite acquire the character of genteel disinterestedness essential for full acceptance as political leaders, and that is why most colonial merchants were not active in public life.[41]

John Hancock and Henry Laurens knew this, and during the imperial crisis each shed his mercantile business and sought to ennoble himself. Hancock spent lavishly, bought every imaginable luxury, and patronized everyone. He went through a fortune, but he did become the single most popular and powerful figure in Massachusetts politics during the last quarter or so of the eighteenth century. Laurens especially was aware of the bad image buying and selling had among southern planters. In 1764 he advised two impoverished but aspiring gentry immigrants heading for the back-country to establish themselves as planters before attempting to open a store. For them to enter immediately into "any retail Trade in those parts," he said, "would be mean, would Lessen them in the esteem of people whose respect they must endeavour to attract." Only after they were "set down in a Creditable manner as Planters" might they "carry on the Sale of many specie of European and West Indian goods to some advantage and with a good grace." In this same year, 1764, Laurens himself began to curtail his merchant operations. By the time of the Revolution he had become enough of an aristocrat that he was able to sneer at all those merchants who were still busy making money. "How hard it is," he had the gall to say in 1779, "for a rich, or covetous man to enter heartily into the kingdom of patriotism."[42]

For mechanics and others who worked with their hands, being a disinterested gentleman was impossible. Only when wealthy Benjamin Franklin retired from his printing business, at the age of forty-two, did "the Publick," as he wrote in his *Autobiography,* "now considering me as a Man of Leisure," lay hold of him and bring him into an increasing number of important public offices. Other artisans and petty traders who had wealth and political ambitions, such as Roger Sherman of Connecticut, also found that retirement from business was a prerequisite for high public office.[43]

Members of the learned professions were usually considered gentlemen, particularly if they were liberally educated. But were they disinterested? Were they free of the marketplace? Were they capable of virtuous public service? Hamilton for one argued strongly that, unlike merchants, mechanics, or farmers, "the learned professions … truly form no distinct interest in society"; thus they "will feel a neutrality to the rivalships between the different branches of industry" and will be most likely to be "an impartial arbiter" between the diverse interests of the society. But others had doubts. William Barton thought "a few individuals in a nation may be actuated by such exalted sentiments of public virtue, … but these instances must be rare." Certainly many thought lawyers did not stand above the fray. In fact, said Barton, "professional men of every description are necessarily, as such, obliged to pursue their immediate advantage."[44]

Everywhere, men struggled to find a way of reconciling this classical tradition of disinterested public leadership with the private demands of making a living. "A Man expends his Fortune in political Pursuits," wrote Gouverneur Morris in an introspective unfinished essay. Did he do this out of "personal Consideration" or out of a desire to promote the public good? If he did it to promote the public good, "was he justifiable in sacrificing to it the Subsistence of his Family? These are important Questions; but," said Morris, "there remains one more," and that one question of Morris's threatened to undermine the whole classical tradition: "Would not as much Good have followed from an industrious Attention to his own Affairs?" Hamilton, for one, could not agree. Although he knew that most people were selfish scavengers, incapable of noble and disinterested acts, he did not want to be one of them. Thus he refused to make speculative killings in land or banking "because," as he put it in one of his sardonic moods, "there must be some *public fools* who sacrifice private to public interest at the certainty of ingratitude and obloquy—because my *vanity* whispers I ought to be one of those fools and ought to keep myself in a situation the best calculated to render service." Hamilton clung as long and as hard to this classical conception of leadership as anyone in post-Revolutionary America.[45]

Washington too felt the force of the classical ideal and throughout his life was compulsive about his disinterestedness. Because he had not gone to college and acquired a liberal education, he always felt he had to live literally by the book. He was continually anxious that he not be thought too ambitious or self-seeking; above all, he did not want to be thought greedy or "interested." He refused to accept a salary for any of his public services, and he was scrupulous in avoiding any private financial benefits from his governmental positions.

Perhaps nothing more clearly reveals Washington's obsession with these classical republican values than his agonized response in the winter of 1784–1785 to the Virginia Assembly's gift of 150 shares in the James River and Potomac canal companies. Acceptance of the shares seemed clearly impossible. The shares might be "considered in the same light as a pension," he said. He would be thought "a dependant," and his reputation for virtue would be compromised. At the same time, however, Washington believed passionately in what the canal companies were doing; indeed, he had long dreamed of making a fortune from such canals. He thought the shares might constitute "the foundation of the *greatest* and most *certain* income" that anyone could expect from a speculative venture. Besides, he did not want to show "disrespect" to his countrymen or to appear "ostentatiously disinterested" by refusing the gift of the shares.[46]

What should he do? Few decisions in Washington's career called for such handwringing as this one did. He sought the advice of nearly everyone he knew. Letters went out to Jefferson, to Governor Patrick Henry, to William Grayson, to Benjamin Harrison, to George William Fairfax, to Nathanael Greene, to Henry Knox, even to Lafayette—all seeking "the best information and advice" on the disposition of the shares. "How would this matter be viewed then by the eyes of the world[?]" he asked. Would not his reputation for virtue be tarnished? Would not accepting the shares "deprive me of the principal thing which is laudable in my conduct?"—that is, his disinterestedness.

The story would be comic if Washington had not been so deadly earnest. He understated the situation when he told his correspondents that his mind was "not a little agitated" by the problem. In letter after letter he expressed real anguish. This was no ordinary display of scruples such as government officials today show over a conflict of interest: in 1784–1785 Washington was not even holding public office.[47]

These values, this need for disinterestedness in public officials, were very much on the minds of the founding fathers at the Philadelphia Convention, especially James Madison's. Madison was a tough-minded thinker, not given to illusions. He knew that there were "clashing interests" everywhere and that they were doing great harm to state legislative politics. But he had not yet given up hope that it might be possible to put into government, at the national if not at the state level, some "proper guardians of the public weal," men of "the most attractive merit, and most diffusive and established characters." We have too often mistaken Madison for some sort of prophet of a modern interest-group theory of politics. But Madison was not a forerunner of twentieth-century political scientists such as Arthur Bentley, David Truman, or Robert Dahl. Despite his hardheaded appreciation of the multiplicity of interests in American society, he did not offer America a pluralist conception of politics. He did not see public policy or the common good emerging naturally from the give-and-take of hosts of competing interests. Instead he hoped that these clashing interests and parties in an enlarged national republic would neutralize themselves and thereby allow liberally educated, rational men, "whose enlightened views and virtuous sentiments render them superior to local prejudices, and to schemes of injustice," to promote the public good in a disinterested manner. Madison, in other words, was not at all as modern as we make him out to be.[48] He did not expect the new national government to be an integrator and harmonizer of the different interests in the society; instead he expected it to be a "disinterested and dispassionate umpire in disputes between different passions and interests in the State." Madison even suggested that the national government might play the same superpolitical, neutral role that the British king had been supposed to play in the empire.[49]

The Federalists' plans for the Constitution, in other words, rested on their belief that there were some disinterested gentlemen left in America to act as neutral umpires. In this sense the Constitution became a grand—and perhaps in retrospect a final desperate—effort to realize the great hope of the Revolution: the possibility of virtuous politics. The Constitution thus looked backward as much as it looked forward. Despite the Federalists' youthful energy, originality, and vision, they still clung to the classical tradition of civic humanism and its patrician code of disinterested public leadership. They stood for a moral and social order that was radically different from the popular, individualistic, and acquisitive world they saw emerging in the 1780s.

## IV

The Antifederalists, of course, saw it all very differently. Instead of seeing enlightened patriots simply making a Constitution to promote the national good, they saw groups of interested men trying to foist an aristocracy onto republican America. And they said so, just as the Federalists had feared, in pamphlets, newspapers, and the debates in ratifying conventions. Fear of aristocracy did become the principal shibboleth and rallying cry of the opponents of the Constitution. Already during the 1780s the classical demand that government should be run by rich, leisured gentlemen who served "without fee or reward" was being met by increasing contempt: "Enormous wealth," it was said even in aristocratic South Carolina, "is seldom the associate *of pure* and *disinterested virtue.*"[50] The Antifederalists brought this popular contempt to a head and refused to accept the claim that the Federalists were truly disinterested patriots. In fact, many of them had trouble seeing anyone at all as free from interests. If either side in the debate therefore stood for the liberal, pluralistic, interest-ridden future of American politics, it was the Antifederalists. They, not the Federalists, were the real modern men. They emerged from the confusion of the polemics with an understanding of American society that was far more hardheaded, realistic, and prophetic than even James Madison's.

There were, of course, many different Antifederalist spokesmen, a fact that complicates any analysis of the opposition to the Constitution. Yet some of the prominent Antifederalist leaders, such as Elbridge Gerry, George Mason, and Richard Henry Lee, scarcely represented, either socially or emotionally, the main thrust of Antifederalism. Such aristocratic leaders were socially indistinguishable from the Federalist spokesmen and often were as fearful of the excesses of democracy in the state legislatures as the Federalists. Far more representative of the paper money interests of the 1780s and the populist opposition to the "aristocracy" of the Federalists was someone like William Findley— that pugnacious Scotch-Irishman from western Pennsylvania. Gerry, Mason, and Lee did not really point the way to the liberal, interest-ridden democracy of nineteenth-century America, but Findley did. Until we understand the likes of William Findley, we won't understand either Antifederalism or the subsequent democratic history of America.

Findley came to the colonies from northern Ireland in 1763, at age twenty-two, in one of those great waves of eighteenth-century emigration from the northern parts of the British islands that so frightened Dr. Johnson. After trying his hand at weaving, the craft to which he had been apprenticed, Findley became a schoolmaster and then a farmer—until he was caught up in the Revolutionary movement, moved through the ranks to a militia captaincy, and became a political officeholder in Pennsylvania. Findley was the very prototype of a later professional politician and was as much a product of the Revolution as were the more illustrious patriots like John Adams or James Madison. He had no lineage to speak of, he went to no college, and he possessed no great wealth. He was completely self-taught and self-made, but not in the manner of a Benjamin Franklin who acquired the cosmopolitan attributes of a gentleman: Findley's origins showed, and conspicuously so. In his middling aspirations, middling achievements, and middling resentments, he represented far more accurately what America was becoming than did cosmopolitan gentlemen like Franklin and Adams.[51]

By the middle eighties this red-faced Irishman with his flamboyant white hat was becoming one of the most articulate spokesmen for those debtor-paper money interests that lay behind the political turbulence and democratic excesses of the period. As a representative from the West in the Pennsylvania state legislature, he embodied that rough, upstart, individualistic society that eastern squires like George Clymer hated and feared. In the western counties around Pittsburgh, gentry like Clymer could see only avarice, ignorance, and suspicion and a thin, weak society where there were "no private or publick associations for common good, every Man standing single."[52] Findley never much liked Clymer, but he reserved his deepest antagonism for two others of the Pennsylvania gentry— Hugh Henry Brackenridge and Robert Morris.

Findley's political conflicts with these two men in the Pennsylvania legislature in the 1780s foreshadowed and, indeed, epitomized the Antifederalists' struggle with the Federalists. It is perhaps not too much to say that Findley came to see the Constitution as a device designed by gentry like Brackenridge and Morris to keep men like himself out of the important affairs of government. This was especially galling to Findley because he could see no justification for the arrogance and assumed superiority of such men. Brackenridge and Morris were in reality, he believed, no different from him, and during the 1780s he meant to prove it.

Hugh Henry Brackenridge, born in 1748, was seven years younger than Findley. He was a Princeton graduate who in 1781 moved to western Pennsylvania because he thought the wilds of Pittsburgh offered greater opportunities for advancement than crowded Philadelphia. As the only college-educated gentleman in the area, he saw himself as an oasis of cultivation in the midst of a desert. He wanted to be "among the first to bring the press to the west of the mountains," so he helped establish a newspaper in Pittsburgh for which he wrote poetry, bagatelles, and other things.[53] He was pretty full of himself, and he never missed an opportunity to sprinkle his prose with Latin quotations and to show off his learning. This young, ambitious Princeton graduate with aristocratic pretensions was, in fact, just the sort of person who would send someone like William Findley climbing the walls.

William Findley was already a member of the state legislature in 1786 when Brackenridge decided that he too would like to be a legislator. Brackenridge ran for election and won by promising his western constituents that he would look after their particular interests, especially in favoring the use of state certificates of paper money in buying land. But then his troubles began. In Philadelphia he inevitably fell in with the well-to-do crowd around Robert Morris and James Wilson, who had cosmopolitan tastes more to his liking. Under the influence of Morris, Brackenridge voted against the state certificates he had promised to support and identified himself with the eastern establishment. He actually had the nerve to write in the *Pittsburgh Gazette* that the "eastern members" of the assembly had singled him out among all the "Huns, Goths and Vandals" who usually came over the mountains to legislate in Philadelphia and had complimented him for his "liberality." But it was a dinner party at Chief Justice Thomas McKean's house in December 1786, at which both he and Findley were guests, that really did him in. One guest suggested that Robert Morris's support for the Bank of North America seemed mainly for his own personal benefit rather than for the people's. To this Brackenridge responded loudly, "The people are fools; if they would let Mr. Morris alone, he would make Pennsylvania a great people, but they will not suffer him to do it."[54]

Most American political leaders already knew better than to call the people fools, at least aloud, and Findley saw his chance to bring Brackenridge down a peg or two. He wrote a devastating account of Brackenridge's statement in the *Pittsburgh Gazette* and accused him of betraying the people's trust by his vote against the state certificates. It was all right, said Findley sarcastically, for a representative to change his mind if he had not solicited or expected the office, "which is the case generally with modest, disinterested men." But for someone like Brackenridge who had openly sought the office and had made campaign promises—

for him to change his vote could only arouse the "indignation" and the "contempt" of the people. Brackenridge may have professed "the greatest acquired abilities, and most shining imagination," but he was in fact a self-seeking and self-interested person who did not have the public good at heart.

Brackenridge vainly tried to reply. At first he sought to justify his change of vote on the classical humanist grounds that the people could not know about the "complex, intricate and involved" problems and interests involved in legislation. "The people at home know each man his own wishes and wants." Only an educated elite in the assembly could see the problems of finance whole; it required "the height of ability to be able to distinguish clearly the interests of a state." But was Brackenridge himself a member of this disinterested elite? Did he really stand above the various interests of the state? He admitted under Findley's assault that he had a "strong *interest* to prompt me to *offer* myself" for election, but his private interest was the same interest with that of the western country where he lived. "My object was to advance the country, and thereby advance myself."[55]

It was a frank and honest but strained answer, a desperate effort by Brackenridge to reconcile the presumed traditional disinterestedness of a political leader with his obvious personal ambition. The more he protested, the worse his situation became, and he never recovered from Findley's attack. The two men crossed swords again in the election of delegates to the state ratifying convention in 1788, and Brackenridge as an avowed Federalist lost to the Antifederalist Findley. Brackenridge then abandoned politics for the time being and turned his disillusionment with the vagaries of American democracy into his comic masterpiece, *Modern Chivalry.*

Findley sent Brackenridge scurrying out of politics into literature by attacking his pretensions as a virtuous gentlemanly leader. He attacked Robert Morris in a similar way, with far more ruinous consequences for Morris. Findley and Morris first tangled while they were both

members of the Pennsylvania legislature in the 1780s. During several days of intense debate in 1786 over the rechartering of the Bank of North America, Findley mercilessly stripped away the mask of superior classical disinterestedness that Morris had sought to wear. This fascinating wide-ranging debate—the only important one we have recorded of state legislative proceedings in the 1780s—centered on the role of interest in public affairs.

Findley was the leader of the legislative representatives who opposed the rechartering of the bank. He and others like John Smilie from western Pennsylvania were precisely the sorts of legislators whom gentry like Madison had accused throughout the 1780s of being illiberal, narrow-minded, and interested in their support of debtor farmers and paper money. Now they had an opportunity to get back at their accusers, and they made the most of it. Day after day they hammered home one basic point: the supporters of the bank were themselves interested men. They were directors or stockholders in the bank, and therefore they had no right in supporting the rechartering of the bank to pose as disinterested gentlemen promoting the public good. The advocates of the bank "feel interested in it personally." Their defense of the bank, said Findley, who quickly emerged as the principal and most vitriolic critic of the bank's supporters, revealed "the manner in which disappointed avarice chagrins an interested mind."

Morris and his fellow supporters of the bank were embarrassed by these charges that they had a selfish interest in the bank's charter. At first, in George Clymer's committee report on the advisability of rechartering the bank, they took the overbearing line that the proponents of the bank in the general community "included the most respectable characters amongst us," men who knew about the world and the nature of banks. But as the charges of their selfishness mounted, the supporters of the bank became more and more defensive. They insisted they were men of "independent fortune and situations" and were therefore "above influence or terror" by the bank. Under the relentless criticism by Findley and others, however, they one by one grew silent, until their defense was left almost entirely in the hands of Robert Morris, who had a personal, emotional involvement in this debate that went well beyond his concern for the bank.[56]

Morris, as the wealthiest merchant in Pennsylvania and perhaps in all of North America, had heard it all before. The charges of always being privately interested had been the plague of his public career. No matter that his "Exertions" in supplying and financing the Revolution were "as disinterested and pure as ever were made by Mortal Man," no matter how much he sacrificed for the sake of the public, the charges of using public office for personal gain kept arising to torment him. No prominent Revolutionary leader had ever been subjected to such "unmeritted abuse," such bitter and vituperative accusations of selfishness, as he had.[57]

Now in 1786 he had to hear it all over again: that his support of the bank came solely from his personal interest in it. What could he do? He acknowledged that he was a shareholder in the bank, but he tried to argue that the bank was in the interest of all citizens in the state. How could he prove that he was not self-interested? Perhaps if he sold his bank stock? If he did, he assured his fellow legislators that he would be just as concerned with the bank's charter. At one point he gave up and said he would leave the issue of his self-interestedness to the members of the house to determine. But he could not leave it alone, and was soon back on his feet. Members have said "my information is not to be trusted, because I am interested in the bank: but surely," he pleaded, "I am more deeply interested in the state." He hoped, "notwithstanding the insinuation made, that it will never be supposed I would sacrifice the interest and welfare of the state to any interest I can possibly hold in the bank." Why couldn't his arguments for the bank be taken on their merits, apart from their source? he asked. Let them "be considered, not as coming from parties interested, but abstractedly as to their force and solidity."

Such nervous arguments were symptoms of his mounting frustration, and he finally exploded in anger and defiance. Once more he stated categorically: "I am not stimulated by the consideration of private interest, to stand forth in defence of the bank." If people supposed that he needed this bank, they were "grossly mistaken." He was bigger than the bank. If the bank should be destroyed, he on his "own capital, credit, and resources" would create another one; and even his enemies ("and God knows I seem to have enough of them") would have to deal with him, if only "for the sake of their own interest and convenience."[58]

It was an excruciating experience for Morris. At one point in the debate he expressed his desire to retire from office and become a private citizen, "which suits both my inclination and affairs much better than to be in public life, for which I do not find myself very well qualified." But the lure of the public arena and what it represented in the traditional aristocratic terms of civic honor were too great for him, and instead he retired once and for all from his merchant business and like Hancock and Laurens before him sought to ennoble himself. In the late eighties and early nineties, he shifted all his entrepreneurial activities into the acquisition of speculative land—something that seemed more respectable for an aristocrat than trade. He acquired a coat of arms, patronized artists, and hired L'Enfant to build him a huge, marble palace in Philadelphia. He surrounded himself with the finest furniture, tapestry, silver, and wines and made his home the center of America's social life. Like a good aristocrat, he maintained, recalled Samuel Breck, "a profuse, incessant and elegant hospitality" and displayed "a luxury ... that was to be found nowhere else in America." When he became a United States senator in 1789, he—to the astonishment of listeners—began paying himself "compliments on his manner and conduct in life," in particular "his disregard of money." How else would a real aristocrat behave?[59]

For Morris to disregard money was not only astonishing, however; it was fatal. We know what happened, and it is a poignant, even tragic story. All his aristocratic dreams came to nothing; the marble palace on Chestnut Street went unfinished; his dinner parties ceased; his carriages were seized; and he ended in debtors' prison. That Morris should have behaved as he did says something about the continuing power of the classical aristocratic ideal of disinterestedness in post-Revolutionary America. It also says something about the popular power of William Findley, for it was Findley, more than anyone else in the debate over the bank, who had hounded Morris into renouncing his interests in commerce.

Findley in the debate knew he had Morris's number and bore in on it. "The human soul," Findley said, "is affected by wealth, in almost all its faculties. It is affected by its present interest, by its expectations, and by its fears." All this was too much for Morris, and he angrily turned on Findley. "If wealth be so obnoxious, I ask this gentleman why is he so eager in the pursuit of it?" If Morris expected a denial from Findley, he did not get it. For Findley's understanding of Morris's motives was really based on an understanding of his own. Did he love wealth and pursue it as Morris did? "Doubtless I do," said Findley. "I love and pursue it—not as an end, but as a means of enjoying happiness and independence," though he was quick to point out that he had wealth "not in any proportion to the degree" Morris had. Not that this made Morris in any way superior to Findley. Indeed, the central point stressed by Findley and the other western opponents of the bank was that Morris and his patrician Philadelphia crowd were no different from them, were no more respectable than they were. Such would-be aristocrats simply had "more money than their neighbours." In America, said Findley, "no man has a greater claim of special privilege for his £100,000 than I have for my £5." That was what American equality meant.

Morris, like all aspiring aristocrats in an egalitarian society, tried to stress that social distinctions were not based on wealth alone. "Surely," he said in desperate disbelief, "persons possessed of knowledge, judgment, information, integrity, and having extensive connections, are not to be classed with persons void of reputation or character." But Morris's claims of superiority were meaningless as long as he and his friends were seen to be interested men, and on that point Findley had him. Findley and his western legislative colleagues had no desire to establish any claims of their own to disinterestedness. In fact they wanted to hear no more spurious patrician talk of virtue and disinterestedness. They had no objection to Morris's and the other stockholders' being interested in the bank's rechartering: "Any others in their situation … would do as they did." Morris and other legislators, said Findley, "have a right to advocate their own cause, on the floor of this house." But then they could not protest when others realize "that it is their own cause they are advocating; and to give credit to their opinions, and to think of their votes accordingly." In fact, said Findley, such open promotion of interests meant an end to the archaic idea that representatives should simply stand and not run for election. When a candidate for the legislature "has a cause of his own to advocate, interest will dictate the propriety of canvassing for a seat." Who has ever put the case for special-interest elective politics any better?[60]

These were the arguments of democratic legislators in the 1780s who were sick and tired of being told by the aristocratic likes of James Madison that they were "Men of factious tempers" and "of local prejudices" and "advocates and parties to the causes which they determine." If they were interested men, so too were all legislators, including even those such as Morris and Brackenridge who were supposed to be liberal-thinking genteel men of "enlightened views and virtuous sentiments." "The citizens," Findley later wrote, by which he meant citizens like himself, "have learned to take a surer course of obtaining information respecting political characters," particularly those who pretended to disinterested civic service. They had especially learned how to inquire "into the local interests and circumstances" of such characters and to point out those with "pursuits or interests" that were "inconsistent with the equal administration of government." Findley had seen the gentry up close, so close in fact that all sense of the mystery that had hitherto surrounded aristocratic authority was lost.[61]

The prevalence of interest and the impossibility of disinterestedness inevitably became a central argument of the Antifederalists in the debate over the Constitution. Precisely because the Constitution was designed to perpetuate the classical tradition of disinterested leadership in government, the Antifederalists felt compelled to challenge that tradition. There was, they said repeatedly, no disinterested gentlemanly elite that could feel "sympathetically the wants of the people" and speak for their "feelings, circumstances, and interests." Would-be patricians like James Wilson, declared William Findley, thought they were "born of a different race from the rest of the sons of men" and "able to conceive and perform great things." But despite their "lofty carriage," such gentry could not in fact see beyond "the pale of power and worldly grandeur." No one, said the Antifederalists, however elevated or educated, was free of the lures and interests of the marketplace. As for the leisured gentry who were "not ... under the necessity of getting their bread by industry," far from being specially qualified for public leadership, they were in fact specially disqualified. Such men contributed nothing to the public good; their "idleness" rested on "other men's toil."[62]

But it was not just the classical tradition of leisured gentry leadership the Antifederalists challenged. Without realizing the full implications of what they were doing, they challenged too the whole social order the Federalists stood for. Society to the Antifederalists could no longer be a hierarchy of ranks or even a division into two unequal parts between gentlemen and commoners. Civic society should not in fact be graded by any criteria whatsoever. Society was best thought of as a heterogeneous mixture of "many different classes or orders of people, Merchants, Farmers, Planter Mechanics and Gentry or wealthy Men," all equal to one another. In this diverse egalitarian society, men from one class or interest could never be acquainted with the *"Situation* and Wants" of those from another. Lawyers and planters could never be "adequate judges of trademens concerns." Legislative representatives could not be just *for* the people; they actually had to be *of* the people. It was foolish to tell people that they ought to overlook local interests. Local interests were all there really were. "No man when he enters into society, does it from a view to promote the good of others, but he does it for his own good." Since all individuals and groups in the society were equally self-interested, the only "fair representation" in government, wrote the "Federal Farmer," ought to be one where "every order of men in the community ... can have a share in it." Consequently any American government ought "to allow professional men, merchants, traders, farmers, mechanics, etc. to bring a just proportion of their best informed men respectively into the legislature." Only an explicit form of representation that allowed Germans, Baptists, artisans, farmers, and so on each to send delegates of its own kind into the political arena could embody the pluralistic particularism of the emerging society of the early Republic.[63]

Thus in 1787–1788 it was not the Federalists but the Antifederalists who were the real pluralists and the real prophets of the future of American politics. They not only foresaw but endorsed a government of jarring individuals and interests. Unlike the Federalists, however, they offered no disinterested umpires, no mechanisms at all for reconciling and harmonizing these clashing selfish interests. All they and their Republican successors had was the assumption, attributed in 1806 to Jefferson, "that the public good is best promoted by the exertion of each individual seeking his *own good* in his own way."[64]

As early as the first decade of the nineteenth century it seemed to many gentlemen, like Benjamin Latrobe, the noted architect and engineer, that William Findley and the Antifederalists had not really lost the struggle after all. "Our representatives to all our Legislative bodies, National, as well as of the states," Latrobe explained to Philip Mazzei in 1806, "are elected by the majority *sui similes,* that is, *unlearned.*"

For instance from Philadelphia and its environs we send to congress not *one* man of letters. One of them indeed is a lawyer but of no eminence, another a good Mathematician, but when elected he was a Clerk in a bank. The others are plain farmers. From the next county is sent a Blacksmith and from just over the river a Butcher. Our state legislature does not contain one individual of superior talents. The fact is, that superior talents actually excite distrust, and the experience of the world perhaps does not encourage the people to trust men of genius.[65]

This was not the world those "men of genius," the founding fathers, had wanted. To the extent therefore that the Constitution was designed to control and transcend common ordinary men with their common, ordinary pecuniary interests, it was clearly something of a failure. In place of a classical republic led by a disinterested enlightened elite, Americans got a democratic marketplace of equally competing individuals with interests to promote. Tocqueville saw what happened clearly enough. "Americans are not a virtuous people," he wrote, "yet they are free." In America, unlike the classical republics, "it is not disinterestedness which is great, it is interest." Such a diverse, rootless, and restless people— what could possibly hold them together? "Interest. That is the secret. The private interest that breaks through at each moment, the interest that moreover, appears openly and even proclaims itself as a social theory." In America, said Tocqueville, "the period of disinterested patriotism is gone … forever."[66]

No wonder the founding fathers seem so remote, so far away from us. They really are.

## Notes

1. Gladstone, quoted in Douglass Adair, "The Tenth Federalist Revisited," in Trevor Colbourn, ed., *Fame and the Founding Fathers* (New York, 1974), 81.

2. Henry Steele Commager, *Jefferson, Nationalism, and the Enlightenment* (New York, 1975), xix.

3. Thomson to Jefferson, Apr. 6, 1786, in Julian P. Boyd *et al.*, eds., *The Papers of Thomas Jefferson* (Princeton, N.J., 1950–), IX, 380. On the demographic explosion of the 1780s, see J. Potter, "The Growth of Population in America, 1700–1860," in D. V. Glass and D.E.C. Eversley, eds., *Population in History: Essays in Historical Demography* (Chicago, 1965), 640.

4. For examples of the various historians who have minimized the criticalness of the 1780s, see Charles A. Beard, *An Economic Interpretation of the Constitution of the United States* (New York, 1913), 48; E. James Ferguson, *The Power of the Purse: A History of American Public Finance, 1776–1790* (Chapel Hill, N.C., 1961), 337; Merrill Jensen, *The New Nation: A History of the United States during the Confederation, 1781–1789* (New York, 1950), 348–349; Bernard Bailyn, "The Central Themes of the American Revolution: An Interpretation," in Stephen G. Kurtz and James H. Hutson, eds., *Essays on the American Revolution* (Chapel Hill, N.C., 1973), 21.

5. "Amicus Republicae," *Address to the Public …* (Exeter, N.H., 1786), in Charles S. Hyneman and Donald S. Lutz, eds., *American Political Writing during the Founding Era, 1760–1805* (Indianapolis, Ind., 1983), I, 644; Rush to David Ramsay, [Mar. or Apr. 1788], in L. H. Butterfield, ed., *Letters of Benjamin Rush* (Princeton, N.J., 1951), I, 454; Washington to John Jay, Aug. 1, 1786, May 18, 1786, in John C. Fitzpatrick, ed., *The Writings of George Washington …* (Washington, D.C., 1931–1944), XXVIII, 503, 431–432.

6. Jackson Turner Main, *The Antifederalists: Critics of the Constitution, 1781–1788* (Chapel Hill, NC, 1961), 177–178.

7. Findley to Gov. William Plumer of New Hampshire, "William Findley of Westmoreland, Pa.," *Pennsylvania Magazine of History and Biography,* V (1881), 444; Jerry Grundfest, *George Clymer: Philadelphia Revolutionary, 1739–1813* (New York, 1982), 293–294; John Bach McMaster

and Frederick D. Stone, eds., *Pennsylvania and the Federal Constitution, 1787–1788* (Philadelphia, 1888), 115.

8.  On this point, see Robert A. Feer, "Shays's Rebellion and the Constitution: A Study in Causation," *New England Quarterly,* XLII (1969), 388–410.

9.  Washington to Jay, May 18, 1786, in Fitzpatrick, ed, *Writings of Washington,* XVIII, 432; Madison to Jefferson, Oct. 24, 1787, in Boyd *et al.,* eds., *Papers of Jefferson,* XII, 276.

10. Robert A. Rutland, editorial note to "Vices of the Political System of the United States," in William T. Hutchinson *et al.,* eds., *The Papers of James Madison* (Chicago, Charlottesville, 1962–), IX, 346.

11. Jefferson quoted in Ralph Ketcham, *James Madison: A Biography* (New York, 1971), 162; Drew R McCoy, "The Virginia Port Bill of 1784," *Virginia Magazine of History and Biography,* LXXXIII (1975), 294; Madison to Edmund Pendleton, Jan. 9, 1787, to Washington, Dec. 24, 1786, in Hutchinson *et al.,* eds., *Papers of Madison,* IX, 244, 225; A. G. Roeber, *Faithful Magistrates and Republican Lawyers: Creators of Virginia Legal Culture, 1680–1810* (Chapel Hill, N.C., 1981), 192–202.

12. McCoy, "Virginia Port Bill" *VMHB,* LXXXIII (1975) 292; Madison to Washington, Dec. 7, 1786, to Pendleton, Jan. 9, 1787, to Washington, Dec. 24, 1786, to Jefferson, Dec. 4, 1786, in Hutchinson *et al.,* eds., *Papers of Madison,* IX, 200, 244, 225, 191; Ketcham, *Madison,* 172.

13. "Vices," in Hutchinson *et al.,* eds., *Papers of Madison,* IX, 354, 355–356.

14. Washington to Henry Lee, Apr. 5, 1786, in Fitzpatrick, ed., *Writings of Washington,* XXVIII, 402; Grundfest, *Clymer,* 165, 164; E. Wayne Carp, *To Starve the Army at Pleasure: Continental Army Administration and American Political Culture, 1775–1783* (Chapel Hill, N.C., 1984), 209; Knox quoted in William Winslow Crosskey and William Jeffrey, Jr., *Politics and the Constitution in the History of the United States* (Chicago, 1980), III, 420, 421.

15. Rush to Jeremy Belknap, May 6, 1788, in Butterfield, ed., *Letters of Rush,* I, 461; Elbridge Gerry in Max Farrand, ed., *The Records of the Federal Convention of 1787* (New Haven, Conn., 1911, rev. ed., 1937), I, 48.

16. The best study of wartime mobilization in a single state is Richard Buel, Jr., *Dear Liberty: Connecticut's Mobilization for the Revolutionary War* (Middletown, Conn., 1980). For an insightful general assessment of the effects of mobilization, see Janet Ann Riesman, "The Origins of American Political Economy, 1690–1781" (Ph.D. diss., Brown University, 1983), 302–338.

17. Laurens quoted in Albert S. Bolles, *The Financial History of the United States from 1774 to 1789: Embracing the Period of the American Revolution,* 4th ed. (New York, 1896), 61–62 (I owe this citation to Janet Riesman); Carp, *To Starve the Army,* 106.

18. Nathanael Greene to Jacob Greene, after May 24, 1778, in Richard K. Showman ed., *The Papers of General Nathanael Greene* (Chapel Hill, N.C., 1976–), II, 404; Richard Buel, Jr., "Samson Shorn: The Impact of the Revolutionary War on Estimates of the Republic's Strength," in Ronald Hoffman and Peter J. Albert, eds., *Arms and Independence: The Military Character of the American Revolution* (Charlottesville, Va., 1984), 157–160. On the growth of commercial farming in the middle of the 18th century, see especially Joyce Appleby, "Commercial Farming and the 'Agrarian Myth' in the Early Republic," *Journal of American History,* LXVIII ( 1982), 833–849. There is nothing on 18th-century America's increased importation of "luxuries" and "comforts" resembling Neil McKendrick *et al., The Birth of a Consumer Society: The Commercialization of Eighteenth-Century England* (Bloomington, Ind., 1982). But see the articles of Carole Shammas, especially "The Domestic Environment in Early Modern England and America," *Journal of Social History,* XIV (1980), 3–24; Lois Green Carr and Lorena S. Walsh, "Inventories and the Analysis of Wealth and Consumption Patterns in St. Mary's County, Maryland, 1658–1777," *Historical Methods,* XIII ( 1980), 81–104; and Gloria L. Main, *Tobacco Colony: Life in Early Maryland, 1650–1720* (Princeton, N.J., 1982).

19. For examples of the new thinking about luxury as an inducement to industry, see Drew R. McCoy, *The Elusive Republic: Political Economy in Jeffersonian America* (Chapel Hill, N.C., 1980), 97.

20. [William Barton], *The True Interest of the United States, and Particularly of Pennsylvania Considered…* (Philadelphia, 1786), 12.

21. *Ibid.,* 4, 25–26.

22. [William Smith], *The Independent Reflector ... by William Livingston and Others,* ed. Milton M. Klein (Cambridge, Mass., 1963), 106. See J. E. Crowley, *This Sheba, Self: The Conceptualization of Economic Life in Eighteenth-Century America* (Baltimore, 1974), 38–39, 44, 49, 87, 97–99.

23. *Remarks on a Pamphlet, Entitled, "Considerations on the Bank of North-America"* (Philadelphia, 1785), 14; Madison to Monroe, Apr. 9, 1786, in Hutchinson *et al.,* eds., *Papers of Madison,* IX, 26; [Barton], *True Interest,* 20; Pa. Statute of 1785, cited in E.A.J. Johnson, *The Foundations of American Economic Freedom: Government and Enterprise in the Age of Washington* (Minneapolis, Minn., 1973), 43 n.

24. Jefferson, *Notes on the State of Virginia,* ed. William Peden (Chapel Hill, N.C., 1955), Query XXII, 175; Jefferson to G. K. van Hogendorp, Oct. 13, 1785, in Boyd *et al.,* eds., *Papers of Jefferson,* VIII, 633.

25. Madison to Monroe, Oct. 5, 1786, in Hutchinson *et al.,* eds., *Papers of Madison,* IX, 141; *Carlisle Gazette* (Pa.), Oct. 24, 1787, quoted in Herbert J. Storing, ed., *The Complete Anti-Federalist* (Chicago, 1981), II, 208; Washington to James Warren, Oct. 7, 1785, in Fitzpatrick, ed., *Writings of Washington,* XXVIII, 291; Hamilton, in Farrand, ed., *Records of the Federal Convention,* I, 378. On the nature and role of interests in 18th-century British politics, see Michael Kammen, *Empire and Interest: The American Colonies and the Politics of Mercantilism* (Philadelphia, 1970).

26. Pauline Maier, *The Old Revolutionaries: Political Lives in the Age of Samuel Adams* (New York, 1980), 3–50, quotation at 47.

27. Washington, quoted in Lester H. Cohen, *The Revolutionary Histories: Contemporary Narratives of the American Revolution* (Ithaca, N.Y., 1980), 273.

28. Joseph Lathrop (1786), in Hyneman and Lutz, eds., *American Political Writing,* I, 660; Wilson, in Farrand, ed., *Records of the Federal Convention,* I, 605; Jefferson to Edward Carrington, Jan. 16, 1787, in Boyd *et al.,* eds., *Papers of Jefferson,* XI, 49. See also Ralph Ketcham, *Presidents above Party: The First American Presidency, 1789–1829* (Chapel Hill, N.C., 1984).

29. Jefferson, "Summary View of the Rights of British America" (1774), in Boyd *et al.,* eds., *Papers of Jefferson,* I, 134.

30. Johnson, *A Dictionary of the English Language ...* (London, 1755); Charles Royster, *A Revolutionary People at War: The Continental Army and American Character, 1775–1783* (Chapel Hill, N.C., 1979), 22–23.

31. John Brewer, *Party Ideology and Popular Politics at the Accession of George III* (Cambridge, 1976), 97.

32. Washington to John Hancock, Sept. 24, 1776, in Fitzpatrick, ed., *Writings of Washington,* VI, 107–108.

33. Adam Smith, *An Inquiry into the Nature and Causes of the Wealth of Nations,* ed. R. H. Campbell and A. S. Skinner (Oxford, 1976) (V.i.f. 50–51), II, 781–783; [John Trenchard and Thomas Gordon], *Cato's Letters; or, Essays on Liberty, Civil and Religious, and Other Important Subjects,* 5th ed. (London, 1748), III, 193; Phillips Payson, "A Sermon Preached before the Honorable Council ... at Boston, May 27, 1778," in John Wingate Thornton, ed., *The Pulpit of the American Revolution ...* (Boston, 1860), 337; Jefferson, "A Bill for the More General Diffusion of Education" (1779), in Boyd *et al.,* eds., *Papers of Jefferson,* II, 527. On the 18th-century British developments out of which "Cato," Smith, and others wrote, see the illuminating discussion in John Barrell, *English Literature in History, 1730–80: An Equal, Wide Survey (London,* 1983), 17–50.

34. The best discussion of the distinctiveness of the gentry in colonial America is Rhys Isaac, *The Transformation of Virginia, 1740–1790* (Chapel Hill, N.C., 1982), esp. 131–132.

35. Royster, *Revolutionary People at War,* 86–95; John B. B. Trussell, Jr., *Birthplace of an Army: A Study of the Valley Forge Encampment* (Harrisburg, Pa., 1976), 86.

36. Francis Hutcheson, *A System of Moral Philosophy in Three Books ...* (London, 1755), II, 113. "Let not your Love of Philosophical Amusements have more than its due Weight with you," Benjamin Franklin admonished Cadwallader Colden at mid-century. Public service was far more important. In fact, said Franklin, even "the finest" of Newton's "Discoveries" could not have excused his neglect of serving the commonwealth if the public had needed him (Franklin to Colden, Oct. 11, 1750, in Leonard W. Labaree *et al.,* eds., *The Papers of Benjamin Franklin* [New Haven, Conn., 1959–], IV, 68).

37. Jack N. Rakove, *The Beginnings of National Politics: An Interpretative History of the Continental Congress* (New York, 1979), 216–239, quotation by William Fleming to Jefferson, May 10, 1779, at 237; George Athan Billias, *Elbridge Gerry, Founding Father and Republican Statesman* (New York, 1976), 138-139.

38. See William R. Taylor, *Cavalier and Yankee: The Old South and American National Character* (New York, 1961).

39. Wilson, "On the History of Property," in Robert Green McCloskey, ed., *The Works of James Wilson* (Cambridge, Mass., 1967), II, 716; Dickinson, "Letters of a Farmer in Pennsylvania" (1768), in Paul Leicester Ford, ed., *The Writings of John Dickinson*, Vol. I, *Political Writings, 1764–1774* (Pennsylvania Historical Society, *Memoirs*, XIV [Philadelphia, 1895]), 307 (hereafter cited as Ford, ed., *Writings of Dickinson*).

40. "We have found by experience, that no dependence can be had upon *merchants,* either at *home,* or in *America"* Charles Chauncy told Richard Price in 1774, "so many of them are so mercenary as to find within themselves a readiness to become slaves themselves, as well as to be accessory to the slavery of others, if they imagine they may, by this means, serve their own private separate interest" (D.C. Thomas and Bernard Peach, eds., *The Correspondence of Richard Price* [Durham, N.C., 1983], I, 170). For Adam Smith's view that the interest of merchants and indeed of all who lived by profit was "always in some respects different from, and even opposite to, that of the publick," see Smith, *Wealth of Nations,* ed. Campbell and Skinner, (I.xi.p.l0) I, 267.

41. Jackson to Franklin, June 17, 1755, in Labaree *et al., eds., Papers of Franklin,* VI, 82. On the colonial merchants' "detachment from political activity," see Thomas M. Doerflinger, "Philadelphia Merchants and the Logic of Moderation, 1760–1775," *William and Mary Quarterly,* 3d Ser., XL (1983), 212–213; and Edward Countryman, *A People in Revolution: The American Revolution and Political Society in New York, 1760–1790* (Baltimore, 1981), 113.

42. William M. Fowler, Jr., *The Baron of Beacon Hill: A Biography of John Hancock* (Boston, 1980); Charles W. Akers, *The Divine Politician: Samuel Cooper and the American Revolution in Boston* (Boston, 1982), 121, 128, 130, 141, 176, 311; Laurens to Richard Oswald, July 7, 1764, in Philip M. Hamer *et al.,* eds., *The Papers of Henry Laurens* (Columbia, S.C., 1968–), IV, 338 (see also Rachel N. Klein, "Ordering the Backcountry: The South Carolina Regulation," *WMQ,* 3d Ser., XXXVIII [1981], 667); David Duncan Wallace, *The Life of Henry Laurens …* (New York, 1915), 69–70, quotation at 335. In the 1780s Elbridge Gerry likewise retired from mercantile business and "set himself up as a country squire" (Billias, *Gerry,* 135–136).

43. Leonard W Labaree *et al.,* eds., *The Autobiography of Benjamin Franklin* (New Haven, Conn., 1964), 196; Christopher Collier, *Roger Sherman's Connecticut: Yankee Politics and the American Revolution* (Middletown, Conn., 1971), 14, 21–22.

44. Jacob E. Cooke, ed., *The Federalist* (Middletown, Conn., 1961), No. 35; [Barton], *True Interest,* 27. For arguments in pre-Revolutionary Virginia whether lawyers were practicing "a grovelling, mercenary trade" or not, see Roeber, *Faithful Magistrates and Republican Lawyers,* 156–157. Some conceded that lawyers were members of one of the "three genteel Professions," but that they were guilty of more "petit Larceny" than doctors and clergymen. Madison was not convinced of the disinterestedness of lawyers (*ibid.,* 157, 147; Ketcham, *Madison,* 145). On the efforts of some 19th-century thinkers to make professional communities the repositories of disinterestedness against the selfishness and interestedness of businessmen, see Thomas L. Haskell, "Professionalism *versus* Capitalism: R H. Tawney, Emile Durkheim, and C. S. Peirce on the Disinterestedness of Professional Communities," in Thomas L. Haskell, ed., *The Authority of Experts: Studies in History and Theory* (Bloomington, Ind., 1984), 180–225.

45. Morris, "Political Enquiries," in Willi Paul Adams, ed., "'The Spirit of Commerce, Requires that Property Be Sacred': Gouverneur Morris and the American Revolution," *Amerikastudien/American Studies,* XXI (1976), 329; Hamilton to Robert Troup, Apr. 13, 1795, in Harold C. Syrett *et al.,* eds., *The Papers of Alexander Hamilton* (New York, 1961–1979), XVIII, 329.

46. Washington to Benjamin Harrison, Jan. 22, 1785, to George William Fairfax, Feb. 27, 1785, in Fitzpatrick, ed., *Writings of Washington,* XXVIII, 36, 85.

47. Washington to Benjamin Harrison, Jan. 22, 1785, to William Grayson, Jan. 22, 1785, to Lafayette, Feb. 15, 1785, to Jefferson, Feb. 25, 1785, to George William Fairfax, Feb. 27, 1785, to Gov. Patrick Henry, Feb. 27, 1785, to Henry Knox, Feb. 28, 1785, June 18, 1785, to Nathanael Greene, May 20, 1785, in Fitzpatrick, ed., *Writings of Washington,* XXVIII, 36, 37, 72, 80–81, 85, 89–91, 92–93, 167, 146. The only friend whose advice on the disposition of the canal shares Washington did not solicit was Robert Morris, perhaps because he feared that Morris might tell him to keep them. Instead he confined his letter to Morris to describing the commercial opportunities of the canals. To Morris, Feb. 1, 1785, *ibid.,* 48–55.

48. Cooke, ed., *The Federalist,* No. 10; Gordon S. Wood, "Democracy and the Constitution," in Robert A. Goldwin and William A. Schambra, eds., *How Democratic Is the Constitution?* (Washington, D.C., 1980), 11–12. On the tendency to misread Madison, see Robert J. Morgan, "Madison's Theory of Representation in the Tenth Federalist," *Journal of Politics,* XXXVI (1974), 852–885; and Paul F. Bourke, "The Pluralist Reading of James Madison's Tenth *Federalist,*" *Perspectives in American History,* IX (1975), 271–295.

49. Madison to Washington, Apr. 16, 1787, to Edmund Randolph, Apr. 8, 1787, in Hutchinson *et al.,* eds., *Papers of Madison,* IX, 384, 370; John Zvesper, "The Madisonian Systems," *Western Political Quarterly,* XXXVII (1984), 244–247.

50. Jerome J. Nadelhaft, "'The Snarls of Invidious Animals': The Democratization of Revolutionary South Carolina," in Ronald Hoffman and Peter J. Albert, eds., *Sovereign States in an Age of Uncertainty* (Charlottesville, Va., 1981), *77.*

51. On Findley, see his letter to Gov. William Plumer of New Hampshire, Feb. 27, 1812, "William Findley of Westmoreland, Pa.," *PMHB,* V (1881), 440–450; and Russell J. Ferguson, *Early Western Pennsylvania Politics* (Pittsburgh, Pa., 1938), 39–40.

52. Grundfest, *Clymer,* 141.

53. Claude Milton Newlin, *The Life and Writings of Hugh Henry Brackenridge* (Princeton, N.J., 1932), 71.

54. *Ibid.,* 80–81, 78; Ferguson, *Early Western Pennsylvania,* 66–69.

55. Newlin, *Brackenridge,* 79–80, 83–84; Ferguson, *Early Western Pennsylvania,* 70–72.

56. Mathew Carey, ed., *Debates and Proceedings of the General Assembly of Pennsylvania on the Memorials Praying a Repeal or Suspension of the Law Annulling the Charter of the Bank* (Philadelphia, 1786), 19, 64, 10, 30.

57. Morris to Washington, May 29, 1781, E. James Ferguson *et al.,* eds., *The Papers of Robert Morris, 1781–1784* (Pittsburgh, Pa., 1973–), I, 96; Ellis Paxson Oberholtzer, *Robert Morris, Patriot and Financier* (New York, 1903), 52–56, 70–71.

58. Carey, ed., *Debates,* 33, 79–80, 98 (quotations on 80, 98).

59. *Ibid.,* 81; Oberholtzer, *Morris,* 285–286, 297–299, 301–303; Eleanor Young, *Forgotten Patriot: Robert Morris* (New York, 1950), 170; Barbara Ann Chernow, *Robert Morris, Land Speculator, 1790–1801* (New York, 1978); H. E. Scudder, ed., *Recollections of Samuel Breck …* (Philadelphia, 1877), 203; *The Journal of William Maclay* (New York, 1927 [orig. pub. 1890]), 132.

60. Carey, ed., *Debates,* 66, 87, 128, 21, 130, 38, 15, 72–73.

61. Cooke, ed., *The Federalist,* No. 10; [William Findley], *A Review of the Revenue System Adopted at the First Congress under the Federal Constitution …* (Philadelphia, 1794), 117.

62. Jonathan Elliot, ed., *The Debates in the Several State Conventions on the Adoption of the Federal Constitution …* (Philadelphia, 1896), II, 260, 13; [Findley], "Letter by an Officer of the Late Continental Army," *Independent Gazette* (Philadelphia), Nov. 6, 1787, in Storing, ed., *Complete Anti-Federalist,* III, 95; Ruth Bogin, *Abraham Clark and the Quest for Equality in the Revolutionary Era, 1774–1794* ( East Brunswick, N.J., 1982), 32.

63. Philip A. Crowl, "Anti-Federalism in Maryland, 1787–88," *WMQ,* 3d Ser., IV (1947), 464; Richard Walsh, *Charleston's Sons of Liberty: A Study of the Artisans, 1763–1789* (Columbia, S.C., 1959), 132; [James Winthrop], "Letters of Agrippa," *Massachusetts Gazette,* Dec. 14, 1787, in Storing, ed., *Complete Anti-Federalist,* IV, 80; "Essentials of a Free Government," in Walter Hartwell Bennett, ed., *Letters from the Federal Farmer to the Republican* (University, Ala., 1978), 10.

64. Benjamin Latrobe to Philip Mazzei, Dec. 19, 1806, in Margherita Marchione *et al.,* eds., *Philip*

*Mazzei: Selected Writings and Correspondence* (Prato, Italy, 1983), III, 439 (I owe this reference to Stanley J. Idzerda).

65. *Ibid.*

66. James T. Schleifer, *The Making of Tocqueville's "Democracy in America"* (Chapel Hill, N.C., 1980), 242, 243; Tocqueville to Ernest de Chabrol, June 9, 1831, in Roger Boesch, ed., *Alexis de Tocqueville: Selected Letters on Politics and Society* (Berkeley, Calif. 1985), 38; Tocqueville, *Democracy in America*, ed. Phillips Bradley (New York, 1954), I, 243. It was not, of course, as simple as Tocqueville made it out to be. The ideal of disinterested politics did not disappear in the 19th century, and even today it lingers on here and there. It formed the basis for all the antiparty and mugwump reform movements and colored the thinking of many of the Progressives. For Theodore Roosevelt in 1894 "the first requisite in the citizen who wishes to share the work of our public life … is that he shall act disinterestedly and with a sincere purpose to serve the whole commonwealth" (Roosevelt, *American Ideals and Other Essays, Social and Political* [New York, 1897], 34 [I owe this reference to John Patrick Diggins]). Of course, at almost the same time, John Dewey was telling Americans that it was psychologically impossible for anyone to act disinterestedly. See John Patrick Diggins, *The Lost Soul of American Politics: Virtue, Self-interest, and the Foundations of Liberalism* (New York, 1984), 341–343. See also Stephen Miller, *Special Interest Groups in American Politics* (New Brunswick, N.J., 1983).

# 13
# CONSTITUTIONAL RECOGNITION OF A FREE RELIGIOUS MARKET

*Frank Lambert*

## Introduction

Among the most pressing issues in the United States so-called "culture wars" has been the constitutional meaning of the separation of church and state and whether the country was founded as a "Christian nation." It might come as a surprise to the partisans in these battles to find that revolutionary Americans debated these questions too and that they, no less than us, were not of a single opinion. Conspicuously, the Constitution makes no mention of God or Christianity and explicitly prohibits religious tests for office holding. Yet revolutionary Americans attributed different meanings to the first feature, and some of them were mightily offended at the second. Indeed, one of the most common criticisms of the Constitution among Antifederalists who opposed its ratification was that it seemed at best indifferent and at worse hostile to Christianity. Frank Lambert, one of our most prominent historians of religion in early America, sees other forces at work at the Constitutional Convention.

Lambert argues that the framers of the Constitution, whatever their various individual beliefs, avoided religious issues out of fear that they would derail ratification in an America divided into more than a dozen religious denominations. In today's ecumenical environment, few Americans can appreciate just how prejudicial and even hostile revolutionary Americans from different denominations could be toward one other. Even among Protestants, there were sometimes fierce rivalries between Congregationalists, Presbyterians, Baptists, Anglicans, Dutch Reformed Calvinists, Huguenots, Quakers, Moravians, and Lutherans, never mind Catholics and Jews. Religion was not a source of unity. Sensitive to that fact, the framers agreed to avoid the issue of religion altogether.

Most of the framers looked favorably on religion and thus answered religious critics of the Constitution by arguing that they had safeguarded religion from the federal government's interference. Without such interference, there would be a robust religious marketplace. They argued, in short, that religion stood to lose more than gain from a close association of church and state. Their argument ultimately won the day with one important caveat: under pressure from Baptists and Jews alike, the First Federal Congress passed a Bill of Rights guaranteeing that the federal government would not favor one denomination over another, thus preventing the establishment of anything akin to an American Church of England.

- Americans often characterize "the Founders" as a monolithic group. Do you see a consensus among the Constitution's framers on the issue of religion?
- What criticisms did Americans voice over the Constitution's handling of religious matters? Did that criticism tend to come from large denominations which wanted to impose their beliefs on others, small denominations who feared discrimination, or both? What was the range of these criticisms?

- Where did Antifederalist criticisms about the Constitution's ignoring of religion fall into their broader concerns about government power, as discussed in the essay by Saul Cornell?
- To what extent do modern American debates over religion and the founding capture or ignore the complexity of the story as told by Lambert? What does Lambert's account stand to teach us? Be sure to consider what constitutional issues the framers did not address, such as the right of the states, as opposed to the federal government, to erect religious establishments.

When he first read a draft of the proposed new federal constitution in 1787, William Williams of Connecticut was dismayed. Nowhere did the document affirm faith in God. Not only did this New Light merchant call for the omission of the sentence categorically debarring a federally mandated religious test for officeholders; he also wanted a religious test for officeholders that would "require an explicit acknowledgment of the being of a God, his perfections and his providence." Indeed, what Williams desired was a strong affirmation of religious beliefs to introduce the entire document. He proposed a preamble that began: *"We the people of the United States, in a firm belief of the being and perfections of the one living and true God, the creator and supreme Governour of the world, in his universal providence and the authority of his laws; that he will require of all moral agents an account of their conduct; that all rightful powers among men are ordained of and mediately derived from God "*[1] Citizens of a Christian nation, Williams believed, should not allow the historic moment of constitution making to pass without acknowledging their faith in God.

In Williams's opinion, the framers of the Constitution, the Founding Fathers, had betrayed their forebears, especially the Puritan Fathers. Those earlier divines had brought to New England a determination to establish not only a Christian nation but one whose beliefs and practices would so conform to Scripture that future generations would look on it as a "City upon a Hill." The most cursory comparison between the Constitution's preamble and John Winthrop's *Model of Christian Charity* reveals the fundamentally different orientations between the two blueprints. First, the Constitution took its authority from "the People," whereas the *Model* rested on a "special overruling Providence" and the "Churches of Christ." Second, the Constitution pursued secular goals: "to form a more perfect union, establish justice, insure domestic tranquility, provide for the common defense, promote the general welfare, and secure the blessings of liberty to ourselves and our posterity." Winthrop's goals were sacred, his concern less about this world than about preparing for the next. The Puritans of Massachusetts sought to "improve our lives to do more service to the Lord and to comfort and increase the body of Christ of which we are members, so that ourselves and our posterity may be better preserved from the common corruptions of this evil world in order to serve the Lord and work out our salvation under the power and purity of His holy ordinances."

Relations between religious and civil duties were also very different. In the state the Puritan Fathers erected, freemen took an oath as Christians, swearing by "the great and dreadful name of the ever-living God that I will be true and faithful to the same ... . So help me God, in the Lord Jesus Christ." Now, 150 years later, the Constitution fashioned by the Founding Fathers made no mention of God or Christ. And one's religious persuasions had nothing to do with citizenship and officeholding. In its only reference to religion, the Constitution declared that "no religious test shall ever be required as a qualification to any office or public trust under the United States." Moreover, according to Luther Martin, one of the few delegates who favored a religious test, the clause had occasioned little debate or dissension. Indeed, only North Carolina voted against the ban, and Martin's Maryland delegation split on the issue.

The pacific atmosphere in Philadelphia stands in sharp contrast to the rancor that had characterized the debate over religious freedom in Virginia two years earlier. In that historic moment, Baptist and Presbyterian Dissenters fought Episcopalians who insisted on continuing their colonial tradition of an established religion. Recognizing that the state was too pluralistic to make the Episcopal Church the official body, some delegates suggested that Christianity in general be established. Thomas Jefferson described what happened when someone moved to add Christ's name to the law's preamble, so that it would read "a departure from the plan of Jesus Christ, the holy author of our religion." He said that "the insertion was rejected by a great majority, in proof that they meant to comprehend within the mantle of its protection the Jew and the Gentile, the Christian and Mahometan, the Hindoo and infidel of every denomination."[2] Like Virginia's constitution, the United States Constitution created the framework for a secular state open to all persons regardless of religion.

Rather than viewing religion as an integrative force, the Founding Fathers considered it to be divisive, threatening their desire to form a "more perfect union."[3] American society had grown more pluralistic and sectarian from the Great Awakening to the Revolution. As dissenters grew in numbers and confidence, they became bolder in defying authority, in both church and state. Some splintered from existing denominations and went their separate ways. Then, at the state constitutional conventions, they agitated for disestablishment in bitter battles pitting Protestant sects against each other. Religious passions were intense, and they emphasized sectarian differences rather than Christian unity. Indeed, Madison cited "a zeal for different opinions concerning religion" as one of the powerful passions that have "inflamed [men and women] with mutual animosity, and rendered them much more disposed to vex and oppress each other, than co-operate for their common good."[4]

The Founders' solution to the problem of how to keep religion from undermining union was to ignore it. That is, they gave it no place

in the Constitution. They delegated to the federal government no power whatever over religion, leaving matters of faith and practice in the hands of the people and the states. Such separation represented a radical departure from other governments around the world, where the state promoted and defended an official religion. The creation of a secular state resulted from the enlightened conviction of many leading Founders who thought that, by natural right, church and state ought to be separate. But the framers were also practical politicians who, recognizing the growing numbers and influence of dissenters, decided to put contending sectarians on equal footing by giving special status to none.

Just how radical the Founders' religious settlement was became apparent in 1797 when the United States declared emphatically to the world that it was not a "Christian" state. On Monday, June 26, the lead story in the *Boston Price-Current and Marine Intelligencer* was that of the "Treaty With Tripoli," running under the heading "Important State Papers" and prominently located at the head of the first column of the front page. Because many of the paper's subscribers were involved in Boston's shipping industry, which sent vessels to the Mediterranean, any news about that region was of interest, especially matters bearing on the pirates from the Barbary States. Indeed, since losing the protection of the British navy following the American War of Independence, American ships were regularly seized and tribute demanded of their owners. Thus, with more than a little attention, Boston's merchants and investors read the "Treaty of Peace and Friendship Between the United States of America and the Bey and Subjects of Tripoli of Barbary." The second of the twelve articles told the good news: "If any goods belonging to any nation with which either of the parties is at war shall be loaded on board of vessels belonging to the other party they shall pass free, and no attempt shall be made to take or detain them." Article 11, however, told news of a different sort. It contained a pledge from the United States that must have brought up short some readers whose forefathers had planted the "City upon a Hill":

> As the government of the United States of America is not in any sense founded on the Christian Religion, – as it has in itself no character of enmity against the laws, religion or tranquility of Musselinen, – and as the said States never have entered into any war or act of hostility against any Mehomitan nation, it is declared by the parties that no pretext arising from religious opinions ever produce an interruption of the harmony existing between the two countries.[5]

Boldly stated for all Americans and the world to see, "the government of the United States of America is not in any sense founded on the Christian Religion." Moreover, this was no declaration uttered by one of the radical Deists such as Thomas Paine or Ethan Allen who regularly attacked Christianity and its leaders. This was a treaty negotiated by an agent of the federal government, presented by the president of the United States to the Senate, which, after due deliberation, had ratified it with a two-thirds vote. And the government had been at pains to make the treaty known. Philadelphia's *Porcupine Gazette* explained the route that the treaty took in reaching the newspapers: "Now be it known, That I John Adams, President of the United States of America, having seen and considered the said treaty do, by and with the advice and consent of the senate accept, ratify, and confirm the same, and every clause and article thereof. And to the end that the said treaty, may be observed and performed with good faith on the part of the United States, I have ordered it to be made public."[6]

Reprinted and prominently displayed throughout the United States, the treaty, and in particular its remarkable Article 11, elicited almost no public comment. William Cobbett, editor of the *Porcupine,* was an exception. Following the reprint of the treaty, Cobbett editorialized within brackets as follows:

The 11th article of this treaty certainly wants some explanation. That "the government of the United States of America is not in any sense founded on the Christian Religion," is a declaration that one might have expected from Soliman Kaya, Hassan Bashaw, or the sans-cu-lotte Joel Barlow; but it sounds rather oddly from the President and the Senate. If it will admit of satisfactory explanation, it ought to receive it, for it certainly looks a little like trampling upon the cross.[7]

Taken aback, Cobbett first tried to pass the statement off as the creation of the Muslim negotiators or perhaps the insertion of Joel Barlow. Barlow was a republican ally of Thomas Jefferson, and Cobbett viewed him as a Deist at best and a pro-French infidel at worst. But the editor finally acknowledged that Article 11 was no private statement. It came from the "President and the Senate." It was the deliberate product of discussion that allowed ample opportunity for objections and time to remove objectionable clauses. The editor was stunned by the statement's bold and public nature.

Upon close analysis, however, the clause is entirely consistent with the Constitution. Ten years earlier, the delegates to the Constitutional Convention had crafted a secular state, one that established, supported, and defended no religion. Indeed, the end result of the Founding Fathers' deliberations was the acknowledgment that religion was not under government jurisdiction, remaining one of those natural rights that the people retained for themselves. Article 11 of the 1797 treaty affirmed that the *"government* [my emphasis] of the United States of America is not in any sense founded on the Christian Religion." Under the Constitution, church and state were separate. But the Founders differentiated between the state and the nation. The former was the political power that bound the people together, and the latter was their cultural unity, including their common beliefs, aspirations, and principles. By no means did the separation of church and state mean that Americans were not a religious people. Nor did it preclude the possibility that the nation was already or could become a Christian nation; that would be determined by the voluntary decisions of men and women in a free religious market, not by government coercion.

## Religious Factions and the Threat to Union

James Madison has with good reason been called the Father of the Constitution. Introduced in the opening days of the convention, it was his Virginia Plan that provided the framework for debate, and after four months of line-by-line scrutiny and a couple of major compromises, his draft held up. Underlying the diminutive Virginian's plan was his concern that the United States under the Articles of Confederation was weak and therefore subject to internal rebellion and external invasion. Shays's Rebellion in Massachusetts in 1786 fueled fears of the former, while British trade wars against the new republic and the continued presence of British troops in frontier forts fed anxieties about the latter. Like George Washington, Madison believed that as long as states controlled the central government, the country was at the mercy of the special interests that dominated them. As commander of the Continental Army, Washington had seen firsthand the reluctance of some states to supply their share of men and money for the war effort. After the war, states continued to hold the national Congress hostage under the Articles of Confederation, which called for the unanimous consent of all the states for passage of any tax measure. When Rhode Island refused to agree to an excise tax to keep the new republic afloat, the United States faced bankruptcy.

As he contemplated a new and stronger national government, Madison was therefore most concerned about special interests and "factions," among which he numbered the nation's many religious groups. By faction, Madison meant "a majority or minority of the whole, who are united and actuated by some common impulse of passion, or of interest, adverse to the rights of other citizens, or to the permanent and aggregate interests of the community." Along with politics and property, he considered religion to be among the greatest sources of factions. As a participant in Virginia's struggle over the place of religion, Madison had witnessed firsthand the passions religious differences inflamed. And he knew that delegates from other states, such as Massachusetts, had faced similarly emotional battles. Madison knew that factional conflict could not be avoided at Philadelphia; indeed, he believed that factions resulted from human nature and therefore could never be eliminated. People would always divide into contending parties and sects. He concluded, then, that factions must be controlled so that no one interest group could impose its will on all of society, so that an emergent majority could not oppress others.[8] How to do that was the biggest question facing the Founders in Philadelphia during the summer of 1787. How can a society of great diversity and pluralism govern itself so that the public interest is optimally served while the rights and property of private citizens are protected?

At first, Madison thought that the enormous size of the republic made representative government unworkable. Historically, he knew, the republics that worked best were those in small territories where representatives were close to those they represented and shared their interests. Inspired by reading David Hume, Madison eventually concluded that a large area could actually promote republican government by preventing factions from dominating the whole. "Extend the sphere," he wrote in *Federalist* No. 10, "and you take in a greater variety of parties and interests; you make it less probable that a majority of the whole will have a common motive to invade the rights of other citizens."[9] He reasoned that America's factionalism and pluralism were assets in securing liberty. Throughout the whole republic there would be "so many parts, interests and classes of citizens, that the rights of individuals or of the minority, will be in little danger from interested combinations of the majority." He concluded that "in a free government, the security for civil rights must be the same as for religious rights. It consists in the one case in the multiplicity of interests, and in the other, in the multiplicity of sects. The degree of security in both cases will depend on the number of interests and sects; and this may be presumed to depend on the extent of country and number of people comprehended under the same government."[10] Religious pluralism in fact promised religious freedom. Thus Madison, like Adam Smith, realized that with no single religion able to impose its views on the whole, all religious sects must compete in a free marketplace of ideas, therein providing a check against religious tyranny.

Madison's strong convictions against civil and religious tyranny date from his college days. In 1769, he left Virginia, electing to attend the College of New Jersey (later Princeton University), known for its hostility to episcopacy, over the Anglican-controlled College of William and Mary. The year before Madison arrived at Princeton, John Witherspoon had become the college's president, bringing with him a passion for the Enlightenment and a firm opposition to Parliament's oppression of the colonies. Under his leadership, Princeton became more than a college to train Presbyterian ministers. He expanded the curriculum, offering students a much more liberal education with a focus on the arts and sciences. Then, protest against the Stamp Act converted Princeton into a "cradle of liberty." A decade before Madison's arrival, "religion held the dominant place in the minds and hearts of faculty and students," but political protest changed the atmosphere. Groups of undergraduates discussed the "injustice of the Stamp Act … in the refectory, on the campus, and in the chambers of Nassau Hall." Moreover, beginning in the mid-1760s, commencements became occasions "for harangues on patriotism, or debates on the thesis that 'all men are free by the law of nature.'" In September 1765, the assembled graduating class "were attired in cloth

of American manufacture, an act of patriotism which brought forth warm praise from the public and the press."[11] President Witherspoon added his fervor to the Patriot cause when he arrived in 1768.

As a delegate to the Second Continental Congress, John Witherspoon expressed views that James Madison would echo a dozen years later at the Constitutional Convention. Witherspoon was the only minister to sign the Declaration of Independence, in part because he understood that the issue of independence was a political, not a religious, matter. Another Presbyterian minister, John Zubly of Georgia, had preceded him at the Congress. Noting that Zubly was the "first Gentleman of the Cloth who has appeared in Congress," John Adams quickly added that "I can not but wish he may be the last."[12] Zubly wanted to make the question of American independence a theological, not a political, issue. Out of step with his fellow delegates, he wanted the Congress to focus on making America a "Christian" nation rather than an independent state. A staunch Calvinist, he believed that God's grace, not human laws, was of ultimate importance. In fact, he considered it an "extreme absurdity" to struggle for "civil liberty, yet continue slaves to sin and lust." Through his otherworldly preachments, Zubly made himself irrelevant at the Congress; he simply was not a factor in the proceedings. Far more influential was Witherspoon, who, though a Calvinist, understood that the issue before the Congress was that of civil liberty. Furthermore, he knew that civil liberty and religious liberty were connected. "There is not a single instance in history," he noted, "in which civil liberty was lost, and religious liberty preserved entire."[13] Witherspoon and his fellow delegates believed that they, and not Parliament, were the proper guardians of American liberties, civil and religious.

In 1787, Madison brought to Philadelphia a strong conviction as to how religious freedom would best be protected: church and state must be separate. He arrived at that position in part through his understanding of natural rights, in part through the Enlightenment ideas he learned at Princeton, and in part through his role in the struggle for religious liberty in Virginia. In arguing for the adoption of Jefferson's Statute for Religious Freedom (1785), Madison had premised his remarks on the "undeniable truth, 'that religion or the duty which we owe to our Creator and the manner of discharging it, can be directed only by reason and conviction, not by force or violence.'" He therefore opposed on principle any kind of religious establishment, no matter how mild it might be. In an obvious reference to the current political tyranny, he warned "that the same authority which can force a citizen to contribute threepence only of his property for the support of any one establishment may force him to conform to any other establishment in all cases whatsoever." To him, religious establishments were like parliamentary taxes: they were unconstitutional powers imposed on free citizens without consent. He denied that a civil magistrate was a "competent judge of religious truths," and he feared that magistrates would "employ religion as an engine of civil policy." Further, he thought that government support of religion belittled the Christian faith. He reminded his fellow Virginians that for centuries Christianity "both existed and flourished, not only without the support of human laws but in spite of every opposition from them."[14]

In 1785, the same year Madison and Jefferson fought for separation of church and state in Virginia, the issue of religious liberty confronted the national Congress. The question surfaced in the debate over the Land Ordinance, a measure setting forth a system for surveying the land between the Appalachians and the Mississippi River known as the Northwest Territory. A group of Massachusetts land speculators had urged Congress to make federal land available to them at low prices for the purpose of developing the region. Reflecting the sponsors' Puritan backgrounds, the proposed bill contained a provision for federally supported religion in the

territory: "There shall be reserved the Central section of every township for the maintenance of public schools and the [section] immediately to the Northward for the support of religion, the profits arising therefrom in both instances to be applied for ever according to the will of the majority of male residents of full age within the same." The clause for the support of religion touched off in Congress a debate over church and state. Charles Pinckney of South Carolina moved that the paragraph be amended by the deletion of the words "for the support of religion" and the insertion of "for religious and charitable uses." But, wishing to expunge any mention of religion whatever, William Ellery of Rhode Island moved that the lawmakers amend the amendment by striking out the words "religious and," so that it read "for charitable uses." Ellery's motion passed, thereby expressing the principle of separation of church and state for the first time at the federal level.[15]

Locked in Virginia's battle for religious liberty, Madison was delighted to learn about Congress's stand. In a letter to his friend James Monroe, Madison wrote, "It gives me much pleasure to observe by 2 printed reports sent me by Col. Grayson that, in the latter Congress had expunged a clause contained in the first for setting apart a district of land in each Township for supporting the Religion of the majority of inhabitants." He expressed his strong opposition to any government support of religion, even if it were the religion of the majority of citizens: "How a regulation so unjust in itself, foreign to the Authority of Congress, so hurtful to the sale of the public land, and smelling so strongly of an antiquated Bigotry, could have received the countenance of a Committee is truly a matter of astonishment." He concluded with the hope that the ringing victory of separation of church and state at the federal level would influence lawmakers in Virginia to embrace the same principle to guarantee religious freedom in the state.[16]

Thus when the Constitutional Convention convened on May 14, 1787, James Madison was well prepared to take the lead in proposing a totally new framework for government. Like George Washington, Madison had been an outspoken critic of the Articles of Confederation, which rendered the country weak by granting sovereignty to thirteen jealous states that were often more concerned about local than about national interests. In Madison's view, the states, controlled by powerful interest groups, were not the best guardians of civil and religious freedom. Determined to transfer power from the states to the federal government, he brought with him a plan designed to protect individual liberty by dividing power.

## The "Godless" Constitution[17]

In designing a frame of government, the delegates to the Constitutional Convention in Philadelphia appealed primarily to secular, not sacred, authority. An analysis of citations in American political pamphlets and treatises in the late eighteenth century indicates that almost 90 percent of the references are to European writers who wrote on Enlightenment or Whig themes or who commented on the English common law. Only about 10 percent of the citations were biblical, with most of those coming from writings attributed to Saint Paul. Framers of the United States Constitution were steeped in political theory and history, and they had seen firsthand how unchecked power undermined freedom. Because of the abuse of constitutional power by the king and Parliament, Americans sought to preclude future tyranny by making a "fixed Constitution" the supreme law against which no civil or religious authority could transgress. The task for American lawmakers was one of law, not theology, and raised two fundamental questions: "First, what shall the form of government be? And Secondly, What shall be its power?"[18]

Unlike the Puritan Fathers, the Founding Fathers gave Christianity no privileged place of authority in their deliberations regarding a frame of government. While religion offered insights into the means and ends of human fulfillment,

no single sect possessed exclusive insights. "All sober inquirers after truth," wrote John Adams in 1776, "ancient and modern, pagan and Christian, have declared that the happiness of man, as well as his dignity consists in virtue. Confucius, Zoroaster, Socrates, Mahomet, not to mention authorities really sacred, have agreed in this." But when considering how government should be structured to provide for the greatest human happiness, Adams appealed not to truths lodged in various documents claiming divine revelation but to "the minds of people." For principles of republican government, he recommended not Jesus, Saint Paul, Augustine, Luther, Calvin, Wesley, the Mathers, or Edwards, but "Sidney, Harrington, Locke, Milton, Nedham, Neville, Burnet, and Hoadly."[19]

Though relying on secular authorities to structure the Constitution, many of the Founders did believe that religion, particularly Protestant Christianity, was essential for a law-abiding nation. During the Revolution, Whig spokesmen frequently linked Christianity and citizenship. In a typical sermon, the congressional chaplain Jacob Duche reminded the legislators that American freedom rested on twin foundations: "the charter of TEMPORAL FREEDOM, and the records of ETERNAL TRUTH." One could not separate the civil from the religious liberty of a people where the "banners of CHRISTIAN and BRITISH Liberty were at once unfolded." In a 1776 review of the colonists' "present calamities," Duche blamed Britain, whose "merciless and unhallowed hands" had choked her colonists, but he also reminded his constituents that the "present chastisements have … been drawn down upon us by a gross neglect of our SPIRITUAL PRIVILEGES." The only solution was "the revival of every private and public virtue, which can adorn and dignify the citizen and the christian."[20]

Delegates to the Constitutional Convention were concerned primarily with "temporal freedom" – specifically, the problem of how to allocate and restrain power in a way that best assured liberty. The pursuit of "eternal truth" they left to individuals and churches. The delegates wrestled with mundane but important questions, like that of sovereignty, or whether the states or the national government should have ultimate authority. In the end they decided on a strong central government organized on federalist principles whereby sovereignty was split between the national and state governments. Delegates also debated the vexing issue of representation, determining that for the House of Representatives "the people" should elect their own representatives, the number to be proportionate to each state's population, and in the Senate the states should have equal representation. And they argued over which powers should be assigned to each branch of the federal government, and which powers should remain with the states. During four months of deliberation, those big structural and functional issues concerning the distribution and balance of power predominated. Within the context of those broader discussions, religion rarely surfaced. As historian John Murrin concluded, while the delegates were not antireligion, they were humanists determined to create a secular state based on sound constitutional principles, such as the separation of powers and "checks and balances," designed to provide a republicanism that optimally protected citizens' property and rights.[21]

The delegates knew that social concord in a republic depended on a virtuous citizenry, but the question was how to ensure public virtue. The Puritan Fathers had believed that God through divine Election produced men who could be trusted with the franchise and officeholding. Leaders of the Great Awakening had agreed, emphasizing the necessity of a spiritual conversion to transform willful, selfish people into obedient servants of God and man. Though many delegates expressed their belief that religious instruction promotes morality and thus good citizenship, few had faith that religion alone would produce virtuous citizens. Ancient and recent history testified to the fact that religious people sometimes engaged in irreligious behavior. And with so many different

sects in America insisting that they represented the one true religion, no delegate proposed establishing any one of them as the nation's official religion. Followers of the Enlightenment thought that the ideal social order was one where reason prevailed and rational men discerned and obeyed the "laws of nature and nature's God." The problem was that too many Americans allowed tradition and superstition, rather than informed reason, to guide them. Some followers of the Scottish Enlightenment, like Jefferson, believed that all people possessed a "moral sense," an inner compass that could be relied upon for virtuous behavior.

In the end, the delegates agreed with Madison that men and women could not be relied upon to act always as virtuous citizens. But they could be relied upon to act out of self-interest, and the great diversity of competing interests presented a fair prospect of preventing any one interest from oppressing the others. By framing a constitution that divided power and checked its abuse, self-interested people could pursue their own ends without turning the republic into an engine of tyranny. Rather than relying upon virtuous people to pursue the common weal, the delegates hoped that they could construct a constitution that would promote virtue.

Though religion was not at the center of the delegates' deliberations, it nevertheless had to be considered. Like their counterparts at the various state constitutional conventions, the men who gathered in Philadelphia faced two issues regarding religion. First, they had to define church-state relations as they pertained to the federal government. They could follow Massachusetts's model, establishing religion in the sense of insisting that every person must have the benefit of religious instruction by a "Protestant" minister, appointed and remunerated by the government if the people in a specific location did not undertake this responsibility. Such an arrangement would ensure that all citizens received public religious and moral instruction deemed by many to be the cornerstone of a peaceful, law-abiding society. And they could protect the rights of dissenters by guaranteeing the free exercise of religion according to the dictates of each person's conscience. The delegates to the federal convention knew however, that the Massachusetts religious clause had touched off heated controversy in that state. As dissenters in Massachusetts pointed out, the state constitution imposed a narrow establishment whereby the Congregational churches were deemed to be the orthodox and privileged churches and all others were subject to government restrictions.

If delegates to the Philadelphia convention opposed such a narrow establishment, they could have adopted the more expansive provision in the South Carolina Constitution. After much wrangling over whether a single denomination should be preferred above all others, the South Carolina delegates affirmed that "the Christian Protestant religion shall be deemed, and is hereby constituted and declared to be, the established religion of this State." They then defined a set of beliefs that any religious group must subscribe to in order to be "incorporated and esteemed as a church of the established religion of this State":

> 1st. That there is one eternal God, and a future state of rewards and punishments.
> 2nd. That God is publicly to be worshipped.
> 3nd. That the Christian religion is the true religion.
> 4th. That the holy scriptures of the Old and New Testaments are of divine inspiration, and are the rule of faith and practice.
> 5th. That it is lawful and the duty of every man being thereunto called by those that govern, to bear witness to the truth.[22]

The delegates at Philadelphia in fact chose, or at least endorsed, the Virginia model of a free marketplace of religion, refusing to grant any power whatever to the federal government concerning religion, thereby leaving religion as a voluntary pursuit of individuals and their churches. While some embraced the view out of conviction, the prevailing sentiment was a desire to avoid dissension that would undermine union. To these delegates, religion was a divisive, not a unifying, force in pluralistic America. Any hope of obtaining ratification would be dashed if the new constitution attempted to define or support religion, because one or more sects would construe any formulation as violating their freedom of conscience. Better to make no mention of religion at all. Thus the enumerated powers of the federal government set out in the Constitution omitted any discussion of religion. During the ratification debates, many people in fact feared that the Constitution's silence on religion opened the door for the federal government at some future point to establish religion or otherwise interfere in its free exercise. But as Madison argued, that was not the case. The Constitution delegated specific powers to the federal government, prohibiting all others, including that of religious establishment.[23]

The second issue the delegates faced with regard to religion was that of a religious test for officeholders.[24] Again, the state constitutions offered several models. The idea behind a religious test was that government officials ought to be men of high moral stature, and that sound religion – namely, Protestant Christianity – was the foundation of that morality. The Massachusetts Constitution required the governor and legislators to swear that they believed the "Christian religion, and have a firm persuasion of its truth." Maryland officeholders were required to make "a declaration of a belief in the Christian religion." The New Hampshire Constitution declared that "no person shall be capable of being elected a senator, who is not of the protestant religion." Delaware's oath of office was even more restrictive, reading like a Christian creed: "I, ..., do profess faith in God the Father, and in Jesus Christ His only Son, and in the Holy Ghost, one God, blessed for evermore; and I do acknowledge the holy scriptures of the Old and New Testament to be given by divine inspiration." Similarly, North Carolina's constitution held "That no person, who shall deny the being of God or the truth of the Protestant religion, or the divine authority of either of the Old or New Testaments, or who shall hold religious principles incompatible with the freedom and safety of the State, shall be capable of holding any office or place of trust or profit in the civil department within this State."[25] In light of diverse formulations, the delegates at Philadelphia were well aware of the many distinctions Americans made regarding religious faith and the potential that religious questions posed for contentious debate.

On Tuesday, May 29, 1787, the Constitutional Convention began its substantive work by hearing two proposed drafts of constitutions that would replace the Articles of Confederation. Edmund Randolph of Virginia introduced Madison's Virginia Plan, which was heard and referred to the Committee of the Whole House for consideration of its specific provisions. That draft was silent on religious matters, reflecting Madison's views of religion's place in society. He contended that government is a compact between the governed and their governors, and that the former retain all rights that they do not explicitly grant to the latter. He considered religion to be a natural right that the governed did not cede to the government; it remained secure with the people themselves. Delegates would not have been surprised at the silence, because the Articles of Confederation were also mute on the subject. Charles Cotesworth Pinckney of South Carolina also offered a proposed constitution that day similar in structure to the Virginia Plan, but his was explicit in prohibiting the federal government from having any positive role concerning religious matters, stating, "The legislature of the United States shall pass no law on the subject of religion."[26] At least on this point the delegates in Philadelphia apparently agreed. There is no record of any delegate's proposing a positive role for government in supporting religion.

The only mention of religion at all was in the negative, the prohibition against religious tests. On August 20, Pinckney proposed that "no religious test or qualification shall ever be annexed to any oath of office under the authority of the U.S." Ten days later the measure was brought before the convention for debate and a vote. Madison's notes suggest that the debate was limited. Roger Sherman of Connecticut thought that the proscription was unnecessary, with "the prevailing liberality being a sufficient security agst such tests." A majority of his fellow delegates had less faith than he that such liberality could be counted on in succeeding decades, and voted to include the clause. Only North Carolina opposed.[27]

Several possibilities explain the exclusion of positive language regarding religion. First, the delegates could have subscribed to the view that religion was beyond the purview of government because it was a natural right, the Madisonian position. Second, others could have placed it outside the state's jurisdiction by viewing religion as a spiritual matter whose authority rests with God and not with man at all. Third, some no doubt considered religion to be under state, not federal, control. This meant that if the people in any given state desired some sort of religious establishment, they were free to secure it within their own constitution. Fourth, some were confident that the establishment of Christianity was unnecessary because most Americans were Christians, and Christianity, by virtue of its own perceived superiority, would always prevail in the marketplace of ideas. Many, Deists as well as Christians, expressed confidence that "true religion" needed no coercive support from the government and would emerge victorious because of the force of its tenets. A final explanation for the absence of any federal government role in supporting religion was the pluralistic nature of religion in America. Scores of sects existed in the new republic, each claiming that its teachings and practices represented "true" Christianity. To many of these competing groups, any establishment, no matter how broadly conceived, was offensive. They were unwilling for any government, comprising unholy as well as holy men, to make any binding statements regarding religion. Given these reasons against the inclusion of a positive statement regarding religion, the delegates, more interested in union than uniformity, took the path least likely to offend any sect or church and said nothing at all.

The Founders' religious settlement thus stood in sharp contrast to the Elizabethan Settlement, which had since the sixteenth century maintained a "national church under royal and parliamentary authority." Instead of a national state church like the Church of England, wherein all English inhabitants were regarded as being members, America would have voluntary churches gathered by individuals subscribing to similar beliefs and practices and joined by those who shared those views. And while the Church of England received "financial support, the right to hold ecclesiastical courts, and political privileges secured by the Test and Corporation Acts," American churches would receive only the right to worship freely and to use all legal means of persuasion to maintain themselves and woo new members.[28]

On Monday, September 17, the delegates completed their work. Benjamin Franklin, who had said little during the deliberations, rose with a speech endorsing the Constitution. He acknowledged that there were parts of the draft that he did not approve, but that he consented because "I expect no better, and because I am not sure, that it is not the best." Franklin warned against the delegates' insisting on a constitution that conformed in every part to their own individual preferences and biases. In seeking compromise and agreement, he turned to religion for an instructive analogy.

> Most men indeed as well as most sects in Religion, think themselves in possession of all truth, and that wherever others differ from them it is so far error. Steele a Protestant in a Dedication tells the Pope, that the only difference between our Churches in their opinions of the certainty of their doctrines is, the Church of Rome is infallible and the Church of England is never in the wrong. But though many private persons think almost as highly of their own infallibility as of that of their sect, few express it so naturally as a certain french lady, who in a dispute with her sister, said "I don't know how it happens, Sister, but I meet with no body but myself, that's always in the right."[29]

Franklin no doubt anticipated the heated debates that would rage in the various state ratifying conventions as individuals and groups tore the Constitution apart. He certainly knew that people would view the document through lenses tinted by self-interest as well as high principle. Indeed, every aspect came under intense scrutiny, including the Constitution's silence on religion and its ban on religious tests.

## Ratification Contingent Upon Religious Freedom

The debate over church-state questions begun by the delegates to the Constitutional Convention reached the states even before the document proposed for ratification did. Those voicing concerns fell into two categories. Some hoped that the federal Constitution would reflect the faith of the Puritan Fathers. That meant some level of government support for the Christian religion and the assurance that only Christians would hold offices in the new government. Others, including the Constitution's principal architects, envisioned a secular state built on Enlightenment and Whig principles. They feared that a powerful, unchecked federal government would do as monarchies had done through the centuries: establish an official religion for political purposes, one that could become powerful enough to demand special governmental favor and so threaten liberty of conscience.

Once the Constitution became public, its silence on religion became a matter of public debate. An Anti-Federalist, the designation by which Madison and others referred to those who opposed the Constitution, warned in a Boston newspaper on January 10, 1788, that because God was absent from the Constitution, Americans would suffer the fate that the prophet Samuel foretold to Saul: "because thou hast rejected the word of the Lord, he hath also rejected thee."[30] Another letter-writer argued that civic virtue depended upon governmental encouragement of the Christian faith. He compared Massachusetts's constitutional provision requiring public officials to be Protestants with the federal Constitution's "public inattention" to religion and found the latter flawed. He charged the framers with "leaving religion to shift wholly for itself," and he predicted that the new nation was headed toward disaster, for "it is more difficult to build an elegant house without tools to work with, than it is to establish a durable government without the publick protection of religion."[31] A delegate to the Massachusetts ratifying convention, Amos Singletary, voiced his objection to the absence of a religious test. Upset that the Constitution did not require men in power to be religious, he noted that "though he hoped to see Christians [in office], yet by the Constitution, a papist, or an infidel was as eligible as they."[32] All of these protesters proceeded from the same assumption: America was a Christian nation and its constitution must reflect that fact by supporting the "true faith."

No one voiced that position more eloquently than did Ezra Stiles, the president of Yale, who from the beginning of the Revolution envisioned the United States as "God's American Israel." Stiles, like John Adams and others, believed that the American Revolution was as much about religion as it was about politics. Indeed, he thought that the new republic's unprecedented religious freedom would become a model for all nations, inspiring other countries to rid themselves of persecution. Writing in 1783, Stiles looked back to his Puritan Fathers and hailed John Winthrop as an "American Nehemiah" who had established the importance of founding a society on the principles of "true religion."[33] As Winthrop had deemed Massachusetts a "City upon a Hill,"

a beacon for future generations, Stiles saw the United States as a land of the "most ample *religious liberty,*" which, he ventured, "will also be the basis for making America a new Israel." He acknowledged that the new republic started with natural advantages, especially its vast stretches of productive land and a growing population. But, he warned, those assets alone were insufficient to guarantee happiness. He claimed that "our system of dominion and CIVIL POLITY would be imperfect, without the TRUE RELIGION." Indeed, Stiles argued, "Holiness ought to be the end of all civil government." But "true religion" and "holiness" must come from the people; they cannot be imposed by any government. Of all polities, he favored the one he considered to be best suited to the "nature of man" and that which withstood the "comparison of ages": a "well-ordered DEMOCRATICAL ARISTOCRACY standing upon the annual elections of the people, … revocable at pleasure." Predicting that that polity would "approve itself the most equitable, liberal, and perfect," Stiles argued that the acid test of its liberality would be in how it handled religious differences.[34] European countries had long histories of religious oppression whereby the monarch or ruling oligarchy favored one religion in order to secure the political support of its adherents. Stiles envisioned a very different America, a Christian nation that guaranteed religious freedom for all.

In the republic Stiles envisioned, no religious group would be excluded, nor would one body be favored over another. Rather, "the united states will embosom all the religious sects or denominations in Christendom. Here they may all enjoy their whole respective systems of worship and church government, complete." Further, he added, "all religious denominations will be independent of one another … , and having, on account of religion, no superiority as to secular powers and civil immunities, they will cohabit together in harmony." The absence of a state religion would create an atmosphere for a "candid and liberal disquisition" of religious ideas and issues that Stiles maintained would set

America apart from all other nations. "Removed from the embarrassment of corrupt systems, and the dignities and blinding obedience connected with them," he explained, "the unfettered mind can think with a noble enlargement, and with an unbounded freedom, go wherever the light of truth directs." Unlike in other nations, "here will be no bloody tribunals, no cardinals inquisitors-general, to bend the human mind, foreceably to control the understanding, and put out the light of reason, the candle of the Lord, in man; ... Religion may here receive its last, most liberal, and impartial examination."[35]

An unfettered search for the truth, Stiles believed, would demonstrate that Protestant Christianity was the "true religion." Moreover, he foresaw the day when the United States was "increased to 40 or 50 millions": then, "while we see all the religious sects increased into respectable bodies, we shall doubtless find the united body of the *congregational* and *consociateci* and *presbyterian* churches, making an equal figure with any of them." By that prediction he meant that denominations with hierarchical structures – such as the Church of England – which had done well during the colonial period, would not fare as well after the War of Independence. Stiles was also projecting his New England bias and expressing his hope that the rest of the American religious landscape would soon look like that in the northernmost states. While admitting that there had been imperfections and controversies, nonetheless, in his mind, New Englanders had indeed created a spiritual "City upon a Hill" that the new republic should view as a model.[36]

As Stiles contemplated what kind of nation the United States might become, he thought it would be well served if led by men like the Founding Fathers of Puritan New England. In his mind, they had returned Christianity to its primitive, unadulterated form, without the "mutilated artificial forms of the pontifical or patriarchal constitutions, of the middle and present ages." He had little hope that such leaders would emerge from the present generation, which he characterized as "the present period of

deism and sceptical indifferentism in religion, of timidity and irresolution in the cause of the great *Emmanuel*." But perhaps in the future "there may arise a succession of civil magistrates, who will not be ashamed of the cross of Christ, nor of patronizing his holy religion." In that day, Stiles, exclaimed, "the *religious* as well as the *civil* patriot will shine in the faces of the future *Moses's* and *Joshuas* of the land."[37]

Stiles summed up his review of idolatry, Deism, and Christianity by asking which would "most contribute to the secular welfare," and which would be "most subservient to eternity and its momentous concerns."

He then guaranteed the right response by asking, "Which of these empires would be the favorite of Jesus? Or is he indeed an unconcerned spectator of human affairs? If not, why should we doubt or hesitate to give the preference to the *christian republic*?"

While Stiles wished the Founders had constructed a *"christian republic,"* other Christians applauded their work.[38] While they agreed with Stiles on the superiority of Christianity to all other religions, they disagreed with his belief that the new republic would be best served by its being framed on the Massachusetts model. Dissenters, a broad category that included all American Christians who did not subscribe to an established religion, believed that Stiles's representation of Massachusetts's church-state relations was grossly distorted. Isaac Backus, a delegate to the Massachusetts ratifying convention, expressed the sentiments of Dissenters everywhere when he rose to defend the framers' exclusion of religious tests:

> Many appear to be much concerned about it; but nothing is more evident, both in reason and the Holy Scriptures, than that religion is ever a matter between God and individuals; and, therefore, no man or men can impose any *religious test,* without invading the essential prerogatives of our God Jesus Christ. Ministers first assumed this power under the Christian name;

and then Constantine approved of the practice, when he adopted the profession of Christianity, as an engine of state policy. And let the history of all nations be searched from that day to this, and it will appear that the imposing of *religious tests* hath been the: greatest engine of tyranny in the world. And I rejoice to see so many gentlemen, who are now giving in their rights of conscience in this great and important matter. Some serious minds discover a concern lest, if all *religious tests* should be excluded, the Congress would hereafter establish Popery, or some other tyrannical way of worship. But it is most certain that no such way of worship can he established without any *religious test*.[39]

Supporters of a constitutional religious test raised the specter of all sorts of undesirables being elected to the highest offices. Some couched their objections in general terms. Patrick Calhoun told his fellow delegates to the South Carolina convention that "too great latitude [was] allowed in religion."[40] Others were more specific. Reverend David Caldwell of North Carolina feared that the open "invitation to Jews and pagans" carried political as well as religious dangers. In supporting Caldwell's position, a like-minded delegate expanded the list of undesirables. The failure to exclude non-Christians, which he defined more narrowly as non-Protestant Christians, meant that it "is most certain, that Papists may occupy that chair [i.e., the presidency], and Mahometans may take it."[41]

One pamphleteer attempted to allay such concerns by expressing his confidence that voters would impose their own tests and consequently never elect persons other than Christians. Samuel Langdon, pastor at Hampton Falls, New Hampshire, called on his readers to select for their officials "men who fear God, and hate covetousness; who love truth and righteousness." He claimed that only men who fear God could rule well. Moreover, "will not the example of their impiety and immorality

defeat the efficacy of the best laws which can be made in favour of religion and virtue?" Langdon warned voters against being seduced by sectarians, saying, "regard not men who are continually crying up their own sect, and employing their utmost zeal and art to proselyte men to their party: they aim to strengthen themselves by your numbers and purses, more than to save your souls." He also warned against "imbibing the licentious principles of men who affect to render all religion doubtful, by persuading you that every kind of religion is equally acceptable to God if a man is but sincere in it."[42] Langdon urged citizens to impose their own religious test on officeholders and select only those whose beliefs and practices met the electors' standards.

While some expressed support for religious tests, many others voiced concern over the lack of a Bill of Rights that would safeguard the individual's rights of conscience from federal government coercion. It became apparent in some of the largest states' conventions, including those of Massachusetts and Virginia, that the Constitution would not be ratified without amendments guaranteeing certain rights. Religious freedom was one of the rights that delegates were uneasy about, fearing that the Constitution's silence on religion was insufficient protection against government "mischief' in religious affairs. Dissenters in particular were concerned that future governments might establish an official religion and thereby interfere with the free exercise of religion according to one's conscience. Accordingly, delegates drafted bills of rights, or lists of expressed rights that individuals held without interference from the federal government. The Virginia convention approved the following amendment regarding religion:

> That religion, or the duty which we owe to our Creator, and the manner of discharging it, can be directed only by reason and conviction, not by force or violence; and therefore all men have an equal, natural,

and unalienable right to the free exercise of religion, according to the dictates of conscience, and that no particular religious sect or society ought to be forced or established, by law, in preference to others.[43]

James Madison opposed the measure because he feared that any constitutional or legislative attempt to define religious freedom would result in narrowing its scope. In a letter to Jefferson, who was in Paris as minister to France, Madison expressed his concern: "I am sure that the rights of conscience in particular, if submitted to public definition would be narrowed much more than they are ever to be by an assumed power." As an example, he noted that New Englanders opposed the Constitution's prohibition of religious tests because it "opened a door for Jews Turks and infidels."[44] Liberty of conscience was a natural right that all should enjoy, not a grant of positive law.

Madison was a practical politician, and he recognized that to win ratification, he must support a Bill of Rights. Therefore, he pledged his support in getting the amendments passed in the first Congress. While Madison may have been satisfied with the absence of an explicit guarantee of religious liberty, dissenters were not. Several groups appealed to George Washington, already regarded as father of his country and protector of citizen rights.[45]

In May 1789, the General Assembly of Presbyterian Churches sought assurance from Washington that their religious rights would be honored. In his reply, Washington first reiterated his belief that the pious practice of sound religion was essential to good citizenship. He opined that "the general prevalence of piety, philanthropy, honesty, industry, and oeconomy seems, in the ordinary course of human affairs, particularly necessary for advancing and conforming the happiness of our country." He expressed his hope that civic responsibility would accompany religious freedom in the new republic. "While all men within our territories are protected in worshipping the Deity according to the dictates

of their consciences," he wrote, "it is rationally to be expected from them in return, that they will be emulous of evincing the sanctity of their professions by the innocence of their lives and the beneficence of their actions; for no man, who is profligate in his morals, or a bad member of the civil community can possibly be a true Christian, or a credit to his own religious society." He concluded by asserting that churches, though separated from government, played an important role in promoting republican virtue. He asked the Presbyterians to accept his gratitude for their "laudable endeavors to render men sober, honest, and good Citizens, and the obedient subjects of a lawful government."[46] In short, churches were to provide the moral foundation necessary for good government.

Virginia Baptists expressed to Washington their lingering concern that without an explicit prohibition against religious establishment in a Bill of Rights, the government could erect and maintain an official church, thereby undermining religious liberty. He replied that he was convinced that the Constitution, even without a Bill of Rights, barred any religious establishment. He explained, "if I could have entertained the slightest apprehension that the Constitution framed in the Convention, where I had the honor to preside, might possibly endanger the religious rights of any ecclesiastical society, certainly I would never have placed my signature to it." He added that "if I could now conceive that the general government might ever be so administered as to render the liberty of conscience insecure, I beg you will be persuaded that no one would be more zealous than myself to establish effectual barriers against the horrors of spiritual tyranny and every species of religious persecution." He repeated his oft-stated sentiment "that every man, conducting himself as a good citizen, and being accountable to God alone for his religious opinions, ought to be protected in worshipping the Deity according to the dictates of his own conscience."[47] He extended that same idea to Catholics, wishing them "every temporal and spiritual felicity" in a liberal republic where all "are equally entitled to the protection of civil government."[48]

In addition to Christians, Jews viewed Washington as a champion of freedom, and they, too, sought his assurances that all people, non-Christians as well as Christians, would enjoy complete religious freedom. He responded by declaring America's revolution in religion to be an example for the rest of the world. "The citizens of the United States of America," he wrote, "have a right to applaud themselves for having given to mankind examples of an enlarged and liberal policy – a policy worthy of imitation. All possess alike liberty of conscience and immunities of citizenship." He made clear that religious liberty in the United States was not mere toleration; the government simply had no positive role in religion. In a commentary on what the Founders had done in Philadelphia, Washington declared, "It is now no more that toleration is spoken of as if it were the indulgence of one class of people that another enjoyed the exercise of their inherent natural rights, for, happily, the Government of the United States, which gives to bigotry no sanction, to persecution no assistance, requires only that they who live under its protection should demean themselves as good citizens in giving it on all occasions their effectual support."[49]

True to his word, Madison provided leadership in the passage of a Bill of Rights. In a speech to the House of Representatives on June 8, 1789, Madison enunciated the amendments that he would like to see made to the Constitution. Rather than grouping them as a Bill of Rights, he advocated incorporating the changes within the text of the main body. Regarding the place of religion in the republic, he made two proposals. First, he recommended the insertion of the following clause in Article 1, section 9, which prohibited specific measures that Congress could pass:

> The civil rights of none shall be abridged on account of religious belief or worship, nor shall any national religion be established, nor shall the full and equal rights of conscience be in any manner, or on any pretext infringed.

In his analysis of the text, Chief Justice William Rehnquist attempts to draw Madison into the accommodationist interpretation. First, he views Madison as preeminent in defining church-state relations, not Jefferson, whose metaphor of a "wall" separating church and state lies at the center of the separationist perspective. "On the basis of the record of these proceedings in the House of Representatives," Rehnquist wrote in *Wallace v. Jaffree,* "James Madison was undoubtedly the most important architect among the Members of the House of the Amendments which became the Bill of Rights." But, he adds, "it was James Madison speaking as an advocate of sensible legislative compromise, not as an advocate of incorporating the Virginia Statute for Religious Freedom into the U.S. Constitution."[50] Rehnquist fails to note, however, that Madison also proposed language that would, in fact, prohibit the states from interfering with individuals' rights of free exercise. Madison's preference was indeed to extend Virginia's guarantee of complete religious freedom to all states, including those in New England that continued to restrict dissenters' rights. He therefore proposed inserting the following clause in Article 1, Section 10, which placed certain prohibitions on the states:

> No state shall violate the equal rights of conscience, or the freedom of the press, or the trial by jury in criminal cases.[51]

Had they been passed, Madison's measures would have banned religious regulation by any government act – state or federal.

After considerable debate, the House rejected Madison's format and his proposals. On August 24, 1789, the representatives passed a series of constitutional amendments that would stand as a Bill of Rights as opposed to being incorporated into the Constitution's body. The third article dealt with religion, and stated that:

Congress shall make no law establishing religion or prohibiting the free exercise thereof, nor shall the rights of Conscience be infringed.[52]

Though a categorical prohibition against religious establishment by the federal government, the wording was silent regarding the states. The Senate debated the House proposal and proposed a change in the wording. The senators sent the following version to the House:

Congress shall make no laws establishing articles of faith, or a mode of worship, or prohibiting the free exercise of religion.[53]

A narrow reading of the first two clauses could give Congress some role in establishing religion. As one historian has noted, there was the suggestion that "Congress was barred only from enacting laws supporting particular points of doctrine (for example, belief in the Holy Trinity or the divinity of Jesus or the reality of transubstantiation) or requiring certain forms of worship. Legislation supporting (or establishing) religion in other ways would presumably be acceptable." In the conference committee appointed to resolve differences between the House and Senate versions, Madison succeeded in reinstating language that "flatly commanded Congress to 'make no law respecting an establishment of religion.'"[54]

Religious freedom resulted from an alliance of unlikely partners. New Light evangelicals such as Isaac Backus and John Leland joined forces with Deists and skeptics such as James Madison and Thomas Jefferson to fight for a complete separation of church and state. Influenced by the Great Awakening, the former believed that individuals were free to make religious choices among competing claims to truth. God alone was governor of the conscience, and only he could judge the choices individuals made. Moreover, they believed that Christianity had stood on its own without government assistance in the past and would do so in the future. Indeed,

they pointed to the historical evils resulting from a union of church and state. The latter argued from Whig and Enlightenment principles but came to the same end. They held that reason, not force, should determine religious beliefs and practices. And they thought that religion was a voluntary matter and should be sustained by voluntary means.

For Madison and his supporters, the Constitution's guarantee of religious freedom represented a triumph of the spirit of 1776. The Declaration of Independence had upheld the great principles of natural and "unalienable" rights, and the Founders numbered religion among those. In 1787, they explicitly barred the federal government from violating that sacred freedom. The Constitution also reflected Adam Smith's notions that religion should operate within a free marketplace of ideas, notions set forth in his *Wealth of Nations*, published in 1776. The idea was that if left free to operate without governmental establishment or restraint, numerous competing sects would be placed on an equal footing such that they could woo followers on the strength of their respective beliefs and practices. The Founders, then, crafted a constitutional solution that gave the fullest expression to the expansive dreams of freedom set form in 1776. America would have a secular state wherein all persons would be free to pursue their religious preferences in open competition.

Both Jefferson and Madison lived long enough to observe how well the Founders' religious settlement worked in practice. Adhering to the Constitution's proscription of an establishment, Jefferson instituted a competitive religious marketplace at the University of Virginia. He rejected the traditional practice of appointing a professor of divinity from a particular church, yet he believed that religious instruction was an important part of a young person's education and vital to the nation's good order. His solution was to open the campus to all sects, thereby offering the students choice. In 1822, he and the Board of Visitors encouraged "the different religious sects to establish, each for itself a professorship of their own tenets, on the confines of the university, so near as that their students may attend the lectures there." He expressed his confidence that the plan would promote "peace, reason, and morality."[55]

Throughout their deliberations, the Founders indicated that they were thinking about future generations. They acknowledged that their generation was a particularly liberal one, meaning that it was attuned to the dangers of any form of tyranny including that of a majority. But they knew that if proper constitutional safeguards were not in place, an imaginable political tyrant of the future could make a play for power by giving a popular religious group a position of favor in the eyes of the state. They also knew that without the separation of church and state, religious leaders would do as they had in the past and try to promise political support to the regime that would grant them privileges. They could not have foreseen, however, that the very first time candidates of opposing parties vied for the presidency, the combustible question of religion and politics would once again be kindled.

## Notes

1. Kurland and Lerner, *The Founders' Constitution*, 4:643.
2. Thomas Jefferson, *Autobiography*, in *The Writings of Thomas Jefferson*, ed., Andrew Lipscomb, 20 vols. (Washington, D.C., 1905), 1:67.
3. Wood, *Radicalism of the American Revolution*, 329–331, 443.
4. Madison made his remarks in *Federalist* No. 10. See Jacob Cooke, ed., *The Federalist* (Middletown, Conn., 1961), 56–65.
5. *The Boston Price-Current and Marine Intelligencer,* June 26, 1797.
6. *Porcupine* Gazette, June 23, 1797.
7. Ibid., 351–352.
8. Cooke, *The Federalist*, 56–65 and 347–353.
9. Ibid., 64.
10. Ibid., 351–352.
11. Thomas J. Wertenbaker, *Princeton, 1746–1890* (Princeton, 1946), 55–56.
12. Cited in Jim Schmidt, "The Reverend John Joachim Zubly's 'The Law of Liberty' Sermon:

13. Cited in ibid., 368.
14. Gaillard Hunt, ed., *The Writings of James Madison,* 9 vols. (New York, 1901), 2:184, 186–187.
15. *Journals of the Continental Congress,* 28:291–296.
16. Hunt, *The Writings of James Madison,* 2:143–145.
17. See Isaac Kramnick and Laurence Moore, *The Godless Constitution: The Case against Religious Correctness* (New York, 1997).
18. See Donald Lutz, "The Relative Importance of European Writers on Late Eighteenth Century American Political Thought," *American Political Science Review* 189 (1984): 189–197.
19. John Adams, *Thoughts on Government* in Charles Francis Adams, *The Works of John Adams,* 4:193–194.
20. Jacob Duche, *The American Vine, A Sermon Preached in Christ-Church, Philadelphia, Before the Honourable Continental Congress, July 20, 1775* (Philadelphia, 1775), 18, 20–21.
21. John Murrin, "Religion and Politics in America from the First Settlements to the Civil War," in Noll, *Religion and American Politics,* 19–43.
22. Poore, *The Federal and State Constitutions,* 2:1626.
23. Studies of the Constitutional Convention include Derek Davis, *Religion and the Continental Congress, 1774–1789: Contributions to Original Intent* (New York, 2000), and Bette Evans, *Interpreting the Free Exercise of Religion: The Constitution and American Pluralism* (Chapel Hill, 1998).
24. On religious tests, see Edwin Gaustad, "Religious Tests, Constitutions, and 'Christian Nation,'" in Hoffman and Albert, *Religion in a Revolutionary Age,* 218–235.
25. Poore, *The Federal and State Constitutions,* 1:276, 1:828, 1:970, 2:1286, 2:1418.
26. Jonathan Elliot, ed., *The Debates in the Several State Conventions on the Adoption of the Federal Constitution,* 5 vols. (Philadelphia, 1888), 1:148.
27. *Notes of Debates in the Federal Convention of 1787, Reported by James Madison* (New York 1987).
28. H. T Dickinson, "Britain's Imperial Sovereignty: The Ideological Case against the Colonies," in Dickinson, *Britain and the American Revolution,* 92–93.
29. Ibid., 653.
30. Kramnick and Moore, *The Godless Constitution,* 34–35.

Calvinist Opposition to the American Revolution," *Georgia Historical Quarterly* 82 (Summer 1998): 354.

31. Ibid., 36.

32. Ibid., 32.

33. Ezra Stiles, *The United States Elevated to Glory and Honor. A Sermon Preached before His Excellency Jonathan Trumbull, Governor and Commander in Chief, And the honorable The General Assembly of the State of Connecticut Convened at Hartford at the Anniversary Election May 8th, 1783* (New Haven, 1783), 7, 53.

34. Ibid., 20–21.

35. Ibid., 56.

36. Ibid., 58.

37. Ibid., 67, 72.

38. Ibid., *79*, 84.

39. Elliot, *Debates,* 2:148–149.

40. Ibid., 4:312.

41. Ibid., 199, 215.

42. Samuel Langdon, *The Republic of the Israelites* (Exeter, N.H., 1788), 35, 45.

43. Elliot, *Debates,* 3:659.

44. Cited in Kammen, *Origins of the American Constitution,* 369.

45. See Jay Fliegelman, *Prodigals and Pilgrims: The American Revolution against Patriarchal Authority, 1750–1800* (Cambridge, Eng., 1982).

46. George Washington, letter to the General Assembly of Presbyterian Churches, May 1789, in *The Writings of George Washington,* ed., Jared Sparks, 12 vols. (Boston, 1834–1837), 12:152–153.

47. Ibid., 154–155.

48. Ibid., 178–179.

49. George Washington, letter to the Hebrew Congregation in Newport, August 1790, in *The Papers of George Washington: Presidential Series,* ed. Dorothy Twohig, 9 vols. (Charlottesville, 1996), 6:284–285.

50. Terry Eastland, ed., *Religious Liberty in the Supreme Court: The Cases That Define the Debate over Church and State* (Washington, D.C., 1995), 356.

51. Jack Rakove, *Declaring Rights: A Brief History with Documents* (Boston, 1998), 173–174.

52. Ibid., 184. See Derek Davis, *Original Intent: Chief Justice Rehnquist and the Course of American Church-State Relations* (New York, 1991).

53. Ibid., 187.

54. Ibid., 187–188.

55. H. A. Washington, ed., *The Writings of Thomas Jefferson,* 9 vols. (New York, 1859), 7:267.

# 14
# ARISTOCRACY ASSAILED
*The Ideology of Backcountry Anti-Federalism*

## *Saul Cornell*

## Introduction

Americans often think of the Constitution as the natural capstone to the American Revolution. This view diminishes the voices of Antifederalists who believed that the Constitution violated revolutionary principles. During the ratification debate, Antifederalists formed a critical mass in practically every state and a majority in several of them. In the face of this opposition, proponents of the Constitution reluctantly agreed to pass a Bill of Rights once ratification was secured. Only this concession convinced enough Antifederalists to support the Constitution that the requisite nine states finally ratified the document and put it into effect. This essay's author Saul Cornell contends that the Antifederalists, as the driving force of the Bill of Rights, should be considered "the other Founders."

Cornell argues that the Antifederalists offer an important perspective on the meanings of the Revolution and the challenges of the early republic to Americans who lived through those times. Many and perhaps most white Americans considered a powerful central government with close ties to high finance, funded by high taxes, and backed by a strong military, to be antithetical to the principles of the Revolution. These Antifederalists associated centralized power with corruption and, not the least of all, the very empire from which they had just won their independence. Antifederalists wanted a government in which voters knew their representatives and in which representatives voted as their constituents wanted. They saw the states, not the nation, as the embodiment of the popular will.

Antifederalists believed the Constitution was a ruse to concentrate power in the hands of the moneyed, educated, eastern elite, which was at best indifferent and at worse disdainful of common people's interests. This elite, Antifederalists predicted, would raise and collect taxes with a bureaucracy staffed by its own kind, then channel the revenues toward elite enterprises, thus enabling the powerful to become yet more powerful. The indirect election of the president and senators, large electoral districts for representatives, an appointive Supreme Court, and presidential veto of congressional legislation all seemed designed to make the federal government unresponsive to the average voter. This kind of government was not what had driven Antifederalists to take up arms against Britain.

Such ideas were widespread, and yet Federalists, the supporters of the Constitution, triumphed anyway.

- Cornell argues that Antifederalists were more divided than their Federalist opponents, particularly along class lines. How was that the case?
- Antifederalists were right that the framers of the Constitution wished to concentrate power in elite hands and make the federal government less responsive than the states to voters. Given this goal, how did the Federalists manage to win public support for the Constitution? In what ways did Antifederalist arguments fail to address the issues of the mid 1780s?
- In your view, was the Bill of Rights an Antifederalist triumph or just a partial victory?

Historical accounts of the ratification of the federal Constitution have viewed Anti-Federalism through the eyes of the leading political figures who opposed adoption of the new frame of government. By focusing too narrowly on the delegates to the state ratifying conventions and leading Anti-Federalist politicians, studies of ratification have underestimated the depth of hostility to the new Constitution characteristic of grass-roots Anti-Federalism. Discussions of Anti-Federalist political thought have also been obscured by the tendency to treat Anti-Federalism as a monolithic ideology.[1]

Since the Progressive Era, historians have vigorously debated who was more democratic: the Anti-Federalists or their Federalist opponents. Neo-progressive historians like Jackson Turner Main have cast the Anti-Federalists as the first genuine democratic populists and the Federalists as opponents of further democratization of American society. Against this view, consensus historians have generally followed the lead of Cecelia M. Kenyon who claimed that the Anti-Federalists were "men of little faith" who distrusted the common people as much as their elected representatives.[2]

To understand the thinking of the opponents of the Constitution, especially their attitude toward democracy, we must abandon the idea that Anti-Federalists were united by a single, homogeneous political creed. Instead, we must identify the various subgroups within the Anti-Federalist ranks and explore the various ideologies that led individuals to oppose the Constitution.

Gouverneur Morris, an ardent nationalist member of the Constitutional Convention, confided in George Washington, "I dread the cold and sour temper of the back counties" toward the new frame of government.[3] Contemporaries on both sides of the ratification debate readily conceded that hostility toward the new Constitution was most intense among the farmers who populated the interior regions of the country.[4]

While east/west tensions accounted for much of the animosity felt by back-country folk toward the Constitution, it is also important to acknowledge the role of class antagonisms in shaping a distinctive populist variant of Anti-Federalist ideology. Even among backcountry opponents of the Constitution there were important divisions. While traveling in western Pennsylvania, Thomas Rodney, a leading Delaware Anti-Federalist, noted that "the better sort. … seem much afraid of the Foederal constitution in its present form without a bill of rights" while "the inferior class are totally against it, from their current Sentiment against proud & Lordly Idea's." Rodney's distinction between the attitudes of the Anti-Federalist elite and those of the popular opposition to the Constitution provides an important starting point for any interpretation of Anti-Federalist ideology.[5]

The leading Anti-Federalist representatives of the western interests, individuals like William Findley, were among the most democratic figures in Pennsylvania politics. Yet despite their democratic sympathies, men like Findley were members of a recognizable political elite, even if they were far closer to the social status of the people they represented than were members of the more established eastern political elites. The individuals who served in state government were members of a mediating class that stood well above the common folk. To uncover grass-roots Anti-Federalist thinking it is essential to move beyond the lesser elite who dominated politics in the backcountry and to restore a voice to a segment of Anti-Federalism that has been rendered mute by the elitist bias of previous scholarship.[6]

The Carlisle Riot of 1788 affords a rich occasion for comparing the ideology of Anti-Federalists of the better and inferior sorts. Since violence in backcountry Pennsylvania attracted the attention of prominent Anti-Federalist politicians, the riot and its aftermath provide an unusual opportunity to contrast popular and elite attitudes among the opponents of the new Constitution. Furthermore, since events in Carlisle were often linked to Shays's Rebellion in the minds of contemporaries, rural unrest in backcountry Pennsylvania can also reveal the depth of concern over anarchy that united the Federalist and the Anti-Federalist political elites.

## The Carlisle Riot

Located roughly a third of the way across Pennsylvania, the town of Carlisle had, during the 1760s, marked the state's western boundary. During the subsequent years the town became a major settlement in the interior of Pennsylvania. Although it had ceased to mark the frontier and could by the mid-1780s boast both a newspaper and a college, leading gentlemen still expressed concern over the town's continuing frontier character.

Local politics in Carlisle were colored by the intensity of partisan conflict throughout Pennsylvania. The area west of the Susquehanna, including Carlisle, was a stronghold of the egalitarian political traditions associated with the state constitution of 1776. Much of the controversy in Pennsylvania politics during the decade after the Revolution revolved around proposals to revise the state constitution and replace its unicameral legislature with a bicameral system. At the root of this conflict was an argument about the role of representation in a republican government.[7] The debate turned on the question of how much democracy could be sustained in a republic before it would degenerate into mobocracy, tyranny, or aristocracy. Leading citizens in Carlisle, like many notable political figures throughout the United States who would support the Federalist cause, were concerned about the destabilizing impact of the more democratic aspects of revolutionary ideology on American society. Like their counterparts in other parts of the country, nationalists in Carlisle sought to counter the forces of democratization by championing the idea of ordered liberty, a deferential conception of politics, and the ideal of disinterested republican virtue. These positions set them against the popular traditions of egalitarianism that had played a crucial role in the revolutionary straggle against Britain and that

typified grass-roots Anti-Federalism. The debate over ratification of the federal Constitution brought the two opposing political cultures into direct conflict in the streets of Carlisle.[8]

At about five o'clock in the evening on December 26, 1787, a group of Federalists gathered in Carlisle's center for a celebration marking Pennsylvania's ratification of the new federal Constitution. The mood was festive: drums beat and bells rang as Federalists awaited the cannon salute that would honor the new Constitution. The celebratory mood shifted, however, when an angry crowd of Anti-Federalists came on the scene and ordered the Federalists to disband. Confident in the superiority of their cause and undaunted by their opponents, the Federalists resolutely stood their ground. One of the Federalist organizers of the event responded to the provocations of the Anti-Federalists with the charge "that he hoped people so pregnant with liberty as they appeared to be would not wish to hinder their neighbors." His pleas were brushed aside by the Anti-Federalists, who refused to allow the opposition to proceed with their victory display. The leaders of the Anti-Federalist crowd warned the Federalists "that their conduct was contrary to the minds of three-fourths of the inhabitants, and must therefore produce bad consequences if they persisted."[9]

Although the Federalists had won a resounding victory in the state ratifying convention, the area west of the Susquehanna was an acknowledged Anti-Federalist stronghold. Carlisle itself was divided; the town's elite was strongly Federalist while popular sympathies lay largely with the Anti-Federalists. As one observer noted, "in Cumberland county all are against it, except a small group in Carlisle."[10]

When the two groups met in the streets of Carlisle, tensions were already high. The Anti-Federalists were angry and easily provoked; they were still smarting from their recent defeat in the state convention. Federalist arrogance exacerbated matters. When confronted by local Anti-Federalist opposition, Federalists insisted that "they would fire the cannon in spite of any who would oppose them; and if they would not clear the way, they would blow them up." The Anti-Federalists responded by pelting Federalists with pieces of wood and the confrontation escalated into a full-scale riot. Armed with staves and bludgeons, the Anti-Federalists easily routed the Federalists and drove them from the scene.

At noon the next day, the Federalists gathered once more to celebrate; this time the heavily armed group succeeded in hailing the new government with a volley of musket fire and an artillery salute. Afterwards, the Federalists retired to a tavern where they toasted leading Federalists, the new frame of government, and the future prosperity of the United States. Carlisle Federalists raised their glasses to demonstrate their respect for order and their deference to their leaders, men like George Washington and James Wilson. They praised the prospects of greatness awaiting a powerful federal union, when "the flag of the United States" would "fly triumphant in all the ports of the world." The Federalists attacked the actions of the "vile rabble," decried the unruly behavior of their opponents, and proclaimed "that every lover of good order" would lament the actions of the Anti-Federalist mob.[11]

In response to the Federalist demonstration, the Anti-Federalists mounted a counter-demonstration. Led by a local militia captain, the opponents of the Constitution staged a procession complete with effigies of James Wilson and of Pennsylvania's chief justice, Thomas McKean, men who had helped secure ratification in Pennsylvania. The Federalist leaders were treated as the leaders of a conspiracy to foist an aristocratic government on the people. Such treachery demanded severe punishment, and the Anti-Federalist crowd overlooked no detail in preparing the figures for public judgment. The two effigies were dressed in garb appropriate to their high stations. A local Federalist reported that "the Effigie of the Chief Justics was pretty well Dressed a good Coat but not black a pretty good hat & wig & Rufld

Shirt." The crowd jeered as the figures of the two Federalists were paraded through town in a cart and repeatedly lashed. After being humiliated before the assembled crowd, the two effigies were hanged and then delivered to a funeral pyre while "the dead bell tolled until they were totally consumed to ashes."[12]

One Anti-Federalist explained the actions of the rioters as a natural reaction to the Federalists' refusal to call "a town meeting, to take the sense of the people on the subject." In the view of Anti-Federalists, the supporters of the Constitution had disregarded the feelings of local inhabitants, acted contrary to the will of the local majority, and revealed their own arrogant contempt of the people.[13]

Anti-Federalists in Carlisle showed little interest in the vision of national greatness that inspired many Federalists. Rather than accept the Federalist ideal of a large republican empire administered by a small elite, Anti-Federalists defended the ideal of a confederation of small republics in which republican liberty and popular participation were the defining characteristics of political life. The nature of the Anti-Federalists' political protest provides one measure of the ideological distance separating them from Federalists. Not content to defer to their social betters, local Anti-Federalists drew upon popular traditions of "rough music" to express their resentment against the elitism of their opponents. An essential feature of the plebeian cultural traditions of the Anglo-American world, the rituals of rough music, such as tarring and feathering, were usually administered to individuals who had violated commonly accepted community values.[14]

The ritual use of effigies by the rioters was designed to affirm the values of community, equality, and democracy. The public humiliation of the figures of Wilson and McKean provided a focus for popular animosity and allowed the protesters in Carlisle to identify two individuals who, they believed, were leaders in the Federalists' attempt to foist an aristocratic government on the people. The two Federalist leaders were subjected to a symbolic trial and executed for conspiring to undermine the liberty of the people. Like legal punishment, the ritual was designed to reaffirm the values of the community and to provide a warning. In the minds of the protesters, the battle to defeat the Constitution was not yet over. Their actions sent a message to others who might contemplate similar betrayals of the people's trust.

The colorful plebeian rituals of status reversal enacted by Anti-Federalists also served to undercut the deferential political message implicit in Federalist ideology. Anti-Federalists reacted angrily to the aristocratic leanings of their opponents and took every opportunity to berate Federalists for their "proud and Lordly" ideas. Many Anti-Federalists resented the attempt by the Federalists to use the prestige of great men to gain support for the Constitution. One participant in the riot, sarcastically assuming the voice of his Federalist opponents, suggested that "the names of Washington and a Franklin, must be rung in the people's ears." He further advised that "it must be declared a crime bordering on blasphemy, to say any thing against the production of such men as these."[15]

The actions of the rioters were an explicit rejection of Federalist pleas for deference. The men who took to the streets in Carlisle accepted the warning of the influential Anti-Federalist author "Centinel," who noted that "the wealthy and ambitious … in every community think they have a right to lord it over their fellow creatures." Indeed, they followed his advice quite literally and refused "to yield an implicit assent to the opinions of those characters." Anti-Federalists in Carlisle would not defer to their "betters." The rioters proudly asserted that they "would pay no respect to their rank, nor make any allowance for their delicate constitutions," adding that "it was laughable to see Lawyers, Doctors, Colonels, Captains & c. & c. leave the scene of their rejoicing in such haste."[16]

With the community bitterly divided by the riot, local authorities faced a difficult problem: Should the instigators of the riot, the Anti-

Federalists, be prosecuted to the full extent of the law or should the incident be forgotten in the hope of restoring harmony to the community? The prospect of a divisive trial did not appeal to a number of leading Federalists. A prominent Philadelphia merchant, Walter Stewart, warned William Irvine, a Carlisle Federalist, that they should not be so "very Ridiculous as to blow up a Coal which Now seems expiring; by Investigating them, or Calling to Account any of the People concern'd in the Affair at Carlisle." Nonetheless, depositions were taken, and on January 23, 1788, a warrant for the arrest of the leaders of the Anti-Federalist mob was issued.[17]

The twenty-one men named in the writ were rounded up for prosecution and charged with assembling "in a riotous, routous, and unlawful manner" and fomenting "great terror and disturbance on the inhabitants of the said borough of Carlisle." The presiding judge in the case offered the defendants the opportunity to leave jail on bail. Seven prisoners refused the offer, proclaiming that since "they were prosecuted to gratify party spite, they were determined not to enter bail on the occasion."[18]

Local Anti-Federalists turned to the community for support. Organizing themselves through the militia, the Anti-Federalists elected representatives to meet with local Federalist leaders and negotiate the release of the jailed Anti-Federalists. A number of respectable persons on both sides of the question, fearful of further violence, signed a petition to release the prisoners. After the agreement was formally ratified, a contingent of militia numbering between two hundred and fifty and fifteen hundred men marched to the jail to secure the release of the prisoners, singing a song composed by the rioters that mocked the Federalists' aristocratic bearing. Once released, the prisoners joined the front of the procession and "marched through town huzzaing, singing, hallooing, firing and the like." Federalists breathed a sigh of relief; a violent confrontation had been averted and they contented themselves by expressing their contempt for the "dirty, raga-muffin-looking blackguards" in private. Anti-Federalists rejoiced at their symbolic victory. The huge crowd that marched on the jail to secure the release of prisoners was a visible affirmation of the strength of the Anti-Federalist cause. The parade provided another occasion to humiliate their opponents and thereby to demonstrate popular hostility toward the Federalist vision of order and deference.[19]

Political rituals provide one set of clues that help reveal the underlying political dynamic at work in Carlisle. While Federalists engaged in rituals of deference, the Anti-Federalists employed rituals of status reversal. Contemporary observers on both sides of the ratification debate were struck by the clear class divisions that separated Federalists from Anti-Federalists in the Pennsylvania backcountry. The hostility to the new Constitution was most acute among men of the "lower and middling sort." One hostile observer noted that rioters were small property holders who "have but few lots."[20]

Anti-Federalists did not deny their humble origins and modest wealth. Anti-Federalists in Carlisle stressed the nobility and dignity of simple farmers and artisans against the attempts by Federalists to assert the superiority of gentlemen of wealth and education.

Evidence obtained from the 1787 tax lists for Carlisle provides an unusual opportunity to assess the social origins of Anti-Federalism in one backcountry locality. (See Table 14.1.) The Carlisle rioters represented a cross section of the population that ranged from freemen to moderately prosperous yeomen. Anti-Federalists who signed petitions to gain the release of the rioters tended to be somewhat better-off and were concentrated within the ranks of the middling and the prosperous yeomanry. Anti-Federalism in Carlisle, however, drew its most vocal support from the lower and middling inhabitants of the town. By contrast, Federalists who signed the same petition were largely drawn from the wealthiest stratum of Carlisle society. The median assessed tax for those Federalists was roughly four times as much as that of Anti-Federalist petitioners and roughly seven times that of the jailed rioters. Both the striking class-conscious rhetoric of the rioters and the tax lists suggest that there was an important class dimension to the struggle between Federalists and Anti-Federalists in Carlisle.[21]

## Anti-Federalism and Plebeian Populism

Opposition to aristocracy was a central concern in the rhetoric and symbolism of the Anti-Federalist Carlisle rioters. The charge that the Constitution was an aristocratic document was among the accusations most often repeated in the Anti-Federalist press. One astute, but admittedly sarcastic, Federalist commentator felt that Anti-Federalist writing could be reduced to a simple recipe that included the following proportions: "WELL-BORN, nine times – *Aristocracy,* eighteen times ... *Great Men,* six times." The author reminded readers that "these

*Table 14.1* Median Level of Assessed Tax for Selected Taxpayers in Carlisle, 1787

| Group | Median Tax (£) | Interquartile Range (£) | N |
|---|---|---|---|
| All taxpayers (includes freemen and householders) | 68.6 | 19.7–176.2 | 281 |
| Householders | 100.0 | 50.0–229.35 | 226 |
| Federalist petitioners | 749.1 | 322.8–802.69 | 9 |
| Anti-Federalist petitioners | 187.0 | 93.6–245.6 | 8 |
| Anti-Federalist rioters | 103.8 | 27.5–125.3 | 14 |

Source: Cumberland County Tax Lists 1787, microfilm copy (Historical Society of Pennsylvania, Philadelphia).
Note: The assessment was made in pounds; I have converted shillings to a decimal figure in pounds. The interquartile range represents the range over which the central 50 percent of the data is spread.

*Table 14.2*  Frequency of Selected Accusations in Anti-Federalist Rhetoric[a]

| Category | % |
| --- | --- |
| Aristocracy | 49 |
| Well born | 35 |
| Great names | 23 |

Source: These figures are based upon content analysis of 80 Anti-Federalist attacks on the Constitution or its supporters published in the Pennsylvania press between September 26 and December 26, 1787, appearing in Merrill Jensen et al., The Documentary History of the Ratification of the Constitution (16 vols., Madison, 1976–), and its microform supplement.
a Since each article usually contained more than one epithet, the percentages listed above add up to more than 100%.

*words* will bear … being served, after being once used, a dozen times to the same table and palate." A survey of the popular press in Pennsylvania in the four months between the publication of the Constitution in September and the Carlisle riot confirms the observations of that anonymous Federalist. (See Table 14.2.)[22]

The author of the mock recipe for an Anti-Federalist essay distinguished between attacks on the Constitution's tendency to promote an aristocracy and a crudely formulated class critique directed at the "well born" and "great men." He thereby implicitly acknowledged a distinction that contemporaries often made between the concepts of aristocracy and natural aristocracy.

The difference between attacks on aristocracy and those on natural aristocracy illustrates an aspect of the ratification debate that has often been confused in recent scholarly discussions. One could attack the new Constitution for concentrating too much power in the hands of government and thus establishing an aristocracy of governmental officials, or one could attack the Constitution for favoring the interests of a specific social class, loosely defined as the natural aristocracy. The difference between the two critiques is crucial to understanding Anti-Federalism as a heterogeneous ideology. Concern about the dangers of aristocracy was a republican commonplace and was closely

tied to the fear of corruption that was central to republican discourse. Virtually all Americans accepted the legitimacy of that concern even if they disagreed about how to guard against such danger. The problem of natural aristocracy was far more complicated and politically divisive.[23]

The most systematic discussion of the interrelated concepts of aristocracy and natural aristocracy by any Anti-Federalist can be found in the writings of the "Federal Farmer," who observed that:

> There are three kinds of aristocracy spoken of in this country – the first is a constitutional one, which does not exist in the United States … the second is an aristocratic faction; a junto of unprincipled men, often distinguished for their wealth and abilities, who combine together and make their object their private interests and aggrandizement.[24]

The third category in the "Federal Farmer's" scheme, natural aristocracy, was far more difficult to define. The "Federal Farmer" acknowledged that the exact composition of this class "is in some degree arbitrary; we may place men on one side of this line, which others may place on the other." The "Federal Farmer" estimated that the class numbered about "four or five thousand men," including high-ranking politicians like state governors; the most important officers of Congress; state senators; the officers of the army and militia; superior judges; and the most eminent professional men, wealthy merchants, and large property holders. In large measure this class was defined against the middling sort, which included the yeomanry, subordinate officers of the military and militia, mechanics, and many of the traders and merchants. The bottom category in the Anti-Federalist's scheme was the inferior sort, which included the dependent poor and unskilled laborers. Although few Anti-Federalists were as systematic in their thinking as the "Federal Farmer," many shared his belief that natural aristocracy was best understood as a distinctive, if ill-defined, social class, which the Constitution clearly favored.

The concept of natural aristocracy also figured prominently in Federalist thinking. The most detailed analysis occurred in John Adams's *Defence of the Constitutions of Government of the United States of America*. Adams identified a class of natural aristocrats whose wealth, education, reputation, and talents set them apart from the common people. Adams defended the salutary effects that this class would have on government if its members were sequestered in an upper house of the legislature and allowed to play their natural role as a check on a popularly elected lower house.

When Adams and other Federalists discussed natural aristocracy they often blurred two distinct interpretations of who ought to be included as its members: society's social and political elite or men of wisdom, talent, and virtue. His use of the term included both an aristocracy of privilege and an aristocracy of merit. Virtually all Federalists supported the notion of natural aristocracy and were successful at deflecting Anti-Federalist criticisms of the concept in public debate. Federalists exploited the ambiguous meaning of the term by arguing that republicanism required a government composed of a natural aristocracy of virtuous leaders. When pressed in public debate, most Federalists followed the example of James Wilson who argued that a government ruled by a natural aristocracy was "nothing more or less than a government of the best men in the community … most noted for wisdom and virtue."[25]

A reliance on the so-called natural aristocracy was compatible with the Federalist belief that the new Constitution's system of representation should effectively filter out men with parochial views and elevate men of refined views who would best discern the common good. To promote the election of "men of intelligence and uprightness," Federalists followed Wilson's recommendation that "experience demonstrates that the larger the district of election, the better the representation. It is only in remote corners

of a government, that little demagogues arise. Nothing but real weight of character can give a man real influence over a large district." Wilson's views were shared by James Madison (writing as "Publius") who counseled the necessity of enlarging the "public views, by passing them through the medium of a chosen body of citizens, whose wisdom may best discern the true interest of their country." In practice, Madison's "chosen body of citizens," the men who possessed "the weight of character" discussed by Wilson, were more likely to be found among the educated, affluent, and leisured elite.[26]

At the root of the Anti-Federalist critique of that elite, and of the ideology of natural aristocracy, lay a distinctive vernacular sociology. Anti-Federalist radicals, such as the Carlisle rioters, sought to ensure that representatives would do more than serve as spokesmen for the interests of individual localities. The radicals argued that true representation required that legislators actually resemble their constituents. When populists suggested that the legislature ought to be an exact mirror of society, they were speaking in a literal, not a figurative, sense. Since no one class possessed an exclusive monopoly on virtue, they reasoned, representative bodies ought to include a wide range of individuals from different social classes.

Anti-Federalists sought to demonstrate that when Federalists used the idea of natural aristocracy they were not discussing virtue but merely defending the interests of an identifiable social class. While Anti-Federalists thundered against natural aristocracy, Federalists countered with the claim that they were proponents of an aristocracy of merit, what we would now call meritocracy. Federalists argued that the Anti-Federalist alternative to an aristocracy of merit, the idea of the legislature as an exact mirror of society's diverse interests and classes was incompatible with the republican ideal of virtue. Implicitly this debate turned on whether the necessary qualities of virtue, talent, and wisdom were evenly distributed throughout the various classes in society. Federalists believed that these qualities were disproportionately found in the upper stratum of society, while the populists among the Anti-Federalists maintained that there were enough virtuous men within the different classes to warrant broader representation. Federalists sought to frame the debate in terms of representativeness versus merit, while Anti-Federalist populists hoped to show that these two goals were not mutually exclusive.

The vernacular sociology of Anti-Federalists presented an inverted mirror image of the Enlightenment political sociology of Federalists like Madison and Wilson. Anti-Federalist populists and Federalists were in essential agreement about the impact of the Constitution's new scheme of representation: it would, both sides believed, enhance the prospects for electing members of the society's natural aristocracy and diminish the power of local politicians.[27]

In the Anti-Federalists' assault on natural aristocracy, John Adams became a favorite target. The connections between Adams's theory of government and Federalist ideas were made quite explicit by the "Centinel," who feared that "the principles of government inculcated in Mr Adams treatise" permeated the Constitution. The "Centinel" drew a sharp contrast between the aristocratic qualities of the federal Constitution and the more democratic elements of the 1776 Pennsylvania Constitution.[28]

The Carlisle Anti-Federalists did not need the "Centinel" to remind them of the similarity between Adams's thinking and that of other Federalists. Carlisle Anti-Federalists did not have to look very far to find ardent supporters of Adams's theory of natural aristocracy. Charles Nisbet, president of nearby Dickinson College, took every opportunity to remind local inhabitants of the necessity of an educated governing elite drawn from the ranks of society's natural aristocracy.

A recent immigrant from Scotland and a staunch Presbyterian, Nisbet saw the world quite differently than did the Carlisle rioters. While they fulminated at lawyers, clergymen, and university men, Nisbet extolled the virtues of governance by a leisured and learned elite. Where the rioters saw an overbearing elite in control of political life, Nisbet saw a society that veered dangerously close to a Hobbesian state of nature. In Nisbet's view, "This new world ... is unfortunately composed, like that of epicurus, of discordant atoms, jumbled together by chance and tossed by inconstancy in an immense vacuum, it greatly wants a principle of attraction and cohesion."[29] According to Nisbet's view, the New World threatened to level all distinctions and thus plunge society into anarchy.

To offset the leveling tendency of the frontier, Nisbet regularly intoned the sober principles of traditional republicanism to his students at Dickinson College. While the Constitutional Convention met, Nisbet reminded students in his class on public law that "it is certain that men of learning, leisure and easy circumstances ... if they are endued with wisdom, virtue & humanity, are much fitter for every part of the business of government, than the ordinary class of people." It is hardly surprising that Anti-Federalists felt that "Dickinson Coledge will be a Choice nursery for Federal officers and rulers." The commencement services held at the college during the spring of 1788 confirmed their suspicions. As one Anti-Federalist observed, "the great Drift of all their discourses was to prove the mass of the people to be void of every liberal Sentiment" and "destitute of understanding and integrity."[30]

The concept of natural aristocracy articulated by Federalists was embedded within an ideology that posited a strong link between education, knowledge, and republican virtue. In addition to the martial and yeoman ideals of the citizen, republicanism also accorded a special role to the "republican man of letters" whose extensive reading habits conferred on him a cosmopolitan sensibility.[31] In his role as the president of Dickinson College, Charles Nisbet became the leading spokesman for the concept of natural aristocracy within Carlisle and served as a model of the "republican man of letters." Nisbet was not the only Federalist who espoused that ideal. One of its most ardent exponents was Federalist Benjamin Rush, a leading supporter of the Constitution in Pennsylvania and a trustee of Dickinson College. Rush hoped to use education and the popular press to mold the character of citizens and believed that it was "possible to convert men into republican machines" so that they might "perform their parts properly in the great machine of government."[32] The choice of a mechanical metaphor was especially appropriate since it captured the essentially hierarchical nature of the Federalist vision of politics.

The most outspoken critic of the concept of natural aristocracy in Carlisle was William Petrikin, a leader of the Anti-Federalist election riot. Petrikin was the embodiment of a different, radical egalitarian, version of the "republic of letters." Unlike Nisbet, Petrikin was schooled in the popular press and proudly proclaimed that he was a "mechanic … who never spent an hour in coledge."[33] He eagerly consumed the popular political literature of his day. The popular press did not, however, convert Petrikin into a "republican machine." The egalitarian vision of the "republic of letters" that Anti-Federalists like Petrikin rallied around encouraged an active role for common folk who would exercise their own capacity for civic virtue by reading popular political literature, writing for the popular press, and even seeking public office. In fact, Petrikin was sufficiently inspired by what he read to take up his own pen to denounce the proponents of natural aristocracy in Carlisle. By examining Petrikin's own Anti-Federalist ideas and his use of other Anti-Federalist writers we can gain important insights into the complex process by which common folk read the rhetoric of ratification and appropriated it to formulate their own populist ideology.[34]

Petrikin clearly favored the writings of the "Centinel," one of the most egalitarian and democratic Anti-Federalist writers.[35] In one of the first pieces he published after the riot, he adopted the name the "Scourge," defended the actions of the "friends of liberty," and

attacked the Federalists for "having the learned professions on their side." He charged that Federalists in Carlisle had the support of "all the attorneys then in town and all the auxiliaries they could procure" and compared their ideas to those of a "Solon, a Lycurgus … or an Adams."[36]

Since formal education was clearly a prerogative associated with wealth and social standing, the "Scourge" saw the invocation of venerable republican figures such as Solon and Lycurgus as yet another attempt by the affluent to equate formal education with virtue. Unlike his Federalist opponents, Petrikin felt that politics required no recourse to classical allusion. Like the other participants in the Carlisle riot, he proudly asserted that virtue and knowledge were not the sole possessions of a small elite class of natural aristocrats. Anti-Federalists did not believe that figures from the republican past monopolized political wisdom any more than they believed that education or wealth signaled greater wisdom in their own society. When Anti-Federalists did invoke classical republican figures, they favored the defenders of the late Roman republic, such as Brutus, men who symbolized the battle against tyranny. In marked contrast, Federalists favored figures such as Publius, the great founders and lawgivers of republican antiquity.[37]

Although Anti-Federalists admired Brutus, the historical figure depicted in Plutarch's *Lives* mattered less to Anti-Federalist populists than the spirit of "Brutus" dwelling in all stalwart republicans.[38] When Carlisle Anti-Federalists praised the dissenting members of the state ratifying convention who voted against adoption of the Constitution, they took great pride in noting that "scholastic learning and erudition" were set against the "simple reason" of "a very few country farmers and mechanics." The dissenting Anti-Federalist members of the state convention, "it will be said … were the … Bruti, the Cato's of America." The modern heirs of Brutus did not need 2 class of educated leaders to interpret his message.[39] The literary conventions of the popular press, particularly the rules governing the use of pseudonyms, made popular participation possible. Any citizen concerned about the state of the republic could author a piece, assume the pen name "Brutus," and alert his fellow citizens that the republic or liberty was jeopardized. The tradition of pseudonymous writing closed the distance between readers and authors, allowing any concerned citizen to step forward and enter an ongoing debate as an equal participant. Thus one can readily understand Anti-Federalists' outrage when a number of Federalist printers sought to abandon the convention of printing anonymous or pseudonymous pieces. "Philadelphiensis" thought that the Federalist effort to abolish the use of pseudonyms embodied "the genius and spirit of our new government" and that it would please the "well born." In opposition, he championed the belief that "it is of no importance whether or not a writer gives his name; it is with the illustrations and arguments he affords us, and not with his name," that "we have any concern." Requiring authors to sign their names would discourage "men of ability, of a modest, timid, or diffident cast of mind … from publishing their sentiments."[40]

Anti-Federalist hostility to men of learning did not signal a hostility to education or knowledge. Following the lead of the "Centinel," the Anti-Federalists argued that "liberty only flourishes where reason and knowledge are encouraged." For that reason they encouraged the growth of the popular press, which they viewed as a powerful weapon to combat patterns of deference.

By championing the popular press, Anti-Federalist populists signaled their desire to increase their contact with the wider world of print culture. As the "Centinel" noted, "in a confederated government of such extent as the United States, the freest communication of sentiment and information should be maintained." The progress of the ratification campaign was proof that without such a network, liberty itself was at risk. "For want of this intercommunity of sentiment and information," "Centinel" observed, "the liberties of this country are brought to an awful crisis." In his view, it was precisely the Federalists' ability to dominate the press that had allowed supporters of the Constitution to isolate and "overwhelm the enlightened opposition."[41]

Although several modern commentators have acknowledged that the opponents of the Constitution were wedded to an intensely localistic ideology, most scholars have mistakenly viewed Anti-Federalist localism as the polar opposite of Federalist cosmopolitanism.[42] Anti-Federalist localism was not an expression of a narrow parochial and insular world view. Localist ideology owed much to whig oppositional thought, especially the rhetoric of country ideology. The pervasive fears of centralized authority, standing armies, and excessive taxation were only the most obvious instances of Anti-Federalism's debt to this older whig tradition. It would, however, be a mistake to view Anti-Federalist ideology as a mere echo of an older English straggle between "court and country."[43] The emergence of a distinctively American localist ideology was conditioned by the structure of imperial relations between the American colonies and Britain. The essence of Anti-Federalist localist ideology was captured by the ardent states' rights advocate Luther Martin, who argued that the American people were accustomed to "have their seats of government near them, to which they might have access, without much inconvenience." Martin's vision of localism was congruent with that of Massachusetts Anti-Federalist James Winthrop, who saw localism as the natural consequence of the diversity of American society. It is hard to maintain that Anti-Federalist localists were narrow-minded provincial politicians while recognizing Winthrop, the librarian of Harvard College, and Martin, a respected figure in the Maryland legal community, as leading theorists of Anti-Federalist localism.[44] Both men illustrate the existence of an important strain of cosmopolitan localism among the Anti-Federalist elite.

A simple localist/cosmopolitan dichotomy not only fails to capture the complexity of many leading Anti-Federalists, but it also obscures the nature of the popular Anti-Federalist ideology espoused by such individuals as William Petrikin and the Carlisle rioters. The localism of the Carlisle rioters was closely tied to their egalitarian populist ideas. Although distinctly localistic in outlook, Anti-Federalists were not provincial in their cultural views; they did not envision localities as isolated and insular communities. Their localism stressed the importance of face-to-face relationships and the values of neighborliness even as they defended the necessity of expanding communication between individual communities. In this way, local autonomy could be maintained without fostering provincialism. Even the localism of the most populist-minded Anti-Federalists was closely tied to their own egalitarian defense of the "republic of letters."

The most forceful expression of Petrikin's egalitarian populism came in a pamphlet he authored under the pseudonym "Aristocrotis." Even the choice of pseudonym was intended to parody Federalist ideas of natural aristocracy. Petrikin's sardonic tone mocked Federalist elitism and in the process he provided a forceful statement of his own populist ideals. "Aristocrotis" addressed his pamphlet to the "well born," and "the full blooded gentry," who have the "necessary qualifications of authority; such as the dictatorial air, the magesterial voice, the imperious tone, the haughty countenance." At several points, "Aristocrotis" seemed to echo the words of Charles Nisbet, who would have undoubtedly agreed that "nature hath placed proper degrees and subordinations amongst mankind, and ordained a few to rule, and many to obey." For Petrikin, the Constitution was designed to elevate the members of an identifiable class of natural aristocrats to preeminence.[45]

"Aristocrotis" took the logic of the Federalist defense of disinterestedness to its final conclusion by claiming that "a government ... agreeable to nature must be entirely independent." According to the satire of "Aristocrotis," the Revolution had given the people "exorbitant power ... of electing their rulers" tending to "the subversion of all order and good government." The greatest evil flowing from the excess of democracy was the necessity of pandering to the mob, which "Aristocrotis" described as the vulgar practice of "electioneering." The Constitutional Convention had, according to his view, successfully rolled back these democratic excesses, restoring the legislative branch to its proper position of independence from the will of the people. To facilitate this goal the convention had wisely decided against annual elections, allowed Congress to determine the manner and place of holding elections, and provided for taxes that would insure that the people would be forced to "attend to their own business; and not be dabbling in politics."[46]

Petrikin's satire echoed the Federalist sentiments voiced at the Dickinson College commencement, where Nisbet, and his students attacked the people as "dupes of selfish demagoge[s]." Nisbet like many other Carlisle Federalists, would have agreed with "Mentor," who observed that after the Revolution, representatives had allowed "local situations bias them to act contrary to the general good." "Mentor" recommended electing men of property and education who were not "confined, by their domestic concerns." Once again, the notion of a leisured, gentlemanly elite was set against a localistic and decidedly populist conception of representation.[47]

The Federalist hostility to "electioneering" that Petrikin parodied as "Aristocrotis," like the charges made by "Mentor" blended together two distinct concerns. Federalists feared that postrevolutionary politics had become too interest-oriented and that representatives had become too parochial. Federalists also feared that the Revolution had eroded the traditional deference accorded gentlemen.

Anti-Federalist populist localism was based on a "mandate" or "actual" of representation.

According to it, representatives were to act as agents of their constituents. In the view of most Anti-Federalists, members of the legislature had to be sufficiently steeped in the values of the locality, immersed in its economic and social life, to serve as true spokesmen for community interests. To achieve that goal, populists argued, representatives had to resemble those they represented. The ideology of localism rejected the republican ideal of disinterestedness. Only by guarding the many diverse local interests in society, Anti-Federalists believed, could Americans maintain liberty.[48]

Challenges to the claim that disinterested gentlemen of refined views were more capable of representing the people than were the people themselves resonated in the minds of backcountry folk. Such ideas were not unique to the backcountry of Pennsylvania. Indeed, similar ideas could be found throughout the backcountry from Maine to Georgia. Amos Singletary, an Anti-Federalist from Sutton, Massachusetts, in the heart of Shaysite Worcester County, warned that "these lawyers, and men of learning, and moneyed men, that talk so finely, and gloss over matters so smoothly," would "get into Congress themselves" and would become "the managers of this Constitution, and get all the power and all the money into their own hands, and then they will swallow up all us little folks."[49]

The rhetoric of populists in Carlisle was tinged with similar inchoate class consciousness. At the root of their crudely formulated class critique was the claim that an identifiable class of natural aristocrats that included lawyers, men of learning and monied men were engaged in a systematic plot to increase their own power and dilute the influence of the people in government. John Montgomery, a Carlisle Federalist, observed that Anti-Federalists feared that the Constitution would make the farmers "dependents … who will be reduced to a sort of vassalage."[50]

The plebeian populism that motivated so much of the popular opposition to the Constitution created an important division within the ranks of the Anti-Federalists. It divided

those (such as Petrikin) hostile to the concept of natural aristocracy from those whose fear that the Constitution promoted aristocracy did not lead them to challenge the ideal of natural aristocracy.

Anti-Federalists like Virginia's George Mason feared that the government created by the Constitution would "commence in a moderate Aristocracy" and would probably degenerate into an "oppressive Aristocracy." Mason is quite properly thought of as a "man of little faith." He did not, however, fear natural aristocracy. A wealthy cosmopolitan planter like Mason expected society's leaders to be drawn from the gentlemanly elite. What worried Mason was the traditional republican fear of corruption. In his mind, any group of men who were given too much power would seek aggrandizement and elevate their own interests above those of society. The solution to Mason's objections was a more effective system of checks on government and a written bill of rights to protect individual liberty. Hardly a populist democrat, Mason was a critic of the democratic excess that characterized American politics during the Confederation period. At the Constitutional Convention, Mason acknowledged "that we had been too democratic," but he also cautioned against moving too far "into the opposite extreme."[51] Mason's elitist republicanism stood in stark contrast to the populist sentiments of the Carlisle rioters. The debate over natural aristocracy was only one instance of a basic rift separating elite Anti-Federalists from grass-roots Anti-Federalists.

## Liberty versus Order: Responses to Backcountry Violence

If the issue of natural aristocracy divided Anti-Federalists, the plebeian traditions of protest enacted by the Carlisle rioters were even more divisive. Events like the Carlisle riot touched a sensitive nerve in leading figures on both sides of the ratification struggle. It is hardly surprising that Federalists viewed such events as signs of the need for a stronger union. What is surprising is the reaction of leading Anti-Federalists to those events. Anti-Federalist reactions were often indistinguishable from those of Federalists. The fear of aristocracy and concern for liberty that inspired elite opposition to the Constitution paled when the Anti-Federalists were presented with the specter of anarchy. For Anti-Federalists of the better sort, the actions of the rioters were a sobering reminder of the necessity and difficulty of balancing liberty and order.[52]

Shays's Rebellion left a profound imprint on the minds of many Americans, and the fear of anarchy and disorder created by the western Massachusetts insurgents influenced members of political elites on both sides of the ratification struggle. The climate of fear created by Shays's Rebellion accounts for the coverage of the Carlisle riot in the press as far south as Georgia and as far north as Maine. Many Federalists viewed the rioters as "mobites" and "levellers."[53]

The horror of Federalists was more than matched by the reactions of leading Anti-Federalists, especially in Massachusetts, where Shays's Rebellion had left an especially deep impression. To an experienced politician like Elbridge Gerry, a man of the "better sort," the Carlisle riot was a bitter reminder of the leveling tendencies among the populace. Although an outspoken opponent of the Constitution, Gerry shared the Federalist belief that the nation's political problems stemmed from an "excess of democracy." His commitment to republican ideas stopped well short of the democratic leanings of the Carlisle rioters. In the Constitutional Convention he admitted that he "had been taught by experience the danger of the levilling spirit." When he learned that the "people threatend the Justice in Carlisle to pull down his House, & the houses of the federalists," Gerry expressed grave concern that "we shall be in a civil War," but he hoped that God would "avert the evil." Rather than solidifying opposition to the Constitution, the Carlisle riot drove a wedge between the majority of backcountry Anti-Federalists and the most respected Anti-Federalist leaders.[54]

Despite the fears of prominent Anti-Federalists, popular support for the rioters was strong in the Pennsylvania backcountry. William Petrikin observed that in the aftermath of the riot "almost every day … some new society … [is] being formed" to oppose "this detastable Fedrall conspiracy." Anti-Federalist Richard Baird noted that "on the West side of the Susquehanna in this state there is at least nine out of every ten that would at the risk of their lives & property" oppose the new Constitution.[55]

In the wake of the peaceful resolution of events in Carlisle, backcountry Anti-Federalists mounted a petition campaign to void the actions of the state ratifying convention. In the short space of twelve days, Anti-Federalists gathered more than six thousand signatures to petitions in six counties. Leading Federalists in Huntingdon County sought to frustrate the campaign by destroying Anti-Federalist petitions. The actions of the "federal junto" aroused the indignation of local inhabitants who turned to the traditions of rough music to vent their anger. "A number of people … collected, and conducted upon the backs of old *scabby* ponies the EFFIGIES of the principals of the junto." When this procession passed the local courthouse, officers of the court apprehended the "effigy-men." The response of the local community was decisive. "Immediately the county took the alarm, assembled, and liberated the sons of liberty, so unjustly confined." The release of the prisoners was greeted with "loud huzzas and repeated acclaimations of joy from a large concourse of people." These self-styled sons of liberty re-enacted the same traditions of direct community action that inspired Anti-Federalists in Carlisle. Once again Anti-Federalists took to the streets, marched to the jail, and forced the release of their fellow citizens who had been unjustly imprisoned by an "aristocratic junto."[56]

Backcountry Anti-Federalists did not limit their actions to petition campaigns and street demonstrations. Events like the Carlisle and Huntingdon riots gave additional impetus to the move to call a second convention to revise the federal Constitution. Encouraged by the plans for a convention in Harrisburg, Carlisle Anti-Federalists offered up the following toast in celebration: "may such amendments be speedily framed … as may render the proposed Constitution of the United States truly democratical."[57] Leading Anti-Federalists from throughout Pennsylvania and several newcomers to Pennsylvania politics did convene in Harrisburg to discuss the future of their opposition to the new Constitution. One of the newcomers was a feisty representative from Carlisle, William Petrikin.[58]

Petrikin wanted the convention to adopt a radical program to unite Anti-Federalists throughout the country and to call a new convention to amend the Constitution. Petrikin's more radical position was defeated by the moderate forces led by a Philadelphia merchant, Charles Pettit. Like most other Anti-Federalist leaders, Pettit sought to distance himself from events such as the Carlisle riot. Men like Pettit were alarmed by the depth of hostility in the backcountry and feared the prospects of anarchy. Pettit felt that to "reject the New Plan and attempt again to resort to the old would … throw us into a State of Nature, filled with internal Discord." Pettit captured the view of many leading Anti-Federalists when he later confided to George Washington that "even after the vote of adoption by the State Convention, a large proportion of the people, especially in the western counties, shewed a disposition to resist the operation of it, in a manner which I thought indicated danger to the peace of the State."[59]

Ironically, the very success of the Carlisle rioters ultimately proved their own undoing. The fear of anarchy aided the moderates at Harrisburg and effectively ensured the demise of the second convention movement. Rather than encourage extralegal action on the part of backcountry populists, leading Anti-Federalists opted to compromise and take up their role as a "loyal opposition party."[60]

Elbridge Gerry, George Mason, and Charles Pettit were representative of Anti-Federalists of

the "better sort." They interpreted events like the Carlisle riot as a reminder of the precarious balance between liberty and order. The Anti-Federalism of these men had little to do with any populist notions of democracy. Such "men of little faith" sought to steer a political course between unfettered democracy and tyranny. The fear of popular anarchy was as intense among the Anti-Federalist political elite as among the Federalist leadership.[61]

The irony surrounding events in Carlisle was not lost on local Federalist leaders. John Montgomery, a leading Carlisle Federalist, astutely noted that the unintended consequence of public disturbances like the Carlisle riot was to strengthen the position of Federalists and moderate Anti-Federalists at the expense of more radical elements among the opponents of the Constitution. After expressing his relief that "horrors of civil war" had been averted, Montgomery, observed that events in Carlisle, like so much "seeming evil … since the Revolution" had "been productive of real good in our public affairs."[62]

## The Legacy of Plebeian Populism

If we are to understand why popular antagonism to the Constitution spilled into the streets we must attempt to see the struggle through the eyes of the men who risked their lives to oppose a form of government that, they thought, veered toward a new aristocratic order.

The rioters in Carlisle, like the supporters of Shays and many Anti-Federalists throughout the backcountry, were extremely hostile toward the federal Constitution. Although the eruption of violence in Carlisle grew out of local circumstances and events, the ideology that inspired this violent outburst and the rhetoric evoked to articulate local grievances were hardly unique to Carlisle. The rhetoric and symbols of protest appropriated by the rioters filled the popular press. Similar indictments of the new Constitution could be found in every major Anti-Federalist newspaper. Backcountry

Anti-Federalists of the "lower and middling sort" articulated a vision of populist democracy that was decidedly egalitarian and localistic. They challenged the idea that wealth, education, or prestige were appropriate measures of civic virtue and resisted the attempt by Federalists to frame a political system that shifted political power away from local communities. This position set backcountry opponents of the Constitution against Federalists who championed a vision of representative government that sought to encourage deference for men of "refined views" who would transcend local interests.

The ideological divide separating Federalists from Anti-Federalists cannot, however, be understood solely in terms of a battle between populist democrats and supporters of deference and order. Not everyone within the Anti-Federalist ranks championed populist democratic sentiments. Many leading Anti-Federalists were as concerned about the dangers of democratic excess as were leading Federalists. Many Anti-Federalists of the better sort were "men of little faith," who saw the federal Constitution as a threat to individual liberty and a dangerous departure from traditional whig opposition to powerful centralized governments. Anti-Federalists of the better sort, like the young John Quincy Adams, took great pains to make clear that their "strong *antifederalist*" sentiments were based upon "very different principles than those of your Worcester insurgents [Shaysites]." Indeed, it was precisely because of the popularity of Anti-Federalist sympathy among former Shaysites, that men like John Quincy Adams felt that continuing opposition to the Constitution "would be productive of much greater evils," no matter how "dangerous the tendency" of the new frame of government.[63]

As for Anti-Federalist populists, although they did not succeed in their efforts to block ratification, their political vision should not be ignored. The populist sentiments that inspired backcountry Anti-Federalists would continue to be a potent force in American political culture. A scant few years would pass before the anger

and frustrations of common folk would again lead men into the streets to vent their hostility against the new federal government. The reverberations of Anti-Federalism can clearly be heard in the Whiskey Rebellion. In fact, the Anti-Federalist challenge to the Constitution, like the Whiskey Rebellion, was only the first of many populist challenges that shaped the course of American politics. Localism and egalitarianism, the cornerstones of Anti-Federalist populism, provided inspiration for a distinctly American style of radical politics, one fashioned around the idea of participatory democracy and equality. Similar ideas would echo in the rhetoric of Jacksonian democracy and the Populist movement of the late nineteenth century.[64]

## Notes

Saul Cornell is NEH postdoctoral fellow at the Institute of Early American History and Culture and assistant professor of history, College of William and Mary.

I would like to thank the staff of the Documentary History of the Ratification of the Constitution for making their files available to me. Additional research was made possible by grants from the University of Pennsylvania, the John Carter Brown Library, and the American Antiquarian Society. Earlier drafts of this essay were presented at the Philadelphia Center for Early American Studies in 1986 and at the annual meeting of the Organization of American Historians at Philadelphia in April 1987. The final version of the essay benefited from the sound advice of my teachers at the University of Pennsylvania and of innumerable colleagues in and outside the university. I would like to thank the staff and referees of the *Journal of American History* for advice and encouragement.

1 For a useful corrective to treatment of the Anti-Federalists as a monolithic entity, see John P. Kaminski, "Antifederalism and the Perils of Homogenized History: A Review Essay," *Rhode Island History*, 42 (Feb. 1983), 30–37. On the different connotations of the hyphenated and unhyphenated spellings (Antifederalist or anti-Federalist), see Forrest McDonald, "The Anti-Federalists, 1781–1789," *Wisconsin Magazine of History*, 46 (Spring 1963), 206–14. The former

usage implies substantial uniformity among opponents of the Constitution; the latter suggests little unity beyond a common antipathy to the Federalists' scheme of government. I have not followed McDonald's use of the lowercase *a* in "anti" because I believe that it has the effect of denying commonalities among opponents of the Constitution. In this article I have adopted the term *Anti-Federalist* as middle position between the two poles. When considering an abstract political theory derived from the opposition I have employed the term *Anti-Federalism*.

2 Although the Anti-Federalist elite may have been no more democratic than leading Federalists, rank-and-file Anti-Federalists were democrats according to Jackson Turner Main, *The Antifederalists: Critics of the Constitution, 1781-1788* (Chapel Hill, 1961). On the need to separate elite from popular political thought in the ratification struggle, see Lee Benson, *Turner and Beard: American Historical Writing Reconsidered* (Glencoe, 1960). For the consensus view that Anti-Federalists were no more democratic than the Federalists, see Cecelia M. Kenyon, "Men of Little Faith: The Anti-Federalists on the Nature of Representative Government," *William and Mary Quarterly*, 12 (Jan. 1955), 3–43; Martin Diamond, "Democracy and *The Federalist*: A Reconsideration of the Framers' Intent," *American Political Science Review*, 53 (March 1959), 52–68; and James H. Hutson, "Country, Court, and Constitution: Antifederalism and the Historians," *William and Mary Quarterly*, 38 (July 1981), 337–68. Herbert J. Storing, *What the Anti-Federalists Were For* (Chicago, 1981), argues that the Anti-Federalists were somewhat more democratic than their opponents since they feared society's rulers more than they feared the people.

3 Many of the most important documents relating to ratification in Pennsylvania have been reprinted in Merrill Jensen et al., eds., *The Documentary History of the Ratification of the Constitution* (16 vols., Madison, 1976– ). See esp. II, 206–7. See also the sources in the microform supplement to the Pennsylvania volume.

4 Orin Grant Libby, *The Geographical Distribution of the Vote of the Thirteen States on the Federal Constitution, 1787–8* (Madison, 1894), demonstrated that Anti-Federalist strength

was concentrated in the interior of the country. Besides the backcountry violence in Pennsylvania, discussed in this article, there were other back-country protests during the battle over ratification, including incidents in South Carolina, North Carolina, and Rhode Island. Opposition in the South Carolina backcountry is described in Aedanus Burke to John Lamb, June 23, 1788, John Lamb Papers (New-York Historical Society, New York, New York). The Dobbs County, North Carolina, election riot is discussed by Robert A. Rutland, *The Ordeal of the Constitution: The Antifederalists and the Ratification Struggle of 1787–1788* (Norman, 1966), 271–274. On backcountry Anti-Federalist protest in Rhode Island, see *Providence Gazette and Country Journal*, July 12, 1788. The relative lack of interest in backcountry Anti-Federalism in recent scholarship contrasts with the proliferation of studies about other aspects of backcountry political culture. For an overview of those studies, see Gregory H. Nobles, "Breaking into the Backcountry: New Approaches to the Early American Frontier, 1750–1800," *William and Mary Quarterly*, 46 (Oct. 1989), 641–70.

5 Thomas Rodney Journal, May 10, 1788, in *Documentary History of the Ratification*, ed. Jensen et al., II, microform supplement, doc. no. 676.

6 On William Findley's political thought, see Gordon S. Wood, "Interests and Disinterestedness in the Making of the Constitution," *Beyond Confederation: Origins of the Constitution and American National Identity*, ed., Richard Beeman et al. (Chapel Hill, 1987), 69–109.

7 On Pennsylvania politics, see Robert L. Brunhouse, *The Counter-Revolution in Pennsylvania, 1776–1790* (Harrisburg, 1942); Douglas M. Arnold, "Political Ideology and the Internal Revolution in Pennsylvania: 1776–1790" (Ph.D. diss., Princeton University, 1976); and Richard A. Ryerson, "Republican Theory and Partisan Reality in Revolutionary Pennsylvania: Toward a New View of the Constitutionalist Party," in *Sovereign States in an Age of Uncertainty*, eds., Ronald Hoffman and Peter J. Albert (Charlottesville, 1981), 95–133.

3 Most of the important documents relating to the Carlisle riot are reprinted in Jensen et al., eds., *Documentary History of the Ratification*, II, 670–708. Many additional sources relevant to

the riot appear in the microform supplement to the Pennsylvania volume.

9 Jensen et al., eds., *Documentary History of the Ratification,* II, 671, 675.

10 *Pennsylvania Gazette,* March 26, 1788.

11 Jensen et al., eds., *Documentary History of the Ratification,* II, 672–73, 681.

12 *Ibid.,* 675, 678; see also microform supplement, doc. nos. 271, 409.

13 Jensen et al., eds., *Documentary History of the Ratification,* II, microform supplement, doc. no. 409.

14 Popular plebeian traditions are discussed by E. P. Thompson, "The Moral Economy of the English Crowd in the Eighteenth Century," *Past & Present,* 50 (Feb. 1971), 76–136; E. P. Thompson, "Patrician Society, Plebeian Culture," *Journal of Social History,* 7 (Summer 1974), 382–405; and Alfred F. Young, "English Plebeian Culture and Eighteenth-Century American Radicalism," in *The Origins of Anglo-American Radicalism,* ed. Margaret Jacob and James Jacob (London, 1984), 185–212. On the crowd in America, see Pauline Maier, *From Resistance to Revolution: Colonial Radicals and the Development of American Opposition to Britain, 1756–1776* (New York, 1972); Edward Countryman, "The Problem of the Early American Crowd," *Journal of American Studies,* 7 (April 1973), 77–90; and Paul Gilje, *The Road to Mobocracy: Popular Disorder in New York City, 1763–1834* (Chapel Hill, 1987).

15 Aristocrotis [William Petrikin], *The Government of Nature Delineated; or, An Exact Picture of the New Federal Constitution* (1788), in *The Complete Anti-Federalist,* ed. Herbert J. Storing (6 vols., Chicago, 1981), III, 196–213. Storing failed to identify the author as William Petrikin. For evidence supporting the attribution, see Jensen et al., eds., *Documentary History of the Ratification,* II, 674.

16 [Samuel Bryan], "Centinel," in *Complete Anti-Federalist,* ed. Storing, II, 137. The "Centinel" was among the most widely distributed Anti-Federalist works and was especially popular among Carlisle Anti-Federalists. William Petrikin, a leader of the riot, wrote to a prominent Pennsylvania Anti-Federalist to request "a few of the Centinals" since "they are much admired here." William Petrikin to John Nicholson, Feb. 24, 1788, in *Documentary History of the Ratification,* ed. Jensen et al., II, 695; *ibid.,* microform supplement, doc. no. 409.

17 Walter Stewart to William Irvine, Jan. 30, 1788, in *Documentary History of the Ratification,* ed., Jensen et al., II, microform supplement, doc. no. 380.

18 Pennsylvania Supreme Court to Sheriff Charles Leeper, Jan. 23, 1788, in *Documentary History of the Ratification,* ed., Jensen et al., II, 685. The prisoners' statement is reprinted, *ibid.,* 700.

19 For the petition signed by respectable persons, see *ibid.,* 708. For details of the prisoners' release, see *ibid.,* 699. Estimates of the crowd that marched to the jail to secure the release of prisoners vary from 250 to 1500, see *ibid.;* John Montgomery to James Wilson, March 2, 1788, *ibid.,* 701–6; John Shippen to Joseph Shippen, March 3, 1788, *ibid.,* 706–7; and *ibid.,* microform supplement, doc. nos. 491, 544, 554, 556, 629, 652.

20 "John Penn's Journal of a Visit to Reading, Harrisburg, Carlisle, and Lancaster in 1788," *Pennsylvania Magazine of History and Biography,* 3 (1879), 284–95, esp. 292. Montgomery to Benjamin Rush, June 12, 1787, in *Documentary History of the Ratification,* ed., Jensen et al., II, microform supplement, doc. no. 691.

21 Cumberland County Tax Lists 1781, microfilm copy (Historical Society of Pennsylvania, Philadelphia). Only 14 of 21 rioters were found on the Carlisle tax lists. The 7 missing individuals may have been either too poor to make it onto the evaluations or nonresidents. The names of Federalist and Anti-Federalist petitioners were obtained from a petition signed by respectable persons associated with each side, and the names of the rioters were obtained from the arrest warrant, see notes 16 and 15 above. Figures for householders were obtained by excluding from the tax lists the figures for freemen (that is, nonhouseholders).

22 Jensen et al., eds., *Documentary History of the Ratification,* XIV, 103. Several charges often appeared within a particular text. In discussing Anti-Federalist rhetoric, I have attempted to remain faithful to the categories outlined in the "Anti federal Recipe." Anti-aristocratic sentiment was defined by attacks on the tendency of the Constitution to promote the creation of an aristocracy composed of elected officials. Attempts to portray the new government as a system designed to favor the interests of a

distinctive social class of natural aristocrats or the better sort were grouped under accusations against the "well born." Objections to Federalist appeals for deference to prominent gentlemen, such as George Washington or Benjamin Franklin, were classified under appeals to "great names." These numbers do not tell us about the impact of various ideas on readers. Among the Carlisle rioters, it is possible to determine that they greatly esteemed "Centinel." All of the themes noted above were forcefully articulated by "Centinel" who conformed to the "Anti federal Recipe" with particular success. On the popularity of this essay among Carlisle Anti-Federalists, see Petrikin to Nicholson, Feb. 24, 1788, *ibid.,* II, 695.

23　Anti-Federalist attacks on the "well born," and "natural aristocracy" are excellent examples of E. P. Thompson's notion that class struggle may occur even if a modern social class structure is not yet fully formed; see E. P. Thompson, "Eighteenth-Century English Society: Class Struggle without Class," *Social History,* 3 (May 1978), 133–66. The ambiguity of eighteenth-century terms like lower, middling, and better sort is an index of the inchoate nature of class formation in this period. On Thompson's notion of class, see Craig Calhoun, *The Question of Class Struggle: Social foundations of Popular Radicalism during the Industrial Revolution* (Chicago, 1982). For a disputing of the claim that Anti-Federalists used the term *aristocracy* as an indictment of a specific social class, see Gary J. Schmitt and Robert H. Webking, "Revolutionaries, Antifederalists, and Federalists: Comments on Gordon Wood's Understanding of the American Founding," *Political Science Reviewer,* 9 (Fall 1979), 195–229, esp. 216–18. Both meanings of *aristocracy* are to be found in the writings of Anti-Federalists. The task for historians is to determine whether different social groups used *aristocracy* in distinctive ways.

24　"Federal Farmer," in *Complete Anti-Federalist,* ed. Storing, II, 267.

25　"John Adams, *A Defence of the Constitutions of Government of the United States of America* (2 vols., London, 1787–1788). The first volume appeared shortly before the Constitutional Convention. See John R. Howe, Jr., *The Changing Political Thought of John Adams* (Princeton, 1966);

Gordon S. Wood, *The Creation of the American Republic, 1776–1787* (Chapel Hill, 1969), 567–92; Joyce Appleby, "The New Republican Synthesis and the Changing Political Ideas of John Adams," *American Quarterly,* 25 (Dec. 1973), 578–95; and Peter Shaw, *The Character of John Adams* (Chapel Hill, 1976). James Wilson, speech in the Pennsylvania State Convention, in *Documentary History of the Ratification,* ed., Jensen et al., II, 488–89.

26　Jensen et al., eds., *Documentary History of the Ratification,* II, 488–89. For similar statement by Wilson, see Adrienne Koch, ed., *Notes of the Debates in the Federal Convention of 1787 Reported by James Madison* (Athens, Ohio, 1966), 74, 85. For Madison's comment, see James Madison, Alexander Hamilton, and John Jay, *The Federalist,* ed. Jacob Cooke (Middletown, 1961), 62. On the important but often subtle differences among Federalists on the issue of representation, see Lance Banning, "The Hamiltonian Madison: A Reconsideration," *Virginia Magazine of History and Biography,* 92 (Jan. 1984), 3–28. See also Robert J. Morgan, "Madison's Theory of Representation in the Tenth *Federalist,*" *Journal of Politics,* 36 (Nov. 1974), 852–85; Jean Yarbrough, "Representation and Republicanism: Two Views," *Publius,* 9 (Spring 1979), 77–98; and Gordon S. Wood, "Democracy and the Constitution," in *How Democratic Is the Constitution?* ed. Robert A. Goldwin and William A. Schambra (Washington, 1980), 1–17.

27　On the convergence of Federalist hopes and Anti-Federalist fears regarding representation under the new Constitution, see Jack Rakove, "The Structure of Politics at the Accession of George Washington," in *Beyond Confederation,* ed. Beeman et al., 261–94.

28　On the connection between Adams and the new Constitution, see "Centinel," *Complete Anti-Federalist,* ed. Storing, II, 138–39. For a different view, see *Carlisle Gazette,* Oct. 24, 1787.

29　James Smylie, "Charles Nisbet: Second Thoughts on a Revolutionary Generation," *Pennsylvania Magazine of History and Biography,* 98 (April 1974), 189–205, esp. 193. See also "Charles Nisbet to the Students after Vacation," in *Documentary History of the Ratification,* ed., Jensen et al., II, microform supplement, doc. no. 182; Charles Nisbet to Alexander Addison, Dec.

7, 1787, *ibid.,* 259; Nisbet to the Earl of Buchan, Dec. 25, 1787, *ibid.,* XV, 87–90.

30 Smylie, "Charles Nisbet," 193; Petrikin to Nicholson, May 8, 1788, in *Documentary History of the Ratification,* ed., Jensen et al., II, microform supplement, doc. no. 675.

31 On the centrality of the militia and yeomanry to traditional republicanism, see Edmund S. Morgan, *Inventing the People: The Rise of Popular Sovereignty in England and America* (New York, 1988), 153–208. On the ideological significance of education, print, the press, and the notion of the "republic of letters," see Richard D. Brown, "From Cohesion to Competition," in *Printing and Society in Early America,* ed., William Joyce et al. (Worcester, 1983), 300–309, esp. 304; and David Paul Nord, "A Republican Literature: Magazine Reading and Readers in Late-Eighteenth-Century New York," in *Reading in America: Literature and Social History,* ed., Cathy N. Davidson (Baltimore, 1989), 114–39.

32 Benjamin Rush, "Thoughts upon the Mode of Education Proper in a Republic," in *Essays on Education in the Early Republic,* ed., Frederick Rudolph (Cambridge, Mass., 1968), 9–23, esp. 17. In addition to Rush, several other prominent Federalists served as trustees of Dickinson College during this period, including John Dickinson and James Wilson, and among local Federalists, John Armstrong and John Montgomery. For a list of the college's trustees, see Charles C. Sellers, *Dickinson College: A History* (Middletown, 1973), 481–84.

33 Jensen et al., eds., *Documentary History of the Ratification,* II, microform supplement, doc. no. 675. Little is known about Petrikin's early life; see the biographical sketch in John Blair Linn, *History of Centre and Clinton Counties, Pennsylvania* (Philadelphia, 1883), 219. Petrikin was an ideal person to represent local Anti-Federalist sentiment. Like many other Carlisle residents, he was not a large property holder but a man of modest means who rented a small house lot. Like many in this region, Petrikin was a recent immigrant from Scotland. On the prevalence of tenancy, see Lucy Simler, "Tenancy in Colonial Pennsylvania; The Case of Chester County," *William and Mary Quarterly,* 43 (Oct. 1986), 542–69. On the growing class stratification in western Pennsylvania, see R. Eugene Harper,

"The Class Structure of Western Pennsylvania in the Late Eighteenth Century, 1783–1796" (Ph.D. diss., University of Pittsburgh, 1969). On the importance of immigration, especially of the Scots and Scotch-Irish, see Thomas L. Purvis, "Patterns of Ethnic Settlement in Late-Eighteenth-Century Pennsylvania," *Western Pennsylvania Historical Magazine,* 70 (April 1987), 107–22; and Bernard Bailyn, *Voyagers to the West: A Passage in the Peopling of America on the Eve of the Revolution* (New York, 1986), 25–27, 176–85, 204–38. On the ethnocultural roots of Pennsylvania politics, see Owen Ireland, "The Crux of Politics.' Religion and Party in Pennsylvania, 1778–1789," *William and Mary Quarterly,* 42 (Oct. 1985), 453–75. For suggestive attempts to link ethnocultural politics with variants of republicanism, see Robert Kelley, *The Cultural Pattern in American Politics: The First Century* (New York, 1979); and Forrest McDonald, *Novus Ordo Seclorum: The Intellectual Origins of the Constitution* (Lawrence, 1985), 157.

34 For theoretical works that have influenced my attempt to explore the different interpretive communities within Anti-Federalism, see Stanley Fish, *Is There a Text in This Class? The Authority of Interpretive Communities* (Cambridge, Mass., 1980); and, on the importance of moving beyond authorial intent to consider the response of readers, Roger Chartier, "Intellectual History or Sociocultural History? The French Trajectories," in *Modern European Intellectual History: Reappraisals and New Perspectives,* ed. Dominick La Capra and Steven L. Kaplan (Ithaca, 1982), 13–46; and Janice Radway, "American Studies, Reader Theory, and the Literary Text: From the Study of Material Objects to the Study of Social Processes," in *American Studies in Transition,* ed., David E. Nye and Christen Kold Thomsen (Odense, Denmark, 1985), 29–51.

35 On "Centinel," see Saul Cornell, "Reflections on the 'Late Remarkable Revolution in Government': Aedanus Burke and Samuel Bryan's Unpublished History of the Ratification of the Federal Constitution," *Pennsylvania Magazine of History and Biography,* 112 (Jan. 1988), 103–30, esp. 113–16.

36 Jensen et al., eds., *Documentary History of the Ratification,* II, 685–92.

37 On the differences between Anti-Federalist and Federalist pseudonyms, see McDonald, *Novus Ordo Sechrum,* 67–70.

38  On the importance of Plutarch to eighteenth-century American perceptions of classical political history, see McDonald, *Novus Ordo Seclorum,* 67–70. Writing as "Aristocrotis," William Petrikin remarked that New York's Brutus was one of the more influential writers on plebeian Anti-Federalists. See Storing, ed., *Complete Anti-federalist,* III, 198. On the influence of classical authors on Federalist and Anti-Federalist writing, see Donald S. Lutz, "The Relative Influence of European Writers on Late Eighteenth-Century American Political Thought," *American Politicai Science Review,* 78 (March 1984), 189–97.

39  "Jensen et al., eds., *Documentary History of the Ratification,* II, 661–63.

40  On the ideological significance of Federalist attempts to stifle debate by requiring authors to publish their names, see Robert Gross. "The Authority of the Word: Print and Social Change in America, 1607–1880," 1984, (in Saul Cornell's possession), 125–35; and "Philadelphiensis," *Complete Anti-Federalist,* ed. Storing, III, 103–4.

41  "Centinel," *Complete Anti-Federalist,* ed. Storing, II, 159, 205. For a radical version of the "republic of letters" similar to the one espoused by Petrikin, see Samuel Eliot Morison, ed., "William Manning's *The Key to Libberty,*" *William and Mary Quarterly,* 13 (April 1956), 202–54.

42  On the localist/cosmopolitan dichotomy, see Jackson Turner Main, *Political Parties before the Constitution* (Chapel Hill, 1973), 32.

43  On republicanism, whig politics, and "country ideology," see Bernard Bailyn, *The Ideological Origins of the American Revolution* (Cambridge, Mass., 1967); J. G. A. Pocock, *The Machiavellian Moment: Florentine Political Thought and the Atlantic Republican Tradition* (Princeton, 1975); J. G. A. Pocock, ed., *Three British Revolutions: 1641, 1688, 1776* (Princeton, 1980); J. G. A. Pocock, *Virtue, Commerce, and History* (Cambridge, Eng., 1985); and Wood, *Creation of the American Republic.* Useful review articles that treat the problem of republicanism in early American history include Robert Shalhope, "Toward a Republican Synthesis: The Emergence of an Understanding of Republicanism in American Historiography," *William and Mary Quarterly,* 29 (Jan. 1972), 49–80; Robert Shalhope, "Republicanism and Early American Historiography," *ibid.,* 39 (April 1982),

334–56; and the special issue "Republicanism in the History and Historiography of the United States," ed., Joyce Appleby, *American Quarterly,* 37 (Fall 1985), 461–598. For contrasting views of the relevance of that literature to Anti-Federalist thought, see Hutson, "Country, Court, and Constitution," and Richard Beeman "Introduction," in *Beyond Confederation,* ed., Beeman et al., 3–19, esp. 16.

44  On the relationship between localism and the structure of politics within the British Empire, see Jack P. Greene, *Peripheries and Centers; Constitutional Development in the Extended Politics of the British Empire and the United States, 1607–1788* (Athens, Ga., 1986); [Luther Martin], "The Genuine Information," *Complete Anti-Federalist,* ed. Storing, II, 48; [James Winthrop], "Agrippa," *ibid.,* IV, 76–77, 93.

45  [Petrikin], *Government of Nature,* in *Complete Anti-Federalist,* ed. Storing, III, 197–98, 204–5.

46  *Ibid.,* 199, 202.

47  Petrikin to Nicholson, May 8, 1788, in *Documentary History of the Ratification,* ed. Jensen et al., II, microform supplement, doc. no. 675; "Mentor," *Carlisle Gazette,* Sept. 27, 1786.

48  See Hanna F. Pitkin, *The Concept of Representation* (Berkeley, 1967), 60–61, 146–47.

49  Jonathan Elliot, ed., *The Debates in the Several State Conventions …* (5 vols., Philadelphia, 1836–1845), II, 102.

50  Montgomery to Wilson, March 2, 1788, in *Documentary History of Ratification,* ed., Jensen et al., II, 705.

51  "George Mason's Objections to the Constitution of Government Formed by the Convention, 1787," in *Complete Anti-Federalist,* ed. Storing, II, 13; Koch, ed., *Notes of the Debates in the Federal Convention of 1787 Reported by James Madison,* 39.

52  Gordon S. Wood's discussion of a struggle between the "worthy and licentious" captures the essential political dynamic of the battle between Anti-Federalist populists and Federalists. However, Wood treated "aristocratic" Anti-Federalists as unrepresentative, whereas I see them as representative of an elite strand of Antifederalism. See Wood, *Creation of the American Republic,* 471–518. For evidence that many prominent Anti-Federalists worried about the dangers of Shaysism, see Robert A. Feer,

"Shays's Rebellion and the Constitution: A Study in Causation," *New England Quarterly,* 42 (Sept. 1969), 388–410. One suggestive attempt to place the tension between liberty and order at the center of the history of this period is Thomas P. Slaughter, *The Whiskey Rebellion: Frontier Epilogue to the American Revolution* (New York, 1986).

53 The Federalist description of the riot by an "Old Man" was reprinted thirty-seven times by March 10, 1788, in papers from Georgia to Maine. On the distribution of the piece, see Jensen et al., eds., *Documentary History of the Ratification,* XV, 225; *ibid.,* microform supplement, doc. nos. 392, 334.

54 For Gerry's statements about the dangers of too much democracy, see Koch, ed., *Notes of the Debates in the federal Convention,* 39. On Gerry's view of events in Carlisle, see Elbridge Gerry to S. R. Gerry, Jan. 28, 1788, Samuel R. Gerry Papers (Massachusetts Historical Society, Boston, Mass.).

55 Petrikin to Nicholson, Feb. 24, 1788, in *Documentary History of the Ratification,* ed. Jensen et al., II, 695–96; Richard Baird to Nicholson, Feb. 1, 1788, *ibid.,* 712.

56 On the petition campaign, see *ibid.,* 709–25. On the riot in Huntingdon County, Pennsylvania, see *ibid.,* 718.

57 Merrill Jensen and Robert A. Becker, eds., *The Documentary History of the first federal Elections, 1788–1790* (3 vols., Madison, 1976– ), I, 242.

58 Documents relating to the Harrisburg Convention have been reproduced *ibid.,* I, 257–81. For historical discussion of the Harrisburg convention, see Paul Leicester Ford, *The Origin, Purpose, and Result of the Harrisburg Convention of 1788: A Study in Popular Government* (Brooklyn, 1890); Linda Grant DePauw, "The Anticlimax of Antifederalism: The Abortive Second Convention Movement, 1788–89," *Prologue, 2* (Fall 1970), 98–114; and Steven R. Boyd, *The Politics of Opposition: Antifederalists and the Acceptance of the Constitution* (Millwood, 1979), 142–44.

59 Charles Pettit to Robert Whitehill, June 5, 1788, Robert Whitehill Papers (Hamilton Library, Cumberland County Historical Society). See also Pettit to George Washington, March 19, 1791, in *Documentary History of the Ratification,* ed., Jensen et al., II, microform supplement, doc. no. 706.

60 For a slightly different explanation of Anti-Federalism's transition into a loyal opposition, see Lance Banning, "Republican Ideology and the Triumph of the Constitution, 1789 to 1793," *William and Mary Quarterly,* 31 (April 1974), 167–88.

61 Kenyon, "Men of Little Faith."

62 Montgomery to Wilson, March 2, 1788, in *Documentary History of the Ratification,* ed. Jensen et al., II, 703, 704.

63 John Quincy Adams to Oliver Fiske, Feb. 17, 1788, Adams folder, Miscellaneous Manuscripts (American Antiquarian Society, Worcester, Mass.).

64 On unrest in Carlisle during the Whiskey Insurrection, see Slaughter, *Whiskey Rebellion,* 205–11. On the ideological continuity between Anti-Federalism and the Whiskey Rebels, see Dorothy Fennell, "Herman Husband's Antifederalism and the Rebellion in Western Pennsylvania," paper presented at the annual meeting of the Organization of American Historians, Philadelphia, April 1987 (in Cornell's possession). On the Anti-Federalists' vision of participatory democracy, see Jennifer Nedelsky, "Confining Democratic Politics: Anti-Federalists, Federalists, and the Constitution," *Harvard Law Review,* 96 (Dec. 1982), 340–60. Many of the ideas essential to Anti-Federalist populism played an important role in Jacksonian thought. See Richard Ellis, "The Persistence of AntiFederalism after 1789," in *Beyond Confederation,* ed., Beeman et al., 295–314. On the radical democratic character of much Jacksonian rhetoric, see John Ashworth, *'Agrarians' & 'Aristocrats': Party Political Ideology in the United States, 1837–1846* (Cambridge, Eng., 1983). On the Populist movement, see Lawrence Goodwyn, *The Populist Moment: A Short History of the Agrarian Revolt in America* (New York, 1978). On the rediscovery of Anti-Federalism by modern populists, see Saul Cornell, "The Changing Historical Fortunes of the Anti-Federalists," *Northwestern University Law Review* (forthcoming).

# 15
# "TO MAN THEIR RIGHTS"
*The Frontier Revolution*

## Alan Taylor

### Introduction

The United States faced a number of critical issues following its victory over Britain in the Revolution, including an economic depression, ongoing wars with Indian nations, and an ineffective federal government. Alan Taylor points to yet another of the era's crises: independence movements in the West (and, as New Englanders would put it, Down East). In places as varied as Maine, Vermont, the Wyoming Valley of Pennsylvania, Kentucky, and Tennessee, white settlers tried to establish new states in areas claimed by old ones. In some cases, when they did not get their way, they formed armed militias and threatened to seek annexation by foreign empires like Britain and Spain. With greater effectiveness, they used generous land grants to buy the support of political grandees like Alexander Hamilton, John Jay, and John Witherspoon. Such tactics ultimately led to the creation of some of the early republic's first new states.

Taylor argues that these secessionist movements involved more than just poor white settlers seeking cheap and even free land. Also driving these contests was competition between eastern elites and opportunistic land speculators whose ambitions had been thwarted through conventional political means. Both sides claimed western land through a number of competing sources, such as Indian purchases and grants from the crown, colonies, and states. However, ultimately their claims turned on whether they could enlist the support of white squatters who flooded into western regions. Those squatters represented military might and votes. To earn their support and undercut well-established elite speculators, upstart land speculators offered squatters land on the cheap. They also used land to bribe politicians into supporting their campaigns to separate from eastern states. Though a number of these schemes failed, as in the would-be state of Franklin and in the Wyoming Valley of Pennsylvania, still others paid off, at least for the squatter-speculator combinations.

Such developments threatened the political stability of several eastern states and the federal government, thus providing the impetus for the Northwest Ordinances of 1785 and 1787. Thereafter, upstart speculators were forced to turn to elections and lobbying, rather than the arming of militias, to make their fortunes. Squatters lost their leverage.

- Read alongside Saul Cornell's essay, in what ways does Taylor's account help explain public support for the new federal Constitution? What course would the backcountry have taken without that Constitution?

- Taylor focusses on divisions among white Americans in the contest for frontier land, but do you also see a consensus at work? What was the position of these various interests in relation to Indians and the government's responsibility to protect private property? How do the answers to these questions affect your reading of Colin G. Calloway's essay on Indians during the revolutionary era?

- In what ways did these western schemes reflect earlier American grievances against Britain such as the Proclamation Line of 1763 and the Quebec Act of 1774?
- Was western unrest yet another example in which the argument for independence gave rise to demands for substantial social change, as discussed in essays by Gary B. Nash, Ira Berlin, and Rosemarie Zagarri?

In November 1787 Col. Timothy Pickering lamented his inability to maintain Pennsylvania's legal authority over the rebellious Yankee settlers of Luzerne County in the upper Susquehanna Valley. Pickering blamed the local settler insurgency on "the natural instability of the common people" compounded by frontier isolation from established authority and well stirred by populist demagogues. And he detected a national pattern. "The discontents in the county of Luzerne are not the result merely of disaffection to the government of Pennsylvania. The peculiar circumstances of the United States have encouraged bad men in several of them to throw off their allegiance to excite the common people to rebellion & to attempt the erecting of New States." Pickering regarded the "bad men" as class traitors: rogue gentlemen "of talents, but of desperate fortunes," who, for want of restraining virtue, recklessly pursued their self-interest by encouraging popular turmoil. Pickering worried that "no one can say what would be the final issue of the contest, in the present weak state of the federal union and general discontent and spirit of revolt so prevalent among the people of these states."[1]

Pickering's alarm about the extent of backcountry unrest during the 1780s was widely shared and well founded. In Maine, aggrieved settlers and frustrated local politicians combined to agitate for separation from Massachusetts. They found inspiration in Vermont, where the settlers had seceded from New York and used force to keep their independence. Hundreds of Massachusetts and New Hampshire farmers resisted the collection of taxes and debts during Ely's Rebellion of 1782 and Shays's Rebellion of 1786–87. The tenant farmers living along the New York–New England border frequently rioted against their landlords and in favor of

secure freehold land. In Western New York unscrupulous land speculators sought to preempt the region by leasing it for 999 years from a few compliant Iroquois sachems; these speculators meant to evade a New York state law that forbade private purchases of land from the Indians in western New York. To uphold their brazen deal, the leaseholders encouraged the settlers in western New York to secede and organize their own state. Western Pennsylvania was also rife with squatters, secessionist schemes, and tax resistance. Meanwhile squatters in the Ohio country defied federal troops and made plans to organize their own state. George Washington dubbed them "a parcel of banditti, who will bid defiance to all authority." In Kentucky hundreds of settlers seeking free lands hoped to escape Virginia's jurisdiction and its landlords by supporting separatist proposals hatched by some competing land speculators. In Tennessee, dissident settlers and speculators cooperated to secede from North Carolina and to form the state of Franklin. Surveying the whole frontier, a Connecticut newspaper aptly concluded in 1787, "We see *banditties* rising up against law and good order in all quarters of our country." Washington worried that "the Western Settlers … stand, as it were, on a pivet – the touch of a feather would almost incline them any way"[2]

As Pickering noted, most of the frontier separatist movements of the 1780s were alliances between two distinct but compatible groups: penurious settlers seeking free or cheap homesteads *and* aggressive land speculators who lacked the proper connections to realize their ambitions through the existing state governments. The two groups allied to defy the legal and political establishments and the old-money land speculators who had invested in more reputable land titles. In sum, the scramble for wilderness lands newly wrested from the Indians generated a series of triangular contests from Maine to Tennessee involving settlers and two competing sets of speculators – well-established gentlemen and aspiring, opportunistic new men. Ultimately, the contending speculator camps struggled for the power to collect payments from the settlers; but in the short run, the competition created opportunities for the first settlers in a given district to demand free or cheap homesteads in return for their support. In general, the first settlers found it in their interest to enlist with the opportunists who needed armed force to circumvent the established legislatures and courts that favored the land titles of more reputable men of entrenched wealth and status.

But we should be careful not to equate settlers and opportunists, not to regard the latter as exemplifying the behavior and aspirations of the former. In fact, the settlers had their own agenda and readily deserted or sought new allies as circumstances shifted. Nor should we regard the settlers as simply the pawns of the opportunists. The upstart speculators responded to opportunities created by settlers of more modest means and aspirations. Indeed, settler resistance could exist without speculator allies, as was the case in Maine. This essay will examine the triangular contests for the frontier with special attention to the related conflicts in Vermont and in northern Pennsylvania's Susquehanna Valley.[3]

## Disaffection and Opportunism

In eighteenth-century America, men acquired fortunes and political power by obtaining titles to lands on the fast-settling frontier. No other path to wealth and power was more promising on a continent of fertile soil and fecund people. Access to extensive lands conquered from the Indians encouraged colonists to marry relatively young (four to five years younger than in Europe) and to bear additional children. Consequently, even apart from immigration, the population

grew at a rate of about 3 percent annually, a doubling by natural increase every twenty-five years. Because almost every family sought a farm, each new generation doubled the demand for land, putting increased pressure on the beleaguered Indians. Given the demographic facts of North American life, those men who acquired titles to large tracts of unsettled land could reap rich profits by retailing farms as the tide of settlement reached their domains. In a detailed memorandum meant to shape his extensive land speculations, Gen. Henry Knox noted, "The price of any commodity whatever may be raised in two ways, either by diminishing the quantity for sale, or by increasing the demand. But the extension of settlements and the increase of wealth and population operate at once in both these ways upon American lands: not only diminishing the quantity for sale, but increasing the means and the eligibility of making further purchases and settlements." Titles were licenses to collect payments from whoever wanted to use the land; they were valuable only to the degree that their owners could induce actual settlers to buy them. A settler found it in his interest to buy a title when the landlord could resort to a court of law and prevail in a lawsuit for trespass or ejectment. So, in the last analysis, the power of the courts to enforce their will gave titles their value. And the courts favored the titles created by governors and legislatures and awarded to their political favorites rather than titles asserted by squatters or by those who bought deeds from the Indians without official license.[4]

Ordinarily, colonial settlers accepted that they had to pay a landlord to obtain a piece of the forest. But when landlords behaved in a blatantly predatory manner, they aroused the ordinarily dormant but always potent fear that the rich were hoarding the wilderness in order to "enslave" the common people. At such moments, settlers imagined themselves as verging on the degradation of European peasants, for they knew that without secure property they were ripe for exploitation by the powerful. The settlers of Orange County, North

Carolina, anticipated a dreadful life of "wooden shoes and uncombed hair" for want of secure homesteads. William Prendergast, a leader in the New York tenant rebellion of 1766, said that "it was hard they were not allowed to have *any property.*" He knew that people without property could not long keep their liberty. When alarmed by impending domination, rural Americans suddenly could imagine the better society of equal rights and justice that Hermon Husband of the North Carolina Regulators called a "new government of liberty" or a "New Jerusalem." Both alarmed and inspired, settlers strove to secure the property that endowed liberty. They denounced their landlords as parasites, rallied around the cheapest alternative titles they could obtain, and organized militias to defend themselves from eviction and to oust anyone who assisted the landlord.[5]

Growing settler unrest encouraged the emergence of a new brand of land speculator – less reputable and less well connected men ready to proffer quasi-legal and cut-rate land titles. The opportunists capitalized on the growing number of settlers who felt cheated and who wanted cheap lands. The opportunists concocted alternative titles either by extending the bounds of bordering colonies and states or by plying cooperative Indian sachems with alcohol and trade goods. Then the opportunists retailed their titles to farm-sized lots at reduced rates in order to fill their lands with supportive settlers prepared forcefully to repel the law officers of the established courts in the existing states. Opportunists appealed to the poorest settlers, those least able to pay the higher prices demanded by the holders of the more reputable titles created by colonial and state governments. In a pamphlet written to support the Indian-deed claim of Col. John Henry Lydius to about one million acres in what is now Vermont, Dr. Thomas Young insisted that such cheap titles furnished "many poor families with the means of a very comfortable living, who must otherwise groan with poverty." In an "Invitation to the Poor Tenants of New York," Thomas Rowley

of Rutland County, Vermont, promoted the suspect titles based on New Hampshire grants; by recruiting settlers among New York's tenants, Rowley hoped simultaneously to undermine the economic base of that colony's landlord class and strengthen the numbers committed to resisting their claims to Vermont. He urged,

> Come all you laboring hands that toil below,
> Among the rocks and bands, that plow and
>     so;
> Upon your hired lands, let out by cruel
>     hands,
> 'Twill make you large amends to Rutland go.
> Your patroons forsake, whose greatest care
> Is slaves of you to make, while you live
>     there;
> Come, quit their barren lands, and leave
>     them in their hands,
> 'Twill ease of[f] you your bands to Rutland
>     go.

The opportunists gambled that once they had placed a body of well-armed settlers on the land, the governments would have to bow to the fait accompli, and the gentry would have to welcome the victors to their club. By undercutting the titles manufactured by governors and their councils and upheld by the courts, the opportunists threatened the entire basis of political authority in eighteenth-century America, the dispensation of land grants to construct networks of interest binding influential men together in support of the established institutions of governance.[6]

During the 1760s and early 1770s innovative landgrabs proliferated along the entire frontier arc. Small-scale speculators from New England exploited suspect titles created by New Hampshire's unscrupulous governor, Benning Wentworth, to lay claim to northeastern New York (present-day Vermont). To defy New York's posses and surveyors, the claimants recruited well-armed settlers by offering free grants to the first comers and prices as low as two cents per acre to subsequent arrivals. "They are crowding up to this Country as if all New England was set on fire," one Vermont resident observed in 1771. To retain their bargains, the settlers in western Vermont organized a de facto government of local committees and a militia known as the Green Mountain Boys. Meanwhile aspiring land speculators from Connecticut meant to seize northern Pennsylvania; they organized the Susquehannah Company in 1753, negotiated a treaty of purchase with some intoxicated Iroquois Indians, and began to sell titles for nominal amounts to settlers who came from Pennsylvania, New Jersey, and New York, as well as from New England. Farther south, Judge Richard Henderson of North Carolina and his partners financed transappalachian exploration by Daniel Boone, organized the Transylvania Company, and in March 1775 negotiated a purchase of twenty million acres – nearly all of present Kentucky and much of northern Tennessee – from a group of Cherokee Indians for trade goods worth £10,000, the equivalent of two to three cents an acre. Henderson won over most of the region's new settlers by offering them lands at the low price of twenty shillings per hundred acres; he meant to wrest the region away from Virginia and establish a distinct colony. Another cartel based in North Carolina and known as the Watauga Association pursued a similar strategy to secure eastern Tennessee for £2,000 and to bring the local settlers into their scheme.[7]

## Vermont

The frontier opportunists became even more daring and formidable after the outbreak of the Revolutionary War in 1775. Exploiting the Revolutionary upheaval, opportunists from Maine to Tennessee went into the state-making business. The elimination of royal authority over the wilderness added to the uncertainty over who could create legitimate land titles. And the colonists' Declaration of Independence from Great Britain set a precedent for aggrieved frontiersmen and canny opportunists to cite in their efforts to break away from the regimes of the eastern seaboard. The would-be leaders of projected frontier states built popular support by promising the first settlers better terms (often free land) than those offered by the land speculators of the established states. Once the new leaders had secured their new state, they meant amply to reward themselves from the offices of government and from the remaining stock of unsettled lands within their jurisdiction. In effect, through state-making, the opportunists meant to seize the most important path to wealth and power on the North American continent – the authority to build an "interest" by making, selling, and enforcing land titles. For ambitious men with few scruples, Revolutionary state-making promised meteoric social mobility.[8]

Vermont was the prototype for the opportunistic state-making associated with the Revolution. In January 1777 a convention of delegates from seventeen townships established the republic of Vermont, independent of both New York and New Hampshire. Six months later another convention adopted a populist constitution for the republic. The new government was dominated by a group of opportunists known as the Arlington Junto because most resided in that town during the war: Ethan Allen, his brother Ira, and their friends Thomas Chittenden and Matthew Lyon. The popular and pliable Chittenden presided over the new republic's council of state; the shrewd and secretive Ira Allen filled most of the other major posts – treasurer, secretary of state, and surveyor general; Lyon served as Ira Allen's chief deputy and as clerk of the Vermont assembly; Ethan Allen rarely held formal office but influenced the government through his three allies.[9]

The Arlington Junto exercised their control over Vermont's land to build an "interest," or faction, that would keep them in office so that they could ultimately enrich themselves from the residue of the republic's unsettled forest. In the short run, they had to dispense land generously to cultivate men who would help them weather the threats of British invasion, internal disaffection, and New York's continuing efforts to suppress the Vermont republic. In the long run, the Arlington Junto meant to secure their own wealth and social preeminence by speculating in New Hampshire land grant titles to over 75,000 acres of Vermont's very best land, principally in the then unsettled Onion River Valley (now the Winooski River Valley) around present-day Burlington. Over the course of their dozen-year stewardship of Vermont, they accumulated thousands of additional acres farther north. If Vermont survived and prospered, the Junto would reap fortunes from their extensive, albeit legally dubious, land claims.[10]

The Junto's first task was to curry support among the settlers and thereby obtain the militia needed to repel the British and to intimidate New York's authorities and their local supporters. To that end, Vermont abrogated the claims of New York's landlords and endorsed the New Hampshire grants that most settlers relied upon for title. Settlers without any titles could obtain cheap grants to "public lands" from the Vermont assembly. This policy promised settlers that they need make no additional payments for purchase or for quit-rents to New Yorkers so long as Vermont remained independent. Consequently, the interest of most settlers as freeholders depended on the survival of the Junto's republic. Moreover, the Junto sustained popularity by minimizing taxes, financing their regime virtually without taxes through 1780 by confiscating and auctioning the lands of alleged loyalists. The Junto's broad definition of "loyalist" extended to anyone who supported New York's jurisdiction or land titles. Junto members often profited from their positions by purchasing the best properties at bargain prices. The regime also minimized the costs of defense (postponing the introduction of significant taxes) by entering secret negotiations with the British authorities in Canada. The Vermont leaders purchased a de facto state of neutrality during the war's later years by promising (perhaps disingenuously) to persuade their constituents to rejoin the British empire. A reputation for cheap land and for low taxes made Vermont a haven for hard-pressed

New England yeomen who flocked to the region during the war, swelling the ranks of the militia that the Junto needed to stay in power. By serving the ambitions of rogue gentlemen, common yeomen eased their own access to freehold prosperity, leaving the landlords and rulers of New York to fume in futility. The Junto sustained their republic because it offered the common yeomanry better access to cheap, fee-simple homesteads than did New York's authorities and landlords.[11]

The Junto's second task was to use their land titles to counteract New York's influence in Congress and to buy the goodwill of leading men in other state governments. The land committee of the Vermont assembly allocated generous grants of wild land in fifty new townships at token prices to useful and powerful outsiders: members of Congress, Continental army generals, and the leaders of state governments. The grantees included John Paul Jones, John Adams, Oliver Wolcott, generals John Sullivan and Horatio Gates, and President John Witherspoon of Princeton. The grantees' interest in their new townships merged with the interest of the Arlington Junto because the township grants would prove valuable only if the republic preserved its independence from New York. Into the bargain, members of the Junto sought further enrichment by naming themselves and their allies partners in many of the grants. Thomas Chittenden, for example, held interests in at least forty-two new townships.[12]

By securing the support of both resident yeomen and many nonresident gentlemen, the Arlington Junto weathered the war and remained in control of their republic until Ethan Allen's death in 1789. New York could never secure a congressional commitment to suppress the Junto, in part because of Vermont's growing "interest" in Congress and in part because of fears that coercion would drive the rogue republic into the British embrace. In 1791 the Junto's successors negotiated peace with New York. In return for an indemnity of $30,000, New York surrendered its claims and permitted

Vermont to enter the Union. Following the Junto's example, the new state government used land grants to reward the New York politicians – including Alexander Hamilton, John Jay, and William Duer – who had consummated the deal over the bitter opposition of their state's governor, George Clinton. The Arlington Junto had retained power long enough to secure Vermont's statehood and to consolidate their private claims to substantial landholdings.[13]

The success of the Arlington Junto attests to the new avenues to wealth and authority opened by the Revolution and exploited by men of great ambition but of only middling property and without patronage from the established elite. Short on the social graces, family ties, and literary education necessary for acceptance among the nation's gentility (who included New York's landlords), the members of the Junto had made a virtue of necessity, obtaining Vermont leadership and estates by cultivating popular suspicion of prominent and wealthy outsiders. Before squandering his fortune on unwise investment in foreign commerce and political intrigue, Ira Allen had become one of the richest men in Vermont. The other members of the Junto were more fortunate. Matthew Lyon had come to America an Irish immigrant and an indentured servant, but he obtained in Fairhaven, Vermont, a four-hundred-acre tract unusually rich in iron, lumber, and water-power. During the 1780s and early 1790s he established a profitable complex with a sawmill, gristmill, paper mill, ironworks, tavern, store, newspaper, and farm. He also became a United States congressman who won notoriety as an extreme Jeffersonian. Ethan Allen secured a fourteen-hundred-acre farm of choice riverside land in Burlington and another 12,000 acres of fast-appreciating forest land in new townships. It was less than the great estates of the New York grandees he had contended with – men like James Duane and Philip Schuyler – but it was far more than he had begun with as the son of a Connecticut yeoman. Thomas Chittenden also achieved new wealth and power from his

leadership in Vermont's revolution. In 1789 the Rev. Nathan Perkins, the Congregationalist pastor of orderly West Hartford, Connecticut, expressed distaste after he visited Governor Chittenden and toured his frontier estate. Perkins found anomalous and disquieting the new wealth of a man of humble origins and crude manners. "A low poor house, – a plain family – low, vulgar man, clownish, excessively parsimonious, – made me welcome, – hard fare, a very great farm, – 1000 acres, – hundred acres of wheat on the Onion River – 200 acres of extraordinary interval land. A shrewd, cunning man – skilled in human nature and in agriculture – understands extremely well the mysteries of Vermont, apparently and professedly serious." Men of established standing were uneasy that the Revolution had enriched clusters of new men without the cultured, genteel tone and without the established patrons previously expected as prerequisites for admission to the eighteenth-century American elite. It profoundly alarmed the genteel that upstarts could grow rich and influential by abetting popular unrest.[14]

## Extending Vermont

The Arlington Junto's success and the new nation's postwar turmoil combined to encourage other ambitious opportunists to make other Vermonts. During the 1780s and early 1790s in Maine, western New York, northern and western Pennsylvania, Ohio, Kentucky, and Tennessee, aggrieved settlers and canny opportunists spoke of adopting the "Vermont plan" or of establishing "a Second Vermont," to the profound alarm of entrenched gentlemen. As late as 1801 a Susquehanna opportunist "referr'd to the success of Govr. Chittendon and the Aliens in forming the State of Vermont and gave his opinion that the same thing might be effected here with greater ease."[15]

The recent Revolution and the weakness of the new state governments and their confederation created a sense of uncertainty and possibility during the 1780s and early 1790s.

People questioned every form of allegiance to authority. Widespread discontent among the yeomanry with the taxes and debts collected by their betters inspired in most states a spate of riots that escalated into overt rebellions in parts of New England and Pennsylvania. While established gentlemen dreaded the disorders as harbingers of violent, leveling anarchy, opportunists dispassionately calculated how they could profit from the turmoil. One of those opportunists was Dr. Timothy Hosmer, a Connecticut land speculator determined to profit by wresting the upper Susquehanna country away from Pennsylvania. In early February 1787, while the New England Regulators commanded by Daniel Shays waged an insurgency against the state troops of Massachusetts, Hosmer wrote to the Susquehanna settlers,

> Will it not be Advantageous to the Susquehannah Settlement, let the event Go which way it will. If Government succeeds those opposers must look for some other Place to make their Residence and I have no doubt but numbers of them will flee to your Goodly Country: If they Fail (the Government Troops) we Shall be Flung into a State of Anarchy, from which a new form of Government must Grow, from the Feebleness of the present Foederal Government, … a Monarchical (government) of some kind will it is most probable Grow out of it. If so, we have all the reason to draw this Conclusion That the holders of the Lands will have it secured to them after the Revolution for undoubtedly there will be an anihilation of State lines under a one Headed Government. That we shall not have to Quarell with a State but have a Tryal before Majesty which I had rather Submit to Tho' it were a Nero or Caligula Than to the Land Jobing Jockying State of Pennsylvania.

It seemed that bold and resourceful men could take advantage of the Revolutionary flux to pursue interest in defiance of any government, republican or monarchical.[16]

The leaders of the Susquehannah Company were opportunists bent on obtaining the northern third of Pennsylvania despite a December 1782 ruling by a special federal tribunal at Trenton in favor of that state's claim to the long-contested region. Most of the old guard among the company shareholders accepted the Trenton decision and gave up the contest. But in 1784 the Susquehanna Valley's Yankee settlers, led by Col. John Franklin, independently organized a militia that drove out the soldiers and tenants sent by Pennsylvania to occupy the region. The settlers' success inspired a few daring, ambitious, and unscrupulous investors to revive the moribund Susquehannah Company during the summer of 1785. But for the settlers' initiative, there would have been no opportunity for upstart speculators to advance their counterclaim to the Susquehanna country.[17]

The new leaders of the Susquehannah Company were remarkably akin to the Arlington Junto. Both sets of opportunists were aggressive, entrepreneurial, and daring men of middling property, and most members of both groups came from the Connecticut-New York borderland, a region known for land speculation and controversy. Dr. Joseph Hamilton, Col. John McKinstry, Capt. Solomon Strong, Zerah Beach, Dr. Caleb Benton, and Maj. William Judd of the Susquehannah Company all embodied the stereotype of the crafty, calculating, self-righteous Yankee speculator so disliked and distrusted by their New York neighbors. Some of the new leaders had inherited small interests in the pre-Revolutionary Susquehannah Company, but none had been prominent in company affairs until the reorganization of 1785. Their initial bond came from shared membership in freemasonry, which in late eighteenth-century Connecticut was synonymous with political and religious free-thinking. Joseph Hamilton, the company's preeminent new leader, inherited his penchant for aggressive and contentious land speculation from his father, David Hamilton, one of the first settlers and proprietors of Sharon in northwestern Connecticut, near the New York border. Father Hamilton had invested in the New Hampshire Grants and in the Susquehannah Company, banking in both cases on settler resistance to make good his suspect titles. The youngest of three sons, Joseph Hamilton moved across the border to Hudson, Columbia County, New York, and became a doctor and innkeeper – careers often associated in Revolutionary America with religious and political unorthodoxy. He also became a leading freemason. John McKinstry was another Hudson freemason and innkeeper who joined Hamilton in the new company's leadership. Solomon Strong was a Connecticut-born sawmill owner in nearby Claverack, New York, until obliged to flee from a counterfeiting indictment to the Susquehanna country. Zerah Beach was a storekeeper and Caleb Benton was a doctor; both were residents of Amenia, Dutchess County, New York, near the Connecticut line, and both were sons of Yankee fathers. William Judd of Plainville, Connecticut, was a man of more established connections – a Yale graduate (1763), successful lawyer, and Continental army officer. But he was prone to bursts of relentless, reckless ardor, as in September 1775 when he led a provocative and foolhardy raid against Pennsylvania, only to land in a Philadelphia jail. And he was an avid freemason who became master of Connecticut's grand lodge in 1792. Alienated from Connecticut's religious and political establishment, he became a leading Jeffersonian.[18]

The one new leader who did not fit the opportunist mold was the one who was an actual Susquehanna settler, John Franklin. He shared little with the nonresident leaders besides birth in northwestern Connecticut to the son of a petty investor in the Susquehannah Company. Principled, pious, and fearless, Franklin devoted his life to the settlers' cause and rarely availed himself of his opportunities, as the company's clerk and treasurer, to become rich through land speculation. He was content with a modest farm and sawmill and with his fellow settlers'

esteem. He used the nonresident leaders to obtain needed funds for the settler resistance, as they used him to advance their ambitions. Dr. Hamilton understood that Franklin was the key figure in the Susquehanna resistance. On behalf of the nonresident speculators, Hamilton assured Franklin that "we have got the money chest in possession, we are very sensible of, but then you have the key, no righteous wheel will move until you move and that in such manners as to make the world know you are in earnest."[19]

By attaching themselves to the settlers' resistance led by Colonel Franklin, the company's new directors hoped to intimidate Pennsylvania's rulers into a quick compromise. If that failed, the Susquehannah Company's upstart leaders planned to follow Vermont's precedent and declare their claim an independent state. Franklin explained, "We must sweep in settlers to make ourselves strong; then if a writ of ejectment under Pennsylvania is served, we will rise and beat off the sheriff; and if Pennsylvania sends out a party against us, we will embody and drive them out; and then we will openly proclaim a new state, comprehending the Susquehannah Purchase." Several of the Susquehannah Company's new leaders – Benton, Hamilton, and McKinstry – also speculated in an equally brazen sister scheme by the "New York Lessees" to rob New York, their home state, of its western lands by obtaining Indian leases for 999 years and by declaring that region a new state. Apparently the opportunists hoped to merge their two overlapping companies and their two projected states, one extracted from New York and the other from Pennsylvania.[20]

In search of the necessary expertise in Revolutionary state-making, the company leaders turned to Ethan Allen. Aware that interest was Allen's god, Joseph Hamilton recruited him by offering a gratuity of twelve full shares in the company in August 1785. The son of an original Susquehannah Company proprietor, Allen was flattered by the company's offer and delighted by the new stage on which to strut in pursuit of more adventure, acclaim, and property. Speaking from experience, he advised the Susquehannah settlers, "Crowd your settlements, add to your numbers and strength; procure fire-arms, and ammunition, be united among yourselves … . Liberty & Property; or slavery and poverty; are now before us." In April 1786 Allen toured the upper Susquehanna to boost settler morale. He seems to have taught the settlers the violent profanity that was his chief stock-in-trade. In the wake of Allen's visit, a shocked Pennsylvania supporter named Obadiah Gore reported, "Men Up the river are breathing out Threatnings … . [They] make use of the most Blasphemous Expressions that I ever heard being Uttered from any person." Thereafter old age, a new marriage, and his Vermont affairs diverted Allen's attention from the Susquehanna. Nonetheless, until his death in 1789, rumors persisted among the settlers that Allen would soon return with one thousand armed Green Mountain Boys.[21]

The violent contest between the competing speculators of opposing states created an opportunity for poor men to obtain free homesteads. In July 1785 the new leaders promised a half-share in the company to "every Able bodied and effective Man" who settled in the valley and agreed to "submit himself to the Orders of this Company." A half-share entitled every new settler to a homestead of at least one hundred, and as many as two hundred, acres that he could retain only if the company defeated Pennsylvania. By 1786 about half of the upper valley's five hundred adult male settlers were newcomers – "Half-Share Men" – and the other half were pre-1783 "Old Settlers." By all accounts, the Half-Share Men were refugees from poverty. In August 1786 Timothy Pickering toured the Susquehanna country and described the newcomers as "men destitute of property, who could be tempted by the gratuitous offer of lands, on the single condition that they should enter upon them armed, 'to man their rights,' in the cant phrase of those people." Another Pennsylvania official, Thomas Cooper, later characterized the resistance as a coalition of "the unprincipled speculators in half share rights, and

the poor, industrious, but obstinate and deluded people who confide in these men."[22]

The company leaders put great stock in the power of interest to sustain settler resistance. Hamilton advised, "Men thus Planted and desperate The angels from Heaven, unless Divinely Commissioned, could not disposses … . my Friends go on, go on, but for God sake preserve rule and good order among yourselves, but let no man be among you but who feels himself Interested, let him be pleased with his situation if possible. This is the only true Policy." John McKinstry insisted "that the Pennsylvanians would never fight like those who are particularly concerned." By giving away a small part of their vast claim to armed settlers, the company leaders meant to obtain the forces needed to wrest the rest of the region away from Pennsylvania; the leaders expected subsequently to profit by retailing farms to later settlers.[23]

Most of the Half-Share Men came from the Yankee borderland bisected by the boundary line between eastern New York and western New England. The Yankee borderlanders were experienced in organized extralegal violence meant to protect their small homesteads from the taxes, rents, and purchase payments sought by New York's landlords and Massachusetts' magistrates. In the 1750s and in 1766 those on the New York side of the line had organized a violent resistance against the rents charged by that colony's landlords. Defeated, many Yankee tenants subsequently migrated north to participate as Green Mountain Boys in Vermont's rebellion against some of the same landlords. During the Revolution and the 1780s, the Yankees on the Massachusetts side of the line resisted the collection of taxes and debts by massing in armed force to close down the courts. When one state's authorities triumphed over resistance, the most disgruntled yeomen sought refuge on the other side of the border. New York tenants sought succor in Massachusetts and Connecticut during the 1750s and 1760s, and the defeated Regulators of Massachusetts found havens in Vermont and New York in 1787. The region was also notorious for harboring counterfeiters who evaded arrest by shifting back and forth across the legal borders. By the mid-1780s, Vermont could no longer satisfy the hunger for cheap land among borderlanders frustrated by the defeats of the tenant uprisings and of the New England Regulation. The disaffected began to spill over into the Susquehanna country, bearing with them a readiness "to man their rights" with armed force.[24]

The Susquehannah Company's new leaders were well placed to recruit the borderland's disaffected yeomen. Most of the new leaders were transplanted Connecticut Yankees dwelling in eastern New York's Columbia or Dutchess counties, the cockpits of violent antirentism. Moreover, many of those new leaders were doctors or innkeepers, men especially well positioned to know the area and to communicate with its inhabitants. Joseph Hamilton's tavern lay by an important ferry across the Hudson River, a strategic location for recruiting and directing Yankee emigrants. With tempting offers and populist rhetoric, the speculators tapped the borderland's growing surplus of defiant families. In November 1787, in the immediate wake of the defeat of Shays's Rebellion, one emigrant to the Susquehanna reported, "In order to incourage Settlers to come into their country & settle, I see a writing … signifying that Each settler should have a certain Quantity of Land gratis, &c., &c. Subtill arguments are made use of to persuade the people to repair to a New Country to avoid the heavy Taxes their new Masters lay on them."[25]

In addition to wooing actual settlers with free homesteads, the Susquehannah Company also tried to buy support among America's leading men. Once again the Arlington Junto provided the model. In 1794–95 the company authorized 234 new townships, each five miles square, and embarked on an aggressive program of surveying and promotion. Shares in the new townships were sold cheap, or given away, to influential men like Theodore Sedgwick, a United States

senator from Massachusetts. Settler resistance made this program of creating new land titles possible, as the Half-Share Men chased away the surveyors for Pennsylvania's landlords and protected those working for the Susquehannah Company.

In the Susquehanna scheme, settler strength and speculator interest supported one another. On the one hand, a formidable settler commitment to an upstart title attracted the attention of outside investors on the alert for a promising speculation. On the other, the accumulation of speculator interest in a landgrab bolstered settler confidence in ultimate victory, for they knew the importance of wealth and influence in a political struggle. To boost morale, Colonel Franklin and other local leaders actively circulated among their neighbors the letters of support received from influential gentlemen living in other states. In September 1796 Clement Paine, a Susquehanna settler leader exulted, "The title of our land is growing in repute; many persons of respectability and influence, particularly in Connecticut, Massachusetts, New York, Rhode Island, and Vermont, have purchased and made themselves interested in the business."[26]

But Paine spoke too soon, for few outsiders of significant standing bought Susquehannah titles, and almost all who did quickly lost interest. Although successful in the first half of their program – to establish a settler constituency – the company failed in the second – to develop a substantial interest among the nation's leaders. In large part this was because of the countercampaign waged by Tench Coxe, a Pennsylvania land speculator and the state's land office secretary, for the hearts and minds of America's elite. In 1801 he vigorously denounced the Susquehannah Company in a pamphlet freely distributed to the "Governors, Senators, and Representatives, Judges, Members of the State legislatures, Lawyers, Landed men, &c, the Attorney general of the United States, and every other public Man from … Washington to Massachusetts." Coxe effectively warned them that they would reap nothing but trouble and expense by assisting the Susquehannah rebels. Moreover, the American elite had begun to reach a new consensus that it was dangerous and unseemly to carry their competition for wealth and power to extremes that empowered men of little property. After the reformation of the federal government with the ratification of a new Constitution in 1788, gentlemen had reunited in support of established legal institutions; they became loath to undermine another state's jurisdiction and land titles. Consequently, after 1788 the Susquehannah Company failed to attract as much support among America's political leaders as Vermont had enjoyed during the preceding decade. The company's inability to match the wealth and prowess of their Pennsylvania competitors discouraged the resisting settlers. To highlight their advantage, the Pennsylvania speculators formed an association and published a broadside meant to intimidate the settlers: "The Associators are highly respectable in number and character. The property they have at stake is immense. Their Committee is active and industrious. Council of eminence in the law have been applied to, for the support of prosecutions against offenders." An effective argument, it cracked the settler confidence; within five years most of the settlers came to terms and agreed to buy Pennsylvania titles.[27]

## Conclusion

All of the coalitions of opportunists and settlers formed during the 1780s fell short in their schemes to create additional Vermonts. When Kentucky and Tennessee won separate statehood and admission to the Union in 1792 and 1796, it was with the consent of their mother states, Virginia and North Carolina. That consent came after the new regimes promised to preserve the status quo in land titles. Maine did not win separate statehood until 1820, and again only after it had become clear that the new leaders would not tamper with the land titles already created by Massachusetts and already

sold to regular land speculators. Secessionist schemes in western New York and northwestern Pennsylvania also crumbled.[28]

The post-Revolutionary alliances of settlers and opportunists ultimately failed because they frightened the established gentlemen into creating a federal government capable of stifling frontier disaffection. Peter S. Onuf has demonstrated that jurisdictional conflicts between the states during the 1780s built a new consensus among America's gentlemen in favor of vesting sovereignty in a central government that could guarantee the territorial integrity of every member state. Those jurisdictional conflicts originated in the efforts by settlers and upstart speculators to create and uphold alternative land titles. After the ratification of the federal Constitution in 1788, state-making ceased to be a viable option for opportunists. Frontier dissidents, like the Susquehannah Yankees, who looked to federal courts or Congress for succor against state authorities, invariably had their hopes blasted. Pro-Spanish and secessionist intrigues persisted in Kentucky and Tennessee, but ultimately they came to nothing. During the 1790s frontier dissidents who violently defied federal authority, like the Whiskey Rebels of western Pennsylvania, were vigorously suppressed. As a result, the disaffected within states had to seek compromises from their state legislatures. For example, during the first decade of the nineteenth century, Pennsylvania mollified the Yankee settlers within the fifteen oldest and most populated Susquehanna townships by selling them titles for an average of thirty-two cents per acre. But most of the Half-Share Men lived in newer settlements excluded from the compromise legislation; they had to pay more – two to three dollars per acre – to Pennsylvania's land speculators or give up and move on. Their abettors, the Susquehannah Company, gained nothing from the long and expensive struggle.[29]

Moreover the new federal government assumed control of the vast domain of wilderness land lying west of Pennsylvania and north of the Ohio River. There the federal government enforced the Northwest Ordinances of 1785 and 1787, a program of land sales and territorial government specifically designed to preclude further trouble from combines of squatters and opportunists. By mandating a relatively high minimum price for land (one dollar per acre) and by insisting upon government surveys in advance of sale and settlement, the Northwest Ordinance of 1785 encouraged compact, orderly settlement by commercial farmers who could be relied upon to support the federal government as the source of their titles. The Northwest Ordinance of 1787 mandated hierarchical territorial governments dominated by a governor, a secretary, and three territorial judges all appointed by the distant national government. The ordinance delayed statehood until a territory's population topped 60,000 in the expectation that the previous period, if supervised by gentlemen landlords and governors, would teach the inhabitants, in the words of Arthur St. Clair, Ohio's first territorial governor, "habits of Obedience and Respect."[30]

With the Northwest Ordinances, Congress acted to restore the primacy of true gentlemen in retailing, settling, and governing frontier lands. The restrictive policy appealed to prestigious gentlemen like George Washington who were appalled at the competition from upstart speculators of limited means but aggressive ambition. In 1784 he had complained, "Men in these times talk with as much facility of fifty, a hundred, and even 500,000 Acres as a Gentleman formerly would do of 1000 acres. In defiance of the proclamation of Congress, they roam over the Country on the Indian side of the Ohio, mark out Lands, Survey, and even settle them." In 1787 Congress agreed to make a special sale at reduced rates of 1,500,000 acres to the Ohio Company, a cartel of great men, principally Continental army officers from New England and their friends in Congress. The company members impressed Congress as "men of very considerable property and respectable characters." Their spokesman, Manasseh Cutler, promised that they would "begin *right*" by carefully screening prospective settlers so that

there would be "no *wrong* habits to combat, and no inveterate systems to overturn … no rubbish to remove." Impressed with that promise, Washington's administration drew upon leading members of the Ohio Company to command Ohio's territorial government.[31]

For the moment, the federal government stifled the symbiosis of squatter and petty speculator in the Ohio territory. But it would revive in a new form after 1800 through the vehicle of state politics, when Jeffersonian "friends of the people" cast out the Federalist "fathers of the people" throughout the West. The Jeffersonian leaders of Ohio, who ousted St. Clair and his Ohio Company allies from office in 1802, were small-scale speculators who knew how to win votes among the common people insulted by Federalist paternalism. The new Ethan Aliens and John Franklins of the West were men like Nathaniel Massie and Thomas Worthington of Ohio who, as surveyor-speculators and Jeffersonian politicians, had found that they could profitably work within and dominate the new system of federal land sales and state governments. But the common settler got little more than the catharsis that came from electoral crusades against the haughty Federatosi "aristocrats." The common settlers had lost their leverage for want of any further demand for their services as militias on behalf of upstart titles.[32]

## Notes

1   Col. Timothy Pickering to George Clymer, Nov. 1, 1787, Julian P. Boyd and Robert J. Taylor, eds., *The Susquehannah Company Papers,* 11 vols. (Wilkes-Barre, Pa., and Ithaca, N.Y., 1930–71), 9:255–59.

2   Ronald F, Banks, *Maine Becomes a State: The Movement to Separate Maine from Massachusetts, 1785–1820* (Portland, Maine, 1973), 3–25; Robert E. Moody, "Samuel Ely: Forerunner of Daniel Shays," *New England Quarterly* 5 (1932):105–34; David P. Szatmary, *Shays' Rebellion: The Making of an Agrarian Insurrection* (Amherst, Mass., 1980); Oscar Handlin, "The Eastern Frontier of

New York," *New York History* 18 (1937): 50–75; Thomas P. Slaughter, *The Whiskey Rebellion: Frontier Epilogue to the American Revolution* (New York, 1986), 29–60, 86 (second Washington quotation); Andrew R. L. Cayton, *The Frontier Republic: Ideology and Politics in the Ohio Country, 1780–1825* (Kent, Ohio, 1986), 2–11 (first Washington quotation, 7); Patricia Watlington, *The Partisan Spirit: Kentucky Politics, 1779–1792* (New York, 1972), 46–78; Thomas Perkins Abernethy, *Western Lands and the American Revolution* (New York, 1959), 288–310; extract from the *Connecticut Courant,* Sept. 10, 1787, in Boyd and Taylor, eds., *Susquehannah Company Papers,* 9:188.

3  Historians of the early American frontier disagree in how they describe the relationship of settlers and land speculators. Frederick Jackson Turner and his intellectual heirs, the Progressive historians, depict an adversarial relationship; revisionists, such as Charles S. Grant and Bernard Bailyn, insist that settlers and large-scale speculators were inclined to cooperate in a shared pursuit of the profits from rising land values. Both cases can be sustained because at different times in separate places each scenario was true. I mean to argue that neither the bipolar nor the unitary concept of the settler-speculator relationship works well for the American Revolutionary generation. See Ray Allen Billington, "The Origins of the Land Speculator as a Frontier Type," *Agricultural History* 19 (1945): 204–12; Charles S. Grant, *Democracy in the Connecticut Frontier Town of Kent* (New York, 1961), 1–65; Bernard Bailyn, *The Peopling of British North America: An Introduction* (New York, 1986), 65–86. The latter conflates settlers and speculators. For a work that treats resisting settlers simply as pawns of petty speculators, see Sung Bok Kim, *Landlord and Tenant in Colonial New York: Manorial Society, 1664–1775* (Chapel Hill, 1978), 281–345.

4  Jim Potter, "Demographic Development and Family Structure," in Jack F Greene and J. R. Pole, eds., *Colonial British America: Essays in the New History of the Early Modern Era* (Baltimore, 1984), 136, 149; Henry Knox, "Facts and Calculations Respecting the Population and Territory of the United States of America," Henry Knox Papers, vol. 53, 138, Massachusetts

Historical Society, Boston. For a fuller discussion of titles see Alan Taylor, "'A Kind of Warr': The Contest for Land on the Northeastern Frontier, 1750–1820," *William and Mary Quarterly,* 3d ser. 46 (1989): 3–26.

5  Richard Maxwell Brown, "Back Country Rebellions and the Homestead Ethic in America, 1740–1799," in Richard Maxwell Brown and Don E. Fehrenbacher, eds., *Tradition, Conflict, and Modernization: Perspectives on the American Revolution* (New York, 1977), 79; Prendergast quotation in Edward Countryman, *A People in Revolution: The American Revolution and Political Society in New York, 1760–1790* (Baltimore, 1981), 50; Orange County settlers' quotation in A. Roger Ekirch, *"Poor Carolina": Politics and Society in Colonial North Carolina, 1729–1776* (Chapel Hill, 1981), 190; idem, "'A New Government of Liberty': Hermon Husband's Vision of Backcountry North Carolina, 1755," *William and Mary Quarterly,* 3d ser. 34 (1977):632–46; Ruth N.. Bloch, *Visionary Republic: Millennial Themes in American Thought, 1756–1800* (New York, 1985), 72–73, 183–84; Taylor, "A Kind of Warr,'" 3–26; Kim, *Landlord and Tenant,* 281–415; Countryman, *A People in Revolution,* 36–71; Thomas L. Purvis, 'Origins and Patterns of Agrarian Unrest in New Jersey," *William and Mary Quarterly,* 3d ser. 39 (1982): 613–21.

6  Dr. Thomas Young, *Some Reflections on the Dispute between New-York, New-Hampshire, and Col. John Henry Lydius of Albany* (New Haven, 1764), 14–15; Thomas Rowley quotation in John C. Williams, *The History and Map of Danby, Vermont* (Rutland, 1869), 240.

7  Chilton Williamson, Sr., *Vermont in Quandary, 1763–1825* (Montpelier, 1949), 12–18; Charles A. Jellison, *Ethan Allen: Frontier Rebel* (Syracuse, N.Y., 1969), 18–38; Matt Bushnell Jones, *Vermont in the Making, 1750–1777* (Cambridge, Mass., 1939), 20–66, 225–26; Florence May Woodward, *The Town Proprietors in Vermont: The New England Proprietorship in Decline* (New York, 1936), 45–55; John Munro to Gov. William Tryon, Nov. 6, 1771, in Edmund Bailey O'Callaghan, ed., *The Documentary History of the State of New York,* 4 vols. (Albany, 1850–51), 4:453; Boyd and Taylor, eds., *Susquehannah Company Papers,* 1:lxiv–lxxxvii; Malcolm J. Rohrbough, *The Trans-Appalachian Frontier: People, Societies, and*

*Institutions, 1775–1850* (New York, 1978), 21–25; Abernethy, *Western Lands and the American Revolution,* 123–34.

8  Peter S. Onuf, *The Origins of the Federal Republic: Jurisdictional Controversies in the United States, 1775–1787* (Philadelphia, 1983), 131.

9  Ibid., 127–45; Aleine Austin, *Matthew Lyon: "New Man" of the Democratic Revolution, 1749–1822* (University Park, Pa., 1981), 20–22; Countryman, *A People in Revolution,* 156; Jellison, *Ethan Allen,* 178–93; Jones, *Vermont in the Making,* 347–93.

10  Jellison, *Ethan Allen,* 178–93; Williamson, *Vermont in Quandary,* 26–27, 75–76.

11  Jellison, *Ethan Allen,* 196–200, 247–49; Austin, *Matthew Lyon,* 22–24; Michael A. Bellesiles, "The Establishment of Legal Structures on the Frontier: The Case of Revolutionary Vermont," *Journal of American History* 73 (1987): 899–900; Michael A. Bellesiles, *Revolutionary Outlaws: Ethan Allen and the Struggle for Independence on the Early American Frontier* (Charlottesville, Va., 1993); Williamson, *Vermont in Quandary,* 67–74; Onuf, *Origins of the Federal Republic,* 135–38; Woodward, *Town Proprietors in Vermont,* 111–13.

12  Jellison, *Ethan Allen,* 208–35; Austin, *Matthew Lyon,* 25–29; Woodward, *Town Proprietors in Vermont,* 114–16, 129–31; Williamson, *Vermont in Quandary,* 76.

13  Alfred F. Young, *The Democratic Republicans of New York: The Origins, 1763–1797* (Chapel Hill, 1967), 57; Williamson, *Vermont in Quandary,* 165–82; E. Wilder Spaulding, *His Excellency, George Clinton, Critic of the Constitution* (New York, 1938), 142–45; Edward Porter Alexander, *A Revolutionary Conservative: James Duane of New York* (New York, 1938), 202–3; Austin, *Matthew Lyon,* 61–62.

14  Gordon S. Wood, "Interests and Disinterestedness in the Making of the Constitution," in Richard Beeman et al., eds., *Beyond Confederation: Origins of the Constitution and American National Identity* (Chapel Hill, 1987), 69–109; Rev. Nathan Perkins, *A Narrative of a Tour through the State of Vermont from April 27 to June 12, 1789* (Woodstock, Vt., 1920), 17; Austin, *Matthew Lyon,* 26, 30–33; John Page, "The Economic Structure of Society in Revolutionary Bennington," *Vermont History* 49 (1981):76–79; Williamson, *Vermont in Quandary,* 26–27; Jellison, *Ethan Allen,* 322–24; Alexander, *A Revolutionary Conservative,* 70–73, 84–85.

15  For endorsements of Vermont see [Samuel Ely], *The Appeal of the Two Counties of Lincoln and Hancock from the Forlorn Hope, or Mount of Distress* (Portsmouth, N.H., 1796), 20, 23; Maj. William Judd to Zebulon Butler, Feb. 1, 1782, "Extract of a Letter from Wayne County," July 21, 1801, Boyd and Taylor, eds., *Susquehannah Company Papers,* 7:97–98, 11:139. For fears of Vermont, see David Cobb to William Bingham, Sept. 7, 1797, Frederick S. Allis, Jr., ed., *William Bingham's Maine Lands,* 2 vols. (Boston, 1954), 2:859; George Washington to James Madison, Mar. 31, 1787, John C. Fitzpatrick, ed., *The Writings of George Washington,* 39 vols. (Washington, D.C., 1931–44), 29:192; and Peter S. Onuf, "Settlers, Settlements, and New States," in Jack P Greene, ed., *The American Revolution: Its Character and Limits* (New York, 1987), 181. For backcountry disaffection during the 1780s and 1790s see Onuf, *Origins of the Federal Republic,* 149–72; Slaughter, *Whiskey Rebellion,* 28–44; Watlington, *Partisan Spirit,* 36–78; and Abernethy, *Western Lands,* 288–310.

16  Timothy Hosmer to John Paul Schott, Feb. 2, 1787, in Boyd and Taylor, eds., *Susquehannah Company Papers,* 9:21–22; see the similar sentiments in Judd to Butler, Jan. 11, 1787, ibid., 9:5–6. Circulating widely among the receptive settlers of the upper Susquehanna, Hosmer's words quickly became an article of faith among the inhabitants. See Joseph Sprague to Pickering, Feb. 20, 1787, ibid., 9:64.

17  Introduction, ibid., 5:xxi–lii; Oscar Jewell Harvey, *A History of Wilkes-Barre, Luzerne County, Pennsylvania* (Wilkes-Barre, Pa., 1927), 3:1476–78.

18  Harvey, *History of Wilkes-Barre,* 3:824–25n, 1498n, 1569n; Dorothy A. Lipson, *Freemasonry in Federalist Connecticut, 1789–1835* (Princeton, 1977), 69–71, 88: George Clinton to Benjamin Franklin, Dec. 13, 1786, in Boyd and Taylor, eds., *Susquehannah Company Papers,* 8:423; James H. Smith, ed., *History of Dutchess County, New York* (Syracuse, N.Y., 1882), 339; Stephen B. Miller, *Historical Sketches of Hudson* (Hudson, N.Y., 1862), 77. Connecticut's freemasons opposed that state's congressional religious establishment and most became leading Jeffersonians at odds with the state's governing Federalists. On medicine's association with unorthodoxy see Pauline Maier,

*The Old Revolutionaries: Political Lives in the Age of Samuel Adams* (New York, 1980), 131–34.

19  Louise Welles Murray, *A History of Old Tioga Point and Early Athens* (Athens. Pa., 1907), 492; James Edward Brady, "Wyoming: A Study of John Franklin and the Connecticut Settlement into Pennsylvania," Ph.D. diss., Syracuse University, 1973, 11, 308–12: Harvey. *History of Wilkes-Barre* 3:1227–30; David Craft. *History of Bradford County, Pennsylvania* (Philadelphia, 1878), 102. 107: Dr. Joseph Hamilton to Col. John Franklin, Sept. 10, 1787, in Boyd and Taylor, eds., *Susquehannah Company Papers,* 9:187.

20  John Franklin quotation in John J. AcModer deposition, Dec. 22, 1788, Boyd and Taylor, eds., *Susquehannah Company Papers,* 9:524–25; Samuel Gordon to Obadiah Gore, Oct. 15, 1787, ibid., 9:240–41; Orsamus Turner, *History of the Pioneer Settlement of Phelps and Gorham's Purchase, and Morris' Reserve* (1851; reprint ed., Geneseo, N.Y., 1976), 106–10. New York's Gov. George Clinton reacted quickly before the Lessees could establish more than a few dozen settlers on the land; at Clinton's orders, Herkimer County's sheriff dispossessed the Lessees' settlers, burned their cabins, and arrested their leaders. The pretensions of the New York Lessees collapsed.

21  Jellison, *Ethan Allen,* 316–19; Ethan Allen's receipt, Aug. 19, 1785, in Boyd and Taylor, eds., *Susquehannah Company Papers,* 8:256; Ethan Allen to Butler et al., Oct. 27, 1785, ibid., 8:270–71; William Montgomery to Pennsylvania's Council, May 17, 1786, ibid., 8:329; "An Address from the Inhabitants of Wyoming," Sept. 12, 1786, ibid., 9:394–401; William Hooker Smith to Charles Biddle, Aug. 10, 1786, ibid., 8:380; Gore to Pickering, Nov. 12, 1787, ibid., 9:267; Harvey, *History of Wilkes-Barre,* 3:1498–1500.

22  Pickering quotation in Octavius Pickering and Charles W. Upham, *The Life of Timothy Pickering,* 2 vols. (Salem, Mass., 1829), 2:259, 266; Susquehannah Company Minutes, July 13, 1785, in Boyd and Taylor, eds., *Susquehannah Company Papers,* 8:247–50; Thomas Cooper to Tench Coxe, July 13, 1801, ibid., 11:118. For other accounts of settler poverty on the upper Susquehanna see Craft, *Bradford County,* 87–90, 438; and Johann David Schoepf, *Travels in the Confederation [1783–1784],* trans, and ed., Alfred J. Morrison, 2 vols. (Philadelphia, 1911), 1:170–74, 186.

23  Col. John McKinstry, quoted in Thomas Wigton deposition, Sept. 8, 1787, in Boyd and Taylor, eds., *Susquehannah Company Papers,* 9:183; Hamilton to John Franklin, Mar. 24, 1786, ibid., 8:311–12.

24  Staughton Lynd, *Anti-Federalism in Dutchess County, New York: A Study of Democracy and Class Conflict in the Revolutionary Era* (Chicago, 1962), 37–54; David J. Goodall, "New Light on the Border: New England Squatter Settlements in New York during the American Revolution," Ph.D. diss., State University of New York at Albany, 1984; Handlin, "The Eastern Frontier of New York"; Countryman, *A People in Revolution,* 5–71; Robert J. Taylor, *Western Massachusetts in the Revolution* (Providence, 1954).

25  Zerah Beach to Butler, Sept. 21, 1785, in Boyd and Taylor, eds., *Susquehannah Company Papers,* 8:262; Hamilton to John Franklin, Mar. 24, 1786, ibid., 8:310; Gordon to Nathan Dennison, Nov. 24, 1787, ibid., 9:305.

26  Susquehannah Company Minutes, Feb. 20, 1795, ibid., 10:214–16; Dr. Caleb Benton to John Jenkins, Oct. 26, 1795, ibid., 10:329; Clement Paine to Seth Paine, Sept. 20, 1796, ibid., 10:381. For the circulation of letters see Pickering to Samuel Hodgdon, Mar. 16, 1788, ibid., 9:338.

27  Coxe to Cooper, June 26, 1801, ibid., 11:88; Broadside of the Pennsylvania Landholders' Association, Apr. 14, 1801, ibid., 11:53; Jacob E. Cooke, *Tench Coxe and the Early Republic* (Chapel Hill, 1978), 366 n. 51.

28  Paul W. Gates, *Landlords and Tenants on the Prairie Frontier: Studies in American Land Policy* (Ithaca, N.Y., 1973), 13–47; Rohrbough, *Trans-Appalachian Frontier,* 56–63; Alan Taylor, *Liberty Men and Great Proprietors: The Revolutionary Settlement on the Maine Frontier, 1760–1820* (Chapel Hill, 1990).

29  Onuf, *Origins of the Federal Republic;* Introduction, in Boyd and Taylor, eds., *Susquehannah Company Papers,* 11:xxix–xxx; Rosewell Welles and Alexander Scott to Gov. Thomas McKeen, Mar. 4, 1808, ibid., 11:524.

30  Peter S. Onuf, "Liberty, Development, and Union: Visions of the West in the 1780s," *William and Mary Quarterly,* 3d ser. 43 (1986): 179–213; Onuf,

"Settlers, Settlements, and New States," 171–96; Cayton, *Frontier Republic,* 12–50, St. Clair quotation, 35; Malcolm J. Rohrbough, *The Land Office Business: The Settlement and Administration of American Public Lands, 1789–1837* (New York, 1968), 4–23.

31  Onuf, "Liberty, Development, and Union," 184–93, Washington quotation, 192; Onuf, "Settlers, Settlements, and New States," 171–96, Cutler quotation, 185; Cayton, *Frontier Republic,* 17.

32  Rohrbough, *Land Office Business,* 44–48; Cayton, *Frontier Republic,* 51–94.

PART V

# A SOCIAL REVOLUTION?

# 16
# THE REVOLUTION IN BLACK LIFE
*Ira Berlin*

## Introduction

Ira Berlin argues that the Revolution was a watershed in black American life for both good and bad. He makes this case by carefully distinguishing between developments in the North, Upper South, and Lower South, and between rural and urban areas. Berlin finds that black freedom grew considerably in the post-revolutionary North and Upper South, particularly in urban areas. At the same time, whites in the post-revolutionary era imported more slaves and subjected them to a harsher labor regime than ever before, driven by the newfound profitability of cotton. Moreover, whites in the North, in a backlash to the growth of the free black population, instituted the country's first Jim Crow laws. In this, the Revolution had a mixed and consequential legacy for black Americans.

Berlin challenges students who assume that American patterns of slavery and freedom during the antebellum era were holdovers from the colonial period. Rather, they were creations of the Revolution. All of the colonies, northern and southern, had slaves, as was true for colonies throughout the Atlantic World. Yet the Revolution challenged this shared commitment to slavery. From the earliest days of the imperial crisis, black slaves and whites alike used egalitarian revolutionary principles to challenge the righteousness of slavery. This criticism sparked a crisis of conscience among white slaveholders and the non-slaveholding white public and stiffened the resolve of slaves themselves to resist their bondage. Once the war began, manpower shortages put pressure on the states to offer blacks freedom in exchange for military service, particularly in light of the Britain's effective use of such a strategy. Whites in the North and South began to reexamine their commitment to slavery in light of these developments and blacks everywhere began forcing the issue.

The results were mixed. The states north of Delaware, where slavery was relatively unimportant economically and socially, either immediately freed their slaves (as in the cases of Vermont and Massachusetts) or, in most cases, phased it out over several years. This process was the birth of the free North. Similar forces, combined with the diminishing profitability of tobacco growing, also encouraged manumission in the Upper South states of Virginia and especially Maryland. Yet the Upper South's slave population also grew during this same period. The Lower South experienced no such tensions. Though the Revolution dealt a mighty blow to slavery there, with tens of thousands of blacks escaping to the British lines, whites made up for these losses by purchasing slaves at an unprecedented rate following independence. They had newfound incentive to do so because the technological breakthrough of the cotton gin in the 1790s made the mass production of cotton possible. The Cotton South, no less than the Free North, was a post-revolutionary development.

- Berlin emphasizes that black people themselves were active agents in winning their own freedom even as he acknowledges the importance of other forces like economics and military strategy. In what ways did black slaves and freemen advocate for themselves despite their lack of power in a white-dominated society?

- Where did blacks fit into the military strategies of Britain and the United States during the Revolution? How did those strategies evolve following Dunmore's Proclamation of 1775, as discussed in the essay by Woody Holton?
- Freedom did not mean equality for blacks in the early republic. Yet Berlin contends that they experienced freedom as a marked improvement over slavery. What are the bases for his argument?
- It is easy to conclude that the northern states phased out slavery only because their economies did not depend on it. Does this argument do full justice to the complexity of slavery's end in the northern states? What was the constellation of factors that ended slavery in a region where it had existed for over a century?
- Some historians contend that the Revolution was a missed opportunity to end slavery throughout the United States. Drawing on Berlin's account of the economic and social conditions of the revolutionary era, what do you think?

The years between 1770 and 1810 were a formative period for Afro-American culture. The confluence of three events – freedom for large numbers of blacks with the abolition of slavery in the North and large-scale manumission in parts of the South; the maturation of a native-born Afro-American population after more than a century of American captivity; and a new, if short-lived, flexibility in white racial attitudes – made these years the pivot point in the development of black life in the United States. The social patterns and institutions established during the revolutionary era simultaneously confirmed the cultural transformation of the preceding century and shaped black life well into the twentieth century. In many ways, the revolutionary era, far more than the much studied Reconstruction period, laid the foundation for modern Afro-American life.

The events and ideas of the revolutionary years radically altered the structure of black society and the substance of Afro-American culture. The number of blacks enjoying freedom swelled under the pressure of revolutionary change, from a few thousand in the 1760s to almost two-hundred thousand by the end of the first decade of the nineteenth century. Freedom, even within the limited bounds of white domination, enhanced black opportunities by creating new needs and allowing blacks a chance to draw on the rapidly maturing Afro-American culture to fulfill them. But the revolution in black life was not confined to those legally free. The forces unleashed by the American Revolution soon reached beyond the bounds of free black society and deeply influenced the course of slave life in the critical years before the great migration to the Lower South. Most importantly, the revolution in black life created new and enlarged older regional distinctions between the black populations, free and slave, of the North, the Upper South, and the Lower South. In each of these regions, differences in the size, character, and dynamics of development of the free and slave black populations bred distinctive patterns of relations with whites and among blacks, shaping the development of black life and American race relations during the nineteenth century and beyond.

# I

The growth of the free Negro population was one of the most far reaching events of the revolutionary era. Before the Revolution only a tiny fraction of the black population enjoyed liberty in English mainland North America. A 1755 Maryland census, one of the few enumerations of colonial freemen, counted slightly more than 1,800 free Negroes. who composed about 4 percent of the colony's black population and less than 2 percent of its free population. Moreover, over 80 percent of these freemen were of mixed racial origin, and more than one-fifth were cripples or old folk deemed "past labour." Few full-blooded Africans found their way to freedom. Maryland's tiny free Negro population was composed almost entirely of the descendants of mixed racial unions – freed after a term of service if their mothers were white, or perhaps liberated by their white fathers – and bondsmen who, through age or circumstance, had become liabilities to their masters. Although colonial freemen demand further study, it appears that Maryland's free Negroes typified those found throughout the mainland English colonies. In 1805, Virginians recalled that "less than thirty years ago, the number of free negroes was so small that they were seldom to be met with." Some years later, William Gaston, the chief justice of North Carolina, investigated the subject and found "that previous to the Revolution there were scarcely any emancipated Slaves in this State; and that the few free men of color that were here at that time, were chiefly Mulattoes, the children of white women." Unsure of his judgment, Gaston queried "some aged persons"; they too confirmed that before the 1770s "scarcely an instance could be found at that time, either in Virginia or this State of an emancipated Slave."[1]

Although few in number and much like whites in appearance, free Negroes raised white fears of subversion. During the colonial years, lawmakers steadily gnawed at the freemen's liberty, taxing them with numerous proscriptions on their civil, political, and social rights.[2] On the eve of the Revolution, few whites, even those who opposed slavery, showed any inclination to increase the number of Negro freemen. But the events of the revolutionary years moved in unpredictable and uncontrollable ways. As the war dragged on, military necessity forced the British and then, more reluctantly, Americans to muster black slaves into their armies by offering them freedom in exchange for their services.

The British, who had no direct interest in slavery, first offered the exchange. In November 1775, Lord Dunmore, the royal governor of Virginia, declared martial law and freed all slaves that were able and willing to bear arms in His Majesty's service. Even though this declaration shook colonial Virginians, it came as no surprise. Dunmore and other British officials had been threatening such action for several months. Slaves, ever alive to the possibilities of liberty, quickly picked up these first rumblings of freedom. Some months earlier, a group of blacks had visited Dunmore and offered to join him and take up arms. At that time, Dunmore brusquely dismissed them. But the blacks would not be put off, and when Dunmore officially tendered the promise of liberty, they flocked to British headquarters in Norfolk harbor.

Defeat deflated Dunmore's promise of liberty. In December, about a month after his proclamation, patriot troops routed Loyalist forces, including a large number of blacks wearing sashes emblazoned with the words "Liberty to Slaves." The loss broke the back of Dunmore's attempt to discipline rebellious Virginians, and thereafter the colonials limited him to foraging raids from his seaborne headquarters. Despite military defeat and patriot propaganda that he would sell his black followers to the West Indies, Dunmore's promise stirred slaves throughout the Chesapeake region. Whenever his flotilla neared the coast, slaves, as one dejected master put it, began "flying to Dunmore." Slaveholders became so desperate to stop their flight that they addressed an article directly to their slaves in the *Virginia Gazette,* in which they alternately denied complicity in the slave trade, threatened death to runaways, and enjoined slaves to "be content with their situation, and expect a better condition in the next world."

Dunmore used his black recruits to raid the Virginia coast; and in August 1776, when he retreated to Bermuda, 300 blacks sailed north for future military service and freedom. All told, perhaps 800 slaves escaped to join Dunmore, and more important, hundreds more heard of his promise of freedom and were infected with the dream of liberty.[3]

The manpower shortage that forced Dunmore to use black troops worsened as the war dragged on. British commanders, despite popular opposition in England, increasingly followed Dunmore's lead and recruited slaves. When the war turned south in 1778, thousands of blacks flocked to the British standard. General Henry Clinton, the British commander-in-chief, officially promised liberty to all slaves who deserted their masters for British service. In the years that followed, British reliance on black manpower increased, and the proponents of utilizing black military might on a massive scale grew ever more vocal. Dunmore, now in Charleston, South Carolina, urged the formation of a black army of ten thousand men to end the rebellion swiftly, and other British officers dickered over the creation of a southeastern sanctuary for black Loyalists. No attempt was made to implement these proposals or even give them a full hearing, but their continued presence during the last years of the war suggests the mode of warfare that the British might have adopted had they continued to prosecute the rebellion.[4]

Colonial commanders and policymakers were considerably more chary about accepting slave recruits. Many were large slaveholders who had much to lose from any disruption of slavery. Most feared that a servile revolt or a mass defection of slaveholders would follow the arming of blacks. Although blacks had occasionally served in colonial militias and distinguished themselves in the first battles of the Revolution, the Continental Congress, at South Carolina's instigation, barred them from the Continental army. But patriots proved no more immune to the exigencies of war than the British. As the struggle for independence lengthened and manpower grew critically short, the patriot policy shifted. The northern states, led by New England, began to solicit black recruits, and Rhode Island created a black regiment. When the war moved south, Upper South states grudgingly adopted a similar course of action, in spite of their larger black populations and greater dependence on slave labor. Maryland authorized slave enlistments and eventually

subjected free Negroes to the draft. Virginia allowed black freemen to serve in its army and navy, and Delaware and North Carolina, following Virginia, occasionally permitted slaves to stand as substitutes for their masters. In the Lower South, however, white resistance to arming blacks stiffened. The numerical superiority of blacks in the lowland rice swamps, the large numbers of newly arrived African slaves, and the commonplace absenteeism bred an overpowering fear of slave rebellion. Despite the pleas of the Continental Congress and the urgings of commanders in the field, South Carolina and Georgia rejected the hesitant measures adopted in the Upper South. Yet, even in the Lower South, the pressures of the war produced at least one native son, John Laurens, who argued eloquently for a black soldiery as the only means of securing independence. The "howlings of a triple-headed monster, in which prejudice, avarice, and pusillanimity were united," easily defeated Laurens's proposal, but its presence suggests the potential transforming force of revolutionary warfare on slavery – even where it was most deeply entrenched.[5]

Almost everywhere, the war widened opportunities for blacks to gain their liberty. When the British left America at the end of the war, they carried thousands of blacks to freedom in Great Britain, the West Indies, Canada, and, eventually, Africa. Hundreds, perhaps thousands, of others that were freed by British wartime policy eluded their masters and remained in the United States. There is "reason to believe," petitioned angry white Virginians in 1781, "that a great number of slaves which were taken by the British Army are now passing in this Country as free men." Many blacks who fought with the patriots also secured their liberty. Some grateful masters freed their slaves, and occasionally state legislatures liberated individual bondsmen by special enactment. Most whites seemed to think this was right. The Virginia General Assembly drew back in horror at reports that slaveholders had reenslaved black military substitutes, and ordered their emancipation. In other states, a slave who served in his master's place had only a verbal promise of freedom. Some masters kept their word, others did not. Doubtless most bondsmen did not wait around long enough to find out.[6]

Whatever the effects of official British and American policy, the chaos created by rampaging armies did even more to expand a slave's chances for liberty. The actions of soldiers of both belligerents, and the often violent disputes between patriot and Tory militiamen, created near anarchic conditions, revealed the limits of slaveholder authority, and encouraged slaves to take their freedom. Runaways, previously few in number, increased rapidly in the confusion of the war. This was especially true in the Upper South, where the nature of agriculture had allowed second and third generation Afro-Americans to gain broad familiarity with the countryside.[7] At war's end, these fugitives also passed into the growing free black population.

## II

The war did not last long enough to destroy slavery, but the libertarian ideology that patriots used to justify their rebellion continued to challenge it when the war ended. If all men were created equal, why were some men still slaves? Lockean ideology protected slavery, even as it commended universal liberty, and that duality allowed slave-owners to fashion a defense of chattel bondage out of America's first principles. But, in the context of the Revolution, the impetus to universal liberty could not be easily ignored. "How is it," asked Samuel Johnson, "that we hear the loudest *yelps* for liberty among the drivers of negroes?" Those stinging words, like similar indigenous charges of hypocrisy, made it impossible for Americans to escape the confrontation between their ideology and their reality. However narrow its bounds, and whatever its internal flaws and ambiguities, revolutionary equalitarianism forced large numbers of men and women to question slavery for the first time, thereby subverting slavery

throughout the new republic. Some of these men and women freed their slaves, and others, taking the ideology of the Revolution to heart, demanded liberty for all and pushed for a general emancipation. Even more important, the persistent questioning of slavery allowed blacks and white emancipationists to push slavery on to the defensive. Plantation slavery expanded greatly during the postrevolutionary years, and there were many more enslaved blacks in 1800 than in 1776; but slavery was no longer a national institution, and its routine acceptance could no longer be taken for granted. By the beginning of the nineteenth century, chattel bondage had become the South's "peculiar institution."[8]

Slavery fell first in New England, where blacks were few in number and never an important part of the labor force or a threat to white dominance. In the Middle Atlantic states, where blacks were more numerous and bondage more deeply entrenched than in New England, slavery proved more resistant to revolutionary change. But an influx of white immigrant workers assured employers of an adequate supply of labor, and undermined the most persuasive argument against abolition. By 1804, every northern state had provided for eventual emancipation.[9]

Still, slavery died hard. In 1810, almost 30,000 blacks – almost a quarter of the region's black population – remained in chattel bondage. Although that number fell dramatically in succeeding decades, slavery continued. There were over 1,000 bondsmen in the "free" states in 1840. Moreover, in many of the new northern states, slaveholders and their allies tried to overthrow the antislavery provisions of the Northwest Ordinance and reinstate the peculiar institution. Failing that, they enacted various forms of long-term indentureships, which allowed chattel bondage to flourish covertly until the Civil War.[10] Nevertheless, slavery was doomed, and the mass of Northern black people had been freed.

South of Pennsylvania, emancipation faced still greater obstacles, and, in the long run, these difficulties proved insuperable. But the

Christian equalitarianism unleashed by the evangelical revivals of the mid-eighteenth century complemented and strengthened the idealism of the Revolution in many parts of the South. Like revolutionary ideology, the religious awakenings transcended sectional boundaries. Methodists and Baptist evangelicals crisscrossed the southern states and, in hundreds of camp meetings, made thousands of converts. Propelled by the revolutionary idea that all men were equal in the sight of God, they frequently accepted black and white converts with equal enthusiasm. The equality of the communion table proved contagious, and some evangelicals broke the confines of other-worldly concerns to make the connection between spiritual and secular equality. Methodists, Baptists, and other evangelical sectarians joined with Quakers to become the mainstays of the southern antislavery movement. Like their northern counterparts, they organized antislavery societies, petitioned legislatures, and aided freedom suits.[11]

Economic changes in the Upper South, especially in Maryland, Delaware, and northern Virginia, offered emancipationists an opening wedge. Beginning in the 1760s, the increased worldwide demand for foodstuff encouraged planters to expand cereal production. Dislocations in mercantile ties, resulting from the war and the depression that accompanied independence, further speeded the shift from tobacco to cereal agriculture in many parts of the Chesapeake region. This change reduced the demand for slaves, since wheat culture on small units under the existing technology thrived on free labor. Many farmers found themselves burdened with a surplus of slaves. Moreover, the agricultural transformation and the resultant establishment of new methods of processing and development of new patterns of marketing quickened the pace of commerce, stimulated the growth of light industry, and swelled urban centers. Baltimore, Richmond, Fredericksburg, and Petersburg grew as never before. In all, changes in the agricultural landscape increased commercial activity, and nascent urbanization

and industrialization profoundly altered the region. Many Americans believed that the Upper South would follow the pattern of development exemplified by Pennsylvania, and not the states farther south. As the price of slaves sagged under the weight of these changes, the future of slavery became an open question.[12]

The combined force of revolutionary and Christian equalitarianism pressed on slavery in the Upper South and allowed abolitionists to score impressive, if fleeting, gains. Legislatures and courts, under emancipationist pressure, liberalized manumission codes and relaxed strictures against freedom suits, greatly increasing the slave's opportunity for liberty. Emancipationist principles also profited from the drop in slave prices and the general insecurity of slave property. Although most slaveowners profitably sold their excess slaves to the South, masters burdened with surplus bondsmen were susceptible to abolitionist rhetoric. Throughout the region, the number of manumissions rose sharply. Moreover, since most manumitters were motivated by ideological and economic concerns, they tended to free their slaves relatively indiscriminately. Field hands as well as house servants, unskilled laborers as well as skilled artisans, and blacks as well as mulattoes passed from slavery to freedom.[13]

Economic changes in the Upper South affected the nature of slavery as well as its future. The seasonal demands of wheat farming, especially when compared to the year-long routine necessitated by tobacco cultivation, made it profitable for farmers to hire their slaves out to the growing industrial and commercial enterprises in the region.[14] Hiring out greatly enlarged the slaves' occupational opportunities and widened their knowledge of the world. Some slaves, encouraged by the self-esteem that accompanied their new skills, reached beyond their new status as artisans and saved enough money to buy their way out of bondage. Masters, sympathetic to the libertarian spirit of the age, but unwilling to free their slaves outright, encouraged self-purchase because it satisfied their conscience as well as their purse. But as slave artisans passed from job to job and town to town, their confidence grew and their tolerance for slavery waned. Many eschewed the onerous task of buying liberty. More than a few used their sanctioned time away from their masters' homesteads to make good their escape.[15]

The economic transformation of the Upper South supported freedom in other less direct ways. The growing number of tenant farmers and independent tradesmen in the region, often in need of an extra hand and rarely in a position to purchase slaves, frequently employed blacks, with few questions asked. The ability to find a safe haven, even for a few days, could make the difference between a successful flight and a return to bondage. The success of many fugitives, like relatively indiscriminate manumission, not only enlarged the free black population, but darkened it as well.[16] The larger, darker-skinned free Negro population camouflaged fugitives, increased their chances of success, and encouraged still other blacks to make their way from slavery to freedom. The increase in runaways begun during the tumult of the Revolution continued into the postwar years.

Slavery easily survived the increase of manumissions and runaways, recovered its balance, and in most places continued to grow. But the social changes of the revolutionary era profoundly altered the size and character of the free Negro population in the Upper South, and sent reverberations of liberty into the region's slave quarters.

The growth of the free Negro population can be most clearly viewed in Maryland. Between 1755 and 1790, the number of free Negroes in that state increased almost 350 percent, to about 8,000, and in the following decade it again more than doubled. By 1810, almost a quarter of Maryland's blacks were free, numbering nearly 34,000.[17] Although not immediately apparent, slavery in Maryland had been dealt a mortal blow.

Free Negroes registered similar gains throughout the Upper South. In 1782, the year

*Table 16.1* Free Negro Population, 1790–1810

|                | 1790   | 1800    | 1810    |
|----------------|--------|---------|---------|
| United States  | 59,466 | 108,395 | 186,466 |
| North          | 27,109 | 47,154  | 78,181  |
| South          | 32,357 | 61,241  | 108,265 |
| Upper South    | 30,158 | 56,855  | 94,085  |
| Lower South    | 2,199  | 4,386   | 14,180  |

* Increase in the Lower South between 1800 and 1810 is largely due to the accession of Louisiana.
Source: *Population of the United States in 1860* (Washington, D.C.,1864), 600–601.

Virginia legalized private manumissions, St. George Tucker estimated the number of freemen in his state at about 2,000.[18] By 1790, Virginia's free Negroes had increased to 12,000. Ten years later, Negro freemen numbered 20,000, and by 1810, the total stood at over 30,000. During the twenty years between 1790 and 1810, the free Negro population of Virginia more than doubled. In all, the number of Negro freemen in the Upper South grew almost 90 percent between 1790 and 1800, and another 65 percent in the following decade, so that freemen now composed more than 10 percent of the region's black population.

In 1810, the nearly 100,000 freemen were the fastest growing element in the Upper South's population. Although the number of whites and slaves also grew rapidly during the early years of the republic, the growth of the free Negro population outstripped both. In Virginia, for example, the number of free Negroes doubled between 1790 and 1810, while whites increased 24 percent, and slaves 31 percent. Maryland during the same period presented an even more startling comparison. Maryland's free Negroes increased fourfold, while the white population grew 12 percent, and the slave population a mere 8 percent. In Delaware, the expansion of freedom undermined slavery. In 1790 there were 4,000 free Negroes in Delaware, a smaller total than the state's slave population. Twenty years later, that state's 13,000 free Negroes outnumbered slaves more than three to one, and Delaware slavery was permanently impaired.

Moreover, relatively indiscriminate manumission and the increase of successful fugitives added large numbers of blacks – as opposed to mulattoes – and young folk to the free Negro population. Free Negroes, whose thin ranks had previously been filled largely by mulattoes and a disproportionate number of cripples and old people, were now a considerably larger, darker, and more vigorous group.

The social forces that transformed black society in the North and in the Upper South met stern resistance in the Lower South. There, economic and demographic considerations countered the ideology of the Revolution and the great revivals. During the war, Lower South whites had rejected the pleas of the Continental Congress to arm slaves in the patriot cause. With independence, no antislavery societies appeared, and few masters freed their slaves. Instead, the increased demand for slaves caused by enormous wartime losses, the expansion of rice production in the low country, and the spread of cotton culture in the up-country hardened the Lower South's commitment to slavery. Under such circumstances, abolition, as one Savannah, Georgia, newspaper observed, was simply "not a prudent subject for discussion." Following the war, Lower South whites imported thousands of slaves from the states to the north and, in 1803, South Carolina reopened the slave trade with Africa.[19] Not until the 1790s, when the successful black revolution in Saint Domingue sent hundreds of light-skinned *gens de couleur* fleeing for American shores, did the number of free Negroes increase significantly in the Lower South.[20] Thus, unlike northern and Upper South freemen, Lower South free people of color remained a tiny mulatto fragment of the larger population.

In transforming the structure of black society, the events of the revolutionary years created new, and enlarged older, regional distinctions between the black populations of the North, the Upper South, and the Lower South. By the end of the century, northern whites had committed themselves to emancipation, and the great

majority of blacks enjoyed freedom. Upper South slavery, on the other hand, withstood the challenges of the revolutionary years, but its free black population expanded rapidly during the period, so that better than one black in ten was free by 1800. Slavery in the Lower South, although greatly disrupted by the war, never faced the direct emancipationist pressures present in the North or even the Upper South. It stood almost unchallenged throughout the postwar period, quickly recouped its wartime losses, and entered into a period of its greatest expansion. Lower South free people of color remained as they had been in the colonial era, a small appendage to a rapidly increasing slave population. While the northern and Upper South free Negro population grew darker in color with emancipation and relatively indiscriminate manumission, most Lower South freemen continued to display the somatic attributes of their mixed racial origins. An influx of West Indian coloreds following the Haitian Revolution reinforced the mulatto bias of the Lower South free Negro population, without significantly altering its share of the black population. These regional distinctions in the structure of both slave and free black societies reflected and influenced white racial attitudes and shaped the development of black life in the years to come.

## III

It was not only the structure of black society that changed during the revolutionary era. By the eve of the American Revolution, black people had been living in English mainland North America for more than 150 years. After a century of American captivity, they were not the same people whom John Rolfe had watched march down the gang-plank at Jamestown in 1619. The transplanted Africans were no longer an alien people whose minds were befogged by the horrors of the Middle Passage, whose tongues were muted by the strange language of their enslavers, and whose senses were confused by the unfamiliar landscape that everywhere surrounded them. By the 1770s, if not earlier, the vast majority of blacks were native Americans with no firsthand knowledge of Africa. Increasingly, secondhand accounts of the "great land across the sea" were losing their meaning to new generations of American-born blacks – just as the fading memories of English life were losing their meaning for new generations of American-born whites. Beyond their master's eyes many tried to maintain the ways of the old country, difficult though that was. But since adapting to the conditions of the New World was literally a life and death matter, most of them changed. Slowly, almost imperceptibly, transplanted Africans became a new people. They spoke English, worked with English tools, and ate foods prepared in the English manner. On the eve of the Revolution, many blacks had done so for two or three generations, and sometimes more.

But black acculturation was more than a leeching process whereby an English culture, modified by New World conditions, replaced an African one. To the emerging Anglo-American culture, transplanted Africans added their own heritage, a way of thinking and acting that had survived the Middle Passage. And this was not just a single African heritage. A mélange of African cultures, some compatible, some antagonistic, had been thrown together in the barracoons of Africa, and continued to blend under the pressures of New World enslavement. The African melting pot – unlike the European one – melted. The diverse heritage of Africa and the dominant Anglo-American culture, in turn, were molded and shaped by the peculiar status and circumstances of black people to create a new cultural type: the Afro-American.[21] The maturation of Afro-American culture gave added force to the transformation of black society during the revolutionary era, deeply affecting those who slipped out of slavery as well as those who remained locked in bondage.

Structural and cultural changes in black society profoundly influenced white attitudes and behavior. In the long run, they stiffened white racism. With so many blacks in possession of freedom, whites could no longer rely on their status alone to distinguish themselves from a people they despised. They began to grope for new ways to subordinate Negro freemen and set themselves apart from all blacks. Thus as the free Negro population grew, whites curbed their mobility, limited their economic opportunities, all but obliterated many of their political rights, and schemed to deport freemen from the country. Yet, the Revolution, with its emphasis on equality, forced whites to reconsider their racial values. This reconsideration produced a new flexibility in the racial attitudes of some whites and a brief recession in the color line. The liberalization of manumission codes, the passage of antikidnapping laws, the increased number of free Negroes, and the challenge to slavery all reflected small, but real, changes in white racial attitudes. These changes allowed blacks some room to maneuver in a society that was often hostile to their very being. Nevertheless, racism remained a potent force in revolutionary America.[22] The society and culture that emerged from this first attempt to remake black life in America represented an easing of white racial hostility within a system of continued racial oppression.

## IV

The cumulative impact of freedom, cultural maturation, and the new flexibility in white attitudes unleashed the creative energies of black people. Newly freed blacks moved at once to give meaning to their freshly won liberty and form to the cultural transformation of black life in America. They took new names, established new residential and occupational patterns, reconstructed their family life, chose the first recognizable leadership class, and developed new institutions and modes of social action.

Blacks commonly celebrated emancipation by taking new names. A new name was both a symbol of personal liberation and an act of political defiance; it reversed the enslavement process and confirmed the freemen's newly won liberty, just as the loss of an African name had earlier symbolized enslavement. Emancipation also gave blacks the opportunity to strip themselves of the comic classical names that had dogged them in slavery, and to adopt common Anglo-American names. Few Caesars, Pompeys, and Catos remained among the new freemen. In bondage, most blacks had but a single name; freedom also allowed them the opportunity to take another. Robert Freeman, Landon Freeland, and Robin Justice chose names that celebrated their new status. Many, like Tom, who took the name "Toogood" when he ran off, flaunted the increased self-esteem that accompanied liberty. Others, following an ancient tradition, borrowed names from their trades or skills: James Carter was a drayman, Henry Mason a bricklayer, Charles Green a gardener, and Jacob Bishop a preacher with obvious aspirations. Similarly, James Cook took his name "from his being skilled in the art of cooking and house service," and the origins of Jockey Wheeler's cognomen can be safely surmised. More significantly, some identified themselves by their pigment and origin and took names like "Brown," "Coal," "Africa," and "Guinea." But slave society, which identified wealth, power, and authority with whites, was not easily denied. Some blacks called themselves "White," and others borrowed the name of some local notable, more often than not a slaveholder. But only a few took the name of their emancipator.[23]

Newly manumitted bondsmen also tried to escape the stigma of bondage by deserting the site of their enslavement. Runaways did it as a matter of course, and some newly liberated freemen were no longer welcome on their masters' homesteads. But even when invited to stay, many free blacks gladly left. The expectations generated by emancipation encouraged freemen to venture out on their own. Bondage had limited the physical mobility of blacks, and now amity seemed determined to compensate for their confinement. "Negro Soloman," one manumitter ruefully observed,

"now free, prefers to mould bricks than serve me." In snubbing their former masters, free Negroes demonstrated their liberty. Some freemen seemingly went out of their way to break the bonds of dependence that weighed so heavily in slavery. Much to the displeasure of one Delaware mistress, her former servant ignored her offer of a "a good place" with a Philadelphia friend and found a job on her own. "I cannot help thinking," complained the rejected aristocrat, that "it is too generally the case with all those of colour to be ungrateful."[24] Throughout the South, emancipated blacks tested their liberty by asserting it.

Fleeing the memory of servitude, looking for new opportunities, searching for loved ones, freemen moved in all directions. Many went north, some to Canada, and some to Haiti, and a few found their way back to Africa. Yet most of those who abandoned the place of their enslavement remained in the United States. Friendless and fearful, some doubtless returned to their old neighborhoods where they had friends and relatives. A few, however, continued to wander aimlessly, living off the land while searching for a new life. As a result, every state had a transient group of free Negroes that encouraged "dangerous" thoughts among restless slaves and frightened, edgy whites. In 1786, for instance, whites in Sussex County, Delaware, complained that large numbers of wandering blacks "under the name and Character of Free Negroes" were residing "thoughout this Country [and] stroll thro' the same."[25] Such bands of freemen were a magnet for runaways and occasionally grew so large that officials called upon the militia to disperse them.

But most migrating free Negroes chose their destination with care. Many sought out loved ones, hoping to reconstruct their shattered families or simply to share the exhilaration of liberty. Some freemen, like whites, searched for new opportunities in the West, but more often free blacks turned to the urban frontier. Cities, where the relative anonymity of urban life provided an additional measure of liberty, were the most important refuges from the memory of plantation slavery. Throughout the nation, municipal officials joined the mayor of Petersburg, Virginia, in lamenting that "large numbers of free blacks flock from the country to the towns …" Although cities added police and passed special ordinances to curb this migration, urban freemen throughout the South increased in numbers more rapidly than did the free Negroes generally. While the free Negro population of Virginia more than doubled between 1790 and 1810, that of Richmond increased fourfold, and of Norfolk tenfold. Similar patterns of growth could be observed in New York, Philadelphia, and Charleston.[26] Most freemen, like most whites and slaves, resided in the countryside, but, by the beginning of the nineteenth century, cities had become centers of free black life.

Migration, no matter how tempting, was never easy. For many newly freed blacks, it meant abandoning enslaved loved ones. Although many free blacks would later attempt to improve their status by distinguishing themselves from slaves, in the formative years free and slave blacks stood together to a large degree.[27] Changes in free black life had a deep and lasting impact on slave society. The extent of this relationship has yet to be fully explored, but it is important to emphasize the close ties between freemen and bondsmen during the revolutionary era. It could hardly be otherwise, with so many free Negroes just a step away from bondage, and so many slaves hopeful of freedom, especially in the North and Upper South. Abolition and relatively indiscriminate manumission in those regions eliminated many of the differences in social origins and color that had existed between freemen and slaves during the colonial era. Free and slave blacks were perhaps closer than they were at any time in the past, and perhaps than they had been at any time in the future. Bonds of friendship and kinship, rooted in common experience and sealed by common expectations, made freemen reluctant to leave their old homes without family and friends.

As a result, the era witnessed a major reconstruction of black family life. Although traditional West African society rested on a powerful familial base, the trauma of the Middle Passage, the diversity of their African heritage, the sexual imbalance of the colonial slave population, and the physical isolation of life on colonial plantations prevented the first generation of enslaved blacks from reconstituting family life as they had known it in Africa. Often these forbidding circumstances subverted the development of stable family relationships of any kind. Not until the second decade of the eighteenth century in many colonies, and still later in others, did the emergence of a more favorable sexual balance and a larger plantation unit allow first generation Afro-Americans to build the family life that had been destroyed by enslavement. That process, which entailed shaping new marital roles, molding new familial structures, and defining anew the relationship between family and society in accordance with the diverse heritage of Africa and the circumstances of American slavery, is little understood at this point. It was influenced by the cultural origins of the first Africans in a particular area, the number and origins of new slaves later brought into that area, the size of the plantation unit, the kind of labor demanded of blacks, the master's example, as well as other factors. Yet whatever the process, it had been completed in most places by the 1770s. By the time of the Revolution, blacks had shaped the most important instrument of their survival in slavery: the family. Yet the master's whim continually threatened the slave family. The forces unleashed by the Revolution offered blacks the opportunity to place their family life on a stronger base, and they quickly took advantage of it.[28]

Many freemen, themselves fresh from bondage, helped family and friends purchase their liberty, and thus rebuilt families separated by slavery. Since most freemen were poor, buying the freedom of a loved one took years of austere living. It was not unusual for a free Negro to save for five to ten years in order to liberate a single bondsman. Despite these obstacles, some free blacks dedicated much of their lives and fortunes to help others escape bondage. Graham Bell, a Petersburg freeman, purchased and freed nine slaves between 1792 and 1805. In 1792, Bell emancipated five slave children (probably his own) whom he had bought three years earlier. In 1801 he purchased and freed a slave woman, who later paid him £15 for the service. The following year, noting "that God created all men equally free," he emancipated two more slaves, and in 1805 he manumitted his brother. Bell's persistence was exceptional, but not unique. In New Bern, North Carolina, John C. Stanly, a successful free Negro barber, purchased and emancipated his wife and children in 1805, and two years later freed his brother-in-law. During the next eleven years, Stanly freed another eighteen slaves. Aletha Tanner of Washington equaled Stanly's benevolence: After purchasing her own freedom, she bought and liberated twenty-two friends and relatives.[29]

Other free Negroes, anxious to reunite their families or friends, had not the patience, money, or inclination to buy liberty. Instead, they plotted to aid fugitives from bondage. So often did newly freed blacks rescue their families from servitude, that masters looked first to them when their slaves ran off. When Jonathan fled slavery, his owner noted he was "related to a family of negroes, who lately obtained their freedom"; Bet's mistress believed she "went off in company with a mulatto free fellow name Tom Turner, who follows the water for a living and calls her his wife"; and Sam's master thought he would go to Baltimore where he had "several relations (manumitted blacks), who will conceal and assist him to make his escape." Little wonder that slaveholders, determined to stop the growing number of fugitives, demanded legislative restraints on free blacks because of the "great number of relations and acquaintances they still have among us, and from the harbours and houses such manumitted Negroes" afford runaways. Although slaveowners found freemen easy scapegoats for slave unrest, their

presumption proved true often enough to sustain their generalized suspicions.[30] Once liberated from bondage, free blacks did not forget those left behind.

Yet even more important than a fast horse or a forged pass, freemen provided fugitives with the example that blacks could be free. The rapid growth of the free Negro population swelled the expectations of those still in bondage. Many who saw their friends and relatives shed the shackles of slavery began thinking about what previously seemed unattainable. "Henny," noted a Maryland slaveholder in 1783, "will try to pass for a free woman as several have lately been set free in this neighbourhood."[31] The increase of successful fugitives not only added to the free Negro population but provided just one more measure of the close ties between freemen and bondsmen during the formative postrevolutionary years.

Selecting a new name and address or helping a friend from slavery to freedom were symbolically important. These acts marked a clean break with bondage and an effort to begin life anew. But whatever psychic satisfaction a freeman received from his new name, address, or reunited family, they provided little of the substance of liberty. Newly emancipated blacks were still black in a society that presumed only whites to be free, and propertyless in a society that measured status mainly in dollars.

Some blacks moved from slavery to freedom in relative comfort. Their masters, partly from necessity and partly out of foresight, provided for them after emancipation. George Washington and Robert Carter, both of whom manumitted several hundred slaves, composed elaborate plans to support their former bondsmen and ensure that they would not burden the community. Washington provided for apprenticeship and tenancy for the able-bodied and lodging and pensions for the aged. But only a few slaveowners furnished their former bondsmen with a means of making a living. Occasionally, some masters gave them small gifts of clothing, a few sticks of furniture, or a little money; rarely did they give more than this.[32] Since most manumitters were motivated by the ideology of the Revolution and since that ideology required nothing more than the bestowal of freedom, slaveholders saw little reason to go beyond emancipation. Certainly there was never a hint of compensation for the long years of bondage. Slaveholders might be compensated, but not slaves. Thus for most blacks, slavery was a poor school for freedom, and emancipation at first added nothing to their inheritance. Once free, they usually found themselves without property or steady work.

Newly freed blacks frequently suffered a sharp decline in occupational status. As slaves, blacks had been the artisans who did much of the skilled labor in colonial society. Indeed, the proportion of slaves engaged in skilled labor had increased during the second half of the eighteenth century. Yet, once freed, blacks found themselves proscribed from many of the trades at which they excelled. The decline of free Negro occupational status took place at an uneven pace during the pre-Civil War years, speeded by competition from newly arrived immigrant workers and retarded by the general demand for labor and the refusal of whites, especially in the slave states, to work at trades deemed "nigger work." But from the outset, whites objected to working alongside blacks, especially free ones. Similarly, many white employers gave preference to white workers, and those who wanted blacks usually preferred slaves, over whose labor they had greater control. Thus freemen were driven from certain jobs because they were black, and they were excluded from others because they were free. This dual proscription allowed whites to limit free Negroes to an ever shrinking range of menial occupations, increasing tensions between white and black workers, and sometimes between freemen and bondsmen as well.[33]

Although accompanied by proscription and exclusion, freedom also created new opportunities, often for slaves as well as freemen. It allowed some blacks to attain positions from which all blacks previously had been barred. Suddenly blacks took the role of a painter, poet, author, astronomer, minister, and merchant. The almanacs of Benjamin Banneker, the poems of Phillis Wheatly and Jupiter Hammon, and the portraits of Joshua Johnston stand not only as tributes to the achievements of talented men and women, but also as symbols of the cultural transformation of the revolutionary era.[34]

The new opportunities of freedom also allowed some freemen to accumulate property and achieve a modicum of economic security. William Flora, a revolutionary veteran, purchased several lots in Portsmouth, Virginia, soon after his discharge from the army. Later he opened a livery stable, served Portsmouth for thirty years, and willed his property to his son. In 1783, James McHenry, a Maryland shoemaker, purchased his freedom, and four years later rented a farm for £35 a year and had "a house and other stock more than sufficient for his farm." Henry Carter, a Virginia freeman, was similarly successful. He was emancipated in 1811, and within six years not only had "funds sufficient to purchase his wife Priscilla but some other property, personal & real." Throughout the nation the growth of a black property-holding class followed the growth of the free Negro population. In some places, freemen controlled sizable businesses. The striking success of sea captain Paul Cuffee of New Bedford, Massachusetts, sail manufacturer James Forten of Philadelphia, and merchant Robert Sheridan of Wilmington, North Carolina, suggests how quickly blacks took advantage of the expanding, if still limited, opportunities created by freedom.[35] Although most blacks remained, as in slavery, poor and propertyless, some freemen rose to modest wealth and respectability.

Slowly, a new black elite emerged: Prince Hall in Boston, Richard Allen in Philadelphia, Daniel Coker in Baltimore, Christopher McPherson in Richmond, Andrew Bryan in Savannah, and a host of others in black communities throughout the new republic. Born in the decade before the Revolution, these men came of age with the emergence of the free Negro population and the maturation of Afro-American culture. Many of them owed their liberty to the changes unleashed by the American Revolution, and they shared the optimism and enthusiasm that accompanied freedom. Wealthier and better educated than most blacks, they moved easily into positions of leadership within the black community and pressed whites to expand black liberty. Pointing to the ideas of the Declaration of Independence, the new black elite provided the leadership in petitioning Congress and state legislatures to abolish slavery and relieve free blacks of the disabilities that prevented them from enjoying their full rights as citizens. Norfolk freemen, in a typical action, requested that they be allowed to testify in court against whites so they could prove their accounts. Boston blacks demanded an equal share of the city's school fund so they might educate their children. South Carolina's free Negroes petitioned for relief from a special head tax that pushed them into a condition "but small removed from Slavery." And from Nashville, Tennessee, came a plea that free Negroes "ought to have the same opportunities of doing well that any Person being a citizen & free … would have, and that the door ought not be kept shut against them more than any other of the Human race." In the North, blacks, themselves but recently liberated, urged an end to the slave trade and the establishment of a universal emancipation. Occasionally, a few bold southern freemen like Baltimore's Daniel Coker added their voices to this public condemnation of slavery.[36]

These freemen protested in vain. Even the most restrained pleas led to harsher repression, further anchoring them to the bottom of free society. The experience of Charleston's free Negroes indicates how vehemently whites opposed any improvement in the status of blacks. In 1791, Peter Mathews, a free Negro butcher, along with several other free black artisans and tradesmen, petitioned the state legislature to expand their rights. The law barred them from testifying in court against whites –

"for which cause many Culprits have escaped punishments," made it difficult and sometimes impossible for them to collect their debts, and subjected them to numerous frauds. At the same time, they were tried without a jury in courts that permitted slaves to testify against them. For many years, according to Mathews, Negro freemen had supported the government, paid their taxes, and upheld the peace. "Your memorialists," he tactfully concluded, "do not presume to hope that they shall be put on an equal footing with free White Citizens of the State in general [but] humbly solicit such dictates in their favor" by repealing the offending laws. Although Mathews measured his words carefully and tailored his request to avoid threatening white dominance in any way, his petition received no hearing from the legislature. Yet it may not have gone unnoticed. Three years later, when fears of insurrection ran high, white vigilantes broke into Mathews's house to search for a cache of arms. Mathews, a substantial tradesman of good repute, had little choice but to try and explain publicly that an "old pistol without flint, a broken sword, and an old cutlass" he kept in his attic were not the beginning of a revolution.[37] Perhaps he convinced Charleston vigilantes, perhaps not; in any case the lot of Peter Mathews was just further proof that whites would tolerate no alteration of their standards of race relations.

## V

Frustrated by unyielding white hostility, freemen took two divergent courses. Some turned away from slaves in an effort to ingratiate themselves with whites, by trying to demonstrate they were more free than black. This strategy was especially evident in – although not limited to – the Lower South, where ties between freemen and slaves had never been strong and where many of the newly arrived *gens de couleur* had suffered heavy losses at the hands of the Haitian slave rebels. During the 1790s, the free people of color in Charleston established the Brown Fellowship Society, an organization limited to free brown people, and one which remained a symbol of mulatto exclusiveness throughout the antebellum period.[38]

Most freemen, especially in the North and Upper South, took a different course. Increasingly, they turned inward and worked to strengthen the black community – free and slave. Freemen, frequently joined by slaves, established institutions where blacks might pray, educate their children, entertain, and protect themselves. African churches, schools, and fraternal societies not only served the new needs of the much expanded free Negro population and gave meaning to black liberty, but they also symbolized the emergence of Afro-American culture and represented the strongest effort to unite the black community.

Yet, even while they shouldered the new responsibilities of freedom, blacks did not immediately form separate institutions. The development of the African church, for example, was not merely a product of the emergence of the free Negro population. At first, most blacks looked to the white-dominated evangelical churches, which made acceptance of the gospel the only criteria for salvation and welcomed blacks into the fold. Free Negroes, along with slaves and poor whites, found this open membership policy, the emotional sermons, and the generous grants of self-expression an appealing contrast to the icy restrictiveness of the older, more staid denominations. Although racially mixed congregations were often forced to meet at odd hours to avoid hostile sheriffs and slave patrols, black membership in these churches grew rapidly. By the end of the eighteenth century, thousands of blacks, free and slave, had joined Methodist and Baptist churches.

The newness of the evangelical denominations together with their Christian equalitarianism fostered new racial patterns. In many such churches, blacks and whites seated themselves indiscriminately. It was not unusual for black churchmen to attend synods and association meetings with whites. In 1794, when

one Virginia church called this practice into question, the Portsmouth Baptist Association firmly announced that "it saw nothing in the Word of God nor anything contrary to the rules of decency to prohibit a church from sending as a delegate, any male member they shall choose." Sometimes blacks served as preachers to a mixed congregation. John Chavis, a black Presbyterian circuit rider, enjoyed his greatest success among whites; Fayetteville whites regarded Henry Evans, a black Methodist, as the "best preacher of his time in that quarter"; and when Richard Allen looked down from his Philadelphia pulpit he saw "Nearly … as many Whites as Blacks."[39]

Yet the old racial patterns had remarkable resilience. Christian equalitarianism momentarily bent the color line, but could not break it. In most churches, membership did not assure blacks of equal participation. Indeed, whites usually placed blacks in a distant corner or gallery and barred them from most of the rights of church members. One Virginia congregation painted some of its benches black to avoid any possibility of confusion.[40]

As blacks found themselves proscribed from white churches or discriminated against in mixed churches, they attempted the difficult task of forming their own religious institutions. In doing so, blacks not only lacked the capital and organizational experience, but they frequently faced fierce white opposition. This was especially true in the South, where whites identified freemen with slaves and seemed to see every meeting of free blacks, no matter how innocuous, as an insurrectionary plot.[41] The abolition of slavery in the North, in large measure, had freed whites from this fear, allowing blacks greater organizational opportunities. Northern whites frequently took a benign view of black institutions and believed, along with Benjamin Rush, that it would "be much cheaper to build churches for them than jails."[42]

Regional differences in white attitudes allowed blacks to act more openly in the North. While northern freemen quickly established their own churches and schools, southern free blacks, frequently joined by slaves, continued to meet intense opposition. The difficulties faced by blacks in Williamsburg, Virginia, typified the problems that confronted blacks throughout the South. In the 1780s, when Moses organized a group of Williamsburg Baptists "composed, almost, if not altogether, of people of colour," he was seized and whipped. Gowan Pamphlet, who succeeded Moses as church leader, also encountered stiff opposition. The local Baptist Association refused to recognize the church, and when Pamphlet persisted, they excommunicated him and some of his congregation. Still, Pamphlet's church continued to meet and expand. In 1791, announcing that they numbered over 500, blacks again petitioned the Dover Baptist Association for membership, and two years later the Association grudgingly received the church, with Pamphlet as its minister. Even then the Association could not resist one last slap. In 1793 Pamphlet was accepted as a delegate from the Williamsburg African Church only "as they could not have done better under the circumstances."[43]

Despite the rising pitch of white opposition, the number of black churches increased steadily throughout the 1780s and 1790s. Whites, who monopolized all the important ecclesiastical offices, controlled church finances, and regulated church discipline, increasingly found themselves confronted by blacks who demanded autonomy or a greater share of power within the church organization. Visiting Baltimore in 1795, Methodist Bishop Francis Asbury issued the common lament of many white churchmen: "The Africans of this town desire a church, which in temporals, shall be altogether under their own direction, and ask greater privileges than the white stewards and trustees ever had the right to claim."[44] When their demands were not met, blacks usually seceded from the white-dominated organizations. In some places, they left after a violent confrontation, as when whites physically removed Absalom Jones from his pew in Philadelphia's St. George Methodist Church.[45] More often, blacks quietly withdrew

when it became obvious that their pleas for greater equality would never be satisfactorily answered.[46] The rank discrimination of white-dominated churches fostered black separatism, but some blacks welcomed the split. It allowed them, for the first time, full control over their own religious life. By the end of the century, black communities from Boston to Savannah boasted their own African churches.[47]

The equalitarian moment had not lasted long, but it was crucial nonetheless. Anglo-American and Afro-American religious styles mixed freely during these years, and when whites and blacks retreated to their separate segregated organizations, they carried much of the other's culture with them. The West African call-response pattern, for example, became a regular part of early Baptist and Methodist services, and the polity and theology of the evangelical denominations became central to the development of the African Baptist and African Methodist Church. The full dimensions of these cultural exchanges have not been fully studied, but it is important to observe that they were part of a larger cultural transformation at a time of relatively easy racial intermingling, especially among the lower classes.[48]

During the early years of the nineteenth century, blacks continued to establish new African churches in the northern and border slave states. In 1816, leading black churchmen from various parts of these regions joined together to form the first independent black denomination, the African Methodist Episcopal (AME) Church.[49] But if the African church flourished in the North, it fell upon hard times in the South. While the abolition of slavery had freed northern whites from the fear of insurrection, those anxieties grew among white southerners. In 1800, when Gabriel Prosser's aborted insurrection in Virginia nearly transformed the worst fears of southern whites into a dreadful reality, the African church came under still greater pressure. Hysterical whites shut many black churches and forced black ministers to flee the South. Even white churchmen found themselves under attack for proselytizing blacks.

When a white circuit rider tried to preach to a mixed congregation in Richmond in 1802, he was threatened with the lash and driven out of the city. Charleston Methodists similarly found themselves "watched, ridiculed, and openly assailed" for allowing blacks to attend their meetings. The growth of the African church in the South was abruptly halted during the first years of the nineteenth century.[50] Later it would revive under very different conditions.[51]

The early development of African schools followed the same tortuous path as that of the independent black churches. In the years immediately following the Revolutionary War, the momentary respite in racial hostility encouraged some freemen and sympathetic whites to establish integrated academies throughout the North and even in some border states. But the emotions and ideals that united poor whites and blacks in evangelical churches were absent from the founding of schools. Schools were middle- and upper-class institutions, and class distinctions alone doubtless excluded most free blacks. Handicapped by a lack of funds and surrounded by increasingly hostile whites, integrated schools languished. By the turn of the century, the ebbing of revolutionary equalitarianism forced those few remaining integrated schools to close their doors or segregate their classrooms. The support of black schools fell largely on black communities. African schools, usually attached to black churches, continued to meet in the North, and in some places increased in size and number. But in the South, they faced intense opposition from whites, who viewed them as nurseries of subversion.[52]

The destruction of the Richmond African school suggests the depth of white hostility to any attempt blacks might make to secure their liberty and improve themselves. In 1811, Christopher McPherson, a free Negro of considerable talent and modest wealth who also styled himself "Pherson, the first son of Christ," hired Herbert H. Hughes, a white schoolmaster, and established a night school for free Negroes and slaves who had obtained the consent of their masters. Classes began at dusk and ran until nine-thirty, and Hughes taught "the English language grammatically, Writing, Arithmetic, Geography, Astronomy, &c. &cc." for a fee of about $.25 per month. Slaves and freemen flocked to Hughes's classroom. The school opened with twenty-five pupils, and McPherson noted "from frequent applications since, 'tis expected the number will shortly be doubled." McPherson was so pleased with his initial success that he boasted of the school in the *Richmond Argus,* and recommended "to the people of colour throughout the United States (who do not have it in their power to attend day schools) to establish similar institutions in their neighbourhoods." Excited over the new possibilities, he hoped "that everyone who loves his Country, and has it in his power will generously further and foster every institution of the kind that may be established throughout this happy Union."[53]

Richmond whites were less enthusiastic. The following day, "several citizens … whose opinions we highly respect" confronted Samuel Pleasants, the editor of the *Argus,* and demanded that McPherson's advertisement be withdrawn. "They deem it," Pleasants reported, "impolitic and highly improper that such an institution should exist in this City." Pleasants dissented, but dutifully withdrew the advertisement. Herbert Hughes, the white schoolmaster, was made of sterner stuff. He took space in the *Argus,* defended the school, and attacked the idea that it was impolitic to educate blacks as Rousseauian sophistry. Reiterating his commitment to the school, Hughes declared that "without Education in some degree *they are* in a state of bastard civilization," and he pledged to teach until "a verdict from a proper tribunal" closed the school.[54]

That apparently was not long in coming, for soon after Hughes made his appeal, Richmond officials summoned McPherson to court to show why his school should not be declared a nuisance. The case was delayed, but the police continued to harass McPherson, and probably drove Hughes out of town. Despite the greater threat implicit in the police action, in April, when the court again delayed his case, McPherson advertised his desire to establish "a seminary of learning of the arts and sciences" as soon as he could find a "proper tutor." But before he could act, police jailed McPherson and then shipped him to the Williamsburg Lunatic Asylum. McPherson doubtless had religious delusions, but these had not prevented him from functioning for years in a manner acceptable to Richmond whites; only when he established a school was he clapped into a madhouse.[55] His lesson was obvious: any black who would attempt to found a school was "crazy."

The dismantling of African churches and schools suggests the intensity of white opposition to the development of independent black institutions wherever slavery continued to exist. Yet, even as whites closed black churches and schools and slapped new proscriptions on black liberty in order to freeze blacks into a place of permanent social inferiority, they could not erase all the gains made in the first flush of freedom. In the North, African churches and schools continued to grow and occasionally flourish, and even in the South some of these institutions limped on, although often forced to accept white supervision or meet clandestinely.

On the surface, African churches and schools and allied benevolent and fraternal societies were but a weak imitation of those of the larger society. Often they reflected white values and mimicked the structure of their white counterparts. But, on closer inspection, they embodied an Afro-American culture that was over a century in the making. Whites who visited black church meetings or attended black funerals almost uniformly observed the striking difference between them and their own somber rituals.[56] It was no accident that blacks called their churches African churches, their schools African schools, and their benevolent societies African benevolent societies.

These organizations provided an institutional core for black life throughout the nineteenth century and well into the twentieth. In African churches and schools, black people baptized their children, educated their youth, and provided for the sick, aged, and disabled. African churches strengthened black family life by insisting that marriages be solemnized, by punishing adulterers, and occasionally by reuniting separated couples. Leaders of these institutions, especially ministers, moved into dominant positions in the black community, and African churches, in turn, provided a means of advancement for ambitious black youth. More than this, these institutions gave the black community a sense of solidarity and common purpose. At no time was this more evident than in the postrevolutionary era, when slaves and freemen joined together to re-form black society and give shape to the cultural transformation of the preceding century. Later, free Negroes and slaves would drift apart, and many of the institutions formed during this earlier era would become identified with the free blacks and urban slave artisans who placed them at the center of black life in the North and urban South. But the new social and institutional forms established during the years after the Revolution were not lost for the mass of enslaved black people. The changes set in motion by the Revolution permeated slave life in ways that are only barely recognized now. The new occupational, religious, and familial patterns and the new social roles and modes of social action established by the convergence of changes in Afro-American and Anglo-American life during the revolutionary era continued to inform slave society, as the great cotton boom pulled slaves out of the seaboard states and into the Lower South. The revolution in black life spread across the continent. On the rich, loamy soils of the cotton South, slaves reshaped the cultural legacy of the revolutionary era to meet the new needs of plantation life. And with the Civil War, the Emancipation Proclamation, and the Thirteenth Amendment, the transformed institutional and cultural legacy of the revolutionary era emerged once again and stood at the center of black life.

## Notes

1. *Gentlemen's Magazine and Historical Chronicle.* 34 (1764): 261: Petition from Petersburg, 11 December 1805, Virginia Legislative Papers, Virginia State Library, Richmond; *Proceedings and Debates of the Convention of North-Carolina Called to Amend the Constitution of the State* (Raleigh. N.C.: J. Gales and Son, 1835), 351; [John S. Tyson], *Life of Elisha-Tyson* (Baltimore: B. Lundy. 1825), 7.

2. Winthrop D. Jordan, *White Over Black: American Attitudes Toward the Negro, 1550–1812* (Chapel Hill. N.C., 1968), 122–28: Edgar J. McManus. *Black Bondage in the North* (Syracuse. N.Y, 1973), 67–70, 122. 161–62; Lorenzo J. Greene, *The Nergro in Colonial New England* (New York, 1942), 298–304.

3. Benjamin Quarles, *The Negro in the American Revolution* (Chapel Hill, N.C, 1961), 19–32; *Williamsburg Virginia Gazette* (Purdie), 17 November 1775, (Dixon & Nicholson) 2 December 1775. For an enlightening comparative perspective on war and slavery, see David Brion Davis, *The Problem of Slavery in the Age of Revolution, 1770–1823* (Ithaca, N.Y, 1975), 72–82.

4. Quarles, *Negro in the American Revolution*, 111–57; Donald L. Robinson, *Slavery in the Structure of American Politics, 1765–1820* (New York, 1971), 98–113.

5. Quarles, *Negro in the American Revolution*, 3–18, 51–67; Robinson, *Slavery in the Structure of American Politics*, 113–22, quote 120–21; Pete Maslowski, "National Policy toward the Use of Black Troops in the Revolution," *South Carolina Historical Magazine* 73 (1972): 1–17.

6. Quarles, *Negro in the American Revolution*, 68–93, 111–57; Petition from Henrico County, 1784, Virginia Legislative Papers; Virginia State Library, Richmond; Luther P. Jackson, "Virginia Negro Soldiers and Seamen in the American Revolution," *Journal of Negro History* 27(1942): 274–75; William W. Hening, comp., *The Statutes at Large; Being a Collection of All the Laws of Virginia,* 13 vols. (Richmond, New York, Philadelphia, 1809–1823), 8:103, 9:308–9.

7. Complaints about the loss of slave property and the growing number of fugitives were rife throughout the war years. For example, see Walter Clark, ed., *The State Records of North Carolina, 1777–1790,* 16 vols. [numbered consecutively after a preceding series] (Raleigh, 1886–1907), 15:138: W. H. Browne et al., eds., *Archives of Maryland,* 71 vols. (Baltimore, 1883–), 45:473; William P. Palmer, ed., *Calendar of Virginia State Papers,* 11 vols. (Richmond, 1875–1893), 1:477–78; and Quarles, *Negro in the American Revolution,* especially, 115–32. The effect of internal dissension of slavery has not yet been fully assayed, but Ronald Hoffman, *A Spirit of Dissension: Economics, Politics, and the Revolution in Maryland* (Baltimore, 1973), 147–48, 152–53, 184–88, is suggestive. Gerald W. Mullin, *Flight and Rebellion: Slave Resistance in Eighteenth-Century Virginia* (New York, 1972) documents the relationship between acculturation and patterns of resistance in the most important Upper South colony and state.

8. An understanding of the relationship between the American Revolution and the ideological opposition to slavery must begin with Jordan, *White Over Black,* 269–475, and Davis, *The Problem of Slavery in the Age of Revolution.* Davis is especially insightful on the ambiguities and limitation of antislavery thought. Robert McColley, *Slavery and Jeffersonian Virginia* (Urbana, Ill., 1964), rightly emphasizes the expansion of slavery during the postrevolutionary period, although he ignores the larger pattern of events which threw slavery on the defensive. The long-range implications of these events on slavery are explored by William W. Freehling, "The Founding Fathers and Slavery," *American Historical Review* 77 (1972): 81–93.

9. Arthur Zilversmit, *The First Emancipation: The Abolition of Slavery in the North* (Chicago, 1967); Jordan, *White Over Black,* 315–74; Gary B. Nash, "Slaves and Slaveowners in Colonial Philadelphia," *William and Mary Quarterly,* 3d ser. 30 (1973): 231–32, 236–56, especially 254, 256; Robert William Fogel and Stanley L. Engerman, "Philanthropy at Bargain Prices: Notes on the Economics of Gradual Emancipation," *Journal of Legal Studies* 3 (1974): 377–82, 385–93. Again, Davis's comparative perspective on emancipation in nonplantation societies is instructive. *The Problem of Slavery in the Age of Revolution,* 86–92.

10. Jacob P. Dunn, Jr., *Indiana: A Redemption from Slavery* (Boston, 1888); Theodore C. Pease, *The Story of Illinois* (Chicago, 1949), 72–78.

11. Wesley M. Gewehr., *The Great Awakening in Virginia, 1740–1790* (Durham, N.C., 1930); John B. Boles, *The Great Revival, 1787–1805: The Origins of the Southern Evangelical Mind* (Lexington, Ky, 1972); McColley, *Slavery and Jeffersonian Virginia,*148–62; Donald G. Mathews, *Slavery and Methodism: A Chapter in American Morality, 1780–1845* (Princeton, NJ, 1965), 3–29; Davis, *The Problem of Slavery in the Age of Revolution,* 203–10: Garnett Ryland, *The Baptists of Virginia, 1699–1926* (Richmond, Va, 1955), 150–55; W. Harrison Daniel, "Virginia Baptists and the Negro in the Early Republic," *Virginia Magazine of History and Biography* 80 (1972): 65–68.

12. Carville Earle and Ronald Hoffman, "The Urban South: The First Two Centuries." *Perspectives in American History,* forthcoming, is the best discussion of economic and demographic changes in the region. Also Lewis C. Gray, *History of Agriculture in the Southern United States to 1860,* 2 vols. (Washington. D.C, 1933). 2:602–17: Mullin. *Flight and Rebellion.* 124–27: John R. Alden, *The First South* (Baton Rouge, La, 1961), 9–10. Although they fail to make regional distinctions, Robert William Fogel and Stanley L. Engerman offer the most accurate information on slave prices during the period. *Time on the Cross: The Economics of American Negro Slavery* (Boston, 1975), 86–89.

13. Ira Berlin, *Slaves Without Masters: The Free Negro in the Antebellum South* (New York, 1974), 29–35.

14. Mullin, *Flight and Rebellion,* 87–88, 117, 156–57; Samuel S. Bradford, "The Negro Iron Workers in Ante Bellum Virginia, *Journal of Southern History* 25 (1959): 195; but see also Charles B. Dew. "David Ross and the Oxford Iron Works: A Study of Industrial Slavery in the Early Nineteenth-Century South," *William and Mary* Quarterly, 3d ser. 31 (1974): 200 n.36.

15. George Drinker to Joseph Bringhurst, 10 December 1804, Pennsylvania Society for Promoting the Abolition of Slavery Papers, Historical Society of Pennsylvania, Philadelphia; Mullin, *Flight and Rebellion,* 83–139 and passim; Berlin, *Slaves Without Masters,* 36–45.

16. The United States census did not distinguish between blacks and mulattoes – meaning, presumably, anyone of mixed African ancestry – until 1850, and at that time about a third of Upper South free Negroes and 22 percent of Maryland's free Negroes were of mixed racial origins. This contrasts sharply with the racial composition of the colonial free Negro population as suggested by the Maryland census of 1755. An enumeration of Negro freemen in the District of Columbia in 1807, soon after it was carved out of Maryland and Virginia, indicates that the shift in the character of the free Negro population from brown to black (although, compared to slaves, still disproportionately brown) took place in the years following the Revolution. *Negro Population of the United States, 1790–1915* (Washington, D.C., 1918), 109, 221: U.S. Commissioner of Education, *Special Report … on the Condition and Improvement of Public Education in the District of Columbia* (Washington, D.C., 1871), 195.

17. Unless otherwise noted, the following statistics are computed from *Population of the United States in 1860* (Washington, D.C., 1864), 195.

18. St. George Tucker, *A Dissertation on Slavery* (Philadelphia, 1796), 72.

19. *Columbian Museum & Savannah Advertiser* 11 March 1796: W. E. B. DuBois, *The Suppression of the African Slave-Trade to the United States of America, 1638–1870* (Cambridge, 1896), 86–87; Patrick S. Brady, "The Slave Trade and Sectionalism in South Carolina," *Journal of Southern History* 38 (1972): 601–20.

20. C. L. R. James, *The Black Jacobins: Toussaint L'Ouverture and the San Domingo Rebellion,* 2d rev. rid. (New York, 1963); Thomas O. Ott, *The Haitian Revolution, 1789–1804* (Knoxville, Tenn., 1973): James G. Leyburn, *The Haitian People* (New Haven. Conn., 1941), chap. 1: Berlin, *Slaves Without Masters,* 35–36.

21. Two original works of scholarship have recently reopened the question of acculturation: Mullin. *Flight and Rebellion,* and Peter H. Wood, *Black Majority: Negroes in Colonial South Carolina from 1670 through the Stono Rebellion* (New York, 1974). An older, but still insightful formulation of the question is Melville J. Herskovits, "The Negro in the New World: The Statement of a Problem," *American Anthropologists* 32 (1930): 145–55, and *The Myth of the Negro Past* (New York, 1941). Also valuable are Norman E. Whitten, Jr. and John F. Sawed, eds., *Afro-American Anthropology: Contemporary Perspectives* (New York, 1970); Roger Bastide, *African Civilisations in the New World* (New

York, 1972); John W. Blassingame, *The Slave Community: Plantation Life in the Ante-Bellum South* (New York, 1972), 1–40.

22. Jordan, *White Over Black,* 269–582; Berlin, *Slaves Without Masters,* 21–35, 79–107.

23. For Tom Toogood, *Annapolis Maryland Gazette,* 18 June 1795; for Carter, ibid., 3 July 1794; for Mason, Petition from Henrico County, 22 December 1847, Virginia Legislative Papers, Virginia State Library, Richmond; for Green, *Virginia Gazette,* 15 July 1795; for Bishop, *Minutes of the Portsmouth Baptist Association,* 1794, 6; for Cook, *Baltimore Federal Gazette,* 14 March 1806; for Wheeler, Anne Arundel County Manumissions, Lib. no. 1, A, 289, Maryland Hall of Records, Annapolis. Other names are taken from a survey of Free Negro Registers at the Maryland Hall of Records, Annapolis, Virginia State Library, Richmond, South Caroliniana Library, University of South Carolina, Columbia, South Carolina Archives, Columbia, Georgia Historical Society, Savannah, and the Georgia Department of Archives and History, Atlanta. For a fuller discussion of naming patterns in the postrevolutionary years, see Berlin, *Slaves Without Masters,* 51–53.

24. Robert Carter to Spenser Ball, 23 April 1796, Carter Letterbooks, Library of Congress; A[nn] Ridgely to Henry M. and George C. Ridgely, 17 November 1796, Ridgely Family Papers, DelHR; Johann D. Schoepf, *Travels in the Confederation,* 2 vols. (Philadelphia, 1911), 2:150.

25. Petition from Sussex County, 1786, Misc. Slavery Collection, Historical Society of Delaware, Wilmington; South Carolina House Journal, 1788, 266–67; Charleston Grand Jury Presentment, November 1792, South Carolina Archives, Columbia.

26. Petition from Petersburg, 11 December 1805, Virginia Legislative Papers, Virginia State Library, Richmond; Charleston Grand Jury Presentment, September 1798, South Carolina Archives, Columbia; *Returns of the Whole Number of Persons Within the … United States* (Philadelphia, 1791); *Aggregate Amount of Persons Within the United States in the Year 1810* (Washington, D.C., 1811).

27. Even during this period, however, black unity was far from perfect. Berlin, *Slaves Without Masters,* 56–58.

28. Russell R. Menard, "The Maryland Slave Population, 1658 to 1730: A Demographic Profile of Blacks in Four Counties," *William and Mary Quarterly,* 3d ser. 32 (1975):31–53. For the development of the slave family in eighteenth-century South Carolina, see the C. C. Pinckney [1789–1865] Plantation Book, 1812–1861, Pinckney Family Papers, Library of Congress.

29. Luther P. Jackson, "Manumission in Certain Virginia Cities," *Journal of Negro History* 15 (1930): 285–86; John Hope Franklin, *The Free Negro in North Carolina, 1790–1860* (Chapel Hill, N.C., 1943), 31–32; Constance McLaughlin Green, *The Secret City: A History of Race Relations in the Nation's Capital* (Princeton, NJ, 1967), 16.

30. *Richmond Virginia Gazette,* 11 December 1793; *Baltimore Maryland Journal,* 25 June 1793; *Annapolis Maryland Gazette,* 6 May 1790; Petition from Accomac County, 3 January 1783, Virginia Legislative Papers, Virginia State Library, Richmond.

31. *Annapolis Maryland Gazette,* 3 April 1783.

32. John C. Fitzpatrick, ed., *The Writings of George Washington,* 39 vols. (Washington, D.C., 1931–1944), 37:267–77; Eugene Prussing, *The Estate of George Washington, Deceased* (Boston, 1927), 154–60; Benjamin Dawson to Robert Carter, 7 September 1793, Robert Carter Papers, Virginia Historical Society, Richmond; Robert Carter to Benjamin Dawson, 22 July 1794, Robert Carter Letterbooks, Library of Congress, Washington, D.C.; Proposal to Prince and others, 13 February 1793, Robert Carter Papers, Virginia Historical Society, Richmond; Louis Morton, *Robert Carter of Nomini Hall* (Williamsburg, 1941), 251–69.

33. McManus, *Black Bondage in the North,* 184–85; Leon F. Litwack, *North of Slavery: The Negro in the Free States, 1790–1860* (Chicago, 1961), 5–6, 101–3, 153–86; Theodore Hershberg, "Free Blacks in Antebellum Philadelphia: A Study of Ex-Slaves, Freeborn, and Socio-economic Decline," *Journal of Social History* 5 (1972): 186, 198–99; Berlin, *Slaves Without Masters,* 60–62, 96–97, 217–49.

34. Silvio A. Bedini, *The Life of Benjamin Banneker* (New York, 1971); Phillis Wheatley, *Poems on Various Subjects, Religious and Moral* (Philadelphia, 1787); Phillis Wheatley, *Memoirs and Poems of Phillis Wheatley, a Native African and a Slave* (Boston, 1834); J. Hall Pleasants, "Joshua Johnston, The First American Negro Portrait

Painter," *Maryland Historical Magazine* 37 (1942): 120–49.

35. Jackson, "Virginia Negro Soldiers and Seamen," 269, 272, 283; Talbot County, Md., Manumission, 1787, Pennsylvania Society for the Abolition of Slavery Papers, Historical Society of Pennsylvania, Philadelphia, Petition from Charles City County, 21 December 1815, from Petersburg, 9 December 1805, Virginia Legislative Papers, Virginia State Library, Richmond; Peter Williams, *A Discourse, Delivered on the Death of Capt. Paul Cuffe* (New York, 1817); George A. Salvador, *Paul Cuffe, the Black Yankee, 1759–1817* (New Bedford, Mass., 1969); *New York Colored American,* 4 August 1838; there is no adequate study of James Forten.

36. Petition from Norfolk, 7 December 1809, Virginia Legislative Papers, Virginia State Library, Richmond; Petition from John and William Morriss, [1783], South Carolina Legislative Papers, South Carolina Archives, Columbia; Petition from William Nodding, 31 August 1803, from Casper Lott, 4 August 1803, Tennessee Legislative Papers, Tennessee State Library, Nashville; *Annals of Congress,* 4th Cong., 2d sess., 2104–2204; ibid., 6th Cong., 2d sess. 229–45; ibid., 8th Cong., 2d. sess., 790; Lorenzo J. Greene, "Prince Hall: Massachusetts Leader in Crisis," *Freedomways* 1 (1961): 244–54; Robert C. Twombly, "Black Resistance to Slavery in Massachusetts," in William L. O'Neill, ed., *Insight and Parallels: Problems and Issues of American Social History* (Minneapolis, 1973), 41–53; Dorothy Porter, ed., *Early Negro Writing, 1760–1837* (Boston, 1971), 13–27, 313–401; Daniel Coker, A *Dialogue Between a Virginian and an African Minister* (Baltimore, 1810).

37. Petition from Thomas Cole, Mathew Webb, P. B. Mathews, and other free Negroes, 1 January 1791, South Carolina Legislative Papers, South Carolina Archives, Columbia; *Charleston City Gazette,* 7 September 1793.

38. WPA, Brown Fellowship Society Papers, South Carolina Historical Society, Charleston; E. Horace Fitchett, "The Traditions of the Free Negro in Charleston, South Carolina," *Journal of Negro History* 25 (1940): 144–45; Kenneth and Anna M. Roberts, eds. and trans., *Moreau de St. Méry's American Journey (1793–1798)* (New York, 1947), 48; John Lambert, *Travels Through Lower*

*Canada and the United States of North America,* 3 vols. (London, 1810), 1:414, 416.

39. Elmer E. Clark et al., eds., *The Journal and Letters of Francis Asbury,* 3 vols. (London and Nashville, Tenn, 1958), l:403; Ryland, *Baptists of Virginia,* 155; *Minutes of the Portsmouth Baptist Association,* 1794, 6, 1798, 3; William Wightman, *Life of William Capers … Including an Autobiography* (Nashville, Tenn., 1858), 124–29; Margaret B. DesChamps, "John Chavis as a Preacher to Whites," *North Carolina Historical Review* 32 (1955): 165–72; Walter H. Brooks, "The Priority of the Sliver Bluff Church and Its Promoters," *Journal of Negro History* 7 (1922), 172–96; Richard Allen and Jupiter Gipson to Ezekiel Cooper, 22 February 1798, Ezekiel Cooper Papers, Garrett Theological Seminary, Evanston, Ill. The pioneering and still invaluable work on the Negro Church is Carter G. Woodson, *The History of the Negro Church* (Washington, D.C., 1921).

40. Roberts and Roberts, eds. and trans., *St. Méry's Journal,* 64.

41. See, for example, Lemuel Burkitt and Jesse Read, *A Concise History of the Kehekee Baptist Association from Its Rise Down to 1803* (Halifax, N.C., 1803), 258–59.

42. Rush quoted in Jordan, *White Over Black,* 424.

43. Robert Semple, *A History of the Rise and Progress of the Baptists in Virginia* (Richmond, Va., 1810), 97, 114–15; *Minutes of the Dover Baptist Association,* typescript, 1793, Virginia Baptist Historical Society, Richmond; Thad W. Tate, Jr., *The Negro in Eighteenth-Century Williamsburg* (Charlottesville, Va., 1965), 158–63. Pamphlet served as a delegate until 1807; *Minutes of the Dover Baptist Association* 1807.

44. Clark et al., eds., *Journal and Letters of Francis Asbury.* 2:65.

45. Richard Allen, *Life, Experience, and Gospel Labors* (Philadelphia, 1888), 14–15; William Douglass. *Annals of the First African Church in the USA now styled the African Episcopal Church of St. Thomas. Philadelphia* (Philadelphia, 1862), 10–11; Charles H. Wesley, *Richard Allen: Apostle of Freedom* (Washington, D.C., 1935), 52–53.

46. See, for example, the establishment of the Baltimore African Methodist Church. James A. Handy, *Scraps of African Methodist Episcopal History,* (Philadelphia, n.d.), 13–16. 22–24; Daniel A. Payne, *A History of the African Methodist*

*Episcopal Church* (Nashville, Tenn., 1891), 5–8; James H. Wright, *The Free Negro in Maryland, 1634–1860* (New York, 1921), 212–13.

47. Woodson, *History of the Negro Church,* 71–99.

48. I hope to address the question of cultural exchanges during the revolutionary era in a separate essay in the near future.

49. Wesley, *Richard Allen*, 124–88.

50. Alexander McCaine to Ezekiel Cooper, 30 September 1802, Ezekiel Cooper Papers, Garrett Theological Seminary, Evanston. Ill.; Mood, *Methodism in* Charleston, 64. Many black ministers were forced out of the South. Burkitt and Read, *Kuhekee Baptist Association*, 258–59; Coker, *Dialogue Between a Virginian and An African Minister*, 40; David Benedict, *A General History of the Baptist Denomination in America and Other Parts of the World,* 2 vols. (Boston, 1813), 2:509; John W. Davis, "George Liele and Andrew Bryan, Pioneer Negro Preachers," *Journal of Negro History* 3 (1918). 120–21.

51. Berlin. *Slaves Without Masters,* 291–96.

52. Caner G. Woodson, *The Education of the Negro Prior to 1861* (New York, 1915); William C. Dunlap, *Quaker Education in Baltimore and Virginia Yearly Meetings with an Account of Certain Meetings of Delaware and Eastern Shore Affiliated With Philadelphia* (Philadelphia, 1936), 173ff; *Special Report of the Commissioner of Education,* passim; "Constitution of the African School Society," in the Minutes of the African School Society, Wilmington, 1809–1835, Historical Society of Delaware, Wilmington: *Raleigh Register,* 25 August 1808; *Baltimore American,* 6 June 1805; *Richmond Virginia* Argus, 12 March 1811; Charles C. Andrews, *The History of the New York African Free-Schools* (New York. 1830), passim.

53. Christopher McPherson, *A Short History of the Life of Christopher McPherson, alias Pherson, Son of Christ, King of Kings and Lard of Lords...* 1st ed., ca. 1811 (Lynchburg, Va., 1855): Edmund Berkeley. Jr., "Prophet Without Honor: Christopher McPherson. Free Person of Color," *Virginia Magazine of History and Biography* 77 (1969): 180–89; quote in *Richmond Virginia Argus,* 12 March 1811.

54. Ibid., 14 March 1811, 16 March 1811.

55. McPherson, *Short History of McPherson,* 6–11, 24.

56. For example, see George Lewis, *Impressions of America and the American Churches* (Edinburg, 1845), 167–70. Frederick von Raumer, *America and the American People* (New York, 1846), 434–35: Frederick Bremer, *The Homes of the New World, 2* vols. (New York, 1853), 2:234–38; *Charleston Patriot* 19 September 1835: *Savannah News* quoted in *Louisville Daily Courier,* 6 March 1855; Lillian Foster, *Way-Side Glimpses, North and South* (New York, 1860), 109.

# 17
# THE CONTINUING REVOLUTION IN INDIAN COUNTRY

*Colin G. Calloway*

## Introduction

Who were the biggest losers of the American Revolution? Probably the first answers that spring to mind are the British or, perhaps, American loyalists. Yet the British Empire continued to enjoy tremendous wealth and power in the century after the Revolution while most loyalists, after a period of difficult transition, managed to reestablish their lives. Colin G. Calloway posits a different answer. American Indians, he argues, suffered the most from the American War for Independence both in the short and long term.

The irony is that Indians had nothing at stake in the constitutional debate over American home rule and Parliamentary sovereignty that produced the conflict. Additionally, when the war broke, practically every Indian nation insisted that it wanted nothing to do with the fighting. Yet, almost invariably, Indians in eastern North America were drawn into the conflict by considerations of trade, politics, and defense. Though most of them allied with the British, including, most notably, the Cherokees and four of the Iroquois nations (Senecas, Cayugas, Onondagas, and Mohawks), a number of Indians took up arms on the American side, including Oneidas, Wampanoags, Mahicans, and Catawbas. Some nations split over which side to support, creating something of an Indian civil war parallel to the American rift with Britain and the patriot/loyalist divide. The tragedy, Calloway contends, was that Indians suffered steep losses of lives, land, and sovereignty no matter which side they took.

Calloway identifies the Revolution as a watershed in American Indian history and American racial history, not just in American national history. Before the war, Indian and colonial societies were deeply intertwined, for good and for ill. After the war, whites wanted all Indians gone, fueled by land lust and a racial hatred stoked by decades of brutal warfare. Indeed, the term "white" became more common and salient following the Revolution as Americans sought to define who was a member of their new nation and, importantly, who was not. For the next century, the nation, its states, and its people made dispossessing Indians by hook and by crook a foundation of national expansion and identity. In this sense, Indians were the big losers of the Revolution.

- What stakes did Indians have in the American Revolution? What factors weighed most heavily on Indians' decision of which side to support?
- What divisions within Indian societies did the American Revolution exacerbate and create?
- What roles did Indians play during the Revolutionary War? How pivotal were those roles?
- Most eastern Indians were not faring well before the Revolution, yet Calloway argues that their fate worsened considerably because of the war. What changes does he see as resulting from the Revolution?
- In what ways does taking Indians seriously change our perspective on the Revolution? For instance, historians often use the Revolution to date the end of the colonial era. Would the Indians under consideration here agree with that periodization?

For many Native Americans, the American Revolution did not end in 1783; it was one phase of a Twenty Years' War that continued at least until the Treaty of Greenville in 1795. Before it was over, a whole generation had grown up knowing little but war. Whether they sided with rebels or redcoats, or neither, or both, Indians during the Revolution were doing pretty much the same thing as the American patriots — fighting for their freedom in tumultuous times. Indian people in the new republic continued their struggles for independence and attempted to adjust to the new world order. But, with the Revolution won, Americans reduced to a single adversarial role the diverse Indian experiences and varying degrees of involvement in that conflict. Native Americans became identified with the enemies of the republic. This image fueled ambivalence about the place of Indian people in the American future. In its simplest terms, while Anglo-Americans could imagine subordinate Indians as friends, they typically equated resistance with a national threat. Native Americans in the new Republic found that the American Revolution not only had created a new society; it also provided the justification for excluding them from it.

The "world turned upside down" for American Indians long before it did for Lord Cornwallis,[1] and many Indian nations were already shadows of their former selves by 1775. European emigration, European diseases, European firearms, and European imperial ambitions had produced political upheaval, economic dislocation, and demographic disaster throughout Indian country. Generations of contact had seen precedents established, attitudes ingrained, and patterns of coexistence worked out and fall apart. Indian communities in colonial America struggled to survive in a chaotic new world, and yet despite massive inroads in Indian country and Indian cultures, Indian people were still virtually everywhere in colonial America.[2]

The forces that had inverted their world intensified with the outbreak of the Revolution.

At first the American Revolution had looked very much like an English civil war to Indian eyes, and most Native Americans tried to avoid becoming entangled in it. Throughout the eastern woodlands, and throughout the war, British and American agents solicited Indian support. An Abenaki woman in western Maine said her tribe was being constantly courted. "O, straing [strange] *Englishmen* kill one another," she said. "I think the world is coming to an end." In the spring of 1777 British agent William Caldwell warned the Senecas not to "regard anything the Bigknife [Americans] might say to them for tho he had a very smooth Oily Tongue his heart was not good." Two years later American commander Daniel Brodhead warned the Shawnees that the British would tell them fine stories but had come three thousand miles only "to rob & Steal & fill their Pockets."[3]

Such competition produced confusion and division in Indian communities as people wrestled with how best to proceed in perilous and uncertain times. Fernando de Leyba told Governor of Louisiana Bernardo de Galvez in the summer of 1778 that the war was "causing a great number of Indian tribes to go from one side to the other without knowing which side to take."[4] Discourse and discord were part of the normal process by which most eastern woodland societies reached consensus, but the issues raised by the Revolution were such that consensus could not always be reached. The divisions of colonial society that John Adams summarized as one-third patriot, one-third loyalist, and one-third neutral were replicated with numerous variations in countless Indian communities in North America, and, as elsewhere on the frontier, the pressures imposed by the Revolution revealed existing fissures as well as creating new ones.[5] The Delawares in 1779 asked Congress to distinguish between their nation as a whole, which was still friendly, and the actions of a few individuals who, like the loyalists in the states, sided with the British and had been obliged to leave the nation.[6] As provocations increased, however, neutrality became increasingly precarious, even impossible, forcing Indians to choose sides.

The national mythology has assigned Indians a minimal and one-dimensional role in the Revolution: they chose the wrong side and they lost. But commitment was never unanimous, and in Indian country the American Revolution often translated into an American civil war. The League of the Iroquois – the confederacy of the Mohawks, Oneidas, Onondagas, Cayugas, Senecas, and Tuscaroras that stretched across upper New York state – had managed to maintain a pivotal position in North American affairs by preserving formal neutrality and essential unity of action in previous conflicts, but was unable to do so now. Samuel Kirkland, the New England Presbyterian missionary who himself generated significant divisions in Oneida society, heard Indians say that "they never knew a debate so warm & contention so fierce to have happened between these two Brothers, Oneidas & Cayugas, since the commencement of their union." The bitter divisions the Revolution produced *within* the Oneidas were "not yet forgotten" by 1796.[7] In 1775 both the Oneidas and Senecas took a neutral stance; two years later they were killing each other at the Battle of Oriskany and the league's central council fire at Onondaga was ritually extinguished. Pro-British warriors burned Oneida crops and houses in revenge; Oneidas retaliated by burning Mohawk homes. Most Tuscaroras also supported the Americans while the Cayugas lent their weight to the British. The Onondagas maintained a precarious neutrality until American troops burned their towns in 1779. For the Iroquois the Revolution was a war in which, in some cases literally, brother killed brother.[8]

In Massachusetts the Stockbridge Indians, a community of Christian Mohican and neighboring groups, had their own scores to settle against the British, having been deprived of lands while warriors were away fighting *for* the Crown in earlier wars and having tried in vain to seek redress.[9] They volunteered at the outbreak of the Revolution and assisted the Americans

steadfastly despite suffering heavy losses.[10] William Apess, a Pequot Indian writing in the next century, said that the small Indian town of Mashpee on Cape Cod furnished twenty-six men for the patriot service, all but one of whom "fell martyrs to liberty in the struggle for Independence." Pequots and Mohegans from Connecticut suffered similar high casualties. Indian women widowed by the war were forced to look outside their communities for husbands, intermarrying with Anglo-American and African-American neighbors.[11]

The situation elsewhere in New England and eastern Canada was less simple. The Abenakis, for generations the shock troops of New France against the New England frontier, displayed ambivalence, despite considerable British coercion. Some served the British; others offered their services to George Washington. About forty-five Abenaki families took up residence near American settlements on the upper Connecticut and supplied scouts and soldiers for the American army. Those who remained in Canada became deeply divided, and some appeared to play both sides of the street. Most Abenakis seem to have restricted their role to watching the woods.[12] Other Canadian tribes displayed similar reluctance and ambivalence, while the village of Caughnawaga (Kahnawake) near Montreal became a hotbed of intrigue in the contest for Indian allegiance in the north.[13] In Maine and Nova Scotia the Passamaquoddies, Micmacs, and Maliseets were not eager to become involved in a war that had little to do with them or to offer them. Many sided with the Americans but then split as British power and British goods exerted increasing influence.[14]

In the strategically crucial Ohio country, the Indians were the prize in a diplomatic tug of war between Henry Hamilton, the British commander at Detroit, and George Morgan, the American Indian agent at Fort Pitt. The Delawares, neutral at the outbreak of the war, soon came under pressure from American and British agents and from other tribes, particularly the pro-British Wyandots under Half King to the north. A group of young Delaware warriors defected, but even General Hand's infamous "squaw campaign" did not destroy the tribe's commitment to peace. The United States signed a treaty with the Delawares in 1778 in an effort to secure their neutrality and right of passage across their lands, but many Delawares complained they had been deceived into taking up the hatchet for the United States. White Eyes and John Killbuck of the Turtle clan displayed continued pro-American sympathies, but Captain Pipe and the Wolf clan moved to the Sandusky River, closer to the Wyandots and the British. The American murder of White Eyes, their strongest supporter in the Delaware National Council, and their failure to provide the trade goods the Delawares needed, allowed Pipe to gain influence among his hungry and disillusioned people.[15]

A detachment of Delawares served the United States through the final years of the war, but in 1780 Daniel Brodhead declared the Delawares had "acted a double part long enough."[16] American troops, guided by Killbuck and his men, burned the Delaware capital at Coshocton.[17] Killbuck's followers took refuge at Fort Pitt, where they not only suffered hunger and hardship but were exposed to danger at the hands of American frontiersmen to whom all Indians were the same. Those Delawares who lived in separate villages under the guidance of Moravian missionaries also clung to a neutrality that cost them dearly. In 1782 American militia marched to the Moravian Delaware town of Gnadenhutten, rounded up the inhabitants, and bludgeoned to death ninety-six men, women, and children.[18]

The neighboring Shawnees had been involved in long resistance against encroachment on their lands and had just fought a costly war against Lord Dunmore and Virginia. Shawnee emissaries were active in efforts to form a confederacy against American expansion, but the Shawnees themselves were divided over the question of further resistance and many migrated west of the Mississippi. The Shawnee chief Cornstalk

tried to preserve his people's fragile neutrality but confessed he was unable to restrain his "foolish Young Men." Moreover, the Americans displayed their peculiar penchant for murdering key friends at key moments. After Cornstalk was killed under a flag of truce at Fort Randolph in 1777, his Maquachake peace party joined the still-neutral Delawares at Coshocton, but most of the Shawnees now made common cause with King George.[19]

In the South the Cherokees had already had grim experience of the consequences of becoming involved in the wars of their non-Indian neighbors, but, with settlers encroaching on their lands, they fought this war for their own reasons. While the older chiefs watched in silent dejection, Dragging Canoe and younger Cherokees accepted a war belt from the northern nations and threw themselves into the fighting early in the Revolution. After expeditions from Virginia and North and South Carolina destroyed Cherokee towns and crops, the older chiefs sued for peace, and refugees fled to the Creeks, the Chickasaws, and to Pensacola. The nation split along generational lines as many younger warriors followed the lead of Dragging Canoe, seceding to form new communities at Chickamauga, which became the core of Cherokee resistance until 1795. Other Cherokees suffered as a result of Chickamauga resistance; some helped the Americans, and the Revolution assumed the look of a civil war in Cherokee country.[20]

Elsewhere in the South, Choctaw towns were divided between Britain and Spain; the majority supported King George, but British agents always feared losing them. The Chickasaws were basically pro-British, while the Catawbas, surrounded by settlers, supported the Americans.[21] At the beginning of the Revolution, the Creeks were at war with the Choctaws, and though the British now took measures to end a conflict they had previously encouraged, the Cherokee experience gave them ample reason to drag their feet. British Indian superintendent John Stuart complained they were "a mercenary

People, Conveniency & Safety are the great Ties that Bind them." Most eventually sided with the British and about 120 Creeks and over 700 Choctaws fought alongside the British in the defense of Pensacola against Spanish attack early in 1781. But the war divided the Creeks into bitter factions.[22]

Any overview of Indian dispositions and allegiances is difficult and hazardous. Most tribes fluctuated in their sentiments, intertribal alliances formed at the cost of increased intratribal disunity, and participation was usually cautious and often relatively brief. One of the first communities to wage war against the Americans was Pluggy's Town, where Chippewas, Wyandots, and Ottawas joined Mingoes (Ohio Iroquois), and where Americans found it was often "difficult to tell what Nation are the Offenders." Pluggy's Mingoes caused consternation among neighboring tribes who blamed them for corrupting their young men and threatening to embroil everyone in the war.[23] In June 1778 Congress found that the nations at war against them in the West included "the Senecas, Cayugas, Mingoes and Wiandots in general, a majority of the Onondagas and a few of the Ottawas, Chippewas, Shawnese & Delawares, acting contrary to the voice of their nations," but the situation was not that simple and was constantly changing. A month later, delegates from the Shawnees, Ottawas, Mingoes, Wyandots, Potawatomis, Delawares, Mohawks, and Miamis accepted a war belt from Henry Hamilton at Detroit. While Delawares, Oneidas, Tuscaroras, and other Indians friendly to the United States gathered "to guard against the impending Storm" and called on the Americans for protection, Thomas Jefferson and others advocated using friendly tribes to wage war against hostile ones.[24]

The American Revolution was not only a civil war for Indian people; it also amounted to a world war in Indian country with surrounding nations, Indian and non-Indian, at war, on the brink of war, or arranging alliances in expectation of war. American history has paid little attention to the impact of this war on the Indians' home front. American campaign strategy aimed to carry the war into Indian country, destroy Indian villages, and burn Indian crops late in the season when there was insufficient time for replanting before winter. American troops and militia tramped through Indian country, leaving smoking ruins and burned cornfields behind them.[25] American soldiers and militia matched their British and Indian adversaries in the use of terror tactics. George Rogers Clark declared that "to excel them in barbarity was and is the only way to make war upon Indians and gain a name among them," and he carried his policy into effect at Vincennes by binding and tomahawking Indian prisoners within sight of the besieged garrison. Pennsylvania offered $1,000 for every Indian scalp; South Carolina £75 for male scalps, and Kentucky militia who invaded Shawnee villages dug open graves to scalp corpses.[26]

Barely had the Cherokees launched their attacks on the backcountry settlements than the colonists carried fire and sword to their towns and villages, bringing the nation to its knees. Even Dragging Canoe's villages were not invulnerable to attack: Evan Shelby burned eleven of them in 1779, forcing the Chickamaugas to relocate in safer locations. John Sevier burned fifteen Middle Cherokee towns in March 1781, and the following summer destroyed new Lower Cherokee towns on the Coosa River. American armies marching through Cherokee country in pursuit of Chickamauga raiders did not always distinguish between Cherokee friends and Cherokee foes, thereby swelling Dragging Canoe's ranks with new recruits. A Cherokee headman summed up the cost of the Revolution for his people: "I … have lost in different engagements six hundred warriors, my towns have been thrice destroyed and my corn fields laid waste by the enemy." British reports claimed Cherokee women and children were butchered in cold blood and burned alive.[27]

In the spring of 1779, Col. Goose Van Schaick marched against the Onondaga settlements, laying waste their towns and crops, slaughtering cattle and horses, and carrying off thirty-three prisoners. In the fall Gen. John Sullivan led his famous expedition into Iroquois country on a campaign of destruction that burned forty towns, 160,000 bushels of corn, as well as beans, squash, orchards, and cattle. Meanwhile, Daniel Brodhead devastated the Seneca and Munsee towns on the Allegheny. The Americans spent whole days systematically destroying Iroquois fields and food supplies.[28] The Iroquois pulled back and sustained minimal casualties, but an Onondaga chief later claimed that when the Americans attacked his town, "they put to death all the Women and Children, excepting some of the Young Women, whom they carried away for the use of their Soldiers & were afterwards put to death in a more shameful manner."[29]

Deprived of food and shelter, Iroquois women and children faced starvation as one of the coldest winters on record gripped North America. Refugees fled to British posts for support, and thousands of Indian men, women, and children huddled in miserable shelters around Fort Niagara.[30] Fearing retaliation from their relatives, many Oneidas abandoned their villages and placed themselves under American protection near Schenectady where, living in wretched refugee camps, they endured the prejudice of the American garrison.[31]

Thomas Jefferson wanted the Shawnees exterminated or driven from their lands, and American invasions of Shawnee country became a regular feature of the war. In 1779 Col. John Bowman attacked the town of Chillicothe on the Little Miami River. In 1780 the Shawnees burned Chillicothe as George Rogers Clark approached and fought a major engagement at Piqua. Clark returned two years later, burning Shawnee villages and orchards. The pattern continued in 1786 when Kentucky militia attacked Maquachake villages – murdering Molunthy as the old chief clutched an American flag and a copy of the treaty he had signed with the Americans just months before – and with Gen. Josiah Harmar's expedition in 1790. Chillicothe was destroyed four times in this

period, but the Shawnees rebuilt it each time in different locations.[32]

American soldiers were impressed by the cornucopia they destroyed in Indian fields and villages; by eighteenth-century frontier standards, Indian communities were rich in agricultural foodstuffs when not disrupted by the ravages of war. Moreover, many Indian towns provided material comforts that were the envy of frontier whites. The Oneidas later submitted to Congress claims for compensation for their losses that included sheep, horses, hogs, turkeys, agricultural implements, wheat, oats, corn, sugar, linen, calico, kettles, frying pans, pewter plates, "10 tea-cups & saucers," "6 punch bowls," tablespoons, wampum, candlesticks, silver dollars, harness, sleighs, plows, "a very large framed house [with a] chimney at each end [and] painted windows," a teapot, ivory combs, white flannel breeches, silk handkerchiefs, mirrors, and scissors.[33] The wealth they found in Indian country gave Americans an economic incentive to go on campaigns and made them eager to seize fertile Indian lands once the war was over.

Even when the war was not fought on the Indians' home ground, it produced disruption and misery in Indian communities. Men who fell in battle were not only warriors. They were "part-time soldiers" who were also husbands, fathers and sons, providers and hunters. Warriors who were out on campaign could not hunt or clear fields; women who were forced to flee when invasion threatened could not plant and harvest. Indians still tried to wage war with the seasons: warriors preferred to wait until their corn was ripe before they took up the hatchet, and according to one observer "quit going to war" when hunting season came.[34] But war now dominated the activities of the community and placed tremendous demands on the people's energy at the expense of normal economic and social practices. Even before Sullivan's campaign, there were food shortages in Iroquois longhouses as "the Young Men were already either out at War, or ready to go," and many Mohawks became sick from eating nothing but salt meat. At a time when the need for food increased greatly, Indians could not cultivate the usual quantities of corn and vegetables, and what they did grow was often destroyed before it could be harvested.[35] Crops also suffered from natural causes in time of war. The late 1770s marked the beginning of a period of "sporadically poor crops" among southeastern tribes. Partial failure of the Creek corn crop in 1776 produced near famine at a time when the influx of Cherokee refugees placed additional demands on food supplies. Choctaw crops failed in 1782, increasing the people's reliance on deer hunting.[36] Hunting became vital to group survival, but fewer hunters were available, and hunting territories could be perilous places in time of war.

As a result, Indian communities became increasingly dependent on British, American, or Spanish allies to provide them with food, clothing, and trade. Rival powers waged economic warfare to compel Indian allegiance, and harsh economic realities increasingly curtailed the tribes' freedom of action and governed their decisions.[37] Dependency on outside supplies of food and clothing rendered the end of the war all the more catastrophic, when allies deserted and supplies dried up.

Those tribes who supported the Americans or remained neutral suffered as much as those who fought with the British. In the spring of 1782, those Cherokees who remained friendly to the Americans were "in a deplorable situation, being naked & defenceless for want of goods and ammunition," besides being caught between loyalists and patriots who assumed they were hostile.[38] In December a group of Cherokees en route to Richmond elicited the sympathy of William Christian, one of the generals who had carried devastation to their towns in the summer of 1776: "The miseries of those people from what I see and hear seem to exceed description; here are men, women & children almost naked; I see very little to cover either sex but some old bear skins, and we are told that the bulk of the nation are in the same naked situation." To make matters

worse, Cherokee crops that year had been "worse than ever was known."[39] The next month the Cherokee chief Oconastota begged Col. Joseph Martin for trade at low prices, adding: "All the old warriors are dead. There are now none left to take care of the Cherokees, but you & myself, & for my part I am become very old."[40]

Disease took an additional toll. Smallpox raged at Onondaga in the winter of 1776–77, among the Creeks and Cherokees in the fall of 1779, and among the Chickamaugas and Georgia Indians in the spring of 1780. It struck the Oneida refugees at Schenectady in December 1780 and hit the Genesee Senecas in the winter of 1781–82. Cold and disease killed 300 Indians in the refugee camps at Niagara in the winter of 1779–80.[41]

The Revolutionary era intensified political changes in Indian communities. War chiefs, who traditionally exercised limited and temporary authority, took advantage of endemic warfare and outside support to elevate their status over village chiefs whose counsel held sway in normal circumstances. The abnormal was now normal, and war captains like Pipe and White Eyes of the Delawares spoke with an increasingly loud voice in their nation's councils. Tenhoghskweaghta, an Onondaga chief, explained: "Times are altered with us Indians. Formerly the Warriors were governed by the wisdom of their uncles the Sachems but now they take their own way & dispose of themselves without consulting their uncles the Sachems – while we wish for peace and they for war." Oneida chiefs agreed: "We Sachems have nothing to say to the Warriors. We have given them up for the field. They must act as they think wise."[42] New leaders like Pluggy, Joseph Brant, and Dragging Canoe attracted followings that cut across village, tribal, and kinship ties. Older chiefs complained increasingly that they could not control their young men – or as was often the case in the polyglot communities created by the Revolution, control somebody else's young men.

The interference of outsiders further complicated tribal politics and undermined traditional patterns of leadership. The British elevated Mohawk Joseph Brant, protégé of Sir William Johnson and friend of the Prince of Wales, to a position in which he exerted tremendous influence in Indian councils during and after the Revolution.[43] The Americans granted a commission to Joseph Louis Gill of the St. Francis Abenakis, and the British offered to make him head chief of his village, even though Gill pointed out that his son had more right to the position.[44] The Americans appear to have interfered to disrupt traditional succession among the Delawares in favor of pro-American individuals and exerted their influence in the choice of a successor to White Eyes.[45] Among the Creeks, Alexander McGillivray's growing power owed as much to British connections as to his membership in the Wind clan.[46] British, Americans, and Spaniards cultivated client chiefs, and the practice of handing out commissions was so common that it became standard practice to identify Choctaw and Chickasaw leaders as "great medal," "small medal," and "gorget" chiefs. Access to guns and gifts was a key to securing the voluntary obedience that underlay so much of Indian political relations. Daniel Brodhead complained that the Indian chiefs appointed by the British commander at Detroit were "clothed in the most elegant manner," while chiefs appointed by Congress went naked and were scorned by the Indians. A Seneca chief warned the British he could not exert any authority over his warriors unless they provided him with goods to distribute to them.[47]

In addition, at a time when non-Indians in London and Philadelphia, Detroit and Fort Pitt, St. Augustine and Pensacola were making decisions that reverberated through Indian country, non-Indians who lived in Indian country played a growing role in Indian councils. Men like Simon Girty, Matthew Elliott, and Alexander McKee among the Ohio tribes, Alexander Cameron among the Cherokees, and James Colbert among the Chickasaws lived in Indian communities but maintained connections elsewhere and functioned as influential intermediaries, interpreters, leaders of expeditions, and conduits of supply and support.[48] White officers often accompanied and sometimes replaced Indian war chiefs on campaign. The end of the war did not end the presence or the influence of British trader agents, and in the South British companies continued their lucrative Indian trade with the grudging blessing of the Spanish authorities.[49]

The Revolution dislocated thousands of Indian people. Mobility was a fundamental feature of Indian life, but seasonal migration for social or subsistence purposes now gave way to flight from the horrors of war. Indian villages relocated to escape American assault; communities splintered and reassembled, sometimes amalgamating with other communities. Many Shawnees migrated from Ohio to Missouri where they took up lands under the auspices of the Spanish government. By the end of the Revolution, those Shawnees who remained in Ohio were crowded into the northwestern reaches of their territory, and in time they joined other Indians in creating a multitribal, multivillage community centered on the Auglaize.[50] Indian refugees flooded into Niagara and Schenectady, Detroit and St. Louis, St. Augustine and Pensacola; Iroquois loyalists relocated to new homes on the Grand River in Ontario.[51] Stockbridge Indians, unable to secure relief from their former allies after the Revolution, joined other Christian Indians from New England in moving to lands set aside for them by the Oneidas. By 1787 "there was a vast concourse of People of many Nations" at New Stockbridge.[52] Hundreds of refugee Indians drifted west of the Mississippi and requested permission to settle in Spanish territory. Abenaki Indians, dispersed by previous wars from northern New England into the Ohio Valley, turned up in Arkansas after the Revolution.[53] Nor were Indian people the only migrants in Indian country. Micmacs in Nova Scotia suffered from the inroads of Loyalist settlers fleeing the Revolution to the south; English refugees fleeing Spanish reprisals following the Natchez rebellion took refuge in Chickasaw country.[54]

Escalating warfare and concomitant economic dislocation reached even into ritual and ceremonial life. Eastern woodland Indians tried to maintain their social and ceremonial calendar tied to the rhythm of the seasons: in 1778 the Creeks frustrated the British by refusing to take the warpath until after the Green Corn Ceremony.[55] But the endemic warfare of the Revolution threw many traditional religious practices and sacred observances into disarray. Not only did the ancient unity of the Iroquois league crumble but many of the ceremonial forms that expressed that unity were lost. Preparatory war rituals were neglected or imperfectly performed, and the Cayuga leader Kingageghta lamented in 1789 that a "Great Part of our ancient Customs & Ceremonies have, thro' the Loss of Many of our principal men during the War, been' neglected & forgotten, so that we cannot go through the whole with our ancient Propriety."[56] The traditional Cherokee year was divided into two seasons, with the winter reserved for war, and returning warriors underwent ritual purification before reentering normal village life. Now war was a year-round activity and Chickamauga communities existed on a permanent war footing. In addition, the Cherokees' six major religious festivals of the year became telescoped into one – the Green Corn festival. Many Cherokees remembered the 1780s as marking the end of the old ways.[57] The loss of sacred power threatened the Indians' struggle for independence, and, according to historian Gregory Evans Dowd, Indian resistance movements of the Revolutionary and post-Revolutionary era drew strength from the recognition that they "could and must take hold of their destiny by regaining sacred power." Indians in the new republic sought to recover through ritual, as well as through war and politics, some of what they had lost.[58] New religious practices also suffered in the Revolution. Missionary work was disrupted and Christian Mohawks devoted less time to their observances because war

occupied their attention. Delaware Moravian communities endured forced relocation at the hands of the British and destruction at the hands of Americans.[59]

For all the devastation they suffered, Indians remained a force to be reckoned with during and after the Revolution. Most survived the destruction of their villages and cornfields. The Shawnees, for example, sustained minimal casualties when the Americans invaded their country, withdrew before the invaders, then returned and rebuilt their villages when the enemy retreated. Untouched food sources beyond the enemy's reach and support from the British at Detroit sustained the Shawnee war effort in the face of repeated assaults. George Rogers Clark recognized the limitations of the American search-and-destroy strategy so long as the Indians could resort to the British supplies at Detroit.[60] Sullivan's campaign too was more effective in burning houses and crops than in killing Iroquois: as one American officer noted, "The nests are destroyed but the birds are still on the wing."[61]

The real disaster of the American Revolution for Indian people lay in its outcome. The Indians were "thunderstruck" when they heard that the British and Americans had signed the Treaty of Paris, without so much as a mention of the tribes. Little Turkey of the Overhill Cherokees concluded, "The peacemakers and our Enemies have talked away our Lands at a Rum Drinking." Alexander McGillivray protested that the Indians had done nothing to permit the king to give away their lands, "unless … Spilling our blood in the Service of his Nation can be deemed so."[62] Americans gloated to the Shawnees: "Your Fathers the English have made Peace with us for themselves, but forgot you their Children, who fought with them, and neglected you like Bastards."[63]

The Treaty of Paris brought Indians no peace. Some wanted to evacuate along with the redcoats. Others fled their homelands rather than come to terms with their former enemies. Most stayed and adjusted to the new situation.[64]

Catawbas derived maximum mileage from their Revolutionary services, but they were an exception.[65] While other Revolutionary veterans were granted land bounties, Indian veterans lost land. Mashpee lost its right of self-government in 1788 when Massachusetts established an all-white board of overseers. Samson Occom and other Indian missionaries at New Stockbridge lamented that "the late unhappy wars have Stript us almost Naked … we are truly like the man that fell among Thieves, that was Stript, wounded and left for dead in the high way."[66] Penobscots found their hunting territories invaded by their former allies, and Massachusetts deprived the tribe of most of its land in a series of post-Revolution treaties.[67] The Oneidas, who suffered mightily in the American cause during the war, fared little better than their Cayuga and Seneca relatives in the post-Revolutionary land-grabbing conducted by the federal government, New York state, and individual land companies.[68]

The end of the Revolution opened the gate for a renewed invasion of Indian lands by a flood of backcountry settlers, who broke arrangements of coexistence that had been built up over generations and knocked the heart out of federal attempts to regulate the frontier.[69] Many were Scotch-Irish immigrants coming from a borderlands heritage of their own, where violence had been a way of life for centuries. They had their own experiences of dispossession and their own understanding of clan and kinship, blood feud, and custom, which they applied with grim determination in their new world.[70] American policymakers were no more capable of controlling such citizens than were Indian chiefs of controlling their young men.

A delegation of 260 Iroquois, Shawnee, Cherokee, Chickasaw, Choctaw, and "Loup" Indians visiting St. Louis in the summer of 1784 told the Spanish governor that the Revolution was "the greatest blow that could have been dealt us, unless it had been our total destruction. The Americans, a great deal more ambitious and numerous than the English, put us out of our lands, forming therein great settlements,

extending themselves like a plague of locusts in the territories of the Ohio River which we inhabit. They treat us as their cruelest enemies are treated, so that today hunger and the impetuous torrent of war which they impose upon us with other terrible calamities, have brought our villages to a struggle with death."[71]

American commissioners demanded lands from the Iroquois at Fort Stanwix in 1784; from the Delawares, Wyandots, and their neighbors at Fort McIntosh in 1785, and from the Shawnees at Fort Finney in 1786, in arrogant confidence that the lands were theirs for the taking by right of conquest. The Treaties of Hopewell, with the Cherokees (1785) and the Choctaws and Chickasaws (1786), confirmed tribal boundaries but did little to preserve them. Cherokee chiefs Corn Tassel and Hanging Maw told Virginian Joseph Martin that "we find your people Settle much Faster on our Lands after A Treaty than Before." Meanwhile, a handful of compliant Creek chiefs made land cessions to Georgia.[72] Confronted with renewed pressures and aggressions, many of the tribes renewed their confederacies. Led by capable chiefs like Brant, Little Turtle, Buckongahelas, Dragging Canoe, and McGillivray, they continued the wars for their lands and cultures into the 1790s and exposed the American theory of conquest for the fiction it was.[73]

In the new world created by the Revolution, new communities emerged, new power blocs developed, and new players called different tunes. Americans in the new republic, like their British and Spanish rivals, were often hard pressed to keep up with it all. Chickamauga Cherokees and militant Shawnees joined hands in common cause even as older chiefs apologized for their behavior. Chickasaws on the Mississippi River had responded to American threats of invasion during the Revolution by offering to meet them halfway: "Take care that we don't serve you as we have served the French before with all their Indians, Send you back without your Heads."[74] Come the end of the Revolution, they sent out very different, and very mixed, signals. By October 1782 Chickasaw headmen were blaming the British for putting "the Bloody Tomahawk" into their hands. In July 1783 they sent word that they were being courted on all sides but would wait to hear from Congress "as it is our earnest desire to remain in peace and friendship with our Br[others] the Americans for ever."[75]

Economic realities dictated political and diplomatic choices. The shutting-off of British trade and supplies had to be made up somewhere, especially as the Chickasaws became embroiled in hostilities with the neighboring Kickapoos. The United States represented one source of trade and protection, but only one: Chickasaw delegates from six villages attended the Mobile Congress in 1784, placing themselves under Spanish protection and promising to trade exclusively with Spanish-licensed traders. Two years later Chickasaws promised the Americans the same trade monopoly at the Treaty of Hopewell.[76] But the appearance of a unified and duplicitous Chickasaw foreign policy obscures more complex realities of division and disunity that both limited and expanded diplomatic choices. Chickasaw "factions" crystallized in the early republic: the pro-British group shifted their allegiance to the United States and remained anti-Spanish; the old French party in the nation consorted with Spain; others were ambivalent.[77] The United States was adept at exploiting factionalism within Indian societies, implementing divide-and-rule strategies, but factionalism could prove an asset in frontier diplomacy. Different parties cultivating good relations with different powers prevented domination by anyone outside force.[78] The United States had to cut through multiple and shifting Chickasaw foreign policies; the Chickasaws had to deal with shrinking foreign policy options as the United States emerged as their only "available" foreign power in the postwar geopolitical contest for the lower Mississippi Valley.

The emergence of the independent United States as the ultimate victor from a long contest of imperial powers reduced Indians to further dependence and pushed them into one of the darkest ages in their history. War, invasion, economic dislocation, political factionalism and fragmentation, disruption of ancient traditions, hunger, disease, and betrayal into the hands of their enemies continued to wreak havoc in Indian country. Seneca communities, in the words of anthropologist Anthony F. C. Wallace, became "slums in the wilderness," wracked by poverty, loss of confidence in traditional certainties, social pathology, violence, alcoholism, witch fear, and disunity.[79]

And yet, in the kaleidoscopic, "all-change" world of the Revolutionary era, there were exceptions and variations. The upheaval generated by the Revolution offered opportunity as well as oppression. Seminole warriors, wearing scarlet coats and British medals, armed with British guns, and executing British strategies, appeared to be dependent on outsiders and vulnerable to a transfer of that dependence to new masters. But the Seminoles fought for their own reasons and maintained their independence against both Spain and the United States.[80] Despite new colors on the map of Florida, political change in Seminole country reflected not new dependence on a foreign power so much as increasing *independence* from the parent Creek confederacy. While Alexander McGillivray continued traditional Creek "playoff" policies with considerable skill, the Seminoles emerged by the new century as a new player and an unknown quantity in the Indian and international diplomacy of the Southeast.[81] Moreover, the American Revolution added to the changing ethnic composition of Seminole and Creek communities as African slaves who had fled to the British lines found refuge in Indian country after Yorktown.[82] Many Indian communities succumbed and some disappeared in the new world produced during the Revolution, but others were in process of formation, asserting their separate identity, and doing some nation-building of their own.

The Revolutionary war destroyed many Indian communities – in Iroquoia, the upper Susquehanna Valley, the Smoky Mountains

– but new communities – at Grand River, Chickamauga, and the Auglaize – grew out of the turmoil and played a leading role in the Indian history of the new republic. The black years following the Revolution saw powerful forces of social and religious rejuvenation in Handsome Lake's Longhouse religion among the Iroquois, political movements like the northwestern Indian confederacy of the 1780s and 1790s, and multitribal unity under the leadership of Tecumseh and the Shawnee Prophet in the early years of the new century.[83] By the end of the eighteenth century, Indian peoples already had plenty of experience suffering and surviving disasters. They responded to the American Revolution as they had to previous cataclysms: they set about rebuilding their world.

In the long run, however, almost as devastating as the burned towns and crops, the murdered chiefs, the divided councils, the shattered lives, and the towns and forts choked with refugees was the legacy that the war produced in the minds of non-Indians. As Kenneth M. Morrison has pointed out, "For many Americans, the story of who they are winds back to the Revolution."[84] It is equally true that for many Americans the story of who the Indians are winds back to that time.

Americans at different times have always invented versions of Indians to suit their particular policies and purposes, but the Revolution had particularly enduring influence.[85] Embodied in the document that marked the nation's birth, the image of Indians as vicious enemies of liberty became entrenched in the minds of generations of white Americans. Siding with the redcoats meant opposing the very principles on which the new nation was founded: having fought to prevent American independence, Indians could not expect to share in the society that independence created.

Looking back from nineteenth- and twentieth-century vantage points, their view obscured by chronicles of border warfare, racist writings of Francis Parkman and Theodore Roosevelt, and romanticized depictions of conflict in paintings like John Vanderlyn's *Death of Jane McCrea* (1804) or Carl Wimar's *Abduction of Daniel Boone's Daughter* (1853), Americans telescoped the Revolution and the colonial wars into one long chronicle of bloody frontier conflict. Periods of peace and patterns of interdependence were ignored as racial war took a dominant place in the national mythology. Responsibility for the brutality and destruction of the Revolutionary War on the frontier was placed squarely on the shoulders of the Indians and their British backers. In American eyes, the Gnadenhutten massacre and reports of American atrocities at Onondaga and Piqua paled in comparison with descriptions of white "Women and Children strip'd, scalped, and suffered to welter in their gore," whole families "destroyed, without regard to Age or Sex," infants "torn from their mothers Arms & their Brains dashed out against Trees."[86] The well-worn story of William Crawford's capture and torture by Delaware warriors in 1782 featured prominently in narratives of border warfare; the more typical peacekeeping efforts and shuttle diplomacy of Cornstalk, White Eyes, and Kayashuta tended to be forgotten.[87] After the war, lurid accounts tended to increase rather than diminish, and the growing popularity of narratives of Indian captivity fueled popular stereotypes. Powerful images and long memories of Indian violence primed subsequent generations for trouble with new Indian groups encountered farther west.[88]

The fiction that all Indians had fought for the British in the Revolution justified massive dispossession of Native Americans in the early republic, whatever their role in the war. As historian Gary B. Nash has pointed out, most Americans were no more willing to extend the Revolution's principles to Indian people than they were to fulfill the Revolutionary ideal of abolishing slavery. Indian land, like African slave labor, was a vital resource for the new republic, and the new republic would not and could not forego its exploitation.[89] A century and a half earlier, Pequot William Apess bitterly understood the extent to which the Revolution excluded African Americans and Native Americans from the republican principles on which it was based. Referring to the guardian system reinstituted by Massachusetts after the war, he wrote, "The whites were no sooner free themselves, than they enslaved the poor Indians."[90] Other groups in American society – women and industrial laborers as well as African slaves – found that the victory in the War for Independence for them meant continued, if not increased, dependence.[91] But most Native Americans found that, as their land became the key to national, state, and individual wealth, the new republic was less interested in their dependence than in their absence.

Having fought against the republic at its birth, Indians continued to fight against the very civilization on which the republic prided itself. Outright military resistance gave way to more subtle forms of cultural resistance, but that only reinforced the inherited view that Indians fought against civilized people and civilized ways. As Bernard W. Sheehan has pointed out, the so-called philanthropists of the new nation were almost more deadly than Indian-hating and land-hungry frontiersmen, since they demanded that Indians commit cultural suicide: "Philanthropy had in mind the disappearance of an entire race."[92] If Indian country were to continue to exist, it must do so beyond the Mississippi. Artistic depictions of Indian people showed them retreating westward, suffused in the heavy imagery of setting suns, as they faded from history.[93]

Confronting the question of where Indian people fit in the new republic, Americans looked back to the Revolution and found their answer to be explicitly negative. Indians belonged to the past, and it was a violent past.[94] A future of peace and prosperity held no place for them. Indian people survived the Revolution and, as they had in the past, proceeded to build new worlds on the ruins of old worlds. But in American eyes their continuing struggles to survive as Indians guaranteed their exclusion from the new nation. The United States looked forward increasingly to a new world without Indians.

## Notes

1 Compare James H. O'Donnell III, "The World Turned Upside Down: The American Revolution as a Catastrophe for Native Americans," in Francis P. Jennings, ed., *The American Indian and the American Revolution* (Chicago, 1983), 80–93.

2 James H. Merrell, "Some Thoughts on Colonial Historians and American Indians," *William and Mary Quarterly,* 3d ser. 46 (1989): 94–119.

3 Letter from Henry Young Brown, May 16, 1775, U.S. Revolution Collection, American Antiquarian Society, Worcester, Mass.; Peter Force, ed., *American Archives,* 4th ser., 9 vols. (Washington, D.C., 1837–53), 2:621; Reuben Gold Thwaites and Louise Phelps Kellogg, eds., *The Revolution on the Upper Ohio, 1775–1777* (Madison, Wis., 1908), 67–70; Robert L. Scribner et al., eds., *Revolutionary Virginia, the Road to Independence: A Documentary Record,* 7 vols. (Charlottesville, Va., 1973–83), 4:129–30; Draper Manuscripts, 1H54, Wisconsin State Historical Society, Madison.

4 Lawrence Kinnaird, ed., "Spain in the Mississippi Valley, 1765–1794," in *Annual Report of the American Historical Association for the Year 1945,* 4 vols. (Washington, D.C., 1946–49), 2:298.

5 Compare Ronald Hoffman, Thad W. Tate, and Peter J. Albert, eds., *An Uncivil War: The Southern Backcountry during the American Revolution* (Charlottesville, Va., 1985), xii.

6 Draper Mss., 1F50 and 1H91–93; Louise Phelps Kellogg, ed., *Frontier Advance on the Upper Ohio, 1778–1779* (Madison, Wis., 1916), 352; Papers of the Continental Congress (microfilm M247), roll 183, item 166, 446, National Archives, Washington, D.C.

7 Samuel Kirkland to Philip Schuyler, Mar. 11, 1776, Kirkland Papers, 64b, Hamilton College, Clinton, N.Y.; John C. Guzzardo, "The Superintendent and the Ministers: The Battle for Oneida Allegiances," *New York History* 57 (1976): 255–83; *Collections of the Massachusetts Historical Society,* 1st ser. 5 (1789):16.

8 Barbara Graymont, *The Iroquois in the American Revolution* (Syracuse, N.Y., 1972); idem, "The Oneidas and the American Revolution," in Jack Campisi and Laurence M. Hauptman, eds., *The Oneida Indian Experience: Two Perspectives* (Syracuse, N.Y., 1988), 39; George F. Stanley,

"The Six Nations and the American Revolution," *Ontario History* 56 (1964): 217–32; James Everett Seaver, *A Narrative of the Life of Mary Jemison* (Syracuse, N.Y., 1990), 49, 52; Papers of Sir Frederick Haldimand, Add. Mss. 21767:104 and 21773:101, British Museum; Draper Mss., 14:248–51; *Papers of the Continental Congress,* roll 183, 387–93; Thomas S. Abler, ed., *Chainbreaker: The Revolutionary War Memoirs of Governor Blacksnake, as Told to Benjamin Williams* (Lincoln, Nebr., 1989), 69, 87, 91, 144.

9 Oscar Handlin and Irving Mark, eds., "Chief Daniel Nimham *v.* Roger Morris, Beverly Robinson, and Philip Philipse – An Indian Land Case in Colonial New York, 1765–1767," *Ethnohistory* 11 (1964): 193–246; William Coates, ed., "A Narrative of an Embassy to the Western Indians, from the Original Manuscript of Hendrick Aupaumut," part 1, *Memoirs of the Historical Society of Pennsylvania* 2 (1827): 128. On the history of Stockbridge, see Patrick Frazier, *The Mohicans of Stockbridge* (Lincoln, Nebr., 1992).

10 Deirdre Almeida, "The Stockbridge Indians in the American Revolution," *Historical Journal of Western Massachusetts* 4 (1975): 34–39; *Journals of the Continental Congress, 1774–1789,* 34 vols. (Washington, D.C., 1904–37), 5:627, 9:840; Papers of the Continental Congress, roll 23, item 12A, vol. 1, 196, vol. 2, 14, roll 50, item 41, vol. 4, 422, roll 55, item 42, vol. 5, 451, roll 170, item 152, vol. 9, 165–66; Force, ed., *American Archives,* 4th ser. 1:1347, 2:315–16, 1002–3, 1060–61; 5th ser., 3 vols. (Washington, D.C., 1848–53), 1:725, 903; John C. Fitzpatrick, ed., *The Writings of George Washington from the Original Manuscript Sources, 1745–1799,* 39 vols. (Washington, D.C., 1931–44), 20:44–45; *Papers of Horatio Gates, 1726–1828* (New York, 1978, microfilm), roll 3:248, roll 6:85, 720.

11 Colin G. Calloway, "New England Algonkians in the American Revolution," in *Annual Proceedings of the Dublin Seminar for New England Folklife, 1991* (Boston, 1993), 51–62.

12 Colin G. Calloway, *The Western Abenakis of Vermont, 1600–1800: War, Migration and the Survival of an Indian People* (Norman, Okla., 1990), chap. 11; idem, "Sentinels of Revolution: Bedel's New Hampshire Rangers and the Abenaki Indians on the Upper Connecticut," *Historical New Hampshire* 45 (1990): 271–95;

Papers of General Philip Schuyler, roll 7, box 14, New York Public library; "List of St. Francis Indians, June 5, 1778," *The Remembrancer or Impartial Repository of Public Events* (London), 1775, 251.

13 Paul Lawrence Stevens, "His Majesty's 'Savage' Allies: British Policy and the Northern Indians during the Revolutionary War: The Carleton Years, 1774–1778," Ph.D. diss., State University of New York at Buffalo, 1984.

14 *Sir Guy Carleton Papers, 1777–1783* (microfilm), roll 5, no. 1690, roll 6, no. 2158; K. G. Davies, ed., *Documents of the American Revolution, 1770–1783,* 21 vols. (Shannon, Ireland, 1972–81), 13:266; Frederic Kidder, ed., *Military Operations in Eastern Maine and Nova Scotia during the Revolution, Chiefly Compiled from the Journals and Letters of Colonel John Allen* (Albany, 1867); *Dictionary of Canadian Biography,* s.v. Saint-Aubin, Ambroise, and Tomah, Pierre; James Phinney Baxter, ed., *Documentary History of the State of Maine: Collections of the Maine Historical Society,* 24 vols. (Portland, Maine, 1869–1916), vols. 14 and 15.

15 On the Delawares in the Revolution and the schisms within the nation, see C. A. Weslager, *The Delaware Indians: A History* (New Brunswick, N.J., 1972), chap. 13; Gregory Evans Dowd, *A Spirited Resistance: The North American Indian Struggle for Unity, 1745–1815* (Baltimore, 1992), 65–89; The Brodhead Papers, Draper Mss., H ser., esp. 1H22–23, 47–48; Reuben Gold Thwaites and Louise Phelps Kellogg, eds., *Frontier Defense on the Upper Ohio, 1777–1778* (Madison, Wis., 1912), 27–29, 95–97, 100–101, 215–20; Kellogg, ed., *Frontier Advance,* esp. 20–21, 117–18; George Morgan Letter-book, esp. 1:18–22, 46, 49–51; 3:149–51, 162–65, Carnegie Library, Pittsburgh. John Heckewelder, *A Narrative of the Mission of the United Brethren among the Delaware and Mohegan Indians* (Philadelphia, 1820), provides a first-hand, pro-American account of developments in Delaware country.

16 Pay Roll of the Delaware Indians in Service of the United States, June 15, 1780–Oct. 31, 1781, Revolutionary War Rolls, 1775–83 (microfilm M246), roll 129, Natl. Arch.

17 Draper Mss., 3H19, 5D80, 86, 99, 142; *Pennsylvania Archives,* 1st ser., 12 vols. (Philadelphia, 1852–56), 8:640; 9:161–62; Kellogg, ed., *Frontier Advance,* 337–43, 353, 376–

81, 399; Neville B. Craig, ed., *The Olden Time,* 2 vols. (Cincinnati, 1876), 2:378–79, 389; Dowd, *Spirited Resistance,* 82–83.

18  Papers of the Continental Congress, roll 73, item 59, vol. 3, 49–51; *Pennsylvania Archives,* 1st ser. 9:523–25; Edmund de Schweinitz, *The Life and Times of David Zeisberger* (1870; reprint ed., New York, 1971), 537–38; Consul Willshire Butterfield, ed., *Washington-Irvine Correspondence* (Madison, Wis., 1882), 99–109, 179.

19  Colin G. Calloway, "'We Have Always Been the Frontier': The American Revolution in Shawnee Country," *American Indian Quarterly* 16 (1992): 39–52; Davies, ed., *Documents,* 12:199–203; Papers of the Continental Congress, roll 180, item 163, 245–47; Draper Mss., 2YY92, 3D 164–73; Thwaites and Kellogg, eds., *Revolution on the Upper Ohio,* 43; idem, *Frontier Defense,* 157–63, 175–77, 188–89, 205–9, 243–47, 258–61; *Remembrancer,* 1780, pt. 1, 154–58; *Collections and Researches Made by the Michigan Pioneer and Historical Society,* 40 vols. (Lansing, Mich., 1874–1929), 25:690; William L. Saunders, ed., *The Colonial Records of North Carolina, 1662–1776,* 30 vols. (Raleigh, 1886–1914), 10:386; Morgan Letterbook, 1:47–49, 57–59; 3:27, 56, 96. The Maquachake division of the Shawnees were consistently most amenable to peace with the Americans. See, for example, Edward G. Williams, ed., "The Journal of Richard Butler, 1775: Continental Congress' Envoy to the Western Indians," *Western Pennsylvania Historical Magazine* 47 (1964): 45, 148.

20  Gary C. Goodwin, *Cherokees in Transition: A Study of Changing Culture and Environment prior to 1775* (Chicago, 1977), 103–4; James Paul Pate, "The Chickamaugas: A Forgotten Segment of Indian Resistance on the Southern Frontier," Ph.D. diss., Mississippi State University, 1969; Saunders, ed., *Colonial Records of North Carolina,* 10:657, 659–61, 763–85; John P. Brown, *Old Frontiers: The Story of the Cherokees from Earliest Times to the Date of Their Removal to the West, 1838* (Kingsport, Tenn., 1938), 163, 171; James H. O'Donnell III, *The Cherokees of North Carolina in the American Revolution* (Raleigh, 1976); idem, "The Virginia Expedition against the Overhill Cherokees, 1776," *East Tennessee Historical Society's Publications* 39 (1967): 13–25; Robert L. Ganyard, "Threat from the West: North Carolina and the Cherokee, 1776–1778," *North Carolina Historical Review* 45 (1968): 47–66; Archibald Henderson, "The Treaty of Long Island of Holston, July 1777," *North Carolina Historical Review* 8 (1931): 55–117; William P. Palmer, ed., *Calendar of Virginia State Papers and Other Manuscripts, 1652–1781,* 11 vols. (Richmond, 1875–83), 1:484–87, 495, 2:24, 679; Draper Mss., 30S66–73, 140–80, 31S170–71, 1U45–48, 12S19, 11S99–100; Davies, ed., *Documents,* 12:190, 200, 205–8, 229–30, 239–40, 247, 14:34–35, 94, 112–15, 194, 15:285 17:181–82; Fred Gearing, "Priests and Warriors: Social Structures for Cherokee Politics in the 18th Century," *American Anthropologist* 64, no. 5, pt. 2 (1962): 102–4.

21  Davies, ed., *Documents,* 11:118, 19:62, 20:59–60, 149–50; James H. Merrell, *The Indians' New World: Catawbas and Their Neighbors from European Contact through the Era of Removal* (Chapel Hill, N.C., 1989), 215–21.

22  David H. Corkran, *The Creek Frontier, 1540–1783* (Norman. Okla., 1967), 316–25; Michael D. Green, "The Creek Confederacy in the American Revolution: Cautious Participants," in William S. Croker and Robert R. Rea, eds., *Anglo-Spanish Confrontation on the Gulf Coast during the American Revolution* (Pensacola, Fla., 1982), 54–75; *Carleton Papers,* roll 3A, no. 925; Haldimand Papers, 21761:134.

23  Draper Mss., 2D122; "In Congress, Dec. 3, 1777," Schuyler Papers, roll 7, box 14; Schweinitz, *Life and Times of Zeisberger,* 445: Thwaites and Kellogg, eds., *Revolution on the Upper Ohio,* 236–37; *Pennsylvania Archives,* 1st ser. 5:260; Morgan Letterbook, 1:23, 47–50, 56–59, 61, 71–73, 76; 2:45.

24  *Papers of Gates,* 7:764–66; *Journals of the Continental Congress,* 11:587–88; *Collections by the Michigan Pioneer and Historical Society,* 9:442–58; Julian P. Boyd et al., eds., *The Papers of Thomas Jefferson,* 28 vols. to date (Princeton, 1950–), 3:276; Clarence W. Alvord, ed., *Kaskaskia Records, 1778–1790* (Springfield, 111., 1909), 147. A better summary of limited tribal commitments is provided in Richard White, *The Middle Ground: Indians, Empires, and Republics in the Great Lakes Region, 1650–1815* (Cambridge, 1991), 399.

25  Fitzpatrick, ed., *Writings of Washington,* 15:189; Kellogg, ed., *Frontier Advance,* 311; *Pennsylvania Archives,* 1st ser. 6:614.

26  Milo M. Quaife, ed., *The Conquest of the Illinois* (Chicago, 1920), 148–49, 167; *Pennsylvania*

*Archives,* 1st ser. 8:167; Force, ed., *American Archives,* 5th ser. 3:32; Calloway, "'We Have Always Been the Frontier,'" 43.

27 Brown, *Old Frontiers,* 173–75, 196; Plate, "Chickamaugas," 93–95, 116, 119, 122–26; Papers of the Continental Congress, roll 85, item 71, vol. 1, 45, 241–42; Carleton Papers, 30/55/60, no. 6742:4–6, Public Record Office; Davies, *ed., Documents,* 17:233, 269, 21:122; C.O. 5/82:287–88, 343, P.R.O.

28 *Remembrancer,* 1779, pt. 2, 273–74, 1780, pt. 1, 152–58; Frederick Cook, ed., *Journals of the Military Expedition of Major General John Sullivan against the Six Nations* (Auburn, N.Y., 1887); Fitzpatrick, ed., *Writings of Washington,* 16:478, 480, 492–93. On Daniel Brodhead, see Draper Mss., 1AA39; Louise Phelps Kellogg, ed., *Frontier Retreat on the Upper Ohio, 1779–1781* (Madison, Wis., 1917), 56–62; *Pennsylvania Archives, 1st* ser. 12:155–58; Craig, ed., *Olden Time,* 2:308–17.

29 Haldimand Papers, 21762:238.

30 Ibid., 21760:220, 244, 21765:140–41, 21770:242–46; *Collections by the Michigan Pioneer and Historical Society,* 19:461.

31 Graymont, *Iroquois in the American Revolution,* 242–44.

32 Calloway, "'We Have Always Been the Frontier,'" 43–44; William Albert Galloway, *Old Chillicothe: Shawnee and Pioneer History* (Xenia, Ohio, 1934); J. Martin West, comp, and ed., *Clark's Shawnee Campaign of 1780* (Springfield, Ohio, 1975); Draper Mss., 8J136–40, 210–12, 265–66, 320–22, 9J61–70, 11J24, 26J3–5, 49J89–90; Haldimand Papers, 21781 :76–77, 21756:91, 21760:147–48.

33 Timothy Pickering Papers, 62:157–74, Massachusetts Historical Society, Boston.

34 Draper Mss., 2AA70; Thwaites and Kellogg, eds., *Revolution on the Upper Ohio,* 190.

35 Haldimand Papers, 21765:34–35, 21774:7, 115–16; Peter C. Mancall, "The Revolutionary War and the Indians of the Upper Susquehanna Valley," *American Indian Culture and Research Journal* 12 (1988): 39–57.

36 Davies, ed., *Documents,* 17:233; Martha Condray Searcy, *The Georgia-Florida Contest in the American Revolution, 1776–1778* (University, Ala., 1985), 110; Richard White, *The Roots of Dependency: Subsistence, Environment, and Social Change among the Choctaws, Pawnees, and Navajos* (Lincoln, Nebr., 1983), 28–29, 98.

37 Davies, ed., *Documents,* 15:67.

38 Draper Mss., 11S77–83.

39 Ibid., 11S10.

40 Ibid., 12S10.

41 Papers of the Continental Congress, roll 73, item 153, vol. 3,59–60, roll 173:551–54; Anthony F. C. Wallace, *The Death and Rebirth of the Seneca* (New York, 1970), 195; Brown, *Old Frontiers,* 182n; Kellogg, ed., *Frontier Retreat,* 189.

42 Weslager, *Delaware Indians,* 291–92; Speech of Tenhoghskweaghta at the Johnstown Conference, Mar. 10, 1778, Schuyler Papers, roll 7, box 14; *Papers of Gates,* 6:191.

43 Haldimand Papers, 21717:39–40. On Joseph Brant see Isabel Thompson Kelsay, *Joseph Brant, 1743–1807: Man of Two Worlds* (Syracuse, N.Y., 1984).

44 *Journals of the Continental Congress,* 15:1263, 16:334; Fitzpatrick, ed., *Writings of Washington,* 17:68–69; Haldimand Papers, 21772:2–4.

45 Weslager, *Delaware Indians,* 298, 324 n: 21; Kellogg, ed., *Frontier Retreat,* 419–20n, 376; Kellogg, *ed., Frontier Advance,* 194.

46 Michael D. Green, "Alexander McGillivray," in R. David Edmunds, ed., *American Indian Leaders: Studies in Diversity* (Lincoln, Nebr., 1980), 41–63; John Walton Caughey, *McGillivray of the Creeks* (Norman, Okla., 1938).

47 C.O. 5/81:111, P.R.O.; Dawes, ed., *Documents,* 15:153–57; Draper Mss., 3H52; Haldimand Papers, 21783:276–79. For information on Choctaw "medal chiefs," see White, *Roots of Dependency,* chaps. 2–3, and idem, *Middle Ground,* esp. 322, 403–6.

48 Reginald Horsman, *Matthew Elliott: British Indian Agent* (Detroit, 1964); Colin G. Calloway, "Simon Girty: Interpreter and Intermediary," in James A. Clifton, ed., *Being and Becoming Indian: Biographical Studies of North American Frontiers* (Chicago, 1989), 38–58; C.O. 5/82:114, P.R.O.; Papers of the Continental Congress, roll 104, item 78, vol. 24, 435, 440–43.

49 William S. Coker and Thomas D. Watson, *Indian Traders of the Southeastern Spanish Borderlands: Panton, Leslie and Company, and John Forbes and Company, 1783–1847* (Pensacola, Fla., 1986).

50 Davies, ed., *Documents,* 12:199–203, 214; Galloway, *Old Chillicothe,* 40–42; Draper Mss., 5D12; Thomas L. McKenney and James Hall, *History of the Indian Tribes of North America,* 3

vols. (Philadelphia, 1836–44), 1:18; Calloway, "'We Have Always Been the Frontier,'" 44–45; Helen Hornbeck Tanner, "The Glaize in 1792: A Composite Indian Community," *Ethnohistory* 25 (1978): 15–39.

51 *Carleton Papers*, roll 17, no. 6742:18, roll 23, no. 6476:3; Charles M. Johnston, ed., *Valley of the Six Nations: A Collection of Documents on the Indian Lands of the Grand River* (Toronto, 1964).

52 Harold Blodgett, *Samson Occom* (Hanover, N.H., 1935), 195.

53 Kinnaird, "Spain in the Mississippi Valley," 3:186, 203–8, 255.

54 Ruth Holmes Whitehead, ed., *The Old Man Told Us: Excerpts from Micmac History, 1500–1900* (Halifax, Nova Scotia, 1991), 77; Kinnaird, ed., "Spain in the Mississippi Valley," 3: xi–xii, 15, 32–33, 60.

55 Davies, ed., *Documents*, 15:180.

56 Graymont, *Iroquois in the American Revolution*, 224; Kingageghta to Col. Guy Johnson, Jan. 25, 1780, quoted in Dorothy V Jones, *License for Empire: Colonialism by Treaty in Early America* (Chicago, 1982), 131.

57 Gearing, "Priests and Warriors," 47, 49, 74, 104; compare Dowd, *Spirited Resistance*, 10: "The warlike state of man [was] an unnatural state that had been ritually prepared."

58 Dowd, *Spirited Resistance*, 27. Compare Joel W. Martin, *Sacred Revolt: The Muskogees' Struggle for a New World* (Boston, 1991).

59 Papers of the Continental Congress, roll 54, vol. 3, 137; Annual Report of the Society for the Propagation of the Gospel (1781), 41. On the Moravian experience see, for example, Earl P. Olmstead, *Blackcoats among the Delaware: David Zeisberger on the Ohio Frontier* (Kent, Ohio, 1991), chap. 2.

60 Calloway, "'We Have Always Been the Frontier,'" 47; Draper Mss., 26J27–28; James Alton James, ed., *George Rogers Clark Papers, 1771–1781* (Springfield, Ill., 1912), 383.

61 Cook, ed., *Journals of Sullivan*, 101.

62 Colin G. Calloway, "Suspicion and Self-interest: British-Indian Relations and the Peace of Paris," *Historian* 48 (1985): 41–60; idem, *Crown and Calumet: British-Indian Relations, 1783–1815* (Norman, Okla., 1987), 3–23; Haldimand Papers, 21717:146–47; CO. 5/82:446–47, P.R.O.; Caughey, *McGillivray of the Creeks*, 92.

63 Haldimand Papers, 21779:117.

64 C.O. 5/82:372–73, P.R.O.; Peter Marshall, "First Americans and Last Loyalists: An Indian Dilemma in War and Peace," in Esmond Wright, ed., *Red, White, and True Blue: The Loyalists in the Revolution* (New York, 1976), 37–38.

65 Merrell, *Indians' New World*, 215–22.

66 Calloway, "New England Algonkians"; William De Loss Love, *Samson Occom and the Christian Indians of New England* (Boston, 1899), 276.

67 Papers of the Continental Congress, roll 71, item 58, 59–63, 67–68, 75–79; Colin G. Calloway, ed., *Dawnland Encounters: Indians and Europeans in Northern New England* (Hanover, N.H., 1991), 128–31.

68 J. David Lehman, "The End of the Iroquois Mystique: The Oneida Land Cession Treaties of the 1780s," *William and Mary Quarterly*, 3d ser. 48 (1990): 524–47.

69 White, *Middle Ground*, chaps. 9–11.

70 Denys Hays, "England, Scotland, and Europe: The Problem of the Frontier," *Transactions of the Royal Historical Society*, 5th ser. 25 (1975): 77–91; David Hackett Fischer, *Albion's Seed: Four British Folkways in America* (New York, 1989); Bernard Bailyn, *Voyagers to the West: A Passage in the Peopling of America on the Eve of the Revolution* (New York, 1986); Forrest McDonald and Ellen Shapiro McDonald, "The Ethnic Origins of the American People, 1790," *William and Mary Quarterly*, 3d ser. 37 (1980): 179–99.

71 Kinnaird, ed., "Spain in the Mississippi Valley," 3:117.

72 All the treaties are reprinted in Colin G. Calloway, ed., *Revolution and Confederation*, Early American Indian Documents: Treaties and Laws, vol. 18 (Frederick, Md., 1993); the Cherokee speech is in Papers of the Continental Congress, roll 69, item 56, 417.

73 Dowd, *Spirited Resistance*, chap. 5, provides details on the post-Revolution confederacy.

74 Papers of the Continental Congress, reel 65, item 51, vol. 2, 41–42; CO. 5/81:139–41, P.R.O.

75 Papers of the Continental Congress, roll 104, item 78, vol 24, 445–49; Palmer, ed., *Calendar of Virginia State Papers*, 3:357, 515–17.

76 Papers of the Continental Congress, roll 69, item 56, 113. The Chickasaw villages represented at Mobile are listed in Kinnaird, ed., "Spain in the Mississippi Valley," 3:102.

77  Arrell M. Gibson, *The Chickasaws* (Norman, Okla., 1971), 75; Caughey, *McGillivray of the Creeks,* 238–40, 265–67, 336–38, 343, 348–49, 351.

78  White, *Roots of Dependency,* 64.

79  Wallace, *Death and Rebirth of the Seneca.*

80  80 C.O. 5/79:37, P.R.O.

81  William C. Sturtevant, "Creek into Seminole," in Eleanor Burke Leacock and Nancy Oestreich Lurie, eds., *North American Indians in Historical Perspective* (New York, 1971), 92–128; Charles H. Fairbanks, "The Ethno-Archaeology of the Florida Seminoles," in Jerald Milanich and Samuel Proctor, eds., *Tacachale: Essays on the Indians of Florida and Southeastern Georgia during the Historic Period* (Gainesville, Fla., 1978), 170–71; Richard Sattler, *"Siminoli Italwa:* Socio-Political Change among the Oklahoma Seminoles between Removal and Allotment. 1836–1905," Ph.D. diss., University of Oklahoma, 1987, 64–84; Brent Richards Weisman, *Like Beads on a String: A Culture History of the Seminole Indians in North Peninsular Florida* (Tuscaloosa, Ala., 1989), 8–10, 80–81.

82  J. Leitch Wright, Jr., *Creeks and Seminoles: The Destruction and Regeneration of the Muscogulge People* (Lincoln, Nebr., 1986), 84–90.

83  Wallace, *Death and Rebirth, of the Seneca;* Dowd, *Spirited Resistance;* R. David Edmunds, *The Shawnee Prophet* (Lincoln, Nebr., 1983).

84  Kenneth M. Morrison, "Native Americans and the American Revolution: Historic Stories and Shifting Frontier Conflict," in Frederick E. Hoxie, ed., *Indians in American History* (Arlington Heights, Ill., 1988), 95.

85  Roy Harvey Pearce, *Savagism and Civilization: A Study of the Indian and the American Mind,* rev. ed., (Baltimore, 1965); Robert F Berkhofer, Jr., *The White Man's Indian: Images of the American Indian from Columbus to the Present* (New York, 1978).

86  *Virginia Magazine of History and Biography* 27 (1919): 316; Palmer, ed., *Calendar of Virginia State Papers,* 2:48.

87  Archibald Loudon, ed., *A Selection of Some of the Most Interesting Narratives, of Outrages Committed by the Indians, in Their Wars with the White People* … (1808; reprint ed., New York, 1971).

88  Compare Peter C. Mancall, *Economic Culture along the Upper Susquehanna, 1700–1800* (Ithaca, N.Y., 1991), 158–59. Russell Bourne's *The Red King's Rebellion: Racial Politics in New England, 1675–1678* (New York, 1990), sees a similar phenomenon in New England after King Philip's War. John D. Unruh, Jr., *The Plains Across: The Overland Emigrants and the Trans-Mississippi West, 1840–1860* (Urbana, Ill., 1979), chap. 5, esp. 120–21, 136.

89  Gary B. Nash, "The Forgotten Experience: Indians, Blacks, and the American Revolution," reprinted in Richard D. Brown, ed., *Major Problems in the Era of the American Revolution* (Lexington, Mass., 1992), 277–83.

90  Barry O'Connell, ed., *On Our Own Ground: The Complete Writings of William Pess, a Pequot* (Amherst, Mass., 1992), lxix, lxxiii, 239–40.

91  For example, Elaine F. Crane, "Dependence in the Era of Independence: The Role of Women in a Republican Society," in Jack P. Greene, ed., *The American Revolution: Its Character and Limits* (New York, 1987), 253–75.

92  Bernard W. Sheehan, *Seeds of Extinction: Jeffersonian Philanthropy and the American Indian* (1973; reprint ed., New York, 1974), 277–78.

93  For example, Rick Stewart, Joseph D. Ketner II, and Angela L. Miller, *Carl Wimar: Chronicler of the Missouri River Frontier* (Fort Worth, Tex., 1991), plates 1–2, 4–15; Brian W. Dippie, *Catlin and His Contemporaries: The Politics of Patronage* (Lincoln, Nebr., 1990), plate 12.

94  Pearce, *Savagism and Civilization,* 154, 160.

# 18
# THE RIGHTS OF WOMAN

*Rosemarie Zagarri*

## Introduction

The American Revolution contributed to the Enlightenment debate about whether women's subservience to men was a product of nurture or nature and whether it was just. During the Revolution, white women gained confidence and political experience by participating in economic boycotts, managing their homes and farms while their husbands were at war, and petitioning for their families and communities. They also accumulated political capital for their innumerable sacrifices. In turn, a number of white women, no less than working-class white men and black slaves, began employing revolutionary principles to call for reforms to their condition. Led by Judith Sargent Murray, a growing chorus of white women called for greater educational opportunities. Abigail Adams wanted women to receive greater property rights and protection against abusive husbands. Still others wanted white women to enjoy the suffrage, which was unheard of in pre-revolutionary America.

In the little-known case of New Jersey, propertied women did get the right to vote, at least for a while. In 1790 and 1797, New Jersey explicitly stated that women owning fifty pounds or more worth of property could cast the ballot. Though this law effectively applied only to widows, its implications were profound. According to Rosemarie Zagarri, New Jersey legislators were taking revolutionary ideas "to their logical, if unexpected and untraditional, conclusion."

The pushback was equally powerful, as it was in every case of a disempowered population demanding its rights. White men, particularly those of property, knew that gender inequality was the most basic of several inequalities structuring American society, including race and class. Granting white women basic rights risked going down a slippery slope of reform that might radically reshape American society. As such, not a single state followed New Jersey's example and even New Jersey rescinded the propertied widows' franchise in 1807.

Nevertheless, the genie was out the bottle. Activists such as Mary Wollstonecraft, author of *A Vindication of the Rights of Woman* (1792), kept up the pressure by calling on American men to follow through on their self-professed egalitarian principles. Their efforts made "women's rights" part of American political debate and, gradually, of American society.

- Zagarri considers revolutionary America's debate over white women's rights to have been of a piece with its reconsideration of working-class white men and black slaves. Do you agree? What explains why white women achieved less progress than did working-class white men in their state constitutions (as discussed by Gary B. Nash) or northern black slaves in receiving their freedom (as discussed by Ira Berlin).
- Can the Revolution be said to have had a causal effect on the expansion of women's rights given that this development took place many decades after the war ended?
- Zagarri attributes great power to revolutionary ideas about natural rights, but she acknowledges that relatively few women politicked for men to apply these rights to them. Consider Zagarri's essay alongside Mary Beth Norton's article to explain why this was the case.

In 1798, less than ten years after the ratification of the U.S. Constitution, the writer Charles Brockden Brown, often considered the country's first professional man of letters, published an article on a controversial topic in his periodical, the Philadelphia *Weekly Magazine*. Entitled "The Rights of Woman," the piece depicted a dialogue between a young man, Alcuin, and his female acquaintance, Mrs. Carter. At one point Alcuin, the namesake of a medieval monk, posed a question to his companion, asking the woman about her preferences in terms of political parties. Instead of deferentially refusing to discuss such an unfeminine topic, Mrs. Carter went on the offensive. "What have I, as a woman, to do with politics?" she asked. "Even the government of our country, which is said to be the freest in the world, passes over women as if they were not [free]. We are excluded from all political rights without the least ceremony. Lawmakers thought as little of comprehending us in their code of liberty, as if we were pigs, or sheep. That females are exceptions to their general maxims perhaps never occurred to them. If it did, the idea was quietly discarded, without leaving behind the slightest consciousness of inconsistency or injustice."[1]

Charles Brockden Brown had gone straight to the heart of a fundamental contradiction in postrevolutionary American society. Although the Revolution had been fought in the name of equality and natural rights, the American political system failed to embody those ideals for substantial portions of its population. It denied equal rights to all black people and to nearly one-half of the white population: women. Although the first organized resistance to slavery began to emerge at this time, there was no comparable movement for women's rights. Most historians, in fact, assume that the first widespread debates about women's rights did not occur until the decade or so preceding the Seneca Falls Convention of 1848. Yet, as Brown's tirade suggests, the first agitation about women's rights can actually be traced to the years immediately following the Revolution,

or even earlier, to Enlightenment discussions about the role of women in history and society. Although the American Revolution was not fought in an effort to promote women's rights, the commitment to equality and natural rights created an unexpected conundrum. Would American women share in what the author Judith Sargent Murray called "the blessings of liberty"?[2] Or would the new country treat its women, as Brown claimed, merely like "pigs, or sheep"?

## Women, Custom, and History

The relationship of women to the polity is part of the ongoing, long-term *querelle des femmes* that began during the Renaissance, continued through the Enlightenment, and gained new momentum after the American and French Revolutions. The Enlightenment, in particular, produced important shifts in the understanding of women's role and status. In 1673 François Poulain de la Barre published a work in France called *The Equality of the Two Sexes*. Building on the Cartesian belief in the centrality of reason, Poulain argued that women's physical traits did not impair their mental faculties. Men's and women's minds were essentially the same; the differences between their bodies were incidental to this more fundamental fact. Over the course of the eighteenth century, Poulain's dictum "The mind has no sex" became widely accepted among the educated classes throughout the transatlantic world. If both men and women had the ability to reason, then women were as capable as men in the arena that mattered most: the realm of the intellect. John Locke's *Essay on Human Understanding* provided a different kind of support for the possibility that men and women might have equal intellectual faculties. He proposed that the mind is a tabula rasa, a blank slate shaped by the environment and education rather than by innate ideas. This explanation helped explain women's apparent intellectual inferiority. Their deficiencies were the result not of inherent incapacity but of the failure to receive adequate educational opportunities. Embracing this notion, the English writer Mary Astell attacked men for their complicity in keeping women in ignorance. "Instead of inquiring why all Women are not wise and good," wrote Astell in 1694, "we have reason to wonder that there are any so. Were the Men as much neglected, and as little care taken to cultivate and improve them, perhaps they wou'd be so far from surpassing those whom they now dispise, that they themselves wou'd sink into the greatest stupidity and brutality." The "Incapacity" of the female mind, "if there be any," she concluded, "is acquired, not natural." Given the same opportunities as men, women would be able to match their male counterparts in intellectual achievement.[3]

Around the same time, other thinkers also began to challenge the belief in women's inherent inferiority. They recounted women's roles and accomplishments in distant times and places. The very earliest women's histories appeared during the Renaissance, beginning with Giovanni Boccaccio's *Concerning Famous Women* (1355–59) and Christine de Pisan's *Book of the City of Ladies* (1404). During the late seventeenth and eighteenth centuries a whole new profusion of women's histories appeared. Usually consisting of a series of biographical sketches, these works listed the accomplishments of notable "female worthies" from ancient times to modern, including women from the Old Testament, Roman matrons, Greek poetesses, famous queens, and female writers and thinkers. Significantly, these women succeeded in areas that were typically thought to be the province of men, such as literature, politics, government, and warfare. Playing to the tastes of an increasingly literate female audience, the women's histories intended to set the historical record straight by recovering a story that had been lost, ignored, or suppressed. Conventional histories focused on men and "Eclipsed the brightest Candor of Female perfection." Their purpose, according to one author, was to enlighten women as to "the history of their own sex." Women, said another,

would receive "a valuable proportion of the praise [they have] merited." Women would have their own past. This would be nothing less than "An Historical Vindication of the Female Sex."[4]

Judging by the pace of publication, the publishers were correct. Readers, especially women, seemed to have a voracious appetite for these works. Thomas Heywood's *Generall History of Women*, published in England in 1657, was followed in 1686 by John Shirley's *Illustrious History of Women, or A Compendium of the Many Virtues that Adorn the Fair Sex*. Others appeared in quick succession: Richard Burton's *Female Excellency or the Ladies Glory* in 1688; and Nahum Tate's *A Present for the Ladies: Being an Historical Account of Several Illustrious Persons of the Female Sex* in 1693. After the turn of the century, the genre gained momentum. James Bland issued his *Essay in Praise of Women* in 1735, while in 1752 the Oxonian George Ballard published *Memoirs of several Ladies of Great Britain, who have been celebrated for their writings and skill in the learned languages, arts, and science*. In 1766 *The Biographium Foemineum: or, Memoirs of the Most Illustrious Ladies of All Ages and Nations* appeared. French authors turned out similar works, some of which were translated into English.[5]

North American British colonists shared the motherland's enthusiasm for women's history. Not only did Americans import a substantial number of volumes, which were quite expensive, but they also began to print their own, cheaper editions. In 1774 a Philadelphia publisher issued William Russell's translation of Antoine-Léonard Thomas's *Essay on the Character, Manners, and Genius of Women in Different Ages*, which had been issued the previous year in London and was originally printed in France in 1772. In 1796 and 1800 Philadelphia editions of the anonymous work *Sketches of the History, Genius, Disposition, Accomplishments, Employments, Customs and Importance of the Fair Sex in All Parts of the World* appeared. In addition, popular periodicals and literary magazines often excerpted portions of the histories, enabling the works to reach a larger audience.[6]

One of the most popular and influential works was William Alexander's two-volume *History of Women, From the Earliest Antiquity, to the Present Time; Giving an Account of Almost Every Interesting Particular Concerning that Sex, Among All Nations, Ancient and Modern*. The work was first issued in London and Dublin in 1779, and excerpts were published in the *Boston Magazine* from December 1784 through July 1785. *The History of Women* appeared in two American editions, one in 1795 and another a year later. The 1796 printing alone listed more than 450 subscribers, including sixty-four women, booksellers such as Matthew Carey, and eminent personages such as General Thomas Craig, Governor Thomas Mifflin, and Supreme Court Justice James Wilson. References to the work abounded. Many American writers, including Judith Sargent Murray and Hannah Mather Crocker, explicitly cited Alexander's history of women in their own writings.[7]

Then as now, however, the lessons of the past were not self-evident or unambiguous. Different readers took away different lessons. For some, the histories provided proof that women could equal men in their intellect and achievements. The past provided a trove of evidence that could be marshaled in women's defense. In 1806, for example, the *Literary Magazine* proclaimed that Sappho, the poetess of ancient Lesbos, "soared above her sex in the wonderful endowments of her mind." Semiramis of Nineveh, it was said, ruled an empire in the ancient Middle East. Queen Christina of Sweden, observed the *New York Weekly Museum,* was noted for her prodigious learning and relinquished her crown rather than marry and "resign [her] liberty." More recently, England and America produced famous women authors, including Hannah More, Susanna Rowson, Charlotte Rowe, and Mercy Warren. Laura Bassi earned a doctorate in mathematics at the Institute of Bologna. Throughout history, it seemed, women had demonstrated the capacity to excel in the same areas as men did.[8]

Other readers, however, came to different conclusions. These observers criticized women from the past who displayed traits that they deemed masculine, such as leadership or learning. An article in the *Weekly Museum,* for example, condemned the female ruler of ancient Assyria, Semiramis, for her "cruelty" in power as well as her hideous murder of her husband. Another author unfavorably compared Elizabeth of England, who exhibited "the foibles of a weak woman," to her sister, Mary, Queen of Scots, who combined "the merit of a literary character [with] every female accomplishment." Their praise was reserved for women who most nearly conformed to contemporary feminine ideals of beauty, purity, modesty, or self-sacrifice. *Port Folio* magazine, for example, celebrated the French writer Madame de Sevigne because she was "always a woman; never an author, never a pedant, never a literary female … . A woman always loses by attempting to be a man." Another author claimed that although "we admire the masculine mind of Elizabeth, we love Mary Queen of Scots." Although women might have the ability to succeed in the same arenas as men did, they should not necessarily aspire to such goals. "It will generally be found," said the *New York Weekly Museum,* "that woman is better calculated to tread in softer and smoother paths; to leave the tumultuous bustle of public life, to spread light, cheerfulness, and felicity in less splendid circles." Thus the early women's histories could be read either to critique the gender status quo or to affirm it.[9]

Whether or not women's past actions gained approval, the histories presented irrefutable evidence of women's past accomplishments and, hence, of their current untapped potential abilities. Even if one believed that women should not aspire to achieve the same accomplishments as men, the histories demonstrated that women were capable of doing so. "The history of women," asserted the *Female Advocate,* "is forever intruding on our unwilling eyes, bold and ardent spirits, who no tyrant could tame, no prejudice enslave." Despite resistance, women in the past had overcome innumerable obstacles in order to succeed. In her *Gleaner* essays, Judith

Sargent Murray noted that there were over 845 Women "writers of eminence" in the past. "If the triumphs and the attainments of THE SEX, under the various oppressions with which they have struggled, have been thus splendid," she said, "how would they have been augmented, had not ignorant or interested men … contrived to erect around them almost insurmountable barriers." The "distinction" between men and women "was artificial, and not *natural*," insisted another author, and "there have always been instances of female intelligence and female merit to prove [it]." Women would not be deterred.[10]

Perhaps most important, the early histories of women revealed the bankruptcy of the belief in women's inherent inferiority. As William Alexander pointed out, women in the eighteenth century had failed to accomplish as much as their forebears had not because they were incapable but because of "all the disadvantages they are laid under by the law, and by custom." This meant that society had developed norms that limited women's role and restricted their choices. "Why," demanded an author writing in the *New-York Magazine,* "are the ladies condemned to remain in ignorance?" The answer, at least to this writer, seemed apparent: "It is because the majority of men have an interest in concealing knowledge from them." Custom and tradition, not nature, limited women's roles and possibilities.[11]

This was a key insight. While inherent differences were immutable, custom could be changed. Hence, as Judith Sargent Murray put it, women "were *naturally* as susceptible of every improvement, as those of men." If women took responsibility for their own condition, they could change society. Women, proclaimed a young woman graduating from a female academy, should throw off "the shackles of custom, and dispel from our minds those clouds of ignorance and darkness, in which our sex has been too long involv'd." Once freed from customary restrictions, women's prospects seemed almost limitless. "The greatest concerns," declared the *Gentleman and Lady's Magazine,* "are not beyond their capacity." Although custom might be what Murray called a "tyrant," it was an oppressor that could be overthrown. Even those who disparaged women's past achievements as "masculine" would have to admit that.[12]

At the same time that the early histories of women were challenging the notion of women's inherent inferiority, Enlightenment thinkers posited a new conception of history, sometimes called "conjectural history," that moved women from the margins of the historical process to the center. Philosophers as diverse as Henry Home (Lord Kames), John Millar, David Hume, the baron de Montesquieu, and Condorcet all employed some version of this approach in their writings. In their view, societies progressed through a series of predictable stages along a continuum from savagery to civilization. Although the precise number of stages, ranging from four to twelve, varied according to each philosopher, the trajectory was similar.

In the first stage, the primitive or savage phase, life was simple, hard, and brutal. Men were hunters who spent most of their time mired in the basic struggle for subsistence. Over time, some societies moved beyond this basic level into the more auspicious pastoral phase of existence. Large numbers of people herded sheep and kept cattle. With their basic needs taken care of, life lost some of its brutality and harshness. An even smaller number of societies moved beyond this point into the agrarian phase. For people living in these societies, material existence became more secure. Inhabitants enjoyed a certain amount of comfort and leisure. Society began to shed some of its rusticity; people became more refined and cultivated. An even smaller number of societies moved into the final phase, the mercantile stage. Having escaped the demands of mere subsistence, commercial societies allowed people to escape the crudities of their earlier existence and cultivate their higher interests and pleasures. Inhabitants could spend time in learning, leisure, or the refined arts. These stages were not regarded merely as abstract theories. The natives of North America represented the primitive end of the spectrum, while modern

Britain exemplified the other extreme, a nation that had reached the pinnacle of civilization, refinement, and achievement.[13]

Significantly, conjectural historians portrayed women as key agents in the development of society and civilization. In their schema, women represented both an index to and an instrument of social advancement. The more a society progressed, the better it treated its women. In the lowest stage of civilization, women were regarded as nothing more than men's slaves, suitable primarily for sexual congress and physical labor. There was, according to William Robertson, "a cruel distinction between the sexes, which forms the one to be harsh and unfeeling, and humbles the other to senility and subjection." As society moved into the pastoral and agrarian phases, however, men treated women with more dignity and respect. "That women are indebted to the refinements of polished manners for a happy change in their state," commented Robertson, "is a point which can admit of no doubt." At the same time, women furthered social progress by cultivating men's higher instincts, refining their manners, and helping them discipline their more unruly passions. "The gentle and insinuating manners of the female sex," said Kames, "tend to soften the roughness of the other sex; and where-ever women are indulged with any degree of freedom, they polish sooner than men." Eventually women gained greater status and better treatment. They emerged from their status as chattel or as simple objects of lust and rose, according to Kames, "out of slavery to possess the elevated state they are justly entitled to by nature." In the highest stage of development, the mercantile phase, women enjoyed "that nearness of rank, not to say equality," as Hume put it, "which nature has established between the sexes." They now took their place as men's friends and companions. According to Millar, women were "encouraged to quit that retirement which was formerly esteemed so suitable to their character, to enlarge the sphere of their acquaintance, and to appear in mixed company, and in public meetings of pleasure." They became the social – though not political – equals of men.[14]

Conjectural histories helped American men and women appreciate women's contributions to society. Women had a crucial role in inculcating virtue, fostering manners, and promoting the civilizing process. "Female manners," observed John Cosens Ogden of New Hampshire, "must and ever will, form those of men. The latter are rude and savage, polished and refined, in proportion as the former are cultivated and softened." Society's treatment of its women would, in turn, reflect its degree of progress toward civilization. "There is no truth more generally admitted," noted the Reverend Samuel Miller, "than that every step in the progress of civilization brings new honour to the female sex, and increases their importance to society." American men and women knew that their own society would be judged by these standards. "It is a fact," the *Weekly Museum* declared, "that in all ages of the world, in proportion as mankind have advanced in civilization, in the same proportion have the softer sex been esteemed and treated with respect." As men's friends and companions, women gained dignity, respect, and a modicum of equality.[15]

Acknowledging women's centrality to society made it easier to envision the possibility that women might contribute to the polity as well. In a monarchy women's place was primarily ornamental. In a republic where the people governed themselves, women could shape the values and ideals of the populace. "[Although] the men possess the more ostensible powers of making and executing the laws," observed an Independence Day speaker, "the women, in even' free country, have an absolute control of manners: and it is confessed, that in a republic, manners are of equal importance with laws." In their role as wives and mothers, women could instill virtue and inculcate patriotism in their children, husbands, and neighbors. Addressing the women attending his lectures on the law in 1790, the lawyer James Wilson emphasized the significance of women's contributions. "To protect and to improve social life," he said, "is, as we have seen, the end of government and law. If, therefore, you [women] have no share in the formation, you have a most intimate connexion with the effects, of a good system of law and government." Through their influence over men, women could have a crucial, if indirect, influence on the polity. They might have a political role to play.[16]

## Women and the American Revolution

The new Enlightenment histories of women and stage theories of social change created new perceptions of women's roles and possibilities. Writing in 1803, the American Presbyterian minister Samuel Miller noted, "One of the most striking peculiarities of the eighteenth century … is the change of opinion gradually introduced into society, respecting the importance, capacity, and dignity of the *Female Sex*." The effect, as he saw it, amounted to nothing less than "a revolution radical and unprecedented with respect to [women's] treatment and character."[17]

Yet this was a revolution of a certain kind – a change in the understanding of women's intellectual capacity and social contributions rather than the achievement of political rights and privileges. Before the American Revolution the popular perception remained that politics and government were exclusively male realms. Although women had certain rights, their status was inferior to that of men. Only men could vote and hold public office. Only men could attend meetings of the colonial assemblies, hold positions of power at court, serve in the military, collect customs duties, or be appointed governor. Men so thoroughly monopolized government and politics that the prevailing belief was that women either had no opinions about these subjects or, if they did, should not express them.

Yet even before the American Revolution, small numbers of elite women in both England and America had already begun to express an interest in politics and a desire to participate in government. Aristocratic women in England attended balls, salons, and court ceremonies, which gave them access to and influence over political figures. The English civil war and Glorious Revolution produced a torrent of works written by women on political subjects ranging from the state of the monarchy, succession, and republican government to the prospect of foreign war. By the early eighteenth century some British women had grown dissatisfied with their inferior legal status and had begun to protest publicly against the system's inequities. In a 1735 petition to Parliament, one group of women condemned the "Hardship of English Laws in Relation to Wives," which, they said, "put us in a worse Condition than Slavery itself." Claiming their privilege as "Free-born Subjects of *England*," they sought redress of their grievances, requesting more equitable treatment in terms of property rights, widows' portions, and physical safety at the hands of their spouses. Writing a few years later, a woman calling herself "Sophia, A Person of Quality," produced the published tract, *Vindication of the Natural Right of the Fair-Sex to a Perfect Equality of Power, Dignity, and Esteem, with Men*. Not only did the author maintain that women were men's intellectual equals, she also claimed that women were as fit as men to govern and hold public office. "I think it evidently appears," she declared, "that there is no science, office, or dignity, which Women have not an equal right to share with Men: Since there can be no superiority but that of brutal strength shewn in the latter, to entitle them to engross all power and prerogative to themselves; nor any incapacity proved in the former to disqualify them of their right, but what is owing to the unjust oppression of the Men, and might be easily removed." Continuing this line of investigation, the 1758 pamphlet called *Female Rights Vindicated* protested against women's exclusion from government and probed the nature of women's "Obligations to civil Society." According to the tract's female author, "women in general are as fit for the offices of state, as those who commonly fill them." By the 1780s and 1790s British radicals such as John Gale Jones, William Hodgson, Thomas Cooper, and Jeremy Bentham, associated with clubs such as the London Corresponding Society and the Manchester Literary and Philosophical Society, were advancing propositions supporting women's equality and natural rights, including women's right to vote.[18]

Women in colonial British North America also experienced political stirrings. Two editions of the British tract *Female Grievances Debated* were printed in the colonies between 1731 and 1758. In fact, the Custis family of Virginia – Martha Washington's family of origin – owned the original English edition. Colonial newspapers sometimes printed pieces that satirized men's treatment of women or challenged women's subordinate status. A poem published in Virginia in 1736 and South Carolina in 1743 declared,

> Then equal Laws let Custom find,
>    And neither Sex oppress;
> More Freedom give to Womankind,
>    Or to Mankind give less.

Other pieces picked up on the theme of women's subjugation. A poem from 1743, subsequently reprinted in other publications, described marriage as woman's "wretched" fate, a condition that changed the man into a "tyrant" and the woman into a creature bound by a "Slave's Fetters." The Englishwomen's 1735 petition to Parliament was reprinted in 1788 in Philadelphia's *Columbian Magazine* under the heading "A Tract on the Unreasonableness of the Laws of England, in regard to Wives." Though it appeared without editorial comment, the implication seemed to be clear.[19]

As in Britain, however, the predominant norm in colonial British America held that women should neither interest themselves in politics nor involve themselves in the business of government. Nonetheless, a long-term growth in women's literacy and the increasing availability of political information, particularly newspapers,

meant that more women in British America could read about politics and form their own opinions. In 1734 during the controversy over the prosecution of the printer John Peter Zenger for seditious libel, a reader of the *New-York Weekly Journal* complained to the editor that women in the colony were "contending about some abstruce Point in Politicks, and running into the greatest Heats about they know not what." Hoping to quell the outburst, he dismissed their comments, saying, "Politicks is what does not become them." Yet some women apparently continued to express political views. "The Men," reported Esther Edwards Burr in 1755, "say … that Women have no business to concern themselves about [politics] but [should] trust to those that know better." Although men complained, women did not always defer to their judgment.[20]

By and large, however, most women remained reluctant to transgress into what was understood to be male territory. Even Mercy Otis Warren, who would become one of the most accomplished women authors of her generation, responded timidly when her friend John Adams first spoke to her about the subject of politics. In a letter written in 1776, Adams asked Warren what form of government she would prefer for the newly independent United States. In reply, she expressed her hesitancy to speak to the issue, fearing that a discussion of "war, politicks, or anything relative thereto" was off-limits to women. She wondered whether his query was "designed to ridicule the sex for paying any attention to political matters." Only after she received his explicit reassurances did she dare "approach the verge of any thing so far beyond the line of my sex."[21]

This state of affairs could have persisted indefinitely if not for the American Revolution. The American Revolution marked a watershed in the popular perceptions of women's relationship to the state. Almost as soon as the controversy began in the 1760s, Whig leaders realized that the effectiveness of their resistance to Britain depended on their ability to mobilize popular support. This included women. Women's support, they knew, would be critical to the resistance movement against Britain and could affect the course of the war. Significantly, patriot leaders did not presume that American women would automatically follow their husbands' lead. Schooled in Enlightenment theories about women, many men believed that women had an equal capacity to reason. Just as skeptical farmers, merchants, artisans, and mechanics would have to be persuaded to aid the resistance movement, women too would have to be won over to the cause.

It is plausible, even likely, that women had played some role, direct or indirect, in determining the outcome of previous wars, conflicts, and rebellions throughout history. What was different about the American Revolution was the nature and extent of the appeals to women. The more extensive use of print media made this change possible. Newspapers, magazines, and broadsides reached out to women in a direct, widespread, and public fashion. Using poems, essays, plays, and orations, male political leaders urged women to join in the effort. During the 1760s they asked women to boycott imported luxury goods, produce homemade textiles and clothing, and give up drinking British tea. Once armed resistance began, they asked them to sacrifice the conveniences of life, take over their husbands' duties at home in their absence, and, if necessary, be willing to offer their men's lives for their country on the field of battle. Printed appeals drew women to the cause.

Women responded with a widespread outpouring of support. During the 1760s women in Boston, Massachusetts, and Edenton, North Carolina, signed formal agreements to abide by the boycotts forbidding the importation of British goods. In other places women organized local chapters of the Daughters of Liberty as female counterparts to the Sons of Liberty, held patriotic spinning bees, or wore homespun as a sign of symbolic sacrifice. Soon after declaring independence, New Yorkers toppled a leaden statue of George III on the Bowling

Green. Seizing the opportunity, the women of Litchfield, Connecticut retrieved the statuary and transformed the broken pieces into over forty-two thousand cartridges to supply the Continental Army with ammunition. Once the war began, some women sewed shirts or knit stockings for Washington's desperately needy troops. Still others took even more direct action. In 1780 Esther DeBerdt Reed spearheaded a drive in Philadelphia to collect funds for the Continental Army. In towns throughout Pennsylvania, Maryland, New Jersey, and Virginia, women went door to door soliciting funds to assist the wavering war effort. Participating in the revolutionary movement in their own ways and on their own terms, women made themselves a political force.[22]

At the grassroots level, women came to realize that their personal response to the Revolution could have an impact on the course of the war itself. The new nation needed thousands of men, year after year, to fill offices in the new state and federal governments, to serve in the militia or the Continental Army, and to represent the country as ambassadors abroad. When men left home to take up arms or serve in government positions, they depended on women to take over their duties on the farm, in business, and within the family. Women often had little prior training or experience in supervising these matters. Economic conditions were difficult; war-time shortages and inflation made matters worse. The trials of family life without a father present caused untold emotional strains.

Women's willingness to shoulder men's burdens and become what Laurel Ulrich has called, in another context, a "deputy husband" gave men the freedom to participate in the war effort. Yet women were well aware of the personal costs. Helen Kortright Brasher of New York City recalled that although she supported the Revolution, she resented her husband's absences from home. "He had formerly been a most domestick man; now he was forever out of his house surrounded with gentlemen conversing on politicks; every evening out at some meeting or other haranguing his fellow citizens, writing for the public prints; in short the whole city experienced the unhappy change and every family was more or less in the same painful situation."[23]

Not all women responded equally willingly to the calls for sacrifice. Differences in women's responses suggest important ways in which women could influence their husbands' political choices and ultimately affect the course of the war. While some women rose to the new challenges, or at least accepted the responsibilities grudgingly, others refused or resisted. This was true even among families of the leaders of the revolutionary cause. Abigail Adams represented a paragon of female revolutionary patriotism. Her husband John was, of course, a stalwart of the resistance movement. Beginning as a young lawyer, he quickly moved into a leadership position in the Massachusetts Assembly and then during the early years of the Revolution became one of the central figures in the new Continental Congress. Beginning in 1778 he went abroad for several years to negotiate treaties, first with France and then with Britain. During these long separations Abigail bore the full burden of managing the house, farm, and family without her husband. Although Abigail proved to be a skillful "farmeress," as she called herself, she always grieved her husband's absence. Anticipating John's arrival for a quick trip home in 1775, she poured out her despair to her friend Mercy Otis Warren: "I find I am obliged to summon all my patriotism to feel willing to part with [John] again. You will readily believe me when I say that I make no small sacrifice to the publick." Warren sympathized with her plight as her own husband was often gone for long periods on public business. "The frequent Absence of the best of friends," she wrote to Abigail, "prevents to you and to me the full injoyment of the Many Blessings providence has kindly showered Down upon us . . . . But while the sword and the pestilence pervade the Land, and Misery is portion of Millions, why should we expect to feel No interruption of Happiness."

Abigail Adams nonetheless repeatedly gave her blessing to her husband's choices and supported his decision to serve the public.[24]

In contrast, Mercy Otis Warren chose not to be as self-abnegating as Abigail Adams was. Both were avid patriots. In the 1770s, Mercy, in fact, had written several satirical plays and numerous poems attacking British tyranny and, in particular, the treachery of Massachusetts lieutenant governor Thomas Hutchinson. Her husband, James, began his political career in the mid-1760s and served for over ten years in the Massachusetts General Court. An early leader of the resistance movement in his hometown of Plymouth, he also served during the war as a member of the state constitutional convention, as an officer in the Massachusetts militia, on the federal navy board, and in various other offices. These duties frequently entailed absences from home lasting anywhere from several weeks to several months. By 1780 Mercy had had enough. She urged her husband to retire from public service and return home to be with her. "I am sometimes Ready," she wrote to James, "to think you could serve the public better unencumbered by anxieties for me, but I am not Hipocrite Enough to conceal the secret Regrets that pray upon my mind and Interrupt my peace." Her entreaties convinced him. Despite the fact that the war had not yet been won and the business of state building had just begun, he essentially withdrew from public service. As Warren's case demonstrates, patriotic appeals to women were not simply rhetorical exercises. If women were unwilling to sacrifice for the cause, their husbands might be less likely to participate as well. Women needed to subordinate their own private happiness for the sake of the common good – and act more like Abigail Adams than Mercy Warren.[25]

Aware of their dependence on women, men realized that they would ignore "the sex" at their peril. Throughout the war, patriot leaders publicly praised women's sacrifices and stoked the fires of female patriotism. By recognizing women's political efforts and contributions, they politicized women, acknowledging their capacity as political agents. Women felt a new sense of empowerment. In a poem on the Townshend boycotts against the British goods, Warren highlighted the importance of women to the plan's success: by "quit[ting] the useless vanities of life," women would "at once … end the great political strife." Their actions would "bless, or ruin all mankind." Similarly, Milcah Martha Moore of Pennsylvania emphasized the ability of women to provide leadership during the crisis over the Tea Act:

> Let the Daughters of Liberty, nobly arise,
> And tho' we've no Voice, but a negative here,
> The use of the Taxables, let us forbear. …
> That rather than Freedom, we'll part with
>     our Tea.

Instead of being simply followers, women would lead the way and "point out their Duty to Men." Having suffered numerous adversities, they came to believe that their patriotism equaled any man's. Carrying on while her husband was a British prisoner, Mary Fish of Connecticut declared, "I have the vanity to think I have in some measure acted the heroine as well as my dear Husband the Hero." American women were, as Esther DeBerdt Reed put it, "Born for liberty."[26]

Once independence was achieved, men reinforced women's newfound sense of themselves as political actors. In public speeches and published articles, they repeatedly acknowledged women's support and praised their contributions to the revolutionary cause. Like men, women had felt the scourge of British tyranny and suffered through a multitude of deprivations and hardships. "Though ruin and desolation pervaded your country, and those to whom you [women] were bound by the dearest ties were insulted, outraged and imprisoned," proclaimed John Fauchereaud Grimké, "still you remained firm and undismayed in the conscientious discharge of your duty." Celebrating women's cooperation, they acknowledged their contribution in achieving

victory over Britain. Both sexes, noted Richard Dinsmore, "gloried in the appellation rebel." Although female patriotism was, as Keating Lewis Simon noted, more "of a kind entirely suited to their sex," women had fully earned the country's esteem. "Our heroines, in their place," concluded Solomon Aiken, "were not a whit behind our foremost heroes."[27]

These appeals had effects that lasted well beyond the war. Print culture established a vehicle through which patriot leaders might reach out to large numbers of women and involve them in the revolutionary cause. Women received public recognition for their activities. In acknowledging women's importance to the cause, men affirmed women's capacity to act as political agents. Their actions not only affected the fates of individual families but also had an impact on the course of the war, politics, and society. Although the Revolution did not necessarily radicalize women, it did politicize them in ways and to an extent that had never before occurred. They started to see themselves – and were seen by others – as political beings. No longer were they politically invisible.

## Rights and Revolution

Before the Revolution, the notion of women's subordination to men permeated American society. The doctrine of coverture assumed that women were not independent legal agents. Before they were married, they were under the guardianship of their fathers. Once married, their husbands acted in their stead. Without a separate legal identity, women could not sue or be sued in court, make contracts, or own property. In addition, the assumption that they lacked an independent identity extended far beyond statutory prescriptions. Young women were supposed to defer to their fathers' opinions; married women, to their husbands. Their lives were defined with reference to home and family. Women were not supposed to travel alone, speak in public to audiences that included men, or become too learned. Their exclusion from political rights was an assumed given, seldom questioned or discussed.[28]

It is undeniably true that at the beginning of the war for independence, most American leaders would never have dreamed that their struggle against Britain would turn into an attack on the gender status quo. Yet, like all revolutions, the American Revolution produced its share of unintended consequences. No single person or group could control the direction of events or the flow of ideas. This was especially true with regard to ideas about women's relationship to the state, their involvement with politics, and their political rights and privileges.

The most crucial development was the growing centrality of the principles of equality and natural rights. Originally, of course, these ideas were meant to pertain primarily, if not exclusively, to men. During the 1760s and 1770s American colonists found themselves in an ongoing political struggle with Britain. Initially they protested against British policies by insisting on their rights as Englishmen. As British subjects, they claimed to share in a long tradition of English rights that included the right to trial by jury, the right to petition, the right to freedom of speech, and a right to be taxed only when they were properly represented in their legislatures. When Britain repeatedly dismissed or ignored Americans' protests, the colonists realized that they must seek other grounds on which to justify their claims. By 1776 many Americans believed that Britain had violated not only their rights as Englishmen but also their God-given natural rights, inscribed in nature. The Declaration of Independence justified independence by asserting men's natural equality and by invoking the "Laws of Nature and of Nature's God." Natural rights commanded assent because they were said to be inalienable, immutable, and universal – possessed by virtue of one's personhood rather than as a result of citizenship, parentage, or wealth. Such claims were hard to refute.

Yet unbeknownst to the revolutionaries, these concepts could take on a life of their own.[29] Equality and natural rights had an elastic quality, capable of almost infinite expansion and extension. If these principles were universal in nature, as was contended, why did they not apply to other dispossessed groups, such as poor white men, black people, or women? One of the first areas to be challenged was the property qualification for voting. As was the case in Britain, the North American British colonies allowed only those who met certain property qualifications to vote for members of their colonial assemblies. Colonists assumed that those who owned property had a greater stake in society and a greater interest in the deliberations of the legislature than those who did not. Property owners, moreover, were believed to be more independent and virtuous than the propertyless masses, who might be susceptible to bribery, manipulation, or corruption. In England electors had to own a forty-shilling freehold to vote for members of Parliament. In most of the colonies a similar requirement was established, sometimes based on acreage rather than land value. In practice, however, the same principle had very different implications in the two places. Whereas in England, due to the shortage of land, no more than 20 percent of adult males could vote, in the colonies, because of the widespread cheapness and availability of land, between 50 percent and 80 percent of all white males could vote. What had been a restrictive requirement in Britain was inconsequential in America. Even before the Revolution, then, a majority of white men were enfranchised.[30]

Even so, once the Revolution began, the very existence of property qualifications for voting started to bother some members of society. As states began to write their first constitutions, agitation for lowering or eliminating property qualifications became a subject of debate. Some commentators pointed out the inconsistency in allowing men to fight and die for their country but not allowing them to vote. Others pointed out that by expanding the franchise, state governments would broaden their base of popular support. Still others noted that if

Americans believed that those who paid taxes should be represented, then all taxpayers, not just owners of real property, should be enfranchised. The most powerful argument, however, was that if all men were truly created equal and shared the same natural rights, then all men should be entitled to vote.[31]

Inspired by these sentiments, William Sullivan wrote a letter in May 1776 to his friend John Adams in which he made the case for universal suffrage. Responding with alarm, Adams pointed out that all societies operate on the basis of "general rules," or commonly agreed-upon conventions. These conventions may or may not have a rational basis. With regard to voting, Adams said, many groups were excluded from the franchise, including women, children, and those who were not mentally sound. Some of these exclusions were somewhat arbitrary. He pointed out, for example, that while a twenty-one-year-old man could vote, an equally qualified man who was only "twenty years eleven months and twenty-seven days old" could not. Such norms and distinctions, Adams claimed, were necessary for society to maintain order and prevent chaos. He defended the property qualification because, among other things, it represented a clear and distinct line of demarcation. Those who possessed enough property could vote, and everyone else was excluded; there was no ambiguity. Adams, however, had a bigger fear – a suspicion that revolutionary ideology might produce a larger movement to eradicate distinctions between the social classes. Without property qualifications, he believed, there would be no sound basis for excluding other groups in society from the franchise, including women. The elimination of property qualifications, he said, would "confound and destroy all distinctions, and prostrate all ranks to one common level." Significantly, Adams instinctively grasped what many other people at the time did not: that the rationale for excluding women from government rested on certain agreed-on social conventions rather than any inherent reason. Thus even before women agitated for the vote, Adams

perceived the direction in which revolutionary ideology might lead.[32]

Before the Revolution, questions had seldom arisen about whether women could or should be able to vote. At the same time, although all voters were men, voting itself was not necessarily defined as an exclusively male prerogative. In fact, fewer than half of the colonies – Pennsylvania, Delaware, Georgia, Virginia, and South Carolina – used the word "male" in their election statutes or otherwise specifically excluded women. Women's exclusion may have been regarded as so self-evident that it did not require a specific prohibition. Because of the legal doctrine of coverture, married women, under the guardianship of their husbands, could not own property. Although widows and single women could own property, they constituted just a small fraction of the population. Hence the question of women voting did not often arise. Even so, it is significant that women were not alone in their disfranchisement. Substantial numbers of white males (from 20 percent to 50 percent) and in most colonies all free black males also did not meet the property qualifications and thus were excluded from the franchise. Thus, while it is true that women did not have the right to vote, neither did a lot of men. Class, not sex, represented the primary basis for inclusion or exclusion.[33]

The issue of female suffrage did not receive a great deal of public attention during the War for Independence itself. A few writers, such as James Otis and Thomas Paine, published articles that mentioned the notion of women voting, but they did not take up the issue in a sustained fashioned. In 1790 in the *Massachusetts Magazine*, Judith Sargent Murray published an essay called "On the Equality of the Sexes," which demanded greater educational opportunities for women. She did not, however, address the question of women's political rights. In private letters and discussions, the issue of female suffrage did start to surface. Individuals such as Rachel Wells, and Mary Willing Byrd, and others began to broach the subject in letters to friends, family, and spouses. Hannah Tee Corbin of Virginia, for example, challenged her brother, the revolutionary leader Richard Henry Lee, as to why she, as a taxpaying woman, was not allowed to vote even though she met the state's property qualifications to do so. Having recently asserted the principle of "no taxation without representation" against the British, Lee was put on the defensive. He admitted that neither "wisdom" nor "policy" offered valid reasons "to forbid widows having property from voting." The best he could offer was to point to custom and tradition: it had "never been the practice either here or in England." Though he promised that he "would at any time give my consent to establish their right of voting," the issue went no further.[34]

Today many historians cite Abigail Adams's letter of March 31, 1776, to her husband as a plea for woman suffrage. In this letter Adams reflected on the imminence of independence and contemplated what that meant for the country. She then proposed to John, who was at that time a member of the Continental Congress, that the members of the new assembly "Remember the Ladies" when they prepared a new code of laws for the nation. "Be more generous & favourable to [women] than your ancestors," she said. "Do not put such unlimited power into the hands of the Husbands. Remember all Men would be tyrants if they could." John responded with a combination of patronizing condescension and weak humor. "As to your extraordinary Code of Laws," he said, "I cannot but laugh .... We know better than to repeal our Masculine systems. Altho they are in full Force, you know they are little more than Theory ... . We have only the Name of Masters." If "we give up this," he continued, men "would be completely subject" to the "Despotism of the Peticoat." In fact, despite the playfully defiant tone of her remarks, Abigail probably was not demanding the vote. She was more concerned with married women's lack of property rights and lack of protection against abusive husbands. Moreover, while the letter is well-known today, it was a private missive intended for John's eyes only. Although

Abigail did mention her concerns at the time to her good friend Mercy Otis Warren, her ideas did not reach a larger public audience at the time. Whatever the case, John's reply indicated that he was resistant even to discussing the issue.[35]

Abigail Adams's letter, however, did make an important point: women understood the principles of the American Revolution and could apply them to their own situation. Thus when John Adams received William Sullivan's letter shortly thereafter raising the question of expanding the male franchise he could clearly see the ultimate implications of the proposal. In fact, in his response to Sullivan, Adams admitted that many women were as intelligent and well-informed about politics as some men were. They possessed "as good judgments, and as independent minds, as those men who are wholly destitute of property." Their abilities raised the stakes for abolishing the property qualifier among males. If women had as much wisdom and virtue as men, then on what basis could women be excluded? John Adams wanted to foreclose such possibilities before they ever became real threats. Unlike Abigail's letter to John, the letter to Sullivan did not remain private; it was published in 1792 in a popular Philadelphia magazine.[36] More than most of his contemporaries, Adams understood the fragile assumptions that underlay the social order and gender hierarchy. Ironically, he was uncannily accurate in predicting how the logic of the debate over both universal male suffrage and the female franchise would ultimately unfold.

## New Jersey Exception

At the very time that Adams was ruminating about the dangers of women voting, one state actually experimented with that possibility. In May 1776, anticipating the coming of independence, the Continental Congress sent out instructions ordering each state to devise a new framework for governing. Meeting in convention, the legislature of New Jersey wrote a new state constitution. Describing who would be entitled to vote, the document stipulated that "all inhabitants of this colony of full age, who are worth fifty pounds … shall be entitled to vote for Representatives in Council and Assembly; and also for all other public officers, that shall be elected by the people of the county at large." The use of gender-neutral language – "all inhabitants" – was not in and of itself significant. In fact, only five of the first state constitutions – those of New York, Georgia, South Carolina, Pennsylvania, and Massachusetts – specified that the vote be limited to men, by using the word "male," or inserting a reference to "sons." Since voting had customarily been a male prerogative, there probably was little need to be more specific.[37]

It soon became clear, however, that the New Jersey legislators had more radical intentions. Their initially ambiguous formulation gave way to more unequivocal assertions. Although in 1777 and 1783 the legislature enacted laws regarding election procedures that used only the male pronoun, beginning in 1790 the assembly passed an election statute, pertaining to seven of the thirteen counties in the state, that explicitly enfranchised women. It said, "No Person shall be entitled to Vote in any other Township or precinct, than that in which *he or she* doth actually reside at the time of the Election" (emphasis added). A 1797 law extended these privileges to all qualified women throughout the state. Voters, the law stated, should "openly and in full view deliver *his or her* ballot." Seldom has the use of a single pronoun effected such a radical change in political practices.[38]

In actuality, the New Jersey law applied only to a small proportion of the women in the state. Because married women could not own property, and voting required ownership of a substantial amount of property, widows who had inherited their deceased husbands' estates were the women most likely to vote. Although single women who had never been married could theoretically exercise the franchise, they were less likely to have accumulated enough wealth to meet the property qualification that the constitution required. As a result, female

suffrage in New Jersey never pertained to more than a small proportion of the state's female population. In any given election, it was likely that not more than a few hundred cast ballots. Nonetheless, among those who qualified, women could vote – and did vote – in both state and federal elections for a time.[39]

Due to the lack of documentary records, we do not know why New Jersey legislators were willing, when no other state was, to extend the vote to women. There is no indication that New Jersey women actively demanded the vote. They did not send petitions to the legislature, hold rallies, or mount campaigns on their own behalf. Some historians speculate that Quaker delegates, grounded in their religion's more egalitarian ideas about women, may have been behind the initial efforts to enfranchise women. Other historians argue that by the 1790s partisan Federalists believed that enfranchising women would give them an edge over their Republican opponents. It is true that the 1790 law applied only to the seven southern New Jersey counties, which were heavily populated by Quakers and more politically conservative. By 1797, however, the legislature had expanded the privilege to all qualified women throughout the state.

In fact, New Jersey legislators seem to have given women the vote because they followed their revolutionary beliefs to their logical, if unexpected and untraditional, conclusion. Reviewing the history of female voting in New Jersey, a Trenton newspaper from the time maintained that the assembly had acted "from a principle of justice, deeming it right that every free person who pays a tax should have a vote." If those who paid taxes should be allowed to vote, there was on the face of it no logical reason why taxpaying women should be excluded. Other newspapers confirmed this rationale. Discussing a debate over a proposed election law in 1800, the *Newark Centinel of Freedom* published a letter that reported, "A motion was made to amend the bill by adding that 'it is the true intent and meaning of this act that the inspectors of elections … shall not refuse the vote to any widow or unmarried woman of full age.'" As it turned out, the legislators defeated the motion – not because they objected to women voting but rather because they found it superfluous: "The House unanimously agreed that this section would be clearly within the meaning of the Constitution and as the Constitution is the guide of inspectors it would be entirely useless to insert it in the law." The conclusion seemed obvious: "Our Constitution gives this right to maids or widows, black or white."[40]

Others outside of New Jersey understood the experiment in similar terms – as an extension of revolutionary ideals. "Single Females in the State of New Jersey, possessed of a certain property, and having paid taxes, are entitled to vote at elections," reported a Boston newspaper in 1800. "We understand that at a late election, there were many [who] exercised this privilege." Abigail Adams also was aware of these developments. Discussing a recent election held in her sister's home parish, Adams declared mischievously, "Tell [your friend that] if our State constitution [in Massachusetts] had been equally liberal with that of New Jersey and had admitted the females to vote, I should certainly have exercised it on his behalf." Adams's plea for women had found an unexpected fulfillment in New Jersey's experiment in female suffrage.[41]

The practice remained extremely controversial. Many people at the time believed that female voting degraded the political process, masculinized women, and undermined male authority. Even critics, however, understood the rationale behind the innovation. At a Fourth of July oration at the local Presbyterian church in Morristown, New Jersey, Henry Ford of Morristown remarked, "Our constitution requires a voter to be possessed of 50 pounds. The prevailing theory is that taxation and representation should go together." Yet he believed that the theory had gone too far and said, "Our practice outstrips them both, in its liberality, and makes no invidious exceptions. It admits to the pole people of all sexes, colors, tongues, characters, and conditions. In our unbounded generosity, we would admit to a participation in our choicest rights the lame, and the halt, and the blind [as well as] … the worthless and the penniless; – as motley a group as the day of Pentecost or the pool of Bethesda ever witnessed." Another critic, William Griffith, admitted the legality of the practice: "If we were to be guided by the letter of the charter, it would seem to place [women] on the same footing in this particular [with men] – ." Nonetheless, he insisted that "it is perfectly disgusting to witness the manner in which women are polled at elections. Nothing can be a greater mockery of this invaluable and sacred right, than to suffer it to be exercised by persons, who do not even pretend to any judgment on this subject." Another skeptic concluded, "The petticoat faction's a dangerous thing." Even as they attacked the practice, however, opponents of female suffrage had conceded the validity of the principle.[42]

Whatever their reservations or objections, members of both political parties in New Jersey courted female voters and sought their support for their candidates. Especially in close elections, women might provide the margin of victory for one side or the other. Because only women who owned a substantial amount of property were entitled to vote, women voters, much to the dismay of the Republicans, tended to favor Federalist candidates. Yet neither side in New Jersey ever lost its doubts about the wisdom of enfranchising women. A poem published in 1797 in a Newark newspaper captures the conflicting feelings surrounding the New Jersey experiment. Called "The Freedom of Election," the poem was to be sung to the tune of "The Battle of the Kegs," which suggests its satirical purpose.[43] The opening stanza appears to celebrate New Jersey's liberality for enfranchising women:

> In freedom's cause you gain'd applause,
>   and nobly spurn'd subjection;
> You're now the *Oracle of Laws*,
>   a and *Freedom of Election*!

A subsequent stanza appears to support women's new opportunities and condemn the "narrow-minded" policies that promoted women's subordination. It even suggests that men's freedom was linked with women's liberty:

That tho' we read, in days of yore,
    The woman's occupation,
Was to direct the wheel and loom,
    Not to direct the nation;
This narrow-minded policy
    By us hath met detection;
While woman's bound, men can't be free,
    Nor have a *fair Election.*

Later stanzas, however, disclose the author's true beliefs. The poem portrays an election scene in which women voters "parade" to the poll, "some marching cheek by jole [jowl], sir!" Women voting presented a sight so "strange" and so unnatural that it seemed a *"Milennial* state was near, sir!" There were other problems as well. While the deluded women went off to vote, predatory men subjected the women who stayed behind to their unwanted sexual advances:

While men of rank, who play'd this prank,
    beat up the widows' quarters;
Their hands they laid on every maid,
    And scarce spar'd wives, or daughters!

Allowing women to vote, then, was nothing more than a sexual "prank" played on women by "men of rank." Yet the practice had opened up the possibility of further trouble. Women would not be satisfied merely with the vote; they would soon seek to pursue other male prerogatives:

To Congress, lo! Widows shall go,
    Like metamorphos'd witches!
Cloth'ed in the dignity of state,
    And eke! in coat and breeches!

Women who sought political privileges abandoned their femininity and literally became like men. "Cloth'ed in the dignity of state," they would dress like men, "in coat and breeches." In the process they would become "metamorphos'd witches," repugnant aberrations of their true feminine selves.

The final stanza appears once again to celebrate female suffrage and proclaim the end of men's oppression of women:

Then Freedom hail – thy powers prevail
    O'er prejudice and error
No longer shall man tyrannize
    And rule the world in terror.

Although the poem recognizes women's claims to political equality with men, its hostility is even stronger. The closing lines reveal the poem to be a vicious satire:

Open wide your throats
And welcome in the peaceful scene
Of Government in petticoats!

Female suffrage would be accepted only if it were literally shoved down people's throats.

Continuing ambivalence meant that the female franchise was constantly under attack from one quarter or another. In session after session the New Jersey legislature considered proposals that would abolish female voting. For a time a sufficient number of members rallied, out of either principle or interest, to preserve the experiment, but this would soon end. The precipitating cause was a local election in 1807 in which the voters of Essex County were to decide on a new location for their county courthouse. Citizens of Newark and Elizabeth each hoped that their town would prevail. A courthouse, they believed, would bring business, economic development, and prestige to their locale. On election day boosters on each side beat the bushes to turn out the vote. Voting was heavy. After the votes were counted, Newark claimed victory. Charging fraud and corruption, the citizens of Elizabeth demanded a recount. When they investigated, state officials found that more votes had been cast than the number of legal voters in the county. Observers claimed that men and young boys had dressed up as women in order to cast multiple ballots for their side. "Their dress favouring disguise," reported one commentator, "it is said that some have repeated the vote without detection."[44]

In the ensuing scandal, the legislature voided the election results. Claiming an opportunity to eliminate voter fraud, Federalists and Republicans in the legislature joined together to make a Faustian bargain. Federalists, who had benefited from the women's vote, and Republicans, who had enjoyed the support of free blacks, each agreed to relinquish the votes of the group that the other considered suspect. The assembly passed a law disenfranchising both women and free blacks, the groups that were least well represented and least able to defend themselves. Significantly, there is no evidence that either free blacks or women publicly protested their loss.[45]

Perhaps, given the circumstances, women may have suspected that any kind of public protest would be fruitless. For women, however, voting presented a host of problems that had never been satisfactorily resolved. At the most practical level, it was inconvenient. Women often lived substantial distances from their polling places. Because respectable women did not travel alone, they always needed male family members or friends to accompany them to the polls. The atmosphere at the election site may have also represented a deterrent. It was not uncommon for voting to occur at taverns or other public places. Riotous drinking was typical. Groups of drunken or disorderly men often mulled about outside. Fights, or even riots, were common. Investigating a 1794 election, one congressman noted casually, "If the committee are to break up every election where persons were seen drunk, they will have a great deal of work upon hand." At every stage women would have felt uncomfortable and out of place, subjected to unwanted scrutiny and possible ridicule. Responding to his sister's query about voting rights for widows, Richard Henry Lee noted that while he supported the idea in principle, he "thought [it] rather out of character for women to press into those tumultuous assemblages of men where the business of choosing representatives is conducted." Only the most determined women – or women goaded on by ambitious male politicians – would have braved such obstacles. Many may have been relieved once they no longer had to do so.[46]

There may have been other reasons as well why women did not object to the loss of the vote. It was understood that New Jersey had pioneered female suffrage by extending to women the principle of no taxation without representation. At this time, voting was considered a privilege of private property. In colonial Anglo-America this was the common and widely accepted understanding of the franchise. In fact, north of the border in lower Canada, from 1791 until 1834 unmarried women with property also were allowed to vote.[47] In neither place did women object when their legislatures reversed this decision and withdrew their privilege. Women may have reasoned thusly: because members of the assembly granted women the vote, they also had the authority to take it away. In later decades, once voting came to be seen as a natural right belonging to all people, the consequences of denying the vote to individuals or groups would be much more severe.

Despite the reversal, New Jersey had taken a profound step. Allowing women to vote had made the unimaginable a reality. Women could behave politically in the same ways and on the same terms as men. Perhaps even more important, the New Jersey legislators appear to have acted out of principle. Those in power – white males – understood that if they took their revolutionary ideals seriously, then they must, in the interest of fairness and consistency, allow women to vote. What had started out as a justification for rebelling against Britain ended in a critique of gender inequality.

## Women as Rights Bearers

Citizenship at this time was understood to encompass privileges much broader than simply the ability to vote. With the coming of independence, all free white inhabitants who had been subjects of the Crown, including white women, were presumed to be citizens. Yet the precise meaning of "citizenship" was vague, subject to changing legal and popular definitions. At various times in American history, "citizen" could refer to all inhabitants, all white inhabitants, all legal nonaliens, white male residents, or just to male voters. Significantly, the language in the new United States Constitution tended to be gender-neutral, employing the term "person" rather than "male" or "men." No provision explicitly excluded women from voting or holding federal office. In fact, only in 1868, with the passage of the Fourteenth Amendment, did the Constitution employ the phrase "male citizen" and explicitly exclude women from certain political rights.[48]

It is not clear whether the earlier use of gender-neutral language was deliberate or accidental. Nonetheless, some people at the time believed that at least some provisions of the Constitution were meant to encompass women. In particular, Article I, Section IV describes who should be counted in the census in order to determine the ratio of people to congressional representatives for each state. While it was clear that only three-fifths of the total number of slaves would be represented, white women were to be counted on an equal basis with white men. Explaining the significance of this point to his wife, Sen. Samuel Mitchill of New York noted, "In the theory of our Constitution women are calculated as political beings. They are numbered in the census of inhabitants … and the Representatives are apportioned among the people according to their numbers, reckoning the females as well as the males. Though, therefore, women do not vote, they are nevertheless represented in the national government to their full amount." As part of the enumerated population, women thus were members of the body politic. They were, as Mitchill said, nonvoting "political beings." In

this sense, women were represented "virtually" in much the same way that the North American British colonists were represented in Parliament before the Revolution.[49]

Even if they could not vote, women actually did enjoy many specific rights and liberties. Widows and single women received the same protections for their property as men did. More importantly, to the extent that the Constitution, and especially the Bill of Rights, shifted the focus away from the rights of property owners and toward the rights enjoyed by all human beings, women were included and protected. They could practice their religion freely, assemble to protest governmental actions, and exercise free speech. If accused of a crime, a woman, like a man, had the right to receive a trial by jury – though the jury would be composed exclusively of men. As the president of Harvard College pointed out in 1798, every citizen, female as well as male, enjoyed "the right to life and personal security, … the right to liberty of action, the right to reputation, the right to liberty of opinion, of speech, and of religious profession and worship." If citizenship was understood to encompass rights besides voting, the Constitution did indeed guarantee a broad array of civil liberties to women as well as men.[50]

For women of the early republic, one of the most important of these liberties was the right to petition. Petitioning the legislature represented a crucial means for women, who lacked the vote, to express their political sentiments directly to their legislators. Petitioning was a powerful and time-honored tradition in the Anglo-American political tradition. For centuries women in both England and the colonies had petitioned their colonial assemblies on a variety of matters. After the Revolution, American women, inspired by notions of popular government, seemed to have seized on the petition as a preferred means of expressing their grievances and asking for redress from their legislators. In Massachusetts, as the historian Nancy Cott has shown, the number of women petitioning the legislature for divorce increased at a far greater rate than the population growth would suggest. In North and South Carolina, as Cynthia Kierner has demonstrated, the number of women's petitions increased tenfold in the last quarter of the eighteenth century. These women were often asking for compensation of some sort: restitution of property, military pensions for widows, payment for confiscated land, or requests for husbands' back pay as the result of military service? Women also believed that the new national legislature should be responsive to their needs. Between 1789 and 1820 at least 246 women submitted petitions to the new U.S. Congress. Among these, the vast majority (83 percent) sought compensation for losses or payment of military pensions related to the American Revolution.[51]

Whether or not their petitions were granted, the very fact that women petitioned their governments revealed the extent to which they felt a stake in or a connection with the formal institutions of governance. Their actions implied that women believed that the government was, in some real sense, their own and accountable to them. Janet Spurgin, for example, had a husband who had been a loyalist during the American Revolution. Afterward his property was confiscated and he fled to Britain, leaving his wife and eight children behind in North Carolina. Asserting her status as a loyal American, Janet Spurgin petitioned the North Carolina Assembly in an effort to recoup some of the property. She had, she asserted, "always behaved herself as a good Citizen and well attached to the government" and believed it "extreamly hard to be deprived of the Common rights of Citizens."[52] Like Spurgin, many women saw themselves as good citizens, a part of the government, not apart from it. In subsequent decades women would frequently turn to petitioning as a vehicle of social reform, appealing to the federal government on a variety of moral, social, or religious issues. Long before that time, however, women had begun to use the petition in order to act as "political beings" in their own right.

The acknowledgment of women's civil liberties also implied something even more significant. Women were understood to be autonomous beings who possessed rights. By recognizing that women had rights, the state acknowledged that it also had a responsibility to protect women – not as adjuncts to their husbands or fathers but as separate and distinct individuals. The fuller meaning of this idea became apparent after the publication in 1792 of Mary Wollstonecraft's incendiary tract *A Vindication of the Rights of Woman*. Wollstonecraft was an unlikely revolutionary. A self-educated young woman who traveled in radical literary circles in London, she followed the early years of the French Revolution with great interest and anticipation. When the French proposed a system of national education for men but ignored the education of women, Wollstonecraft penned her treatise. Deliberately echoing the title of Thomas Paine's *Rights of Man,* published the previous year, Wollstonecraft's work exposed the gendered assumptions behind the revolutionaries' thinking. While Paine had argued that all human beings shared certain basic rights, the specific rights he mentioned – the rights to own property, to vote, to participate in government – were, in fact, limited only to men. Typically for his time, Paine did not even consider whether women had rights or what those rights might be.[53]

In contrast, Wollstonecraft explicitly applied the concept of natural rights to women. Given by God, these rights were universal, inherent in the condition of being human, and they applied to all people, regardless of sex. Women's rights were thus irrevocable and undeniable. "If the abstract rights of man will bear discussion and explanation," she insisted, "those of woman, by parity of reasoning, will not shrink from the same test." Yet while only some men had been denied their rights, all women had been excluded from enjoying their rights simply because of their sex. "The *rights* of humanity have been … confined to the male line from Adam downwards." The greatest social inequity, she claimed, did not exist between or among males but between men and women. The result was that half of the population had been kept from realizing its full human potential. "The tyranny of man" and the perpetuation of a "male aristocracy" had oppressed women in all aspects of their lives, retarding the development of their intellect, hindering the growth of their virtue, and preventing them from making a full contribution to society.[54]

Significantly, Wollstonecraft mentioned but did not emphasize the question of women's political rights. She raised the issue of female suffrage only once, and then only briefly and tentatively. "I may excite laughter," she noted, "by dropping a hint, which I mean to pursue at some future time, for I really think that women ought to have representatives." She never took up the issue again. It was more important, she believed, that women gain greater educational and economic opportunities than to participate in what she considered to be a deeply flawed and corrupt political system. The franchise would presumably come in the wake of other gains.[55]

As in Britain, many Americans at first responded favorably to Wollstonecraft's work. Excerpts from *A Vindication* appeared almost immediately in American periodicals and magazines such as the *Ladies Magazine* published in Philadelphia and the *Massachusetts Magazine* published in Boston. By 1795 three American editions of the volume had been issued. A modern study indicates that Wollstonecraft's treatise appeared in more American libraries of the era than Paine's *Rights of Man* did.[56]

Personal scandal, however, soon tarnished her reputation. In 1798, soon after Wollstonecraft's death, her husband, the freethinking radical philosopher William Godwin, published a memoir of his wife. Committed to an unflinchingly honest portrayal, Godwin mentioned details about Wollstonecraft's life that had not been widely known. During the French Revolution, he said, Wollstonecraft had had an affair with an American man, Gilbert Imlay, and gave birth to an illegitimate child. Subsequently she tried to kill herself not once but twice. After taking

up with Godwin, but before they married, she conceived their daughter (who, as Mary Shelley, would later author the classic work *Frankenstein*), whose birth resulted in her death. These actions represented an assault on the conventional Christian morality of the time and provided ample ammunition for Wollstonecraft's critics. Her "licentious practice," railed the minister Samuel Miller, "renders her memory odious to every friend of virtue."[57]

Despite the scandal, Wollstonecraft's tract popularized the notion of women's rights and introduced the phrase into widespread usage. Whereas the American Revolution had raised the question of women's rights indirectly, Wollstonecraft's work raised the issue directly, in a way that could not be avoided. Numerous pieces of poetry, fiction, humor, and prescriptive essays bore the title "The Rights of Woman" or contained allusions to women's rights. Songs were written on the subject. In 1795, for example, several different periodicals published the same piece "Rights of Woman," written by a "Young Lady" of Philadelphia. Sung to the tune of "God Save America," the piece began:

> God save each Female's right,
> Show to her ravish'd fight
>    Woman is Free;
> Let Freedom's voice prevail,
> And draw aside the veil,
> Supreme Effulgence hail,
>    Sweet Liberty.
> The poem continues,
> Let Woman have a share,
> Nor yield to slavish fear.
> Her equal rights declare,
>    And well maintain.[58]

Although the precise meaning of "women's rights" remained ambiguous Wollstonecraft was claimed as "a friend."

In subsequent years the concept of women's rights took on a life of its own. A widespread public debate ensued over what it meant for women to have rights and whether women shared the same rights, including political rights, as men. Occurring outside of formal legal channels, in venues such as novels, essays, periodicals, and public speeches, the phrase became a staple of popular discourse. As early as 1793 Congressman Elias Boudinot could announce, "The Rights of Women are no longer strange sounds to an American ear; they are now heard as familiar terms in every part of the United States." A 1799 article noted that Wollstonecraft's work had "quickly became a staple commodity at the circulating libraries, saw two editions in the year of its publication, was the manual and vademecum of every romantic Miss." An 1818 article declared that "there are to be found, some females who delight to make the 'Vindication' … their text book."[59] Wollstonecraft became the chief symbol and enduring referent for the notion of women's rights in the United States.

So pervasive was Wollstonecraft's influence that even those who opposed her felt obliged to refute her in her own terms. An 1801 essay entitled "A Second Vindication of the Rights of Women" invoked Wollstonecraft – only to reject her central claims. Another adversary, a Maine orator, minced no words. Speaking to the women in his audience, he insisted, "You will not consult a Wollstonecraft for a code of 'The Rights of Women.' Do not usurp the rights of man; they are essentially distinct. Scorn her principles." In 1818 Hannah Mather Crocker, a descendant of the Puritan minister Cotton Mather, published her own refutation, entitled *Observations on the Real Rights of Women, with their Appropriate Duties, agreeable to Scripture, Reason, and Common Sense.* Although highly controversial and deeply contested, the concept of women's rights could no longer be ignored. By the first decade of the nineteenth century, even a hardened Wollstonecraft hater had to admit that her "ingenious vindication of the *Rights of Woman* [was] universally known."[60]

Acknowledging that women had natural rights opened up other possibilities. If women shared in the same constellation of God-given rights as men did, then women were what modern political theorists call "rights bearers." Implicit in this concept was an understanding that women were separate individuals who were distinct from men and who possessed their own rights and responsibilities. They were, in this sense, equal to men. As rights-bearing individuals, women gained the moral authority to demand that the state protect their God-given natural rights from infringement or usurpation. As Wollstonecraft herself pointed out, if men refused to recognize that women had rights, then "by the same rule, their duties vanish, for rights and duties are inseparable." White women, in particular, enjoyed a privileged status. They were unlike slaves, who were considered to be outside the social compact, and they were different from free blacks, whose race was often invoked to disqualify them from possessing the same rights and privileges that white men enjoyed.[61]

Even when the meaning of the phrase "women's rights" was vague or imprecise, it evoked a whole new world of possibility for women. In 1796 Harvard graduate William Boyd devoted his entire commencement address to the subject of "Woman." After hailing women's contributions throughout world history, he pointed out how little women's status had changed over time: "Still lives this truth, by savage man confess'd *Woman belov'd, yet Women the oppres'd.*" Ending his speech with a solemn vow, another commentator concluded, "I shall always be found among the foremost to contribute my feeble efforts to defend THE RIGHTS OF WOMAN." This insight led some commentators to acknowledge men's role in oppressing women. In 1800 the *National Magazine* quoted the English radical Thomas Cooper, declaring, "Let the defenders of male despotism answer (if they can) *The Rights of Woman,* by Miss Wollstonecraft." To Americans, the analogy was clear. Just as England had stifled America's freedom, so men repressed women. "It appears ever to have been the policy of our sex," a Boston man said, "to arrogate to themselves a superiority over the other, and to treat them with all the spirit of a petty tyranny." Acknowledging the fragile basis of male authority, he noted, "We seemed to have claimed a prescriptive right for calling them our inferiors, and we can give no better account of our authority for treating them as such, than that custom has so established it." Although the solution was vague, the problem was now widely acknowledged.[62]

Others found the prospect of women's rights more troubling. Women's assertion of rights might subvert the gender hierarchy and threaten the subordination of women to men. Even the terminology itself seemed to open up dangerous prospects. Discussions of "equality of right," worried "A Lady," might "excit[e] an insurrection in the female world." A man calling himself "Ignotus" agreed: "If once a man raises his wife to an equality with himself, it is all over, and he is doomed to become a subject for life to the most despotic of governments." Nothing, he decided, "was more dangerous to the rights of man [than] when it took possession in *the home department*." Not only would the relations between the sexes be affected, but the whole family structure might suffer as well. A satirical poem called "The Rights of Both Sexes," originally published in England and republished several times in the United States, warned of the possibility of ludicrous role reversals. Men would "reside at the tea-table, regulate the household, and rule the nursery; while all the offices of state and business of commerce should pass into the hands of the ladies." Men might even end up, the poem warned, as a "wet-nurse" to the baby. As each sex took over the other's "employments, amusements, and cares," the whole world would be turned upside down. What was good for women, then, might be bad for men. "These *Rights of Woman*" concluded a Massachusetts newspaper, "would become the *wrongs* of man."[63]

Long before the American Revolution, Enlightenment conjectural histories and the earliest histories of women challenged the notion of women's inherent incapacity and raised the possibility that custom and tradition explained their apparent inferiority to men. Changed circumstances, it was said, would allow women to achieve as much as men could, perhaps even in traditionally masculine arenas such as philosophy, literature, government, and politics. Over the course of the eighteenth century, these ideas elevated women's status and focused public attention on their standing in society. Women, it seemed, might well be men's social and intellectual equals.

The coming of the American Revolution gave these ideas a political salience and created new opportunities for women to participate in politics. Responding to men's appeals, women engaged in a variety of actions in support of the revolutionary cause, which led women to experience a greater sense of connection to and involvement with the polity. After the war their political contributions were praised, celebrated, and remembered. Instead of political ciphers, women now were seen as political beings who had the capacity to influence the course of war, politics, and history.

Even more important, Wollstonecraft's *A Vindication of the Rights of Woman* changed the terms of the debate, suggesting that women shared in the same natural rights enjoyed by men. As rights-bearing individuals, women were independent beings who enjoyed certain rights simply because they were human. Unlike slaves or free blacks, white women were also understood to have the moral authority to demand that the state protect their rights. Wollstonecraft's work appeared when women in New Jersey were actually casting ballots. Ultimately, it was less significant that New Jersey women lost the franchise than that the experiment in female suffrage had been tried. These developments raised the stakes for women immensely. Whereas the Revolution had addressed the question of women's rights obliquely, now the question arose directly, in a way that could not be avoided. Whether they wanted to or not, American men and women had to confront the meaning of their revolutionary principles for women.

## Notes

1. The piece was one installment in a series called "Rights of Women: A Dialogue," originally published in the *Weekly Magazine of Original Essays, Fugitive Pieces, and Interesting Intelligence* 1 (Philadelphia), March 10, 1798; March 17, 1798; March 24, 1798; and April 7, 1798. The quoted section appears in the April 7, 1798, issue. The series constituted parts 1 and 2 of Brown's novel *Alcuin* and was published anonymously that same year as a pamphlet: [Charles Brockden Brown], *Alcuin: A Dialogue* (New York, 1798). Parts 3 and 4, which contained additional material that was even more incendiary than that in the first sections, celebrated the notion of free love and challenged the institution of marriage. These parts were published in 1815, five years after Brown died. Quotations are from a modern edition of the entire novel: Charles Brockden Brown, *Alaun: A Dialogue,* ed. Lee R. Edwards (New York, 1971), 29–30.

2. Judith Sargent Murray, *The Gleaner,* ed. Nina Baym (Schenectady, N.Y., 1992 [orig. pub. 1798]), 705.

3. Lieselotte Steinbrügge, *The Moral Sex: Woman's Nature in the French Enlightenment,* trans. Pamela F. Selwyn (New York, 1995), 10–18; Siep Stuurman, "The Deconstruction of Gender: Seventeenth-Century Feminism and Modern Equality," in *Women, Gender and Enlightenment,* ed. Sarah Knott and Barbara Taylor (Hampshire, 2005), 371–88; Melissa A. Butler, "Early Liberal Roots of Feminism: John Locke and the Attack on Patriarchy," *American Political Science Review* 72 (March 1978): 135–50; Mary Astell, *A Serious Proposal to the Ladies, for the Advancement of their True and Greatest Interest* (1694), in *Women in the Eighteenth Century: Constructions of Femininity,* ed. Vivien Jones (London, 1990), 198–99.

4. D. R. Woolf, "A Feminist Past?: Gender, Genre, and Historical Knowledge," *American Historical Review* 102 (June 1997): 645–79; Philip Hicks, "The Roman Matron in Britain: Female Political Influence and Republican Response, ca. 1750–1800," *Journal of Modern History* 77 (March 2005): 35–69; Sylvana Tomaselli, "Civilization, Patriotism, and Enlightened Histories of Women," in *Women, Gender and Enlightenment,* 117–35; William Alexander, *History of Women, From the Earliest Antiquity, to the Present Time; Giving an Account of Almost Every Interesting Particular Concerning that Sex, Among All Nations, Ancient and Modern* (Philadelphia, 1796), front-page advertisement; John Shirley, *The Illustrious History of Women, or A Compendium of the many virtues that adorn the Fair Sex* (London, 1686); Nahum Tate, *A Present for the Ladies: Being An Historical Account of Several Illustrious Persons of the Female Sex,* 2nd ed. (London, 1693), 1. For a later period in the development of women's history, see Nina Baym, *American Women Writers and the Work of History, 1790–1860* (New Brunswick, N.J., 1995).

5. Woolf, "A Feminist Past?," 645–79; Julia Cherry Spruill, *Women's Life and Work in the Southern Colonies* (New York, 1998 [orig. pub. 1938]), 228n35; Kevin J. Hayes, *A Colonial Woman's Bookshelf* (Knoxville, 1996), 72–73.

6. Antoine-Léonard Thomas, *Essay on the Character, Manners, and Genius of Women in Different Ages,* trans. William Russell, 2 vols. (Philadelphia, 1774); [By a Friend to the Sex], *Sketches of the History, Genius, Disposition, Accomplishments, Employments, Customs and Importance of the Fair Sex in All Parts of the World* (Philadelphia, 1796); *The American Lady's Preceptor,* 9th ed. (Baltimore, 1821), 26.

7. William Alexander, *History of Women,* 2 vols. (London, 1779; 1779; Philadelphia, 1795; Philadelphia, 1796) – subscribers' list is at the end of the 1796 edition; Murray, *Gleaner,* 709–26; Hannah Mather Crocker, *Observations on the Real Rights of Women, with their Appropriate Duties, agreeable to Scripture, Reason and Common Sense* (Boston, 1818), 22–64; Kate Davies, *Catharine Macaulay and Mercy Otis Warren: The Revolutionary Atlantic and the Politics of Gender* (Oxford, 2005), 233.

8. *Literary Magazine & American Register* (Philadelphia), February 1806, 87; ibid., July 1805, 57; *New-York Weekly Museum,* August 8, 1812; *Mrs. A. S. Colvin's Weekly Messenger* (Washington City, D.C.), June 16, 1827, 320.

9. *Weekly Museum* (New York), February 9, 1805; ibid., August 10, 1816; *Port Folio* (Philadelphia), June 22, 1805, 187–88; *Independent Chronicle and the Universal Advertiser* (Boston), March 10, 1800; *New-York Weekly Museum, or Polite Repository of Amusement and Instruction,* March 19. 1816, 291.

10. [Written by a Lady], *The Female Advocate* (New Haven, Conn.: Thomas Green & Son, 1801), 12; Murray, *Gleaner,* 710; *Boston Monthly Magazine* 1 (August 1825), 129.

11. Alexander, *History of Women,* 2:336; *New-York Magazine,* February 1790, 90.

12. Murray, *Gleaner,* 710; *New-York Magazine; or Literary Repository,* February 1790, 90; Miss Laskey, "The Valedictory Oration," May 15, 1793, in *The Rise and Progress of the Young Ladies' Academy of Philadelphia* (Philadelphia, 1794), 98; *Gentleman & Lady's Town & Country Magazine; or, Repository of Instruction and Entertainment* (Boston), December 1784, 339.

13. For further discussion, see Rosemarie Zagarri, "Morals, Manners, and the Republican Mother," *American Quarterly* 44 (June 1992): 192–215; Sylvana Tomaselli, "The Enlightenment Debate on Women," *History Workshop* 20 (Autumn 1985): 101–24.

14. William Robertson, *The History of America* (1777) (Albany: E. Hosford, 1822), 1:255, 257; Henry Home, Lord Kames, *Six Sketches on the History of Man* (abridged version) (Philadelphia, 1776), 195, 228; David Hume, "Of Polygamy and Divorces" (1742), in *Essays and Treatises on Several Subjects* (Edinburgh, 1825), 1:181; John Millar, *The Origin of the Distinction of Ranks; or, An Inquiry into the Circumstances which give Rise to Influence and Authority in the Different Members of Society* (1771), in *John Millar of Glasgow, 1735–1805,* ed. William C. Lehmann (New York, 1979), 225.

15. John Cosens Ogden, *The Female Guide: or, Thoughts on the Education of That Sex; Accommodated to the State of Society, Manners, and Government, in the United States* (Concord, N.H, 1793), 4; Samuel Miller, *A Brief Retrospect of the Eighteenth Century* (New York, 1803), 2:280; *Weekly Museum* (New York), July 2, 1803.

16. James Tilton, M.D., "An Oration pronounced on the 5th July, 1790," *Universal Asylum & Columbian Magazine* 5 (December 1790), 372; James Wilson, "Lecture on the Study of the Law in the United States" (1790), in *The Works of James Wilson,* ed. Robert Green McCloskey (Cambridge: Harvard University Press, 1967), 1:88.

17. Miller, *Brief Retrospect of the Eighteenth Century,* 2:278–79.

18. Hilda L. Smith, *Reason's Disciples: Seventeenth-Century Feminists* (Urbana, 1982), 57; Katherine M. Rogers, *Feminism in Eighteenth-Century England* (Urbana, 1982), 2–20; Hayes, *Colonial Woman's Bookshelf* 67–68; *The Hardship of English Laws in Relation to Wives* (London, 1735), 1–2; *Woman Not inferior to Man: Or, A Short and Modest Vindication of the Natural Right of the Fair-Sex to a Perfect Equality of Power, Dignity, and Esteem, with Men,* 2nd ed. (London, 1740), 55; [By a Lady], *Female Rights vindicated; or The Equality of the Sexes Morally and Physically Proved* (London, 1758), 43, 67. Anna Clark, "Women in Eighteenth-Century British Politics," in *Women, Gender and Enlightenment;* and Arianne Chernock, "Extending the 'Right of Election': Men's Arguments for Women's Political Representation in Late Enlightenment Britain," in ibid., 570–609.

19. Hayes, *Colonial Woman's Bookshelf,* 67, 159n27; *Virginia Gazette* (Williamsburg), October 22, 1736; *South-Carolina Gazette* (Charles Town), August 15, 1743, November 21, 1743; *Columbian Magazine* (Philadelphia), January 1788, 22–27, February 1788, 61–65, March 1788, 126–29, April 1788, 186–89, May 1788, 243–46.

20. *New-York Weekly Journal,* August 19, 1734; Esther Edwards Burr to Sarah Prince Gill, November 29, 1755 (entry for December 20, 1755), in *The Journal of Esther Edwards Burr, 1754–1757,* ed. Laurie Crumpacker and Carol F. Karlsen (New Haven, Conn, 1984).

21. John Adams to Abigail Adams, November 4, 1775, *Adams Family Correspondence* (Cambridge, 1963), 1:320; Mercy Warren to John Adams, September 4, 1775, in *Warren-Adams Letters, Being chiefly a correspondence among John Adams, Samuel Adams, and James Warren* (Boston, 1917), 1:106–7.

22. Linda K. Kerber, *Women of the Republic: Intellect and Ideology in Revolutionary America* (Chapel Hill, 1980); Mary Beth Norton, *Liberty's Daughters: The Revolutionary Experience of American Women, 1750–1800* (Glenview, Ill., 1980); Joan R. Gundersen, *To Be Useful to the World: Women in Revolutionary America, 1740–1790* (New York, 1996), 149–83; Carol Berkin, *Revolutionary Mothers: Women in the Struggle for America's Independence* (New York, 2005), 12–49, 148–61; Alfred F. Young, "The Women of Boston: 'Persons of Consequence' in the Making of the American Revolution, 1765–76," in *Women and Politics in the Age of Democratic Revolution,* ed.

Harriet B. Applewhite and Darline G. Levy (Ann Arbor, 1990), 118–26.

23. Laurel Thatcher Ulrich, *Good Wives: Image and Reality in the Lives of Women in Northern New England, 1650–1750* (New York, 1982), 9; "Narrative of Mrs. Abraham Brasher [Helen Kortright], Giving an Account of Her Experiences during the Revolutionary War" (1802) MS, 24, New York Historical Society, New York City.

24. Abigail Adams to Mercy Warren, August 27, 1775, in *Warren-Adams Letters,* 1:106; Edith B. Gelles, *Portia: The World of Abigail Adams* (Bloomington, 1992), 30–36; Rosemarie Zagarri, *A Woman's Dilemma: Mercy Otis Warren and the American Revolution* (Wheeling, Ill., 1995), 87–88.

25. Mercy Otis Warren to James Warren, March 12, 1780, Mercy Otis Warren Papers, Massachusetts Historical Society, Box 1 (1779); Zagarri, *Woman's Dilemma,* 104–8.

26. Mercy Otis Warren, "To the Hon. J. Winthrop, Esq.," in *Plays and Poems of Mercy Otis Warren,* ed. Benjamin Franklin V (Delmar, N.Y, 1980 [orig. pub. 1790]), 208; Milcah Martha Moore, "Patriotic Poesy," *William & Mary Quarterly,* 3rd ser., 34 (1977): 307; Mary Fish quoted in Joy Day Buel and Richard Buel, *The Way of Duty: A Woman and Her Family in Revolutionary America* (New York, 1984), 129; Esther DeBerdt Reed, "Sentiments of an American Woman" (1780), supplement to *Columbian Magazine* 3 (Philadelphia), September 1789, 760.

27. John Fauchereaud Grimké, *An Oration Delivered in St. Philip's Church, before the Inhabitants of Charleston, South-Carolina, on Saturday, the Fourth of July, 1807* (Charleston, 1807), 17; Keating Lewis Simon, *An Oration delivered in the Independent Circular Church, before the Inhabitants of Charleston, South-Carolina, on Friday, the Fourth of July, 1806* (Charleston, 1806), 6; Reverend Solomon Aiken, *An Oration, Delivered before the Republican Citizens of Newburyport, and its Vicinity, July 4, 1810* (Newburyport, Mass, 1810), 13.

28. Kerber, *Women of the Republic,* 119–21; Norton, *Liberty's Daughters,* 45–50.

29. For contrasting portrayals of the postrevolutionary era, see Gordon S. Wood, *The Radicalism of the American Revolution* (New York, 1991); Gary Nash, *The Unknown American Revolution: The Unruly Birth of Democracy and the Struggle to Create America* (New York, 2005).

30. Bernard Bailyn, *The Origins of American Politics* (New York, 1967), 86–88; Robert J. Dinkin, *Voting in Provincial America: A Study of Elections in the Thirteen Colonies, 1689–1776* (Westport, Conn., 1977), 28–49; Robert J. Dinkin, *Voting in Revolutionary America: A Study of Elections in the Original Thirteen States, 1776–1789* (Westport, Conn., 1982), 27–43; Alexander Keyssar, *The Right to Vote: The Contested History of Democracy in the United States* (New York, 2000), 3–7.

31. Marc W. Kruman, *Between Authority and Liberty: State Constitution Making in Revolutionary America* (Chapel Hill, 1997), 87–108; Keyssar, *Right to Vote,* 8–25.

32. John Adams to James Sullivan, May 26, 1776, in *Works of John Adams, Second President of the United States,* ed. Charles Francis Adams (Boston, 1854), 9:375–78.

33. Chilton Williamson. *American Suffrage from Property to Democracy, 1760–1860* (Princeton, N.J., 1960), 181; Richard R. Beeman. *The Varieties of Political Experience in Eighteenth-Century America* (Philadelphia, 2004), 293–94; John G. Kolp and Terri L. Snyder, "Women and the Political Culture of Eighteenth-Century Virginia," in *The Many Legalities of Early America,* ed. Christopher L. Tomlins and Bruce H. Mann (Chapel Hill, 2001), 275–76. Even so, there were a few isolated reports that unmarried women with property' may have cast ballots in the colonial period. See Robert J. Dinkin, *Before Equal Suffrage: Women in Partisan Politics from Colonial Times to 1920* (Westport, Conn., 1995), 8–9.

34. [Thomas Paine], "An Occasional Letter on the Female Sex" (1775), in *The Complete Writings of Thomas Paine,* ed. Philip S. Foner (New York, 1945), 1:34–38; James Otis, "The Rights of the British Colonies Asserted and Proved" (1764), in *The Debate on the American Revolution, 1761–1783,* ed. Max Beloff, 3rd ed. (New York, 1949). 48–52; Judith Sargent Murray, "On the Equality of the Sexes," in *Judith Sargent Murray: A Brief Biography with Documents,* ed. Sheila Skemp (Boston, 1998), 176–82; Richard Henry Lee to Mrs. Hannah Corbin, March 17, 1778, in *Letters of Richard Henry Lee,* ed. James Curtis Ballagh (New York, 1911), 1:392–93.

35. Abigail Adams to John Adams, March 31, 1776, in *Adams Family Correspondence,* 1:370; John Adams to Abigail Adams, April 14, 1776, in ibid.,

1:382; Zagarri, *Woman's Dilemma*, 91–92; Gelles, *Portia*, 47–49.

36. "Copy of an Original Letter from Mr. John Adams, to a Gentleman in Massachusetts," *Universal Asylum & Columbian Magazine* (Philadelphia), April 1792, 219–22.

37. Constitution of New Jersey – 1776, in *The Federal and State Constitutions, Colonial Charters, and Other Organic Laws of the States, Territories and Colonies Now or Heretofore Forming the United States of America* (Washington, D.C., 1909), 5:2595; William Smith, *A Comparative View of the Constitutions of the Several States with Each Other, and with that of the United States* (Philadelphia, 1796; Washington, D.C., 1832); Keyssar, *Right to Vote*, 29–52, 55–56, Table A. 1, 328–29.

38. Although some historians claim that women's enfranchisement in New Jersey was an accidental oversight, more careful students of the episode confirm the deliberate nature of the legislature's actions, at least by the 1790s. Prior election laws in 1777 and 1783 used only the male pronoun. In the 1790 and 1797 laws, the phrase "he and she" was used. See "Election Law of 1790," in *Acts of the 15th New Jersey General Assembly, Nov. 18, 1790*, 670; and "An Act to Regulate an election of members of the legislative council and general assembly, sheriffs, and coroners, in this State," in *Laws of New Jersey, 1797*, for the precise wording. See also Judith Apter Klinghoffer and Lois Elkis, "The Petticoat Electors': Women's Suffrage in New Jersey, 1776–1807," *Journal of the Early Republic* 12 (Summer 1992): 159–93; Edward Raymond Turner, "Women's Suffrage in New Jersey: 1790–1807," *Smith College Studies in History* 1 (July 1916): 156–87; Kruman, *Between Authority and Liberty*, 191n85; Carl Prince, *New Jersey's Jeffersonian Republicans: The Genesis of an Early Party Machine, 1789–1817* (Chapel Hill, 1964), 134n7; Irwin N. Gertzog, "Female Suffrage in New Jersey, 1790–1907," in *Women, Politics, and the Constitution*, ed. Naomi B. Lynn (New York, 1990), 47–58.

39. It is difficult to get accurate estimates of how many women actually voted. A poll list from Burlington in 1787 lists two women voters; see Henry C. Shinn, "An Early New Jersey Poll List," *Pennsylvania Magazine of History and Biography* 44 (January 1920): 77–81. To my knowledge, other poll lists have not been systematically examined for women voters. Other evidence

is impressionistic. The *Centinel of Freedom* (Newark) of October 18, 1797, states, "no less than seventy-five women were *polled* at the late election in a neighboring borough." Presumably, more women voted throughout the entire state. The *Boston Independent Chronicle* of October 27, 1800, reporting on "female electors" in New Jersey, simply claimed that at the last election "there were many [who] exercised this privilege."

40. *Trenton True American* (New Jersey), October 18, 1802; *Centinel of Freedom* (Newark), November 7, 11, 1800; Neale McGoldrick and Margaret Crocco, *Reclaiming Lost Ground: The Struggle for Woman Suffrage in New Jersey* (Trenton, 1994), 2–5.

41. *Independent Chronicle* (Boston), October 27, 1800; Abigail Adams to Mary Cranch, November 15, 1797, in *The New Letters of Abigail Adams*, ed. Stewart Mitchell (Boston, 1947), 112.

42. Henry Ford, *An Oration, Delivered in the Presbyterian Church at Morris-Town, July 4, 1806* (Morris-Town, N.J., 1806), 11; William Griffith, *Eumenes: Being a Collection of Papers written for the Purpose of Exhibiting Some of the More Prominent Errors and Omissions of the Constitution of New-Jersey* (Trenton, N.J., 1799), 33; *Centinel of Freedom* (Newark, N.J.), October 18, 1797.

43. *Centinel of Freedom* (Newark, N.J.), October 18, 1797.

44. John Lambert, *Travels throughout Canada, and the United States of North America, in the Years 1806, 1807 & 1808*, 2nd ed. (London: C. Cradock and W. Joy, 1813), 2:315.

45. Edward Raymond Turner, "Women's Suffrage in New Jersey: 1790–1807," in *Smith College Studies in History* 1, ed. John S. Bassett and Sidney B. Fay (July 1916): 165–87; Klinghoffer and Elkis, "Petticoat Electors," 186–91; Gertzog, "Female Suffrage in New Jersey," in *Women, Politics, and the Constitution*, 47–58.

46. "Conducting an Election in Virginia: The Contested Election of Congressman Francis Preston, 1793," in *The Early Republic, 1789–1828*, ed. Noble E. Cunningham, Jr. (New York, 1968), 214; Lambert, *Travels throughout Canada, and the U.S.*, 2:314; Richard Henry Lee to Mrs. Hannah Corbin. March 17, 1778, in *Letters of Richard Henry Lee*, 1:392–93.

47. Allan Greer, *The Patriots and the People: The Rebellion of 1837 in Rural Lower Canada* (Toronto, 1993), 203–10.

48. Linda K. Kerber, "'Ourselves and Our Daughters Forever': Women and the Constitution, 1787–1876," in *One Woman, One Vote: Rediscovering the Woman Suffrage Movement,* ed. Marjorie Spruill Wheeler (Troutdale, Oreg., 1995), 21–36; James H. Kettner, *The Development of American Citizenship, 1608–1870* (Chapel Hill, 1978), 287–88; Rogers M. Smith, *Civic Ideals: Conflicting Visions of Citizenship in U.S. History* (New Haven. Conn., 1997), 115–36; Linda K. Kerber, *No Constitutional Right to Be Ladies: Women and the Obligations of Citizenship* (New York, 1998), 36–37, 128–36.

49. Samuel L. Mitchill to Catharine Mitchill, December 8, 1804, Mitchill Papers, Library of Congress.

50. John Thornton Kirkland, *An Oration, Delivered at the Request of the Society of Phi Beta Kappa, in the Chapel of Harvard College, on the Day of their Anniversary, July 19, 1798* (Boston, 1798), 10: Jan Lewis, "'Of Every Age Sex & Condition': The Representation of Women in the Constitution," *Journal of the Early Republic* 15 (fall 1995): 382n76.

51. Nancy Cott, "Divorce and the Changing Status of Women in Eighteenth-Century Massachusetts," *William and Mary Quarterly,* 3rd ser., 33 (October 1976): 586–614; Cynthia A. Kierner, ed., *Southern Women in Revolution, 1776–1800: Personal and Political Narratives* (Columbia, S.C., 1998), xix–xxviii, 231–32: Ruth Bogin, "Petitioning and the New Moral Economy of Post-Revolutionary America," *William and Mary Quarterly,* 3rd ser. (1 July 1988): 391–425; Alison G. Olson, "Eighteenth-Century Colonial Legislatures and Their Constituents," *Journal of American History* 79 (September 1992): 557–59; Linda Burch, "1789–1820: The Republican Mother Exercises Her Right to Petition," unpublished research paper, George Mason University, May 2, 1997; Kerber, *Women of the Republic,* 93–99.

52. Petition of Janet Spurgin to the North Carolina Assembly, November 28, 1791 in *Southern Women in Revolution.* 180–81; Cynthia A. Kierner, *Beyond the Household: Women's Place in the Early South, 1700–1835* (Ithaca, N.Y., 1998), 124–29.

53. Mary Wollstonecraft, *A Vindication of the Rights of Woman,* ed. M. Brody (London: Penguin Books, 1975 [orig. pub. 1792]); Thomas Paine, *Rights of Man, Common Sense, and Other Political Writings* (Oxford, 1995 [orig. pub. 1791–92]). Useful interpretations of Wollstonecraft include Barbara Taylor, *Mary Wollstonecraft and the Feminist Imagination* (Cambridge, 2003); Mary Poovey, *The Proper Lady and the Woman Writer: Ideology as Style in the Works of Mary Wollstonecraft, Mary Shelley, and Jane Austen* (Chicago, 1984); Virginia Sapiro, *A Vindication of Political Virtue: The Political Theory of Mary Wollstonecraft* (Chicago, 1992); Garry Kelly, *Revolutionary Feminism: The Mind and Career of Mary Wollstonecraft* (New York, 1992).

54. Wollstonecraft, *Vindication,* 87, 88, 188, 326.

55. Ibid., 265.

56. *New-York Magazine, or Literary Repository* (February 1793), 77. For early excerpts from *A Vindication,* see *Ladies Magazine* (Philadelphia), September 1792, 189–98; and *Massachusetts Magazine* (Boston), October 1792, 598–99. See also Marcelle Thiébaux, "Mary Wollstonecraft in Federalist America, 1791–1802," in *The Evidence of the Imagination: Studies of Interactions between Life and Art in English Romantic Literature,* ed. D. H. Reiman, M. C. Jave, and B. T. Bennett (New York, 1978), 195–235; R. M. Janes, "On the Reception of Mary Wollstonecraft's *A Vindication of the Rights of Woman,*" *Journal of the History of Ideas* 39 (1978): 293–302; David Lundberg and Henry F. May, "The Enlightened Reader in America," *American Quarterly* 28 (summer 1976): 262–71 and graphs following.

57. Miller, *Brief Retrospect of the Eighteenth Century,* 2:284. On Wollstonecraft's changing reputation, see William St. Clair, *The Godwins and the Shelleys: The Biography of a Family* (New York, 1989); Chandos Michael Brown, "Mary Wollstonecraft, or, The Female Illuminati: The Campaign against Women and 'Modern Philosophy' in the Early Republic," *Journal of the Early Republic* 15 (1995): 389–424; Patricia Jewell McAlexander, "The Creation of the American Eve: The Cultural Dialogue on the Nature and Role of Women in Late Eighteenth-Century America," *Early American Literature* 9 (1975): 262–64.

58. *Weekly Museum* (New York), April 15, 1795; reprinted in *Philadelphia Minerva,* October 1795.

59. Elias Boudinot, *An Oration Delivered at Elizabeth-Town, New-Jersey, Agreeably to a Resolution of the State Society of Cincinnati on the Fourth of July DCCXCIII* (Elizabethtown, N.J., 1793), 24; *Weekly Magazine of Original Essays, Fugitive Pieces, and Interesting Intelligence* 4 (April 13, 1799): 19; *Philadelphia Magazine, or Weekly Repository of Polite Literature,* May 2, 1818, 89.

60. *Ladies' Monitor* (New York), August 10, 15, 1801, 19–20; Jeremiah Perley, *An Anniversary Oration, Delivered before the Federal Republicans of Hallowell and Its Vicinity* (Augusta, Me., 1807), 23; Crocker, *Observations on the Real Rights of Women;* Miller, *Brief Retrospect of the Eighteenth Century,* 2:284.

61. Wollstonecraft, *Vindication,* 328. On "rights bearers," see Mary Ann Glendon, *Rights Talk: The Impoverishment of Political Discourse* (New York, 1991); Richard Tuck, *Natural Rights Theories: Their Origin and Development* (Cambridge, 1979); Knud Haakonssen, "From Natural Law to the Rights of Man: A European Perspective on American Debates," in *A Culture of Rights: The Bill of Rights in Philosophy, Politics, and Law – 1791 and 1991,* ed. Michael J. Lacey and Knud Haakonssen (Cambridge, 1991); Thomas L. Haskell, "The Curious Persistence of Rights Talk in the 'Age of Interpretation,'" in *The Constitution and American Life,* ed. David Thelen (Ithaca, N.Y., 1988), 324–52; Daniel T. Rodgers, *Contested Truths: Keywords in American Politics Since Independence* (New York, 1987).

62. *National Magazine, or, A Political, Historical, Biographical, and Literary Repository* 2 (1800): 206; William Boyd, *Woman: A Poem, Delivered at a Public Exhibition, April 19, at Harvard University; in the College Chapel* (Boston, 1796), 13; *Columbian Phenix and Boston Review* (May 1800): 267; *Philadelphia Repository, and Weekly Register,* May 21, 1803, 165.

63. *New-York Weekly Museum, or Polite Repository,* March 2, 1816, 276; *Philadelphia Repository and Weekly Register,* March 14, 1801, 5; *Mercury and New-England Palladium* (Boston), September 15, 1801. Originally from a London publication, "The Rights of Both Sexes" was published numerous times in the United States, including in *Lady's Monitor* (New York), October 31, 1801, 88; *Mercury and New-England Palladium* (Boston), August 17, 1802; *Weekly Visitor, or. Ladies' Miscellany* (New York), October 16, 1802, 12; and *Weekly Magazine* (New York), April 13, 1799, 19. Multiple reprintings of the same article, which occurred frequently at this time, indicate how ideas about women's rights were circulated and spread throughout the transatlantic world. Although I have found several printings of many articles that I cite, I do not list every source, unless it helps substantiate a particular point.

# 19

# FROM SLAVES, CONVICTS, AND SERVANTS TO FREE PASSENGERS

*The Transformation of Immigration in the Era of the American Revolution*

## Aaron S. Fogleman

### Introduction

As with the other authors in this part, Aaron S. Fogleman explores the question of just how revolutionary the American Revolution was. In the realm of migration, at least, his answer is very revolutionary. Fogleman shows that nearly three-fourths of all immigrants to the thirteen mainland British American colonies between the founding of Jamestown in 1607 and the outbreak of the American Revolutionary War in 1775 arrived as slaves, servants, convicts, or in some other unfree status. The typical migrant in the colonial era was not a free passenger in control of his or her fate, but a person who was bound to someone else for a period of years or, in the case of slaves, for life.

Migration patterns shifted dramatically after 1776. In the generation after independence, the percentage of free immigrants expanded from one-fourth to almost two-thirds of the total number. By 1820, free immigrants made up more than 90 percent of the total. Why did the character of migration reverse so completely after the Revolution? Fogleman offers several reasons. The Revolutionary War disrupted trade and migration networks, in some cases permanently. Ideology also played a role. The new American citizenry's commitment to social equality contributed to a growing distaste for white servitude and black slavery, especially in the northern states. Yet, tragically, the shift to free migration did not translate immediately to freedom on the ground for African slaves in the southern states. The decision by the United States to close its participation in the transatlantic slave trade in 1808 without abolishing slavery itself meant that, while immigration to America became overwhelmingly free for the first time, millions of its inhabitants would still live in a condition of bondage.

- How did migration patterns during the colonial era help to create and reinforce a hierarchical social order?
- Fogleman acknowledges that it is difficult to pinpoint all the exact reasons for the shift in migration after American independence. Is it possible the change was due to a coincidence in timing? How might historians test such a proposition?
- Fogleman argues vigorously that enslaved Africans should be included in measures of immigration to America. How does including slavery change the overall character of immigration? In what ways did blacks and whites have similar migration patterns? Consider the example of gradual emancipation in the north discussed in Ira Berlin's essay. How was gradual emancipation related to changing migrating patterns during the revolutionary era?

For the first two centuries of the history of British North America, one word best characterizes the status of the vast majority of immigrants – servitude. From the founding of Jamestown until the Revolution, nearly three-fourths of all immigrants to the thirteen colonies arrived in some condition of unfreedom. (See Tables 19.1 and 19.2.) These migrations of slaves, convicts, and servants played a critical role in the demographic, economic, social, and cultural development of the colonies. When they came (or were brought) in large numbers, these strangers often caused a sensation in colonial society. Yet at a time when servitude was considered "normal," few were concerned that their arrival in America meant a temporary or permanent loss of freedom for most of them.[1]

On the eve of the Revolution, these new servant immigrants contributed to a complex world of the free and the unfree, occupying different conditions of liberty and bondage, some tied to masters for brief periods, others viewed as criminal outcasts rightly condemned to forced labor, and many more branded by race and doomed to servitude for life, with no rights of their own. All were interwoven into what Gordon S. Wood has called a "hierarchy of ranks and degrees of dependency" that was simultaneously a pluralistic world of peoples from Europe, Africa, and the Americas.[2] Before

*Table 19.1* Estimated Immigration into the Thirteen Colonies and the United States by Legal Status and Condition of Servitude, 1607–1819 (to the nearest 100 Immigrants)

|  | Unfree by Condition of Servitude | | | | |
|  | *Slaves* | *Convicts and Prisoners*[a] | *Indentured Servants* | *Free* | *Total* |
|---|---|---|---|---|---|
| *Before the American Revolution* | | | | | |
| 1607–1699 | 33,200 | 2,300 | 96,600 | 66,300 | 198,400 |
| 1700–1775 | 278,400 | 52,200 | 103,600 | 151,600 | 585,800 |
| *During and after the American Revolution* | | | | | |
| 1776–1809 | 114,600 | 1,000 | 18,300 | 253,900 | 387,800 |
| 1810–1819 | 7,000 | 0 | 5,300 | 134,300 | 146,600 |
| Total Immigration, 1607–1819 | 433,200 | 55,500 | 223,800 | 606,700 | 1,318,600 |

Note: Adjustments were made for rounding errors.
a Includes political exiles and kidnapping victims.

*Table 19.2* Estimated Immigration into the Thirteen Colonies and the United States, by Legal Status and Condition of Servitude, 1607–1819 (in Percentages)

|  | Unfree by Condition of Servitude | | | | |
|  | *Slaves* | *Convicts and Prisoners*[a] | *Indentured Servants* | *Free* | *Total Percentage* |
|---|---|---|---|---|---|
| *Before the American Revolution* | | | | | |
| 1607–1699 | 17 | 1 | 49 | 33 | 100 |
| 1700–1775 | 47 | 9 | 18 | 26 | 100 |
| *During and after the American Revolution* | | | | | |
| 1776–1809 | 30 | 0 | 5 | 65 | 100 |
| 1810–1819 | 5 | 0 | 4 | 91 | 100 |
| Total immigration, 1607–1819 | 33 | 4 | 17 | 46 | 100 |

Note: Adjustments were made for rounding errors.
a Includes political exiles and kidnapping victims.

1776, for most arrivals, coming to America meant a curtailment of freedom. The literary and historical image of America as the land of unlimited opportunity or as a "best poor man's country" hardly resonates with the realities of servitude for most of the strangers who completed the journey in the colonial period.

But in the late eighteenth and early nineteenth centuries, something fundamentally and permanently altered the nature of North American immigration. When war and independence came after 1775, disruptions in the British Empire forced many involved in the immigrant trade on both sides of the Atlantic Ocean to reconsider how they would do business. Further, many Americans concluded that a large immigration of slaves, convicts, and servants was incompatible with the egalitarian ideas of the Revolution and with the cultural changes occurring in the United States. These developments transformed an immigration primarily of slaves, convicts, and indentured servants into one of free subjects. By the 1820s, when the United States government began keeping official statistics, the transformation was already so complete that it obscured the changes that had occurred before, during, and after the Revolution.

The fundamental transformation in the nature of early American immigration is important for many reasons. First, it reveals significant unfreedom during the early chapters of the "immigrant" story and thus the complicated, changing interaction of freedom, unfreedom, and immigration in American history. Second, a study of this transformation addresses the important question: How (if at all) did the Revolution impact ordinary people in American society? Did the Revolution fundamentally alter the outlook for "freedom" for most Americans? By assessing the extent to which the American Revolution caused a transformation in immigration, study of this little-known aspect of the immigrant story may help answer larger questions about continuity and change in the revolutionary era and about America itself.

## Immigration and Servitude during the Colonial Period

Since the founding of English colonies in the seventeenth century, immigrants – people who came from somewhere else – have shaped and reshaped society and culture in North America. In the first century of settlement, most colonies south of New England depended on large-scale immigration from the English provinces to maintain their populations and allow economic growth. Without such immigration they would have collapsed. Nearly 150,000 English immigrants arrived before 1700, providing labor, markets, and settlers to the developing "immigrant societies" there. They may have brought with them their regional folkways, which in turn shaped the varied cultural development of the colonies.[3]

Not all seventeenth-century immigrants were English, of course. Many other European and African arrivals began to establish the ethnic diversity that became the hallmark of American society. Over 6,000 Dutch, perhaps 5,000 Irish, and smaller numbers of Scots, French, and others had settled on the mainland by 1700. African slave importations did not reach numerically significant levels until after 1680. Indeed, in that year less than 5 percent of the English colonial population on the mainland was of African origin and fewer than 10,000 slaves had been imported. By the end of the century, however, forced African immigration had made a significant impact on the population, culture, and economies of the southern colonies.[4]

In the seventeenth century, servitude played an important role in the immigration of both Africans and Europeans to all the English colonies in North America. In addition to African slaves imported into the colonies, approximately one-half of the European immigrants of this period may have arrived as servants. Some convicts and other prisoners were forced to go to America, where they were sold as indentured servants. They included many Scots banished by Oliver Cromwell for their activities during the English Civil War, the Scottish Covenanters who resisted English rule, and criminals. Irish prisoners taken from 1651 to 1654, English Quakers in the 1660s, and some kidnapping victims were transported involuntarily to the colonies and sold as servants. Some personal servants followed their masters to the colonies. But the majority of unfree arrivals were voluntary migrants who chose America to seek economic improvement and could not afford the costs. Perhaps 70 to 85 percent of the immigrants to colonies on the Chesapeake Bay before 1700 were indentured servants, as were about 16 percent of participants in the Great Migration to New England in the 1630s. Some of the New England immigrants became servants because they were poor, but others were not and allowed their children to become indentured servants as a form of apprenticeship. Perhaps nearly one-half of the Dutch immigrants to New Netherland came as servants. Some signed contracts with the Dutch West India Company or the city of Amsterdam, which were the least restrictive. These immigrants agreed to stay for three years and to repay the advances they had received. Other contracts, for example, those used at the Rensselaerswyck settlement, restricted the immigrants' freedoms more significantly. They were required to remain in the patronship, or domain, for three to four years and to work at a specific job, for which they received a yearly salary, room, and board. Some worked as servants and others as independent producers. Smaller enterprises and private masters also used contracts of this type. None of the contracts used in the colony was negotiable. In short, the majority of seventeenth-century European immigrants to the English North American colonies temporarily forfeited much of their freedom in exchange for passage and employment in America.[5]

Many historians have characterized indentured servitude as a harsh system that mistreated immigrants; however, this view needs to be modified. The system provided opportunities for improvement to many who voluntarily chose to make a go of it in the New World. For many, the system was comparable to servitude and apprenticeship in England. The terms of service were longer in America, and the labor was generally more arduous, but the incentives via freedom dues were greater than in Britain, and those ex-servants who set up as small planters probably did better than if they had stayed at home. In fact, when falling real wages and bad harvests in mid-seventeenth-century England made the overseas option more attractive, and when indenturing oneself to pay transportation costs was the only way to cross the Atlantic, then the indentured servant system actually offered opportunities. Moreover, until about 1660 the chances were high that a young man who completed an indenture in the Chesapeake could achieve a comfortable position in society.[6]

Although indentured servitude offered opportunity to some struggling European migrants, opportunities were even greater for those who traveled as free passengers. In the seventeenth century this included most of the New England and French Huguenot settlers and a small portion of the Chesapeake settlers. Free immigrants came from socially diverse backgrounds, but in general they were of a higher social status than indentured servants. Some came from the lower end of the English social system and were barely distinguishable from the servants, while others came from the middle ranks. The latter included small merchants, petty retailers, craftsmen, and men with modest sums to invest in small-scale merchandising or perhaps a tobacco plantation. Still others were part of the elite – merchants, gentry, and government officials. The free immigrants left for many reasons, but economic improvement was the most common. Some (in both New England and the Chesapeake) combined desire for profit with religious motives for migrating or fled England to escape debt or other trouble. The Huguenots left France because of religious persecution, but many of them chose to go to America only after sojourning in London and deciding that economic opportunities might be better in the colonies. Some who went to the Chesapeake intended to remain there only one or two years, while others intended to stay for good. Kinship networks were important in encouraging and helping maintain migrations and in forging links with the major mercantile centers, especially London.[7]

In the late seventeenth century, the preponderance of immigration to the English colonies in America shifted dramatically from servants and free passengers to slaves. Many historians have emphasized that the planters in the English Caribbean colonies relied on indentured servant labor in the early decades of settlement. Most servants were young English males leaving deteriorating conditions at home. By the late seventeenth century, however, conditions for workers began improving in England, and few wanted to emigrate to America. As prices for lifetime slave workers became competitive with those for short-term servants, planters shifted to the use of African slaves to meet their labor demands. Thus the immigration of indentured servants declined beginning in the late seventeenth century, while that of African slaves increased rapidly.[8]

The shift from servants to slaves occurred later on the mainland than in the Caribbean; the crucial transition occurred between 1680 and 1720. Before 1680 fewer than 10,000 African slaves were imported into the English mainland colonies, while well over 100,000 Europeans settled there, most of whom were servants. From 1680 to 1720, however, over 50,000 slaves were imported into the mainland, and the total number of European immigrants (servants and free passengers) decreased significantly. The transition was most pronounced in the Chesapeake colonies and in South Carolina, where opportunities for new planters in the tobacco market, South Carolina planters' importation of slaves skilled in rice production, and improving conditions for workers in England caused the shift. In 1680 the combined colonial population of Virginia and Maryland was only

7 percent black; in South Carolina it was only 17 percent black. By 1720 the respective figures were 25 percent and 70 percent. Immigration and society in the southern colonies had been transformed, just as they had been in the Caribbean.[9]

The transition from servants to slaves in the late seventeenth century has led many historians to postulate an inverse relationship between the two types of migrations. Not only did large-scale slave importations dominate migrations and labor markets in the late seventeenth and eighteenth centuries but the demise of slavery in the Caribbean during the nineteenth century also revived indentured servitude there. In other words, when indentured servant immigrations were high, slave importations were low, and vice versa. Some historians have modified the model to fit the mainland, emphasizing the gradual decline of indentured servitude there in the eighteenth century, but the perception of an inverse relationship between servant and slave migrations to the mainland is still common.[10]

Yet a model that posits an inverse relationship works for the mainland colonies only during the first century of European settlement. Although the immigration of indentured servants clearly declined after 1680 – just as slave importations increased significantly – the decline was only temporary. After 1720 the immigration of slaves and servants (including convicts) increased to record levels. This corroborates the view that the shift from servants to slaves occurred only in the Caribbean. The mainland colonies still needed both forms of labor, and although improving economic conditions at home meant a decline in the servant pool from England, new supplies came from Germany and Ireland. Indeed, in the half century before independence, indentured servitude, which languished in the French and English Caribbean colonies and in Canada, flourished in the thirteen colonies and played a crucial role in the immigration of tens of thousands of Europeans who helped transform the ethnic, cultural landscape of British North America.[11]

The increase of slave and servant migrations to the thirteen colonies in the eighteenth century was part of an increase in all forms of migration. The volume of eighteenth-century immigration became so large that by midcentury, people born elsewhere may have constituted a larger percentage of the American population than they did later, when the absolute number of immigrants peaked. The percentage of foreign-born inhabitants in the colonial population may have been *increasing* throughout the eighteenth century, after having earlier declined from the skewed levels of early settlement. The demand for labor and settlers became so extreme that record numbers of African slaves, British convicts, indentured servants, and free passengers were imported. Indeed, in the generation before independence, the mechanisms and markets for transporting all four groups flourished in British North America.[12]

The large volume of eighteenth-century migrations to the thirteen colonies has been overlooked by historians who have neglected to consider the African slaves. In the 1970s Peter H. Wood and C. Vann Woodward lamented the exclusion of African slaves from the ranks of "immigrants." They attributed it to racism and the tendency of immigration historians to begin their studies in the nineteenth century, as African immigration into the United States was ending. Too often historians have used the European model to explain immigration and the immigrant story in American history – whatever does not fit that model may not be understood as immigration. In my view, however, immigrants were people who came from somewhere else to the mainland colonies or the United States (as opposed to having been born there). The immigrant story critical to the demographic, economic, and cultural development of the United States is an ongoing, complex, and changing tale that enlists a cast of characters from nearly all parts of the globe. In the past generation that view has become more accepted, as historians have given increasing attention to slaves in the colonial period as

forced African immigrants. But a comprehensive study of immigration into British North America and the United States that includes Africans and takes into account their varied ethnic backgrounds is still lacking, even though the number of slaves imported may have equaled or surpassed that of European immigrants in the eighteenth century.[13]

From 1700 to independence, nearly 300,000 slaves were imported into the thirteen colonies, and they were crucial to the transformation of the economic and social systems in the Tidewater South. As African immigration increased and the slave system expanded, conditions for the new arrivals and their descendants worsened. Slave codes began evolving in the Chesapeake as early as the mid-seventeenth century, and more followed in the eighteenth century. Planters used the codes to help control the black population by restricting their mobility and other legal rights, including the right to hold property. In South Carolina, the shift to rice production in the late seventeenth and early eighteenth centuries led to the large-scale importation of slaves. The large African immigration created a black majority in the colony that heightened anxieties among whites, who responded by strengthening the legal codes to control the slave population. This and the rising mortality resulting from the switch to staple agriculture severely deteriorated conditions for South Carolina slaves. In Georgia slavery was not legal until the mid-eighteenth century, but the colony's Low Country planters quickly caught on and created a slave society that resembled South Carolina's. By the mid-eighteenth century, the number of free blacks in the southern colonies had declined, while the slaves toiled in far harsher working conditions than any other workers endured as they confronted increasingly hierarchical, patriarchal, and racist societies.[14]

Indentured servitude too flourished in the eighteenth century, although it underwent many important changes. Perhaps more than 100,000 of the new arrivals from 1700 to 1775 were indentured servants, and this figure does not include the many convicts, who were often sold as servants. While the number of English servants migrating to the thirteen colonies declined from the high levels of the seventeenth century, these losses were more than offset by the large numbers of non-English servants who came, especially Germans and Irish.[15]

In the 1720s a new form of servitude, the "redemptioner" system, developed among German-speaking immigrants. Philadelphia merchants in the immigrant trade found that Pennsylvania-based relatives, friends, and former fellow villagers of poor immigrants were often willing to redeem their fare costs. The merchants in Philadelphia and Rotterdam (the port of embarkation for most German emigrants) developed a sophisticated system in which immigrants signed contracts in Rotterdam stating how much time they had to get in touch with people in Pennsylvania who might pay their passage. If they did not raise the money within that time, the new arrivals, or redemptioners, were auctioned as indentured servants. In the redemptioner system, the length and terms of service were negotiable, while the prices for servants (that is, passage costs) were fixed. In contrast, the common practice in the English and Irish trade since the early seventeenth century had been to fix the length of servitude, then negotiate the price for servants.[16]

There has been much debate about the conditions immigrant servants endured. Historians have recently corrected earlier views that focused on worst-case scenarios and emphasized the horrors of the servant trade. For example, English servants were fewer and more skilled in the eighteenth than in the seventeenth century, and so they enjoyed better conditions than their predecessors. Some immigrants even used servitude as a "safety net" or apprenticeship to ensure that they would not plunge immediately into poverty upon arrival in America. In other words, they ensured employment and support in America by signing an indenture before departing. This allowed them to save what means they had taken with them and learn the customs

of the country at another's expense. After their period of service they would better know how to invest their money and would have the benefit of their freedom dues. Some immigrant families indentured their children, sparing themselves full passage costs for the entire family and ensuring that someone else paid to raise the children and perhaps to teach them skills during the first, costly years of settlement in America. Parents in Europe and colonial America often apprenticed their children and for similar reasons. In short, according to recent accounts, indentured servitude was a largely successful economic enterprise that helped meet the high demand for labor in the colonies and helped many poorer immigrants establish themselves in America.[17]

While many immigrant servants benefited from the system, many others did not. Indeed, indentured servitude was rarely advertised as one of the attractions America offered. The conditions of immigrant servitude in British North America were generally worse than white servitude in the French colonies or in England. French immigrant servants sometimes received a salary and return passage. A one-year term of service was typical in England and three years in the French colonies, whereas four-year contracts were normal for adult immigrants in the English colonies. Some had to endure beatings (which were not usually allowed in England) and excessive extensions of service as punishment for running away. Further, in the English colonies indentured servants were bought and sold much more frequently than English servants or apprentices. For German indentured servants and redemptioners the worst conditions of overcrowded ships and abusive agents were confined to a few years, 1738, 1749–1754, 1764, and 1773. But well over one-half of all Germans who immigrated through Philadelphia in the colonial period arrived in those years.[18]

Conditions for servants may have improved in the early eighteenth century, but they worsened in the generation before independence. In Philadelphia, the chief port of entry for European immigrants in the eighteenth century, laborers enjoyed generally favorable living and working conditions into the 1740s, but their situation deteriorated badly in the next thirty years. Tens of thousands of Irish and German immigrant servants plunged into this environment. Overcrowded ships and exploitative agents led to some of the worst abuses of the colonial period among voluntary immigrants, and many servants ran away. The Seven Years' War abruptly halted most German immigration, and when it resumed after 1763 conditions were better, but the percentage of passengers who were indentured servants or redemptioners actually increased. At the same time, opportunities for acquiring land declined, and it grew more difficult for freed servants to succeed in the mid-eighteenth-century economy.[19]

An important source reveals the attitudes of the immigrants themselves toward indentured servitude: the letters they wrote home. Although the authors of such letters often exaggerated their successes in order to impress their families and former neighbors, their comments about immigrant servitude are less biased than the propaganda for or against emigration that appeared in public pamphlets, decrees, newspapers, and other printed sources. Letters home written by Scottish immigrants in the 1770s offer mixed evidence, but even one of the most positive assessments suggested that indentured servitude was an obstacle, not a stepping-stone, toward prosperity in America. In 1772 John Campbell, who had recently settled in Maryland, encouraged others to follow him even "at the expense of a few years of servitude," but only if they were still young. Those who were older would find work in a system that ranked them as slaves too oppressive. Baikia Harvey, an indentured servant who had settled near Augusta, Georgia, wrote home in 1775 that he had run away from a cruel master. Although his situation improved when a kind merchant bought his contract, he still felt that it was intolerable. He recommended that none of his relatives come to America unless they could pay their passage. Only then did a poor man have a chance to earn a good living.[20]

The theme of hopeful prospects in America if one avoided servitude also resounded in letters written home by German-speaking immigrants. In their letters from Pennsylvania, many narrated glowing success stories, but they also warned that it was getting harder to make it in America and that one should avoid indentured servitude if at all possible. A Swiss immigrant who arrived in Philadelphia in 1750 could not pay his debts and had to serve "the worst master in all of Pennsylvania" for three years. His fortunes did not improve until, after fourteen months, two friends discovered his plight and purchased him from his master. This immigrant despised Pennsylvania and told others to stay home in Switzerland. Johann Georg Rüdel, who came from Schwaigern (in the northern Kraichgau – an area in modern Baden-Württemberg), was able to purchase land deep in the backcountry of Pennsylvania and avoid servitude. Yet in a letter home written in 1750, Rüdel condemned the system and told others not to come to America. The voyage was too difficult and land too hard to find. Poorer immigrants who could not pay their debts upon arrival did not have a chance in the colony. They were sold and had to work at hard labor for four to ten years.[21]

The tale of Maria Barbara Kober, also of Schwaigern, illustrates how devastating the experience of German redemptioners could be. Kober told her story years later in a letter to her brother. In May 1738, just three months after Kober's marriage to a twenty-four-year-old weaver, Elias Beringer, she and her husband left for Philadelphia with their newborn son and twenty-eight others from Schwaigern. Their son died on the way from Rotterdam to Cowes, England, the major stopover point for Germans emigrating to North America. After a difficult transatlantic voyage lasting sixteen weeks, the group landed in Philadelphia on October 30, 1738. Kober and her husband were redemptioners. For three weeks they wandered the streets of Philadelphia, searching for some opportunity to meet their financial obligations and get started in Pennsylvania. Having no luck,

Kober, on the advice of her husband, indentured herself for four years to some "English" who lived about twenty-six miles from Philadelphia. She left her husband on the ship. Four years later, after working off her debts, Kober returned to Philadelphia to look for him. But she found neither her husband nor any prospects for a better life in Philadelphia, and so she returned to her former master and acquaintances. There she lived and worked for twenty-three more years, never knowing that her husband had died in Philadelphia shortly after she had left him.[22]

The personal experiences of these immigrants suggest that indentured servitude, in spite of the opportunities it offered to poorer migrants, was to be avoided if possible. The statements of such immigrants as John Campbell and Johann Georg Rüdel, who were fortunate enough to avoid servitude yet close enough to observe it and describe it, and the narratives of those who actually endured this status, such as Baikia Harvey, the Swiss immigrant, and Maria Barbara Kober, provide a generally negative image of servitude in late colonial America. Time and time again, the people who were unfree servants condemned the system and warned others to find another way. Free immigrants generally had more opportunities.[23]

Many European servant immigrants in the eighteenth century were transported involuntarily, including kidnapping victims, political exiles, and convicts. Kidnapping cases often received publicity, but the number of such victims forced to go to America was relatively small. The number of political exiles was larger. After the rebellions of 1715 and 1745 in Scotland, nearly 2,000 Jacobites settled in the colonies, most as involuntary exiles. Some went to the West Indies, but the majority settled on the mainland. But by far the largest group of involuntary immigrants from Europe were the convicts. A. Roger Ekirch estimates that Britain banished about 50,000 criminals to North America from 1718 to 1775. Indeed, well over one-half of all English and over one-tenth of all Irish immigrants from 1718 to 1775

were convicts. The number of British convicts arriving in the colonies during the eighteenth century was so large that they did much to replace indentured servants as a source of bound labor from England. Most were sent to Tidewater Maryland and Virginia. Sentenced to seven or fourteen years service in the colonies and transported in chains below deck, this large, peculiar group of "immigrants" constituted an important, though often unwanted, part of the labor force.[24]

Living and working conditions for the convicts worsened in the eighteenth century. After sentencing, British authorities marched groups of convicts through the streets in chains to the ships. Because they made the long voyage to America below deck in cramped quarters, their death rate was high (about 14 percent). Upon their arrival, colonial authorities led them to the auction block – still in chains. (Contemporaries likened these events to livestock auctions.) The majority were probably employed as field workers on plantations. Although convicts received more favorable legal treatment than slaves – their condition was temporary, and they could petition courts for relief from excessive abuse – they steadily lost rights during the eighteenth century. The material conditions under which the convicts lived and labored may not have differed much from those of slaves. Americans treated the convicts as outcasts with little stake in society. In the Chesapeake, where most were sent, they occupied a visible place in society between slaves and white servants – outside the growing racial unity among white planters and servants.[25]

About one-fourth of all immigrants to the thirteen colonies in the eighteenth century arrived as free passengers. The vast majority of these were not English, as they had been in the seventeenth century, but rather German speakers, Irish, and Scots. They came voluntarily and paid for their passage, incurring no contractual obligations or debts that required service in repayment. Upon arrival, assuming they were well enough, they were free to seek employment or land wherever they might find it. That is, they were free to fend for themselves in a competitive labor market where work and wages were often uncertain and land was becoming scarce and more expensive. But for most, freedom was a better choice than servitude, as their own commentaries make clear.

By 1760 the immigrants – slaves, convicts, indentured servants of all sorts, and free passengers – had become quite visible as part of a colonial world characterized by a hierarchy of ranks and degrees of dependency. Slavery flourished in the colonies, challenged only by the Quakers and a few others, and convicts arrived in record numbers. Both the English and the Americans considered indentured labor (including that of apprentices and of adults who bound themselves out in exchange for a lump sum) as a normal form of voluntary labor. Indeed, until the eighteenth century, most labor in England and the colonies was bound, and workers were normally referred to as "servants."[26]

The extent to which immigration directly created the hierarchy of ranks and degrees of dependency varied from region to region. In the eighteenth century, immigration had the least impact on society in New England. There were German, Scots-Irish, and other European settlers in the region, and even some African slave importations, but together they represented only a small portion of either the total New England population or the total number of European and African immigrants arriving in the thirteen colonies. Farther south this was not the case.

Traditionally, historians have emphasized ethnic diversity in the middle colonies, especially southeastern Pennsylvania. Indeed, Philadelphia was the major entrepôt for free and indentured European immigrants in the eighteenth century, and for many convicts and slaves. In 1748 Peter Kalm, a Swedish naturalist touring the colonies, described the effects of the ongoing, ethnically diverse immigration into Pennsylvania society. He carefully delineated many of the degrees of servitude, describing laborers free to serve

by the year (who could leave whenever they wished but forfeited their wages if they did so), indentured servants, and slaves. By 1760 many Scottish, Irish, German, and other immigrants had settled in southeastern Pennsylvania and spread into the northern Chesapeake and the southern backcountry as far south as North Carolina.[27]

Immigration, ethnic diversity, and servitude transformed colonial society in South Carolina as well in the eighteenth century. The forced immigration of many different African ethnic groups after 1680 permanently transformed the colony's Low Country and created a black majority by 1720. Further, many Scots-Irish, Germans, and other Europeans – servant and free – began settling in Charleston and in the backcountry of the colony in the mid-eighteenth century. Indeed, one could argue that South Carolina, more than Pennsylvania, was the center of ethnic diversity in colonial North America.[28]

In the Chesapeake region, immigration in the eighteenth century meant the significant expansion not only of settlement by free people but also of all forms of servitude – that of slaves, convicts, and indentured servants. By 1760 the population of Maryland and Virginia had increased more than eightfold and was 38 percent black – virtually all of the blacks being slaves. In addition, some 40,000 convicts (80 percent of the total sent to America) were transported to Maryland and Virginia, especially to Tidewater areas on the Western Shore, where they labored at the center of the growing commercial economy. In 1755 nearly 10 percent of the white population in Maryland were servants or convicts. In the same year in Baltimore, Charles, Queen Annes, and Anne Arundel counties on Maryland's Western Shore, 12 percent of productive adult laborers (a category defined as those working for others and excluding slaves too young or infirm to work) were convicts, 22 percent were hired and indentured servants, and 66 percent were slaves. Moreover, in the eighteenth century many free and indentured Europeans immigrated directly to Chesapeake ports such as Baltimore, which grew rapidly and developed a close economic relationship with southeastern Pennsylvania. Many European immigrants from Pennsylvania also spilled across the blurred boundary with the Chesapeake.[29]

But the changing immigration patterns and the resulting transformation in Chesapeake society during the eighteenth century went beyond percentages discernible only by historians studying population figures centuries later: As in Pennsylvania, the effects of the "new" immigration were *visible* to observers at the time. A French traveler in Virginia in 1765 touched upon every one of the immigrant groups, servant and free. He wrote that "the number of Convicts and Indented servants imported to virginia [is] amazing, besides the numbers of Dutch and Germans which is also Considerable." Shortly thereafter he commented on seeing three slaves hanging from the gallows in Williamsburg. A travel journal kept in 1747 by two Moravian missionaries on a preaching tour in the Chesapeake reveals the effects of the new immigration in a hierarchical society. Here, where the heaviest influx of bound immigrants of all categories occurred, the missionaries reported to the authorities whenever they entered a new county and received a pass before attempting to preach. This was done for their own protection – otherwise local people might believe that the two white strangers passing through their community were runaway servants or convicts. Indeed, on the Western Shore of Maryland a man accosted the two Moravians and attempted to take them into custody, but they escaped. Convicts and indentured servants were so omnipresent in these areas that even white strangers passing through had to be on their guard lest they be regarded as unfree – and thus outside the law and dangerous. Richard S. Dunn describes the formation of this society, writing that from the 1680s to the 1750s the Chesapeake tobacco planters created an "elaborately tiered social and economic hierarchy with slave laborers at the base, convict and indentured servants ranked next, then tenant farmers, then small landholders,

then middling planters, and a handful of large planters – one to five in each county." I would argue that immigration in the eighteenth century contributed significantly to this development and that the hierarchical immigration itself closely resembled the society that evolved.[30]

This predominantly servant immigration into the British North American colonies, part of a trend in migrations to all the Americas during the early modern period, was a complex and changing one. In the seventeenth century, servant immigration from England meant opportunity for many, but in the eighteenth century, it normally reflected the forced migration of convicts in chains. Many Irish, Scots, and Germans found opportunity as servants in the the half-century before independence, but a significant number of one group, the Irish, were also convicts, and all of them faced generally worsening conditions. Free immigrants too often had a rough go of it, but in the rapidly growing colonial economies and societies of the eighteenth century, free immigrants controlled their own labor and had a much better chance of making it than indentured servants and convicts.

Thus immigration played a critical role not only in population growth in early America but also in the development of hierarchical social and economic relationships there. The forced transportation of slaves and convicts in the eighteenth century created new dimensions in an immigration and a society already characterized by servitude. In the decades before the Revolution, immigration reached record levels, and it became more identified with servitude. In the revolutionary era, however, this trend would quickly change.

## The Transformation to a Free Immigration in the Revolutionary Era

When war broke out between Britain and the thirteen colonies in the spring of 1775, immigration of all kinds suddenly ended. When it resumed in the 1780s, it took on a different character. Free immigrants, not slaves, convicts, and servants, dominated the ranks of strangers entering the new republic. Whereas in the decades before the Revolution free immigrants made up only about one-fourth of all immigrants, during the thirty-five years after independence, free passengers made up nearly two-thirds of the total. And from 1810 to 1819, after the importation of African slaves was banned, free immigrants made up more than 90 percent of the total. (See Table 19.2.)

Why did this happen, and why did it happen when it did? For nearly two centuries most immigrants arrived in British North America in some condition of unfreedom, and the colonists considered this normal. Yet in the late eighteenth and early nineteenth centuries, the trend suddenly reversed. After 1808 few immigrants were servants or slaves, and by 1820 immigrants in servitude were numerically insignificant. The character of American immigration had permanently changed.

The most important factor causing this transformation in immigration into North America was the American Revolution, which involved war, forced removals of populations, disruptions in trade of all kinds, egalitarian ideas and impulses, new constitutions, independence, and the political maneuverings that typically accompany such upheavals. The war that broke out in 1775 disrupted the transatlantic British Empire. Long-standing trade and credit networks were destroyed. Many merchants on both sides of the Atlantic Ocean, who had provided essential links between Europe, Africa, and America, suffered tremendous losses or went bankrupt. At the conclusion of the war, the merchants who survived could not simply return to business as usual – they were now former enemies in two different countries. These events also directly affected immigration to North America, which had been closely associated with overseas trade and credit throughout the colonial period. For example, when the war temporarily ended immigration and most trade, the Scottish mercantile community, especially

in Glasgow, switched from a heavy emphasis on trade in Virginia tobacco to West Indian sugar and cotton. This led to increased immigration of Scots to the Caribbean. Moreover, the Revolution affected trade in other transatlantic empires, as the war disrupted not only the British but also the French slave trade.[31]

The politics and ideas of the Revolution influenced immigration most clearly in the case of the African slaves, who were nearly one-half of all immigrants from 1700 to 1775. The egalitarian impulses of the Revolution led many to challenge the renewal of African slave importations after the war, and the ensuing debate at the Constitutional Convention of 1787 in Philadelphia led to a compromise that forbade Congress to prohibit slave importations prior to 1808. The compromise at Philadelphia did not reflect a general conversion in white Americans' attitudes toward slaves and slavery. The southern delegates at the convention knew that the abolition of the Atlantic trade would not directly threaten the institution of slavery, since the slave populations in the South (unlike those in Latin America) had well-established positive natural growth rates by the late eighteenth century. Carolina planters did not press harder for more slaves because they had not yet discovered how to gin cotton. Forced African immigration soared during the 1780s, 1790s, and 1800s as planters sought to replace their losses during the war and to improve their holdings before the 1808 deadline. Pennsylvanians who freed their slaves frequently, if not generally, put them into very long-term indentures. Thus for many northern black people, indentured servitude began rather than ended after 1775. And while Europeans began pouring into the United States in the nineteenth century, freed of servile restrictions, many white Americans debated how to get rid of the unwanted free black population by shipping its members back to Africa. Although relatively few went to Africa, a second forced migration did occur: Nearly one-third of a million slaves were transported overland from the Chesapeake, the Carolinas, and Georgia to the southwest territories between 1790 and 1820. Another three-quarters of a million were forced to migrate from 1820 to 1860. Given the less than revolutionary, indeed inegalitarian, attitudes held by the majority of whites, slave imports boomed after the war. It was only the constitutional ban – caused by the "Revolution" – that cut them off after 1808. The events of the American Revolution, then, all but ended the critical role that slave importations had played in colonial immigration.[32]

The demise of the British convict trade shows how American independence per se led to a decline in servant migrations to the new republic. The war threw the British criminal justice system into chaos. When immigration resumed in the mid-1780s, the British tried to send convicts disguised as indentured servants to the former colonies (and sometimes they succeeded). The American authorities quickly caught on to the practice, however, and ended it. Thus American independence forced the British to redirect convict transportations to their new colony in Australia.[33]

The American Revolution, broadly understood, led not only to the decline of the slave and convict trades, but also to the demise of the indentured servant migrations. Gordon Wood argues that acceptance of indentured servitude began to erode shortly before independence. "Everywhere ordinary people were no longer willing to play their accustomed roles in the hierarchy," and as a sequel to the "revolutionary attack on patriarchal monarchy," "servitude of any sort (for white males) suddenly became anomalous and anachronistic." Roben J. Steinfeld emphasizes social and cultural change. The American Revolution, he argues, had no sudden, direct impact on indentured servitude, but it advanced processes that made the system seem abnormal. After the Revolution, Americans repudiated traditional hierarchical forms of subordination (at least for white males). As they began to perceive all forms of bound labor as involuntary rather than voluntary servitude, they began to take steps to end them.[34]

The decline of apprenticeship after the Revolution also reflects this gradual ideological change. The absence of guilds in colonial America had meant that anyone could get started in a craft, become a journeyman, and hire apprentices. It had also meant that apprentices could easily walk out on their obligations, as Benjamin Franklin did when he left Boston. Franklin's *Autobiography* describes a runaway apprentice who made good, and thus his widely read work contributed to the decline of the institution. The Revolutionary War also undermined apprenticeship. The British occupations of Boston, New York, and Philadelphia, along with the action of many young men who went off to war, led to soaring labor demand. Some apprentices began running off, while others demanded journeymen's wages. Colonial traditions of apprenticeship required stability, yet the war disrupted life in the cities and raised questions about such traditions. The economic fluctuations of the postwar period led to a reluctance on the part of masters and apprentices to commit themselves to long-term contracts. Moreover, after the Revolution the authority of masters to manage apprentices came under increasing challenge. The masters had to contend with a generation of apprentices who, "having absorbed Revolutionary rhetoric, spouted claims to liberty and equality." Relations between masters and apprentices became strained, and runaways increased. The masters cracked down in the courts, but eventually the courts began favoring the apprentices – the law could not save the master's authority, and there was no social pressure to do so. Thus attitudes toward bound white labor in all forms were changing during the revolutionary era, as Americans came to reject it.[35]

The egalitarian ideology of the Revolution stimulated some direct attacks on indentured servitude, but the effects of ideology should not be exaggerated. Thomas Jefferson's second draft of the Virginia constitution in 1776 opposed all forms of servitude, including indentured servitude. In 1784 a group of New Yorkers protested the arrival of a shipload of servants because the "traffick of White People" was contrary to "the idea of liberty this country has so happily established." Yet during this time at least one founding father had no qualms about keeping white servants. In 1784 George Washington tried to buy skilled immigrant servants in Philadelphia and Baltimore. In short, just because Jefferson and a few conscience-stricken New Yorkers decided that placing white male immigrants in a servant status was a bad idea, it does not follow that this caused the immediate end of the practice.[36]

It is likely that the Revolution had some long, slow impact on the decline of indentured servitude, but one should not overemphasize the ambiguous gradualism of this important event in transatlantic history. In the early 1770s the system flourished. Nearly one-half of English and Scottish emigrants to America in the London register of 1773 to 1775, an official list of persons leaving for the colonies, were servants, and more than one-half of German arrivals in Philadelphia in 1772 were servants. The system remained important for German immigration until 1820, but Germans made up less than 10 percent of all voluntary immigrants during the period. Bar the other 90-plus percent of voluntary immigrants, primarily the Irish, Scots, and English, the system had all but ended before 1800. The longevity of indentured servitude among the Germans was an exception that may obscure the timing of and the reasons for the decline of the institution throughout the new republic.[37]

The rapid demise of the immigrant servant system in the 1780s and 1790s among all but the Germans suggests that the American Revolution, broadly understood to include not just ideology and politics but also the impact of the war and independence on the British Empire, may have been a direct cause of the change. The breakup of a significant portion of the British Empire – one of the many effects of the American Revolution – changed migration,

trade, and credit patterns for the English, Scots, and Irish. After 1783 all those involved in the immigrant trade, as well as the immigrants themselves, had to reevaluate whether and how they would participate in the new migrations. Irish immigration increased dramatically after the war, but the servant trade declined because British ship captains no longer believed that American courts would enforce contracts. According to Maurice Bric, independence redefined the "Atlantic umbrella under which people moved between the old and new worlds" and led to reorganization of the Irish passenger trade and change in the composition and nature of the immigration. When immigration resumed after 1783, it included many indentured servants, but the institution's days were numbered. Irish newspapers emphasized its cruelties and reported that the United States Congress was planning to forbid it. By 1789, according to one report, few Irish servants were arriving in Philadelphia. Others reported that so many Irish who were coming could pay for their passage that ship captains no longer needed to take on those who could not pay. In short, independence led to an altered perception of America by the Irish, which led to a different kind of immigration, no longer dependent on indentured servitude.[38]

The disruptions of war and independence certainly played a critical role in the sudden decline of the British and Irish servant trades in the 1780s and 1790s, but were other factors, notably conditions in Europe, more important? The outbreak of the French Revolution did lead to a new wave of free immigrants to the United States in the 1790s. For the first time since the late seventeenth century, there was a significant number of French immigrants. In the late eighteenth and early nineteenth centuries, nearly 13,000 free French immigrants came, thus contributing to the transformation in early American immigration. But the French immigration represents less than 3 percent of European immigration and less than 2 percent of total immigration from 1776 to 1809.

(See Table 19.1.)[39] The only other significant Continental immigrants were the German speakers, and indentured servitude in the United States continued for them, in spite of the French Revolution. Similarly, the impact of the industrial revolution in Britain should not be exaggerated. Most British immigrants came from Ireland and Scotland, where the effects of industrialization were less significant than in England at this early date. Further, the decline of indentured servitude in the British immigrations (including the Irish) occurred so quickly that it is difficult to explain it by industrialization. In short, conditions in Europe did little to cause the transformation in American immigration that is reflected in Tables 19.1 and 19.2.

Clearly we must look to conditions in the United States, especially to the American Revolution, to explain not only the rapid decline in indentured servitude but also the entire shift from an immigration characterized by degrees of servitude to one characterized by freedom. The war, independence, and the ideas of the Revolution had a tremendous impact on the transatlantic British Empire; in this context indentured servitude all but disappeared. From 1607 to 1699, almost one-half of all immigrants were indentured servants, and from 1700 to 1775, when record numbers of immigrants arrived, about three-fourths of all immigrants (including those from Europe and Africa) were slaves, indentured servants, redemptioners, or convicts. But in the generation after the war, less than 5 percent of immigrants were indentured servants and by the 1810s less than 4 percent. The indentured system, which had appeared a normal form of voluntary labor to most Americans before the Revolution, which had helped 200,000 Europeans make it to America the hard way – sometimes the only way – came to a relatively sudden end after the Revolution. Together with the abolition of slave imports and the end of convict transportations, the demise of indentured servitude ensured that formal, legal servitude would never again characterize American immigration.

# The Significance of the Transformation for American History

This study deals with the relationship between two of the most important factors in American history: the American Revolution and immigration. Since the guns of the Revolution fell silent and its leaders ceased to pronounce its lofty declarations, historians of each generation have asked the crucial questions: Did the Revolution really make a difference in the lives of ordinary people? Did permanent, significant change in American history result from the political, military, ideological, and other upheavals of that era? The debate over those large questions will surely continue, but the evidence presented here suggests that in the context of immigration, the Revolution certainly did make a difference.

Since the beginning (and until this very day), immigrants have shaped and reshaped American history and culture. The old seventeenth-century pattern of an inverse relationship between the demand for indentured servants and the demand for slaves was replaced in the eighteenth century by a strong demand for all kinds of servant and free immigrants. After the Revolution yet another trend developed – Americans no longer wanted overseas immigrants unless they were free. The Revolution had transformed immigration and hence transformed how immigration would continue changing America in the future. Much of the saga of American immigration as it is known to us today could not have come about without the transformation from a largely unfree to a free immigration. Discovering the meaning and limitations of that freedom became part of the immigrant story, but we should not let that story, so well known to us, obscure what was once there.

The significance of the transformation of immigration in the era of the Revolution even transcends the borders of the United States. The shift in North American immigration patterns was part of larger contemporaneous changes in transatlantic migrations. In addition to the United States, many other countries banned the slave trade in the early nineteenth century. But when the legal slave trade ended in the Caribbean, the slave population began to decline. West Indian planters relied in part on the revival of indentured servitude and the illegal slave trade (much larger and more important in Latin America than in the United States) to replace their lost labor supply. In the nineteenth century, slaves, convicts, and indentured servants still crossed the Atlantic in large numbers, but no longer to the United States. Even Chinese immigrants, who were an important part of the indentured servant population in the Caribbean, came to the United States in the mid-nineteenth century voluntarily as free laborers. Thus while unfree people (indentured servants, smuggled slaves, and convicts) were transported to the Caribbean and Australia, immigration into the United States remained one almost exclusively of free passengers, and the migration of millions of Europeans to the United States that followed dominated transatlantic migrations for over a century.[40]

Within the borders of the United States, as many Americans began preaching equality and arguing over its meaning, the people entering that society – many of whom ultimately contributed to the debate and the changing immigrant saga – were more free and equal than immigrants had ever been in American history. Slavery was extended and promoted by different kinds of migrations in the new republic, but transatlantic immigration was no longer one of its sources. Other forms of hierarchy and dependency continued to flourish in the United States, but after a long history before the Revolution, formal, legal servitude in all its forms permanently disappeared as a characteristic of American immigration.

## Notes

Aaron S. Fogleman is associate professor of history at the University of South Alabama.

I would like to thank the members of the International Seminar on the History of the Atlantic World, 1500–1800, at Harvard University (1996) for their comments on an earlier draft of this paper, especially Rosalind Beiler, Maurice Bric, Jon Butler, Willem Klooster, Jennifer Morgan, Bertrand Van Ruymbeke, Claudia Schnurmann, and Bernard Bailyn. I would also like to thank Stephen Behrendt, David Eltis, Stanley Engerman, and the readers for the *Journal of American History,* who made invaluable comments on the revised draft.

1  For summations of recent literature on transatlantic migrations to early America, see P. C. Emmer, ed., *Colonialism and Migration: Indentured Labor before and after Slavery* (Dordrecht, 1986); Susan E. Klepp, ed. *The Demographic History of the Philadelphia Region, 1600–1860* (Philadelphia, 1989); Bernard Bailyn and Philip D. Morgan, eds., *Strangers within the Realm: Cultural Margins of the First British Empire* (Chapel Hill, 1991); Ida Altman and James Horn, eds. *"To Make America": European Emigration in the Early Modem Period* (Berkeley, 1991); and Nicholas Canny, ed., *Europeans on the Move: Studies on European Migration, 1500–1800* (Oxford, Eng., 1994).

2  Gordon S. Wood, *The Radicalism of the American Revolution* (New York, 1992), 3–8, esp. 6.

3  On the transfer of regional folkways, see David Hackett Fischer, *Albion's Seed: Four British Folkways in America* (New York, 1989).

4  In 1680 only 7% of the population in the South was black. By 1700 the figure had risen to 21%. See U.S. Bureau of the Census, *Historical Statistics of the United States, Colonial Times to 1970,* vol. II (Washington, 1975), 1168.

5  David Dobson, *Scottish Emigration to Colonial America, 1607–1785* (Athens, Ga., 1994), 1–80; Abbot Emerson Smith, *Colonists in Bondage: White Servitude and Convict Labor in America, 1607–1776* (Chapel Hill, 1947), 89–203; David Cressy, *Coming Over: Migration and Communication between England and New England in the Seventeenth Century* (Cambridge, Eng., 1987), 52–63; James Horn, "'To Parts beyond the Seas': Free Emigration to the Chesapeake in the Seventeenth Century," in *"To Make America,"* ed. Alunan and Horn, 85–103, esp. 91; Virginia DeJohn Anderson, *New England's Generation: The Great Migration and the Formation of Society and Culture in the Seventeenth Century*

(Cambridge, Eng., 1991), 24–26, 108–12; Richard S. Dunn, "Servants and Slaves: The Recruitment and Employment of Labor," in *Colonial British America: Essays in the New History of the Early Modem Era,* ed. Jack P. Greene and J. R. Pole (Baltimore, 1984), 157–94, esp. 159; Ernst van den Boogaart, "The Servant Migration to New Netherland, 1624–1664," in *Colonialism and Migration,* ed. Emmer, 55–82, esp. 59–65.

6 See, for example, Dunn, "Servants and Slaves," 157–94; and Russell R. Menard, "British Migration to the Chesapeake Colonies in the Seventeenth Century," in *Colonial Chesapeake Society,* ed. Lois Green Carr, Philip D. Morgan, and Jean B. Russo (Chapel Hill, 1988), 99–132, esp. 103–17.

7 Horn, "'To Parts beyond the Seas,'" 85–103; Cressy, *Coming Over,* 37–73; Jon Butler, *The Huguenots in America: A Refugee People in New World Society* (Cambridge, Mass., 1983), 41–67.

8 Edmund S. Morgan, *American Slavery, American Freedom: The Ordeal of Colonial Virginia* (New York, 1975); Russell R. Menard, "From Servants to Slaves: The Transformation of the Chesapeake Labor System," *Southern Studies,* 16 (1977), 355–90; Russell R. Menard, "Migration, Ethnicity, and the Rise of an Atlantic Economy: The Re-Peopling of British America, 1600–1790," in *A Century of European Migrations, 1830–1930,* ed. Rudolph J. Vecoli and Suzanne M. Sinke (Urbana, 1991), 58–77; David Galenson, *White Servitude in Colonial America: An Economic Analysis* (Cambridge, Eng., 1981), 141–68; David Eltis, "Free and Coerced Transatlantic Migrations: Some Comparisons," *American Historical Review,* 88 (April 1983), 251–80, esp. 260–61; Henry A. Gemery, "Markets for Migrants: English Indentured Servitude and Emigration in the Seventeenth and Eighteenth Centuries," in *Colonialism and Migration,* ed. Emmer, 33–54; Donald R. Wright, *African Americans in the Colonial Era: From African Origins through the American Revolution* (Arlington Heights, 1990), 49–61. For a summary of arguments on why the English servant migration declined rapidly in the late seventeenth century, see Dunn, "Servants and Slaves," 159–64.

9 For percentages of whites and blacks in the colonial populations, see Bureau of the Census, *Historical Statistics of the United States,* II, 1168.

10 For the argument that the substitution of slaves for servants on the mainland began in the late seventeenth century but was not complete by the Revolution, see David W. Galenson, "The Rise and Fall of Indentured Servitude in the Americas: An Economic Analysis," *Journal of Economic History,* 44 (March 1984), 1–26, esp. 11–13. See also Stanley L. Engerman, "Servants to Slaves to Servants: Contract Labour and European Expansion," in *Colonialism and Migration,* ed. Emmer, 263–94; and Ida Altman and James Horn, "Introduction," in *"To Make America,"* ed. Altman and Horn, 1–29, esp. 5–6. On the revival of indentured servitude in the Caribbean after the abolition of slavery, see David Northrop, *Indentured Labor in the Age of Imperialism, 1834–1922* (Cambridge, Eng., 1995); and Walton Look Lai, *Indentured Labor, Caribbean Sugar: Chinese and Indian Migrants to the British West Indies, 1838–1918* (Baltimore, 1993).

11 Richard S. Dunn argues that a complete shift from servants to slaves occurred only in the Caribbean. See Dunn, "Servants and Slaves," 159–64. On similar developments in the French colonies, see Frédéric Mauro, "French Indentured Servants for America, 1500–1800," in *Colonialism and Migration,* ed. Emmer, 83–104; Leslie Choquette, "Recruitment of French Emigrants to Canada, 1600–1760," in *"To Make America,"* ed. Altman and Horn, 131–71; Christian Heutz de Lemps, "Indentured Servants Bound for the French Antilles in the Seventeenth and Eighteenth Centuries," *ibid.,* 172–203; Peter Moogk, "Manon's Fellow Exiles: Emigration from France to North America before 1763," in *Europeans on the Move,* ed. Canny, 236–60.

12 On the number of foreign-born in the population, see Aaron Spencer Fogleman, *Hopeful Journeys: German Immigration, Settlement, and Political Culture in Colonial America, 1717–1775* (Philadelphia, 1996), 1–4, 155–62, esp. tables A.l, A.2, and A.3. A. Roger Ekirch argues that Americans in general did not want convicts and often protested to the British authorities for sending so many, yet planters in the Chesapeake found them desirable because they were much cheaper than slaves, served longer terms than indentured servants, and received no freedom dues. See A. Roger Ekirch, *Bound for America: The Transportation of British Convicts to the Colonies, 1718–1775* (Oxford, Eng., 1987), 124–25.

13  See Peter H. Wood, *Black Majority: Negroes in Colonial South Carolina from 1670 through the Stono Rebellion* (New York, 1974), 167–68; and C. Vann Woodward, *American Counterpoint: Slavery and Racism in the North-South Dialogue* (Boston, 1964), 5. A highly influential work from the 1940s does not consider Africans in its chapter on the colonial period. See Marcus L. Hansen, *The Atlantic Migration, 1607–1860: A History of the Continuing Settlement of the United States* (Cambridge, Mass., 1940), 25–52.

14  See, for example, Morgan, *American Slavery, American Freedom*, 293–387; Wood, *Black Majority*; Allan Kulikoff, *Tobacco and Slaves: The Development of Southern Culture in the Chesapeake, 1680–1800* (Chapel Hill, 1986); and Wright, *African Americans in the Colonial Era*, 56–69.

15  See Table 19.1 for estimated numbers of servants arriving in the eighteenth century.

16  For a comparison of the "redemptioner" system with traditional "indentured servitude," see Marianne Wokeck, "Harnessing the Lure of the 'Best Poor Man's Country': The Dynamics of German-Speaking Immigration to British North America, 1683–1783," in *"To Make America,"* ed. Altman and Horn, 204–43, esp. 217–18. See also Günther Moltmann, "The Migration of German Redemptioners to North America, 1720–1820," in *Colonialism and Migration*, ed. Emmer, 105–22; and Farley Grubb, "German Immigration to Pennsylvania, 1709 to 1820," *Journal of Interdisciplinary History*, 20 (Winter 1990), 417–36.

17  Galenson, *White Servitude in Colonial America*, 51–64; Galenson, "Rise and Fall of Indentured Servitude in the Americas," 1–26; Nicholas Canny, "English Migration into and across the Atlantic during the Seventeenth and Eighteenth Centuries," in *Europeans on the Move*, ed. Canny, 39–75, esp. 63; Bernard Bailyn with Barbara DeWolfe, *Voyagers to the West: A Passage in the Peopling of America on the Eve of the Revolution* (New York, 1986), 172–73; Wokeck, "Harnessing the Lure," 217–18; Sharon V. Salinger, *"To Serve Well and Faithfully": Labor and Indentured Servants in Pennsylvania, 1682–1800* (Cambridge, Eng., 1987).

18  For a comparison of servant labor in England and its North American colonies, see Robert J. Steinfeld, *The Invention of Free Labor: The Employment Relation in English and American law and Culture, 1350–1870* (Chapel Hill, 1991), esp. 15–54; and Galenson, *White Servitude in Colonial America*, 7–8, 102–13. For a comparison between indentured servitude and apprenticeship in the colonies, see Bailyn with DeWolfe, *Voyagers to the West*, 167n17. For conditions of indentured servitude in the French colonies, see Moogk, "Manon's Fellow Exiles," 236–60; Choquette, "Recruitment of French Immigrants to Canada," 131–71; Heutz de Lemps, "Indentured Servants Bound for the French Antilles," 172–203; and Mauro, "French Indentured Servants for America," 83–104. On the dates of the worst conditions for Germans arriving in Philadelphia, see Marianne S. Wokeck, "A Tide of Alien Tongues; The Flow and Ebb of German Immigration to Pennsylvania, 1683–1776" (Ph.D. diss., Temple University, 1983), 176.

19  Salinger, *"To Serve Well and Faithfully,"* 1–4; Dunn, "Servants and Slaves," 181; Wokeck, "Tide of Alien Tongues," 137–201, esp. 176, 202–43; Fogleman, *Hopeful Journeys*, 69–99; Hans-Jürgen Grabbe, "Das Ende des Redemptioner-Systems in den Vereinigten Staaten" (The end of the redemptioner system in the United States), *Amerikastudien / American Studies* (Munich), 29 (1984), 277–96, esp. 282.

20  Bailyn with DeWolfe, *Voyagers to the West*, 173–74.

21  Fogleman, *Hopeful Journeys*, 73.

22  For Maria Barbara Kober's story, see *ibid.*, 77–79.

23  On the difficulties facing newly arrived German immigrants (including servants) in colonial America, see *ibid.*, 69–99.

24  On convict transportations, see Ekirch, *Bound for America*; Peter W. Coldham, *Emigrants in Chains: A Social History of Forced Emigration to the Americas of Felons, Destitute Children, Political and Religious Non-Conformists, Vagabonds. Beggars, and Other Undesirables, 1607–1776* (Baltimore, 1992); Smith, *Colonists in Bondage*; Patrick Fitzgerald. "A Sentence to Sail: The Transportation of Irish Convicts to Colonial America in the Eighteenth Century," Working Paper 96–22, 1996 (International Seminar on the History of the Atlantic World, 1500–1800, Harvard University, Cambridge, Mass.): and Dobson, *Scottish Emigration to Colonial America*, 92. 125. On kidnapping, see *ibid.*, 93; and Bailyn with DeWolfe, *Voyagers to the West*, 307–12.

25 Coldham, *Emigrants in Chains,* 79, 99–133; Ekirch, *Bound for America,* 99, 123, 140–56.

26 Wood, *Radicalism of the American Revolution,* 11–92; Steinfeld, *Invention of Free Labor,* 3–121.

27 Pehr Kalm, *Peter Kalm's Travels in North America: The English Version of 1770,* ed. Adolph B. Benson (New York, 1987), 204–11. On ethnic group settlement in southeastern Pennsylvania, see James T. Lemon, *"The Best Poor Man's Country": A Geographical Study of Early Southeastern Pennsylvania* (Baltimore, 1972).

28 Wood, *Black Majority.* For European immigration into South Carolina after 1763, see Jane Reveill, ed., *A Compilation of the Original Lists of Protestant Immigrants to South Carolina, 1763–1773* (Columbia, S.C., 1939).

29 Populations and percentages that were black in 1760 were calculated from Bureau of Census, *Historical Statistics of the United States,* II, 1168. The Maryland census of 1755 enumerates 98,357 free whites, 6,871 servants, 1,981 convicts, 3,592 mulattoes, and 42,764 blacks. See Smith, *Colonists in Bondage,* 324. On transportations of convicts to the Chesapeake, see Ekirch, *Bound for America,* 116, 140–43.

30 "Journal of a French Traveller in the Colonies, 1765, I," *American Historical Review,* 26 (July 1921), 726–47, esp. 744–45; "Journal of a French Traveller in the Colonies, 1765, II," *ibid.,* 27 (Oct. 1921), 70–89. The travel journal was written in English by Jasper Payne. See Jasper Payne and Christian Fröhlich, Description of Their Journey to Maryland, Oct. 26 to Nov. 27, 1747, Journals Box JD III 1 (Moravian Archives, Bethlehem, Pa.). For the quote from Richard Dunn, see "Servants and Slaves," 176. On the importance of servitude in the Chesapeake and its meaning for American history, see Jack P. Greene, *Pursuits of Happiness: The Social Development of Early Modern British Colonies and the Formation of American Culture* (Chapel Hill, 1988).

31 On the relationship between trade and immigration in the colonial period, see Horn, "'To Parts beyond the Seas,'" 85–103; and Wokeck, "Harnessing the Lure," 204–43. On Scottish immigration to the Caribbean, see Dobson, *Scottish Emigration to Colonial America,* 7–8. On disruptions in the French slave trade, see Philip Curtin, *The Atlantic Slave Trade: A Census* (Madison, 1969), 177–78.

32 I am indebted to Richard S. Dunn for many of the ideas presented here. On freed slaves becoming indentured servants in Pennsylvania, see Gary B. Nash and Jean R. Soderlund, *Freedom by Degrees: Emancipation in Pennsylvania and Its Aftermath* (New York, 1991), 167–93. On the second forced migration of slaves to the Old Southwest from 1790 to 1860, see Allan Kulikoff, "Uprooted Peoples: Black Migrants in the Age of the American Revolution, 1790–1820," in *Slavery and Freedom in the Age of the American Revolution,* ed. Ira Berlin and Ronald Hoffman (Charlottesville, 1983), 143–71.

33 Patrick Fitzgerald, "Sentence to Sail," 3; Coldham, *Emigrants in Chains,* 151–57; Ekirch, *Bound for America,* 227–38.

34 Wood, *Radicalism of the American Revolution,* 145, 184; Steinfeld, *Invention of Free Labor.*

35 See W. J. Rorabaugh, *The Craft Apprentice: From Franklin to the Machine Age in America* (New York, 1986), 3–56, esp. 32.

36 Julian P. Boyd, ed. *The Papers of Thomas Jefferson* (27 vols., Princeton, 1950– ), I, 353; *New York Independent Gazette,* Jan. 24, 1784, quoted in Samuel McKee Jr., *Labor in Colonial New York, 1664–1776* (Port Washington, 1935), 175–76; W. W. Abbot, ed. *The Papers of George Washington: Confederation Series* (6 vols., Charlottesville, 1983– ), I, 473, 529.

37 On high levels of servitude among British and German immigrants in the early 1770s, see Bailyn with DeWolfe, *Voyagers to the West,* 166–69; and Farley W. Grubb, "The End of European Immigrant Servitude in the United States: An Economic Analysis of Market Collapse, 1772–1835," *Journal of Economic History,* 54 (Dec. 1994), 794–824, esp. 818–19. On the decline of servitude among Germans, see Grabbe, "Ende des Redemptioner-Systems"; Grubb, "End of European Immigrant Servitude"; and Farley W. Grubb, "The Disappearance of Organized Markets for European Immigrant Servants in the United States: Five Popular Explanations Reexamined," *Social Science History,* 18 (Spring 1994), 1–30.

38 Kerby A. Miller, *Emigrants and Exiles: Ireland and the Irish Exodus to North America* (Oxford, Eng., 1985), 169; Maurice Bric, "Irish Emigration to America, 1783–1800," Working Paper 96–21, 1996 (International Seminar on the History of the

Atlantic World, 1500–1800, Harvard University), esp. 1.

39  For French immigration during this period, see Hans-Jürgen Grabbe, "European Immigration to the United States in the Early National Period, 1783–1820," in *Demographic History of the Philadelphia Region,* ed. Klepp, 194.

40  Denmark abolished the slave trade to its West Indian colonies in 1803, followed by Britain in 1808, the Netherlands in 1814, and France in 1815. On the abolition of the trade, see David Eltis, *Economic Growth and the Ending of the Transatlantic Slave Trade* (New York, 1987); and David Eltis and James Walvin, eds. *The Abolition of the Atlantic Slave Trade: Origins and Effects in Europe, Africa, and the Americas* (Madison, 1981). On indentured servitude in the Caribbean, see Northrup, *Indentured Labor in the Age of Imperialism;* and Look Lai, *Indentured labor, Caribbean Sugar.* On Chinese immigrants in the United States, see Ronald T. Takaki, *A Different Mirror. A History of Multicultural America* (Boston, 1993), 192–94. For a good overview, see Engerman, "From Servants to Slaves to Servants," 263–94.

PART VI

# LEGACIES

# 20

# THE OTHER SIDE OF REVOLUTION
*Loyalists in the British Empire*

## Maya Jasanoff

### Introduction

Perhaps it is understandable that Americans typically focus on the most immediate and obvious consequence of the American Revolution – the creation of the United States of America. In this essay, Maya Jasanoff encourages students of the Revolution to recognize one of its forgotten legacies, the exodus of tens of thousands of whites, blacks, and Native Americans who remained loyal to the British crown. As a percentage of their respective populations, the American Revolution produced five times the number of refugees as did the French Revolution. Jasanoff masterfully traces this human movement to all reaches of the globe, from Canada and the Caribbean to Britain, Africa, India, and Australia.

From the perspective of these loyalist émigrés, the American Revolution had an ironic outcome: it reinvigorated Britain's global empire. In past generations, it was common for historians to use the Revolution as a dividing marker between the "first" British Empire, which focused primarily on settlement colonies in the West, and the "second" British Empire, which was concerned more with extracting goods and materials from nonwhite colonial territories in the East, particularly India. Jasanoff rejects this distinction largely because the Revolution did not act so much as a barrier as a bridge for British imperial activity before and after American independence. Among other influences, the Revolution helped to set in motion (literally) the population base for several of Canada's English-speaking provinces. Loyalists recovered from the bitter defeat and losses, especially in property, of the Revolution to become founders in their own right of new communities and territories in the British Empire.

- Jasanoff defines the American Revolution as a civil war. What insights can be gained by using this framework as opposed to the traditional perspective of political revolution? What, if anything, can be missed with this perspective?
- Jasanoff and Mary Beth Norton each make heavy use of records from the Loyalist Claims Commission in their respective essays in this volume. How do they approach the records in similar and different ways? What are the different historical questions that each uses the records to help answer?
- According to Jasanoff, the one common factor that linked white, black, and Native American loyalists was continuing allegiance to the British monarch. What did each group broadly gain by remaining loyal to a hierarchical system of royal government versus joining the new American republic, which, at least on its face, promised social equality? Consider essays by Alan Taylor, Ira Berlin, Colin G. Calloway, and Aaron S. Fogleman on the social consequences of the American Revolution.

On the first day of summer 1779, a small merchant vessel bobbed around Chebucto Head, drifting past Micmac canoes and the fortifications of George's Island into the crowded port of Halifax, Nova Scotia. It had survived a buffeting two-week voyage from Maine across the Bay of Fundy, and its passengers – the Reverend Jacob Bailey and his family – were grateful to touch land again. They were especially relieved to reach a land where they saw "the Britanic colours flying" because the Baileys were refugees from revolutionary America: loyalists who had fled to Nova Scotia after years of persecution. They reached British safety with just the rags on their backs. Bailey vividly described his costume of rusty black trousers speckled with lint and pitch stains, stockings a threadbare lattice, an oversize coat swinging loose around his ankles, and a "jaundise coloured" wig topped by a limp beaver cap. So many people came to gape at the strange party that Bailey delivered an impromptu speech from the deck: "Gentlemen, we are a company of fugitives … driven by famine and persecution to take refuge among you, and therefore I must intreat your candor and compassion to excuse the meaness and singularity of our dress." He thanked God, he later wrote, for guiding "me and my family to this retreat of freedom and security from the rage of tyranny and the cruelty of opposition." But he had also "landed in a strange country, destitute of money, clothing, dwelling or furniture," and his future was in the hands of chance.[1]

Bailey belonged to a large yet little-studied group of British subjects in revolutionary North America: loyalists who were exiled or fled from the thirteen colonies and sought a haven in Britain and its empire. Loyalists have long been relegated to the margins of mainstream history; they are often seen as losers, backward, and wrong. Books on the American Revolution usually mention that one in five members of the white colonial population sympathized with Britain during the war, passing over them with little further notice. Even the number of loyalists will likely always remain elusive, since "loyalism meant different things to different persons in different situations." Though academic interest in loyalism seems to be on the rise, the bulk of scholarship on the topic was produced in the bicentennial 1970s and tends to focus on the ideology of well-known figures such as Thomas Hutchinson and Joseph Galloway rather than the everyday experiences of ordinary loyalists. Similarly, though the labels applied to them – Tory and loyalist – emanated from British politics (like so much American revolutionary discourse) and continued to resonate on the eastern side of the Atlantic, loyalists have figured little in the major treatments of British politics and identity in the war. (Nor, as David Armitage justly laments, have British historians engaged with American historiography in anything like the way that historians of colonial America have with that of contemporary Britain.) To bend Gary B. Nash's label for the Revolution-era slave population, the loyalists constitute another, perhaps even more "forgotten fifth" in the history of these years.[2]

Indeed, for all that scholars have attempted to correct bluntly patriotic portrayals of American independence, it remains surprisingly controversial in the United States today to count loyalists among the victims of republican chauvinism. It must be remembered, though, that the American Revolution really was a civil war and was clearly seen as such by contemporaries on both sides of the Atlantic, some of whom experienced its divisive effects within their own families, as in the conspicuous example of William Franklin, loyalist governor of New Jersey, and his patriot father, Benjamin. Loyalists expressed their views passively and actively: they refused to swear loyalty oaths to the new assemblies; they moved to cities and regions under British control; and nineteen thousand joined loyalist regiments to fight for their vision of British colonial America. In retaliation they faced harassment from their peers – most vividly, if rarely, by tarring and feathering – and sanctions from state legislatures, which could strip them of their land and possessions or imprison or formally banish them.[3]

Ultimately, at least sixty thousand loyalists with fifteen thousand slaves in tow left the thirteen colonies to build new lives elsewhere in the British world. This figure represents roughly one in forty members of the population (compared with one in two hundred who emigrated from revolutionary France). Seven thousand or so went to Britain, often to find themselves strangers in a strange land. By far the largest group, more than half the total, fled to Canada and settled in the present-day provinces of the Maritimes, Ontario, and Quebec. Notably, about three thousand black loyalists moved to Canada, some of the thousands of former slaves who had gained freedom by fighting for the British. Among the immigrants to the north were also several hundred of Britain's longstanding Indian allies, the Mohawk of upstate New York. Another large contingent of loyalists traveled to the Caribbean, chiefly Jamaica, and to the Bahamas. In perhaps the most intriguing migration, nearly twelve hundred black loyalists moved a second time in 1792 from Nova Scotia to the experimental free black colony of Sierra Leone. Loyalists scattered as far afield as India: the East India Company army would soon be sprinkled with American-born officers, including two of Benedict Arnold's sons. And some black loyalists would even travel to the end of the earth, among the first convicts transported to Australia's Botany Bay. Following Bernard Bailyn's observation that "Atlantic history is the story of a world in motion," loyalist refugees remind readers that the history of the modern British Empire involved an even wider world in motion.[4]

Some have explored these individual episodes. Mary Beth Norton's *The British-Americans* offers an unsurpassed account of the loyalist exiles in Britain; Simon Schama and Cassandra Pybus have traced the black loyalist movements to Nova Scotia and Sierra Leone; and the loyalist experience in Canada – where loyalists are hailed by some as founding fathers – has been the subject of numerous works since the mid-nineteenth century. Yet no comprehensive study has ever been made of the diaspora as a whole.

The result is that historians of this period have not yet appreciated the full imperial extent of these migrations around and beyond the Atlantic. Nor have scholars looked in detail at white, black, and Indian loyalists together to consider where their experiences converged or differed. Only one recent essay, by Keith Mason, has placed the loyalist exodus in a wider, Atlantic context. As Mason rightly observes, "outside Canada" the loyalists' place in the historiography resembles that of the Jacobites: "a people whose story merits inclusion in the larger narrative but who are usually represented as having little impact on the course of Anglo-American history"[5]

Loyalist émigrés demand a larger, more significant narrative of their own that extends, as the refugees did, across the globe. They had a transformative effect on those parts of the empire where they constituted the majority of the population – the Maritimes, the Bahamas, and Sierra Leone – and shared parallel experiences across those domains. Their greater value as historical subjects lies in the perspective they grant onto the wider British world in a moment of crisis and change. For American historians the loyalist diaspora should offer an important reminder that the story of American independence cannot be confined within the borders of the nation. As such it extends the argument made by Alan Taylor, whose work on "the late loyalists" has situated the early Republic in its continental context.[6] Simply acknowledging the scale of the postrevolutionary exodus emphasizes that American independence was messy, with rippling international and human consequences.

At the same time, loyalist migrants help shed new light on an old question in British imperial historiography: how did the American Revolution affect the British Empire? Historians no longer routinely view the Revolution as marking a neat dividing line between a first, largely Atlantic, empire of trade and settlement and a second territorial empire of direct rule, anchored in India and encompassing millions of nonwhite subjects. Indeed, as P. J. Marshall has compellingly demonstrated, the collapse of British rule in the thirteen colonies was underpinned by the same metropolitan policies that encouraged the creation of that multiethnic land empire, which survived and grew after 1783. Most imperial historians would agree, however, that the loss in America clarified and strengthened empirewide impulses toward increasingly authoritarian rule, as well as supplying new rhetoric and in some cases new means of accommodating non-British subjects. "Never again," Eliga H. Gould has observed, "would the British think of any part of their empire as an extension of their own nation." Colonial subjects were henceforth to be embraced in a humanitarian, ostensibly inclusive empire but subordinated to metropolitan Britons, partly by elaborate hierarchies of difference.[7]

Loyalist émigrés offer a concrete population through which to see how these changes developed across the British world. How neatly did they actually conform to the new metropolitan ideas of colonial subjecthood? As migrants from one part of the British Empire to others – at home neither in the United States nor for the most part in Britain – loyalist refugees constitute an especially intriguing group through which to think about the meanings of imperial belonging. By explicitly affiliating themselves with Britain, they help illuminate a defining peculiarity of Britishness: its unusually portable and flexible quality. The loyalists, like millions of imperial subjects well into the twentieth century, laid claim to being British though they did not live within the British nation-state. This is why Bailey's heart swelled when he saw the British flags in Halifax harbor. But what did loyalists mean and expect by associating themselves with the empire and how did the British respond? Looking at loyalists suggests that, though the 1780s marked a decided refashioning of the empire's extent, population, and self-image, the decade also laid the groundwork for persistent tensions within that empire. Enduring contests about how far to incorporate and how far to assimilate, about who did and did not count as British and how to make such a determination

would inflect conceptions of British subjecthood and imperial governance for at least a century to come.

Following the loyalists into the British Empire affords the chance to consider how Britain coped with this mass migration and how successful it was at accommodating different types of refugees. Fitting the picture many scholars have drawn of the late-eighteenth-century empire, the benevolent treatment of some loyalists certainly bolsters an image of the British Empire as a diverse, multiethnic entity. Yet the experiences of other loyalists point to the limits and self-contradictions built into such an empire: differences between who mattered and who did not and questions of how British rights and liberties at home might differ from rights and liberties abroad. Though Britain made an effort to reach out to blacks, white loyalists, and Indians in some areas, in others it appeared to fall short of its seemingly inclusionary mission. Meanwhile loyalists in several settings explicitly challenged imperial authority in terms uncannily like those of their rebel peers. This political disposition was the most striking of several American (or provincial) inheritances they brought with them to their new British (and also provincial) homes. Significant as it was in aggregate, this migration was composed of thousands of individual lives disrupted, dispossessed, or displaced. Probing one family's experiences on the move demonstrates how this migration affected the people caught up in it. Attachment to Britain cost thousands their homes and livelihoods, but might they have gained anything from their British affiliations as well? Losses are intrinsically depressing, and British historians have traditionally painted the immediate aftereffects of the American Revolution in dismal colors: sunk morale, spiraling deficits, and a king reduced to blubbering madness. Yet, as Linda Colley has shown, the loss in America encouraged a stronger sense of British national unity and a similar strengthening of imperial purpose, as British administrators concluded that government authority in the colonies had if anything been too weak. In keeping with the emerging scholarly consensus that discards a tidy division between first and second British empires, the diffusion of loyalist refugees underscores how the war reinvigorated a global empire that was at once Atlantic and Pacific, American and Asian, and was supervised increasingly from a British center.[8]

As a forceful reminder of why the American Revolution should be set in global context, consider the astonishing range of imperial reforms that unfolded in its wake. The end of the war was rapidly followed by a remarkable series of changes in British imperial policy and public perceptions of empire. In 1782 the Irish Patriots, led by Henry Grattan, successfully established a measure of parliamentary independence for Ireland. In 1784 Parliament undertook a major overhaul of Indian administration, aimed in part at staving off the abuses of power that Edmund Burke and others had identified at the heart of the American crisis. Continuing anxieties about the nature of imperial rule in India were played out a few years later in the dramatic impeachment trial of Warren Hastings, governor of Bengal. In 1787 the British antislavery movement consolidated with the founding of the Society for the Abolition of the Slave Trade. American independence cut the number of slaves in the British Empire in half, but equally important, as Christopher Leslie Brown has splendidly demonstrated, the Revolution allowed abolitionists to draw a moral contrast between Britain and the United States.[9] Meanwhile, in 1788, an entirely new arena of imperial activity opened with the arrival of the first convicts in Australia. Taken together these developments demonstrated a turn toward centralized authority coupled in places with the promotion of humanitarian inclusiveness.

The loyalist migration not only took place against this backdrop but also directly intersected with it, most tangibly across Canada, whose population, political structures, and civic institutions were transformed. Americans and Britons easily forget that the loss of America was actually the making of Anglophone Canada, a demographic and cultural shift clearly expressed in the 1791 Canada Constitutional Act, which divided formerly French-majority Quebec into two parts and extended the reach of English law and Protestantism. Elsewhere in the empire, loyalists doubled the population of the Bahamas and the arrival of black loyalists in Sierra Leone revived the fortunes of the faltering colony. And it seems no coincidence that an early proponent of Australian settlement was himself a loyalist who suggested relocating his fellow refugees there.[10] Mapping out the loyalist migration emphasizes how Britain responded to the lost war with expansion, restructuring, and renewed senses of national and imperial purpose.

It is possible to gauge these effects in detail by inspecting how Britain coped with the mass migration. Though it was not the first such episode, the loyalist exodus constituted the widest-ranging and probably the largest refugee crisis Britain had ever faced. The word "refugee" entered the English language with the arrival of up to fifty thousand Huguenots in England after 1685; thousands more immigrated to Ireland and North America. A more concentrated refugee influx descended on England in the summer of 1709, when more than ten thousand "Poor Palatines" sought to settle in Britain under a new law allowing easy naturalization to foreign Protestants. They were supported by ad hoc government and private charity – some were housed in army tents pitched on the various commons south of the Thames – before being mostly dispersed to Ireland and the transatlantic colonies. The naturalization act was repealed soon thereafter.[11]

Where these earlier refugee populations had made their way to England from the Continent, often to settle or emigrate from there, most loyalist migrants began and ended their journeys on British colonial soil. Many of the loyalist exiles in England had left the colonies in 1775 with the fall of Boston. But tens of thousands of civilians had moved during the war, either fleeing over northern and southern borders like Jacob Bailey or traveling to the British strongholds of New

York, Charleston, Savannah, and Saint Augustine. With the evacuations of those cities from 1782 to 1784, British authorities decided to assume responsibility for the loyalists' relocation. While Commander in Chief Guy Carleton coordinated this massive effort from his headquarters in New York, officials on the receiving end, from Nova Scotia to Jamaica, struggled to produce shelter and food for the new and impending arrivals. In Quebec, for instance, more than fifty-six hundred loyalists settled in townships formed so hastily they were known only by number. Government-appointed inspectors regularly mustered the refugees (a practice followed across Canada as well as in Florida and the Bahamas), tallied them by gender and age, and distributed rations with parsimonious exactitude. One inspector was urged never to give excess supplies unless "necessities *absolutely* require it" and advised that considerable savings might be made "by striking off many young people who ought to earn their Livelyhood and Girls who marry." Such savings had their own price; the end of a long winter found many Quebec refugees "very sickly," and "several died owing as they think for the want of provision & Cloathing."[12]

A longer-term challenge of apportionment concerned distributing land, which the Crown had promised to loyalist settlers. Ex-soldiers received lots according to rank, ranging from one hundred acres for a private to seven hundred for a captain. In an almost direct reversal of the enclosures of common lands occurring in contemporary Britain, Canadian land was escheated from large absentee owners and redistributed to thousands of small proprietors. Faced with some thirty thousand applications for lots, the surveyor general of Nova Scotia unsurprisingly saw his job as "next to Egyptian Slavery." During the long winters of the mid-1780s, teams of surveyors struggled through woods clogged by snow to assess the forests, measure lots, and issue warrants of survey. Whitehall dispatched nails and hammers as well as wood rasps and hoes by the hundreds. New sawmills churned out boards and shingles for

houses. By the spring of 1785, refugees such as New Yorker Henry Nase had rediscovered their old lives as farmers, sowing rye, "blue nose" potatoes, butter beans, and cabbages in the Canadian soil.[13]

The hardest consideration was what to do about the property losses, from vast estates to humble oxcarts, that nearly every loyalist refugee had sustained. In hundreds if not thousands of instances, the American states had officially confiscated loyalist property. To what extent could or should the United States indemnify loyalists? This question turned out to be a major stumbling block in the Treaty of Paris peace talks. The heavily negotiated result, enshrined in article 5 of the provisional Anglo-American treaty, determined that "Congress shall earnestly recommend it to the Legislatures of the respective States, to provide for the Restitution of all Estates, Rights, and Properties, which have been confiscated, belonging to Real British Subjects."[14] In other words Congress would ask the states nicely to restore British property, but it was entirely up to the states to decide whether to comply.

In Westminster, which had been fiercely factionalized throughout the war, this article struck many as a complete betrayal of British interests, proving so controversial that it helped bring down the Earl of Shelburne's government in the winter of 1783. But even those sympathetic to the loyalists soon found that pushing the matter further would lead to a total breakdown of negotiations. The article stood. Instead, in a rare (and quite possibly unprecedented) assumption of financial responsibility for overseas subjects, Parliament undertook to supply British government compensation for the loyalists. In June 1783 a commission of five members of Parliament was set up "to Enquire into the Circumstances and former Fortunes of such Persons as are reduced to Distress by the late unhappy Dissentions in America." The Loyalist Claims Commission, as it was known, took oral and written evidence from loyalists and determined appropriate recompense. Within its first nine months, it received more than two thousand claims amounting to property losses of just more than £7 million – "an alarming sum," recalled one of the commissioners, John Eardley-Wilmot – and more loyalists were waiting to file. Parliament extended and widened the commission's brief: in 1785 two of the commissioners even traveled to Nova Scotia and Quebec to take evidence there. An agent was also dispatched to the United States to research property values. The commission's work ended up consuming more than six years, in which time it had received 3,225 claims, examined 2,291 in detail, and awarded more than £3 million, or about one-third the total amount of losses claimed, with the funds supplied in part by national lotteries.[15]

Historians are indebted to the Loyalist Claims Commission for the testimony it gathered. Now housed in two huge series in the British National Archives, the evidence accumulated by the commission forms the biggest single collection of material on loyalist refugees. Most of the loyalist claimants were less grateful: unhappiness at the small amounts most of them received forms a sad thread through their writings. "If you have one that is satisfied with his dividend on your side of the Water," reported one loyalist in London to his brother in New Brunswick, "it is more than I can say on this, the pittance is so small to many that they refuse, & despise it with contempt, while others die with broken hearts … Some have run mad with dispair & disappointment."[16]

But the point is what the very existence of this institution suggested about how the British state conceived of its responsibilities. It deserves note simply as an early example of state welfare at a time when pension schemes, for instance, were only just beginning to take shape. Even more strikingly than the distribution of overseas land, the Loyalist Claims Commission reflected a sense that Crown and Parliament had a duty to protect British subjects and their property at home and abroad. As such the commission foreshadowed the kind of Pax Britannica later

envisioned by Victorian Liberal Henry John Temple, 3rd Viscount Palmerston, who asserted the rights of British subjects to receive British protection no matter where in the empire they were or of what background. (For Commissioner Eardley-Wilmot, it also foreshadowed later relief efforts on behalf of French revolutionary émigrés: he established a committee that raised more than £400,000 for French refugees.) The Loyalist Claims Commission pulled a sort of victory from the jaws of defeat. In Eardley-Wilmot's words, "Whatever may be said of this unfortunate war, either to account for, to justify, or to apologize for the conduct of either Country; all the world has been unanimous in applauding the justice and the humanity of Great Britain … in compensating, with a liberal hand, the Losses of those who suffered so much for their firm and faithful adherence to the British Government."[17] Britain may have lost the war, but its treatment of the loyalists showed that, in principle at least, it would try to protect its overseas subjects from the consequences.

In 1812, about the time he wrote his *Historical View of the Commission* and some twenty-five years after concluding his work on it, John Eardley-Wilmot sat for a portrait by renowned American-born history painter Benjamin West. For historians the most striking feature of the Eardley-Wilmot portrait is a picture on the wall behind him: an allegorical painting, also by West, titled *Reception of the American Loyalists by Great Britain in the Year 1783*. The painting itself no longer survives (and may never have existed), but a contemporary engraving appears as the frontispiece to Eardley-Wilmot's memoir (Figure 20.1). It shows Britannia – big, bland, benevolent – extending her hand to a throng of loyalists led by William Franklin and Sir William Pepperell of Massachusetts. To Britannia's left stand West and his wife, their protected position perhaps reflecting that they had established themselves in Britain well before the war began. Allegories usually need explanation, and the average viewer probably would not guess that the figures holding Britannia's mantle

**Figure 20.1** Benjamin West pictures the loyalists in British care. Engraving by H. Moses, circa 1815, after an insert in the portrait of John Eardley-Wilmot from 1812. Frontispiece from John Eardley-Wilmot, *Historical View of the Commission for Enquiring into the Losses, Services, and Claims of the American Loyalists, at the Close of the War between Great Britain and Her Colonies, in 1783* (London, 1815). Courtesy of The Library Company of Philadelphia.

represent "Religion" and "Justice" or that the cherubs at the top left are binding up the fasces of the Anglo-American relationship. (This image was created in 1812.) Another emblem speaks for itself: a crown, lodged prominently beneath Britannia's shield, represents that focal point of imperial loyalty, the king. Equally legible on the engraving's central axis is the preferred eighteenth-century representation of America: a statuesque Indian chief, in this case resembling someone jolted by an electric shock. He shelters a "Widow and Orphans, rendered so by the civil war" and behind him huddle figures apparently of African origin, "looking up to Britannia in grateful remembrance of their emancipation from Slavery."[18] One presumes they also remembered, gratefully, the abolition of the slave trade in 1807.

An Indian chief, war widows, and former slaves all under the looming protection of Britannia and the Crown: it is hard to imagine a more straightforward image of an inclusive British Empire that had managed to mint moral capital out of its wartime defeat. At some level this allegory corresponds with documented reality. The identifiable white loyalists in this picture, for instance, each got money from the Loyalist Claims Commission. Hundreds of widows and orphans got material support from the British government. The Mohawk received their land and black loyalists made their exodus, however much against the odds, from American slavery to British freedom. In all these ways, as West's image celebrates, the British Empire held out a tangible promise of life, liberty, and the pursuit of happiness to whites, blacks, and

Indians excluded from the political life of the nascent United States.[19]

But self-images can be misleading, and West's image of Britannia was itself a construct. If the treatment of some loyalists shows British conduct as humanitarian and liberal, the fates of others demonstrate ways in which it rested on and perpetuated forms of exclusion. Scholars have not fully explored these cases. Consider the figure of the Indian. If West had any individual in mind for this image, it was likely Joseph Brant, the Mohawk chief who presided over his tribe's Canadian relocation and whom West may well have met when Brant visited London in 1776. Brant was an effective negotiator, and his success demonstrates the importance of indigenous leadership in extracting concessions from the British. Yet the Mohawk experience was not shared by Britain's southern Indian allies. West could not have had them in mind because Britannia did not "receive" those loyalists at all. At a conference in Saint Augustine in May 1783, Creek and Cherokee chiefs were horrified to learn that, according to the terms of the peace, Britain had agreed to cede Florida to their enemy Spain. "We took up the Hatchett for the English … The King and his Warriors have told us they would never forsake us," lamented one chief. "Is the Great King conquered? Or does he mean to abandon Us? … Do you think we can turn our faces to our Enemies[?] … No. If he has any Land to receive us (We will not turn to our Enemies) but go [to] it with our friends in such ships as he may send for us." So vigorous was Indian opposition to the cession that the British briefly floated the idea of relocating them to the Bahamas, though Sir Guy Carleton scotched the scheme on the grounds that the islands would not suit their way of life. Unfortunately for the southern Indians, their loyalty to Britain, unlike that of the Mohawk, ended in relative abandonment to the pressing encroachments of the United States.[20]

A similar reality needs to be exposed regarding the other nonwhite group featured by West: African Americans. Eight to ten thousand

black loyalists went on to enjoy their freedom in the British world; hundreds even received small acreages in Nova Scotia. Though historians have justly celebrated these remarkable tales of freedom, it should be stressed that at least as many blacks also discovered firsthand how slavery was preserved if not reinforced in the British Caribbean domains where it mattered most. As many as two thousand blacks were even taken to Canada as slaves, offering a moving counterpoint to those black loyalists digging out their shelters in the frozen ground. Far more slaves were exported to Florida, the Caribbean, and the Bahamas. Records of British evacuations suggest that at least fifteen thousand blacks were removed from the former colonies, most as slaves. Up to eight thousand went to Jamaica, and the slave population of the Bahamas, according to contemporary figures, increased by at least thirty-six hundred with the loyalist influx. A list of 129 loyalists who filed for tax exemption in Jamaica under a 1783 law gives a telling insight into patterns of loyalist slave exportation. Of these loyalists, 51 slave owners brought a total of 1,522 slaves from the colonies; that is, an average of 30 slaves per white slave owner, a ratio due in part to the fact that some of these slaves had been consigned to loyalists by their friends for sale.[21]

Even by conservative estimates, 50 percent more blacks left the colonies as slaves of loyalists than as loyalist freemen. Moreover the British government sanctioned and facilitated the export of slaves by loyalists, giving them passage on ships, granting the slave owners land, and maintaining slavery in the West Indies. (When Lord Dunmore, whose 1775 proclamation as governor of Virginia had inspired many slaves to run to the British for freedom, became governor of the loyalist-dominated Bahamas in 1787, however, he promptly managed to alienate some white loyalists by honoring the claims of black loyalists who had been wrongly reenslaved.) For every case of British Freedom (the stunningly self-named black loyalist featured in Simon Schama's *Rough Crossings*), the loyalist emigrants carried with them more than one human reminder of persisting British slavery.[22]

Britons could (and did) congratulate themselves that slavery had been effectively abolished in Britain proper in 1772, as it would be in Canada by the century's end. But comparing different sites of exodus makes clear that though the expanding British Empire may in some ways have acted inclusively – granting land to the Mohawk and freedom to black loyalists – it also practiced forms of exclusion: neglecting its subjects and allies in Florida; enabling continued slave ownership; and even, for that matter, failing to meet the expectations of so many petitioners to the Loyalist Claims Commission. Local imperatives could explain such differences between British practices in various domains. The Mohawk lived on the new Anglo-American frontier, so their allegiance remained of palpable strategic importance, whereas the Creek and Cherokee, however much British agents wanted to retain their goodwill in general and the valuable Indian trade in particular, now lived in a Spanish province bordering the United States. By the same token, slavery operated on a vastly greater scale in the West Indies than it ever had in Canada, and sending free blacks to Canada or to Sierra Leone did not seriously compromise the institution in the islands where it mattered to Britain most. Indeed one could interpret the hasty export of poor black loyalists from London to Sierra Leone as a somewhat self-serving attempt to remove an awkward, conspicuous minority from mainland British soil.

As these examples imply, image and reality, like theory and practice, do not always match up. British policy was not an either-or proposition: either Britain was as West showed it – liberal, tolerant, and accommodating – or it was not. It was both. Such apparent contradictions between inclusion and exclusion resurfaced time and again in nineteenth-century British history, and scholars have identified them as a central paradox of British liberalism from the 1830s.[23] Yet as mapping out the loyalist diaspora indicates, similar tensions were already evident

in the aftermath of the American Revolution. They emerged in tandem with the postwar empire, suggesting that the competing pressures of imperial liberty and authority boast a long genealogy.

And what of the white loyalists? They tend to be portrayed as either bad citizens or good subjects, as British counterrevolutionaries and subversives or as good Americans who refused to betray the British Crown. Leaving value judgments to one side, these characterizations correctly indicate that loyalists were two things at once, both British and American. Formally, they were British subjects in their own eyes, in British opinion, and even in some American courts.[24] As natives or long-term residents of the American colonies, they were also American, following widespread late-eighteenth-century usage, and often referred to themselves as such. This double identification meant that loyalist refugees carried a mixed legacy with them, infusing their new British colonial settlements with inheritances from their former American colonial homes.

Loyalist imports extended from the material to the spiritual. In Nova Scotia they ranged from the pancake and codfish recipes used by the governor's wife (who had come from New Hampshire with her husband) to the founding of Canada's first chartered university by emigrants from King's College in New York. Some loyalist transmissions can be traced back to single points of origin. The Wells brothers, loyalist printers of Charleston, South Carolina, fled with their printing press to Saint Augustine, where William Charles Wells published the region's first newspaper, and then to Nassau, where John Wells did the same; their brother-in-law Alexander Aikman settled in Kingston and became the publisher of the *Royal Gazette* and printer to the Jamaica House of Assembly. Another remarkable mini-diaspora emanated from the black Baptist community that later coalesced into the First African Baptist Church in Savannah. This single flock produced black loyalist preachers including David George,

George Liele, and Moses Baker, who went on to establish congregations in Canada and Sierra Leone and founded the first Baptist churches in Jamaica and the Bahamas some twenty years before the arrival of white missionaries.[25]

The most striking and perhaps unexpected American legacy concerned politics. As Bernard Bailyn has demonstrated, American debates of the 1760s and 1770s echoed contemporary British contests about virtual representation, arbitrary power, and perceived tyranny.[26] Loyalists were accordingly styled Tories in contrast to the radical rebel Whigs. They shared some basic traits with Tories across the ocean: Anglican clergy in America (such as Jacob Bailey) were overwhelmingly loyal and, fundamentally, all loyalists upheld the supremacy of the king and Parliament. Allegiance to the monarch, in particular, formed a consistent link – probably the only one – among white, black, and Indian loyalists and joined educated elite loyalists with the humble rank and file, whose expressions of support for the king survive in their sometimes barely literate petitions pleading for support. The Crown sits prominently in Benjamin West's picture for a reason. Just as the Revolution ultimately strengthened the image of the king in Britain proper, so it bolstered the role of the monarch as emperor, a position that if anything outpaced and outlasted the monarch's significance as a figurehead at home.

Yet "Tory," still widely used as a synonym for loyalist, is a misleading designation. (It was also "always the term of reproach," as Thomas Hutchinson observed, and its negative connotations meant that loyalists rarely applied it to themselves.) Most people's choices in times of stress do not come down to pure ideologies alone, and the political label Tory tends to obscure the personal, pragmatic factors that may have influenced their decisions. It also corresponds only loosely with the diverse range of opinions loyalists held. For evidence of the variations in loyalist thought and practice, one need only point to that majority of loyalists who did not leave the United States or to those who returned to the United States in later years. Among loyalist refugees who left, pledging loyalty to the king was just about the only thing they could be counted on to accept. Even in Shelburne, Nova Scotia – the veritable loyalist capital, founded by refugees and settled by more than ten thousand of them – an oath of allegiance to the king had to be "explained as not to extend to taxation," suggesting some rather un-Tory principles among the town's residents. In the long run, as Alan Taylor has acutely observed, "Although we cast the Loyalists as losers, they ultimately won the original goal of the colonial resistance: exemption from British taxation while remaining within the empire."[27] And in many settings, the American loyalists turned out to be far from English Tories, as imperial governors learned to their peril.

The most pronounced contest between loyalists and imperial authorities unfolded in the Bahamas. Not long after arriving from East Florida, a group of refugee "Gentleman Loyalists" beset Governor John Maxwell with demands for more provisions, better land allocation, and greater political voice. How appropriate that the motto of loyalist John Wells's *Bahama Gazette* should be "not bound in loyalty to any masters," since the loyalists evinced little allegiance to Maxwell. Forming a committee "to preserve and maintain those Rights and Liberties, for which they left their Homes and their Possessions," they proceeded to circulate libelous handbills, run riot through the streets of Nassau (ringing the church bell at eleven o'clock at night "as if the Town had been on Fire"), and let loose "a Torrent of Billingsgate Language" when challenged in court. Driven to his wit's end by these "most tormenting, dissatisfied People on Earth," Maxwell may have been relieved to hand over the governorship to James Powell at the end of 1784. Powell fared no better with the loyalists, whose mounting demands for political representation he found as "seditiously mad" as ever those of the American colonists had been. Only under Lord Dunmore did the "violent spirit of Party" in the islands begin to subside, and the loyalists gained seats in the assembly. By the early 1790s, they had helped introduce racial laws on par with those in the old southern American colonies; in 1807, Bahamian loyalists vehemently opposed the ending of the slave trade.[28]

Severe clashes between loyalist settlers and government also took place in New Brunswick, a new province split off from Nova Scotia in 1784. If the American Revolution inspired an authoritarian turn among imperial administrators, that turn was personified by New Brunswick's first governor, Sir Guy Carleton's decidedly unpopulist brother Thomas, who believed "that the American Spirit of innovation should not be nursed among the Loyal Refugees" and held off on calling elections until the fall of 1785. Whereas the rowdy loyalists in the Bahamas were primarily well-off slave owners from the American South, Carleton's opponents were chiefly, in his words, "motly" ex-soldiers, "habituated" to "disorderly conduct … during a long Civil war." A "violent party Spirit" erupted among them, cultivated by agitators who plied them with liquor, promised redress "for all their former Grievances & supposed wrongs," and triggered riots, or at least so Carleton saw it. But another observer, William Cobbett, later recalled the election as an all-too-familiar effort by a ruling elite to suppress the voices of ordinary people. Cobbett, who had just arrived in New Brunswick as an army corporal, went on to be one of the leading British radicals of his generation. In the event the Carleton faction won, and the new assembly promptly passed a bill suppressing mass petitions and, by extension, public dissent. So it was that Britain's newest colonial province dealt with a confrontation between political ideals that were at once emphatically American and familiarly British.[29]

Even in utopia loyalists struggled with British authority. The black loyalists who traveled from Nova Scotia to Sierra Leone in 1792 landed in a mock-Saxon polity dreamed up by abolitionist Granville Sharp where they were represented by community-chosen "hundredors" and

"tithingmen." In practice, however, they were governed by the London-based Sierra Leone Company and its agents, which repeatedly failed to make good on promises. From their first months on African soil, settlers plagued the colony's superintendent, John Clarkson, with demands to honor their "civil rights" and the promise that "all should be equal." Extended delays about land allotment sparked a riot in 1794, competently suppressed by twenty-six-year-old Governor Zachary Macaulay, who set up cannon outside his house and offered free passage back to Nova Scotia – on a former slave ship – for anybody who wished to go. (None did.) Discontent mounted again with the imposition of quitrents in 1796. Then a dispute over the appointment of judges in 1800 triggered what amounted to a loyalist coup. Some of the hundredors and tithingmen issued their own legal code, setting themselves up as a government independent from the company-appointed governor and council. An armed uprising followed and for one steamy week in September black loyalists had to choose again between staying loyal or joining the rebels. But the British company soon prevailed; a month later, a formal charter strengthened the imperial grip in the colony. Among the rebel leaders banished was one Henry Washington, who had run away from George Washington's Mount Vernon twenty years earlier.[30]

The great abolitionist William Wilberforce snidely commented that black loyalists in Sierra Leone were "as thorough Jacobins as if they had been trained and educated in Paris," a reminder that by 1800 the consuming contest with France superseded the American Revolution in British consciousness. (Wilberforce might better have pointed to Saint Domingue: one of the ex-slave leaders of the Haitian Revolution, Henri Christophe, had been armed by the French to fight in the American war.) Nevertheless the African rebellion, echoing the disturbances in New Brunswick and the Bahamas, reflected an important and enduring colonial legacy among these British subjects. The loyalists had chosen to remain British and were happy where possible to reap the "passive benefits of British subjects: cheap land and low taxes."[31] But as these incidents showed, they continued actively to demand or assert what they saw as the rights of British subjects too.

The theme of loss hangs heavily over the loyalists' story: Britain lost the colonies and the loyalists lost their possessions and homes. Great histories are made up of small ones, and to understand the full effects of the loyalist migration, those small stories deserve examination. One of the many documented lives disturbed by this war was that of a middle-class refugee from Georgia named Elizabeth Johnston, who wrote up her experiences in 1836. Johnston's narrative is a valuable source not only because it is one of relatively few refugee accounts by a woman to survive but also because she experienced the trauma of migration in more places than most by moving to Florida, Scotland, Jamaica, and finally Nova Scotia. And yet, mirroring the way that in a larger sense Britain bounced back from the loss, the fortunes of the Johnston family suggest how, for some individual loyalists, the empire for which they had lost so much could also supply longer-term rewards.

Johnston spent most of the war in Savannah while her husband, William, fought in a loyalist regiment. When Savannah was evacuated in July 1782, she moved to Charleston with a toddler son in tow, eight months pregnant and just eighteen years old. Six months later Charleston was evacuated, and the Johnstons moved again, south to Saint Augustine, among twelve thousand loyalists and slaves who had flocked to the British province of East Florida expecting it to be a permanent new home. So when news reached them in the spring of 1783 that Florida was to be handed over to Spain – that they would have to move yet again – they felt utterly betrayed. "The war never occasioned half the distress which this peace has done, to the unfortunate Loyalists," she wrote to her husband. Loyalists frantically tried to sell off their houses and land, glutting the market when there were only a few Spanish buyers. Some dismantled their houses hoping to carry them to the Caribbean, only to find there was not enough room on the crammed transport ships to accommodate them. So the twice-over refugees sailed away from beaches strewn with the lumber of their broken homes.[32]

The Johnstons were comparatively lucky: Elizabeth's father-in-law, Lewis Johnston, formerly speaker of the Georgia House of Assembly, successfully sold his and William's slaves and was able to evacuate with at least some money in hand. The family returned to "his native land," Scotland, not least because it was the best place in the Anglophone world for William to resume the medical training he had commenced in Philadelphia before the war. But like so many loyalists, the Johnstons found life in Britain expensive, uncomfortable, and depressing. Old Dr. Johnston, "a poor Loyalist who had lost so much by the war," could not even afford a carriage to take him to church. And when William finished his training, he does not even seem to have considered practicing in Scotland. Instead he accepted an offer from one of his wartime patrons to go to Jamaica. (He turned down an offer to go to India from another patron, Archibald Campbell, just appointed governor of Madras.) The Johnstons moved to Kingston in 1786, leaving their eldest children to be educated in Scotland, and William became the attending physician on the estates of prominent planter James Wildman.[33]

Elizabeth had by now given birth to four children in four places – Savannah, Charleston, Saint Augustine, and Edinburgh – and would bear five more in Jamaica. But alongside this living record of exodus would come a trail of gravestones. A son died of thrush in Scotland at three months. A two-year-old daughter died of scarlet fever in Jamaica, and another baby girl died of smallpox. These losses weighed severely on Elizabeth, who felt profoundly isolated in Jamaica's alien environment. "I was much exhausted in mind and body," she recalled, "having no female relation to be with me, only black servants." In 1796 the Johnstons made the difficult decision for William to stay in Jamaica while Elizabeth returned to Scotland with the children. "On the morning of that sad day when I heard that the boat was come to take us on board … I hardly think I was in my senses," she wrote. "I uttered screams that distressed my poor husband to such a degree that he … begged me … to let him go on board and bring our things back, but all I could say was, 'It is too late!'"[34]

Separation had become a defining feature of the Johnstons' family life. It also cast long, unanticipated shadows. Elizabeth was reunited in Edinburgh with her two eldest children, who were eighteenth-century-style wayward teenagers. Andrew was now fifteen and had run off to join the navy only to be marched home again by a family friend and cajoled into studying medicine, but his heart was not in it, and he regularly cut classes to go ice skating. Elizabeth packed him off to his father in Jamaica for disciplining. Her daughter Catherine, meanwhile, was now fourteen and had developed a "wild and giddy" streak encouraged, according to her mother, by unfettered access to a lending library and an unsuitable taste for novels.[35]

In 1801 Elizabeth returned to Jamaica to join William, whose health was failing. Back in the family house at Halfwaytree, their Jamaican travails began again. Two daughters barely survived yellow fever, the Caribbean killer. William's own health was so bad that they arranged this time for him to leave; he stayed away two years. For once the family was all together in December 1805, when Andrew, now a qualified doctor, traveled from his practice in the mountains of Clarendon Parish to visit. But the day before he arrived he felt unwell, and he vomited black in the night, the fatal sign of advanced yellow fever. Within a week he was dead. Shortly afterward Catherine lapsed into a complicated "nervous illness, combined also with symptoms of yellow fever," for which the only cure was a change of climate. "Worn down as I was with sorrow of various and trying kinds,"

wrote Elizabeth, "I told her father that … hard as another separation from him and my beloved boys was, I myself would go."[36]

William went to the docks and arranged a passage for his family to Nova Scotia, much to Elizabeth's alarm: "Send us to Nova Scotia! What, to be frozen to death?" Jamaica was one thing; Canada really seemed like exile. What she had not considered, however, was that Nova Scotia had become home to so many loyalist exiles that it would be the most congenial haven she had yet encountered. Though they arrived there nearly "perfect strangers to every one in that place," they promptly made friends among the large community of fellow loyalists. William died in Jamaica in 1807 while the rest of the family flourished in Canada. Two of Elizabeth's younger daughters soon married loyalists and produced seventeen children between them, many of whom went on to enjoy successful professional careers and hold offices in provincial government. Elizabeth's three surviving sons also came to Nova Scotia, where they traced glittering paths in medicine and the law; one ascended briefly to the position of governor.[37]

"Little did I … think that I and all my children would ultimately settle in Nova Scotia," Elizabeth later observed. After decades on the move, she had reason to be surprised. What comes through clearly in Johnston's narrative – as in the writings of other loyalist women – is the sheer physical and psychological hardship of migration. Whereas four male members of her family detailed their property losses to the Loyalist Claims Commission, Elizabeth's memoir illuminates the extended emotional consequences of losing a home and a homeland.[38] Moving affected the relationships between parents and children and precipitated illness and death. The Johnstons' story also foregrounds a feature of refugee life that may not occur to readers at first glance, namely the multigenerational consequences of upheaval. War and its aftermath reverberated across three generations of the family. Their parents had propelled them into the loyalist cause, yet Elizabeth and William's children, especially the two eldest, born during the war, paid the price of migration at least as heavily as they had.

It is easy when reading loyalist letters, petitions, and memoirs to be overwhelmed by the tragedies of refugee lives and to get caught up in the emotional language loyalists used to describe their plight. Johnston's narrative, like Jacob Bailey's, speaks to migration as the loyalists felt it: vivid, poignant, and real. And yet many tales of loyalist loss, especially those of middle-class families, had constructive, even happy, endings. The Johnston family unquestionably attained a degree of prominence in Nova Scotia they would not have had if they had remained in Britain or returned to the United States. Even Bailey was recognized in his rags within moments of his arrival, taken in by friends, and awarded a Nova Scotia parish by the Society for the Propagation of the Gospel. This contrast between the vicissitudes of empire and its rewards is reminiscent of the way that imperial servants in the nineteenth and twentieth centuries often talked about suffering for the empire when that empire was the source of their family's success. By moving on to other British colonies and rebuilding lives, these loyalist imperial pioneers paralleled and in some cases contributed to the larger arc of Britain's postrevolutionary ascent.

All aspects of these loyalist migrations – how Britain materially coped with the exodus; how it incorporated, and saw itself incorporating, various kinds of others; how the refugees responded to new settings – offer insight into how Britain and the empire rebounded from the lost war. All underline the value of a global and comparative study of this topic. Only by looking at the exodus across different settings can one fully appreciate the innovations that the Revolution sparked in British state conceptions of responsibility. Only by comparing regions such as Canada and the Caribbean can one identify the coexistence of inclusive multiculturalism in some places with exclusive

practices in others or fully see the collision of provincial and metropolitan political ideas. Only by taking a global approach can one account for and describe the intrinsically transnational experiences of many loyalist refugees, such as Elizabeth Johnston. In all these respects, the loyalist migrants are an unusually valuable group through which to investigate imperial history in this decade of change, particularly as it was lived and experienced.

They also suggest two ways in which the historiography of the American Revolution and the British Empire needs revisiting. One concerns the global nature of the Revolution, which has for so long been treated by Americanists in an almost exclusively national context or at best a transatlantic one. Loyalist refugees direct attention, rather, to the repercussions of American ideology elsewhere in the British world and to the circulation of colonial political, religious, and cultural influences around the British Empire. Looking forward into the nineteenth century, it seems plausible to speculate that such connections might have relevance for understanding the resilience of the Anglo-American relationship and the emergence of the concept of a greater Britain that would include Americans as well as Anglophone subjects overseas.

The other area for reappraisal involves the nature of the British imperial state. The treatment of loyalist refugees appears at one level to support the picture of an increasingly authoritarian, centralized, and expansionist imperial regime, trends that the French Revolutionary-Napoleonic Wars would magnify. Indeed the existence and extent of the loyalists' empire-wide diaspora call attention to the widening networks of war, commerce, culture, peoples, and opportunities that linked the colonies to one another as well as to Britain. Yet the ad hoc and varied receptions loyalists encountered also signal the continued significance of contingency and local circumstance in the modern British Empire, which could behave differently in different places as metropolitan policies confronted colonial realities. And as the clashes between loyalists and British authorities suggest, imperial rule was no more an uncontested top-down affair after the American Revolution than it had been previously. Historians of the British Empire interested in power relationships have tended to look at forms of resistance posed by nonwhite subjects. Yet templates for home rule and decolonization as well as for the idea of a federal greater Britain were established not in Ireland or India but in Canada, the American loyalist stronghold.[39]

The degree to which loyalist claims to British rights echoed those of their American patriot peers points to another important line of continuity between the pre- and postwar British empires. White, black, and Indian loyalists together encountered several emerging contradictions in the British Empire: gaps between liberal promises and paternalist realities, competing impulses toward liberty and authority, and tensions between what it meant to be British at home or abroad. As twentieth-century historical events would demonstrate, the multiethnic empire championed after 1783 proved no more able to overcome such internal contradictions than that older empire, with its struggle over "how to reconcile the exercise of authority over the empire with the aspiration that it be free."[40] So perhaps it is no wonder that these émigrés – postcolonial migrants of the eighteenth century – should have voiced concerns that anticipated those of a wide range of other imperial subjects. As they lived out the consequences of Britain's first major imperial defeat, it seems only too apt that the loyalist refugees should alert modern readers to oppositions in the greater British world that would contribute to the larger anti-imperial and postcolonial movements to come.

## Notes

Maya Jasanoff is an associate professor in the History Department at Harvard University. She would like to thank the anonymous readers for the *William and Mary Quarterly*, colleagues who offered suggestions on earlier versions of this piece, and audiences at Cornell University, Harvard University, Johns Hopkins University, the New School for Social Research, and the New York Public Library for their comments. The author is also grateful to her former colleagues and graduate students at the University of Virginia for many illuminating conversations on this topic.

1  Jacob Bailey, "A Journal containing a variety of incidents," vol. 4: 4–31, in Jacob Bailey Fonds, MG 1, vol. 95 (reel 14900), Provincial Archives of Nova Scotia, Halifax. On Bailey's persecution in Maine, see "Letters to Various Persons March 21st 1777 to Decr 30 1778," ibid., vol. 91, item no. 21 (reel 14895); "Rev. J. Bailey's explanation of his conduct in sending political notice," Mar. 1, 1775, in Jacob Bailey Papers, Library of Congress, Washington, D.C.

2  Paul H. Smith, "The American Loyalists: Notes on Their Organization and Numerical Strength," *William and Mary Quarterly*, 3d ser., 25, no. 2 (April 1968): 259–77 (quotation, 261). Smith uses the strength of loyalist regiments to develop a plausible estimate that 19.8 percent of the white population remained loyal. For the Nash label, see Gary B. Nash, *The Forgotten Fifth: African Americans in the Age of Revolution* (Cambridge, Mass., 2006). The marginal status of the topic of loyalism is underscored by the predominance of antiquarian and genealogically oriented studies. Some are gold mines, however, from the first serious study of the loyalists, Lorenzo Sabine's *Biographical Sketches of the Loyalists of the American Revolution with an Historical Essay* (Boston, 1864), to "The On-Line Institute for Advanced Loyalist Studies," maintained by Nan Cole and Todd Braisted, http://www.royalprovincial.com.

Major scholarly treatments include Bernard Bailyn, *The Ordeal of Thomas Hutchinson* (Cambridge, Mass., 1974); Carol Berkin, *Jonathan Sewall: Odyssey of an American Loyalist* (New York, 1974); John E. Ferling, *The Loyalist Mind: Joseph Galloway and the American Revolution* (University Park, Pa., 1977); Janice Potter, *The Liberty We Seek: Loyalist Ideology in Colonial New York and Massachusetts* (Cambridge, Mass., 1983); and the indispensable work of Robert McCluer Calhoon, including Calhoon, *The*

*Loyalists in Revolutionary America* (New York, 1973); Calhoon et al., *The Loyalist Perception and Other Essays* (Columbia, S.C., 1989); Calhoon, Timothy M. Barnes, and George A. Rawlyk, eds., *Loyalists and Community in North America* (Westport, Conn., 1994). But there is little on loyalists in works that have looked in detail at the British response to the war: H. T. Dickinson, ed., *Britain and the American Revolution* (Harlow, Eng., 1998); Stephen Conway, *The British Isles and the War of American Independence* (Oxford, Eng., 2000); Eliga H. Gould, *The Persistence of Empire: British Political Culture in the Age of the American Revolution* (Chapel Hill, N.C., 2000). More work has addressed British radicalism in this period than British conservatism, such as John Sainsbury, *Disaffected Patriots: London Supporters of Revolutionary America, 1769–1782* (Kingston, Ontario, 1987), but see Linda Colley, "The Apotheosis of George III: Loyalty, Royalty and the British Nation, 1760–1820," *Past and Present,* no. 102 (February 1984): 94–129; Kathleen Wilson, *The Sense of the People: Politics, Culture and Imperialism in England, 1715–1785* (Cambridge, 1995); J. C. D. Clark, *English Society, 1660–1832: Religion, Ideology and Politics during the Ancien Regime,* 2d ed. (Cambridge, 2000). For David Armitage's lament, see Armitage, "Greater Britain: A Useful Category of Historical Analysis?" *American Historical Review* 104, no. 2 (April 1999): 427–45, esp. 435.

3  See for instance a published response by G. Fiske Brown to my essay, "Loyal to a Fault" (*New York Times Magazine,* July 1, 2007), taking issue with the attempt "to foment sympathy for what amounted to America's first losers" (Letters, *New York Times Magazine,* July 15, 2007). On Benjamin Franklin and William Franklin, see Gordon S. Wood, *The Americanization of Benjamin Franklin* (New York, 2004), 160–63. On contemporary perceptions of the Revolution as a civil war, see among others T. H. Breen, "Ideology and Nationalism on the Eve of the American Revolution: Revisions *Once More* in Need of Revising," *Journal of American History* 84, no. 1 (June 1997): 13–39; Dror Wahrman, "The English Problem of Identity in the American Revolution," *American Historical Review* 106, no. 3 (October 2001): 1236–62; Linda Colley, *Captives: Britain, Empire, and the World, 1600–1850* (New

York, 2003), chap. 7; Edward Larkin, "What Is a Loyalist? The American Revolution as Civil War," *Common-Place* 8, no. 1 (October 2007), http://www.common-place.org/vol-08/no-01/larkin. An estimated nineteen thousand loyalists served in forty-two different provincial regiments and militias. See Smith, *WMQ* 25: 266; Calhoon, *Loyalists in Revolutionary America,* 502; Stephen Conway, *The War of American Independence, 1775–1783* (London, 1995), 46. Legal measures against the loyalists are summarized in Claude Halstead Van Tyne, *The Loyalists in the American Revolution* (1902; repr., Bowie, Md., 1989), app. B–C.

4  Bernard Bailyn, *Atlantic History: Concept and Contours* (Cambridge, Mass., 2005), 61 (quotation). Standard estimates of the loyalists who left range from sixty to one hundred thousand. My research thus far has allowed me to document the migration of roughly thirty thousand loyalists to the Maritimes (including three thousand black loyalists), six thousand to Quebec (including several hundred Mohawk), five thousand to Florida (from whence many would later move to the Bahamas or the Caribbean), three thousand to Jamaica, one thousand to the Bahamas, and seven thousand to Britain; to this total must be added a further five to seven thousand black loyalists not included in these tallies. I have also found evidence to support an estimate of fifteen to seventeen thousand slaves exported by loyalists. Slaves were not loyalists but should be counted in aggregate figures of the number of people dislocated by the war. (I will supply full documentation for my estimates in my forthcoming book on the loyalist diaspora.) For comparison with France, see R. R. Palmer, *The Age of the Democratic Revolution: A Political History of Europe and America, 1760–1800: The Challenge* (Princeton, N.J., 1959), 188. For black loyalist numbers, see Cassandra Pybus, "Jefferson's Faulty Math: The Question of Slave Defections in the American Revolution," *WMQ* 62, no. 2 (April 2005): 243–64. The *Book of Negroes* recorded nearly three thousand black loyalists embarking from New York for Nova Scotia, whereas Simon Schama indicates that thirty-five hundred blacks ultimately settled there. See Schama, *Rough Crossings: Britain, the Slaves and the American Revolution* (London,

2005), 223. For Mohawk loyalists, see Alan Taylor, *The Divided Ground: Indians, Settlers, and the Northern Borderland of the American Revolution* (New York, 2006). On the loyalist immigration to the Caribbean, see Wilbur H. Sieben, *The Legacy of the American Revolution to the British West Indies and Bahamas: A Chapter Out of the History of the American Loyalists* (Columbus, Ohio, 1913); Michael John Prokopow, "'To the Torrid Zones': The Fortunes and Misfortunes of American Loyalists in the Anglo-Caribbean Basin, 1774–1801" (Ph.D. diss., Harvard University, 1996). The black loyalist migration to Sierra Leone has most recently been studied by Schama, *Rough Crossings*; Pybus, *Epic Journeys of Freedom: Runaway Slaves of the American Revolution and Their Global Quest for Liberty* (Boston, 2006). Benedict Arnold's sons Edward and George appear in V. C. P. Hodson, *List of the Officers of the Bengal Army, 1758–1834* (London, 1927), 1: 52. Arnold's son Edward Shippen Arnold went to India "under the Patronage of Lord Cornwallis," and his son James (born just after the Revolution in Saint John) followed three years later. See Benedict Arnold to Jonathan Bliss, Sept. 19, 1800, in Benedict Arnold Papers, New Brunswick Museum, Saint John. For loyalists in Australia, see Pybus, *Epic Journeys*.

5  Keith Mason, "The American Loyalist Diaspora and the Reconfiguration of the British Atlantic World," in *Empire and Nation: The American Revolution in the Atlantic World*, ed., Eliga H. Gould and Peter S. Onuf (Baltimore, 2005), 239–59 (quotation, 239). For loyalists in Britain, see Mary Beth Norton, *The British-Americans: The Loyalist Exiles in England, 1774–178?* (London, 1974). For loyalists in Canada, see Alan Skeoch, *United Empire Loyalists and the American Revolution* (Toronto, Ontario, 1982); Neil MacKinnon, *This Unfriendly Soil: The Loyalist Experience in Nova Scotia, 1785–1791* (Kingston, Ontario, 1986); Janice Potter-MacKinnon, *While the Women Only Wept: Loyalist Refugee Women* (Montreal, Quebec, 1993); Norman Knowles, *Inventing the Loyalists: The Ontario Loyalist Tradition and the Creation of Usable Pasts* (Toronto, Ontario, 1997).

6  Alan Taylor, "The Late Loyalists: Northern Reflections of the Early American Republic," *Journal of the Early Republic* 27, no. 1 (Spring 2007): 1–34.

7  Gould, *Persistence of Empire*, 181–214 (quotation, 214). P. J. Marshall's argument is laid out in Marshall, *The Making and Unmaking of Empires: Britain, India, and America, c. 1750–1783* (Oxford, Eng., 2005), esp. 353–79. On authoritarianism and inclusion, see Linda Colley, *Britons: Forging the Nation, 1707–1837* (New Haven, Conn., 1992), chap. 3; Wilson, *Sense of the People*, chap. 5; Eliga H. Gould, "A Virtual Nation: Greater Britain and the Imperial Legacy of the American Revolution," *American Historical Review* 104, no. 2 (April 1999): 476–89; Christopher Leslie Brown, *Moral Capital: Foundations of British Abolitionism* (Chapel Hill, N.C., 2006). Brown argues that the American Revolution played a key role in crystallizing British abolitionism. On the notion of difference in the empire, see esp. Catherine Hall, *Civilising Subjects: Colony and Metropole in the English Imagination, 1830–1867* (Chicago, 2002); Kathleen Wilson, *The Island Race: Englishness, Empire and Gender in the Eighteenth Century* (London, 2003); Wilson, "Introduction: Histories, Empires, Modernities," in *A New Imperial History: Culture, Identity, and Modernity in Britain and the Empire, 1660–1840*, ed., Wilson (Cambridge, 2004), 1–26.

8  Colley, *Britons*, esp. 132–45. For an excellent concise analysis of the war's effects, see John Cannon, "The Loss of America," in Dickinson, *Britain and the American Revolution*, 233–57.

9  Andrew Jackson O'Shaughnessy, *An Empire Divided: The American Revolution and the British Caribbean* (Philadelphia, 2000), xii, 238; Brown, *Moral Capital*, 26–27.

10  James Mario Matra, "A Proposal for establishing a Settlement in New South Wales," Aug. 23, 1783, in Alan Frost, *The Precarious Life of James Mario Matra: Voyager with Cook, American Loyalist, Servant of Empire* (Carlton, Australia, 1995), 111–16.

11  Robin D. Gwynn, *Huguenot Heritage: The History and Contribution of the Huguenots in Britain* (London, 1985), 1 ("refugee"), 5, 24; H. T. Dickinson, "The Poor Palatines and the Parties," *English Historical Review* 82, no. 324 (July 1967): 464–85. I am grateful to Noah McCormack for the Dickinson reference. Loyalist émigrés also routinely referred to themselves as refugees. Their status conforms to the *Oxford English Dictionary's* first definition of refugee as "one who, owing to religious persecution or political

troubles, seeks refuge in a foreign country" (*OED*, s.v. "refugee").

12 Robert Mathews to Abraham Cuyler, Quebec, Nov. 18, 1782, in Haldimand Papers, British Library, Add. MSS 21825, fol. 25 ("necessities *absolutely* require it"); Stephen DeLancey to Mathews, Apr. 26, 1784, ibid., fols. 233–234 ("very sickly"). Some lucky refugees were equipped with supplies in advance: wool and linen, shoes and mittens, and an ax and spade for men. See "Memorandum by Brook Watson, commissary general," June 14, 1783, in Wallace Brown, *The Good Americans* (New York, 1969), 199–201. In Jamaica local authorities' efforts to cope with the refugee influx are reflected in the Kingston Parish Vestry's expenditures of £2131 8s. 2d. in 1783 and 1784 in pensions and other support for loyalists. See Kingston Vestry Minutes 2/6/6, fol. 118, Jamaica Archives, Spanish Town. For loyalist settlement in Quebec, see "Return of disbanded Troops & Loyalists settled upon the King's Lands in the Province of Quebec in the Year 1784," in Haldimand Papers, Add. MSS 21828, fol. 141.

13 MacKinnon, *This Unfriendly Soil,* 96 ("next to Egyptian Slavery"); Diary of Henry Nase, 20 ("blue nose"), in Nase Family Papers, New Brunswick Museum. For acreage allotments, see "Muster Roll of the following Disbanded officers, Discharged and Disbanded soldiers and their respective families of His Majestys late First Battalion of Kings Rangers that are now settled and preparing to settle in the Island of Saint John, taken 12th day of June 1784," in RG 1, vol. 376, pp. 83–87 (reel 15436), Provincial Archives of Nova Scotia. A list of escheats in Nova Scotia and New Brunswick can be found enclosed in a letter from Governor John Parr to Lord Sydney, June 3, 1786, in National Archives, CO 217/58, fol. 159. The travails of surveying are documented in the letters of Sir John Wentworth, Surveyor General of the King's Woods, in Letter-book of Sir John Wentworth, 1783–1808, RG 1, vol. 49 (reel 15237), Provincial Archives of Nova Scotia. For supplies from Britain, see "List of items sent out to Nova Scotia" (accompanies Lord North's letter to Parr of May 1783), in Carleton Papers, box 32, item no. 7631, New York Public Library.

14 John Eardley-Wilmot, *Historical View of the Commission for Enquiring into the Losses, Services,*

*and Claims of the American Loyalists, at the Close of the War between Great Britain and Her Colonies, in 1783* (1815; repr., Boston, 1972), 38.

15 Eardley-Wilmot, *Historical View of the Commission,* 37–40 ("Enquire into the Circumstances," 40), 50 ("alarming sum"), 90–91.

16 William Jarvis to Munson Jarvis, July 9, 1787, in Jarvis Family Papers, folder 27, New Brunswick Museum.

17 Eardley-Wilmot, *Historical View of the Commission,* 98–99 (quotation). A parallel may be drawn, however, with the distribution of £60,000 among more than five thousand "indigent" Royalist officers in the Restoration. See P. R. Newman, "The 1663 List of Indigent Royalist Officers Considered as a Primary Source for the Study of the Royalist Army," *Historical Journal* 30, no. 4 (December 1987): 885–904. On John Eardley-Wilmot's later support for French refugees, see Robert Tombs and Isabelle Tombs, *That Sweet Enemy: The French and the British from the Sun King to the Present* (New York, 2007), 213.

18 On the portrait of Eardley-Wilmot and the *Reception of the American Loyalists* image depicted on the wall behind him, see Helmut von Erffa and Allen Staley, *The Paintings of Benjamin West* (New Haven, Conn., 1986), 219–22 (quotations, 219), 565–67.

19 John Eardley-Wilmot said that pensions were granted to 588 people, "chiefly Widows, Orphans, and Merchants, who had no means of livelihood, but had lost no real or personal Estate." See Eardley-Wilmot, *Historical View of the Commission,* 95. Keith Mason and Christopher Leslie Brown interpret the image in much the sense conveyed by Eardley-Wilmot. See Mason, "American Loyalist Diaspora," 245–46; Brown, *Moral Capital,* 313.

20 On the treatment of the southern Indians, see "Substance of Talks delivered at a conference by the Indians to His Excellency Governor Tonyn, Colonel McArthur, and the Superintendent," May 15, 1783, in National Archives, CO 5/560, pp. 617–18 (quotations). Compare with the report in Bernardo del Campo to Conde de Floridabianca, London, Aug. 9, 1783, in Joseph Byrne Lockey, *East Florida, 1783–1785: A File of Documents Assembled, and Many of Them Translated,* ed., John Walton Caughey (Berkeley, Calif., 1949), 138–39. Joseph Brant sat for a portrait by

George Romney, and his Mohawk companion David Hill appeared in West's portrait of Guy Johnson. See Leslie Kaye Reinhardt, "British and Indian Identities in a Painting by Benjamin West," *Eighteenth-Century Studies* 31, no. 3 (Spring 1998): 283–305. On the misbegotten Bahamas scheme, see Wilbur Henry Sieben, *Loyalists in East Florida, 1774 to 1785: The Most Important Documents Pertaining Thereto, Edited with an Accompanying Narrative* (Deland, Fla., 1929), 1: 139. Many Iroquois, too, were abandoned on the American side of the border. See Taylor, *Divided Ground,* 111–13.

21  Slaves were listed on musters as "servants" to help stave off possible property claims from the United States. Incomplete records suggest that loyalists brought some 300 slaves to Upper Canada, 1,269 to Nova Scotia, and 441 to Saint John. See Robin W. Winks, *The Blacks in Canada: A History,* 2d ed. (Montreal, Quebec, 1997), 34–43 (quotation, 37). Wilbur H. Siebert says that about 5,000 blacks went to Jamaica from Savannah and 2,613 from Charleston. See Siebert, *Legacy of the American Revolution,* 7–8, 15. A report presented to the Bahamas House of Assembly in April 1789 estimated that twelve hundred whites and thirty-six hundred blacks arrived in the Bahamas in 1784 and 1785. See Journal of the House of Assembly of the Bahamas, Apr. 28, 1789, p. 248, in Department of Archives, Nassau. I draw figures for Jamaica loyalist slave owners from "A List of Loyalists in Jamaica, prepared by George F. Judah," in MS 1841, National Library of Jamaica, Kingston. The list appears to have been prepared for Wilbur H. Siebert.

22  Loyalists also tried to smuggle slaves out of the United States, which was one of the points of conflict between Governor John Maxwell and the loyalists in the Bahamas. Maxwell feared that runaway slaves were being sold in the Bahamas to loyalists, when "the poor Slave [had] obtained his Freedom by doing an Act, which all Nations protect, which is, most of these Wretches deserted from their masters in the Field: our General gave them Protections, and in Shifting for themselves, the Masters deceive them." He also worried that the slaves' true American owners would cause trouble trying to get them back. See Maxwell to Assembly, "Message," May 10, 1784, in National Archives, CO 23/25, fol. 205. On Dunmore

in the Bahamas, see Whittington B. Johnson, *Race Relations in the Bahamas, 1784–1834: The Nonviolent Transformation from a Slave to a Free Society* (Fayetteville, Ark., 2000), 4, 42, 69. Lord Dunmore's rampant self-aggrandizement did nothing to restore his popularity. See Michael Craton, *A History of the Bahamas* (London, 1968), 173–80.

23  See for example Catherine Hall, "The Nation Within and Without," in *Defining the Victorian Nation: Class, Race, Gender and the British Reform Act of 1867,* ed., Hall, Keith McClelland, and Jane Rendali (Cambridge, 2000), 179–233.

24  On the citizenship status of loyalists, see James H. Kettner, "The Development of American Citizenship in the Revolutionary Era: The Idea of Volitional Allegiance," *American Journal of Legal History* 18, no. 3 (July 1974): 208–42. For more perceptual distinctions, see Stephen Conway, "From Fellow-Nationals to Foreigners: British Perceptions of the Americans, circa 1739–1783," *WMQ* 59, no. 1 (January 2002): 65–100.

25  "Memorandum of Cash Expended for the use of Mrs. Wentworth's House," September 1786, in "Records Relating to the Town of Halifax, 1758–1828," RG 1, vol. 411, item no. 10 (reel 15457), Provincial Archives of Nova Scotia. On the Wells family, see Siebert, *Loyalists in East Florida,* 1: 189, 205; Louisa Susannah Wells, *The Journal of a Voyage from Charlestown to London* (New York, 1968), 87, 111–12. For Baptists, the central figures in Jamaica were George Liele and Moses Baker. See David Benedict, *A General History of the Baptist Denomination in America, and Other Parts of the World* (Boston, 1813), 2: 189–92, 194–206; Clement Gayle, *George Liele: Pioneer Missionary to Jamaica* (Kingston, Jamaica, 1982); John W. Pulis, ed., *Moving On: Black Loyalists in the Afro-Atlantic World* (New York, 1999). In Nova Scotia Baptist congregations were established by David George, who moved to Sierra Leone (George had been baptized by, and taken his name from, George Liele). John Marrant, a free black who had been a missionary to the Cherokee before the war and pressed into naval service as a musician during it, founded Methodist congregations. See Marrant, *A Narrative of the Lord's wonderful Dealings with John Marrant, A Black …* , 6th ed. (London, 1788). See also Alexander Pringle, *Prayer for the*

*Revival Of Religion In All The Protestant Churches, and for The Spread Of The Gospel Among Heathen Nations, Recommended …* (Edinburgh, Scotland, [1796]), 101–11, 127–50.

26  Bernard Bailyn, *The Ideological Origins of the American Revolution* (Cambridge, Mass., 1967).

27  Thomas Hutchinson, in Brown, *Good Americans,* 30 ("Tory"); Benjamin Marston, in MacKinnon, *This Unfriendly Soil,* 118 ("explained"); Taylor, *Journal of the Early Republic* 27: 7 ("we cast the Loyalists").

28  Gail Saunders, *Bahamian Loyalists and Their Slaves* (London, 1983), 58 ("not bound"); printed handbill enclosed in John Maxwell to Lord Sydney, June 29, 1784, in National Archives, CO 23/25, fol. 154 ("to preserve and maintain"); Maxwell to Sydney, Aug. 26, Sept. 4, Oct. 9, 1784, ibid., fols. 165 ("as if the Town"), 171 ("Torrent"), 229; Maxwell to Sydney, May 17, 1784, ibid., fol. 111 ("most tormenting"); James Powell to Grey Elliott, May 11, 1785, ibid., p. 193 ("seditiously mad"); Sydney to Maxwell, June 1786, ibid., fol. 418 ("violent spirit"). On the loyalists' political demands, see their petition to Powell, enclosed in Powell to Sydney, May II, 1785, ibid., pp. 321–24. "It is not a little extraordinary," replied Sydney, "that Men who profess to have suffered for their Loyalty to the Crown, and adherence to the British Constitution, should so far forget themselves, and the Duty they owe to His Majesty, as to be guilty of the most daring attempts against His Royal authority, and that Constitution" (Sydney to Maxwell, June 1786, ibid., fols. 418–19). On loyalists and race laws, see Sieben, *Legacy of the American Revolution,* 31–32; Saunders, *Bahamian Loyalists and Their Slaves,* 45, 68–69.

29  Thomas Carleton to Lord Sydney, June 25, 1785, in Thomas Carleton Letterbooks, ser., A, RG 1, RS33, Provincial Archives of New Brunswick ("American Spirit"); Carleton to Sydney, Nov. 20, 1785, ibid. ("motly"). For William Cobbett in Saint John, see D. G. Bell, *Early Loyalist Saint John: The Origin of New Brunswick Politics, 1783– 1786* (Fredericton, New Brunswick, 1983), 130– 31, 142–44. The election is treated in detail on 104–15. Neighboring Nova Scotia also suffered considerable disruption in its November 1785 elections; the first result was nullified, the second conducted in an environment of great "bitterness

[and] rancour," though the central line of tension in that province was between loyalists and preloyalists (settlers who were there before the loyalists). See MacKinnon, *This Unfriendly Soil,* 120–21 (quotation, 120).

30  "Clarkson's Mission to Africa," pp. 222 ("civil rights"), 319 ("all should be equal"), in John Clarkson Manuscripts, New-York Historical Society. On Sierra Leone government and rebellion, see Fyfe, *History of Sierra Leone,* 38–87; Pybus, *Epic Journeys,* xiii–xvi, 169–202.

31  Fyfe, *History of Sierra Leone,* 87 ("thorough Jacobins"); Taylor, *Journal of the Early Republic* 27: 18 ("passive benefits"). On Henri Christophe, see O'Shaughnessy, *Empire Divided,* 181.

32  Elizabeth Johnston to William Martin Johnston, Apr. 20, 1783, in Elizabeth Lichtenstein Johnston, *Recollections of a Georgia Loyalist* (New York, 1901), 211 (quotation). The original manuscript of this book, along with many letters between Elizabeth and William (only some of which are published, in abbreviated form, with the memoir), can be found in Almon Family Papers, reel 10362, Provincial Archives of Nova Scotia. The letters document their wartime travails, which were compounded by William's gambling problem. For the evacuation of Saint Augustine, see Siebert, *Loyalists in East Florida,* 1: 177. Siebert's description is wonderfully evocative, though, alas, not footnoted.

33  Johnston, *Recollections of a Georgia Loyalist,* 75 ("his native land"), 78 ("poor Loyalist"). The Johnstons' departure from Florida is described in Elizabeth Johnston to William Martin Johnston, Jan. 2, 15, Feb. 3, 12, 1784, in Almon Family Papers, reel 10362. William's slaves were sold for £450 (ibid.). Among the convoys leaving Saint Augustine in 1784 and 1785 for Nova Scotia, England, Jamaica, and the Bahamas, Admiralty records list one ship headed for Glasgow with the property of Lewis Johnston aboard. See Carole Watterson Troxler, "Loyalist Refugees and the British Evacuation of East Florida, 1783–1785," *Florida Historical Quarterly* 60, no. 1 (July 1981): 1–28, esp. 28. The list indicates "Lewis Johnston, Jr.," but given that Lewis Johnston Jr. went to the Bahamas and Lewis Johnston Sr. went to Glasgow, the entry must surely be an error. William Johnston's subsequent journey to Jamaica was clearly not unique. Another

Scottish doctor in Jamaica complained in 1787 about the "overabundance of physicians," which he attributed to the "vast number of Medical people who were … *refugees.*" See Alan L. Karras, *Sojourners in the Sun: Scottish Migrants in Jamaica and the Chesapeake, 1740–1800* (Ithaca, N.Y., 1992), 55.

34 Johnston, *Recollections of a Georgia Loyalist,* 85 ("much exhausted"), 90 ("On the morning").

35 Ibid., 91–95, 105–7 (quotation, 105).

36 Ibid., 107, 108 ("nervous illness"), 110 ("Worn down").

37 Ibid., 108–111 (quotations, 111). The *Dictionary of Canadian Biography* includes detailed entries on Elizabeth Johnston's sons-in-law Thomas Ritchie and William Bruce Almon (and their fathers) as well as several of their sons and grandsons; there are also entries for Elizabeth herself (s.v. "Elizabeth Lichtenstein") and for her son James William Johnston.

38 Johnston, *Recollections of a Georgia Loyalist,* 110. For loyalist women's responses to migration, see Mary Beth Norton, "Eighteenth-Century American Women in Peace and War: The Case of the Loyalists," *WMQ* 33, no. 3 (July 1976): 386–409. The Johnston family members who presented claims to the Loyalist Claims Commission were Elizabeth's father, John Lightenstone; her father-in-law, Lewis Johnston Sr.; her husband, William Martin Johnston; and her brother-in-law Lewis Johnston Jr., who settled in the Bahamas and filed the largest claim of all, for a house in Savannah, 1,650 acres, and 400 cattle. See Peter Wilson Coldham, *American Loyalist Claims* (Washington, D.C., 1980), 263–64, 288–89.

39 On Canada's role as a template for decolonization, see Robin W. Winks, *The Relevance of Canadian History: U.S. and Imperial Perspectives* (Toronto, Ontario, 1979). 38–39.

40 Marshall, *Making and Unmaking of Empires,* 161.

# 21
# THE GREATNESS OF GEORGE WASHINGTON

*Gordon S. Wood*

## Introduction

Remarkably, the end product of the American Revolution – a revolt against a strong centralized, monarchical government – was a governing system that featured a strong chief executive modeled on the monarchy. This turn of events, according to Gordon S. Wood, was only possible because of one man: George Washington. The American people had such faith in Washington that they were willing to entrust their republican experiment to his leadership. Wood argues that Washington garnered this trust neither through military heroics nor a great intellect, but because of his character. Specifically, Washington's greatness came from his willingness to surrender power. Twice, once after the Revolutionary War and again after his second term as president, he gave up effective control over the country. In so doing, Washington's greatest legacy was preserving and extending the American republic for future generations.

- Wood unapologetically practices what is sometimes termed the "great man theory of history." This school of thought holds that individuals, not simply broad historical forces, have the power to shape historical events. Does Wood make a persuasive case for Washington's centrality to the founding of the United States? Put another way, is it possible to imagine the American Revolution succeeding without Washington?
- Wood argues that Washington was America's greatest president. What evidence does he present to support this contention? What does Wood mean by the term "republican monarch" to describe Washington's presidency?
- Consider this selection along with Wood's other essay in this volume, on "interests and disinterestedness" in early American politics. How did Washington embody the principles of "disinterested" leadership? By his own admission, Washington was frustrated with the direction of the country, particularly the onset of party politics, by the time of his death in 1799. How should we assess Washington and the other leading founders given the many unintended consequences of the American Revolution?

George Washington may still be first in war and first in peace, but he no longer seems to be first in the hearts of his countrymen. A recent poll asking who was America's greatest president showed that only 6 percent of those polled named Washington. He was ranked seventh among presidents. Young people in particular did not know much about Washington.

Polls of presidential greatness are probably silly things, but if they are to be taken seriously, then Washington fully deserves the first place he used to hold. He certainly deserved the accolades his contemporaries gave him. And as long as this Republic endures, he ought to be first in the hearts of his countrymen. Washington was truly a great man and the greatest president we ever had.

But he was a great man who is not easy to understand. He became very quickly, as has often been pointed out, more a monument than a man. Even his contemporaries realized that he was not an ordinary accessible human being. Every passing year made him less of a real person. By the early decades of the nineteenth century he had already become statuesque and impenetrable. "Did anyone ever see Washington nude?" Hawthorne asked. "It is inconceivable." Washington "was born with his clothes on, and his hair powdered, and made a stately bow on his first appearance in the world."

Of course, as Emerson once said, "Every hero becomes a bore at last," and Washington was no exception. By the middle of the nineteenth century the eulogies of Washington had become so conventional and so prevalent that a humorist like Artemus Ward could not resist parodying them: "G. Washington was about the best man this world ever set eyes on … . He never slopt over! … He luved his country dearly. He wasn't after the spiles. He was a human angil in a 3 kornered hat and knee britches."[1]

Despite the continued popularity of Parson Weems's biographical attempt to humanize Washington, the great man remained distant and unapproachable, almost unreal and unhuman. There were periodic efforts to bring him down to earth, to expose his foibles, to debunk his fame, but he remained massively monumental. By our time in the early twenty-first century he seems so far removed from us as to be virtually incomprehensible. He seems to come from another time and another place, from another world.

That's the whole point about him: He did come from another world. And his countrymen knew it almost before he died in 1799. Washington was the only truly classical hero we have ever had. He was admired as a classical hero in his own lifetime. Among his fellow Americans only Franklin rivaled him for international acclaim, and Franklin's reputation was confined to science and philosophy. Washington was much more of a traditional hero. And he knew it. He was well aware of his reputation and his fame earned as the commander in chief of the American revolutionary forces. That awareness of his heroic stature was crucial to Washington. It affected nearly everything he did for the rest of his life.

Washington was a thoroughly eighteenth-century figure. Like Samuel Adams, he was "one of Plutarch's men," and like Adams, he quickly became an anachronism.[2] He belonged to the predemocratic and pre-egalitarian world of the eighteenth century, to a world very different from the one that followed. No wonder he seems to us so remote. He really is. He belonged to a world we have lost, one we were losing even while he lived.

In many respects Washington was a very unlikely hero. To be sure, he had all the physical attributes of a classical hero. He was very tall by contemporary standards, six feet three or so, and was heavily built and a superb athlete. Physically he had what men and women admired. He was both a splendid horseman at a time when that skill really counted and an extraordinarily graceful dancer, and naturally he loved both riding and dancing. He always moved with dignity and looked like a leader.

Yet those who knew him well and talked with him were often disappointed. He never seemed to have very much to say. He was almost certainly not what we today would call an intellectual. We cannot imagine his expressing his views over the uses and abuses of grief in the world in the way Jefferson and John Adams did in their old age. Adams was contemptuous of Washington's intellectual abilities. It was certain, said Adams, that Washington was not a scholar. "That he was too illiterate, unlearned, unread for his station and reputation is equally past dispute." Adams's judgment is surely too harsh. Great men in the eighteenth century did not have to be scholars or intellectuals. But there is no doubt that Washington was not a learned man, especially in comparison with the other founders. He was very ill at ease in abstract discussions. Even Jefferson, who was usually generous in his estimates of his friends, said that Washington's "colloquial talents were not above mediocrity." He had "neither copiousness of ideas nor fluency of words."[3]

Washington, then, was a man of few words and no great thoughts. Obviously he was not a great mind; he was not in the class of Bacon, Locke, Newton, or even Jefferson or Franklin. He was not an intellectual; he was a man of affairs. He knew how to run his plantation and make it pay. He certainly ran Mount Vernon better than Jefferson ran Monticello; indeed, he was one of the most successful of planter businessmen in all of Virginia. Washington's heart was always at Mount Vernon, but also more than his heart: a good part of his mind too. He thought about it all the time. Even when he was president, he devoted a great amount of his energy worrying about the fence posts of his plantation, and his letters dealing with the details of running Mount Vernon were longer than those dealing with the running of the federal government.

But being a man of affairs and running his plantation or even the federal government efficiently were not what made him a world-renowned hero. What was it that lay behind his extraordinary reputation, his greatness?

His military exploits were of course crucial. Still, Washington was not really a traditional military hero. He did not resemble Alexander, Caesar, Cromwell, or Marlborough; his military achievements were nothing compared with those Napoleon would soon have. Washington had no smashing, stunning victories. He was not a military genius, and his tactual and strategic maneuvers were not the sort that awed men. Military glory was not the source of his reputation. Something else was involved. What was it?

Washington's genius, Washington's greatness, lay in his character. He was, as Chateaubriand said, a "hero of an unprecedented kind."[4] There had never been a great man quite like Washington before, and after Napoleon emerged in 1800 as a Caesar-like world-shattering imperialistic hero, it seemed there might never be another like him again. Washington became a great man and was acclaimed as a classical hero because of the way he conducted himself during times of temptation. It was his moral character that set him off from other men.

Washington epitomized everything the revolutionary generation prized in its leaders. He had character and was truly a man of virtue. This virtue was not given to him by nature. He had to work for it, to cultivate it, and everyone sensed that. Washington was a self-made hero, and this impressed an eighteenth-century enlightened world that put great stock in men's controlling both their passions and their destinies. Washington seemed to possess a self-cultivated nobility.

Washington was a child of the Enlightenment. He was very much a man of his age, and he took its moral standards more seriously than did most of his contemporaries. Washington's Enlightenment, however, was never precisely that of, say, Jefferson or Franklin. It did not involve high philosophy or abstract reasoning. To be sure, he was conventionally liberal on matters of religion ("being no bigot myself to any mode of worship"), and though he went to church regularly to keep up decorum, he was not an emotionally religious person. He rarely mentioned Christ in his writings, and he usually referred to God as "the great disposer of human events." But Washington had no dislike of the clergy or of organized Christianity as Jefferson did.[5] He would never have said, as Jefferson did, that "our civil rights have no dependence on our religious opinions, any more than our opinions in physics or geometry."[6] He came to believe devoutly that God or Divine Providence was looking after man's affairs, including his participation in the Revolutionary War. He was also convinced, as he declared in his Farewell Address, that religion was an indispensable prop for both morality and republican government. Although he admired learning, he was not a man of science like Franklin; in fact, like many eighteenth-century gentlemen, he did not believe that "becoming a mere scholar was a desirable education for a gentleman."[7] Washington's Enlightenment was a much more down-to-earth affair, concerned with social behavior and with living in the everyday world of people. His Enlightenment involved civility.

Sometime before his sixteenth birthday Washington copied 110 maxims from a popular seventeenth-century English translation of a 1595 Jesuit etiquette book, *Bienséance de la conversation entre les hommes,* which in turn was borrowed from an Italian volume first published in 1558–59. These *Rules of Civility and Decent Behaviour in Company and Conversation,* which is the first document we have of Washington's papers, dealt with everything from how to treat one's betters ("In speaking to men of Quality do not lean nor Look them full in the Face … ") to how to present one's countenance ("Do not Puff up the Cheeks, Loll not out the tongue, rub the Hands, or beard, thrust out the lips, or bite them or keep the Lips too open or too Close") and how to eat with company ("Cleanse not your teeth with the Table Cloth Napkin Fork or Knife… ").[8]

All the founders were aware of these conventions of civility, and all in varying degrees tried to live up to them. But no one was more serious in following them than Washington. He wanted desperately to know the proper rules of behavior for a liberal gentleman, and when he discovered them, he stuck by them with an earnestness that awed his contemporaries. It is this purposefulness that gave his behavior such a copybook character. He loved Joseph Addison's play *Cato* and saw it over and over and incorporated some of its lines into his correspondence. The play, very much an Enlightenment tract, helped teach him what it meant to be liberal and virtuous, what it meant to be a stoical classical hero.[9]

Washington was obsessed with having things in fashion and was fastidious about his appearance to the world. It was as if he were always onstage, acting a part. Indeed, he always thought of life as "the Stage" on which one was a "Character" making a mark.[10] He was very desirous not to offend, and he shaped his remarks exquisitely to fit the person to whom he was writing, so much so that some historians have accused him of deceit.[11] He worked on his penmanship, spelling, and grammar, and following the Revolutionary War, when he knew he would be a famous man, he went back and corrected what he took to be deficiencies in his earlier writings.[12] "So anxious was he to appear neat and correct in his letters," recalled Benjamin Rush, that he was known to "copy a letter of 2 or [3?] sheets of paper because there were a few erasures on it."[13] His remarkable formality and stiffness in company came from his very self-conscious cultivation of what was considered proper genteel classical behavior.

Precisely because Washington had not attended college and received a liberal arts education, he became punctilious and literal-minded about observing and adopting what he had formally missed. Colleges like William and Mary were always an "Object of Veneration" to him, and he repeatedly expressed his "consciousness of a defective education."[14] He was forever embarrassed that he had never learned any foreign languages. In the 1780s he refused invitations to visit France in part because he felt it would be humiliating for someone of his standing to have to converse through an interpreter. He said that it was his lack of a formal education that kept him from setting down on paper his recollections of the Revolution. It was even widely rumored that his aides composed his best letters as commander in chief. His lack of a college education, however, did not keep him from expressing his hard-earned gentility in other ways. He loved attending tea tables; during the months of deliberations over the new constitution in 1787 his diary entries note little more than his continual attendance at tea.[15]

He was apt to remain quiet in the presence of sharp and sparkling minds. Some called his diffidence shyness, but whatever the source, this reticence was certainly not the usual characteristic of a great man. "His modesty is astonishing to a Frenchman," noted Jacques Pierre Brissot de Warville. "He speaks of the American War, and of his victories, as of things in which he had no direction." This modesty only added to his gravity and severity. "Most people say and do too much," one friend recalled. "Washington ... never fell into this common error." Washington may not always have been a great dinner party companion, but he certainly had what John Adams ruefully lacked: the "gift of silence."[16]

Washington sometimes may have moved diffidently in the social world, but in the political world he knew how to make a dramatic move. One of his most impressive acts was his freeing of his slaves in his will. Of all the well-known founders who were major slaveholders, including Jefferson, Madison, and Patrick Henry, Washington was the only one who actually ended up freeing his slaves. He was of course no fiery abolitionist, and in his lifetime he never spoke out publicly against the institution of slavery. Instead he arrived at his conclusion that slavery was immoral and inconsistent with the ideals of the Revolution gradually, privately, and with difficulty.

Prior to the Revolution Washington, like most eighteenth-century Americans, especially Virginians, took slavery very much for granted. Eighteenth-century society was composed of many degrees of inequality and unfreedom, and slavery seemed to be merely the most base and degraded status in a hierarchy of dependencies. Although we today can scarcely imagine one person's owning another, that was certainly not the case in early-eighteenth-century America. After all, slavery had existed for thousands of years without any substantial criticism, and this was still true in early-eighteenth-century America.

On the eve of the Revolution all the colonies were implicated in African slavery in one way or another. Of the total American population of 1.5 million in 1760, at least one-fifth – over 300,000 men, women, and children – was enslaved. Washington's Virginia, the largest and richest colony, had the most slaves, more than 140,000, or 40 percent of its population. During the first half of the eighteenth century Virginian planters, even educated and sensitive ones like William Byrd, showed no guilt or defensiveness over their holding hundreds of slaves on their plantations. It was a cruel and brutal age, and the life of the lowly everywhere seemed cheap.

The American Revolution changed all this. The revolutionaries did not need Dr. Johnson ("How is it that we hear the loudest yelps for liberty among the drivers of negroes?") to tell them about the glaring inconsistency between their appeals to liberty and their owning of slaves. In the new republican society of equal citizens dedicated to liberty, slavery suddenly became an anomaly, a "peculiar institution" that, if it were to continue, now needed defending and justifying. It was no accident that the first antislave society in the world was organized in Philadelphia in 1775. All the revolutionary leaders became aware of the excruciating contradiction between their revolution on behalf of liberty and American slavery. Washington was no exception.

But Washington's awakening to the evils of slavery did not come suddenly or easily. It was no simple matter for him to come to question what he had unquestioningly accepted or to challenge what was after all the very basis of his and Virginia's way of life. As a civic-minded southern planter deeply immersed in his society and its culture, he held views on slavery before the Revolution that were indistinguishable from those of his fellow Virginia planters. As he sought to increase the wealth and productivity of Mount Vernon, he bought more and more slaves, selling some only on rare occasions. By 1774 he had over a hundred slaves on his plantation. Although he was a good master, constantly concerned with the health and welfare of his slaves, he did not agonize over his holding human beings in bondage. When he criticized the institution, as he did on several occasions prior to the Revolution, he did so because he believed that slavery made his workers inefficient and lazy, not that it was immoral or inhumane. In 1774 he endorsed the Fairfax Resolves, which included a recommendation that no more slaves should be imported into the British colonies. Many Virginians wanted to end the slave trade because they had more slaves than they knew what to do with. Washington, however, was at the time purchasing additional slaves from the West Indies.

When Washington became commander in chief of the Continental army, he was forced by military circumstances to change his original view that blacks not become soldiers. Finding African Americans among the New England troops in 1775 was an eye-opening experience for him, and he began advocating the recruitment of free blacks into the Continental army. In 1778 he allowed Rhode Islanders to raise an all-black regiment of soldiers, and in 1779 he cautiously approved a plan to grant slaves their freedom in return for military service. Since he understood only too well the deeply rooted fears and prejudices of his fellow southerners, he was not surprised when the plan failed. Still, through the years of the war Washington had led a racially integrated army composed of as many as five thousand African American soldiers. Although as commander in chief he did not speak out publicly against slavery, he was slowly and privately rethinking the issue of black bondage.

By the time he returned to Mount Vernon at the end of the war, he had concluded that slavery needed to be abolished, not simply because it was an inefficient labor system but, more important, because it violated everything the Revolution was about. Reluctant as he was to confront the society and culture in which he had to live, he said nothing publicly against slavery. But privately he vowed in 1786 not to purchase any more slaves; at the time he had over two hundred, nearly half of whom were too young or too old to work. As he told a fellow Virginian, he had come to hope against hope that some plan could be adopted by which slavery could be eliminated "by slow, sure, & imperceptible degrees."[17] He knew only too well that any other plan would be politically impossible.

By 1794, as he contemplated retirement from the presidency, he was seriously considering freeing what he called "a certain species of property which I possess, very repugnantly to my own feelings."[18] But there were problems. Not only did the difficulty of translating his immense land-holdings into ready cash stymie his efforts to liberate his slaves, but the fact that a majority of his slaves, who now numbered close to three hundred, did not belong to him but were dower slaves who belonged to Martha and her heirs complicated matters. In the summer of 1799, six months before his death, he decided to deal with the problem as best he could from beyond the grave. He drew up a new will, composed secretly in his own hand, probably because what he wanted to do with his slaves was opposed by his neighbors, his family, and perhaps even Martha. This will is one of the most important documents he ever wrote. Because his and Martha's slaves had so intermarried, he stated that only upon the death of his wife would all his slaves be freed. But he did not just throw his slaves out into the world. Not only did he forbid any of the freed slaves from being transported out of Virginia "under any pretense whatsoever," but he directed that all the freed slaves who were too young or too old to be independent should be supported for as long as necessary. Not only were the young to be cared for until age twenty-five, but they were to be taught to read and write and prepared for "some useful occupation." Knowing the feelings of his family, not to mention the larger Virginia world, he loaded his will with imperatives, "most pointedly and most solemnly" enjoining his executors "religiously" to fulfill his commands "without evasion, neglect, or delay."[19]

Washington's will was almost immediately printed in pamphlet form and circulated throughout the country. However the country, or at least the southern portion of it, was not yet ready for the message it contained. His legacy regarding emancipation died aborning.

That was not true of another bequest that Washington had earlier left to the nation. In 1783 Washington, consummate actor that he was, made his most theatrical gesture, his most moral mark, and the results were monumental. The greatest act of his life, the one that made him internationally famous, was his resignation as commander in chief of the American forces. This act, together with his circular letter to the states in which he promised his retirement, was what he called his legacy to his countrymen. No American leader has ever left a more important legacy.

Following the signing of the peace treaty and British recognition of American independence, Washington stunned the world when he surrendered his sword to the Congress on December 23, 1783, and retired to his farm at Mount Vernon. As Garry Wills has shown, this was a highly symbolic act, a very self-conscious and unconditional withdrawal from the world of politics.[20] In order to enhance the disinterestedness of the political advice he offered in the circular letter to the states he wrote six months before his actual retirement, he promised not to take "any share in public business hereafter." He even resigned from his local vestry in order to make his separation from the political world complete.

His retirement from power had a profound effect everywhere in the Western world. It was extraordinary; a victorious general's surrendering his arms and returning to his farm was unprecedented in modern times. Cromwell, William of Orange, Marlborough — all had sought political rewards commensurate with their military achievements. Though it was widely believed that Washington could have become king or dictator, he wanted nothing of the kind. He was sincere in his desire for all his soldiers "to return to our Private Stations in the bosom of a free, peaceful and happy Country," and everyone recognized his sincerity. It filled them with awe. Washington's retirement, said the painter John Trumbull, writing from London in 1784, "excites the astonishment and admiration of this part of the world. Tis a Conduct so novel, so unconceivable to People, who, far from giving up powers they possess, are willing to convulse the empire to acquire more." King George III supposedly predicted that if Washington retired from public life and returned to his farm, "he will be the greatest man in the world."[21] Jefferson was not exaggerating when he declared in 1784 that "the moderation and virtue of a single character ... probably prevented this revolution from being closed, as most others have been, by a subversion of that liberty it was intended to establish."[22]

Washington was not naive. He was well aware of the effect his resignation would have. He was trying to live up to the age's image of a classical disinterested patriot who devotes his life to his country, and he knew at once that he had acquired instant fame as a modern Cincinnatus. His reputation in the 1780s as a great classical hero was international, and it was virtually unrivaled. Franklin was his only competitor, but Franklin's greatness still lay in his being a scientist, not a man of public affairs. Washington was a living embodiment of all the classical republican virtue the age was eagerly striving to recover.

Despite his outward modesty, Washington realized he was an extraordinary man, and he was not ashamed of it. He lived in an era when distinctions of social rank were still accepted.

He took for granted the differences between him and more ordinary men. When he could not take those differences for granted, he cultivated them. He used his natural reticence to reinforce the image of a stern and forbidding classical hero. His aloofness was notorious, and he worked at it. When Gilbert Stuart had uncharacteristic difficulty in putting Washington at ease during a sitting for a portrait, the artist in exasperation finally pleaded, "Now, sir, you must let me forget that you are General Washington and that I am Stuart, the painter." Washington's reply chilled the air: "Mr. Stuart need never feel the need of forgetting who he is, or who General Washington is." No wonder the portraits look stiff.[23]

Washington had earned his reputation, his "character," as a moral hero, and he did not want to dissipate it. He spent the rest of his life guarding and protecting his reputation and worrying about it. He believed Franklin made a mistake going back into public life in Pennsylvania in the 1780s. Such involvement in politics, he thought, could only endanger Franklins already achieved international standing. In modern eyes Washington's concern for his reputation is embarrassing; it seems obsessive and egotistical. But his contemporaries understood. All gentlemen tried scrupulously to guard their reputations, which is what they meant by their honor. Honor was the esteem in which they were held, and they prized it. To have honor across space and time was to have fame, and fame was what the founders were after, Washington above all.[24] And he got it, sooner and in greater degree than any other of his contemporaries. Naturally, having achieved what all his fellow revolutionaries still anxiously sought, he was reluctant to risk it.

Many of his actions after 1783 can be understood only in terms of this deep concern for his reputation as a virtuous leader. He was constantly on guard and very sensitive to any criticism. Jefferson said no one was more sensitive. Washington judged all his actions by what people might think of them. This sometimes makes him seem silly to modern minds, but not to those of the eighteenth century. In that very suspicious age in which people were acutely "jealous" of what great men were up to, Washington thought it important that people understand his motives. The reality was not enough; he had to appear virtuous. He was obsessed that he not seem base, mean, avaricious, or unduly ambitious. No one, said Jefferson, worked harder than Washington in keeping "motives of interest or consanguinity, of friendship or hatred" from influencing him. He had a lifelong preoccupation with his reputation for "disinterestedness."[25]

This preoccupation explains the seemingly odd fastidiousness and caution of his behavior in the 1780s. In 1783 he welcomed the formation of the Order of the Cincinnati and agreed to be its first president. Nothing was dearer to him than this fraternity of retired revolutionary army officers, until a great popular outcry was raised against it. Washington was bewildered and shaken, and he appealed to his friends for advice. Jefferson got Washington to put pressure on the order to reform itself and eliminate its hereditary character by appealing to the one argument that Washington could not resist: that his leadership of this aristocratic society would tarnish his reputation for classical virtue.

In the winter of 1784–85 Washington was led into temptation once again, and it was agony. The Virginia Assembly presented him with 150 shares in the James River and Potomac canal companies in recognition of his services to the state and the cause of canal building. What should he do? He did not believe he could accept the shares. Acceptance might be "considered in the same light as a pension" and might compromise his reputation for virtue. Yet he believed passionately in what the canal companies were doing and had long dreamed of making a fortune from such canals. Moreover, he did not want to show "disrespect" to the assembly or to appear "ostentatiously disinterested" by refusing this gift.[26]

Few decisions in Washington's career caused more distress than this one. He wrote to everyone he knew – to Jefferson, to Governor Patrick Henry, to William Grayson, to Benjamin Harrison, to George William Fairfax, to Nathanael Greene, even to Lafayette in France – seeking "the best information and advice" on the disposition of the shares. "How would this matter be viewed then by the eyes of the world?" he asked. Would not his reputation for virtue be harmed? Would not accepting the shares "deprive me of the principal thing which is laudable in my conduct?" – that is, his disinterestedness.

The story would be comic if Washington had not been so deadly earnest. He certainly understated the situation when he told his correspondents that his mind was "not a little agitated" by the problem.[27] In letter after letter he expressed real anguish. This was no ordinary display of scruples such as government officials today show over a conflict of interest; in 1784 and 1785 Washington was not even holding public office.

Once again Jefferson found the key to Washington's anxieties and told him that declining to accept the shares would only add to his reputation for disinterestedness. So Washington gave them away to the college that eventually became Washington and Lee.

Washington suffered even more anguish over the decision to attend the Philadelphia Convention in 1787. Many believed that his presence was absolutely necessary for the effectiveness of the convention, but the situation was tricky. He implored friends to tell him "confidentially what the public expectation is on this head, that is, whether I will or ought to be there?" How would his presence be seen? How would his motives be viewed? If he attended, would he be thought to have violated his pledge to withdraw from public life? But if he did not attend, would his staying away be thought to be a "derilection to Republicanism"? Should he squander his reputation on something that might not work?[28]

What if the convention should fail? The delegates would have to return home "chagrined at their ill success and disappointment. This would be a disagreeable circumstance for any one of them to be in; but more particularly so for a person in my situation." Even Madison had second thoughts about the possibility of misusing such a precious asset as Washington's reputation; What finally convinced Washington to attend the convention was the fear that people might think he wanted the federal government to fail so that he could then manage a military takeover. He decided, as Madison put it, "to forsake the honorable retreat to which he had retired and risk the reputation he had so deservedly acquired." No action could be more virtuous. "Secure as he was in his fame," wrote Henry Knox with some awe, "he has again committed it to the mercy of events. Nothing but the critical situation of his country would have induced him to so hazardous a conduct."[29]

When the convention met, Washington was at once elected its president. Although the convention usually turned itself into a committee of the whole, meaning that Washington did not have to preside over the debates, he apparently said very little during its deliberations. Perhaps he recognized that anything he said or proposed would stymie debate since no one would dare contest him. Only at the very end of the convention did he speak out in favor of reducing the minimum number of people for a representative from forty to thirty thousand. It was an exceedingly minor point, and with Washington's backing, it was agreed to unanimously. It was his way of saying to his colleagues that he favored the Constitution.

No doubt Washington's presence and his leadership gave the convention and the proposed Constitution a prestige that they otherwise could not have had. His backing of the Constitution was certainly essential to its eventual ratification. "Be assured," James Monroe told Jefferson, "his influence carried this government."[30] Washington, once committed to the Constitution, worked hard for its acceptance. He wrote letters to friends and let his enthusiasm for the new federal government be known.

Once he had identified himself publicly with the new Constitution he became very anxious to have it accepted. Its ratification was a kind of ratification of himself.

After the Constitution was established, Washington still believed he could retire to the domestic tranquility of Mount Vernon. But everyone else assumed that he would become president of the new national government. Once again this widespread expectation aroused all his old anxieties about his reputation. He had promised the country that he would permanently retire from public life. How could he now assume the presidency without being "changeable with levity and inconsistency; if not with rashness and ambition?" His protests were sincere. He had so much to lose and so little to gain. But he did not want to appear "too solicitous for reputation." He was certain, he told his friend Henry Lee, "whensoever I shall be convinced the good of my country requires my reputation to put at risque; regard for my own fame will not come in competition with an object of so much magnitude."[31]

But Washington could not continue to pose the issue starkly in this way as one between duty and reputation. For the more he thought about it, the more that both accepting and not accepting the presidency became matters of reputation, especially after Hamilton suggested to him that there might be "greater hazard to that fame, which must be and ought to be dear to you, in refusing your future aid to the system than in affording it." It was not easy to make decisions when a concern for one's virtue was viewed as unvirtuous. Nothing could make him abandon his retirement, Washington told Benjamin Lincoln, "unless it be a *conviction* that the partiality of my Countrymen had made my services absolutely necessary, joined to a *fear* that my refusal might induce a belief that I preferred the conservation of my own reputation & private ease, to the good of my Country."[32]

Washington's apparent egotism and his excessive coyness, his extreme reluctance to get involved in public affairs and endanger his reputation have not usually been well received by historians. Douglas Southall Freeman, his great biographer, thought that Washington in the late 1780s was "too zealously attentive to his prestige, his reputation and his popularity – too much the self-conscious national hero and too little the daring patriot."[33] Historians might not understand his behavior, but his contemporaries certainly did. They rarely doubted that Washington was trying always to act in a disinterested way. His anxious queries about how would this or that look to the world, his hesitations about serving or not serving, his expressions of scruples and qualms – all were part of his strenuous effort to live up to the classical idea of a virtuous leader. He had never accepted a salary as commander in chief of the Continental army, and although the Congress made him accept a salary as president, he wanted it understood that he had tried to refuse it. He seemed to epitomize public virtue. Even if John Adams was not all that impressed with George Washington, Adams's wife, Abigail, was certainly taken with him. She admired his restraint and trusted him. "If he was not really one of the best-intentioned men in the world," she wrote, "he might be a very dangerous one." As historian Garry Wills has so nicely put it, Washington "gained power from his readiness to give it up."[34]

The pressure on Washington to serve as president was immense, and he gave way; naturally, he was elected with every possible electoral vote, the only president in American history so honored. As the first president he faced circumstances that no other president has ever faced, and he was the only person in the country who could have dealt with them. The American people had been reared in monarchy and had never known a distant chief executive who had not been a king. Somehow Washington had to satisfy their deeply rooted yearnings for patriarchal leadership while creating a new elective republican president. Since the United States had never had an elected chief executive like the one created by the Constitution of 1787, Washington had virtually no precedents to follow. Not only did he have to justify and to flesh out the new office of the presidency, but he also had to put together the new nation and prove to a skeptical world that America's grand experiment in self-government was possible. That he did all this in the midst of a revolutionary world at war and did it without sacrificing the republican character of the country is an astonishing achievement, one that the achievements of no other president, however great, can begin to match.

There is no doubt that many American leaders in 1789 thought that there had been too much democracy in the states in the 1780s and that this excessive democracy needed to be curbed without doing violence to republican principles. That had been one of the reasons behind the making of the new Constitution. All the Federalists, as the supporters of the new Constitution called themselves, knew that if democracy were to be curbed, then what was needed in the new government was more power. And power in eighteenth-century Anglo-American political theory essentially meant monarchy. According to the conventional conception of an eighteenth-century balanced or mixed constitution, too much democracy required the counterbalancing of some more monarchy.

But by 1789 the Federalists knew only too well that they could not speak openly about the need for more monarchy in the government. Nevertheless, many of them privately shared the opinion of Benjamin Rush that the new government was one "which unites with the vigor of monarchy and the stability of aristocracy all the freedom of a simple republic."[35] Even Madison, as devoted to republicanism as any of the founders, expected the new federal government to play the same superpolitical neutral role that the British king had been supposed to play in the empire.[36]

Other Federalists like Alexander Hamilton were even more disillusioned with the democratic consequences of the Revolution and wanted even stronger doses of monarchy

injected into the body politic. In fact Hamilton and other high-toned Federalists, who in the 1790s clung to the name of the supporters of the Constitution, wanted to create a centralized fiscal-military state that would eventually rival the great monarchical powers of Europe on their own terms. Yet they knew that whatever aspects of monarchy they hoped to bring back into America would have to be placed within a republican framework. Perhaps, as has been suggested, the Federalists really intended to create another Augustan age, but they never openly declared this to be their aim.[37] Augustus after all had sought to incorporate elements of monarchy into the Roman Empire while all the time paying lip service to republicanism.

If some monarchical power were to be instilled in the new system, the energetic center of that power would be the presidency. For that reason it was the office of the president that made many Americans most suspicious of the new government. The executive or chief magistracy was after all the traditional source of tyranny and, as Benjamin Franklin pointed out, the source in America from which monarchy would naturally emerge.

Although Americans were used to congresses, an independent presidency was a new office for them. A single strong national executive was bound to remind them of the king they had just cast off. When James Wilson in the Philadelphia Convention moved that the executive "consist of a single person," a long uneasy silence had followed. The delegates knew only too well what such an office implied. John Rutledge complained that "the people will think we are leaning too much towards Monarchy." The creation of the presidency, warned Edmund Randolph, "made a bold stroke for monarchy."[38] But the convention had resisted these warnings and had gone on to make the new chief executive so strong, so kinglike, precisely because the delegates expected George Washington to be the first president.

Indeed, Washington was the only American in 1789 who possessed the dignity, patience, restraint, and reputation for republican virtue that the untried but potentially powerful office of the presidency needed at the outset. Many people, including Jefferson, expected that Washington might be president for life, that he would be a kind of elective monarch.[39] Indeed, we shall never understand events of the 1790s until we take seriously, as contemporaries did, the possibility of some sort of monarchy's developing in America. Republicanism was new and untried. Monarchy still prevailed almost everywhere; it was what much of the world was used to, and history showed that sooner or later most republics had tended to develop into kingly governments.

As the theory of four stages of social development showed (and the story of what had happened to ancient Rome was a prime example), the natural evolution of societies and states seemed to be from simple agrarian republican youth to complex commercial monarchical maturity. William Short, viewing the new Constitution from France, was not immediately frightened by the power of the executive. But he thought that "the President of the eighteenth century" would "form a stock on which will be grafted a King in the nineteenth." Others, like George Mason of Virginia, believed that the new government was destined to become "an elective monarchy," and still others, like Rawlins Lowndes of South Carolina, assumed that the government so closely resembled the British form that everyone naturally expected "our changing from a republic to monarchy."[40] To add to the confusion, Vice President John Adams, honest to the core and with little sense of political correctness, was already speaking publicly of America's being a monarchical republic or a republican monarchy.

From the outset Washington's behavior often savored of monarchy. His journey from Mount Vernon to the capital in New York in the spring of 1789, for example, took on the air of a royal procession. He was saluted by cannons and celebrated in elaborate ceremonies along the way. Everywhere he was greeted by triumphal

rejoicing and acclamations of "Long live George Washington!" With Yale students debating the advantages of an elective over a hereditary king, suggestions of monarchy were very much in the air. "You are now a King, under a different name," James McHenry told Washington in March 1789 and wished that the president "may reign long and happy over us."[41] It was not surprising therefore that some people referred to Washington's inauguration as a "coronation."[42]

So prevalent was the thinking that Washington resembled an elected monarch that some even expressed relief that he had no heirs.[43] Washington was sensitive to these popular anxieties about monarchy, and for a while he had thought of holding the presidency for only a year or so and then resigning and turning the office over to Vice President Adams. In the initial draft of his inaugural address he pointed out that "the Divine Providence hath not seen fit, that my blood should be transmitted or my name perpetuated by the endearing though sometimes seducing channel of immediate offspring." He had, he said, "no child for whom I could wish to make a provision – no family to build in greatness upon my country's ruins." Madison talked him out of this draft, but Washington's desire to show the public that he harbored no monarchical ambitions remained strong.[44] His protests testified to the widespread sense that monarchy was a distinct possibility for America.

Sensitive to charges that he had royal ambitions, Washington was often uncertain about the role he ought to play as president. He realized that the new government was fragile and needed dignity, but how far in a monarchical European direction ought he to go to achieve that dignity? Aware that whatever he did would become a precedent for the future, Washington sought the advice of those close to him, including the vice president and the man he soon made his secretary of the treasury, Alexander Hamilton. How often should he meet with the public? How accessible should he be? Should he dine with members of Congress? Should he host state dinners? Could he ever have private dinners with friends? Should he make a tour of the United States? The only state ceremonies that late-eighteenth-century Americans were familiar with were those of the European monarchies. Were they applicable to the young Republic?

Hamilton thought that most people were "prepared for a pretty high tone in the demeanour of the Executive," but probably not as high a tone as was desirable. "Notions of equality," he said, were as "yet ... too general and too strong" for the president to be properly distanced from the other branches of the government. In the meantime, suggested Hamilton, the president ought to follow the practice of "European Courts" as closely as he could. Only department heads, high-ranking diplomats, and senators should have access to the him. "Your Excellency," as Hamilton referred to Washington, might hold a half hour levee no more than once a week and then only for invited guests. He could give up to four formal entertainments a year but must never accept any invitations or call on anyone. Vice President Adams for his part urged Washington to make a show of "Splendor and Majesty" for his office. The president needed an entourage of chamberlains, aides-de-camp, and masters of ceremonies to conduct the formalities of his office.[45]

Washington realized that he had to maintain more distance from the public than the presidents of the Confederation Congress had. They had reduced their office, he said, to "perfect contempt," having been "considered in no better light than as a maître d'hôtel ... for their table was considered as a public one and every person who could get introduced conceived that he had a right to be invited to it." He knew that too much familiarity was no way "to preserve the dignity and respect that was due to the first magistrate."[46]

As uncomfortable as he often was with ceremony, Washington knew that he had to make the presidency "respectable," and when he became president, he spared few expenses in doing so. Although he was compelled to accept his twenty-five-thousand-dollar presidential

salary – an enormous sum for the age – he spent nearly two thousand dollars of it on liquor and wine for entertaining. In his public appearances he rode in a elaborately ornamented coach drawn by four and sometimes six horses, attended with four servants in livery, followed by his official family in other coaches. "When he travels," declared a British observer, "it is in a very kingly style."[47] In Washington's public pronouncements he referred to himself like a king in the third person, and he sat for dozens of state portraits, all modeled on those of European monarchs. Indeed, much of the iconography of the new nation, including its civic processions, was copied from monarchical symbolism.[48]

Washington may have been a simple republican, at heart just a country gentleman who was in bed every night by nine-thirty, but there is no doubt that he was concerned with what he called "the style proper for the Chief Magistrate." He conceded that a certain monarchical tone had to be made part of the government, and he was willing up to a point to play the part of a republican king. Although he may not in fact have been a king, he certainly managed to look like one. Throughout his life people repeatedly remarked upon his natural "dignity" and his "gallant bearing and commanding figure." He was, as John Adams later caustically remarked, "the best actor of presidency we have ever had."[49]

Obsessed with the new government's weakness, other Federalists were even more eager than Washington to bolster its dignity and respectability. Most believed that this could be best done by adopting some of the ceremony and majesty of monarchy – by making, for example, Washington's birthday celebrations rival those of the Fourth of July. Like the king of England speaking to Parliament from the throne, the president delivered his inaugural address personally to the Congress, and like the two houses of Parliament, both houses of Congress formally responded and then waited upon the president at his residence. The English monarchy was the model for the new republican government in other respects as well. The Senate, the body in the American government that most closely resembled the House of Lords, voted that writs of the federal government ought to run in the name of the president, just as writs in England ran in the name of the king. Although the House refused to go along, the Supreme Court did use the Senate's form for its writs. The Senate also tried to have all American coins bear the head of the president, as was the case with the European monarchs.

Although the high-toned Federalists eventually lost this proposal to put the president's impression on the coins, they made many such attempts to surround the new government with some of the trappings of monarchy. They drew up elaborate monarch-like rules of etiquette at what soon came to be denounced as the "American Court."[50] They established excruciatingly formal levees for the president that resembled those held by kings in Europe. In these levees, critics charged, Washington was to be "seen in public on Stated times like an Eastern Lama."[51]

If the president was to resemble a European monarch, what should his title be? Led by Vice President Adams, the Senate debated for a month in 1789 the proper title for the president. He could not be called simply His Excellency, for governors of the states were called that. "A royal or at least a princely title," said Adams, "will be found indispensably necessary to maintain the reputation, authority, and dignity of the President." Only something like "His Highness, or, if you will, His Most Benign Highness" would do.[52] Eventually, under Adams's prodding a Senate committee reported the title "His Highness the President of the United States of America, and Protector of their Liberties." When Jefferson learned of Adams's obsession with titles and the Senate's action, he could only shake his head and recall Benjamin Franklin's now-famous characterization of Adams as someone who means well for his country, is always an honest man, often a wise one, and sometimes and in some things is absolutely out of his senses.[53]

Perhaps in this respect not really out of his senses, for apparently Washington himself had initially favored for a title "His High Mightiness, the President of the United States and Protector of Their Liberties."[54] But when the president heard the criticism that such titles smacked of monarchy, he immediately changed his mind and was relieved when the House of Representatives under Madison's leadership succeeded in fixing the simple title of Mr. President.

Still, the talk of royalizing the new Republic continued and heightened the fears of many Americans. Monarchy after all implied much more than simply the presence of a single ruler. It meant a large bureaucracy, a standing army, authority exercised from the top down, and numerous devices for extracting men and money from the society in order to wage war. The financial program of Secretary of the Treasury Hamilton, with its funded debt and Bank of the United States, was modeled on that of the British monarchy. Indeed, like the British ministers of His Majesty George III's government, Hamilton sought to use patronage and every other source of influence to win support for his and Washington's programs. To many other Americans, however, it looked as if British monarchical corruption had spread to America.

Because of these very real apprehensions of monarchy and monarchical corruption, the first decade or so under the new American Constitution could never be a time of ordinary politics. In fact the entire period was wracked by a series of crises that threatened to destroy the national government that had been so recently and painstakingly created. The new expanded Republic of the United States was an unprecedented political experiment, and everyone knew that. No similar national republic in modem times had ever extended over such a large extent of territory. Since all theory and all history were against the success of this republican experiment, the political leaders worried about every unanticipated development. With even Washington's having suggested at the conclusion of the Constitutional Convention that the new federal government might not last twenty years, most political leaders in the 1790s had no great faith that the Union would survive.[55] In such uneasy and fearful circumstances politics could never be what we today regard as normal.

The parties that emerged in the 1790s, the Federalists and the Republicans, were not modern parties, and competition between them was anything but what some scholars used to call the first party system. No one thought that the emergence of parties was a good thing; indeed, far from building a party system in the 1790s, the nation's leaders struggled to prevent one from developing. The Federalists under the leadership of Washington, Adams, and Hamilton never saw themselves as a party but as the beleaguered legitimate government beset by people allied with revolutionary France out to destroy the Union. Although the Republicans under the leadership of Jefferson and Madison did reluctantly describe themselves as a party, they believed they were only a temporary one, designed to prevent the United States from becoming a Federalist-led British-backed monarchy. Since neither the Federalists nor the Republicans accepted the legitimacy of the other, partisan feelings ran very high, making the bitter clash between Hamilton and Jefferson, for example, more than just personal. The 1790s became one of the most passionate and divisive decades in American history, and we came as close to civil war as we would come until the actual Civil War in 1861.

More than any other person Washington held this divided country together. With the leaders of these two hostile parties, Hamilton and Jefferson, in the cabinet, Washington was able to use his immense prestige and good judgment to restrain fears, limit intrigues, and stymie opposition that otherwise might have escalated into serious violence. In 1794 he delicately combined coercion and conciliation and avoided bloodshed in putting down the Whiskey Rebellion, an uprising of hundreds of farmers in western Pennsylvania. Despite the intense partisan feelings that existed throughout the country, he never entirely lost the respect of all the party leaders, and this respect allowed him to reconcile, resolve, and balance the clashing interests.

It was the people's trust in Washington that enabled the new government to survive. And it was Washington acting as a republican monarch who was most responsible for making the presidency the powerful national office it became. Even an unsympathetic British observer was forced to admit that Washington possessed "the two great requisites of a statesman, the faculty of concealing his own sentiments, and of discovering those of other men."[56] He always understood the exercise of authority; he had led an army and indeed had more people working for him at Mount Vernon than he initially did in the new federal government. He was a systematic and energetic administrator. He kept careful records and communicated regularly with his department heads, to whom he delegated considerable authority. Yet he always made it clear that they were merely his assistants and responsible to him alone. Although he surrounded himself with brilliant advisers, including Hamilton as secretary of the treasury and Jefferson as secretary of state, he was always his own man and determined that the government speak with a single voice. Lacking the genius and the intellectual confidence of his advisers, he consulted them often and moved slowly and cautiously to judgment, but when ready to act, he acted decisively, and in the case of controversial decisions, such as his acceptance of Hamilton's Bank of the United States or his Proclamation of Neutrality in 1793, he did not second-guess himself. By filling out the executive and making it efficient and responsible, he made the presidency the dominant branch of the new government.

Washington knew that whatever he did would set precedents for the future. "We are a young Nation," he said, "and have a character to establish. It behooves us therefore to set out right for first impressions will be lasting."[57] He was particularly concerned with the relations between the president and the Senate. He envisioned the Senate's role in advising and consenting to appointments and treaties as that of a council, similar to what he had been used to as commander in chief, and thus he assumed that much of the Senate's advice and consent, if not with appointments, at least with treaty making, would be done orally.

In August 1789 the president went to the Senate to get its advice and consent to a treaty he was negotiating with the Creek Indians. Instead of offering their advice and consent in the way Washington's senior officers had during the Revolutionary War, the senators began debating each section of the treaty, with the president impatiently glaring at them. When one senator finally moved that the treaty be submitted to a committee for study, Washington jumped to his feet in exasperation and cried, "This defeats every purpose of my coming here." He calmed down, but when he finally left the Senate chamber, he was overheard to say he would "be damned if he ever went there again."[58] He did return two days later, but neither he nor the Senate enjoyed this personal confrontation. The advice part of the Senate's role in treaty making was more or less permanently forgotten. When the president issued his Proclamation of Neutrality in 1793, he did not even bother to ask for the consent of the Senate, and thus he further established the executive as the nearly sole authority in the conduct of foreign affairs.

In dealing with the world, Washington was an utter realist. He always sought, as he put it in 1775, at the outset of the war against Britain, to "make the best of mankind as they are, since we cannot have them as we wish."[59] In the great struggle over acceptance of the treaty with Great Britain negotiated by John Jay in 1794 and ratified by the Senate in 1795, Washington made a series of courageous decisions. With the United States and Britain on the verge of war because of British seizures of neutral American ships, sending Jay to England in the first place was one, and signing the treaty amid an outcry

of popular opposition was another. Standing up to the attempt by the House of Representatives in March 1796 to scuttle the ratified treaty by refusing to vote funds to implement it was still another. Washington refused to recognize a role for the House in the treaty-making process. To do so, he said, not only "would be to establish a dangerous precedent" but also would violate the Constitution, which allowed only the president and Senate to make treaties."[60]

If any single person was responsible for establishing the young Republic on a firm footing, it was Washington. He was nearly as much of an aristocrat as the United States ever produced, in his acceptance of social hierarchy and in his belief that some were born to command and most to obey. Although he trusted the good sense of the people in the long run, he believed that they could easily be misled by demagogues. He was a realist who had no illusions about human nature. "The motives which predominate most human affairs," he said, "are self-love and self-interest." The common people, like the common soldiers in his army, could not be expected to be "influenced by any other principles than those of interest."[61]

With these assumptions he realized only too keenly the fragility of the new nation. As president he devised a number of schemes for creating a stronger sense of nationhood. He understood the power of symbols; the reason he was willing to sit for long hours to have his portrait painted was to encourage respect for the new national government. In the absence of long-existing feelings of nationalism in the 1790s, popular celebrations of Washington became a substitute for patriotism; commemorations of his birthday did in fact come to rival those of the Fourth of July. It is not too much to say that for many Americans he stood for the Union.

As president he was always acutely sensitive to the varying interests of the country and fervent in his efforts to prevent the nation from fragmenting and falling apart. After he became president, he exchanged salutations with twenty-two leading religious groups and made a practice of attending the church services of a variety of denominations, including that of Roman Catholicism, and in a remarkable display of liberality for the age he assured the Jews of Newport, Rhode Island, that America was an enlightened place where "everyone shall sit in safety under his own vine and fig tree, and there shall be none to make him afraid." He undertook his two long royal-like tours of the country in 1789 and 1791 in order to bring the government to the farthest reaches of the land and reinforce the loyalty of people who had never seen him.[62] He promoted roads and canals and the post office – anything and everything that bound the different states and sections together. He spent so much time considering appointments to offices because he wanted not only to get the best men available but also to build local support throughout the country for the new federal government. He thought constantly about the future of the nation and those he called the "unborn Millions."[63] More than any other person he was responsible for backing Pierre L'Enfant in designing the magnificent federal city that was to bear his name. Since he hoped that the United States would eventually become a great nation rivaling, if not surpassing, the powerful states of Europe, he wanted a capital that would suit this potentially great nation. If Jefferson had had his way the national capital would have been the size of a college campus, fifteen hundred acres.

Washington never took the unity of the country for granted. He knew that if the Union broke apart, it would be between the northern and southern sections. In fact he told his secretary of state Edmund Randolph in 1795 that if the United States dissolved, he had made up his mind to join the North – understandable given his evolving attitude toward slavery.[64] But he wanted nothing more than for the United States to stay together, and he remained preoccupied throughout his presidency with creating the sinews of nationhood. Even in the social life of the "republican court" at the capital in New York and then after 1790 in Philadelphia, he and his wife, Martha, acted as matchmakers

in bringing together couples from different parts of the United States. With their own marriage and those of other Virginia families as examples, the Washingtons tended to think of marriage in dynastic terms, as a means of building alliances and consolidating a ruling aristocracy for the sprawling extent of America. He and Martha arranged sixteen marriages, including that between James Madison and Dolley Payne.[65] More than anyone in the country, Washington promoted the sense of Union that Lincoln and others later upheld.

As in the case of his career as commander in chief, Washington's most important act as president was his giving up of the office. The significance of his retirement from the presidency is easy for us to overlook, but his contemporaries knew what it meant. Most people assumed that Washington might be president as long as he lived. Hence his persistent efforts to retire from the presidency enhanced his moral authority and helped fix the republican character of the Constitution. He very much wanted to retire in 1792, but his advisers and friends thought otherwise. Madison admitted that when he first urged Washington to accept the presidency, he had told him that he could protect himself from accusations of overweening ambition by "a voluntary return to public life as soon as the state of the Government would permit," but the state of the government, said Madison, was not yet secure. Washington sought to discover what others thought, and everywhere the answer was the same: He must stay on. Hamilton even tried the ultimate argument: that retirement when he was needed would be "critically hazardous to your own reputation." But it was left to a female friend, Eliza Powel, to develop this point and hammer it home. If Washington followed his inclinations and retired from the presidency, she wrote, his enemies would attack his reputation. They would say "that Ambition had been the moving spring of all your Actions" and that now when the going was tough and his fame could not be enhanced, he "would run no further Risque" for the public.[66] How to preserve one's reputation without at the same time allowing concern for that reputation to overcome one's duty was a peculiar dilemma of the eighteenth century. Washington stayed on for another term.

However, in 1796 he was so determined to retire that no one could dissuade him, and his voluntary leaving of the office set a precedent that was not broken until FDR secured a third term in 1940. But so strong was the sentiment for a two-term limit that the tradition was written into the Constitution in the Twenty-second Amendment in 1951. Washington's action in 1796 was of great significance. That the chief executive of a state should willingly relinquish his office was an object lesson in republicanism at a time when the republican experiment throughout the Atlantic world was very much in doubt.

Washington's final years in retirement were not happy ones. The American political world was changing, and he struggled to comprehend it. During his final years in office he and his administration had been subjected to vicious partisan criticism, and he felt the criticism deeply; indeed, Jefferson thought that Washington took such public attacks to heart "more than any person I ever yet met with."[67] Washington watched with dismay what he believed was the growing interference of the French government in American politics. For him the Republican party had become "the French Party." It was, he said, "the curse of this country," threatening the stability and independence of the United States.[68] He saw plots and enemies everywhere and became as much of a high-toned Federalist as Hamilton.

His fear was real; his sense of crisis was deep. He and other Federalists thought that the French might invade the country and together with the Republican party, "the French Party," overthrow the government. "Having Struggled for eight or nine years against the Invasion of our Rights by one Power, & to establish an Independence of it," he wrote in 1798, "I could not remain an unconcerned Spectator of the attempts of another Power to accomplish the same object, though in a different way, with less pretensions – indeed without any at all."[69] He thus listened attentively to all the urgent Federalist calls that he come out of retirement and head the army that the Congress had created to meet the French invasion.

Though he again expressed reluctance and asked whether becoming commander in chief would not be considered "a restless Act, evincive of my discontent in retirement," he was far more eager in 1798 to step back into the breach and do his duty than he ever had been before. It was a measure of his despair with this "Age of Wonders!"[70]

Before he could actually commit himself, President John Adams acted and appointed him commander of all the military forces of the United States. Washington accepted but scarcely comprehended how it had come about. The next thing he knew he was on his way to Philadelphia to organize the army. Events were outrunning his ability to control them or even to understand them, and he more and more saw himself caught up in "the designs of Providence."[71] His command was a disaster. He wrangled over the appointments of the second-in-command, intrigued against Adams, and interfered with his cabinet. When neither the French invasion nor the American army materialized, Washington crept back to Mount Vernon thoroughly disillusioned with the ways of American politics.

In June 1799 Governor Jonathan Trumbull, Jr., of Connecticut with the backing of many Federalists urged Washington once again to stand for the presidency in 1800. Only Washington, Trumbull said, could unite the Federalists and save the country from "a French President." Finally Washington had had enough. In his reply he no longer bothered with references to his reputation for disinterestedness and his desire to play the role of Cincinnatus. Instead he talked about the new political conditions that made his candidacy irrelevant. In this new democratic era of party politics, he said, "personal influence," distinctions of character, no longer mattered. If the members of the Jeffersonian Republican party "set up a broomstick" as candidate and called it "a true son of Liberty" or "a Democrat" or "any other epithet that will suit their purpose," it still would "command their votes in toto!" But even worse, the same was true of the Federalists. Party spirit now ruled all, and people voted only for their party candidate. Even if he were the Federalist candidate, Washington was "thoroughly convinced I should not draw a *single* vote from the Anti-federal side." Therefore his standing for election made no sense; he would "stand upon no stronger ground than any other Federal character well supported."[72]

Washington wrote all this in anger and despair, but though he exaggerated, he was essentially right. The political world was changing, becoming democratic, and parties, not great men, soon became the objects of contention. To be sure, the American people continued to long for great heroes as leaders, and right up through Eisenhower they have periodically elected military leaders, Washington's manqué, to the presidency. But democracy made such great heroes no longer essential to the workings of American government. Although Washington had aristocratic predilections and never meant to popularize politics, he nonetheless was crucial in making this democracy feasible. He was an extraordinary man who made it possible for ordinary men to rule. There has been no president quite like him, and we can be sure that we shall not see his like again.

## Notes

This chapter is a much revised and longer version of my article in the *Virginia Quarterly Review,* 68 (1992), 189–207, which is used with permission.

1. Hawthorne, Emerson, and Ward, quoted in James Morton Smith, ed., *George Washington: A Profile* (New York: Hill and Wang, 1969), xii.

2. Pauline Maier, *The Old Revolutionaries: Political Lives in the Age of Samuel Adams* (New York: Knopf, 1980), 47.

3. JA to Benjamin Rush, March 19, 1812, in Barry Schwartz, *George Washington: The Making of an American Symbol* (New York: Free Press, 1987), 5; TJ to Dr. Walter Jones, January 2, 1814, *Jefferson: Writings,* 1319.

4. Chateaubriand, in Gilbert Chinard, ed., *George Washington as the French Knew Him* (Princeton: Princeton University Press, 1940), 96.

5. GW to Lafayette, August 15, 1787, to Henry Knox, February 20, 1784, Fitzpatrick, ed., *Writings of Washington* 29: 259; 27:341. See Paul Boller, Jr., *George Washington and Religion* (Dallas: Southern Methodist University Press, 1963), 94; Jay Fliegelman, *Prodigals and Pilgrims: The American Revolution Against Patriarchal Authority, 1750–1800* (Cambridge, England: Cambridge University Press, 1982), 212.

6. TJ, A Bill for Establishing Religious Freedom, 1779, *Jefferson: Writings,* 346.

7. GW to Reverend Jonathan Boucher, July 9, 1771, Fitzpatrick, ed., *Writings of Washington,* 3:50.

8. Charles Moore, ed., *George Washington's Rules of Civility and Decent Behaviour in Company and Conversation* (Boston, 1926), 9, 5.

9. Frederic M. Litto, "Addison's *Cato* in the Colonies," *WMQ,* 3d Ser. (1966), 431–449.

10. GW to George Steptoe Washington, March 23, 1789, in *Papers of Washington: Presidential Ser.,* 1: 438.

11. Bernard Knollenberg, as noted by James Thomas Flexner, *George Washington: The Forge of Experience (1732–1775)* (Boston: Little, Brown, 1965), 254.

12. W. W. Abbot et al., eds., *The Papers of Washington: Colonial Series,* 10 vols. (Charlottesville: University Press of Virginia), 1: xvii.

13. Rush to JA, September 21, 1805, in John A. Schutz and Douglass Adair, eds., *The Spur of Fame: Dialogues of John Adams and Benjamin Rush, 1805–1813* (San Marino, CA: Huntington Library, 1980), 37.

14. GW to David Humphreys, July 25, 1785, Fitzpatrick, ed., *Writings of Washington,* 28: 203.

15. David S. Shields, *Civil Tongues and Polite Letters* (Chapel Hill: University of North Carolina Press, 1997), 116.

16. Brissot de Warville, in Chinard, ed., *Washington as the French Knew Him,* 87; JA to Rush, November 11, 1807, in Schutz and Adair, eds., *Spur of Fame,* 98.

17. GW to John Francis Mercer, September 9, 1786, *Washington: Writings,* 607.

18. GW to Tobias Lear, May 6, 1794, Fitzpatrick, ed., *Writings of Washington,* 33: 358.

19. GW's Last Will and Testament, July 9, 1799, *Papers of Washington: Retirement Ser.,* 4:480. On Washington's attitudes toward slavery and his will, see Robert F. Dazell and Lee Baldwin Dalzell, *George Washington's Mount Vernon: At Home in Revolutionary America* (New York: Oxford University Press, 1998), and Henry Wiencek, *An Imperfect God: George Washington, His Slaves and the Creation of America* (New York Farrar, Straus and Giroux, 2003).

20. Garry Wills, *Cincinnatus: George Washington and the Enlightenment* (New York, 1984), 3–16.

21. GW, Circular Letter to the States, June 8, 1783, in Fitzpatrick, ed., *Writings of Washington,* 26: 486; Wills, *Cincinnatus,* 13.

22. TJ to GW, April 16, 1784, *Washington: Writings,* 791.

23. James Thomas Flexner, *George Washington and the New Nation (1783–1793)* (Boston: Little, Brown, 1965), 3: 419.

24. See AH, *The Federalist,* No. 72, Jacob E. Cooke, ed. (Middletown, CT: Wesleyan University Press, 1961), 488.

25. TJ to Dr. Walter Jones, January 2, 1814, *Jefferson: Writings,* 1319.

26. GW to Benjamin Harrison, January 22, 1785, to William Grayson, January 22, 1785, to George William Fairfax, February 27, 1785, Fitzpatrick, ed., *Writings of Washington,* 28: 36, 85.

27. GW to Benjamin Harrison, January 22, 1785, to William Grayson, January 22, 1785, to Lafayette, February 15, 1785, to George William Fairfax, February 27, 1785, to Governor Patrick Henry, February 27, 1785, to Henry Knox, February 28, 1785, June 18, 1785, to Nathanael Greene, May 20, 1785, Fitzpatrick, ed., *Writings of Washington,* 28: 36, 37, 72, 80–81, 85, 89–91, 92–93, 167, 146.

28. GW to Henry Knox, March 8, 1787, to David Humphreys, March 8, 1787, Fitzpatrick, ed., *Writings of Washington,* 29:172.

29. GW to Humphreys, December 26, 1786, Fitzpatrick, ed., *Writings of Washington,* 29, 128; Flexner, *Washington and the New Nation,* 3:108.

30. Monroe to TJ, July 12, 1788, *Papers of Jefferson,* 13: 352.

31. GW to Henry Lee, September 22, 1788, in Fitzpatrick, ed., *Writings of Washington,* 30: 97, 98.

32. AH to GW, September 1788, *Papers of Hamilton,* 5: 221–222; GW to Lincoln, October 26, 1788, *Papers of Washington: Presidential Ser.,* 1: 71.

33. Douglas Southall Freeman, *George Washington: A Biography* (New York: Scribner's, 1954), 6: 86.

34. Abigail Adams, quoted in Flexner, *Washington and the New Nation,* 220; Garry Wills, *Cincinnatus: George Washington and the Enlightenment* (Garden City, NY: Doubleday, 1984), 23.

35. Rush, "To ——: Information to Europeans Who Are Disposed to Migrate to the United States," April 16, 1790, Lyman H. Butterfield, ed., *Letters of Benjamin Rush* (Princeton: Princeton University Press, 1951), 2: 556.

36. JM, "Vices of the Political System of the United States," in *Papers of Madison,* 9: 352, 357.

37. Washington declared that "the Augustan age is proverbial for intellectual refinement and elegance," but he never suggested that it had any anti-republican political significance. GW to Lafayette, May 28, 1788, *Washington: Writings,* 681. On the Federalists and the Augustan age, see Linda Kerber, *Federalists in Dissent: Imagery and Ideology in Jeffersonian America* (Ithaca, NY: Cornell University Press, 1970).

38. Max Farrand, *The Records of the Federal Convention of 1787* (New Haven: Yale University Press, 1937), 1:65, 119; 2:513.

39. TJ to David Humphreys, March 18, 1789, in *Papers of Jefferson,* 14: 679.

40. Louise B. Dunbar, *A Study of "Monarchical" Tendencies in the United States from 1776 to 1801,* in *Illinois Studies in the Social Sciences,* 10 (1922), 99–100.

41. James McHenry to GW, March 29, 1789, in *Papers of Washington: Presidential Ser.,* 1: 461.

42. Winifred E. A. Bernard, *Fisher Ames: Federalist and Statesman, 1758–1808* (Chapel Hill: University Press of North Carolina, 1965), 92.

43. David W. Robson, *Educating Republicans: The College in the Era of the American Revolution, 1758–1800* (Westport, CT., 1985), 149; Thomas E. V. Smith, *The City of New York in the Year of Washington's Inauguration, 1789* (New York, 1889, reprint ed., Riverside, CT: Chatham Press, 1972), 217–19.

44. GW, undelivered first inaugural address, January 1789, *Papers of Washington: Presidential Ser.,* 2: 162.

45. AH to GW, May 5, 1789, in *Papers of Hamilton,* 5:335–37, JA to GW, May 17, 1789, *Papers of Washington: Presidential Ser.,* 2: 314.

46. Flexner, *Washington and the New Nation,* 195.

47. Leonard D. White, *The Federalists: A Study in Administrative History* (New York: Macmillan, 1948), 108; S. W. Jackman, "A Young Englishman Reports on the New Nation: Edward Thornton to James Bland Burges, 1791–1793," *WMQ,* 18 (1961), 111.

48. David Waldstreicher, *In the Midst of Perpetual Fetes: The Making of American Nationalism, 1776–1820* (Chapel Hill: University of North Carolina Press, 1997), 120–22.

49. GW to JM, March 30, 1789, in *Papers of Washington: Presidential Ser.,* 1: 484; Don Higginbotham, *George Washington: Uniting a Nation* (Lanham, MD: Rowman and Littlefield, 2002), 10; JA to Benjamin Rush, Schutz and Adair, eds., *Spur of Fame,* 181.

50. Kenneth R. Bowling and Helen E. Veit, eds., *The Diary of William Maclay and Other Notes on Senate Debates: Documentary History of the First Federal Congress of the United States of America, 4 March 1789–3 March 1791* (Baltimore: Johns Hopkins University Press, 1988), 9: 21; Schwartz, *Washington,* 62.

51. Bowling and Veit, eds., *Diary of Maclay,* 21.

52. Page Smith, *John Adams* (New York: Doubleday, 1962), 2: 755.

53. TJ to JM, July 29, 1789, in *Papers of Jefferson,* 15: 316.

54. White, *Federalists,* 108.

55. Abraham Baldwin, November 30, 1806, in James H. Hutson, ed., *Supplement to Max Farrand's the Records of the Federal Convention of 1787* (New Haven: Yale University Press, 1987), 305.

56. S. W Jackman, "A Young Englishman Reports on the New Nation: Edward Thornton to James Bland Burges, 1791–1793," *WMQ,* 18 (1961), 104.

57. GW to John Augustine Washington, June 15, 1783, *Washington: Writings,* 527.

58. Bowling and Veit, eds., *Diary of Maclay,* 130; Glenn A. Phelps, *George Washington and American Constitutionalism* (Lawrence, KS: University Press of Kansas, 1993), 170.

59. GW to Philip Schuyler, December 24, 1775, in *Papers of Washington: Revolution Ser.,* 2: 599–600.

60. GW to the House of Representatives, March 30, 1796, in *Washington: Writings,* 931.

61. GW to JM, December 3, 1784, *Papers of Madison,* 12: 478; GW to John Hancock, September 24, 1776, in Fitzpatrick, ed., *Writings of Washington,* 6:107–108.

62. Higginbotham, *Washington,* 53, 59–60, 55.

63. GW, Circular Letter to State Governments, June 8, 1783, *Washington: Writings,* 518.

64. TJ, notes of a conversation with Edmund Randolph [after 1795], *Papers of Jefferson,* 28: 568.

65. Higginbotham, *Washington,* 62, drawing on the work of David Shields and Fredrika Teute.

66. JM's conversations with GW, May 5–25, 1792, AH to GW, July 30–August 3, 1792, *Papers of Washington: Presidential Ser.,* 10: 351, 594; Elizabeth Willing Powel to GW, November 17, 1792, ibid., 11: 396.

67. TJ to JM, June 9, 1793, James Morton Smith, ed., *The Republic of Letters: The Correspondence Between Thomas Jefferson and James Madison 1776–1826* (New York: Norton, 1995), 781.

68. GW to Timothy Pickering, February 6, 1798, to Charles Carroll of Carrollton, August 2, 1798, *Papers of Washington: Retirement Ser.,* 2: 76; 483.

69. GW to the Marquis de Lafayette, December 25, 1798, *Papers of Washington: Retirement Ser.,* 3: 284.

70. GW to James McHenry, July 4, 1798, to JA, July 4, 1798, *Papers of Washington: Retirement Ser.,* 2: 378; 369.

71. GW to John Quincy Adams, January 20, 1799, *Papers of Washington: Retirement Ser.,* 3: 321.

72. Jonathan Trumbull, Jr., to GW, June 22, 1799, GW to Trumbull, July 21, 1799, *Papers of Washington: Retirement Ser.,* 4:143–44, 202.

# CONTRIBUTORS

Ira Berlin is Distinguished University Professor at the University of Maryland.

T.H. Breen is the William Smith Mason Professor of American History at Northwestern University.

Colin G. Calloway is John Kimball, Jr. 1943 Professor of History and Professor of Native American Studies at Dartmouth College.

Saul Cornell is Paul and Diane Guenther Chair in American History at Fordham University.

Aaron S. Fogleman is Professor of History at Northern Illinois University.

Eliga H. Gould is Professor of History at the University of New Hampshire.

Woody Holton is McCausland Professor of History at the University South Carolina.

Maya Jasanoff is Professor of History at Harvard University.

Frank Lambert is Professor of History at Purdue University.

Ned C. Landsman is Professor of History at Stony Brook University.

Wayne E. Lee is Professor of History at the University of North Carolina, Chapel Hill.

Michael A. McDonnell is Associate Professor of History at the University of Sydney.

John M. Murrin is Professor Emeritus of History at Princeton University.

Gary B. Nash is Professor Emeritus of History at the University of California, Los Angeles.

Mary Beth Norton is Mary Donlon Alger Professor of American History at Cornell University.

Robert G. Parkinson is Ray and Madeline Johnston Associate Professor at Shepherd University.

John Shy is Professor Emeritus of History at the University of Michigan.

Alan Taylor is Distinguished Professor at the University of California, Davis.

Gordon S. Wood is Alva O. Way University Professor and Professor of History Emeritus at Brown University.

Rosemarie Zagarri is Professor of History at George Mason University.

# PERMISSION ACKNOWLEDGMENTS

Ira Berlin, "The Revolution in Black Life," in Alfred F. Young, ed., *The American Revolution: Explorations in the History of American Radicalism* (DeKalb, IL., 1976), 349–82. Used with permission of Northern Illinois University Press.

T.H. Breen, "'Baubles of Britain': The American and Consumer Revolutions of the Eighteenth Century," *Past and Present*, vol. 119 (1988), 73–104. Reprinted by permission of Oxford University Press.

Colin G. Calloway, "The Continuing Revolution in Indian Country," in Frederick E. Hoxie, Ronald Hoffman, and Peter J. Albert, eds., *Native Americans and the Early Republic* (Charlottesville, VA, 1999), 3–33. ©1999 by the Rector and Visitors of the University of Virginia. Reprinted by permission of the University of Virginia Press.

Saul Cornell, "Aristocracy Assailed: The Ideology of Backcountry Anti-Federalism," *Journal of American History*, vol. 76 (1990), 1148–72. Reprinted by permission of Oxford University Press Journals.

Aaron S. Fogleman, "From Slaves, Convicts, and Servants to Free Passengers: The Transformation of Immigration in the Era of the American Revolution," *Journal of American History*, vol. 85 (1998), 43–76. Reprinted by permission of Oxford University Press Journals.

Eliga H. Gould, "The Nation Abroad: The Atlantic Debate over Colonial Taxation," in *The Persistence of Empire: British Political Culture in the Age of the American Revolution* (Chapel Hill, NC, 2000), 106–47. Published by the Omohundro Institute of Early American History and Culture. Copyright © 2000 by the University of North Carolina Press. Used by permission of the publisher.

Woody Holton, "'Rebel against Rebel': Enslaved Virginians and the Coming of the American Revolution," *Virginia Magazine of History and Biography*, vol. 105 (1997), 157–92. Reprinted by permission of *Virginia Magazine of History and Biography*.

Maya Jasanoff, "The Other Side of Revolution: Loyalists in the British Empire," *William and Mary Quarterly*, 3rd ser., vol. 65 (2008), 205–32. Reprinted by permission of the Omohundro Institute of Early American History and Culture.

Frank Lambert, "Constitutional Recognition of a Free Religious Market," in *The Founding Fathers and the Place of Religion in America* (Princeton, NJ, 2003), 236–64, 316–18. © 2003 by Frank Lambert. Reprinted by permission of Princeton University Press.

Ned C. Landsman, "Liberty, Province, and Empire," in *From Colonials to Provincials: American Thought and Culture, 1680–*

*1760* (Ithaca, NY, 1997), 149–75, 203–7. Copyright © 1997 by Twayne Publishers. Used by permission of the publisher, Cornell University Press.

Wayne E. Lee, "Restraint and Retaliation: The North Carolina Militias and the Backcountry War of 1780–1782," in John Resch and Walter Sargent, eds., *War and Society in the American Revolution: Mobilization and Home Fronts* (De Kalb, IL, 2007), 163–190. Used with permission of Northern Illinois University Press.

Michael A. McDonnell, "Class War? Class Struggles during the American Revolution in Virginia," *William and Mary Quarterly*, 3rd ser., vol. 63 (2006), 305–44. Reprinted by permission of the Omohundro Institute of Early American History and Culture.

John M. Murrin, "1776: The Countercyclical Revolution," in Michael A. Morrison and Melinda Zook, eds., *Revolutionary Currents: Nation Building in the Transatlantic World* (Lanham, MD, 2004), 65–90. Reprinted by permission of Rowman and Littlefield Publishing Group.

Gary B. Nash, "Writing on a Clean Slate: The Struggle to Craft State Constitutions, 1776–1780," originally titled, "Writing on the Clean Slate, 1776–1780," in *The Unknown American Revolution: The Unruly Birth of Democracy and the Struggle to Create America* (New York, 2005), 264–305. © 2005 by Gary B. Nash. Used by permission of the author and Viking Penguin, a division of Penguin Group (USA) Inc.

Mary Beth Norton, "Eighteenth-Century American Women in Peace and War: The Case of the Loyalists," *William and Mary Quarterly*, 3rd ser., 33 (1976), 386–409. Reprinted by permission of the Omohundro Institute of Early American History and Culture.

Robert G. Parkinson, "Twenty-seven Reasons for Independence," in Christian Y. Dupont and Peter S. Onuf, eds., *Declaring Independence: The Origin and Influence of America's Founding Document* (Charlottesville, VA, 2008), 11–18. Reprinted by permission of the author and the University of Virginia Library.

John Shy, "The Military Conflict Considered as a Revolutionary War," in *A People Numerous and Armed: Reflections on the Military Struggle for American Independence*, rev. ed. (Ann Arbor, MI, 1990), 215–244, 327–36. Copyright © 1973 by the University of North Carolina Press. Used by permission of the publisher.

Alan Taylor, "'To Man Their Rights': The Frontier Revolution," in Ronald Hoffman and Peter J. Albert, eds., *The Transforming Hand of Revolution: Reconsidering the American Revolution as a Social Movement* (Charlottesville, VA, 1995), 231–57. ©1996 by the Rector and Visitors of the University of Virginia. Reprinted by permission of the University of Virginia Press.

Gordon S. Wood, "Interests and Disinterestedness in the Making of the Constitution," in Richard Beeman, Stephen Botein, and Edward C. Carter II, eds., *Beyond Confederation: The Origins of the Constitution and American National Identity* (Chapel Hill, NC, 1987), 69–109. Copyright © 1987 by the University of North Carolina Press. Used by permission of the publisher.

Gordon S. Wood, "The Greatness of George Washington," in *Revolutionary Characters: What Made the Founders Different* (New York, 2006), 29–63, 279–83. Copyright © 2006 by Gordon S. Wood. Used by permission of the author and The Penguin Press, a division of Penguin Group (USA) Inc.

Rosemarie Zagarri, "The Rights of Woman," in *Revolutionary Backlash: Women and Politics in the Early American Republic* (Philadelphia, PA, 2007), 11–45, 188–96. Used by permission of the University of Pennsylvania Press.